S0-BDT-649

# *Encyclopedia of* WAR & American Society

## Peter Karsten

Peter Karsten is professor of history at the University of Pittsburgh with a joint appointment in the Sociology Department. He attended Yale on an NROTC scholarship and served three years on the USS *Canberra*. He received his Ph.D. from the University of Wisconsin in 1968. His first book, *The Naval Aristocracy: The Golden Age of Annapolis and the Emergence of Modern American Navalism* (Free Press, 1972), and his most recent book , *Between Law and Custom* (Cambridge University Press, 2003), won Phi Alpha Theta Best Book Awards. He also has written *Soldiers and Society: The Effects of Military Service and War on American Life* (1978); *Law, Soldiers and Combat* (1978); *Military Threats* (1984); *Heart versus Head: Judge-Made Law in 19th Century America* (1997); and served as editor of *The Military in America from Colonial Times to the Present* (1986), and of a five-volume set of essays, *The Military and Society* (1998). From 1985 to 1998, Karsten served as co-director (with Peter Stearns) of the Pittsburgh Center for Social History.

## Associate Editors

***Mark Grimsley***, Associate Professor, Department of History at The Ohio State University. Mark is the author of *The Hard Hand of War: Union Military Policy Toward Southern Civilians, 1861–1865* (Cambridge University Press, 1995) and *And Keep Moving On: The Virginia Campaign, May–June* (University of Nebraska Press, 2002) .

***Jennifer D. Keene***, Associate Professor and Chair, Department of History at Chapman University. Jennifer is the author of *The United States and the First World War* (Longman, 2000), and *Doughboys, the Great War and the Remaking of America* (Johns Hopkins University Press, 2001).

***Wayne Lee***, Assistant Professor and Vice Chair, Department of History at University of Louisville. Wayne is the author of *Crowds and Soldiers in Revolutionary North Carolina: The Culture of Violence in Riot and War* (University Press of Florida, 2001), and "Fortify, Fight, or Flee: Tuscarora and Cherokee Defensive Warfare and Military Culture Adaptation" (*Journal of Military History*, 2004).

***Mark Parillo***, Director of the Institute for Military History and 20th Century Studies at Kansas State University. Mark is the author of *The Japanese Merchant Marine in World War II* (Naval Institute Press, 1993), and editor of "*We Were in the Big One:" Experiences of the World War Two Generation* (Scholarly Resources, 2002).

# *Encyclopedia of* WAR & American Society

PETER KARSTEN, Editor
*University of Pittsburgh*

A SAGE Reference Publication

445 West 23rd Street, #1D
New York, N.Y. 10011
www.mtmpublishing.com



**Sage Reference**
Publisher: Rolf Janke

**MTM Publishing**
Publisher: Valerie Tomaselli
Executive Editor: Hilary W. Poole
Project Editors: Paul Schellinger, Stephanie Schreiber
Editorial and Research Assistants: Kimberly George, Maureen Noble
Chief Copyeditor: Carole A. Campbell
Additional Copyediting: Kate Stevenson, Catherine Carter, Concord Editorial and Design
Proofreading: Paul Scaramazza and Eleanora von Dehsen
Design and Layout: Annemarie Redmond Design, Inc.
Index: A E I O U, Inc.

For Information:
Sage Publications, Inc.
2455 Teller Road
Thousand Oaks, California 91320
Email: order@sagepub.com

Sage Publications Ltd.
6 Bonhill Street
London EC2A 4PU
United Kingdom

Sage Publications India Pvt. Ltd.
M-32 Market
Greater Kailash I
New Delhi 110 048 India

Printed in the United States of America

Library of Congress Cataloging-in-Publication Data
Encyclopedia of war and American society / editor, Peter Karsten.
p. cm.
"A Sage reference publication."
Includes bibliographical references and index.
ISBN 0-7619-3097-3 (cloth)
1. United States--History, Military--Encyclopedias. 2. War and society--United States--History--Encyclopedias. I. Karsten, Peter.
E181.E634 2006
973.03--dc22

2005025579

# Contents



## Encyclopedia of War and American Society



## Supplemental Material

# List of Entries

## LIST OF ENTRIES

# List of Documents

## LIST OF DOCUMENTS

# LIST OF DOCUMENTS

# Reader's Guide

### Environment, Health, and Medicine

Agent Orange
American Red Cross
Barton, Clara
Chemical Warfare
Doctor Draft
Environment and War
Influenza Pandemic of 1918–19
MASH Units
Medicine and War
Military Psychiatry
Nurses, Military
Psychiatric Disorders, Combat Related
Smallpox and War
U.S. Sanitary Commission
Victory Gardens

### Gender

Barton, Clara
Camp Followers
Commission on Training Camp Activities
Families, Military
Gays and Lesbians in the Military
Mahan, Dennis Hart
Nurses, Military
Pinups
Rosie the Riveter
Sampson, Deborah
Sexual Abuse and Harassment
Stratton, Dorothy C.
Tailhook Convention
Victory Gardens
War Brides
Women in the Military
Women in the Workforce in World War I and World War II
Women's International League for Peace and Freedom

### Media and Journalism

Brady, Mathew B.
Censorship and the Military
CNN
Combat-Zone Photography
Committee on Public Information
*Enola Gay* Controversy
Frontline Reporting
Greeley, Horace
Mauldin, Bill
Media and War
Militant Liberty
My Lai Massacre
Newsreels
Office of Censorship
Office of War Information
Pentagon Papers
Political Cartoons
Propaganda and Psychological Operations
Pyle, Ernie
Radio in World War II
Radio Free Europe
Recruiting Advertisements
Television and War
Voice of America

### Law and Justice

American Civil Liberties Union
Andersonville
Articles of War
Court of Military Appeals
Customs of War
Desertion
Doolittle Board
Draft Evasion and Resistance
Espionage and Sedition Acts
Executive Order 8802
Fort Pillow Massacre
General Orders, No. 100
Geneva and Hague Conventions
Genocide
Impressment
Just War Theory
My Lai Massacre
Posse Comitatus Act
Prisoners of War
Quantrill's Raiders
Tiger Force Recon Scandal
Uniform Code of Military Justice
*United States v. Seeger* and *Welsh v. United States*

### People-Military Leaders and Figures

Arnold, Henry Harley
Brant, Joseph and Margaret "Molly" Brant
Butler, Smedley Darlington
Chief Joseph
Crazy Horse
Custer, George Armstrong
Davis, Jefferson
Eisenhower, Dwight D.
Forrest, Nathan Bedford
Geronimo
Grant, Ulysses S.
Halsey, William F., Jr.
Hitchcock, Ethan Allen
Jones, John Paul
Lee, Robert E.
LeMay, Curtis Emerson
Lynch, Jessica
MacArthur, Douglas
Mahan, Alfred Thayer
Marshall, George Catlett
Mitchell, William "Billy"
Murphy, Audie
Nimitz, Chester William
Osceola
Patton, George
Pershing, John Joseph
Pontiac
Powell, Colin

### Planning, Strategy, and Command and Control



### Politics



### Race and Ethnicity

### Religion



### Science and Technology



### Soldiering and Veterans' Affairs



### Wars

## Veteran Status and Electability

Whit Ayres, a Republican pollster commenting before the 2002 Senate races, claimed that "ever since Sept. 11, we've noticed that a military background—particularly combat experience—is one of the most prominent positives for candidates," whereas "in the past, it was not a significantly positive factor." It is premature to assess Ayres's statement about a shift in the importance of military background post-September 11. But it is the case that military background, or veteran status, has played an important role, historically, on the perceived electability of presidential candidates and of members of the House of Representatives. Data as to the actual effect of veteran status on electability are unsupportive of that presumption but not conclusive. More research is called for; what does appear clear, however, is that over time party leaders have favored nominating veterans for top federal elected offices.

### Nominations, Elections, and Veteran Status

The office of the president is a logical one to examine in terms of veteran status and electability because of the president's role as commander in chief and in policy decisions that affect the military. In presidential races from 1788 to 2004, veterans were chosen to run 46 times while nonveterans were chosen and ran 62 times (a 3:4 ratio). In the period prior to the Civil War (1788–1860), veterans ran 14 times, nonveterans 27 times. From the Civil War to the year before U.S. entry into World War I (1864–1916), a period during which the veteran to nonveteran ratio was higher than in previous decades owing to the vast numbers of Civil War vets, veterans and nonveterans were candidates for the presidency in equal numbers (13 times). Between the election following World War I and the last election during World War II (1920–44), only one veteran ran for the presidency while nonveterans ran 13 times. During the Cold War years (1948–88), however, veterans outnumbered nonveteran presidential candidates 12 to 7. Since the end of the Cold War (1992–2004), a veteran ran six times, a nonveteran twice.

In 24 presidential races, a veteran faced another veteran or a nonveteran faced another nonveteran. Three races were uncontested (the first two, in 1788 and 1792, when George Washington had no opposition, and in 1820, when James Monroe ran unopposed). Hence, 27 races involved a veteran vs. a nonveteran. Of these, veterans won 17, nonveterans, 10. These data seem to suggest that veterans had an advantage over nonveterans in running for president. But if the extent of combat experience is weighted (a combat veteran counting as 1, one who saw no combat one-half), the balance shifts to 14 with combat experience and 12 without combat experience or without military service at all—not a significant difference.

Why, then, did political party leaders choose veterans for presidential races at rates that, for most of these years, were higher than the proportion of veterans in the adult male population? In the only research of its kind, Albert Somit (1948) explored the possibility of whether "military hero" status aided the electability of presidential candidates. Somit noted that a number of individuals had military careers of such distinction and glory that their careers were the central factor contributing to their nomination for president. More than 40 percent of the presidential nominees between 1828 and 1916 could be styled military heroes. Using this classification, Somit found that military heroes received a greater percentage of the popular vote than others, whether they won or lost, and tended to win by larger margins when running against nonheroes. Somit concluded that a political party that nominated a military hero increased its chance of winning the election.

Somit and Joseph Tanenhaus (1957) also conducted a unique investigation of whether veteran status enhanced a House of Representative candidate's chances of winning a seat during congressional elections in 1950, 1952, and 1954. They concluded that the overrepresentation of veterans in the primary process (and consequently in slight accretions in the House itself across the six-year period) was attributable to the way in which the parties nominated candidates. They found that both parties nominated a substantially higher percentage of veterans than their percentage in the adult male population (nearly 50 percent higher), which eventually resulted in an overrepresentation of veterans in the House (55 percent, versus their percentage in the adult male population of 40 percent). Nonetheless, they found that in these three elections, voters, when confronted with a veteran facing a nonveteran, showed absolutely no disposition to favor the veteran!

### A Contemporary Case Study

While evidence suggests that veteran status does not significantly help the electability of those who run for the highest elected offices, it is evident that party leaders continue to think that military experience will make a difference. Indeed, the importance placed on military service was born out in the 2004 presidential election. One of the most effective advertising campaigns in that race was that of the Swift Boat Veterans for Truth (SBVT). In 2004 the SBVT ran ads as a 527 group (so named for the tax code allowing them to collect campaign donations without the same limits as political action committees) against Democratic presidential nominee John Kerry. The SBVT's mission was to call Kerry's war record into question with a focus on his tours of duty in Vietnam and the injuries that garnered him three purple hearts and bronze and silver stars. The SBVT also took issue with Kerry's 1971 statements that war crimes were being committed by American soldiers in Vietnam. SBVT was funded and assisted in 2004 by supporters of George W. Bush and led by John O'Neill, who had been hired in the early 1970s by Nixon White House staffer Charles Colson in an explicit attempt to "take down" Kerry after his testimony against the Vietnam War before the Senate. Colson orchestrated press conferences so that O'Neill could attack Kerry's antiwar stance and created Vietnam Veterans for a Just Peace, featuring O'Neill as the primary spokesperson.

The Colson–O'Neill Vietnam Veterans for a Just Peace plan is an example of attacking a candidate's military service to undermine his appearance of heroic virtue and hence electability. Indeed, political pundits have suggested that Republicans are typically seen as stronger on security and national defense than Democrats and that Democratic candidates can bolster their image by having a military background. The truth of the charges levied by O'Neill and the SBVT were found to be contrary to evidence the media uncovered in Navy records and in interviews with other Swift Boat commanders who had served with Kerry, including a *Chicago Tribune* editor who had served with Kerry. Kerry's silence in the face of their criticism may have damaged his credibility and hence his electability. George W. Bush, Kerry's opponent, remained on the outskirts of the controversy— possibly to divert attention from questions about his own military service. Bush, who was enlisted in the Texas National Guard and then transferred to the Alabama National Guard, appears to have been absent from his Alabama unit between 1972 and 1973 according to available records.

Adding to the diversion of attention was the news story aired by CBS that contained forged documents supporting the inconsistencies in Bush's National Guard record—a story for which CBS later fired four executives. These documents gave the impression that allegations about Bush's absence from the Alabama National Guard were false. The process of diverting attention from his own service and allowing the SBVT to attack's Kerry's record could have given Bush the small lead that he needed in order to win against Kerry (exit polls reported that veterans alone voted for Bush over Kerry by a 58 percent to 42 percent margin).

### Veteran Status and War Policy

While veteran status has historically given presidential candidates only a slight edge and has given no edge to House candidates, differences in the ways in which veterans govern might contribute to their greater electability. Chris Gelpi and Peter Feaver examined the proportion of policy makers

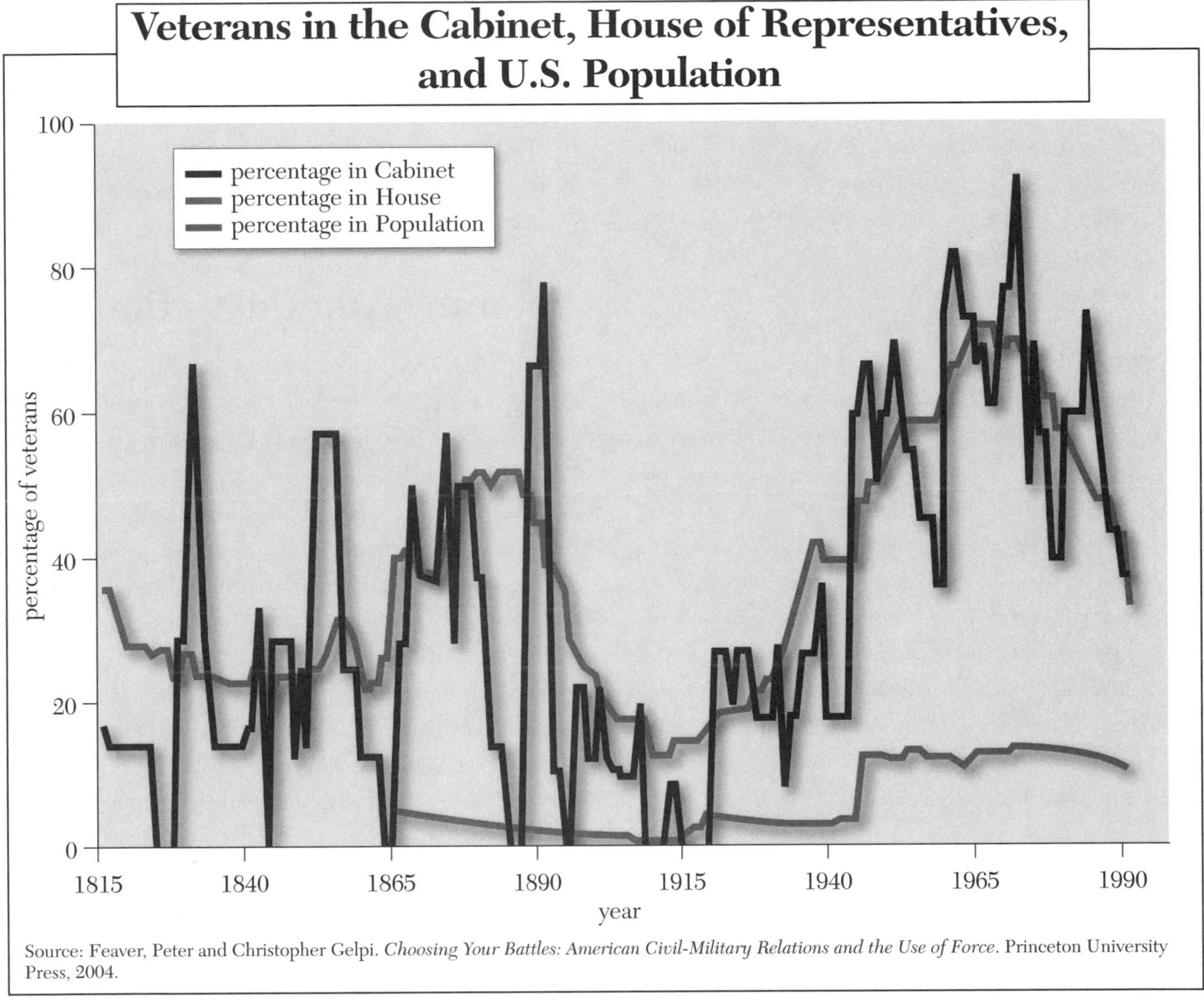


*A chart comparing the percent of veterans in Congress and the Cabinet to the percent of veterans in the general population.*

(members of the House of Representatives and the president's Cabinet, including the president and vice president) with military experience and examined military conflicts from 1816 to 1992. The percentage of veterans in the Cabinet and House rose at rates greater than those of veterans in the general population after the conclusion of the Civil War, World War I, and World War II (see figure). During the course of the 176 years represented in this study, the percentage of veterans in the House ranged from 13 to 72 percent of total membership, those of veterans in the Cabinet from 0 to 92 percent.

Gelpi and Feaver examined conflicts during these 176 years to determine whether, controlling for relevant variables, veteran policy makers were more inclined to initiate military action during disputes with other countries. They divided the disputes into those they labeled "interventionist," against countries where their military had at least a 99:1 disadvantage against the United States and were not allied with a major power. They labeled as "realpolitik" those disputes against countries that did not meet either of the two criteria for an interventionist dispute. In general, they found that the higher the proportion of policy makers having military experience, the lower the probability that the United States would initiate a military dispute; the higher the proportion of policy makers with military experience, the more likely the United States was to initiate a realpolitik rather than an interventionist military dispute. Of particular note was the fact that the greater the number of policy makers with military experience, the greater the level of force used once a conflict had been initiated. That is, historical data show differences in the way that veterans decide to engage in military actions: veterans are more likely to be cautious about entering into conflicts, especially those in which vital U.S. security interests are not at play; but once they decide to engage in war, they use more force. This propensity is consistent with the military-crafted Weinberger–Powell Doctrine.

Historical data confirm that veteran status may not actually influence the electability of a political candidate and that military intervention has been lowest when the proportion of veterans in the Cabinet and in the House is highest. Contemporary pundits have suggested that candidates can enhance their image if they draw attention to their military background in a post–September 11 world. Certainly, a race as close as the 2004 presidential election, ultimately decided by 120,000 votes in the state of Ohio, could have been influenced by military service. In any event, it remains to be seen whether veteran status will continue to be regarded as important in the decades to come.

**Bibliography**

Feaver, P. D., and C. Gelpi. *Choosing Your Battles: American Civil–Military Relations and the Use of Force.* Princeton, N.J.: Princeton University Press, 2004.

Somit, A. "The Military Hero as Presidential Candidate." *The Public Opinion Quarterly* 12, no. 2 (1948): 192–200.

———, and J. Tanenhaus. "The Veteran in the Electoral Process: The House of Representatives." *The Journal of Politics* 19, no. 2 (1957): 184–201.

**Further Reading**

Key, V. O. *Politics, Parties and Pressure Groups.* 5th ed. New York: Crowell, 1964.

**Related Entries**

Civil–Military Relations; Public Opinion and Policy in Wartime; Weinberger–Powell Doctrine.

*—Reynol Junco and Peter Karsten*

# Veterans

See Bonus March; Combat, Effects of; GI Bills; Memory and War; Psychiatric Disorders, Combat Related; Tomb of the Unknown Soldier; Veteran Status and Electability; Veterans Administration; Veterans Day; specific groups.

# Veterans Administration

Military service inevitably involves some sort of sacrifice on the part of those who serve. In addition to risking loss of life or suffering a debilitating injury, military personnel typically have to devote several years of their lives to military service, time that could have been spent pursuing an education, a career, or starting a family. The realization of these sacrifices has prompted the U.S. government to offer benefits to those who have served, varying in type and substance since the end of the Revolutionary War. These benefits, which have included mustering out pay, medical care, insurance, and education benefits, are intended as both a reward for service and as compensation for time lost from civilian life. As the wars of the 20th century demanded that increased numbers of civilians be conscripted for service, the government began to offer a more comprehensive set of benefits. Several different agencies were charged with the task of administering these benefits until the creation of the Veterans Administration (VA) in 1930. Since its inception, the VA has evolved into a vast organization dedicated to administering the multitude of benefits on offer to the nation's veterans. It has aided the millions of returning soldiers in the transition back to civilian life and offered invaluable help in lessening the burden of service.

The principle that all citizens have a special obligation to care for their veterans has existed in America from the beginning of the country's history: indeed, the founders of the Plymouth colony pledged to take care of their disabled soldiers. During the Revolutionary War, the Continental Congress promised soldiers, among other things, mustering out pay and pensions for the disabled. During the first half of the 19th century, benefits were extended to widows of deceased soldiers and their surviving dependents. In addition, individual states offered medical assistance to injured veterans.

The devastating nature of the Civil War left the nation with an unprecedented number of veterans. This ultimately led to pressure on Congress, in a year when there was a federal budget surplus (1890), to increase its efforts to assist veterans. The lobbying efforts of the nationwide veterans' organization The Grand Army of the Republic ensured that Civil War veterans received the most generous and widely available pensions the government had yet offered. In addition to offering pensions to almost 1.9 million former Union Army soldiers (Confederate soldiers were denied such privileges until 1958, when only a handful remained alive), the government offered aid to disabled veterans through the National Home for Disabled Soldiers. By 1930, the government administered 10 such homes in addition to more than 50 veterans' hospitals. Veterans of the Indian Wars and the Spanish–American War received similar benefits at the end of the 19th century. But the total wars of the 20th century forced the government to create a more structured and permanent benefits system.

America's entry into World War I led to an unprecedented mobilization of manpower for an overseas conflict. More than 5 million veterans, including some 200,000 with injuries, reentered society after service. In 1917, the government for the first time recognized the need to compensate veterans for time lost from civilian life by offering World War I veterans vocational rehabilitation and insurance, as well as compensation for the disabled. As a further reward for service, the government also authorized the payment of a one-time cash bonus to be paid in 1945. But because of the financial pressures brought on by the Great Depression, veterans descended on Washington in June and July of 1932 demanding early payment of those bonuses in what would be known as the Bonus March.

Despite an increase in the scale and nature of veterans' benefits after World War I, administration of these benefits proved problematic. Responsibility for distributing the appropriate benefits fell to three different agencies: the Bureau of Pensions of the Interior Department; the National Home for Disabled Volunteer Soldiers; and the Veterans Bureau. Pres. Warren G. Harding signed the Veterans Bureau into existence in 1921, but almost immediately the agency encountered problems. Financial scandals forced Charles Forbes, the first head of the Veterans Bureau, to leave his post after only two years. Moreover, many veterans complained that having to go through three separate agencies meant wading through a lot of unnecessary bureaucracy.

To avoid administrative overlap and to save on costs in the midst of the Depression, Pres. Herbert Hoover created the Veterans Administration in July 1930. The VA assumed responsibility for the distribution of benefits and the medical care of veterans. To head the VA, Hoover chose Frank T. Hines, Charles Forbes's successor at the Veterans Bureau. Hines gained respect as a hard working and efficient VA head. But he conceived of the VA as little more than a service agency, dedicated only to enacting federal policies regarding veterans. As a consequence, the VA remained an essentially conservative agency under his tenure, administering benefits and aid but rarely promoting specific policies or a pro-veteran agenda. World War II challenged this limited mandate.

The problems experienced by returning World War I veterans, combined with the economic exigencies of massive demobilization, convinced many of the need to offer World War II veterans a more comprehensive slate of benefits. The result was the much-heralded Servicemen's Readjustment Act of 1944, or "GI Bill of Rights," signed into law by Pres. Franklin D. Roosevelt on June 22, 1944. The GI Bill offered nearly 16 million veterans unemployment compensation; home, business, and farm loans; and education benefits. More than any other act or event, the GI Bill solidified the principle that the federal government had an obligation to address the needs of both its able-bodied and disabled veterans after service.

The VA assumed responsibility for administering the new benefits. But the vast number of veterans returning and the unprecedented levels of benefits on offer demanded that the VA become a more extensive and efficient organization. Frank Hines resigned amid allegations of substandard care in some VA hospitals. Pres. Harry S. Truman appointed Gen. Omar Bradley to replace him. Bradley, the successful and well-respected World War II general, brought far more dynamism to the role of VA head. Although Bradley headed the VA for only three years, the agency increased its staffing levels and pay scale, and it played a more active role in policy making under his tenure. In addition, the establishment of a VA Department of Medicine and Surgery in 1946, headed by a chief medical director, ensured that VA hospitals proved more capable of meeting the needs of the multitude of returning injured veterans. The administrative demands of the GI Bill forced the VA to become a far more modern and efficient organization. To aid the distribution of benefits, the VA increased greatly the number of regional veterans' centers. By becoming more decentralized, the VA became much more responsive to veterans' needs. Contact with VA became a regular feature of post-service life for many veterans.

The passage of later versions of the GI Bill meant that veterans of both the Korean and Vietnam conflicts continued to receive education benefits, loans, and medical assistance through the VA. Under the Veterans Readjustment Assistance Act of 1952, Korean War veterans received benefits comparable to those of World War II, except for unemployment payments. Vietnam veterans received benefits similar to Korean veterans under the Veterans Readjustment Benefits Act of 1966 and the Vietnam Era Veterans Readjustment Assistance Acts of 1972 and 1974. The continuation of GI Bill benefits and the millions of additional veterans created by the Korean and Vietnam conflicts ensured that the VA continued to grow both in size and significance.

During the early 1970s, however, the VA drew considerable criticism from Vietnam veterans who believed that the agency was not meeting their educational and medical needs. Media reports of substandard hospital care led to an inquiry on Capitol Hill. The educational benefits offered Vietnam veterans did, at first, fall short of those offered to their World War II predecessors until Congress enacted a series of increases throughout the 1970s. Donald Johnson headed the VA from 1969 through 1974. His attitude about benefits levels in particular infuriated many Vietnam veterans. Despite the best efforts of veteran advocacy groups and numerous congresspersons and senators, Johnson repeatedly rejected calls to increase veterans benefit levels, claiming that veterans were adequately cared for. Many accused him of adhering too closely to the fiscal retrenchment of the Richard Nixon and Gerald Ford administrations and ignoring the real problems faced by Vietnam veterans. Johnson's failure to fight on behalf of veterans served as a reminder that the VA functioned primarily as an agency dedicated to administering federal policy regarding medical aid and benefits rather than as a veterans' advocacy group.

Despite its problems during the Vietnam era, the VA remained a vitally important agency within the government and in the lives of veterans. In 1973, the VA assumed control of the National Cemetery System from the Department of the Army, providing gravesites for veterans, their spouses, and dependents. Since 1979, the psychological needs of veterans suffering from combat trauma as a result of their service have been addressed by more than 200 Readjustment Counseling Service centers throughout the country. The VA established these centers essentially to help the many Vietnam veterans who suffered from post-traumatic stress disorder. Although for some these centers came too late, many more found the counseling to be an indispensable part of their readjustment to civilian life.

The VA continued to administer benefits and medical assistance to post-Vietnam era veterans. The 1976 Veterans Educational Assistance Program first offered education benefits to the all volunteer force established after 1973. Vietnam veteran Max Cleland oversaw much of this program as head of the VA under Pres. Jimmy Carter. Since 1985, veterans have received benefits under the Montgomery GI Bill. Efforts have also been made to help homeless veterans with transitional housing and aid.

The wars of the 20th century produced millions of veterans and many more dependents in the United States. By the century's end, more than 70 million Americans were eligible for a wide range of benefits from the VA. Consequently, since its inception in 1930, the agency has expanded into a vast bureaucracy. The heightened role and significance of the VA resulted in its elevation to cabinet level status when, on March 15, 1989, Pres. George H.W. Bush signed into existence the Department of Veterans Affairs. Edward Derwinski served as the first secretary of Veterans Affairs until 1992. In terms of employees, the VA ranks second only to the Department of Defense among cabinet agencies. Its budget request for the fiscal year 2006 stood at 70.8 billion dollars. It oversees more than 120 national cemeteries, 163 hospitals, and more than 850 medical clinics. The VA medical system provides for the largest medical training program in the United States and is responsible for some of the most important research currently underway on treatments for mental health, AIDS, and age-related illnesses.

As increasing numbers of personnel were needed for military service during the 20th century, there existed a clear need for a comprehensive package of benefits and a bureaucratic system modern enough to oversee their distribution. The creation of the Veterans Administration ensured that veterans could receive their appropriate benefits in an efficient manner. Because of measures such as the GI Bill, the VA—and later the Department of Veterans Affairs—has been able to assist veterans with the often difficult transition back to civilian life. It has ensured that the long-held principle that veterans deserve some form of compensation for their service has become a reality for the millions of servicemen and women who put their lives on hold in service of the nation.

**Bibliography**

Fact Sheets, Programs & Issues. Department of Veterans Affairs. <http://www1.va.gov/opa/fact> (July 26, 2005).

Knight, Amy W., and Robert L. Worden. *Veterans Benefits Administration: An Organizational History, 1776–1994.* Washington, D.C.: Veterans Benefits Administration, 1995.

Levitan, Sar A., and Joyce Zickler. *Swords Into Ploughshares: Our G.I. Bill.* Salt Lake City, Utah: Olympus Publishing, 1973.

Ross, David. *Preparing For Ulysses: Politics and Veterans During World War II.* New York: Columbia University Press, 1969.

Taussig, Michael K. *Those Who Served: Report of the Twentieth Century Fund Task Force on Policies Toward Veterans.* Millwood, N.Y.: Kraus Reprint, 1975.

V.A. History. Department of Veterans Affairs. <http://www.va.gov/about_va/vahistory.asp> (July 26, 2005).

**Further Reading**

Keene, Jennifer. *Doughboys, the Great War, and the Remaking of America.* Baltimore, Md.: Johns Hopkins University Press, 2001.

Severo, Richard, and Lewis Milford. *The Wages of War: When America's Soldiers Came Home, from Valley Forge to Vietnam.* New York: Simon & Schuster, 1989.

Skocpol, Theda. *Protecting Soldiers and Mothers: The Political Origins of Social Policy in the United States.* Cambridge, Mass.: Belknap Press of Harvard University Press, 1992.

U.S. Veterans Administration. *Annual Reports.* Washington, D.C.: U.S. Government Printing Office.

**Related Entries**

American Legion; American Veterans Committee; AMVETS; Bonus March; GI Bills; Grand Army of the Republic; Jewish War Veterans; Veterans of Foreign Wars; Vietnam Veterans of America

**Related Documents**

1833; 1932

*—Mark Boulton*

# Veterans Day

Veterans Day, formerly known as Armistice Day, officially received its name in America in 1926 through a congressional resolution. In 1917, Pres. Woodrow Wilson proclaimed that the World War I would be the "War to End All Wars." If these idealistic hopes had succeeded, November 11 might still be called Armistice Day. Within years of the holiday's proclamation, however, war broke out again in Europe. Millions more Americans were called to fight and many died in battle; in order to honor them and those who would serve in future wars, Armistice Day was renamed Veterans Day. A day reserved for remembrance and reflection was not immune, however, to the political debates surrounding most American wars, and Veterans Day often became a time when conflicting views about the necessity of specific wars were aired.

At 11:00 A.M. on November 11, 1918, World War I came to an end with the signing of the cease-fire agreement at Rethondes, France. One year later, November 11 was set aside as Armistice Day in the United States to remember the sacrifices made by men and women during the war. Veterans' parades and political speeches throughout the country emphasized the peaceful nature of the day, echoing the theme of national unity against tyranny. Since the Civil War, Memorial Day (originally Decoration Day) had traditionally been a day when the dead of all conflicts were honored during reverent ceremonies, and their graves decorated with flags and flowers. Veterans of the Civil War and the

Spanish–American War continued to honor their dead on Memorial Day in May (April in some southern states), whereas Armistice Day was designated as a national day commemorating America's participation in World War I.

Armistice Day ceremonies in the United States were similar to those observed in France and Great Britain, with processions, wreath-laying ceremonies, and a moment of silence to pay homage to those who died in the war. On the 3rd Armistice Day, November 11, 1921, America further followed the example of its allies by burying an Unknown Soldier in an impressive ceremony over an elaborate tomb at Arlington Cemetery in Virginia. The event not only bolstered efforts by the American Legion to make Armistice Day a national holiday but established rituals intended to unify a nation still ambivalent about its involvement in the war.

Although united in their desire to pay tribute to those who fought and died in the war, Americans could not agree on the precise nature and intent of Armistice Day commemorative rituals. The American Legion, the largest veterans' organization to emerge following the war, endeavored to ensure that the achievements of American veterans were remembered. Featuring hymns and prayers in memory of loved ones who had died in the war, ceremonies sponsored by the Legion emphasized the terrible cost of war and the need to work for a new, more harmonious, world order. Despite the strong message of peace, Legion parades often included a military component, including rifle or artillery salutes to the dead.

Others preferred to strip Armistice Day of its militaristic character, emphasizing instead the tragedy of war and the preservation of peace. In the 1920s a series of disarmament treaties and pacifist promises such as those of the Kellogg-Briand Pact of 1928, which outlawed the use of aggressive war by its signatories, created a sense of optimism that there might never be another war. Members of national peace movements believed war could only be stopped through disarmament and pacifism, while the American Legion insisted military preparedness provided the best assurance against future wars. The lack of consensus reflected the ongoing ambivalence Americans felt about the path that led to intervention in World War I and the ultimate purpose of the sacrifice of so many lives.

Despite years of political lobbying and campaigning by the Legion, Congress did not vote to designate Armistice Day a federal holiday until 1938. By this time, it was obvious that another war was imminent and once again Americans risked being called to fight. Emotional memories of the previous conflict stirred isolationists and peace groups to urge the government away from another foreign entanglement and toward stringent neutrality. However, after the unprovoked attack on Pearl Harbor in 1941, patriotic fervor and the perceived need to defend the nation against further attacks proved the decisive factors that united the nation behind another war.

After 1945, Americans continued to observe Armistice Day on November 11 as the Legion opened its membership to a new generation of veterans. Together they joined each year in the same rituals and commemorative ceremonies established previously. In 1954, Pres. Dwight D. Eisenhower signed a bill proclaiming that November 11 would now be called Veterans Day, to honor veterans of all American wars. In 1971 Pres. Richard Nixon declared it a federal holiday on the second Monday in November. Seven years later, however, the nation returned the annual observance of Veterans Day to November 11, regardless of where it fell in the week. Thus, the historical significance of the date was preserved and attention once again was focused on the initial purpose of Veterans Day—to honor the nation's veterans, not to provide Americans with a long weekend.

Despite its origins in World War I, each generation of veterans has embraced Veterans Day as a moment for collective reflection. Each war leaves in its wake a plethora of monuments, holidays, cemeteries, museums, and archives that serve as reminders of the human sacrifice war entails. These remain, like Veterans Day, effective in providing people with a sense of common identity as Americans no matter how divided they may otherwise be by class, region, gender, religion, or race.

**Bibliography**

"The Beginnings and Results of Memorial Day." *The American Legion Weekly* (May 26, 1922): 16–17.

Gillis, John R. *Commemorations, the Politics of National Identity.* Princeton, N.J.: Princeton University Press, 1994.

Piehler, G. Kurt. *Remembering War the American Way*. Washington, D.C., and London: Smithsonian Institution Press, 1995.

Worthington, R.C. "Homecoming." *The American Legion Magazine* (November 1938): 3, 48.

**Further Reading**

Gregory, Adrian. *The Silence of Memory, Armistice Day, 1919–1946.* The Legacy of the Great War series, ed. Jay Winter. Oxford and Providence, R.I.: Berg, 1994.

Keene, Jennifer D. *Doughboys, the Great War, and the Remaking of America.* Baltimore, Md.: Johns Hopkins University Press, 2001.

Krythe, Mayme R. *All About American Holidays*. New York: Harper: 1962.

"Veteran's Day." <http://www.patriotism.org/veterans_day>.

Wecter, Dixon. *When Johnny Comes Marching Home.* Cambridge, Mass.: Houghton Mifflin, 1944.

**Related Entries**

American Legion; Memorial Day; Tomb of the Unknown Soldier

*—Lisa M. Budreau*

# Veterans of Foreign Wars

The Veterans of Foreign Wars (VFW) is an organization open to all American veterans who have earned service badges for participating in overseas military campaigns. Founded after the Spanish–American War, the VFW has served as a fraternal association dedicated to the welfare of American veterans and their families. To that end, the VFW has played an important role as a political lobbyist in furthering veterans' legislative agendas at the federal and state levels. Since its inception, the VFW has also voiced veterans' perspectives on American national security and foreign relations issues. Joining with other patriotic organizations, the VFW has championed unswerving dedication to American political institutions and supported the creation of memorials and commemorations of the nation's wars. Comprised of local units called posts, the VFW reaches into thousands of communities across the United States. At both national and local levels, the organization mediates overseas veterans' relationship with the rest of American society.

### The Origins of the VFW

The VFW traces its origins to two veterans' groups, the National Association of the Army of the Philippines and the American Veterans of Foreign Service, both of which formed in 1899 after the Spanish–American War. These groups operated independently until a merger in 1913. After a referendum in 1914, the original organizations consolidated under the banner of the Veterans of Foreign Wars of the United States. The organization initially competed for members with another group, United Spanish War Veterans. After 1914, the VFW opened its membership to all honorably discharged veterans who served on foreign shores or in hostile waters in any war, campaign, or expedition recognized by Congress with a campaign badge or service clasp. By expanding the organization beyond service in Cuba and the Philippines during the Spanish–American War, the VFW opened its doors to some two million potential new members of the American Expeditionary Force (AEF) sent to France in World War I.

Besides seeing the war as an opportunity to attract new members, the VFW also tried to exert some influence on defense policy. Between 1914 and 1917, while the United States stayed neutral as World War I raged in Europe, the VFW argued for a greater level of military preparedness in the event the United States joined the fighting. The VFW wanted to prevent a repeat of the difficulties caused by the hasty and poorly organized mobilization during the Spanish–American War.

During World War I, the VFW waived membership fees for active duty military personnel and heavily recruited the AEF camps in France for new members. Former president Theodore Roosevelt became one of the VFW's wartime recruits based on his service in the Spanish–American War, thus stimulating publicity for the organization. While the VFW membership grew to 20,000 in 1919, it did not enjoy the same success in the immediate postwar period as the organization's rival for Great War veterans, the American Legion.

During the 1920s, the American Legion eclipsed the VFW in terms of membership and political clout. However, the two organizations worked in tandem throughout the decade to improve benefits, medical care, and pensions for all veterans, widows, and orphans. In addition, both lobbied for the payment of a bonus to World War I veterans as "adjusted compensation" for the meager wages received during the conflict. In 1924, a deferred bonus payment was granted to World War I veterans in the form of interest-bearing certificates, which would mature in 1945.

In 1921, the VFW established a National Service Bureau in Washington, D.C., to promote veterans' interests. In 1922, the VFW initiated the annual Buddy Poppy drive; every Memorial Day, lapel-pin poppies are sold by VFW members to benefit disabled veterans and to remind Americans of the costs of war. Throughout the late 1920s, the VFW also sponsored legislation in Congress to make Francis Scott Key's "The Star-Spangled Banner" the official national anthem of the United States. In 1931, this drive finally succeeded.

In the 1930s, the VFW grew dramatically as a result of the organization's leadership in securing immediate cash payment of the World War I bonus and for helping reverse drastic cuts in veteran benefits enacted by the Economy Act of 1933. The VFW never challenged the primacy of the American Legion as the largest veteran organization. Yet, between 1929 and 1941, the VFW surged from fewer than 70,000 to 214,000 members, more than tripling its membership despite the fact that the Depression wreaked havoc on most dues-paying voluntary associations. The VFW played an important role in the origins of the 1932 Bonus March, in which more than 40,000 World War I veterans marched on Washington to demand early payment of their bonus; the VFW fought persistently for immediate payment of the bonus at a time when the Legion opposed the measure. From 1932 to 1936, the VFW never wavered in its support of immediate cash payment, a position that brought it into direct confrontation with the popular Pres. Franklin D. Roosevelt. On foreign policy matters, the VFW joined with those in favor of American isolationism and promoted strict neutrality in world affairs. The VFW's populist message in the 1930s brought the organization enormous institutional gains and placed it in the middle of Depression-era politics.

World War II brought a new infusion of members into the VFW. While the VFW had supported the slow drift towards war after 1940, after the Japanese attack on Pearl Harbor the organization vigorously joined the war effort. During the war, VFW members served as civil-defense personnel and training camp instructors. Many others renewed their military service at advanced ages. In 1942, the VFW instituted a pilot-training program that prepared desperately needed new recruits for flying duty in the armed services. Moreover, in 1944, the VFW became involved in the legislative battle over the proper manner in which to compensate returning veterans and ease their readjustment into civilian life. The VFW initially opposed the expansive benefits that were outlined in the Servicemen's Readjustment Act, more popularly known as the GI Bill, out of fears that the nation would abandon such an expensive system once wartime patriotism flagged. Ultimately, the VFW joined with the bill's champion, the American Legion, in helping secure legislative victory. With the GI Bill, the United States passed one of the most expansive pieces of social welfare legislation in the country's history and profoundly shaped postwar society by providing education, housing, and job training to millions of veterans.

After World War II, the VFW stood at its greatest political and numerical strength, with some 1.5 million members. During the Cold War, the VFW continued the organization's record of staunch anticommunism begun in the years following the Bolshevik Russian Revolution of 1917. In the waging of the Cold War, from U.S. involvement in Korea to Vietnam, the VFW supported an aggressive and militant foreign policy for the United States in battling communism. Even when public support for the Vietnam War waned, the VFW never wavered in its opinion of the war's merits, nor of American soldiers' honorable service. From World War II through the Vietnam conflict, the VFW attempted to account for and repatriate prisoners of war and soldiers missing in action (POW–MIAs). After the Vietnam War, the search for living POW–MIAs and the attempts to identify the remains of the unidentified dead became an even larger VFW project as it worked with the U.S. government and the governments and private citizens of Korea and Vietnam.

After the Vietnam War, the VFW became an outspoken critic of the Veterans Administration's (VA) handling of veterans' post-traumatic stress disorder and of the physical ailments associated with exposure to the chemical defoliant

Agent Orange. In these battles, the VFW struggled with the uncooperative VA and military bureaucracies before finally securing treatment and compensation, respectively. After the Persian Gulf War in 1991, the VFW supported research into what became known as Gulf War Syndrome, a debilitating but mysterious illness, and challenged the U.S. military to provide information on vaccinations given to the troops and possible other causes of the syndrome. The post-Vietnam era also found the VFW very active in supporting public memorials for the veterans of the Korean and Vietnam wars. The Vietnam War and Korean War memorials on the Washington Mall were dedicated in 1982 and 1995, respectively.

Throughout the history of the organization, the VFW has been an outspoken champion of veterans' benefits, healthcare, and pensions, serving as a vital intermediary between veterans and the federal government. As the VFW brings together veterans in thousands of communities across the country, it also acts as a constant reminder of the long-term impact of war on the American people.

**Bibliography**

Bottoms, Bill. *The VFW: An Illustrated History of the Veterans of Foreign Wars of the United Sates.* Bethesda, Md.: Woodbine House, 1991.

Mason, Herbert Molloy, Jr. *VFW: Our First Century, 1899–1999.* Lenexa, Kans.: Addax Publishing, 1999.

Ortiz, Stephen R. "'Soldier-Citizens': The Veterans of Foreign Wars and Veteran Political Activism from the Bonus March to the GI Bill." Ph.D. diss., University of Florida, 2004.

**Further Reading**

Daniels, Roger. *The Bonus March: An Episode of the Great Depression.* Westport, Conn.: Greenwood, 1971.

Keene, Jennifer D. *Doughboys, the Great War, and the Remaking of America.* Baltimore, Md.: Johns Hopkins University Press, 2001.

Pencak, William. *For God and Country: The American Legion, 1919–1941.* Boston: Northeastern University Press, 1989.

Ross, Davis R.B. *Preparing for Ulysses: Politics and Veterans during World War II.* New York: Columbia University Press, 1969.

The Veterans of Foreign Wars Web Page. <http://www.vfw.org/>.

**Related Entries**

Agent Orange; American Legion; Bonus March; GI Bills; Memorials and Monuments; Preparedness Movement; Prisoners of War; Psychiatric Disorders, Combat Related; Spanish–American War; "Star-Spangled Banner, The"; Veterans Administration

*—Stephen R. Ortiz*

# Victory Gardens

The campaign to encourage Victory Gardens was probably the most successful home front effort waged by the U.S. government during World War II. Victory Gardens were originally intended to supplement the food produced by commercial growers in order to prevent shortages around the country. They became important morale-building and unifying weapons as well, providing emotional support for many Americans, who felt that their participation in the Victory Gardens program helped the country's war effort. Victory Gardens were so successful in supplementing the country's food supply that by 1945 American per capita consumption of fresh vegetables and vitamin C reached its all-time high.

Victory Gardens had their roots in World War I. By the time the United States entered the war in April 1917, government officials had studied how European countries mobilized their nations for war. Preferring voluntary compliance to regulation, as many of the European nations did, the federal government asked citizens to conserve food and to plant gardens to produce as much of their own food as possible. Known as War Gardens, these plots sprang up everywhere and were regarded as testaments to patriotism. Talks by the Committee on Public Information's Four-Minute Men promoted War Gardens to audiences around the country. The National War Garden Commission prepared publications with instructions on planting and caring for vegetable gardens. When World War I ended, the Commission continued to call for individual gardens to meet peacetime needs. After the armistice, the name given to these plots was changed to Victory Gardens. The return of peace, however, led to the virtual disappearance of Victory Gardens by 1920.

## VICTORY GARDENS

During the Great Depression, various governmental bodies called on citizens to return to the World War I tradition in creating gardens to feed the needy. Peacetime Victory Gardens, however, failed to catch on, possibly because many who needed the food lacked money for seeds and gardening tools.

The beginning of World War II, however, saw the resurrection of the Victory Garden program. Before the Japanese attack on Pearl Harbor in December 1941, the United States was supplying food to Great Britain and the Soviet Union. After the United States entered the war, many farm laborers were called into the armed forces. Hence, the demand for food increased, while the labor supply declined. The Department of Agriculture took the lead in calling for individual Americans to plant Victory Gardens to make up for shortfalls in production. Because most foods were rationed during the war, Victory Gardens were also a means of supplementing American diets.

In December 1941, Secretary of Agriculture Claude Wickard arranged a National Defense Garden Conference in Washington, D.C. Representatives of gardening organizations, seed companies, the agricultural press, and other organizations met to discuss how to encourage Victory Gardens. The program they soon developed proved to be very successful. Its goals were defined as increasing the production and consumption of fresh vegetables and fruits, encouraging the preservation of surplus vegetables and fruits by individual families, allowing families to save money by not having to purchase produce, providing opportunities for urban dwellers to garden, and maintaining the morale and spiritual well-being of the nation.

Although voluntary, the Victory Garden program proved to be extraordinarily popular. Local organizations, such as defense councils, arranged for expert gardeners to provide advice to novices. The National Institute of Municipal Law Officers developed model ordinances for city and town governments that would allow Victory Gardens on public property and would discourage theft. Businesses promoted Victory Gardens for their employees. Some, such as Westinghouse, provided land for employees' clubs as well as sponsored advertisements about the program in newspapers and magazines. Millions of Americans dug up their backyards to plant gardens. In urban areas, public gardens were created on municipal property and vacant lots, and city-dwellers were able to reserve a plot for their own planting. Schools created gardens that were worked by the students; the products of these gardens often were served in the cafeterias. Other organizations—from prisons to Catholic convents—created gardens. It was estimated that 22 million families had planted gardens during the 1942 growing season. The U.S. Department of Agriculture hoped that by 1943 there would be 18 million Victory Gardens in the country. Results surpassed that expectation, however. At least 20 million gardens were reported in Gallup polls in the early spring, and *House & Garden* predicted that 25.5 million families would plant gardens in 1943. About 40 percent of the vegetables and fruits consumed by Americans during World War II were produced in Victory Gardens.

Because many Americans had not raised their own vegetables and fruit before, the U.S. Department of Agriculture published a series of pamphlets with directions for creating Victory Gardens. Individual states also formed their own Victory Garden committees and published guidebooks for gardeners. Publications included information about when to plant different crops in different regions and what kind of growing conditions worked best for different plants. Sample layouts for the gardens were popular, as were tips on what kinds of plants would yield the best harvests. Seed companies published instructional booklets and prepared packets of seeds for different areas. Lists of recommended vegetables were published, with an eye toward a balance of vitamins. Authorities cited the health benefits of consuming fresh produce, aiming to prevent malnutrition and foster a healthy population. Recommended vegetables included lettuce, kale, and cabbage in the leafy category, and suggested root vegetables included potatoes, turnips, and carrots. Over one-third of the vegetables produced were tomatoes, since tomato plants could yield abundantly in a limited space. Organizations also published pamphlets with instructions on how best to preserve surplus vegetables and fruits. People dried and froze the produce they grew, but the most popular method of preserving Victory Garden's crops was canning. Americans canned an average of 165 jars of food per family annually during the war.

*A man buying seeds for a Victory Garden in May of 1943, with a government-issue poster supporting the Victory Garden program in the background. (From the collections of the Library of Congress)*

While Victory Gardens produced an enormous amount of food for civilian consumers, they also played an important role in helping morale and building national unity. Gardening helped give families a sense of order in a world that seemed otherwise chaotic. Like the paper and scrap metal drives that were popular during the war, Victory Gardens allowed civilians to feel they were contributing to the war effort. As many posters reminded them, "Our Food is Fighting." Women, children, and the elderly could all take part.

Rationing ended soon after the Japanese surrender, and the immediate need for Victory Gardens disappeared. American society soon returned to its old habits, with only fond memories of a time when everyone pulled together to grow vegetables for victory.

**Bibliography**

Hayes, Joanne Lamb. *Grandma's Wartime Kitchen: World War II and the Way We Cooked.* New York: St. Martin's Press, 2000.

Miller, Char. "In the Sweat of Our Brow: Citizenship in American Domestic Practice During WW II—Victory Gardens," *The Journal of American Culture* 26, no. 3 (2003): 395–409.

**Further Reading**

Bentley, Amy Lynn. *Eating for Victory: United States Food Rationing and the Politics of Domesticity During World War Two.* Urbana: University of Illinois Press, 1998.

Boswell, Victor R. *Victory Gardens*. Washington, D.C.: U.S. Department of Agriculture, 1943.

Kains, M.G. *The Original Victory Garden Book.* New York: Stein & Day, 1978.

**Related Entries**

Civil Defense; Rationing

*—Tim J. Watts*

# Vietnam Veterans Against the War

The Vietnam Veterans Against the War (VVAW) was formed in April 1967 by a handful of American servicemen who had returned to the United States after their tours of duty in Vietnam. It gained national prominence over the next several years for its often radical antiwar activities but faded from public view with the end of the conflict in Vietnam. It regained the spotlight briefly in 2004 when one of its former leaders, John F. Kerry, became the Democratic Party's candidate for the presidency.

VVAW initially cultivated a staid public profile, sending well-groomed spokesmen to lobby elected officials to reduce spending on the war. By late 1967, new chapters were being organized in the Midwest and on the West Coast. The Tet Offensive in January–February 1968, however, prompted a change in VVAW's profile and approach. The Vietnamese communists' display of apparently formidable military resources discredited Pres. Lyndon Johnson's direction of the war. In New England, VVAW chapters supported Johnson's antiwar challenger, Sen. Eugene McCarthy, in the New Hampshire primary, and McCarthy's victory there contributed to Johnson's decision not to seek reelection.

Radicalized by the 1968 assassinations of antiwar presidential candidate Robert F. Kennedy and nonviolent civil rights activist Martin Luther King Jr., VVAW temporarily lost mainstream veterans' support. It was revitalized the following year, when public protests against Pres. Richard M. Nixon's continuation of the war led to increased membership, including urban veterans with links to radical organizations such as the Black Panthers. Revelations about the killing of Vietnamese civilians by U.S. Army units at My Lai further boosted membership by increasing VVAW's appeal to veterans troubled by their experiences in Vietnam. The organization still had only a few hundred members, however, until the late spring of 1970, when antiwar protests accelerated nationwide following the deployment of U.S. combat forces into Cambodia. The subsequent shooting of students by National Guard troops during an antiwar demonstration at Kent State University in Ohio drew more middle-of-the-road Americans to the antiwar movement. VVAW gained hundreds of new members, many with middle- and upper-class backgrounds.

At the same time, however, the organization's leaders began to cooperate more closely with radical political groups. Besides the Black Panthers, VVAW also worked with the Citizens' Commission of Inquiry into War Crimes in Indochina, which, following the publicity surrounding the My Lai massacre, was trying to identify Vietnam War veterans willing to speak openly about Americans' violations of international and military laws in Southeast Asia.

VVAW activists also adopted more militant antiwar tactics, including disrupting meetings of local draft boards. In September 1970, VVAW leaders organized Operation RAW (Rapid American Withdrawal), in which some 150 veterans and supporters, many wearing disheveled military uniforms with service medals and antiwar paraphernalia, marched from Morristown, New Jersey, to Valley Forge, Pennsylvania. On the way they acted out battlefield scenarios, such as the capture and interrogation of civilians, in a chaotic and sometimes dangerous street theater that condemned U.S. involvement in Vietnam. A climactic rally included speeches by actors and prominent antiwar activists Donald Sutherland and Jane Fonda, and by Navy Vietnam veteran, Silver Star recipient, and VVAW member John Forbes Kerry of Massachusetts. Kerry became a spokesman for VVAW and traveled to Paris, where he met with Vietnamese communist representatives.

In early 1971, VVAW organized its own "investigation" of illegal activities by U.S. forces in Vietnam, including alleged crimes against Vietnamese civilians. Modeled on the unofficial International War Crimes Tribunals, VVAW's Winter Soldier Investigation opened in Detroit in February 1971, financed in part by Fonda and musician Graham

Nash. The "investigation" elicited personal testimonies from veterans as well as hearsay about abuses and atrocities committed in Vietnam.

In April 1971, VVAW organized Dewey Canyon III, a reference to the U.S.-supported military incursion into Laos that had begun in January. Some 1,000 veterans participated in Dewey Canyon III. A few hundred marched to Arlington National Cemetery, while others assembled on the steps of the U.S. Capitol to throw down their service medals and ribbons. Congressional hearings were convened, and in nationally televised testimony John Kerry urged the country to turn away from the "'barbaric war'" in Vietnam.

During this period, VVAW pioneered veterans' "rap groups," in which veterans discussed their memories of the war, disenchantment with the military, and hardships in readjusting to civilian life as Vietnam veterans. For many veterans these "rap sessions" provided social and psychological support. Mental health professionals used the "rap group" model in Veterans' Administration initiatives to treat war-related stress and, later, to gain clinical recognition of the post-traumatic stress disorder syndrome.

By the end of 1971, however, VVAW membership was in decline. To regain media attention, VVAW activists undertook several high profile actions, including temporarily seizing the Statue of Liberty in New York harbor. President Nixon's decision to mine North Vietnam's harbors in May 1972 re-energized some VVAW chapters, as did Jane Fonda's visit to Hanoi in July. Even so, the winding down of American involvement in Vietnam left the VVAW without a mission. The organization remained intact, albeit with a substantially decreased membership. It published a newsletter and later a Web site, while continuing to advocate veterans' benefits issues.

The VVAW experienced a renewal of interest during the 2004 presidential campaign when John Kerry, then a U.S. senator from Massachusetts, became the Democratic Party's presidential candidate. A private organization, the Swift Boat Veterans for Truth, which included veterans who had served with Kerry in Vietnam, challenged Kerry's truthfulness about the circumstances surrounding the award of his several Vietnam service medals. Criticism of Kerry's actions also proliferated with the new phenomenon of Internet "blogs," individuals' commentaries posted on political-interest websites. Kerry defended his wartime actions and acknowledged his VVAW activities, including his meetings with communist diplomats in Paris, but also apologized for any distress his antiwar advocacy had caused other veterans. VVAW found new life rebutting the charges made against Kerry by the Swift Boat group and other critics. Even so, Kerry lost the election to incumbent George W. Bush by 3.5 million votes.

**Bibliography**

Moser, Richard. *The New Winter Soldiers: GI and Veterans Dissent During the Vietnam Era.* Piscataway, N.J.: Rutgers University Press, 1996.

Nicosia, Gerald. *Home to War: A History of the Vietnam Veterans' Movement.* New York: Crown Press, 2001.

O'Neill, Robert, and Jerome Corsi. *Unfit for Command: Swift Boat Veterans Speak Out Against John Kerry.* Washington, D.C.: Regnery Publishing, 2004.

Verrone, Richard Burks, and Laura M. Calkins. *Voices from Vietnam.* London: David and Charles, 2005.

**Further Reading**

DeBenedetti, Charles, with Charles Chatfield. *An American Ordeal: The Antiwar Movement of the Vietnam Era.* Syracuse, N.Y.: Syracuse University Press, 1990.

Lifton, Robert Jay. *Home from the War: Vietnam Veterans—Neither Victims Nor Executioners.* New York: Touchstone Press, 1973.

Small, Melvin, and William D. Hoover, eds. *Give Peace a Chance: Exploring the Vietnam Antiwar Movement.* Syracuse, N.Y.: Syracuse University Press, 1992.

Stacewicz, Richard. *Winter Soldiers: An Oral History of the Vietnam Veterans Against the War.* Boston: Twayne, 1997.

Wells, Tom. *The War Within: America's Battle Over Vietnam.* Berkeley: University of California Press, 1994.

**Related Entries**

*Born on the Fourth of July*; Psychiatric Disorders, Combat Related; Race Riots; Selective Service System; Veterans Administration; Vietnam Veterans of America; Vietnam War

*—Laura M. Calkins*

# Vietnam Veterans of America

The Vietnam War enlarged existing mainstream veterans' organizations in the United States and produced many new veterans' associations, among them the Vietnam Veterans of America (VVA). These newer organizations sprang up in part because many of the more than 2.5 million soldiers, sailors, and airmen who served within the borders of Vietnam (and nearly a million more who were stationed in the Southeast Asian theater of operations) felt more comfortable working with groups that better reflected their generation's outlook. The "founding principle" of the Vietnam Veterans of America makes this point crystal clear: "never again shall one generation of veterans abandon another." The organization seeks "to promote and support the full range of issues important to Vietnam veterans, to create a new identity for that generation of veterans, and to change public perception of Vietnam veterans."

Vietnam veterans experienced several outwardly novel situations that seemed to require the creation of supportive organizations to service both traditional wartime problems as well as distinctively Vietnam-related difficulties. Along with such customary troubles as physical disabilities and family or career adjustments that returning veterans of earlier wars faced, Vietnam veterans also had to deal with a host of dreadful, apparently unique circumstances: a lengthy, unpopular war that the United States lost; accusations of widespread atrocities committed by American soldiers upon Vietnamese civilians; a popular perception that large numbers of these soldiers were drug addicted and socially dysfunctional; war-induced psychological damage labeled post-traumatic stress disorder; physical maladies resulting from improper handling of such toxic substances as Agent Orange; ecological devastation; and numerous media images that clearly demonstrated the horrors of that war.

Television coverage of the Vietnam War provided graphic, ghastly, and immediate images that media in prior wars could not convey. Although similar terrible consequences occurred in past wars, the media's ability to chronicle combat had vastly improved by the time of hostilities in Vietnam. Photographs or footage of self-immolated monks, summarily executed Viet Cong, a napalmed girl, and swaths of denuded jungle captured war as it really is, not as it was typically presented in Hollywood recreations, which by the 1960s had become America's chief purveyor of the popular history of previous conflicts. Perhaps the media of earlier, more popular military campaigns were willing to downplay, delay, or overlook reportage of negative incidents, thereby diluting or eliminating their impact. In Vietnam such imagery became defining, damning representations of that Cold War conflict. And all of those images reflected on Vietnam veterans, whom the VVA hoped to redeem.

Bobby Muller formed Vietnam Veterans of America in 1978. It was chartered by Congress in 1986 and claims a membership of more than 50,000. Headquartered in Silver Spring, Maryland, it is managed by a national board of directors. It is funded exclusively by private contributions (cash, household goods donations, etc.) and organized as a not-for-profit corporation. The VVA has 43 state councils and 525 local chapters, and publishes *The VVA Veteran* and several guides to veterans' benefits. VVA Service Representatives are available throughout the nation to assist Vietnam veterans in need. The VVA also engages in nonpartisan research topics "pertaining to the relationship between Vietnam-era veterans and the American society, the Vietnam War experience, the role of the United States in securing peaceful coexistence for the world community and other nations . . .".

The VVA lobbies members of Congress, the president, and other influential Americans to improve the treatment of needy Vietnam veterans. According to the VVA Website, such improvements include "physical and cultural . . . growth and development," as well as the promotion of "self-respect [and] self-confidence . . .". It also involves ending discrimination against Vietnam veterans in general and women and minorities in particular; securing government benefits for Vietnam veterans as a whole and assisting individuals in obtaining them; helping the widows and orphans of deceased veterans; and aiding homeless veterans and those with other war-related disabilities.

Unlike most veteran's organizations, however, the VVA leans a bit to the left on many issues—or, as VVA congressional liaison John Terzano put it, from its early days the organization had "a progressive agenda when it [came] to working on justice issues and war and peace issues, and foreign policy issues." For example, the VVA went to court (*Vietnam Veterans of America, et al. v. Robert S. McNamara, et al.*) to obtain data about veterans who were exposed to chemical and biological agents during the 1950s and 1960s in Shipboard Hazard and Defense (SHAD) testing—just as Korean War-era military personnel were exposed to atomic testing and Vietnam veterans to Agent Orange. Nor did Bobby Muller's trip to Hanoi to investigate issues involving Agent Orange and troops missing in action (MIAs), underwritten by *Penthouse Magazine*, endear the organization to most other veterans' organizations. The VVA also fought with rival veterans' groups for influence, most notably with the Veterans of Foreign Wars (VFW), over Pres. Ronald Reagan's appointment of John Behan as head of the Veterans' Administration in 1981. The VFW successfully opposed Behan's nomination because he had organized veterans who had claimed exposure to Agent Orange. Nonetheless, the VVA did produce successful results, including the creation of Vietnam Veterans Week (May 28–June 3), prompting the study of Agent Orange, and revising the Vietnam Veterans' Act to favor veterans with service-related disabilities.

VVA publications provide an accurate indication of the organization's goals and activities. Thus VVA guides include booklets with such titles as *The Guide on VA* (U.S. Department of Veterans Affairs) *Claims and Appeals*; *Guide on Agent Orange*, *Guide on PTSD* (Post-Traumatic Stress Disorder), and *Guide to Veterans Preference*. Its journal, *The VVA Veteran*, similarly features articles whose topics veterans want discussed. The July 2004 issue, for example, contains an interview with Twyla Tharp, the choreographer of the Broadway play *Movin' Out*. The play deals with the problems of three young Long Island men upon returning home from Vietnam. The issue also reviews *In the Shadow of the Blade*, a documentary that traces the path of a restored OH-1H "Huey" helicopter across America, drawing to it at each stop Vietnam veterans and their loved ones and friends who can reconnect with each other, revitalize old memories, and come to terms with the past. Another article deals with Vietnam Veterans' Park in Nashville, where a wall displays the names of Tennessee's 1,289 soldiers who died in that conflict, and a plaque that recognizes all state veterans "who served with distinction and valor, but often without recognition." The issue also contains a book review by preeminent Vietnam War scholar George Herring, assessing the VVA's own publication, *Inside the Pentagon Papers*, by John Prados (an established specialist of the conflict) and Margaret Porter. Also included are articles and reports touching on PTSD, substance abuse, women veterans, homeless veterans, veterans' benefits, reunions, methods for locating veterans, and health concerns. Other issues investigate the Vietnam Veterans Memorial, Operation Baby Life, MIAs—these and other subjects still vital to the lives of those who served in Vietnam.

By organizing their Vietnam comrades, by publishing pertinent studies relating to veterans' affairs, and by conducting hard-nosed lobbying, the Vietnam Veterans of America became a political force. Though not a traditional veterans' organization, the VVA has likely improved the lot of Vietnam veterans and their families by putting effective political pressure on Washington politicians. The VVA also contributed to the ongoing rehabilitation of the Vietnam veteran's image, from one of pitiable loser to noble warrior.

**Bibliography**

Brende, Joel Osler, and Erwin Randolph Parson. *Vietnam Veterans: The Road to Recovery.* New York: Plenum Press, 1985.

Scott, Wilbur J. *Vietnam Veterans Since the War: The Politics of PTSD, Agent Orange, and the National Memorial.* Norman: University of Oklahoma Press, 2003.

Vietnam Veterans of America. <http://www.vva.org> (July 23, 2005).

**Further Reading**

Bonior, David, Stephen Champlin, and Timothy Kolly. *The Vietnam Veteran: A History of Neglect.* New York: Praeger, 1984.

Burkett, Bernard G., and Glenna Whitley. *Stolen Valor: How the Vietnam Generation Was Robbed of Its Heroes and Its History.* Dallas, Tex.: Verity Press, 1998.

Hunt, Andrew. *The Turning: A History of Vietnam Veterans Against the War.* New York: New York University Press, 1999.

Lifton, Robert Jay. *Home From the War: Neither Victims Nor Executioners.* New York: Basic Books, 1973.

Scruggs, Jan, and Joel Swerdlow. *To Heal a Nation: The Vietnam Veterans Memorial.* New York: Harper and Row, 1985.

Shay, Jonathan. *Odysseus in America: Combat Trauma and the Trials of Homecoming.* New York: Scribner, 2002.

U. S. Congress. House Committee on Veterans' Affairs, Subcommittee on Oversight and Investigations. *Social Services for Vietnam Veterans and Their Families: Current Programs and Future Directions.* Washington, D.C.: Government Printing Office, 1995.

**Related Entries**

Veterans Administration; Veterans Day; Veterans of Foreign Wars; Vietnam Veterans against the War; Vietnam War

—*Thomas D. Reins*

# Vietnam War

(1964–75)

The Vietnam War was perhaps the most important and influential event in American history in the last half of the 20th century. That war, which claimed the lives of more than 58,000 American soldiers and millions of Vietnamese, was certainly not, in human terms, the costliest conflict in American history; the American Civil War and World War II each claimed far more American lives. The Vietnam War was, however, a conflict that divided the nation more deeply than any since the Civil War. Military involvement in Vietnam ignited and exacerbated the profound social and political upheavals of the 1960s and early 1970s, eroded Americans' trust in their political and military leaders, sapped American military and economic strength, and damaged the credibility and prestige of the United States in international affairs.

The Vietnam War also created deep and enduring social and political divisions between those who served in Vietnam or supported the American effort there, and those who opposed the war or avoided military service. The legacy of Vietnam has haunted the American people and deeply influenced American foreign policy since its conclusion in April 1975. The divisions and issues that emanate from the American experience in Vietnam are not likely to subside until the generation that fought in Vietnam or protested the war at home is no longer a significant element in American society.

**Vietnam War (1964–75)**

| |
|---|
| Total U.S. Servicemembers (Worldwide): **9,200,000** |
| U.S. Population (millions): **204.9** |
| Deployed to Southeast Asia: **3,403,000** |
| Battle Deaths: **47,415** |
| Other Deaths (In Theater): **10,785** |
| Other Deaths in Service (Non-Theater): **32,000** |
| Non-mortal Woundings: **153,303** |
| Cost (in $ current billions): **111.00** |

Source: Deaths and Nonmortal Wounds: Department of Veterans Affairs, *America's Wars.* <http://www1.va.gov/opa/fact/amwars.html>

### Background to the War

The roots of America's painful experience in Vietnam can be traced back to the political and economic policies that the United States adopted in an effort to contain the spread of communism after World War II. In the wake of that war, the United States sought to help the Japanese and European economies recover from the devastation of the war and to create politically friendly, militarily strong, and economically prosperous regimes capable of containing and resisting the internal and external threats posed by communists. Vietnam became an important source of raw materials and foodstuffs for these recovering economies, and the United States obtained French cooperation in European affairs by acquiescing to French demands to reassert control of their former colonies in Southeast Asia.

Despite substantial material and financial support from the United States, French forces proved incapable of defeating the Viet Minh during the First Indochina War (1946–54). The issue of Vietnamese independence was to be discussed at a conference among the major powers scheduled for May 1954. French forces were defeated at Dien Bien Phu just days before the conference opened, and the defeat, a bitter humiliation for France, broke French will to continue the war in Indochina. At the Geneva Conference, Vietnam was divided between the communist north, under Ho Chi Minh and the Viet Minh, and the noncommunist South, under the control of Ngo Dinh Diem. The vacuum caused by the departure of the French was soon filled by the United States, which gradually committed increasing amounts of aid and advisers to South Vietnam in an effort to keep communism in Southeast Asia confined to North Vietnam. In supplying aid to the Diem regime, American policy was guided by what Pres. Dwight D. Eisenhower called the "domino theory," which argued that if one country fell to communism in Southeast Asia, others would surely follow, and if the process was left unchecked, India and Japan would eventually be forced into the communist camp. Such an eventuality would, according to Eisenhower, be disastrous to the military and economic security of the free world.

Despite generous amounts of military and economic aid and the presence of several hundred American advisers, the Diem regime had difficulty generating and maintaining support in the Vietnamese countryside and often alienated peasants, Buddhists, and intellectuals. When the agreed-upon elections to reunify the nation were cancelled by the Saigon government, South Vietnamese who favored Ho Chi Minh's regime mounted an insurgency aimed at toppling Diem from power. After 1959, North Vietnam began to assist the rebel forces in the South, which soon became known as the Viet Cong.

### Deepening U.S. Involvement

In early 1961, Pres. John F. Kennedy inherited a deteriorating situation in South Vietnam. Kennedy, young and inexperienced, was determined to stand up to Soviet premier Nikita Khrushchev's advocacy of wars of national liberation. Embarrassed by the failure of the Bay of Pigs invasion and facing dangerous challenges from the Soviets in Berlin, Cuba, and Laos, Kennedy believed the United States had to demonstrate its resolve to thwart communism in Vietnam. Mindful of the domestic political fallout following Mao Zedong's victory in the Chinese Civil War in 1949, Kennedy also feared that a communist victory in Vietnam would destroy any chance at reelection in 1964, unleash a new wave of McCarthyism, and perhaps permit reactionary opponents an opportunity to repeal the progressive domestic programs of Franklin D. Roosevelt and Harry S. Truman.

Kennedy dramatically increased the level of American aid, including the number of advisers. He permitted American advisers to engage in combat, dispatched Special Forces units, and authorized the use of napalm and defoliants. The American advisory contingent, which amounted to only a few hundred during the Eisenhower presidency, peaked at 16,000 at the time of Kennedy's assassination in November 1963.

Although Kennedy did much to deepen American involvement in Vietnam and was determined to stem the spread of communism in Southeast Asia, he expressed serious doubts about the wisdom of an expanded American role in Vietnam and resisted pressure to dispatch U.S. combat units to Vietnam. His attempts to deal with the deteriorating situation in South Vietnam were also complicated by contradictory reports on the nature and strength of the insurgency and by the unpopularity of the Diem regime.

### The Gulf of Tonkin Incident and the Dispatch of U.S. Combat Forces

Upon President Kennedy's assassination on November 22, 1963, Pres. Lyndon Johnson inherited the conundrum of Vietnam. Like Kennedy, Johnson feared the international and domestic repercussions that Vietnam's fall to communism would have on his presidency, his party, and his domestic legislative agenda. In the months following Kennedy's assassination, Johnson managed to postpone any major decision regarding intervention in Vietnam as he sought to win the presidential election of 1964, and concentrate on his legislative programs. These priorities explain Johnson's carefully circumscribed response to a confirmed North Vietnamese naval attack on August 2, 1964, and an alleged attack two days later upon U.S. naval vessels patrolling the waters off North Vietnam. Johnson ordered retaliatory air strikes against North Vietnamese naval installations and also obtained the Gulf of Tonkin Resolution from a pliant U.S. Congress. This resolution, a major step in widening America's role in Vietnam, granted the president the authority to use whatever means necessary to protect South Vietnam and U.S. military forces in Southeast Asia.

Despite his enhanced authority, President Johnson refrained from escalating the war until well after the presidential election of 1964. Discouraged by the growing strength of the Viet Cong and fearing an imminent collapse of the South Vietnamese government, in early 1965 Johnson gradually expanded the scope of American involvement. First, Johnson ordered U.S. warplanes to commence bombing North Vietnamese targets in February 1965 in retaliation for heightened Viet Cong activity. Johnson soon authorized a far more comprehensive air campaign against North Vietnam. Dubbed "Rolling Thunder," this initiative was designed to increase the cost of North Vietnam's support of the insurgency in the South, demonstrate American resolve, and buoy the morale of South Vietnam. The president also ordered U.S. Marines to South Vietnam in March to provide base security for units engaged in Rolling Thunder. Once on the ground, the Marine mission quickly shifted from base security to offensive operations in the northernmost provinces of South Vietnam.

Rolling Thunder and the introduction of a few Marine combat units did nothing to retard the progress of communist forces in South Vietnam or to enhance the determination of South Vietnamese forces. In the summer of 1965, the Pentagon and the American ambassador to South Vietnam warned that the Saigon government would not survive without the immediate introduction of significant numbers of American combat troops. Secretary of Defense Robert McNamara recommended the gradual deployment of 100,000 U.S. troops to undertake large-scale combat operations. President Johnson approved the recommendation and in July ordered the dispatch of 50,000 combat troops. By November 1965, the number of American troops in South Vietnam had risen to 165,000; many of these had already engaged North Vietnamese Army forces in a bitter struggle in the Ia Drang Valley.

### Escalation of the War

President Johnson's decisions in 1965 launched the United States on the longest and most divisive foreign conflict in its history. However, the goals President Johnson wanted to achieve with military force were strictly limited: to avoid a humiliating defeat in South Vietnam and keep it and adjacent territories out of Chinese hands, and, only secondarily, to assist the South Vietnamese people to live in freedom. The military operations themselves were also strictly limited. Johnson, fearful of provoking either China or the Soviet Union, forbade U.S. ground forces from invading North Vietnam and from eliminating communist base areas in Laos and Cambodia. The air campaign against North Vietnam was also carefully designed to preclude any incident that might provoke the two communist superpowers. The hope was that the gradually intensifying air campaign in the north and massive search and destroy operations in the south would impose an unacceptable level of casualties upon communist forces and compel North Vietnam to negotiate an end to hostilities. In order to assuage public concerns and not alarm Beijing and Moscow, Johnson refrained from building public support for the war. He did not ask Congress to commit additional resources, nor did he call up the Reserves or declare a state of emergency.

American troop levels in Vietnam steadily increased, from 184,000 troops in December 1965 to 385,000 a year later and over 500,000 by the end of 1967. Although Johnson placed strict geographic limitations on both air and ground operations, U.S. forces were generally granted a free hand to wage the war in South Vietnam. The Americans used their prodigious firepower to kill thousands of communist troops, but the enemy could always retreat into their Cambodian or Laotian sanctuaries and were never in danger of losing more men than they could replace. The use of massive firepower in South Vietnam was frequently counterproductive, since it often killed Vietnamese civilians, damaged vast areas of the countryside, and generated enormous numbers of refugees, all of which alienated many potential supporters of the Saigon regime.

### Division at Home

As the American ground war in Vietnam intensified, draft calls in the United States increased, and as the flag-draped coffins and wounded veterans returned home, opposition to the war increased dramatically. The proliferation and testing of nuclear weapons and the economic, social, and political consequence of the Cold War arms race had already spawned a broad, multifaceted coalition of peace activists by the early 1960s, and the focus of their efforts shifted to the war in Vietnam beginning in 1965.

Although the peace movement was dedicated to stopping the war, it was by no means united, and no single person or organization orchestrated its activities. There were three broad categories of activists: members of the Old and New Left political organizations; radical pacifists devoted to revolutionary nonviolence; and those who questioned the wisdom of using American military might in Vietnam, whom we might call "peace liberals." There were sharp differences among the factions regarding goals, methods, and tactics. The peace liberals, for example, never questioned the legitimacy of Johnson's authority or the foundations of American power, while the more radical elements not only condemned the war as an imperialist adventure but also argued that it was a symptom of the moral bankruptcy and injustice of the entire political, economic, and social system.

The escalating violence in Vietnam motivated the movement to act despite the deep internal divisions. In the autumn of 1965, more than 25,000 activists descended on Washington, D.C., to protest the war. The following spring, the size and scale of the protests increased, with nationwide protests that numbered upwards of 150,000 people. The antiwar movement gained additional momentum as a result of the Senate Foreign Relations Committee's hearings on the war, during which highly esteemed political figures such as George Kennan and Gen. James Gavin questioned the wisdom of the war and criticized it as a diversion of resources from more important strategic priorities. The public dissension of such figures during the hearings opened the way for many members of the Washington establishment to oppose the war.

In 1966, African American civil rights leaders began publicly questioning the wisdom of the war in Southeast Asia. Dr. Martin Luther King, Jr. and others were concerned that the demands of the Vietnam War would retard the Great Society social programs and civil rights initiatives. African American leaders were also angry over the disproportionately large number of black Americans who were being drafted and serving in Vietnam during the first years of the American ground war. More radical African American leaders even encouraged black youth to refuse military service.

Whatever respectability Gavin, Kennan, and King lent the peace movement's message was lost when a growing number of hippies attached themselves to the cause. "Hippy" is a generic term for a wide variety of youthful activists who rejected American bourgeois values. Hippies shocked middle-class America with their dress and hairstyles and their uninhibited experimentation with mind-altering drugs, sex, and music. They were often highly visible on college campuses and in more liberal regions of the country, such as on the east and west coasts. More strident factions further alienated mainstream Americans with threatening rhetoric and "antiestablishment" actions. Public opinion polls throughout the period from 1965 to 1973 indicated that the only thing more unpopular than the interminable conflict in Vietnam was the antiwar movement.

Despite their inability to convince the majority of middle-class Americans of the wisdom of an immediate end to the war, the antiwar movement continued to attract supporters, especially among American youth, and staged impressive protests in 1967 and 1968. Despite the growing size and number of protests, the war in Vietnam continued. Frustrated by the apparent futility of their methods, some factions of the antiwar movement shifted from protest to active resistance, attempting to shut down draft induction centers, stop military recruiting on college campuses, and prevent universities from doing business with corporations associated with the defense industry or undertaking defense-related research. Those who engaged in resistance also counseled young men to claim conscientious objector status, exploit the various deferments and loopholes of the Selective Service System or defy it outright by burning their draft registration cards, or, as a last resort, flee to Canada. A very small number of extremists even resorted to acts of domestic terrorism; incidents of arson and bombing against government buildings escalated dramatically between 1968 and 1970.

As the peace movement grew larger and more raucous in its demands for an end to the war, the policies of the U.S. Selective Service System during the Vietnam War provided yet another source of lasting division and bitterness for the nation. Approximately 27 million young men became eligible for the draft during the years of direct U.S. military involvement in Vietnam, but only 2.5 million—less than 10 percent—saw service in Vietnam. Of the 2.5 million who served in Vietnam, fewer than 10 percent served as infantrymen. Despite the relatively low odds of being drafted and placed in a combat unit in Vietnam, many young men who opposed the war went to great lengths to avoid military service in Vietnam. A safe and socially acceptable way to avoid duty in Vietnam was by joining the National Guard or the Reserves. Those eligible to be drafted also sought student deferments, conscientious objector status, or a note from a sympathetic doctor indicating one was physically or psychologically unfit for military duty. Some young men even feigned insanity or homosexuality or deliberately injured themselves in order to obtain draft exemption. Manipulation of the Selective Service System was widespread and ultimately meant that a disproportionate share of the fighting and dying in Vietnam fell to rural and working class youths who lacked the desire, ability, or means to avoid the draft. In an effort to correct such inequities, in 1970 a lottery system was instituted that was based on birthdays, replacing the old system of issuing quotas to local draft boards.

As the war continued, the burden of serving and fighting in Vietnam fell on an army made up of increasing numbers of draftees. Moreover, the manpower turnover in combat units was extraordinarily high because the military limited the soldier's tour of duty in Vietnam to one year. As a result of these two factors, the U.S. military began to reflect the values and divisions so evident in American society. Antiwar, antiauthoritarian attitudes among soldiers mushroomed, and troop morale plummeted, especially beginning in 1969 when newly elected Pres. Richard Nixon began to withdraw troops from Vietnam and seek a negotiated end to the war. The military also began to encounter very serious breeches of discipline, as incidents of desertion, mutiny, drug use, and the murder of officers (called "fraggings") escalated.

### 1968: The Turning Point

The turning point of the American military effort in Vietnam occurred in January and February 1968 with the Tet Offensive. North Vietnamese Army and Viet Cong units launched coordinated attacks throughout South Vietnam. The attack was a costly military defeat for the communist forces, as American firepower decimated those who exposed themselves by going on the offensive. However, the scale

*Delegates to the 1968 National Democratic Convention in Chicago march against the Vietnam War, bringing the proceedings in the hall to a stop. (© Bettmann/CORBIS)*

and ferocity of the attacks, coming so soon after an extensive government public relations campaign that had stressed progress in the war and the impending collapse of the communist forces, shocked the American public and seriously eroded the will to continue the war. With public support for the war plummeting, members of the Washington elite began to look for a way out of the quagmire.

The year 1968 became one of the most divisive and chaotic in American history. In March, Sen. Eugene McCarthy, a Democratic peace candidate, nearly won the New Hampshire presidential primary race, and massive "dump Johnson" rallies were organized across the country. Government expenditures for the war and the massive Great Society social programs led to mounting inflation and some panic about the national and world economic outlook. Senior policy makers and advisers began urging the president to negotiate an end to the conflict. In late March, Johnson announced that he would not seek reelection. A few days later, Martin Luther King Jr. was assassinated in Memphis, Tennessee, and riots erupted across the nation. In June, Robert Kennedy, the leading Democratic presidential candidate, was murdered in California. In August, antiwar demonstrators and police engaged in a violent melee outside the Democratic National Convention in Chicago. To many it appeared that the nation was descending into civil war.

### Nixon's Search for "Peace with Honor"

Richard Nixon won the presidency in November 1968 with a campaign that stressed law and order at home and "peace with honor" in Vietnam. President Nixon, as devoted as his predecessors to preserving American prestige, planned to extract the nation from the quagmire in Vietnam by gradually pulling out U.S. troops and handing over responsibility for the war effort to South Vietnamese military forces, a process known as "Vietnamization." Nixon also ordered the secret bombing of communist sanctuaries in Cambodia and attempted to intimidate the leaders of North Vietnam by threatening to use nuclear weapons if a satisfactory settlement could not be formulated. Despite these actions, real progress at the Paris peace talks proved elusive. The talks, which had been underway since May 1968, were deadlocked by the North Vietnamese insistence on concessions, such as a bombing halt, as a precondition to any productive diplomatic activity. North Vietnamese diplomats may also have pursued a strategy of stalling and stalemate, calculating that steadily ebbing American support for the conflict would ultimately force Washington to withdraw from the war. No serious discussions of a settlement occurred until the autumn of 1972.

In April 1970, Nixon, in an effort to destroy communist sanctuaries, buy time to build up the South Vietnamese regime, and reinforce the American negotiating position in Paris, ordered U.S. forces to invade the border areas of Cambodia. The action unleashed a storm of angry protests across the United States. At Kent State University in Ohio and Jackson State University in Mississippi, police and National Guard troops, dispatched to quell student rioting, fired on protestors, killing several students. Unrest on college campuses exploded and forced many campuses to shut down.

In March 1972, when nearly all U.S. combat units had been removed from the South, North Vietnam launched a conventional invasion of South Vietnam in an effort to unify the country. The North's invasion was blunted with massive American air power. Nixon also removed many of the restrictions on targets in North Vietnam and ordered the mining of Haiphong Harbor in an effort to choke off the flow of supplies into North Vietnam. Nixon's efforts to encourage rapprochement with China and the Soviet Union also threatened to isolate the North Vietnamese regime. After the failure of the North's conventional invasion, progress at the peace negotiations improved, and by the autumn of 1972 it appeared as if a settlement was in reach. In Paris secret talks between Henry Kissinger and Le Duc Tho had succeeded in hammering out the basic elements of a settlement. Under the terms of the agreement, the United States would withdraw its remaining troops within 60 days of a ceasefire, the North Vietnamese would return American prisoners of war, and a National Council of Reconciliation and Concord would administer elections and implement the terms of the agreement. The agreement did not compel the withdrawal of North Vietnamese troops from the territory of South Vietnam and permitted the sovereignty of the Viet Cong within specific areas of South Vietnam.

The South Vietnamese regime, however, perceiving the proposed settlement as a fig leaf to cover the American abandonment of their client state, was outraged by the terms of the proposed agreement and demanded changes. In an effort to obtain South Vietnamese acquiescence to the agreement, U.S. officials used a combination of promises and threats. The United States delivered massive amounts of military aid to South Vietnam in advance of the agreement, promised swift and severe retaliation against any future North Vietnamese attempts to use military force against the South, and finally threatened to sign the peace accord with North Vietnam without the South's endorsement. The United States eventually obtained the South's reluctant approval for the peace accord, but not before the North Vietnamese negotiators broke off the talks. It was to convince the North Vietnamese to return to the negotiation table that Nixon, in December 1972, ordered the heaviest bombing of North Vietnam of the war. Negotiations resumed in January, and a peace agreement, similar to the draft completed before the bombing, was signed, formally ending American involvement in the war. The exit of U.S. military forces from Vietnam as outlined in the Paris peace accords was reinforced in July 1973 when the United States Congress passed a law that prohibited U.S. combat activities in Southeast Asia after August 15, 1973.

Without active U.S. military assistance, the prospects for the long-term survival of South Vietnam were poor. The American public was bitterly divided over the war by 1973, and the Watergate scandal that ultimately forced President Nixon to resign further polarized the political landscape. Given the unlikely probability of American military intervention under these conditions, North Vietnam took the opportunity to launch a massive invasion of South Vietnam in the spring of 1975. South Vietnamese forces were quickly overwhelmed, and the South Vietnamese regime collapsed with fantastic speed. So quick was the collapse that American embassy staff and American civilians had to be evacuated from Vietnam in a massive and hastily organized helicopter airlift. The fall of Cambodia and Laos to indigenous communist movements that same month magnified the humiliating American failure in Southeast Asia.

### Aftermath of the War

As a result of the war in Vietnam and the social and political upheavals of the 1960s, the United States was a far different nation in 1975 than it had been when its combat troops entered South Vietnam ten years earlier. Although the United States was still the preeminent superpower, its relative economic and military strength had eroded, in large part due to the enormous resources it had devoted to preserving a non-communist South Vietnamese regime. Politically, the nation was deeply divided. Vietnam veterans took exception to the mistreatment and neglect they received from both the government and American society in general, and resented those who avoided service and protested the war. The "credibility gap," the chasm between official government pronouncements on the war and accounts by journalists and veterans on the progress of the conflict, was exacerbated by the Watergate scandal and President Nixon's resignation. In the years following the Vietnam War, Americans demanded a far more cautious foreign policy and were extraordinarily wary of involving U.S. military forces in Third World conflicts.

A divisive debate also emerged regarding the reasons for the American defeat. Some blamed journalists and peace activists for breaking the nation's will to continue the war, some blamed the restrictions placed on American military operations by civilian leaders, while others saw a flawed military strategy that directed the use of conventional forces against an unconventional enemy as the primary reasons for the defeat. A few pointed to the egregious corruption of the South Vietnamese regime and the impossibility of overcoming the power of Vietnamese nationalism short of exterminating North Vietnam.

Regardless of the reasons for the defeat, the war destroyed Americans' unquestioned devotion to anticommunism. Alongside the sweeping social changes brought about by the Great Society programs, the civil rights movement, the sexual revolution, feminism, and the counterculture, the Vietnam War sharpened the political and ideological divisions within American society. Although the tremendous speed and decisiveness of the Gulf War victory in 1991 diminished the power of the "Vietnam syndrome" among Americans, and perhaps signaled the resurgence of a more confident and assertive use of U.S. military power, the memories of

Vietnam continue to provoke bitterness and division. Since the 1980s, as the generation that fought the war has gradually moved into positions of prominence and power, the issue of who served and who avoided service has emerged as an enduring and divisive remnant of America's longest war.

### Bibliography


Appy, Christian. *Working Class War: American Combat Soldiers and Vietnam.* Chapel Hill: University of North Carolina Press, 1993.

Davidson, Phillip B. *Vietnam at War: The History: 1946–1975.* Novato, Calif.: Presidio Press, 1988.

Ebert, James R. *A Life in a Year: The American Infantryman in Vietnam, 1965–1972.* Novato, Calif.: Presidio Press, 1993.

Gilbert, Marc Jason, ed. *Why the North Won the Vietnam War.* New York: Palgrave, 2002.

Gitlin, Todd. *The Sixties: Years of Hope, Days of Rage.* New York: Bantam Books, 1987.

Herring, George C. *America's Longest War: The United States and Vietnam, 1950–1975.* New York: Alfred K. Knopf, 1986.

Karnow, Stanley. *Vietnam: A History.* New York: Penguin Books, 1997.

MacPherson, Myra. *Vietnam and the Haunted Generation.* New York: Doubleday, 1984.

Record, Jeffery. *The Wrong War.* Annapolis, Md.: Naval Institute Press, 1998.


### Further Reading


Berman, Larry. *Lyndon Johnson's War: The Road to Stalemate in Vietnam.* New York: W.W. Norton, 1989.

Braestrup, Peter. *Big Story: How the American Press and Television Reported and Interpreted the Crisis of 1968 in Vietnam and Washington.* Boulder, Colo.: Westview Press, 1977.

Colby, William. *Lost Victory: A Firsthand Account of America's Sixteen-Year Involvement in Vietnam.* Chicago: Contemporary Books, 1989.

Fitzgerald, Francis. *Fire in the Lake: The Vietnamese and the Americans in Vietnam.* New York: Vintage, 1972.

Halberstam, David. *The Best and the Brightest.* New York: Random House, 1972.

Isaacs, Arnold R. *Without Honor: Defeat in Vietnam and Cambodia.* Baltimore, Md.: Johns Hopkins University Press, 1983.

Palmer, Bruce. *The 25-Year War: America's Military Role in Vietnam.* Lexington, Ky.: University Press of Kentucky, 1984.

Sheehan, Neil. *A Bright Shining Lie: John Paul Vann and America in Vietnam.* New York: Random House, 1988.

Small, Melvin, and William D. Hoover, eds. *Give Peace a Chance: Exploring the Vietnam Antiwar Movement.* Syracuse, N.Y.: Syracuse University Press, 1992.

Snepp, Frank. *Decent Interval: An Insider's Account of Saigon's Indecent End.* New York: Random House, 1977.

Summers, Harry. *On Strategy: A Critical Analysis of the Vietnam War.* Novato, Calif.: Presidio Press, 1982.

Wells, Tom. *The War Within: America's Battle over Vietnam.* Berkeley: University of California Press, 1994.

Young, Marilyn. *The Vietnam Wars, 1945–1990.* New York: Harper, 1991.


### Related Entries

Agent Orange; Ali, Muhammad; All Volunteer Force; Antiwar Movements; *Apocalypse Now*; Berrigan, Daniel and Philip Berrigan; *Born on the Fourth of July;* Clergy and Laity Concerned about Vietnam; Cold War; Conscientious Objection; *Deer Hunter, The*; Disabled American Veterans; Draft Evasion and Resistance; McNamara, Robert S.; My Lai Massacre; Pentagon Papers; *Platoon*; Prisoners of War; Psychiatric Disorders, Combat Related; Public Opinion and Policy in Wartime; Rambo; Selective Service System; Vietnam Veterans against the War; Vietnam Veterans of America; War Powers Resolution

### Related Documents

1965 a, b, c, d, e; 1966 a, b, c, d; 1967 a, b; 1968 a, b; 1969; 1970 a, b, c; 1971 a, b, c, d; 1972; 1973; 1976 a, b; 1977

—*James Ehrman*

# Virginia Military Institute

The Virginia Military Institute was established in 1839 on the site of a state arsenal just outside the Blue Ridge mountain town of Lexington, Virginia. The state government had authorized its creation as a military college that would also provide cadets with a technical education in the sciences and engineering. As such, the Virginia Military Institute became the first state-supported military college in the United States. Unlike its federal counterpart, the United States Military Academy at West Point, its cadets were not entitled to a regular commission in the United States Army. Many early graduates did serve with distinction as military officers, especially during times of national emergency. Many others went into civilian occupations in business, engineering, the law, and education. The school instilled high standards of personal discipline and honor, and provided practical training in leadership.

### Early History

The first years of the institution were marked by frequent upheaval, as had been the case at other academies such as those at West Point and Annapolis. As the federal government had done at those academies, the Commonwealth of Virginia had laid a basic framework of what it expected from the Virginia Military Institute: a four-year curriculum split more or less evenly between military training and a technical education. But it was often vague in defining the details of what that program should specifically entail. As such, early cadets attended classes, participated in infantry drill, and were largely restricted to their barracks, with little coordination among their activities or training. However, just as Sylvanus Thayer had done with the Military Academy or George Bancroft with the Naval Academy, the Virginia Military Institute grew owing to the work and vision of several key figures who expected more out of the institution.

Col. Claudius Crozet was appointed as the first president of the institute's Board of Visitors. Crozet was a Frenchman who had served under Napoleon and later became a professor of engineering at West Point after moving to the United States. In 1839, he was the chief engineer of Virginia, working on several key construction projects for the state. With many graduates not pursuing permanent military careers, Crozet believed the curriculum should be technically focused, but in ways geared towards civilian applications, such as civil engineering or transportation. Based on his experiences with mass conscription in Napoleon's France, he also knew that military training needed to be an important component of the program to prepare cadets to step into officer roles in the event of an emergency.

The institute's first superintendent, Gen. Francis Smith, was also crucial to its development. Smith graduated from the United States Military Academy in 1833 and came to the Virginia Military Institute from Hampden-Sydney College, where he had been a professor of mathematics. Smith held his position at the institute for more than 50 years, an extraordinarily long time for an academy superintendent; most officers rotated out of such positions every four or five years. Smith's tenure was especially important in establishing the institute's professional traditions, many of which resembled those at West Point. The institutional culture valued discipline above all else, a priority demonstrated through the institute's insistence on an unquestioning obedience to orders. Cadets also learned to equate their personal honor with that of the institution and their classmates, and the cadet who brought shame to either one stood to be severely punished. Most of the institute's traditions were instilled during the cadets' rat (freshman) year.

### The Civil War

Unlike the case at the federal service academies, students and faculty of the Virginia Military Institute universally supported the Confederacy after the state's secession in April 1861. Indeed, several senior cadets provided additional security at the execution of abolitionist John Brown in Charles Town, Virginia. Many alumni answered their states' call for service and accepted commissions in the Confederate Army. Without a doubt, the most famous individual associated with the institute to serve in the Civil War was Thomas "Stonewall" Jackson. Jackson was not a graduate, but he had served on the faculty as a professor of natural philosophy since 1851. Contrary to popular opinion, Jackson seems not to have been very popular with the cadets, nor to have distinguished himself as a teacher. In fact, in 1856, a group of alumni petitioned General Smith to have Jackson removed from his position. Smith looked into these issues, but after interviewing other cadets he did not believe that there was enough evidence to warrant Jackson's dismissal.

To some extent, the war resurrected Jackson's military career and standing within the institution. The school played up its association with Jackson as his reputation increased as one of the South's preeminent combat commanders. After his inadvertent death from friendly fire at the battle of Chancellorsville, Jackson's place in the school's pantheon of heroes was established. The Corps of Cadets also won renown for their courage under fire at the battle of New Market in May 1864. The entire student body, a group of approximately 257 cadets minus some of the younger boys, marched in relief of an outnumbered Confederate force under Gen. John C. Breckenridge, the first and only such time in which a service academy's entire student body fought as a single combat unit. Ten cadets were killed in the fighting and 45 others were wounded. Ever since, the institute has commemorated the sacrifice of those fallen cadets in the hope of instilling such values in its current cadets.

## 20th Century Mission

Large portions of the institute's facilities were destroyed during Gen. David Hunter's advance into Virginia. The school reopened its doors to 55 cadets in October 1865. For much of the late 19th century, the Virginia Military Institute languished owing to budgetary problems and low enrollments. However, its plight was similar to that of other colleges in the state. Yet the institute survived and underwent a gradual expansion in the early 20th century, eventually reaching a size of approximately 1,300 cadets. The academic curriculum also changed significantly in step with the new technologies of industrialization. The institute continued, however, to be technically focused. The new century also brought greater opportunities for cadets to pursue full-time military careers. As the United States became more active in the world, the size of its military gradually expanded. The Military Academy at West Point continued to supply the bulk of the army's regular officers, but there were greater opportunities for commissions for students from schools such as the Virginia Military Institute.

The institute's military accomplishments peaked during World War II. Sixty-two graduates achieved flag or general rank in the course of that war. The institute's two greatest heroes were arguably George Patton, one of the war's greatest combat commanders, and George Marshall, the Army chief of staff who created the wartime army, the largest such force in the nation's history. Marshall accomplished this feat in record time; his army was ready to fight in a little over two years, much sooner than most of the Allied and Axis planners had anticipated. He went on to become Pres. Harry Truman's secretary of state and, later, secretary of defense.

The postwar threat from the Soviet Union did not allow the United States to demobilize after World War II. As a result, the army had a greater need for officers, more than could ever be supplied by the Military Academy. A permanent ROTC program provided greater commissioning opportunities for Virginia Military Institute cadets than ever before. Even so, many cadets used their experiences to pursue leadership positions in civilian careers rather than serve in the military.

## Admission of Women

Congress abolished the restriction on women attending the federal service academies in 1976. However, state supported schools like The Citadel and the Virginia Military Institute continued to exclude women well into the 1990s. The idea of female cadets was just as foreign to the culture and traditions of these institutions as it was to that of the federal service academies. And as long as the state schools could resist gender integration, their leaders and alumni chose to do so. As groups promoting the admission of women pressured them to make changes, these institutions could not maintain their stance.

In the hopes of staving off integration, the Virginia Military Institute supported the creation of a comparable program for females in 1995 called the Virginia Women's Institute for Leadership at nearby Mary Baldwin College. This program also focused on character building and leadership development, but was entirely separate from the Virginia Military Institute. The U.S. Supreme Court ruled in 1996 that this halfway measure was unconstitutional for a state-supported school, inasmuch as it did not meet the standards of the equal protection clause of the 14th Amendment. As such, the Virginia Military Institute began accepting its first female cadets in 1997. Unfortunately, these women faced many of the same prejudices that their predecessors had experienced at the federal service academies nearly a generation before.

The objective of the Virginia Military Institute today remains similar to that of the past: to provide a technically based education along with character development programs that allow members of its now co-ed student body to be successful leaders both in the military and in the civilian world.

### Bibliography

Millett, Allan, and Peter Maslowski. *For the Common Defense: A Military History of theUnited States of America.* New York: Simon & Schuster, 1994.

Weigley, Russell. *History of the U.S. Army.* Bloomington: Indiana University Press, 1984.

Wise, Henry. *Drawing Out the Man: The VMI Story.* Charlottesville: University Press of Virginia, 1978.

### Further Reading

Brodie, Laura Fairchild. *Breaking Out: VMI and the Coming of Women.* New York: Knopf, 2001.

### Related Entries

Air Force Academy; Citadel, The; Coast Guard Academy; Marshall, George Catlett; Merchant Marine; Military Academy, United States; Naval Academy; Patton, George S.; Women in the Military

—*Todd Forney*

# Visual Arts and War

Humans use visual frames of reference to rekindle memories and connect with past events. The early history of the United States, including military events, is recalled through an array of forms and structures, especially memorials, paintings, and prints. Prior to the onset of photography and its extensive use in the Civil War and to a far lesser extent in the Mexican War, visual awareness of earlier wars can be directly attributed to paintings and prints of these conflicts. Such pictures excite the imagination and inspire patriotism and devotion.

### Early War Art

One of the earliest practitioners of war art in America was Amos Doolittle, who created four engravings depicting the events at Lexington and Concord in 1775; these were the first eyewitness depictions of war in the country and are among only a handful of contemporaneous images of the Revolution. Later, John Trumbull's grand epic paintings, which appeared after the end of hostilities, were inspired by the success his fellow countryman Benjamin West experienced with his stirring canvas of the death of General Wolfe at Quebec in 1759. West, Trumbull, and John Singleton Copley realized that grand heroic tableaux depicting military events might appeal to the art-buying public and began to produce a series of war-inspired paintings suitable for commercial engravings.

The Revolutionary War, as any other war, was followed by a period of assessment, then one of nostalgic overview. In the first decades of the 19th century, illustrated histories of the Revolution began to appear, aimed at exploiting the groundswell of interest in the beginnings of the new republic. Artists and illustrators such as Alonzo Chappel turned their attention to the task of creating representations of the great battles that shaped the country. Historical painting continued into mid-century, epitomized by Emanuel Leutze's canvas, *Washington Crossing the Delaware.*

### The Civil War and Aftermath, 1861–1900

The Civil War spawned countless paintings and illustrations capturing the four years of fighting. Capitalizing on the public fixation with the war, commercial printmakers including Currier & Ives began to produce popular, highly stylized lithographic prints of the battles and personalities. Some mainstream artists such as Winslow Homer committed to canvas the scenes they had witnessed. It was the era of the "special artist" employed by such illustrated newspapers as *Harper's Weekly* and *Frank Leslie's* and sent to the front to sketch the events. Homer was among this small, select group, which also included Alfred and William Waud. At the same time, Mathew Brady, Alexander Gardiner, and others were exploiting a ready market for photographic images of the war and portraits of the combatants.

A period of nostalgia for the Civil War set in during the 1870s and 1880s, and artists and publishers responded with illustrated histories and paintings popularizing the conflict. The period saw the serialized publication of *Civil War Battles and Leaders* in *Century Magazine*, with sketches by

*Benjamin West's famous painting of the death of General Wolfe in Quebec in 1759, an example of the epic war paintings popular with artists and with the art-buying public at that time. (From the collections of the Library of Congress)*

Edwin Forbes and others. At the same time, academic artists, including Gilbert Gaul, William Trego, and Julian Scott (a veteran of the war) began to exhibit war-related canvases at the National Academy and elsewhere, hoping to attract buyers from among the many veterans.

Simultaneously, the large battle panoramas were touring the major cities. The panorama phenomenon had crossed the Atlantic from Europe along with continental artists accustomed to painting huge 360-degree canvases. "Cycloramas," as they were called in America, became popular entertainments for a decade or two, presenting to a fee-paying public such great battles of the war as those at Gettysburg, Vicksburg, and Atlanta. The growing demand for battlefield monuments and war memorials during the last two decades of the century provided work for numerous sculptors.

Also during this period, the country was engaged in numerous small campaigns against Native Americans. These were duly covered in the press but aroused little interest—with one notable exception: the massacre of the U.S. 7th Cavalry at the Little Bighorn River in Montana in 1876 and especially the death of the expedition's commander, Gen. George Armstrong Custer. Numerous artists attempted to capture the "last stand" of this small group of "brave" white soldiers surrounded by the "heathen" warriors. It was a theme mirrored in European military art of the same period and touched peoples' emotions so much that they clamored for reproductions of the paintings. The subject of the Indian Wars was made popular in the paintings of Frederic Remington in the 1890s, while Howard Pyle at the same time depicted scenes from America's military past.

The war in Cuba in 1898 provided the art media with a similar opportunity to create prints, panoramas, and academic paintings, but the war ended before this market could develop fully, and the continuing conflict in the Philippines failed to capture public imagination. However, a little-known apparatus, the movie camera, which would later revolutionize battle reportage, made an early appearance in the war, and entrepreneurs such as Thomas Edison filmed staged battles in the hope of attracting public attention and money.

## Twentieth Century Developments

When war broke out in Europe in 1914, many in America considered that war to be strictly a European conflict. Beyond the illustrated coverage in the press, few artists were attracted to the campaigns on the Western Front during World War I. Even after official artists began accompanying American troops in 1918, the pictorial coverage beyond the papers back in the States was limited. Some souvenir pictures were published, providing work for such commercial artists as Frank Schoonover and Gail Porter Hoskins. However, one visual medium did gain strong footing during World War I: posters for recruiting and fund-raising appeared on a mass scale and more than any other visual form epitomized the image of war for the home front, establishing the reputations of many leading artists including Howard Chandler Christy. War cartoons were also a mode of expression made popular by Louis Reymaekers and others.

The emergence of cinematic pictures showing the fighting on the Western Front had a profound impact on the visual realizations of subsequent armed conflicts. During World War II, the public got its images of the fighting from the cinema and numerous glossy magazines such as *Life*. Apart from the continued popularity of the poster and the cartoon, however, the more static visual arts took second place. Various private companies, including Abbott Laboratories and Standard Oil, commissioned artists to record various war-related activities for advertising purposes; Abbott also commissioned Thomas Hart Benton to paint a series of allegorical scenes of the horrors of war. In 1943, the War Department sent official painters to the various fronts, but some questioned the need for these artists, arguing that the movie camera and photography had eclipsed painting. Exhibitions of war paintings were held around the country to bolster the war effort, but enthusiasm paled in comparison to that exhibited for the moving images that appeared in movie houses across the country.

Advances in technology over the succeeding decades meant that Cold War conflicts, in particular Vietnam, were brought home to the living room by television. Soldier art, beyond officially sanctioned paintings and drawings, was now produced primarily as a means of personal expression, often by veterans. Some created visual statements opposing the war, while a few sought to make a profit from their art. In the post-Vietnam era, the majority of war art was produced by commercial artists for the print market, although the Defense Department still commissions artists to cover wars involving American forces around the globe.

Often dismissed as merely illustration or anecdotal by art historians, the paintings of war created by Americans over the past 200 years have nonetheless created a lasting record of the military history of the country and represent in many cases the only visual images of conflicts that occurred before the age of photography. Many Americans have been inspired by such art, which has served to foster a sense of pride and nationalism.

### Bibliography

Abrams, Ann Uhry. *The Valiant Hero: Benjamin West and Grand Style History Painting.* Washington, D.C.: Smithsonian Institution, 1985.

Grossman, Julian. *Echo of a Distant Drum: Winslow Homer and the Civil War.* New York: H. N. Abrams, 1974.

Metnick, Barbara J. *The Portraits and History Paintings of Alonzo Chappel: Essays by Barbara J. Metnick and David Meschutt.* Chadds Ford, Pa.: Brandywine Museum, 1992.

Neely, Mark, and Harold Holzer. *Mine Eyes Have Seen the Glory: The Civil War in Art.* New York: Orion Books, 1993.

### Further Reading

Army Artwork (U.S. Army Center of Military History): <http://www.army.mil/cmh-pg/art/A&I/artwork.htm>.

Conn, Steven. "Narrative Trauma and Civil War History Painting, or Why Are These Pictures So Terrible?" *History and Theory* 41 (December 2002): 17–42.

Cornebise, Aldred. *Art from the Trenches: America's Uniformed Artists in World War I.* College Station: Texas A & M University Press, 1991.

Harrington, Peter. "The 1943 War Art Program." *Army History* 55 (spring–summer 2003): 4–19.

———, and Frederic A. Sharf. *"A Splendid Little War": The Spanish–American War, 1898. The Artist's Perspective.* London: Greenhill Books, and Mechanicsburg, Pa.: Stackpole Books, 1998.

Ray, Frederic E. *Alfred R. Waud: Civil War Artist.* New York, Viking: 1974.

**Related Entries**

Brady, Mathew B.; Combat-Zone Photography; Film and War; Memorials and Monuments; Memory and War; Political Cartoons; Propaganda Posters: World War I; Propaganda Posters: World War II; Recruiting Advertisements

—*Peter Harrington*

# Voice of America

The Voice of America (VOA), headquartered in Washington, D.C., is the international broadcaster for the United States to the rest of the world, to the citizens of countries either friendly or hostile to America, in times of peace and in times of war. Since its founding in 1942, it has broadcast news and feature programming over the radio, and it has more recently broadcast as well over television and the Internet. VOA has advanced American interests abroad by broadcasting information about U.S. culture and institutions to audiences around the world.

VOA's charter, which has the force of law, mandates that the agency adhere to principles of accuracy, objectivity, balance, and comprehensiveness. More informally, the agency has characterized at least part of its job as "telling America's story to the world," as broadcaster Edward R. Murrow described it. VOA thus provides a global audience with information it could not otherwise get. Many societies lack access to critical, trustworthy, accurate information about America or even information about human rights abuses, for example, in their own countries. VOA has sought to ensure that people around the world receive reliable information about America, even if it reflects poorly on the United States, in the conviction that such openness would serve America's highest diplomatic interests by demonstrating the value of a free press.

The Voice of America's founding came just months after the United States entered World War II. Its mission was clear from the first VOA broadcast on February 25, 1942, when William Harlan Hale proclaimed, in German, "The Voice of America speaks. Today, America has been at war for 79 days. Daily, at this time, we shall speak to you about America and the war. The news may be good, the news may be bad—we shall tell you the truth."

VOA broadcasts editorials representing the views of the American government, though always clearly labeling them as such. Editorials are the only part of the programming not produced by VOA, but by a separate policy office, which clears the editorials it writes with the State Department. The rest of VOA programming consists of news and information about the United States as well as international and regional news. It also aims to provide alternative views of world events to peoples who may be living in societies where the government monopolizes the media. For example, VOA broadcast detailed coverage from Tiananmen Square in 1989 to its large audience in China. That practice has often put VOA at odds with some individuals and governments overseas, prompting responses ranging from denunciations of VOA as a propaganda organ for the American government to elaborate efforts to block and jam VOA radio and television signals.

VOA's influence around the world has not come exclusively from its news coverage and editorials. During the Cold War, for example, VOA built a huge following in the Soviet Union and Eastern Europe for its broadcasting of American jazz, through programming hosted by long-time VOA music broadcaster Willis Conover. VOA Africa Division's programs for many years featured broadcaster Leo Sarkisian's unique treasury of field-recorded African music.

VOA programming comes from many sources: wire services and independent, commercial news media, as well as its own journalists in the U.S. and abroad. VOA journalists keep their overseas audiences in mind, pursuing stories at home and abroad that will be of interest to them. VOA programming at the beginning of the 21st century broadcast in 44 languages.

From its very early years, VOA has been presented in English, but it has also broadcast in such languages as German, Polish, Russian, Japanese, Tibetan, Kurdish, and Bahasa. American foreign policy interests are evident, particularly in VOA's shifting of broadcasting resources from region to region and from language to language, depending on where policy makers have perceived challenges to American interests.

VOA has correspondents, stringers, and news bureaus all over the world, but its programming is produced in and broadcast via shortwave and satellite from studios in Washington, D.C. In 2004, VOA estimated the weekly audience for its radio and television programming to be almost 100 million. The programming has always relied on shortwave broadcasting from VOA's transmitters around the world, but it has also broadcast regionally via AM and FM frequencies through relationships with foreign affiliate stations. Television programming is delivered by satellite, both to individuals with receiving dishes and to affiliate stations, who rebroadcast it as part of their own programming. VOA has invested itself in establishing a significant Internet presence as well.

As VOA observed its 60th anniversary in 2002, it looked to its future as part of a reorganized U.S. international broadcasting effort. A newly established Broadcasting Board of Governors provided oversight to VOA, as well as to other U.S. broadcasters, such as Radio Free Europe, Radio Liberty, Radio Martí, and Radio Free Asia. VOA also anticipated expanding its services into new technologies, including text messaging and satellite radio, to deliver its programming. Its importance as a representative of American society to the rest of the world continues into the 21st century.

**Bibliography**

Alexandre, Laurien. *The Voice of America: From Détente to the Reagan Doctrine*. Norwood, N.J.: Ablex Publishing Corporation, 1988.

Pirsein, Robert William. *The Voice of America: An History of the International Broadcasting Activities of the United States Government, 1940–1961.* New York: Arno Press, 1979.

Tyson, James L. *U S. International Broadcasting and National Security.* New York: Ramapo Press, 1983.

**Further Reading**

Heil, Alan L. *Voice of America: A History.* New York: Columbia University Press, 2003.

Nelson, Michael. *War of the Black Heavens: The Battles of Western Broadcasting in the Cold War.* Syracuse, N.Y.: Syracuse University Press, 1997.

Shulman, Holly Cowan, *The Voice of America: Propaganda and Democracy, 1941–1945.* Madison: University of Wisconsin Press, 1990.

Voice of America Website <http://www.voanews.com>.

**Related Entries**

Media and War; Radio Free Europe; Radio in World War II

—*John Benedict Buescher*

# Volunteerism

See Conscription and Volunteerism.

# War Brides

Falling in love in the midst of war is not a modern phenomenon. As early as the founding of the first English colonies, American soldiers have met and married foreign brides during times of battle, often despite lack of official approval. But "war brides"—the collective term used to describe foreign-born brides of U.S. servicemen stationed abroad—did not truly enter social consciousness until the end of World War II. The sheer number of American troops spread across the globe during that era, the length of their service, and the close contact with foreign populations, proved a fertile ground for the romantic relationships that would change immigration laws, ethnic and racial relations, and American society forever.

The first of these changes was the War Brides Act of 1945, which loosened immigration laws to expedite the entry of more than 100,000 war brides, predominantly those from Europe. As immigration laws continued to relax over the next two decades—and, in particular, with the end of the Korean and Vietnam wars—another wave of predominantly Asian war brides landed on American soil. Although the most recent wars in the Middle East have seen few marriages, U.S. troops stationed throughout the world during peacetime continue to marry abroad and bring home new wives and families that help shape America's multicultural landscape.

### British War Brides

U.S. troops began to arrive in the United Kingdom in 1942. While a welcome military presence, American troops faced some social resentment in Great Britain. A popular British saying of the time cast them as "overpaid, oversexed, and over here." (U.S. troops, in turn, dismissed British troops as "undersexed, underpaid, underfed, and under Eisenhower.")

Still, the American mystique was powerful in that day. In a 2004 *Orlando Sentinel* article, Mary Weyrauch, a British war bride, recalled, "We thought Americans were always living it up. . . . In the movies we saw, it looked like all they did was go on holidays and drive around on Saturday night." Pamela Winfield, author of two books on war brides—and a British war bride herself—said in a 1986 *New York Times* article, "They were different, and so polite. . . . And they were so handsome in their uniforms, which fit better than the British boys."

The mystique was built on more than Hollywood and manners. U.S. troops were also far better off than their British counterparts—earning three times the income, and dining daily on the equivalent of nearly a week's worth of British wartime food rations. Even American soldiers, many of them children of the Depression, could be overwhelmed by the money and food provided by the War Department. This, combined with the notion of U.S. troops as valiant liberators, set the stage for thousands of budding romances. At the end of the war, the number of troops married abroad prompted Congress to pass the War Brides Act in December 1945, to expedite the entry of new brides to the United States.

Beginning in 1946, 70,000 British war brides set sail for the United States aboard U.S. naval ships and luxury ocean liners, such as the *Queen Mary*, which had been converted for military use. These 70,000 comprised the largest group of immigrants—male or female, from any single country—of the 1940s.

Their arrival was heralded by newspapers, and many were greeted at the docks by open arms and friendly faces. Yet their reception had many negative aspects as well. When the war brides arrived, they were sent to processing centers, where they were often made to undress for medical inspection. Some complained that they were treated like cattle. And even after "processing," many war brides faced hostility in public. One British war bride recalled, in a 1986 *Chicago Tribune* article, being told "go back to your own country!" as she toured New York City in a bus emblazoned with "GI War Bride" on one side.

How well a woman acclimated to the United States depended a lot on her expectations. Those taken by glamorous notions of the United States often felt fooled. Those from cities experienced culture shock upon arriving in their new husbands' rural towns. Others adjusted more easily. Some had preexisting transatlantic ties to extended family and friends. (The British were the least affected by early 20th-century laws restricting European immigration.) Many joined groups to maintain relationships with each other and with their homeland. Almost immediately following the departure of the first war brides in 1946, the Transatlantic Brides and Parents Association was founded. This group helped arrange reduced-rate travel for war brides and their families.

In many ways, the tale of British war brides is a happy one: language barriers and cultural differences were negligible compared to war brides from other parts of Europe, and they did not encounter the racism that would plague Asian war brides of the coming generation. Their history is recalled with a tone of nostalgia—and many war brides themselves speak fondly of their past. As Pamela Winfield recalled in the *Chicago Sun-Times*, "We were a special act of Congress, a moment in history."

### Brides From Throughout Europe

Of course, British women were not the only war brides of World War II. Women throughout Europe—particularly

*German war brides and fiancées arriving in New York on December 14, 1948. (© Bettmann/CORBIS)*

from France, Italy, and Germany—were swept up by whirlwind romances with soldiers come to liberate their countries.

Whereas British war brides slid easily—though not seamlessly—into American society, non-English-speaking war brides faced language barriers and, in many cases, resentment. German and Italian war brides fared the worst. From the beginning, fraternization between U.S. troops and Italian or German nationals was looked down upon socially and was forbidden outright by the military. But U.S. servicemen fell in love and proposed marriage nonetheless.

Prospective brides underwent a tedious interview process. For German brides, both a Nazi and someone persecuted by Nazis had to testify that she had no Nazi ties. Once in the United States, German war brides, in particular, were derided as Nazis.

In all, by 1950, an estimated 150,000 to 200,000 women from across continental Europe had married U.S. servicemen. By the 1960s, however, the number of European war brides decreased as the number of U.S. troops in Europe fell. By then, the next wave of war brides—resulting from other conflicts in which the United States had involved its troops—was well under way.

### Asian War Brides

Asian immigration to the United States had been severely restricted since the end of the 19th century. But the end of Word War II brought, in addition to the War Brides Act and the GI Fiancées Act, the repeal of Exclusion Act and a loosening of the quota system for Asians in particular. Chinese, Indian, and Filipina war brides were among the first to arrive. The largest group of war brides, however, came from Japan and, later, Korea.

Approximately 30,000 Japanese war brides came to the United States in the postwar period. In their homeland, they were often cast as opportunists, traitors, and prostitutes. In a 2000 *Los Angeles Times* article, a Japanese war bride named Miwako Cleeve recalled how she was treated by family and countrymen: cousins threw rocks at her, an uncle removed her name from the family tree, the Japanese government official who processed her exit papers said, "Leave, we don't want you."

The reception in the United States was not altogether better. Like brides from other vanquished countries, Japanese brides were met with resistance and resentment upon arrival in the United States, compounded by fierce racism. Those married to African American soldiers experienced additional prejudice, including disapproval from other Japanese war brides. (Until the late 1960s, it was still illegal in many southern states for blacks to marry other races.)

The product of these mixed marriages—biracial children—also became an issue. A *Saturday Evening Post* article from 1952 reads:

> [T]he effect of these mixed marriages on American life at home is still to come—the arrival of thousands of dark-eyed brides in Mississippi cotton hamlets and New Jersey factory cities, on Oregon ranches or in Kansas country towns. The thousands are on the way, and their bright-eyed children soon will be knocking on school doors in most of the 48 states. The great question of how they will fit in and whether they generally will be welcomed or shunned remains to be answered.

Korean war brides in the postwar period fared similarly. The first Korean war bride arrived in 1950, but most did not come to the United States until after the end of the Korean War in 1953. Continued U.S. military presence means that Korean women are still entering the United States today as spouses of U.S. servicemen. It is estimated that one in four Korean immigrants can trace his or her lineage to the arrival of a Korean war bride.

Like Japanese war brides, Korean brides were disparaged as prostitutes and opportunists by Korean nationals and Americans alike. (These beliefs were not entirely unfounded, since in GI camptowns prostitution was tacitly promoted by the U.S. military, and as with war brides from elsewhere in the world, some women saw life in America as a reprieve from the poverty of their war-torn country.) Korean war brides shared with their Asian peers formidable obstacles with respect to language, culture, custom, and food. (Religion played a smaller role for Koreans, who were often Christian, than for Buddhist Japanese.) Postwar Asian war brides, in particular, found themselves shunned by their home country and marginalized or isolated in their new one. As Korean immigrant communities grew, however, many found comfort and support in community organizations and the Korean–American church.

By the end of the Vietnam War, the number of foreign-born women married to U.S. servicemen was striking: an estimated 67,000 Japanese, 28,000 Korean, and 8,000 Vietnamese. These numbers are based on Immigration and Naturalization Service records; and not all foreign-born wives, particularly those from the Philippines, are considered "war brides." In the years of relative peace that followed, those numbers have continued to grow.

### Twenty-First Century War Brides and Beyond

In a 1991 *Los Angeles Times* article about U.S. troops in Saudi Arabia during the first Gulf War, a diplomat said, "This was probably the first war in history without war brides." Indeed, few war brides have emerged from that war, or from the most recent conflicts in Afghanistan or Iraq. Many attribute this to the changing nature of war in the 21st century and the significant religious and cultural differences—particularly governing interactions between men and women—between the United States and most Islamic countries. Still, love persists in the midst of war. One well-reported case of war brides from Iraq involved two military men who converted to Islam and married Iraqi women in secret. At first, the Army threatened to court-martial both soldiers, and the war brides themselves received death threats and were harassed in public. One soldier eventually agreed to divorce. The other negotiated his discharge from the Army and moved to Jordan to be with his wife.

With U.S. troops continuously stationed throughout the world, war brides (or, to be more accurate, military brides) will continue to change American life, though in different, more subtle ways than the brides of the postwar period. Though by no means a homogenous group, war brides share a particular understanding of military culture, the critical glare of foreign-born parents and American-born in-laws and neighbors, language barriers, and culture shock. Historically, these war brides may be said to have led the way for new immigrants pouring into the U.S. melting pot.

**Bibliography**

Ford, Peter. "Forged in the Heat of World War II." *Christian Science Monitor,* 4 June 2004.

McLeod, Michael. "Soldier Went to Fight in Biggest Battle, Found Love." *Orlando Sentinel,* 6 June 2004.

Moning, Susan. "GI War Brides of '40s See their Britain Again." *Chicago Sun-Times,* 28 September 1986.

Moseley, Ray. "English Brides Recall Days of War, Romance." *Chicago Tribune,* 30 September 1986.

Noriyuki, Duane. "Still Searching for Acceptance." *Los Angeles Times*, 1 May 2000.

Tempest, Rone. "Hordes of Strangers Hardly Touched Culture of Saudi Kingdom." *Los Angeles Times,* 3 September 1991.

Trucco, Terry. "300 War Brides Go Home, to Tea and Tears." *New York Times,* 29 September 1986.

**Further Reading**

Shukert, Elfrieda Berthiaume, and Barbara Smith Scibetta. *The War Brides of World War II.* Novato, Calif.: Presidio Press, 1988.

Virden, Jenel. *Good-Bye, Piccadilly: British War Brides in America.* Urbana: University of Illinois Press, 1996.

Winfield, Pamela. *Sentimental Journey: The Story of the GI Brides.* London: Constable, 1984.

Yuh, Ji-Yeon. *Beyond the Shadow of Camptown: Korean Military Brides in America.* New York: New York University Press, 2002.

**Related Entries**

Families, Military

—*Laura Lambert*

# War Industries Board

The creation of the War Industries Board (WIB) was one example of how World War I transformed the relationship between the government and civilian society when the nation for the first time organized its resources to fight a total war. The WIB functioned as the main government clearing house that coordinated the channeling of civilian resources to meet the military's ever-growing industrial and transportation needs. Despite its lack of a clear legal mandate, the board played a major role in most sectors of the economy during the war, particularly during the latter period of U.S. involvement. Its functions included the prioritization and allocation of raw materials, the formulation of production priorities, price fixing, the establishment of transportation priorities, and intervention into labor markets.

The evolution of the WIB was complex, with several roots. One model and predecessor was the Navy Consulting Board (NCB), founded in July 1915. The NCB formed a partnership among Navy Department staff, industrial leaders, and second tier naval officers. Through this body, production capabilities and priorities were surveyed and discussed, but the NCB never actually set in motion any mobilization plan. A second strand of origin came from the National Defense Act of 1916. The act gave the president the power to make any order for war material obligatory. It also authorized a survey of U.S. industry to determine war production conversion capabilities. Because Pres. Woodrow Wilson campaigned on a moderate peace platform in 1916, little was done to implement these provisions until after the election.

The Council for National Defense (CND) was the forerunner that would most directly evolve into the WIB. The CND was a voluntary organization that brought private sector leaders together with pro-preparedness governmental officials. By the second half of 1916, the government was funding the CND, and the wealthy financier, Bernard Baruch had emerged as a key figure within the organization. Southern born, but deeply entrenched in New York financial circles, Baruch had excellent ties to both industrial leaders and government officials, as well as close links to both the southern and Wall Street forces of the conservative wing of the Democratic Party, including President Wilson.

With the break in diplomatic relations with Germany in February 1917, followed by the declaration of war in April, there was a sudden, rapid increase in war mobilization. Draft notices were sent out in July 1917, and draftees began reporting to their training bases in September 1917. This led to enormous food, clothing, equipment, and transportation needs. At the same time, many branches of the government, particularly the Army and Navy, were placing large orders and sending out frequently conflicting signals or orders about priorities. The General Munitions Board, set up in April 1916, proved inadequate for the coordination of production and purchases. Severe inflation, totaling 85 percent over the two years prior to July 1917, wrecked havoc with budgets and disrupted the economy.

As a result, in June 1917 Sec. of War Newton D. Baker sent to President Wilson, on behalf of the CND, a request to establish a War Industries Board. In his order launching the WIB, Wilson supported Baruch's vision of searching for a middle path between a laissez-faire approach and tight, legally mandated government control.

In its first months of existence, the WIB was a decentralized organization that lacked formal power and adequate funding and staffing. The WIB did not make purchases for the government and had little power in that area. It could merely recommend price levels and lacked the authority to enforce those recommendations. Further, it did not have effective liaisons to many key military sectors, including the shipping and aircraft boards.

The early WIB was not without accomplishments, however. Baruch succeeded in drawing many key industrial leaders into service for the WIB and brought them into contact with the relevant government war agencies. Many businessmen, fearing rigid price controls, greatly preferred the voluntary restraints negotiated through the WIB. The WIB was able to discuss priority issues with industry and helped solve some key raw material allocation problems. The United States Chamber of Commerce threw its support behind the WIB approach.

Yet difficulties in procurement persisted. President Wilson became embroiled in a public conflict with the steel industry over pricing. Gen. John J. Pershing predicted failure for a spring offensive unless production, supply, and transport issues were resolved. Meanwhile, the railroad system, still largely without a coordinated plan, had generated a hopeless tangle that was seriously retarding the war effort, prompting a federal government takeover in December 1917.

After constant prodding from Baruch and others, President Wilson adopted the view that greatly strengthening the WIB was key to an improved war effort. On March 4, 1918, the president issued a new executive order to that effect. The WIB would now function as a distinct agency and in May was formally removed from the aegis of the CND.

The most visible sign of the WIB's new powers was its ability to set war production priorities. Since its power to enforce these priorities remained vague, the group continued to rely heavily on voluntary cooperation. Yet, in an atmosphere of record profits for most military suppliers, strong support for the war effort, and the heavy involvement in the WIB's commodity sections of prominent business leaders, the voluntary support from industrialists and businessmen was generally forthcoming. At the same time, the WIB relied upon cooperation from other government agencies, particularly the Army and Navy, which were fearful that the WIB was too sympathetic to business.

Within the WIB, each commodity section was generally headed by a prominent industrialist from that industry. The section was charged with establishing priorities for output and transportation, addressing the raw materials needs of the industry, coordinating large-scale production, and trying to hold down prices to the government and the public, while meeting the industry's profit needs or desires. As Baruch put it, the powers of the commodity sections "extended only to the point where someone opposed it."

Actual price-fixing or setting policy was not vested in the WIB itself. Instead, Wilson set up a body that consisted of Baruch; two WIB members, including its labor representative; the Federal Trade Commission chairman; the Tariff Commission chairman; and the head of the Fuel Administration. Lacking specific congressional legislative authority, the body functioned primarily through persuasion and pressure, mostly via appeals to patriotism and arguments that specific legislation would be less favorable to business than voluntary restraint.

The WIB also issued 56 circulars, or restrictions on civilian-oriented industries. One example was the limitation of private home construction, except in heavily impacted areas. Another was the automobile industry, in which the WIB mediated the demand of some in the military that all production of private automobiles and other consumer goods cease to counter the demand for these goods fueled by the prosperity of the war years. The outcome was a voluntary restraint on the number of passenger cars produced.

Other WIB policies or functions included establishing priorities for the transport of war material and the inventorying of freight cars and locomotives—something that, amazingly, had not been done prior to 1917. Although these priorities were not always followed, they greatly facilitated the movement of war goods. The WIB attempted a general inventory of industrial capacity and potential in the nation, eventually encompassing some 18,000 factories.

The WIB also worked in the area of conservation of resources, focusing more on efficiency than on ecology. An oft-cited example was ending the practice of retailers returning day-old bread to central bakeries, and the resulting discounted sale and use of the bread.

Responding to the over-crowding and labor shortages of the industrial Northeast, the WIB also pushed for the geographic distribution of war production. In addition, the WIB sent a mission to Europe to coordinate supply issues with the Allies. Finally, in the latter stages of the war, the WIB began exploring labor priorities and restrictions on the recruitment and movement of labor. The war ended before this effort went far.

The WIB had done little planning for postwar reconversion, and the sudden collapse of Germany and the end of the war caught the board by surprise. Wilson's coolness towards a continuation of war-time governmental intervention into the economy and the Republican Congress, elected in November 1918, further convinced Baruch that winding down the WIB would be wise. This was despite the fact that many industrialists, including the majority involved in steel production, urged a continued role for the WIB. Price agreements and priority orders expired at the end of November 1918. In late November, Baruch asked President Wilson to terminate the WIB effective January 1, 1919. In early December, Wilson agreed, and the WIB ceased to function by late December.

The WIB provided the first vivid example of how a governmental agency could organize and rationalize the economy to improve the flow and distribution of goods. Although its existence was short, the agency's influence was widely felt over the next 25 years. Wartime cooperation on the part of business convinced some reformers in the 1920s that a new cooperative ethos between the government and business would replace the earlier progressive emphasis on regulation. The WIB also offered a useful model during the New Deal, when the federal government created the National Recovery Administration (NRA) to establish production standards, price controls, and uniform wages within specific industries. In peacetime, however, the Supreme Court proved unwilling to authorize this kind of government-sponsored coordination and ruled the NRA unconstitutional. When the nation found itself once again embroiled in war in 1941, the WIB offered an important precedent as the country mobilized its economic resources.

### Bibliography

Baruch, Bernard. *American Industry in the War: A Report of the War Industries Board.* New York: Prentice Hall, 1941.

Beaver, Daniel R. *Newton D. Baker and the American War Effort, 1917–1919.* Lincoln: University of Nebraska Press, 1966.

Cuff, Robert D. *The War Industries Board: Business–Government Relations During World War I.* Baltimore, Md.: Johns Hopkins University Press, 1973.

Urofsky, Melvin. *Big Steel and the Wilson Administration.* Columbus: Ohio State University Press, 1969.

Weinstein, James. *The Corporate Ideal in the Liberal State.* Boston: Beacon, 1968.

### Further Reading

Coffmann, Edward M. *The War to End All Wars: The American Military Experience in World War I.* Madison: University of Wisconsin Press, 1966.

Keegan, John. *The First World War.* New York: Alfred A. Knopf, 1997.

Knock, Thomas, J. *To End All Wars: Woodrow Wilson and the Quest for a New World Order.* Princeton, N.J.: Princeton University Press, 1995.

### Related Entries

Economy and War; World War I

*—Mark McCulloch*

# War Labor Board

The National War Labor Board—often referred to simply as the War Labor Board (WLB)—supervised and intervened in many aspects of collective bargaining from 1942 to 1945. During that period, the WLB settled contract disputes and played a major role in establishing wage rates, working hours, and union security provisions. It also intervened directly in a number of strikes. The WLB was at the center of labor relations and labor mobilization during World War II and was instrumental in furthering war production. It also played an instrumental role in lowering inflation and improving the positions of unskilled workers, African Americans, and women. In some important respects, the WLB also helped to shape the world of postwar labor relations.

Immediately following the Japanese attack on Pearl Harbor, Pres. Franklin D. Roosevelt called an emergency meeting of 12 labor and 12 management representatives to discuss the creation of an agency responsible for preventing work stoppages during the war. The meeting issued a no-strike no-lockout declaration and agreed that a new board should be established, but the group deadlocked on the issue of guaranteeing union security. Management wanted to deny any government agency authority over this issue, while the labor representatives pressed for union security to be part of contracts settled by the new board.

By executive order, President Roosevelt established the WLB on January 12, 1942. The new agency took over the caseload of the defunct National Defense Mediation Board (NDMB) and was tripartite in nature, with four representatives each from management, labor, and public sectors. The board was first chaired by William H. Davis, the former head of the NDMB, and George W. Taylor succeeded him in March 1945. The WLB immediately established the principle that it should turn first to independent, collective bargaining in disagreements between management and labor. Only if an impasse persisted would the WLB review a case and settle the contract, while trying to avoid work stoppages.

In its first major cases, the WLB dealt with union security issues. In these cases, the public members generally sided with the labor representatives: first, to agree to consider such cases; and second, to establish a principle known as "maintenance of membership." This was a modified union shop provision, under which any worker who had joined the union would remain as a member for the duration of the contract. If a union shop (one in which all workers had to join the union after employment) or a closed shop (where only union members were hired) were already in effect, the WLB would approve it in lieu of maintenance of membership. A key corporate move towards grudging acceptance of this principle came in May 1942, when U.S. Steel announced that it would comply with the Federal Shipbuilding decision.

In the opening months of its existence, the WLB was fairly free to rule on wage increases as it saw fit. The International Harvester decision, arrived at during this period, established the general principle that wages should keep pace with inflation and be high enough to grant workers decent and healthy lifestyles. Given the low wage levels that prevailed at the end of the Depression, this formulation was broadly favorable to workers.

Almost immediately, however, this position of the WLB began to erode. On April 27, 1942, President Roosevelt sent to Congress a seven-point anti-inflation plan. In this environment, on July 16, 1942, the WLB issued perhaps its most significant decision, the Little Steel Formula. This mandate—arrived at during deadlocked negotiations between the United Steelworkers and Bethlehem, Inland, Republic, and Youngstown Sheet and Tube—determined that wage increases in this case, and all others, would not exceed to a level 15 percent above where they had stood on January 1, 1941.

This formula remained the guiding principle of the WLB on wages for the duration of the war. Labor criticized it on several grounds. First, they argued, the general rate of inflation far exceeded 15 percent, and the increase was particularly steep in manufacturing towns. They further argued that the gap preserved the very low wages that had prevailed as a result of the Depression and the previous absence of mass unionization. Corporations argued that weekly wages had kept pace with inflation, although hourly wages had not. This was true because of the longer hours worked during the war, especially overtime at premium pay. They also argued that higher increases would lead to runaway inflation.

Within the Little Steel Formula, there was substantial room for tinkering, since the WLB allowed for inequity exceptions and for the improvement of "substandard" wages and conditions. The public members of the WLB were generally sympathetic to minimizing regional pay disparities, by lifting southern and rural wage rates, but they were cool to the expansion of shift differentials, since they wanted few barriers to round-the-clock production. The board also allowed for increasing female wage rates to lessen discrimination, even if those increases topped 15 percent, while individual merit raises were excluded from consideration.

In 1942, conservative pressures on the WLB increased with the passage of the Economic Stabilization Act. More significantly, on September 18, 1942, Roosevelt issued an executive order calling for the freezing of wages. For a brief period, it seemed that the WLB would effectively go out of business, but on October 3, Executive Order 9250 was issued, allowing for exceptions along the lines of the Little Steel Formula. The Order, however, also made decisions of the WLB subject to the approval of the Office of Economic Stabilization (OES), headed by conservative Democrat James Byrnes, and ordered the board to limit all wage increases to the Little Steel Formula—even those that did not involve cases of dispute.

During this period, unions concentrated their cases at the WLB on lifting general wage increases up to the Little Steel Formula limits and on pushing for the removal of inequities. The WLB also created regional boards to handle the increasing volume of cases. This period ended, however, in April 1943, when Roosevelt issued Executive Order 9328, the "Hold-the-Line" order. This stripped the board of power to address inequities and strengthened the review and denial powers of the OES. Under this order, very little power remained with the WLB, and labor protested in its strongest terms yet. In May, Roosevelt issued a new order, allowing the WLB to reclaim some powers. In the interim, however, the board had thrown out some 10,000 inequity cases, or 60 percent of its backlogged caseload.

For the remainder of the war, more and more collective bargaining cases ended in impasse, stuck before a WLB that was unlikely to approve across-the-board wage increases. With a restive labor force clamoring for raises to keep pace with inflation, the board turned increasingly towards the acceptance of incentive wage plans to boost actual earnings.

The most important strike of the war years, the 1943 series of walkouts by coal miners, also involved the WLB. In April 1943, United Mine Workers of America (UMWA) Pres. John L. Lewis refused to appear before what he called a "discredited political agency" in a case involving a wage increase and the issue of portal-to-portal pay. The board denied the union's claims and the coal miners struck. A promise by the board to reopen the case brought a temporary return to work, but on June 18 the new WLB ruling made only minor changes. Several more strikes took place, and eventually the WLB was forced to approve a settlement that granted the UMWA its $1.50-a-day wage hike, based on portal-to-portal pay and a shortened lunch period.

The WLB was a major force against wildcat strikes by denying any wage gains they might result in, and by sanctioning—even ordering—the termination of wildcatters by their employers. At the same time, a carrot-and-stick approach was utilized to pressure labor leaders to clamp down on militancy. Unions that complied were rewarded with maintenance of membership and dues check-off, while workers who resisted could find themselves fired and drafted, or their union broken and decertified. The public members of the WLB also strongly favored management prerogatives in issues involving new technology and plant movement and closure, generally acting to restrict labor from involvement in those areas. The WLB urged the immediate settlement of jurisdictional disputes between competing unions, but usually did so on the basis of the status quo, which favored the more entrenched American Federation of Labor at the expense of newer unions.

Labor now centered its attacks on the accuracy of the Bureau of Labor Statistics' (BLS) cost-of-living calculations. The BLS estimated the price hikes since January 1941 at 23.4 percent, when Roosevelt appointed five WLB members in December 1943 to a new panel to come up with a more accurate figure. This panel arrived at an inflation figure of 27 percent; but the report was not completed until late 1944, and then simply sent to Roosevelt for "study."

Cases involving the major mass production industries came before the board in 1944, but dragged on in deadlock. By early 1945, labor frustration began to peak, and the executive board of the United Auto Workers urged withdrawal from the WLB. Textile Workers Pres. Emil Rieve did resign from the board, and pressure grew from other unions to do the same.

Conservative corporate leaders became increasingly restive with the enhanced bargaining power of workers now that full employment levels had been obtained—and by the partial recognition of such bargaining power by the WLB. A notable example of such resistance was Montgomery Ward's chairman Sewell Avery's refusal to comply with a WLB order to extend an expired contract. This defiance resulted in the seizure of the plant by troops (under order from President Roosevelt), one of 40 such wartime examples, most of them in the latter half of the conflict.

As it became clear that the war would soon end, cases brought before the WLB in 1945 were more about positioning for the post-war collective bargaining showdown than they were about hopes that the board would actually settle them.

With the end of hostilities overseas, the WLB began to fade away. On August 18, 1945, President Harry Truman's Executive Order 9599 allowed the WLB to grant wage increases "if they did not affect prices." The board then decided it would only accept new cases if they were jointly submitted by labor and management. In October, the WLB went a step further and refused to take any new cases. It also voted to formally dissolve, effective December 15, 1945.

The WLB maintained a mostly strike free environment during a period when prices outstripped hourly wage rates and in an atmosphere of acute labor shortage. It had, at the same time, greatly assisted in the growth of unions and in the stabilization of collective bargaining patterns. In so doing, the WLB had both greatly assisted the U.S. war effort and set the stage for a massive wave of strikes following the war.

**Bibliography**

Fraser, Steven. *Labor Will Rule: Sidney Hillman and the Rise of American Labor.* New York: Free Press, 1991.

Gerstle, Gary. *Working Class Americanism: The Politics of Labor in a Textile City, 1914–1960.* New York: Cambridge University Press, 1989.

Goulden, Joseph. *Meany*. New York: Atheneum, 1972.

James, Ralph, and Estelle James. *Hoffa and the Teamsters: A Study of Union Power.* New York: Van Nostrand, 1965.

Schact, John. *The Making of Telephone Unionism, 1920–1947.* New Brunswick, N.J.: Rutgers University Press, 1985.

**Further Reading**

Lichtenstein, Nelson. *Labor's War at Home: The CIO in World War Two.* New York: Cambridge University Press, 1982.

Seidman, Joel. *American Labor from Defense to Reconversion.* Chicago: University of Chicago Press, 1953.

Zeiger, Robert. *The CIO: 1935–55*, Chapel Hill: University of North Carolina Press, 1995.

**Related Entries**

Economy and War; Labor Strikes

—*Mark McColloch*

# War of 1812

## (1812–15)

The "Second War for Independence" fought between the United States and Great Britain was the product of already strained relations exacerbated by war in Europe. The war was ostensibly fought for freedom of the seas, to end impressment, and for territory in Canada; yet the eventual peace treaty changed these circumstances little. However, the Battle of New Orleans, fought after the treaty was signed, fostered the perception that the United States won the war and ushered in a new era of American nationalism.

### Origins of the Conflict

In 1783, few European countries, particularly Great Britain, welcomed an independent United States into the community of nations. The outbreak of war between Great Britain and France in 1793 further strained U.S.–European relations. Not only did British troops occupy posts in the Old Northwest until 1796, but both France and England began interfering with American shipping in the Atlantic to prevent the other from gaining an economic advantage from the overseas trade. By 1807, the British were stopping American ships on the high seas and impressing sailors into the Royal Navy. While some impressed sailors were in fact deserters from the Royal Navy, others were British-born, naturalized American citizens, a status ignored by Great Britain. Both Britain and France also enacted naval blockades that hurt American overseas shipping interests.

Having exhausted diplomatic solutions, Pres. Thomas Jefferson announced an embargo that confined American vessels to their ports. When the embargo crippled the American economy, Jefferson reopened trade with all nations but Great Britain and France. Jefferson's successor, James Madison, offered a trade monopoly to the first nation that would stop interfering with American trade. Napoleon Bonaparte seemingly promised an end to French aggression contingent upon an end to the British blockade. Madison, hoping to pressure the British, took advantage of the French offer and imposed nonimportation against Great Britain in November 1810.

In addition to free trade and sailors' rights, frontier troubles appeared to give the United States a *causus belli*. Since 1783, American settlers in the Northwest clashed repeatedly with Indians of the region. In 1808, the Shawnee chief Tecumseh and his brother Tenskwatawa, "The Prophet," began unifying western tribes to prevent further American expansion. Blaming the British for increased Indian activity, Indiana Territory Gov. William Henry Harrison led an army to Prophet's Town, Tecumseh's capital, defeating the Shawnee at the November 7, 1811 battle of Tippecanoe. Demoralized, Tecumseh and his followers looked to the British for aid and support, increasing American calls for war against Canada.

### "Mr. Madison's War"

By 1812, western and southern Republicans concluded that war was necessary to protect American neutral rights and stop impressment. Henry Clay, John C. Calhoun, and the "War Hawks" also argued that the western frontier should be defended. Federalists, concentrated in New England in and the northern mid-Atlantic region, opposed the war, fearing continued commercial losses. Less bellicose Republicans argued that the absence of a stable banking system (as the charter for the First Bank of the United States had expired in 1811), limited tariffs, and inadequate trade revenues, combined with the poor state of the armed forces, left the

| War of 1812 (1812–15) |
|---|
| Total U.S. Servicemembers (Worldwide): **286,730** |
| U.S. Population (millions): **7.6** |
| Battle Deaths: **2,260** |
| Non-mortal Woundings: **4,505** |
| Cost (in $ current billions): **.09** |

Source: Deaths and Nonmortal Wounds: Department of Veterans Affairs, *America's Wars*. <http://www1.va.gov/opa/fact/amwars.html>

nation economically unprepared for a conflict. The Army numbered a mere 6,700 poorly trained men, commanded by aging officers. The Navy was well trained and commanded, but it had only 16 vessels with which to challenge a numerically superior Royal Navy. Congress debated Madison's call for a declaration of war against Great Britain, narrowly approving it for presidential signature on June 18, 1812, unaware that the British Parliament had repealed the provisions the United States found offensive only two days earlier.

### The War in the North

Relying upon militia and unproven officers, the American campaigns of 1812 proved inconclusive and costly, despite Great Britain's inability to commit fully to the conflict. Gen. William Hull's offensive into Upper Canada ended in defeat when he surrendered the 2,000-man Detroit garrison without firing a shot. Gen. Stephen Van Rensselaer's inability to reinforce an invasion that had crossed the Niagara River and stormed Queenston Heights led to comparable disaster. Militia under Gen. William Dearborn remained against orders in Plattsburgh, New York, refusing to march on Montreal on the basis that they were raised to defend New York, not attack Canada.

The 1813 campaigns represented only a slight improvement. By May, U.S. forces sacked York, the capital of Upper Canada. By September, American Naval Commodore Oliver H. Perry had built a fleet on Lake Erie, where the numerical advantages of the Royal Navy were negated. Perry's victory on Lake Erie enabled Hull's replacement, Gen. William Henry Harrison, to retake Detroit and challenge the British and their Indian allies in Upper Canada. In October 1813, the British were defeated at the Battle of the Thames, and Tecumseh was killed, halting plans for an Indian union. Elsewhere, the lack of cooperation among senior officers hindered offensive operations, leaving the United States no closer to victory in 1813 than it was in 1812.

### The War in the South

American forces were more successful in the South. After the August 1813 attack on Fort Mims in Alabama, Maj. Gen. Andrew Jackson of Tennessee conducted a campaign against Creeks in Alabama that culminated in a March 1814 victory at Horseshoe Bend. Defeated militarily, the tribe ceded two-thirds of its territory in the Treaty of Fort Jackson in August 1814. For his efforts, Jackson was commissioned a major general in the U.S. Army and tasked with defending the Gulf Coast.

### The 1814 Offensives

The collapse of Napoleon's empire in 1814 allowed Great Britain to rush fresh troops to the United States. Blockading the East Coast, the British proposed invading the United States via Niagara and Lake Champlain, coupled with an offensive up the Chesapeake Bay and another against New Orleans. Before British troops could arrive, however, U.S. forces launched another offensive across the Niagara. At Chippewa and Lundy's Lane in July 1814, Brig. Gen. Winfield Scott proved the value of well-trained and capably officered regulars, but accomplished little, as a stalemate was reached in the region by the end of the year's campaigning.

### Macdonough and Plattsburgh

In September 1814, British Maj. Gen. Sir George Prevost massed 17,000 veterans in Quebec and Montreal, hoping to seize territory in upper New York. Defending Plattsburgh with 3,500 men, American Gen. Alexander Macomb called upon nearby governors for reinforcements. Electing to await the arrival of the British Fleet, Prevost hoped to pin down Macomb's force and then attack Plattsburgh, following a British naval offensive on Lake Champlain. The British fleet on the lake was blocked by American Naval Lt. Thomas Macdonough, who commanded a small fleet. After the American flagship endured repeated broadsides, it swung its undamaged guns into action, battering the British into submission and gaining control of Lake Champlain. Losing 2,000 men in the attempt to take Plattsburgh, Prevost retreated into Canada, convinced that he could not continue his offensive without gaining control of the lake.

### The Chesapeake Campaign

With American attention focused on the Niagara front and on Lake Champlain, a second British force advanced up the Chesapeake. In early June 1814, Vice Adm. Alexander Cochrane and Maj. Gen. Robert Ross sent one British squadron up the Potomac River towards Washington and another up the Chesapeake towards Baltimore. Targeting the nation's capitol, Gen. William Winder's 6,000-man American militia tried to defend Bladensburg, but was no match for 4,000 battle-hardened British regulars. After defeating Winder's forces, the British captured Washington and burned the Capitol, the White House, and other public buildings in retaliation for the sacking of York in 1813.

Moving on to Baltimore, the British force was slowed by earthworks manned by more than 13,000 American militia and regulars, as well as the star-shaped Fort McHenry, a brick fortification garrisoned by U.S. regulars commanded by Maj. George Armistead. At North Point, Maryland, militia stalled the British land advance in a battle that felled their commander, General Ross. Bombarding Fort McHenry, the Royal Navy hoped to reduce it by shelling before moving on towards Baltimore. The successful defense of the fortress throughout the night of September 13 to 14 inspired Francis Scott Key, a Baltimore lawyer, to write the poem that would become famous as "The Star-Spangled Banner." The strength of Fort McHenry, coupled with other well-fortified positions held by a numerically superior force, caused British Vice Adm. Cochrane to abandon his objective.

**Dissension within the United States**

In the wake of Washington's destruction, 26 delegates from the New England states, angered by raids and trade losses from the British blockade, met in Hartford, Connecticut, in December 1814 and January 1815 to discuss "Mr. Madison's War." Proposing constitutional amendments designed to reduce Republican political influence, the delegates threatened secession—the first time this had occurred in the

*The bombardment of Fort McHenry, near Baltimore, in 1814, as represented in a contemporary drawing from the same year. The defense of the fort was the inspiration for "The Star-Spangled Banner," which was to become the American national anthem.* (*© Bettmann/CORBIS*)

young country's history—if their demands were not met. These included limiting the president to one term, prohibiting successive presidents from the same state, limiting trade embargoes to 60 days, excluding the foreign-born from federal offices, abolishing the three-fifths law for taxes and representation, and requiring a two-thirds vote to declare war and admit new states. But the grievances of the Hartford Convention were soon overshadowed by good news from Europe and New Orleans.

### The Treaty of Ghent

In August 1814, British and American diplomats initiated negotiations in Ghent, Belgium, to end the war. Hoping to end impressments and win indemnities for seized ships, American negotiators were held up by the British, who sought territorial concessions in Maine and New York to create an Indian buffer state; demilitarization of the Great Lakes; access to the Mississippi; and an end to American fishing off the Canadian coast. The British secretly hoped that military victories in North America would strengthen their position; but altering their plans, the British dropped their demand for an Indian state and insisted instead on the retention of occupied territory. The Americans countered with status quo ante bellum, invoking a return to the borders as they existed before the war began, and hoping that setbacks on Lake Champlain would weaken British resolve. Facing war weariness both at home and abroad, the British finally signed the treaty on Christmas Eve, 1814, agreeing to terms of status quo ante bellum, despite the fact that the New Orleans campaign was already underway. The war would end upon ratification, but the issues that had caused the conflict remained to be settled.

### New Orleans and Victory

Setting out from Jamaica in October 1814 with a force of 7,500 veteran soldiers, British Gen. Edward Pakenham had sought to capture New Orleans. Regarding the treaty that transferred the Louisiana territory from Spain to France as invalid, the British hoped to establish a colony and potentially return Louisiana to their Spanish allies, the Treaty of Ghent notwithstanding. On the other side, commanding a hastily assembled force of U.S. regulars, western volunteers, free black men, and Baratarian pirates, Gen. Andrew Jackson prepared defensive positions astride the Mississippi River, blocking the approach to the city by land or water. On the morning of January 8, 1815, Pakenham's forces attacked the American positions in a frontal assault. Defeated by a combination of artillery and musket fire that left Pakenham and 2,000 others killed or wounded, the British withdrew from the Gulf, unable to capture the most important port in the western United States and fulfill their goal of territorial acquisition.

### Aftermath

Because of their victory in the Battle of New Orleans, Americans came away from the war considering themselves victorious, despite the fact that none of the issues that had precipitated the war were resolved. Jackson's victory bolstered the case of those who believed in the efficacy of an army of citizen soldiers, though militia failures elsewhere contributed to the realization that the United States would need a regular army commanded by capable officers to protect itself. While Mr. Madison's War could not be considered particularly successful for the United States, it nonetheless had a lasting influence on the young republic.

#### Bibliography

Barbuto, Richard V. *Niagara 1814: America Invades Canada.* Lawrence: University Press of Kansas, 2000.

Latour, Arsène Lacarrière. *Historical Memoir of the War in West Florida and Louisiana, 1814–1815.* Edited by Gene Smith. Gainesville, Fla.: Historic New Orleans Collection/University Press of Florida, 1999.

Pitch, Anthony S. *The Burning of Washington: The British Invasion of 1814.* Annapolis, Md.: Naval Institute Press, 1998.

#### Further Reading

Elting, John R. *Amateurs to Arms!: A Military History of the War of 1812.* Chapel Hill, N.C.: Algonquin Books, 1991.

Hickey, Donald R. *The War of 1812: A Forgotten Conflict.* Urbana: University of Illinois Press, 1989.

Remini, Robert V. *The Battle of New Orleans: Andrew Jackson and America's First Military Victory.* New York: Viking, 1999.

Skeen, C. Edward. *Citizen Soldiers in the War of 1812.* Lexington: University Press of Kentucky, 1999.

Stagg, J. C. A. *Mr. Madison's War: Politics, Diplomacy, and Warfare in the Early American Republic, 1783–1830.* Princeton, N.J.: Princeton University Press, 1983.

Watts, Steven. *The Republic Reborn: War and the Making of Liberal America, 1790–1820.* Baltimore, Md.: Johns Hopkins University Press, 1987.

**Related Entries**

Impressment; Jackson, Andrew; Scott, Winfield; "Star-Spangled Banner, The"; Tecumseh

**Related Documents**

1814

—*Robert P. Wettemann, Jr.*

# War on Terrorism

**(2001– )**

September 11, 2001, ushered in a new age in America and in America's relations with the world. On that date, terrorists flew hijacked airliners into both of the World Trade Center towers, killing themselves, their fellow passengers, and several thousand people inside the buildings. Another hijacked plane was flown into the western face of the Pentagon—the Arlington, Virginia, headquarters of the U.S. military. Yet another crashed in a field near Shanksville, Pennsylvania, after its passengers, having heard of the earlier attacks at the Pentagon and World Trade Center, stormed their hijackers. This brave but Pyrrhic victory prevented an attack on another prominent American landmark—possibly the U.S. Capitol Building or the White House itself.

As America and the world watched on live television, both of the Trade Center's towers collapsed; many emergency workers and firefighters were killed along with those they had entered the buildings to rescue. The final death toll in New York was over 2,600, with the total number of people killed in the four attacks totaling around 3,000, including all passengers on the aircraft. This tally, while horrifically high, was—considering the fact that over 50,000 people worked at the World Trade Center on a typical day—also mercifully low. That said, the sheer scale and scope of these attacks dwarfed any previous terrorist strike.

Immediately after the attacks, America was a nation in mourning and a nation under siege; for the first time, air traffic was almost totally grounded for three days. The state of alert that followed the attacks in the United States was also mirrored overseas, with flights over London, for instance, barred for several days. The New York Stock exchange closed until September 17, and within a week of its reopening, the Dow Jones Industrial Index experienced its largest drop ever over such a short time period. America was effectively a nation at war, with its leaders vowing vengeance on those responsible for the most serious attack on the continental United States in almost 200 years, and its citizens demanding justice for an outrage they could barely believe had happened. The September 11 attacks impacted U.S. society at a fundamental level, and were viewed by many as not only an attack on America, but as an attack on the civilized world itself.

*Onlookers watching the smoke and flames pouring from the World Trade Center in New York following terrorist attacks on September 11, 2001. (Associated Press/AP)*

### The September 11 Attacks in Context

Suspicion for the attacks quickly fell on al Qaeda—an Islamist terrorist organization headquartered in Afghanistan and commanded by a wealthy Saudi Arabian exile, Osama bin Laden. September 11, 2001, was not the first occasion that the United States had been targeted by al Qaeda. Bin Laden had issued the first of several declarations of war against America as far back as 1996, and al Qaeda, like other Islamist terrorist groups, was behind several attacks against U.S. interests in the preceding decade. The first such attack was believed to have taken place in Aden, Yemen, in December 1992, when a hotel hosting U.S. troops en route to a humanitarian mission in Somalia was bombed; two Austrian tourists were killed in this attack, but the Americans had already left before the bomb exploded. Al Qaeda was also believed to have helped train and arm some of those who fought a pitched battle against American troops in Somalia in October 1993, resulting in 18 American deaths and an eventual U.S. withdrawal from the East African country.

In addition, bin Laden's organization was linked to the February 1993 truck bombing of the World Trade Center in New York that left six dead and a thousand wounded, as well as to a disrupted plan to blow up the city's Holland and Lincoln tunnels, among other landmarks. The group was further implicated in a plot to blow up a dozen U.S. airliners over the Pacific in 1995, as well as a bombing in Riyadh, Saudi Arabia, the same year that killed seven people, five of them American. Al Qaeda also carried out truck bombings at the U.S. embassies in Nairobi, Kenya, and Dar es Salaam, Tanzania, in August 1998, killing more than 250, including 12 Americans, and injuring thousands more. Two years later the group used an explosives-packed motorboat to kill 17 Americans aboard the USS *Cole*. As such incidents illustrate, and as the final report of the commission established to examine the 2001 assaults pointed out, "The 9/11 attacks were a shock, but they should not have come as a surprise."

Bin Laden is believed to have helped found al Qaeda in the 1980s. The organization was initially formed to train, support, and fund the many foreign fighters who flocked to Afghanistan to join the Muslim mujahideen resistance movement after the Soviet Union's invasion of the country in 1979. The al Qaeda leader returned to Saudi Arabia in 1989 after the Soviet withdrawal from Afghanistan. After being confined to Jeddah due to his opposition to the Saudi government's close relationship with America, bin Laden fled to Sudan, where he began to invest in the country's infrastructure, setting up legitimate businesses including farms and a road construction company. By January 1994, bin Ladin was suspected to be financing at least three terrorist training camps in Sudan. The al Qaeda leader's support for Islamist fundamentalist movements led the Saudi government to revoke his citizenship and freeze his assets in 1994. Two years later, bin Ladin moved back to Afghanistan after international pressure caused Sudan to expel him. While there he enjoyed a close relationship with the Taliban regime and continued to run terrorist training camps.

Al Qaeda differs from most terrorist groups in that it is a kind of loose network that works to inspire, support, train, and incite like-minded organizations. This decentralized mode of operations makes it more difficult to counter than more conventional terrorists. Al Qaeda itself also undertakes specific operations on occasion, with such attacks—like those of September 11, 2001—sometimes planned years in advance. Led by an Egyptian, Mohammed Atta, the September 11 attacks were carried out by 19 hijackers, some of whom prepared for their mission with flying lessons in America. All the hijackers—who used knives, box cutters, and pepper spray to gain control of their assigned aircraft—died in the attacks. Such martyrdom is a common characteristic of Islamist terrorist groups; their willingness to die is another factor that makes them particularly difficult to counter.

Bin Laden's self-professed goals included the expulsion of American forces from the Arabian Peninsula and the overthrow of existing secular Muslim governments, to replace them with a new caliphate—a pan-Islamic dominion, ruled by religious law. Al Qaeda's war on the West was likely more nuanced than these aims, baldly stated, suggest. As terrorism expert Jessica Stern argues, this war was probably also partly motivated by what many young Muslims perceived to be their humiliation in the face of Western dominance across many realms. In addition, analyst Michael Scott Doran contends that al Qaeda's attack on America may have constituted an effort to draw the United States and the West into what was effectively a civil war between moderate and extremist interpretations of Islam, with any Western counterattack likely to have swollen the ranks of the Islamists or Islamic extremists.

### Framing the War on Terrorism

The parameters of the War on Terrorism were broadly outlined by Pres. George W. Bush on September 20, 2001. Speaking during an address to a joint session of Congress and the American people, President Bush said of this confrontation that it "begins with al Qaeda, but it does not end there. It will not end until every terrorist group of global reach has been found, stopped, and defeated." The President referred to these actions as a "war on terror"—a term that would remain in sporadic use, despite being effectively replaced by the slightly more semantically correct (but often equally contentious) War on Terrorism. This phrase would spawn its own variation—the Global War on Terrorism—a term sometimes attributed to the first Bush administration's department secretary of defense, Paul Wolfowitz.

During the first State of the Union Address after the September 11 attacks, President Bush spoke of an "Axis of Evil," referring to countries that he considered to be either practitioners or sponsors of terrorism, and which had—or could develop—weapons of mass destruction. Initially, this axis comprised Iran, Iraq, and North Korea; it was later expanded to include Cuba, Libya, and Syria. While military action against any of these countries was not explicitly promised, the "Axis" nations were effectively put on notice that the United States would pursue such action if deemed necessary.

On September 18, 2001, the use of military force against those responsible for the September 11 attacks was sanctioned by the U.S. Congress. The scope of this resolution reflected the sense of outrage that the nature and scale of the September 11 attacks invoked. These assaults—the first significant military strikes against the continental United States since the War of 1812—were viewed not only as blows against the country's military and economic might (quite literally in that they were directed at the Pentagon and the World Trade Center), but as attacks on America's society and way of life itself. A wave of patriotism swept the country; and in the immediate aftermath of the attacks, international sympathy and support for America was generally high. Newspaper headlines across the world expressed revulsion at the attacks, with the French newspaper *le Monde*—not known for its pro-U.S. sympathies—famously declaring on its September 12th front page, "*Nous Sommes Tous Americains*" (We are all Americans). Memorial services were held in many cities across the world. A day after the attacks, the North Atlantic Treaty Organization (NATO) invoked Article 5 of its treaty (which says that an attack on one member is an attack on all) for the first time, with NATO aircraft subsequently taking part in air patrols over American territory.

### America Strikes Back

The U.S. government's response to the September 11 attacks had domestic and overseas components that varied militarily as to the intensity and visibility of operations. The first of the high-intensity/high-visibility operations was Operation Enduring Freedom. It was initially to have been called Infinite Justice, but the operation was reportedly renamed amid fears that it would offend the religious sensibilities of Muslims, who might consider that only God was capable of administering such judgment. The campaign began on October 7, 2001, and was directed against the Taliban regime in Afghanistan and the al Qaeda training camps in the country. The capture of bin Laden was a major American aim. A U.S.-led invasion force, working with the Northern Alliance—a loose network of anti-Taliban rebels—ousted the Afghan government by the end of 2001. However, bin Laden was believed to remain free, possibly hiding in the Afghan–Pakistan border regions; still at large, he continued to issue statements condemning America and promising further terrorist acts from al Qaeda and its supporters. An International Security Assistance Force (subsequently taken over by NATO), made up of a coalition of countries, undertook peacekeeping duties in Afghanistan after the Taliban's ouster, while a U.S.-led effort to eradicate Taliban and al Qaeda remnants continued.

Similarly, efforts to locate, capture, or eliminate al Qaeda leaders continued to form an integral part of the U.S. response. While bin Laden's exact whereabouts and status would remain uncertain for some time, other top al Qaeda operatives were taken prisoner or eliminated relatively early in the campaign. Mohammed Atef, thought to have been one of bin Ladin's top commanders, was believed killed during U.S. bombing in Afghanistan in November 2001; and Khalid Sheikh Mohammed, who was believed to have planned the September 11 attacks, was captured in Pakistan in March 2003. Despite that, al Qaeda proved resilient. It also lived up to its self-proclaimed role as a vanguard for like-minded groups and continued to inspire other Islamist terrorist organizations to follow its example by attacking the United States and its allies. In the years following September 11, al Qaeda or its affiliates were linked to a series of such attacks, as far afield as Bali, Morocco, Madrid, and London. Meanwhile, bin Laden was almost displaced as public enemy number one by a new terrorist bogey-man, Abu Musab al-Zarqawi, after the latter's involvement in resistance to U.S. and coalition forces in Iraq, and in a grisly kidnapping campaign there in which hostages were decapitated on videos distributed via the Internet.

The U.S. led-invasion of Iraq in 2003 was explicitly linked to the war on terrorism by the Bush administration. The administration insisted that the regime of Saddam Hussein not only had links with al Qaeda, but was in possession of weapons of mass destruction (WMD), which—it was claimed—the regime might either use itself or pass on to terrorists. Many specialists questioned whether this was actually the case, pointing out the irreconcilable natures of al Qaeda's brand of religious fundamentalism and the secular regime of Saddam Hussein. Many criticisms were also raised surrounding the subsequent failure to find evidence of Iraqi WMD following this regime's ouster. The invasion itself was said by many regional and terrorism experts to have served as a rallying point for America's foes. Such debates aside, the American-led war in Iraq became inextricably linked to the War on Terrorism in that it diverted U.S. resources away from that wider effort and drew terrorists like al-Zarqawi into the fray.

Other aspects of the War on Terrorism were of a lower intensity and visibility. These included a CIA operation in Yemen in November 2002, in which a Predator unmanned aircraft launched a missile strike, killing six al Qaeda operatives. Other initiatives included the Combined Joint Task Force–Horn of Africa (CJTF–HOA), which was designed to intercept terrorist activity in that region, and training operations undertaken by U.S. troops with local forces in places like the Philippines and Georgia.

**Defending the American Homeland**

Domestically, the United States response to the September 11 attacks revolved largely around the formation of the Department of Homeland Security (DHS), which was tasked with protecting America from future terrorist attacks. This was established on November 25, 2002, and became operational two months later, having begun life as the Office of Homeland Security in October 2001. The new department was headed by Tom Ridge—the former governor of Pennsylvania and the first United States secretary of homeland security. The largest government reorganization since the creation of the Department of Defense in 1949, the DHS's formation consolidated 22 separate government agencies and 180,000 employees under one organization and was made up of four major directorates: Border and Transportation Security; Emergency Preparedness and Response; Science and Technology; and Information Analysis and Infrastructure Protection.

The year 2002 also saw the establishment of U.S. Northern Command (NORTHCOM), which assumed responsibility for the homeland defense aspect of the overall security effort. NORTHCOM distinguishes security from defense, describing homeland security as including "the prevention, preemption, and deterrence of, and defense against, aggression targeted at U.S territory." By comparison, it defines homeland defense as "the protection of U.S. territory, domestic population, and critical infrastructure against military attacks emanating from outside the United States." NORTHCOM's mission thus extends beyond the bounds of the War on Terrorism. According to the Pentagon, the creation of the new command was both a reflection of the post-Cold War strategic situation and a reaction to the September 11 attacks. That said, NORTHCOM—whose area of responsibility encompasses the continental United States, Alaska, Canada, Mexico, and the surrounding water out to approximately 500 nautical miles (as well as the Gulf of Mexico, Puerto Rico, and the U.S. Virgin Islands)—performs a role closely tied to America's antiterrorist campaign.

The command has few permanently assigned forces and is comprised of approximately 500 civil servants and uniformed personnel from all services. As well as countering threats to U.S. territory, NORTHCOM is also authorized to provide military assistance to civil authorities as directed by the president or secretary of defense. This aspect of its operations proved to be particularly controversial, with some saying it dangerously weakens the 1878 Posse Comitatus Act, which prohibits the U.S. military being used for domestic law enforcement.

Similarly controversial was the short-lived Total Information Awareness initiative. Conceived by retired U.S. Adm. John Poindexter—a Pentagon consultant and former National Security Advisor under Pres. Ronald Reagan—this computer surveillance system was intended to trawl through virtually all the personal records of every American citizen and analyze this data in an effort to identify terrorists. The program was renamed Terrorist Information Awareness (TIA)—possibly in an attempt to make it more palatable to the American public and to lawmakers. The program's original logo, which bore the Latin inscription "Scienta est potential" (Knowledge is power) and an all-seeing eye surveying the world from atop a pyramid, was likewise scrapped amid a hail of criticism, in which some detractors described it as "Orwellian." In 2003, the U.S. Senate voted against funding for any "deployment and implementation of the [TIA] program." This restriction did not extend to research, however; and some suspicions remained that the U.S. government was still combing the personal files of American citizens, albeit under other guises than TIA. Another of Admiral Poindexter's antiterrorist proposals involved the creation of a type of futures market in which bets would be placed on potential terrorist operations; this system, it was claimed, could offer clues about the likelihood of real attacks, but was also shelved after it provoked outrage from some U.S. politicians. Equally ill-fated was a scheme to set up an Office of Strategic Influence, intended to coordinate U.S. propaganda operations; like the other proposals, it was shelved after being negatively received.

The U.S. response to al Qaeda's attack on America also included efforts to cut off terrorists' financial resources. Towards that end, measures were taken to block and intercept the flow of monies to al Qaeda and other terrorist groups. If appropriately monitored, it was also believed that this money trail could help uncover enemy operatives, with the financial War on Terrorism considered an important part of the overall campaign. However, with the September 11 attacks believed to have been relatively inexpensive (at approximately $500,000), it appeared unlikely that such measures alone would suffice to defeat al Qaeda or like-minded groups.

### The Legal War

Such initiatives were accompanied by new antiterrorist legislation, including the signing into law of the USAPATRIOT Act by President Bush on October 26, 2001. This allowed for indefinite imprisonment without trial of non-U.S. citizens deemed by the attorney general to pose a threat to America's national security. It absolved the government of any obligation to provide legal counsel to detainees or to announce arrests; permitted activities such as the searching of premises without their occupants being immediately informed; and provided greater lassitude generally in intelligence gathering. Significantly, the bill relating to the act was passed in the U.S. Senate by 98 votes to one and in the House of Representatives by 356 votes to 66. Polls also showed that the U.S. public was, initially, not widely alarmed by the PATRIOT Act (full name: The Uniting and Strengthening America by Providing Appropriate Tools Required to Intercept and Obstruct Terrorism Act of 2001).

However, many civil liberties groups, such as the American Civil Liberties Union, condemned the PATRIOT Act as unconstitutional. Public dissatisfaction with the act grew as grassroots activists across America increasingly voiced their concern over aspects of the legislation. Meanwhile, in January 2004, U.S. District Judge Audrey B. Collins ruled that the PATRIOT Act's ban on providing "expert advice or assistance" to groups judged to be terrorist was overly vague and in violation of the 1st and 5th amendments. The ruling came in a lawsuit filed by the Humanitarian Law Project on behalf of plaintiffs who faced up to 15 years imprisonment if they advised groups on the peaceful resolution on the Kurdish refugee problem in Turkey. Bills designed to limit the powers of the PATRIOT Act were introduced at both the U.S. Senate and House of Representatives, and the act continued to be controversial.

*A demonstration in Buffalo, New York, protesting the USAPATRIOT Act, following a meeting of Att. Gen. John Ashcroft with law enforcement officials on Monday, Sept. 8, 2003. (Associated Press/AP)*

A month after signing the PATRIOT Act, President Bush issued an executive order authorizing those accused of terrorism to be tried by military tribunals. It was initially envisaged that these tribunals would meet in private and could pronounce death sentences by recommendation of a two-thirds majority jury, comprised of military officers. This suggestion met with a mixed response, drawing both support and criticism from the American public and politicians. Advocates of such tribunals claimed they were necessary as America was fighting a war on terrorism, and would help avoid any intimidation of jurors and protect intelligence sources. Critics maintained that many of the protections afforded defendants in civilian courts would be denied them at such tribunals, with secrecy equating to a lack of accountability. Many U.S. allies were similarly opposed to this legislation, which was amended in March 2002.

Under the revisions, sessions would now largely be made public, with defendants allowed to review any evidence amassed against them. The unanimous agreement of the entire panel—comprised of three to seven military officers, rather than the twelve members of the public who served on civilian juries—was now needed to pass a death sentence. However, the tribunals still proved controversial in that they permitted procedures such as admitting second-hand evidence (that would be banned in civil courts) and obliged defendants to accept military lawyers unless they could afford to hire civilian ones themselves. Defendants were also barred from appealing in federal courts, being restricted to petitioning review panels that could include military and civilian members.

The establishment of military tribunals was assisted and justified by the U.S. government's classification of enemy personnel in the War on Terrorism as "unlawful combatants" who, because of the nature of their actions, were not protected as fully by international law as "lawful" belligerents. This stance was strongly criticized by many both within and outside the United States, as were its attendant clauses that allowed American citizens to be considered "enemy combatants." Many feared that this would effectively allow anyone to be indefinitely detained without trial, arguing that the adoption of the term "enemy combatant" refuted the Geneva Conventions and was unprecedented in U.S. legal history. Advocates of the approach denied this, citing a 1942 case against German saboteurs apprehended in the United States.

Some nationals of U.S. allies soon fell foul of America's post-September 11 reading of the Geneva Conventions and other treaties, such as the International Covenant on Civil and Political Rights. Many were detained at the U.S. base at Guantanamo Bay, Cuba, which eventually became notorious after being turned into a holding center for prisoners captured by American forces in the Afghan campaign and then the wider War on Terrorism. Likewise, U.S. citizens such as Yaser Esam Hamdi (captured while fighting against American forces in Afghanistan with the Taliban) and Jose Padilla (arrested on suspicion of being involved in a plot to explode a radiological dispersal device—or "dirty bomb"—in the United States), were denied regular civilian trials. The United States also found itself accused of engaging in torture after pictures of abuse suffered by prisoners being held by American forces at Abu Ghraib prison in Iraq were made public. These accusations spread to include bases like Bagram in Afghanistan and Guantanamo Bay in Cuba. There were also allegations that America was sending prisoners to countries known to practice torture for interrogation—in effect, subcontracting its interrogations while avoiding the use of torture itself.

## The War over the War

Since the War on Terrorism began, there was much debate over whether it is possible or desirable to wage such a conflict at all. Any war on terrorism, went the argument, could only be a war in the sense that a war could be waged on cancer or poverty. Moreover, a war risked putting too much emphasis on military means. To many, the drawn-out nature of the conflict in Iraq was evidence of the folly of such an approach. Because of these issues—only a few years into what was expected to be a long conflict, by whatever name it is known—there were those, both within and without the United States, who questioned the degree to which America's post-September 11 security polices furthered their self-professed goals of fostering relations among the great powers and establishing and maintaining an international coalition against terrorism.

Within America itself, the War on Terrorism became a central issue in the political arena and, together with the conflict in Iraq, a pivotal topic in the 2004 election campaign. Meanwhile, domestic opposition to American antiterrorism legislation grew, while others claimed that such measures were necessary to prevent another September 11—even as debate over whether those attacks could have been prevented through more proactive measures on the part of America's intelligence services continued to reverberate. Many concerns centered around the dangers of inadvertently restricting the very freedoms that the U.S. antiterrorist effort sought to protect. Such dilemmas, it was feared, would only deepen the longer America's so-called War on Terrorism continued.

### Bibliography


Anonymous. *Imperial Hubris: Why the West is Losing the War on Terror.* Washington, D.C.: Brassey's: 2004.

———. *Through Our Enemies' Eyes: Osama bin Laden, Radical Islam, and the Future of America.* Washington, D.C.: Brassey's: 2002.

Benjamin, Daniel, and Simon, Steven. *The Age of Sacred Terror.* New York: Random House, 2002.

Bush, George W. "Address to a Joint Session of Congress and the American People," September 20, 2001. <http://www.whitehouse.gov/news/releases/2001/09/20010920-8.html> (July 19, 2005).

Doran, Michael S. "Somebody Else's Civil War." *Foreign Affairs* 81 (2002).

National Commission on Terrorist Attacks Upon the United States. *The 9/11 Commission Report: Final Report of the National Commission on Terrorist Attacks Upon the United States.* New York: W.W. Norton, 2004.

Stern, Jessica. *Terror in the Name of God: Why Religious Militants Kill.* New York: Ecco, 2003.

United States Northern Command (NORTHCOM). "Homeland Defense." <http://www.northcom.mil/index.cfm?fuseaction=s.homeland> (July 19, 2005).

**Further Reading**

Bergen, Peter L. *Holy War, Inc.: Inside the Secret World of Osama bin Laden*. New York: Free Press, 2001.

Freedman, Lawrence. "The Third World War?" *Survival* 43, no. 4 (2001): 61.

Frontline. "Hunting Bin Laden." <http://www.pbs.org/wgbh/pages/frontline/shows/binladen/>.

Greenwood, Christopher. "International Law and the 'War against Terrorism.'" *International Affairs* 78, no. 2 (2002): 301.

Howard, Michael. "What's in a Name?" *Foreign Affairs* 81, no. 1 (2002): 8.

Laqueur, Walter. *No End to War: Terrorism in the Twenty-First Century*. New York: Continuum, 2003.

Record, Jeffrey. "Bounding the Global War on Terrorism." *Military Technology* 28, no. 6 (2004): 17.

Roth, Kenneth. "The Law of War in the War on Terror." *Foreign Affairs* 83, no. 1 (2004): 2.

Woodward, Bob. *Bush at War*. New York: Simon & Schuster: 2002.

**Related Entries**

American Civil Liberties Union; Homeland Security; Iraq War; Peacekeeping Operations; Posse Comitatus Act

**Related Documents**

2001; 2004 a, b, c

—*Mark Burgess*

# War Powers Resolution

The War Powers Resolution was an attempt by Congress to assert its primacy in war-making policy decisions. Although presidents have often used military force without a resolution for war, Congress felt compelled to correct this situation only during the Vietnam War era. Even then, Congress' actions were a corrective for a problem it had largely created itself.

According to Article I, section 8 of the U.S. Constitution, the power to declare war rests with Congress. The national legislature is also responsible for raising and supporting the armed forces. In Article II, section 2, however, the president is designated commander in chief of the Army and Navy. This establishes something of a war-making partnership between the legislative and executive branches of the government, a provision intended to prevent unnecessary wars.

Early on August 1, 1964, North Vietnamese torpedo boats fired on USS *Maddox* while the destroyer was on a spying mission in the Gulf of Tonkin. Although the attackers were driven away, Pres. Lyndon B. Johnson dispatched USS *C. Turner Joy* to join the *Maddox* in the gulf. On August 4, both ships reported a second attack by the North Vietnamese. Despite serious doubts about whether the vessels were fired upon, Johnson asked Congress for authority to use military force to deter further attacks. With only two dissenting Senate votes, the legislature passed the Gulf of Tonkin Resolution on August 7, authorizing the president "to take all necessary measures to repel any armed attack against the forces of the United States and to prevent further aggression." Through this resolution the president deployed the first combat troops to South Vietnam. Over the next few years, the number of Americans fighting in Vietnam rose, peaking at around 500,000 in 1968. By the time Johnson left office in 1969, dissatisfaction with escalation in Vietnam already had many congresspersons considering ways to keep the executive branch from again engaging the nation in undeclared wars. In 1971, Congress quietly withdrew the president's unrestricted authority to make war by repealing the Gulf of Tonkin Resolution. Furthermore, by 1973, congressional gall at America's continued involvement in Vietnam and the Watergate scandal surrounding Pres. Richard M. Nixon moved Congress to pass the War Powers Resolution. Intended to check presidential interference with Congress' constitutional prerogative to declare war, the resolution was narrowly passed over Nixon's veto on November 7.

The War Powers Resolution was not intended to shut the president out of decisions for war, but rather to make the process more collaborative without obstructing the executive branch's authority to respond promptly during military crises. Indeed, the law is called a resolution rather than an act as a concession to congresspersons who worried that a statute required a constitutional amendment. A resolution also seemed to preserve congressional rights while preventing presidential abuse of war powers. In the event of an emergency, the president was required to inform the legislature that a military response had, or would be, employed, and provide justification for using armed force. The report had to be made within 48 hours of taking action. From that moment, Congress had 60 days to determine whether the president's decision was legal. If congressional approval was not forthcoming, military forces had to return home by the end of the two-month decision window, although the president could request a 30-day extension. Moreover, Congress reserved the right to require the president to bring deployed military forces home at any point during the 60-day period.

Despite the resolution, the line between congressional and presidential authority over war making remains blurry, and the legislature's desire to shoulder its responsibility shaky. During the Persian Gulf War, Public Law 102-1 authorized Pres. George H. W. Bush to use armed force—under the terms of U.N. Security Council resolutions condemning Iraq's occupation of Kuwait—once he had concluded that diplomacy would not resolve the crisis. When Pres. Bill Clinton committed troops to war-torn Bosnia in 1996, Congress ultimately failed to declare war or to require withdrawal of American troops. In October 2002, Public Law 107-243 authorized Pres. George W. Bush to use armed force in any way he considered "necessary and appropriate" to secure the U.S. against an Iraqi threat. In each instance, Congress debated whether the president had met the requirements of the War Powers Resolution, as well as the meaning and intent of the resolution itself, but ultimately left the decision for war in the hands of the executive branch. In the final analysis, the War Powers Resolution did little to enforce Congress's authority to declare war.

**Bibliography**

Boylan, Timothy S., and Glenn A. Phelps. "The War Powers Resolution: A Rationale for Congressional Inaction." *Parameters* (spring 2001): 109–24.

Clark, Robert D., Andrew M. Egeland, Jr., and David B. Sanford. *The War Powers Resolution*. Washington, D.C.: National Defense University Press, 1985.

Sullivan, John H. *The War Powers Resolution: A Special Study of the Committee on Foreign Affairs*. Washington, D.C.: Government Printing Office, 1982.

**Further Reading**

Grimmett, Richard F. "The War Powers Resolution: After Thirty Years." *CRS Report for Congress*, 11 March 2004. <http://www.fas.org/man/crs/RL32267.html>.

Reveley, W. Taylor, III. *War Powers of the President and Congress: Who Holds the Arrows and the Olive Branch?* Charlottesville: University Press of Virginia, 1981.

Stern, Gary M., and Morton H. Halperin, eds. *The U.S. Constitution and Power to Go to War: Historical and Current Perspectives*. Westport, Conn.: Greenwood Press, 1994.

Twine, Robert F. *The War Powers Resolution: Its Implementation in Theory and Practice*. Philadelphia: Foreign Policy Research Institute, 1983.

Westerfield, Donald L. *War Powers: The President, the Congress and the Question of War*. Westport, Conn.: Praeger, 1996.

**Related Entries**

Iraq War; Korean War; Persian Gulf War; Vietnam War

**Related Documents**

1973

—*Janet Valentine*

# War Profiteering

That many businessmen profit unduly during wartime, charging exorbitant prices for scarce goods or services, or that they benefit from close connections to politicians or the military, are charges that go back to before the origins of the republic and have continued through every war the country has ever fought. Some historians believe such charges have been warranted, while others argue that what seems to be price gouging is an unavoidable effect of supply and demand. The question of whether individuals or businesses should profit from war is a key moral quandary that highlights an uncomfortable reality: war can sometimes be economically beneficial for certain segments of the American population.

During the wars against the Pequots in the 1630s, gunsmiths charged what to many settlers seemed to be unconscionably high prices. During the American Revolution, Thomas Paine claimed that rich patriots hoarded grain and only sold this basic necessity when the price had skyrocketed—a charge that some historians dispute. However, popular anger against rising prices was real. In Philadelphia, speculation in grain so near the country's breadbasket led crowds to warn that "hunger will break through stone walls"—that is, into the storehouses of the wealthy.

Probably the most egregious example of speculation during the Revolutionary War was in currency. During the course of the war, the gold value of the Continental government's paper money plummeted and inflation ensued. Towards the end of the war, speculators traveled the country, purchasing seemingly worthless currency or certificates that the government issued to soldiers in lieu of paper money—sometimes exchanging Spanish silver coins for the promissory notes at a rate of ten cents on the dollar. By 1781, the new American government turned to hard currency and redeemed the notes with gold or silver. This provided a windfall to the speculators, who were accused by many of having inside information about the coming change in monetary policy. Public discontent with the hard-money policy contributed to Shays's rebellion in 1786.

During the Civil War, the practice of war profiteering arose again, allowing many businessmen to amass enormous fortunes. As before, a cooperative government helped facilitate the practice. The young J. P. Morgan purchased defective rifles from one federal armory and sold them to another for a profit of more than $100,000. The fact that carbines sometimes blew off the thumbs of the Union soldiers firing them was seemingly a small matter. Another famous millionaire, Cornelius Vanderbilt, added to his fortune by selling the government boats that were completely rotten. Fortunes were made by selling the Army boots made of defective leather, rotten meat, and the like—and not just during the Civil War. Later, during the Spanish–American War of 1898, some historians calculate that many more American soldiers were killed by rancid canned foods than by the Spanish.

During World War I, American manufacturers made enormous sums selling shells, armor, and ships to the Allies. Given the severity of the conflict and the high costs of building new factories, prices soared. In the case of naval armor, the price rose 700 percent in just three years. At the beginning, the Allies paid cash, but soon turned to massive loans, organized through Morgan's bank with the approval of the federal government. When the Russians pulled out of the war in 1917, those loans became riskier. In 1917, the United States intervened on the side of the Allies. After the war, critics charged that munitions companies on both sides of the Atlantic, such as DuPont and Krupps—the so-called Merchants of Death—had manipulated or even caused the conflict for their mutual enrichment.

In response to charges that the United States had entered World War I to secure repayment of war loans to private banks, the federal government adopted measures intended to limit the profits of war contractors during World War II. Charges that some companies engaged in unethical practices arose once again. After the war, the Senate found that several powerful companies, among them Ford, Standard Oil, and General Electric, continued to trade crucial—and therefore lucrative—materials, goods, or technologies with the Axis powers. Trade between the German branches of American firms occurred generally through Swiss or Swedish subsidiaries. In the case of Standard Oil, the sale of patented ingredients enabled German bombers to fly farther into the Atlantic for longer periods, sinking more Allied ships. While the Senate investigated these cases, the government did nothing. The vast majority of wartime contracts went to the largest, and often most politically connected, corporations. While profit levels were regulated, contractors bid on a "cost-plus" profits basis, so contractors had an incentive to boost production costs (salaries, etc.) as a way of padding profits. These practices were investigated by then Sen. Harry Truman, but often continued into the Cold War.

During the Cold War, companies producing goods for the military obtained most or all of their research dollars from the government, which represented a guaranteed market for those goods; consequently, defense contracts were lucrative, and costs on the vast majority of weapons systems grew dramatically. The permanent wartime economy that emerged proved highly lucrative to a number of firms, leading again to a pattern of media criticism and government inaction. For instance, in the era of Ronald Reagan, one defense contractor billed the government hundreds of dollars for a simple hammer. As in the past, companies that were well-connected to either Democratic or Republican politicians won lucrative contracts. The firm of Kellogg, Brown and Root, one of the chief financial backers of Lyndon Johnson, won numerous Vietnam-era contracts. The firm was later purchased by Halliburton, which drew charges during the U.S.-led invasion of Iraq for over-billing to the tune of hundreds of millions of dollars.

While it is difficult for scholars or citizens to know definitively whether companies are engaged in war profiteering or simply enjoying a healthy profit consistent with free-market capitalism, it remains clear that throughout U.S. history the profit motive has often been powerful enough to override patriotic considerations. As Woody Guthrie put it in his 1950s song "Stetson Kennedy," "if we take the profit out of war, we'll all forget what we were fighting for."

**Bibliography**

Brandes, Stuart D. *Warhogs: A History of War Profits in America.* Lexington: University Press of Kentucky, 1997.

Engelbrecht, H. C., and Frank Cleary Hanighen. *Merchants of Death: A Study of the International Armament Industry.* New York: Dodd, Mead & Co., 1934.

Higham, Charles. *Trading with the Enemy: An Expose of the Nazi–American Money Plot, 1933–1949.* New York: Delacorte Press, 1983.

Josephson, Matthew. *The Robber Barons: The Great American Capitalists, 1861–1901.* New York: Harcourt Brace, 1934.

**Further Reading**

Black, Edwin. *IBM and the Holocaust: The Strategic Alliance Between Nazi Germany and America's Most Powerful Corporation.* New York: Crown, 2001.

Briody, Dan. *The Halliburton Agenda: The Politics of Oil and Money.* Hoboken, N.J.: Wiley, 2004.

Phillips, Kevin P. *American Dynasty: Aristocracy, Fortune, and the Politics of Deceit in the House of Bush.* New York: Viking, 2004.

—*John Hinshaw*

# *WarGames*

### Film directed by John Badham, 1983

*WarGames*, a 1983 film about a teenage computer hacker (Matthew Broderick) who accidentally almost triggers World War III, was marketed as a youth-oriented film but became popular with audiences of all ages. Young people enjoyed seeing Broderick's character outwit grown-ups and save the world, while adults viewed the film as a commentary about nuclear war and the role of machines in human affairs.

*WarGames* was just one of a number of theatrical and television movies with nuclear war themes released in the early 1980s. These include *Testament*, a 1983 drama about a family's struggle to survive after a nuclear war; *The Day After,* a 1983 made-for-television movie about the effects of a nuclear attack on a midwest city; *Countdown to Looking Glass,* a 1984 cable "mockumentary" recounting the events leading to a thermonuclear exchange; and *The Manhattan Project*, a 1986 comedy/thriller in which a student builds a working atomic bomb as a school science project. *WarGames* was arguably the most popular and best remembered of these films. In addition to these films, many music videos, a very new art form at the time, featured images of missiles, fireballs, and mushrooms clouds, as did the video arcade game Missile Command.

This proliferation of nuclear-war-themed entertainment in the early 1980s reflected the concerns of the times. Fears of nuclear annihilation increased worldwide after Ronald Reagan won the 1980 American presidential election. The former actor's fierce, anti-Soviet rhetoric, in which he described the Soviet Union as an "evil empire," led many to believe he was an irresponsible "nuclear cowboy" willing to launch a first strike without provocation. Reagan did little to dispel this perception. Just months before his reelection in 1984, he joked about "outlawing" the Soviet Union while testing a microphone: "We begin bombing in five minutes."

Of course, Hollywood produced movies about nuclear war long before the Reagan era. Twenty years earlier, films such as *On the Beach* (1959), *Dr. Strangelove* (1964), and *Failsafe* (1964) had received much popular and critical acclaim. Like *Failsafe*, *WarGames* posits an accidental triggering of nuclear war—leading the *New York Times* to ask "Could it ever happen?"

Despite its title, *WarGames* does not emphasize the "war as game" theme. None of the adult characters believe that war is a competition played for fame, honor, or glory. They are professionals who perceive war as a deadly serious endeavor. The "game" of the title is the simulation they use to practice their skills, hoping that they will never need to apply those skills. However, when Broderick's character plays "global thermonuclear war" with the "War Operations Planning and Response" (WOPR) computer, it initiates a real nuclear countdown. The military officers are horrified when the game turns real.

In contrast with many antiwar films, such as *Dr. Strangelove* and *Catch-22* (1970), *WarGames* does not portray the military officers as warmongering buffoons. The Air Force general played by Barry Corbin is presented sympathetically. He is skeptical of giving WOPR control over U.S. nuclear assets and agonizes over the decision to retaliate when WOPR indicates missiles incoming, not knowing whether the attack is real or a simulation. Nonetheless, the U.S. Air Force objected, albeit quietly, to the movie, saying that it contributed to public fears by misrepresenting the service's nuclear security arrangements.

In addition to its criticism of war, *WarGames* also explores the theme, common in science fiction, of humanity's over-reliance on technology. The WOPR computer that nearly destroys the Earth is intended to relieve humans of the burden of waging nuclear war. Supporters of a computer-controlled launch system argued that, if the president decided that nuclear war was necessary, no individual should be able to compromise its execution. Likewise, this technology would also prevent a disturbed individual (such as Gen. Jack D. Ripper in *Dr. Strangelove*) from beginning a nuclear war without authorization.

Yet technology, intended to serve humanity, can turn on and destroy its creators. In *WarGames*, the completely autonomous WOPR is given the authority and ability to launch a nuclear strike on its own. Like HAL in *2001: A Space Odyssey* (1968), WOPR will fulfill its programming regardless of the consequences. It cannot be overridden and will play its "game" to the end, no matter what the cost.

*WarGames* was released at a time when only a handful of technophiles had computers in their homes and when the computer was still a thing of awe to the general public. (Indeed, for many Americans the movie was their introduction to personal computing and hacking; the film inspired many to seek careers as computer programmers and engineers.) As were HAL and the title machine in *Colossus: The Forbin Project* (1970), WOPR is sentient and can learn—something rarely seen in films anymore, since computers have become so familiar. What distinguishes WOPR from its predecessors is that it can empathize with humanity: when it realizes the destruction that a nuclear war will cause, it is appalled and ends the countdown. "What a strange game," it observes. "The only winning move is not to play."

*WarGames* combines many classic themes of the science fiction and antiwar genres in an entertaining package. It is far more than an artifact of Reagan-era nuclear paranoia. The Cold War may be over, but the film's appeal endures.

**Bibliography**

Halloran, Richard. "Could It Ever Happen?" *New York Times*, June 3, 1983.

O'Brien, Tom. "From HAL to WOPR." *Commonweal*, September 9, 1983.

Sarris, Andrew. "Films in Focus: The Most Dangerous Game." *Village Voice*, June 7, 1983.

**Further Reading**

Palmer, William J. *Films of the Eighties: A Social History*. Carbondale: Southern Illinois University, 1993.

**Related Entries**

Cold War; Computer Technology and Warfare; *Dr. Strangelove*; Film and War; Wargaming

*—Roger Horky*

# Wargaming

Wargames, or conflict simulations, are games that recreate historical and hypothetical wars, campaigns, and battles. Military and government personnel play wargames to practice skills, rehearse for real conflicts and crises, and explore the impact of new technology and weapons. Hobby wargamers play for fun and to learn about military history. Educators use wargames to introduce students to the problems encountered by historical figures.

There are four main categories of wargames: miniatures games, computer simulations, live-action events, and board wargames. The first three types were originally developed for and by military organizations, but all have commercial entertainment applications. In live-action games, players decide what to do as individuals in a particular battle scenario (although they are often guided by a coach). The other formats cast players in the role of commanders who make decisions for all battle units. Professional wargames of all types are usually more elaborate and sophisticated than their commercial counterparts.

Wargaming traces its origins to chess, itself a stylized and abstract representation of medieval warfare. Enthusiasts have long tinkered with the rules of chess to represent real-life combat more "accurately," adding terrain effects, scaled movement rates, ranged weapons, special units, and other "realistic" features. In the early 19th century a Prussian junior officer proposed that the army should use one of these chess-based games for training. His chief of staff was so impressed that he ordered a Kriegspiel ("wargame") kit for every regiment. The original Kriegspiel was a miniatures game, played with wooden blocks that represented units on a sandtable sculpted into a landscape. Combat was originally resolved by a roll of the dice, but "free" Kriegspiel, introduced in 1876, used referees. The many Prussian military successes between 1864 and 1870 prompted other armies and navies to adopt wargaming. Most used adaptations of the original Kriegspiel at first but soon developed their own games, adding rules for logistics, political factors, and advances in military technology and doctrine.

In both world wars and many other 20th-century conflicts, most of the belligerents relied on tabletop games to work out strategic, operational, and technical problems before committing their forces. American admiral Chester Nimitz observed in 1960 that, with the exception of the Japanese kamikazes, every aspect of World War II in the Pacific had been anticipated through wargaming. However, admirals and generals sometimes failed to apply what they learned from wargames. During World War I, the Russians played wargames to test strategies for their advance into Prussia. During these games, they identified several potential problems and developed solutions for them. Yet in the actual campaign, they repeated the mistakes, but not the corrections. Leaders sometimes also drew erroneous conclusions from wargames. While preparing for their 1914 invasion of France, the Germans used wargames to refine their plans. These games almost always predicted a German victory—especially when Kaiser Wilhelm II was playing.

Both the Soviet and American governments and armed forces continued to employ wargames throughout the Cold War, seeking the best ways to fight in Korea, Vietnam, Afghanistan, and other conflicts. However, Robert S. McNamara, secretary of defense under presidents John F. Kennedy and Lyndon B. Johnson, discovered a new application for them. Long a proponent of scientific management techniques, McNamara relied on wargames to determine the cost-effectiveness of new weapons systems. However, wargames are only as useful as the assumptions made when designing them. Many of McNamara's simulations modeled budgetary factors alone and failed to account for political and other issues not easily quantified.

Computerized wargames appeared in 1958 when the U.S. Navy introduced the Navy Electronic Warfare Simulator (NEWS). Conceptually, these games differ little from their tabletop predecessors, although the computer's memory capacity and speed allows a much greater level of detail to be modeled. The computer also transformed flight simulators into wargames. The earliest simulators were simple mechanical devices demonstrating how control inputs affect flight attitude. The introduction of digital technology in the 1970s permitted the development of flight simulators that totally immerse trainees in a virtual environment, complete with enemy forces, equipment malfunctions, and flight characteristics all programmed into the system. Tank crews, ship crews, and even foot soldiers also use simulators.

Armies have conducted training maneuvers for centuries, but live-action wargames with formal rules are a 20th-century innovation. Modern technology permits highly realistic military training exercises. The Army's MILES (Multiple Integrated Laser Engagement System) gear, made for tanks and heavy weapons as well as for individual soldiers, uses light beams to register hits on special sensor equipment. There are similar devices for aircraft. Computer datalinks permit real-time tracking of all participants and replays for postgame assessments.

Another form of live-action conflict simulation is the role-playing exercise. Government officials and military personnel use these to work out policy problems. Participants are assigned different, often incompatible objectives, then try to resolve their differences through negotiation. Law enforcement agencies employ these exercises to train for hostage negotiations and other interpersonal conflicts.

Recreational wargaming emerged in the early twentieth century. The entertainment potential of military wargames inspired a number of commercial adaptations, the best known being Little Wars, published in 1913 by British author H. G. Wells. An ardent pacifist, Wells hoped that games could become a substitute for war; at times, however, the wargaming hobby is criticized for promoting militarism and glamorizing war. Most enthusiasts maintain that they play just for the fun of matching wits with an opponent or, in the case of live-action games, for the physical activity.

Little Wars was a miniatures game, replacing Kriegspiel's wooden blocks with lead figurines. Miniatures battles, with their colorfully painted soldiers maneuvering about a model landscape, complete with buildings and trees, are often grand spectacles. Since the hobby's origins, wargamers have gotten their supplies from toy companies, model manufacturers, and specialty concerns that produce a wide variety of miniature soldiers, vehicles, ships, buildings, and landscape accessories.

Many wargamers also read speculative fiction, which inspired a group of American enthusiasts to add fantasy elements to their tabletop battles in the mid-1970s. Their focus soon changed from engaging in combat to developing characters, and they began writing rules—far more complex than those for professional role-playing exercises—to recreate the lives of individual sorcerers and warriors. The result was Dungeons and Dragons, one of the earliest role-playing games. The role-playing hobby quickly grew more popular than its antecedent, and remains so into the 21st century.

Board wargaming developed as an inexpensive alternative to miniatures. Instead of metal pieces on a sandtable, board wargames use cardboard pieces and cardstock maps, usually overlaid with hexagons to regulate movement. The first board wargames were published in the early 1950s. The hobby's popularity peaked some 20 years later. Board wargamers have always been a minority in the general games market, so mainstream board game publishers produce few wargames. Most board wargame companies are owned and operated by hobbyists, often on a shoestring budget, yet some publish a dozen or more new titles each year.

Commercial computer simulations resemble board wargames more than they do arcade-style video games. The appeal of computer wargames may be attributed to their animated graphics, ease of play (the computer handles all game mechanics), and solo playability—artificial intelligence is usually a tolerable substitute for a human opponent. Since the mid-1990s, most computer games can be played online against multiple opponents. Combat flight simulators always sell well, a computer being far better suited than a two-dimensional gameboard for recreating dogfights.

Most live-action wargames are grown-up versions of children's games such as Capture the Flag. Paintball uses gas-powered guns to fire dye-filled wax projectiles. Lazer Tag (and its poorly remembered predecessor, Photon) uses infrared equipment similar to the Army's MILES gear. Mock dogfighting services allow ace wannabes to fly real airplanes (supervised by licensed pilots) that are equipped with laser targeting and sensing devices adapted from Air Force models.

The equipment for live-action games can be found in toy, sporting-goods, and department stores, while most electronics and software retailers carry computer wargames. Board wargames and the rules, figures, and landscapes for miniatures games, however, are usually available only at specialty hobby shops, though many do business online and by mail order. Most wargamers tend to play only one category of game, all of which have their networks of clubs, conventions, tournaments, and magazines.

The armed forces will rely on wargames long into the future. Prospects for the wargaming hobby, however, are uncertain. Computer and live-action games appeal to many people and are likely to remain popular in the future. Board and miniatures wargaming, however, will probably remain specialty hobbies. They are perceived as too intellectually demanding for the general public, yet are also dismissed as frivolous "kiddie games."

### Bibliography


Caffrey, Matthew. "Toward a History-Based Doctrine for Wargaming." *Aerospace Power Journal* 14 (2000).

Dunnigan, James F. *The Wargames Handbook: How to Play and Design Commercial and Professional Wargames.* San Jose, Calif.: Writer's Club, 2000.

"Wargames: A Study." The Wargames Directory <http://www.wargamesdirectory.com/html/articles/wargames/default.asp> (July 21, 2005).


### Further Reading


Allen, Thomas B. *Wargames: The Secret World of the Creators, Players, and Policy Makers Rehearsing World War III Today.* New York: McGraw Hill, 1987.

Dalkey, Norman Crolee. *Simulation of Military Conflict.* Santa Monica, Calif.: Rand, 1967.

Perla, Peter. *The Art of Wargaming.* Annapolis, Md.: Naval Institute Press, 1990.


### Related Entries


Computer Technology and Warfare; Technology and Revolutionary Changes in Military Affairs; *WarGames*


—*Roger Horky*

# Washington, George

## (1732–99)

## 1st President of the United States, Commander of the Continental Army

As commander of the Continental Army, president of the Constitutional Convention, and first president of the United States, George Washington helped to steer the new American republic from revolution to nationhood. While other statesmen, most notably Thomas Jefferson and James Madison, took the lead in writing the seminal texts that defined the purposes and processes of American government, Washington did more than anyone to establish the character of the new nation's military and political leadership. Firm and impartial, dignified yet selfless, and prudent above all else, his status as an exemplar of the principle that power must be tempered by restraint constitutes his most important contribution to the American experiment in limited government.

### Early Life and Career

Born in Westmoreland County, Virginia, in 1732, Washington was the son of Mary Ball and Augustine Washington, an ambitious tobacco planter. When his father died in 1743, George Washington went to live with his older half brother, Lawrence, who in 1751 took him to Barbados. There he contracted smallpox, developing an immunity to the disease that would later claim the lives of thousands of soldiers in the Continental Army. A year later, when Lawrence Washington died of tuberculosis, his 2,500-acre Mount Vernon plantation became part of Washington's inheritance.

Already Washington had begun work as a surveyor employed by Virginia's influential Fairfax family, into which Lawrence had married. He charted the Fairfaxes' land holdings in the Shenandoah Valley, where he gained a familiarity with the trans-Appalachian West that was further strengthened in 1754 when, as a young officer in the Virginia militia, he journeyed into the Ohio Country to secure his colony's land claims against those of the French. There he surrendered in a battle that helped to ignite in North America the Seven Years' War. Soon afterwards he accepted an appointment as commander of Virginia's frontier militia, a position he held until 1758.

Upon his return to Mount Vernon, Washington solidified his status as a member of the gentry. In 1759 he married Martha Dandridge Custis, a widow whose estate of 18,000 acres, when combined with the lands that he had inherited or purchased, made him one of Virginia's richest men. He enlarged and renovated his house, secured seats as a vestryman and justice of the peace, and won election as a member of the House of Burgesses. He earned a reputation as an able legislator and ardent critic of British imperial policies. In 1774 he collaborated with fellow planter and statesman George Mason on the Fairfax Resolves, which recommended a unified colonial boycott of British imports. With these credentials Washington traveled to Philadelphia as one of Virginia's delegates to the Continental Congress.

### Revolutionary General

There, dressed in the uniform of the Virginia militia, Washington attracted the notice of many peers. Like them, he shared the civilian legislators' disdain for British encroachments on colonists' rights, including Parliament's apparent attempt to intimidate Americans by stationing on their shores an army whose protection their popular assemblies had never requested. Like them, he seemed willing to take great risks to resist British policies. Unlike them, however, he had warfighting experience and a carefully nurtured public reputation as a military man. These facts, combined with the realization that military engagements against the British at Lexington and Concord in Massachusetts probably secured northern support for the resistance movement, made Washington—a delegate from the most populous colony in the South—an easy choice to unite the colonies as commander of the Continental Army in June 1775. Entrusted with building an army powerful enough to secure victory, he could also be trusted to restrain that army from threatening republicanism.

Washington took charge of American forces at Boston, which the British soon evacuated. Poorly supplied and inadequately trained, his troops failed to prevent British capture of New York City in 1776. They withdrew to Westchester County and then New Jersey where, after a string of defeats, victories at Trenton (December 26, 1776) and Princeton (January 3, 1777) bolstered his army's flagging morale. Even so, losses at Brandywine (September 11, 1777) and Germantown (October 4, 1777) allowed British forces to occupy Philadelphia for the winter. Meanwhile, his army endured harsh conditions at Valley Forge, and rumors circulated that critics sought to displace him from command. In 1778, however, Washington's forces began to reap the benefits of increasing professionalism. Earlier in the war, members of his army saw themselves as "citizen–soldiers" destined, after brief enlistments, to return to their farms. Now, thanks to Washington's reforms in training and discipline, an increasing number took pride in their status as "regulars."

With the war in the North essentially a draw, Washington encamped in New York until the vulnerability of British forces in Virginia caused him to improvise a brilliant plan. In the late summer of 1781, Washington's forces, joined by the French, rushed south to engage the British and corner them at the Yorktown peninsula. There, after the arrival of a contingent of French warships, the British Army surrendered on October 19. The victory owed much to French–American coordination, but what made it possible was Washington's success at unifying an army of individuals around a military ethic that placed nation before self and the liberty of America above all else.

Although no major battles followed Yorktown, Britain continued to hold several American cities, and not until September 1783 did all sides sign a peace treaty. In the meantime, Washington encamped with his army near Newburgh, New York. There his officers grew restless. Many feared that the cash-strapped Continental Congress would fail to honor its promises regarding military pay and pensions. Rumors of mutiny circulated, as did anonymous tracts suggesting that, should Congress not satisfy the officers' demands, the army might either march west and leave the United States undefended or, if the war ended, refuse to disband. Interpretations differ over the seriousness of these threats, but few dispute that Washington's March 1783 remarks before his officers—whom he urged to obey civilian authority and place the nation's interests above their own—put an end to any possibility of a widespread military revolt. Such might not have been the case had not Washington, whose wealth allowed him to serve without a salary and who observed great tact and deference in his dealings with Congress and state governors, set such a positive example. Although some feared and more than a few hoped that he would use his position to secure permanent power for himself, in November, after hearing word of the conclusion of peace, Washington bid farewell to his soldiers; then, before Congress in December, he tendered his resignation.

### Nation Builder

By retiring, Washington acted unlike many of the world's previous military leaders. He also secured for himself the adoration and trust of Americans, who compared him to Cincinnatus, the famed Roman warrior who fought for his nation but, after achieving victory, traded his sword for his plow. Named president of the Society of the Cincinnati, a veterans organization that drew criticism for its hereditary system of membership, Washington chose to distance himself from the group rather than sully his reputation. During the next phase of Washington's life, he drew on the public's trust to make the most of opportunities to unify Americans in support of a plan to better secure their liberty.

For him the need was apparent. Under the Articles of Confederation, the central government had little power to raise revenue or compel states to contribute men and money to wage the Revolutionary War. Leadership of the Continental Army also allowed Washington to see beyond regional prejudices and develop a keen sense of nationalism. He agreed to preside over the convention that, in 1787, met in Philadelphia and proposed a new Constitution that placed a strong executive at the head of a more robust national government. Some opposed the Constitution because it curtailed the independence of states from distant authority and created a government capable of threatening Americans' liberty. Others, however, supported its ratification, in part because of the understanding that Washington, who had proven that he could be trusted with power, would serve as the nation's first president.

Unanimously elected, Washington took office on April 30, 1789, and served two four-year terms. As a symbol of the new national government, he sought to cement American unity by visiting every state. In 1789 he toured all of New England except Rhode Island, where he traveled in 1790 after it ratified the Constitution; in 1791 he toured the South. As the principal maker of national policy, he aimed mainly to avoid exacerbating division. From a geographically and ideologically diverse cabinet he often received divergent advice. Virginia's Jefferson, who served as secretary of state, disagreed frequently with New York's Alexander Hamilton, the treasury secretary, over issues relating to finance, foreign policy, and constitutional interpretation. Washington struggled to steer a middle course but drew criticism from some Jeffersonians for decisions to use armed force to confront the 1794 Whiskey Rebellion and, through the 1794 Jay Treaty, avoid an armed confrontation with Great Britain. In the first instance, state militias proved strong enough to quell a tax revolt in western Pennsylvania. In the second, Washington feared that citizen–soldiers would fare poorly against the professional British army. Americans' continuing reluctance to support a military establishment made diplomacy the safest means for resolving with Britain disputes over trade and its continuing occupation of western lands.

Washington declined invitations to seek a third term and retired as president in 1797. Although his policy stances caused a few to question his commitment to liberty, no one failed to notice this final renouncement of power. Two years later he died at Mount Vernon. Americans unleashed an unprecedented outpouring of grief. Henry Lee, a fellow veteran of the Revolution, eulogized Washington as "first in war, first in peace, and first in the hearts of his countrymen" (Ellis, 270).

### Bibliography

Ellis, Joseph J. *His Excellency: George Washington.* New York: Alfred A. Knopf, 2004.

Higginbotham, Don. *George Washington: Uniting a Nation.* Lanham, Md.: Rowman and Littlefield, 2002.

———. *The War of American Independence: Military Attitudes, Policies, and Practice, 1763–1789.* New York: Macmillan, 1971.

Royster, Charles. *A Revolutionary People at War: The Continental Army and American Character, 1775–1783.* Chapel Hill: University of North Carolina Press, 1979.

### Further Reading

Flexner, James Thomas. *George Washington.* 4 vols. Boston: Little, Brown, 1965–72.

Freeman, Douglas Southall. *George Washington.* 7 vols. (Vol. 7 completed by John A. Carroll and Mary Wells Ashworth). New York: Charles Scribner's Sons, 1949–57.

Higginbotham, Don. *George Washington and the American Military Tradition.* Athens: University of Georgia Press, 1985.

———, ed. *George Washington Reconsidered.* Charlottesville: University Press of Virginia, 2001.

Leibiger, Stuart. *Founding Friendship: George Washington, James Madison, and the Creation of the American Republic.* Charlottesville: University Press of Virginia, 1999.

Wills, Garry. *Cincinnatus: George Washington and the Enlightenment.* Garden City, N.Y.: Doubleday, 1984.

**Related Entries**

Civil–Military Relations; Colonial Wars; Continental Army; Revolutionary War; Revolutionary War Pensions; Smallpox and War; Society of the Cincinnati

**Related Documents**

1776 b

*—Robert M. S. McDonald*

# Wayne, John

### (1907–79)

### Actor

For both the World War II and Vietnam generations, the motion picture icon John Wayne embodied the place where American manhood and martial valor met. Whether riding "tall in the saddle" or portraying a no-nonsense soldier, Wayne presented to Americans and moviegoers around the world an image of American manhood that was captured in his nickname "the Duke." As with many men whose image is larger than life, the real life John Wayne was less heroic, more complex, and arguably more interesting than the tough-talking marine who dominated the screen.

Wayne was born Marion Michael Morrison to middle-class parents—his father was a druggist—in 1907. His father moved the family to California, where Wayne learned to ride. He got his start in film in the 1920s and, by 1939, had secured small parts in almost 70 films. John Wayne finally made a break from the B-movie list when the director John Ford, to whom his career would be forever linked, had him play a major role in *Stagecoach* (1939).

Despite the success of *Stagecoach*, Wayne's career began waning as he was getting too old to play the role of a pretty boy, and his rather wooden presence on the screen limited the types of parts he received. But he was saved by World War II. Many major actors joined the service (James Stewart, for instance, saw combat in the Air Force), and Wayne's status improved owing simply to the resulting decrease in competition. This was not Wayne's finest moment, as he essentially avoided service; as one historian put it, "he used every excuse but the dog ate my homework." Nonetheless, on screen Wayne's career took off, and he began to play not just the hero, but the middle-aged leader of men, a persona that catapulted him to iconic status.

During the war, Wayne played soldiers, but now he shifted from young man to the honest, tough-talking father figure in films such as *They Were Expendable* (about the Navy). After the war, Wayne continued to hone this character, headlining such movies as *The Sands of Iwo Jima* (1949). John Ford also cast Wayne in a number of his westerns, including the memorable *She Wore a Yellow Ribbon* (1949).

Wayne was a staunch conservative who reveled in films such as *The Alamo* (1960), which cast Americans as the heroic defenders of freedom against despotism. In this film, Wayne played Davy Crockett, whose interest in preserving the honor of a beautiful Mexican woman led her to believe in the Americans' altruistic motives toward Mexico. Wayne often took pains to ensure that his heroes were considerate to non-whites, although some viewed such relationships as reinforcing stereotypes.

John Wayne's politics arguably got the better of him when he put his own money into making *The Green Berets* (1968), Hollywood's first Vietnam movie. Here Wayne plays Col. Mike Kirby, who leads a band of tough Americans and South Vietnamese against ruthless communists, eventually convincing a liberal journalist (played by David Janssen) of the righteousness of the American cause. The film did not enjoy either box office success or critical acclaim. Wayne's identification with the war effort made him a target of anti-war and counterculture protest, and he remained a target years after his death. For instance, in Stanley Kubrick's *Full Metal Jacket* (1987), the character Joker ironically affects a John Wayne swagger and cowboy accent, often asking those around him, and himself, "Is that you John Wayne? Is it me?" The jazz poet Gil-Scott Heron argued in 1981 that

*John Wayne, as Col. Mike Kirby in the 1968 film* The Green Berets. *(© John Springer Collection/CORBIS)*

America really wanted Wayne to be president, to take them back to the days before "fair was square, when the cavalry came straight away, and all American men were like Hemingway." However, "since John Wayne was no longer available, they settled for Ronald Ray-Gun."

For better and for worse, John Wayne represented the American ideal of martial spirit and manliness in the decades between Pearl Harbor and the evacuation of Saigon. For many Americans, Wayne represented what was best about America: he was not just a great American, but symbolized American determination and idealism in times of war. For the generations raised on "John Wayne westerns" and war movies, Wayne had become the face of the American soldier. One veteran recalled, however, that during World War II, Wayne was booed by soldiers wounded in the Pacific when he toured a hospital in Hawaii in a cowboy outfit. William Manchester claimed that "this man was a symbol of the fake machismo we had come to hate." While Manchester confessed that he, and many marines, hated *The Sands of Iwo Jima*, such views bordered on the treasonous to many veterans and aficionados of popular culture.

Wayne's chain smoking finally got the better of him in 1979, when he died of cancer. That year, Congress honored him with a gold medal in recognition of his service to the country.

**Bibliography**

Campbell, James T. "Print the Legend: John Wayne and Postwar American Culture." *Reviews in American History* 28 (2000): 465–77.

Davis, Ronald L. *Duke: The Life and Image of John Wayne.* Norman: University of Oklahoma Press, 1998.

**Further Reading**

Munn, Michael. *John Wayne: The Man Behind the Myth*. New York: New American Library, 2004.
Roberts, Randy. *John Wayne: American*. New York: Free Press, 1995.
Shepard, Donald, Robert Slatzer, and Dave Grayson. *Duke: The Life and Times of John Wayne.* Garden Center, N.J.: Doubleday, 1985.

**Related Entries**

Film and War

—*John Hinshaw*

# Weinberger–Powell Doctrine

Since 1984, the Weinberger–Powell Doctrine has exerted a significant influence over American foreign policy decision-makers when the deployment of U.S. military forces is under consideration. The Weinberger–Powell Doctrine, originally conceived by Reagan administration Sec. of Defense Caspar W. Weinberger and subsequently reshaped by Chairman of the Joint Chiefs of Staff Gen. Colin L. Powell (who as Weinberger's senior military assistant in 1984 had helped to refine the secretary's ideas), argues that the United States ought to proceed with caution: military forces should be deployed only under narrowly circumscribed conditions and with the expectation that massively superior U.S. forces will be employed in order to overmatch an adversary, allowing the intervention to be concluded quickly and with few American casualties.

On November 28, 1984, Weinberger gave a speech before the National Press Club in Washington entitled The Uses of Military Power in which he outlined six conditions that ought to be met before deploying U.S. troops overseas:

> 1) The United States "should not commit forces to combat overseas unless the particular engagement or occasion is deemed vital to our national interest or that of our allies."
>
> 2) If it was deemed necessary to send troops into combat, "we should do so wholeheartedly, and with the clear intention of winning."
>
> 3) "We should have clearly defined political and military objectives" susceptible to the application of military force.
>
> 4) "The relationship between our objectives and the forces we have committed—their size, composition and disposition—must be continually reassessed and adjusted if necessary."
>
> 5) "[T]here must be some reasonable assurance we will have the support of the American people and their elected representatives in Congress."
>
> 6) "Finally, the commitment of U.S. forces to combat should be a last resort."

While Weinberger's immediate inspiration was the disastrous 1982 to 1984 U.S. intervention in Lebanon (which he had opposed from the beginning), the Weinberger Doctrine—so labeled by the *Washington Post* in an editorial shortly after Weinberger's speech—was very much an outgrowth of the so-called Vietnam syndrome. In the wake of U.S. withdrawal from South Vietnam, many Americans felt a deep reluctance to commit troops abroad as well as uncertainty with regard to foreign policy matters in general. The Doctrine was an effort to lay out conditions that could make military force "usable" again in defense of crucial national interests while avoiding missions of lesser significance; in those circumstances when American troops would be committed to battle, the Doctrine was intended to prevent the gradual escalation, unclear goals, and public discord that had contributed to American failure in Vietnam.

The Weinberger Doctrine was arguably most influential in shaping the 1991 Persian Gulf War. That intervention, motivated by a clear national interest in safeguarding Middle East oil supplies, was supported by the Congress and was prosecuted quickly and with overwhelming force. Many observers viewed the successful results as a dramatic vindication of the Weinberger Doctrine.

## WEINBERGER–POWELL DOCTRINE

During the early 1990s, the "Weinberger Doctrine" evolved into the "Powell Doctrine," as Gen. Colin L. Powell, the chairman of the Joint Chiefs of Staff in the administration of Pres. George H. W. Bush, became a forceful advocate for a recast version of Weinberger's principles. The success of the Gulf War, rather than causing Powell to revise his cautious prewar position with regard to the commitment of U.S. forces, led him to recast Weinberger's conditions with an emphasis on his second and third points: the need to employ overwhelming force and the identification of clear, achievable objectives.

In contrast to Weinberger, who more expressly sought to limit the circumstances under which U.S. forces might be deployed to situations "vital to our national interest," Powell was more concerned with seeking to make sure that military force would be employed in a manner that would ensure swift resolution and low American casualties. That being said, the practical effect of Powell's demand for overwhelming force would be to raise the stakes when military intervention was under consideration, presumably leading to fewer interventions.

The October 1993 battle in the Somali capital of Mogadishu, in which 18 American special operations soldiers were killed in what had begun as a humanitarian relief mission, seemed for a time to give Powell's point of view a dominant position in Washington debate—particularly given the general's great stature and the limited foreign policy credentials of the new Democratic administration of Pres. Bill Clinton. Powell vigorously opposed U.S. military intervention in the brutal civil war raging in Bosnia, which, he feared, would lack several of the elements of the Doctrine. This delayed U.S. and NATO entry into that conflict. For the same reasons, his successors effectively blocked proposals from some within the Clinton administration that the United States intervene quickly to halt the genocide underway in Rwanda in 1994.

By the latter half of the 1990s, however, the dominance of the Weinberger–Powell paradigm was less clear: U.S. troops were deployed as peacekeepers in Bosnia, and the NATO alliance had prosecuted a distinctly "gradualist" air campaign against Serbia in reaction to its policies in its Kosovo province. Increasingly, skeptics suggested that the Doctrine was a means of avoiding intervention rather than a means of ensuring success. A cautious military and a more interventionist Democratic administration seemed to move toward an uneasy truce: rather than foregoing interventions that might not adhere to the Weinberger–Powell criteria, force might be employed with the stipulation that American casualties would be kept to an absolute minimum.

Events following the transformative September 11, 2001 attacks on the United States by the Saudi renegade Osama bin Laden's al Qaeda organization further diminished the relevance of the Weinberger–Powell Doctrine. After the United States was attacked, there was little question that it would respond in some fashion. At the same time, in the Global War on Terrorism, the U.S. faced an unconventional conflict that offered little likelihood of decisive resolution, given the difficulty of bringing military power to bear on a non-state group. During 2002 and 2003, a reluctant military leadership—and Sec. of State Powell himself—were unable to prevail in the George W. Bush administration's debates over the prospect of a second war with Iraq. The war was subsequently launched in the spring of 2003, with smaller ground forces than military leaders had advocated.

While the Weinberger–Powell Doctrine retained a significant presence in the national security arena at the turn of the 21st century, events during the Clinton and George W. Bush administrations suggested that, in practice, civilian leaders of both parties saw the need to keep open the nonconventional military options that the Doctrine sought to rule out. In the end, the Weinberger–Powell Doctrine was more often cited by critics of actual or potential interventions than strictly adhered to by policymakers.

**Bibliography**

Powell, Colin L. "U.S. Forces: Challenges Ahead." *Foreign Affairs* 73 (Winter 1992/1993): 32–45.

———, with Joseph E. Persico. *My American Journey.* New York: Random House, 1995.

Weinberger, Caspar W. "The Uses of Military Power," speech before the National Press Club, November 28, 1984. Full text available on the PBS *Frontline* program's "Give War a Chance" episode Website. <http://www.pbs.org/wgbh/pages/frontline/shows/military/force/weinberger.html> (July 19, 2005).

**Further Reading**

Cassidy, Robert M. "Prophets or Praetorians?: The Uptonian Paradox and the Powell Corollary." *Parameters* 33 (autumn 2003): 130–43. Also available online: <http://carlisle-www.army.mil/usawc/Parameters/03autumn/cassidy.pdf>.

Daalder, Ivo and Michael O'Hanlon. "Unlearning the Lessons of Kosovo." *Foreign Policy* 116 (fall 1999): 128–40.

Halberstam, David. *War in a Time of Peace: Bush, Clinton, and the Generals.* New York: Charles Scribner's Sons, 2001.

Woodward, Bob. *The Commanders.* New York: Simon & Schuster, 1991.

**Related Entries**

Civil–Military Relations; Iraq War; Peacekeeping Operations; Persian Gulf War; Powell, Colin; Vietnam War; War on Terrorism

*—Erik Riker-Coleman*

# Wilson, Woodrow

### (1856–1923)
### 28th President of the United States

Woodrow Wilson served as president of the United States prior to and during World War I. Although remembered as an internationalist, Wilson initially worked to preserve the nation's neutrality, believing that intervention in Europe was not in U.S. interests. Indeed, he won reelection in 1916 on an antiwar platform epitomized by the slogan "he kept us out of the war." The president had reversed this position by April 1917, when he asked Congress to declare war. The late entry into the conflict created a mobilization crisis, which Wilson overcame by expanding government control over society and the economy. President Wilson also saw the war as an opportunity to reshape the international political order, which he elaborated upon in the Fourteen Points. Wilson pursued this agenda at the Versailles Peace Conference, but was unable to persuade the Senate to ratify the treaty.

## Early Life and Political Career

Wilson was born in 1856 in Virginia, the son of a Presbyterian minister. His father held assignments throughout the South, including stints in Georgia and South Carolina during the Civil War. Wilson would become the first Southerner elected to the presidency since 1860. At the time, Wilson was also one of the most highly educated men ever to hold the office. He completed his bachelor's degree from Princeton University, a law degree from the University of Virginia, and eventually his doctorate in political science from the Johns Hopkins University. After completing his education, Wilson embarked upon a career in academia, which culminated in the presidency of Princeton University in 1902.

Wilson began his career as a political and social conservative within the Democratic Party. He adhered to many traditional southern positions, including support for segregation and states' rights. His first public office was the governorship of New Jersey in 1910.

Wilson ran for president in 1912; the other two candidates were the Republican incumbent, President William Howard Taft, and Taft's predecessor, Theodore Roosevelt, who was now affiliated with the Progressive Party. Ironically, all of these candidates claimed to be progressive, but their definitions of what that entailed were different. The campaign became a contest between two versions of progressivism: Wilson's New Freedom and Roosevelt's New Nationalism. Wilson prevailed, but both programs probably would have pursued similar agendas in regard to industrial regulation and social welfare.

## Wilson's First Term

The Wilson Administration secured stricter antitrust legislation, oversaw the creation of the Federal Trade Commission, and passed needed income tax legislation to redistribute the tax burden away from property owners, such as farmers. A Federal Reserve Act created a national banking oversight board and a more elastic currency capable of promoting stability in the money system—and hence the economy. Wilson ordered a limited military intervention in the Mexican Revolution from 1914 to 1916, in an attempt to stabilize the country and steer it towards an American-style democracy. Many Mexicans resented American interference, believing that it was primarily motivated by a desire to protect its economic interests.

Wilson proclaimed American neutrality when war erupted in August 1914. He was disgusted with the European alliances, which he believed had fueled tensions between the major powers. The combination of new military technology and mass conscript armies resulted in a bloodbath. The war quickly turned into a stalemate on the Western Front; both sides were incurring heavy casualties that did little to resolve the conflict. Wilson, like many Americans, was more sympathetic to Britain and France; he abhorred the brutalities of German militarism, most evident in its violation of Belgium's neutrality. However, these concerns did not dissuade Wilson from following the nation's longstanding isolationist path. The majority of Americans agreed with the president's position, as evidenced by his reelection in 1916.

### Mobilizing for War

Wilson gradually abandoned isolationism in favor of intervention. From 1914 to 1916, tensions between Germany and the United States escalated, due to Germany's repeated violations of U.S. neutrality. The Germans did not believe that the United States ever intended to be truly neutral and decided to do whatever was necessary to win the war. The most egregious acts involved submarine attacks on ships bound for Britain and France with Americans onboard. It did not matter to Wilson and other Americans that these merchant ships were supplying Germany's enemies.

Wilson also began viewing the American intervention in more philosophical terms. The actions of Germany and its allies were an assault on the values and traditions of Western liberalism. A German victory would be disastrous to freedom and liberty not only in Europe but also around the world. German militarism perpetuated elites who controlled that country's economy and government. The same was true in many other imperial regimes. As the situation unraveled in Russia, Wilson believed that the oppressed peoples in these empires would choose either to follow the path of the Bolshevik Revolution or take a middle course typified by the Western democracies. American intervention was critical to an Allied victory as well as to the securing of international support for Wilson's vision of a democratic, postwar world.

However, Wilson faced serious challenges in preparing the country for war. The United States Army had to expand dramatically, either through volunteering or the draft, to fight the massive German Army in France. The American economy was the world's largest, but it was not geared towards a wartime production schedule that included supplying the American military and its allies, as well as domestic consumers. Many Americans supported the war, but others, including labor unions, socialists, and recent immigrants did not see the point of participating in a European war. Public resolve would probably be tested once the military began suffering heavy casualties.

Wilson dealt with this crisis by expanding the powers of the federal government. He appointed muckraking journalist George Creel to head the Committee on Public Information (CPI) to promote the war to the American people. CPI's approach was twofold: showcase the high moral purpose of the war and demonize the enemy. Meanwhile, Wilson appointed Wall Street financier Bernard Baruch to lead the War Industries Board (WIB), to oversee the economy's conversion to wartime production. The WIB determined production priorities and distribution schedules, allocated raw materials, and set fair profit levels. It assumed unprecedented regulatory powers, to a degree that historians have sometimes labeled the period "wartime socialism." Further examples of this trend towards government expansion included the Food Administration headed by Herbert Hoover, which encouraged farmers to increase production through a program of subsidies and other incentives, and the Railroad Administration, led by Wilson's son-in-law and secretary of the treasury, Robert McAdoo, which took over the management of the railroads for the duration of the war. Wilson also implemented the Selective Service Act, the first draft since the Civil War. Local officials were entrusted with its administration, which successfully muted most resistance.

### Wilson and the Versailles Treaty

Wilson argued that the goal of the war involved more than just defeating Germany. In an April 2 address to Congress, Wilson argued that "the world must be made safe for democracy." On January 8, 1918, Wilson laid out a utopian postwar scenario, wherein countries might resolve their differences peacefully in what he called the Fourteen Points. He talked about the importance of "open covenants of peace, openly arrived at" instead of the secret alliances that had triggered this war. Wilson described a world in which all countries enjoyed freedom on the high seas, a deliberate rebuke to the Anglo–German naval race that had also precipitated World War I. He also introduced a new principle of ethnic self-determination, which laid the basis for groups such as the Serbs to have their own countries once the older empires, like Austria–Hungary, were dissolved.

The centerpiece of the Fourteen Points was the concept of a "general association of nations," which came to be called the League of Nations, where countries would settle their differences peacefully. The League would also provide collective security to its members. Aggressors would be deterred from attacking smaller countries, like Belgium, because they would not want to oppose the entire international community. Wilson's vision was met with skepticism at the Versailles Peace Conference; and some of his objectives, such as self-determination, were only partially achieved. But through sheer force of will, Wilson persuaded the allies to accept his most important goal, the League of Nations. However, Wilson faced even stiffer resistance at home, in the Republican-controlled Senate.

Several Republican senators hesitated to commit the United States to an organization that might involve it in a war without congressional approval. Already in fragile health, Wilson suffered a stroke while taking the case for the treaty nationwide before the American people. Wilson's efforts ultimately were in vain; the Senate blocked ratification in 1918 by seven votes. Wilson lived until 1924, but was essentially an invalid for the rest of his second term.

To some extent, Wilson's internationalist vision was simply too grand for the times. World War I was not enough of an emergency for Americans to abandon their sense that the country should not become embroiled in Europe's or the rest of the world's crises. It would take another world war, just a decade later, to convince them that the United States ought to play a larger role in the international community.

**Bibliography**

Clements, Kendrick. *The Presidency of Woodrow Wilson.* Lawrence: University of Kansas Press, 1992.

Kennedy, David. *Over Here: The First World War and American Society.* New York: Oxford University Press, 1980.

**Further Reading**

Brands, H. W. *Woodrow Wilson.* New York: Times Books, 2003.

Cooper, John Milton. *The Warrior and the Priest: Woodrow Wilson and Theodore Roosevelt.* Cambridge, Mass.: The Belknap Press of Harvard University Press, 1983.

Link, Arthur. *Wilson.* 5 vols. Princeton, N.J.: Princeton University Press, 1917.

**Related Entries**

Pershing, John Joseph; Preparedness Movement; Roosevelt, Theodore; Selective Service System; War Industries Board; World War I

**Related Documents**

1918 d

—*Todd Forney*

# Women in the Military

## Early Roles

Women have been an integral, if often marginalized, part of the American military since its inception. As early as 1775, the U.S. Congress specified that Army units could enlist one female nurse for every ten sick or wounded men. Throughout the 19th century the linkage between women and military service remained focused on traditional female roles like nursing. By the time of the Spanish–American War in 1898, the U.S. Army had 1,200 female nurses caring for soldiers in Cuba and the United States. With the Army Reorganization Act of 1901, the Army officially created a permanent female nursing corps. Like most early attempts to include women in the defense establishment, this act marginalized women by denying the nurses rank, equal pay, and retirement benefits. In 1908 the Navy went further, establishing the Navy Nurses, the first group of women to formally serve as members of the uniformed services. The first nurses, known as the "sacred twenty," evolved into an organization with 160 members by 1917.

In some rare cases, women attempted to go beyond the traditionally feminine roles that the military tried to assign to them. A small number of women, such as the

Revolutionary War soldier Deborah Sampson, disguised themselves as men and participated in combat operations, sometimes with the tacit approval of their male comrades. Such women clearly violated a widely accepted belief in the United States that, until quite recently, has placed men in the role of warrior and women in the role of those whom the warriors protected. During the Civil War, Union nurse Mary Livermore noted the presence of a "large number" of women who disguised themselves as men to fight in the war. Scholar Linda Grant de Pauw places the number of women who disguised themselves as men at 250 in the Confederate army and 400 in the Union army, although an exact count is impossible to determine.

More traditionally, the military has accepted women into clear second-class roles or into roles more in tune with commonly accepted notions of gender. Nursing fit most obviously into these patterns. During World War I, the Army expanded its unit of nurses from 403 in early 1917 to more than 21,400 by the end of the war. Almost half of these nurses saw overseas service. The Navy added more than 1,000 nurses during the war, building on its already path-breaking "sacred twenty."

The personnel needs of the Army during World War I ran counter to desires to maintain traditional gender roles. Accordingly, the armed services reached a compromise that placed enlisted women in administrative roles under the status of civilian contractors. In October 1917, Gen. John Pershing requested 100 female telephone operators fluent in French. These women were volunteers who, although working directly for the Army, received no military rank and had pay scales similar to those of nurses, not the uniformed, male members of the Army. The Army soon recruited women to serve under an analogous status in several administrative departments in the United States and Europe. The Navy recruited 13,000 yeomen (F), better known as "yeomenettes." Although banned from service at sea, "yeomenettes" received full military status, pay, and retirement benefits.

The end of World War I led to a massive reduction of American military forces, and military women were among the first to be let go. The Navy quickly cancelled its yeomenette program and introduced legislation in the 1925 Naval Reserve Act that limited service in the Navy to male citizens only. Similarly, despite studies showing massive female interest in military service in the event of war, the Army abolished its position of director of women's programs in 1931. Most officers and members of Congress viewed women's military participation during World War I as an exigent act designed to meet a temporary emergency, not as a template for future integration of women into the American military.

### Creating the Women's Auxiliaries

The personnel needs of World War II led to an even greater expansion of women's roles. The U.S. Army's decision to limit the size of military forces to 90 infantry divisions, designed to maximize the number of men who could remain in industrial jobs, created an additional need for women to fill military roles. In May 1941, with the international crisis building, Congresswoman Edith Nourse Rogers, who had served with the Army in England in World War I, and First Lady Eleanor Roosevelt proposed a bill to incorporate female volunteers into the Army. The senior leadership of the Army forced a compromise that enlisted women as part of an auxiliary unit whose members were not part of the larger Army structure and thus did not receive rank and pay in accordance with men.

The creation of the Women's Army Auxiliary Corps (WAAC) set the pattern for women's service in World War II. WAAC members were clearly understood to be volunteers and noncombatants. The Navy moved more slowly, but in July 1942 it introduced a broadly similar organization called the WAVES, whose very name—Women Accepted for Volunteer Emergency Service—underscored its auxiliary and secondary role. WAVES were to occupy positions in the U.S. Navy in order to free male sailors and marines for service on ships and overseas duty. In the words of one recruitment poster for female marines: "Be a marine. Free a marine to fight."

By the middle of the war, Army and Navy senior leaders acquiesced to external pressure and institutional reason, offering women full military status in order to simplify the legal and administrative requirements of military women. In July 1943, the WAAC became the WAC (Women's Army Corps), dropping "auxiliary" and providing full military rank to WAC members. Women remained a small proportion of the armed forces (never more than 2.3 percent), but served in increasingly important roles until the end of the war in 1945. The majority of military women (64 percent) served in administrative positions, but others challenged the definitions of "female work" significantly. Navy scientist and WAVES member Grace Hopper used her Ph.D. in mathematics to help develop the electromagnetic Mark I and Mark II calculating machines. She remained in the Navy until 1986, when she retired as an admiral. Other women assumed commands and performed tasks previously reserved for men, including service on the highly technical LORAN (Long-Range Aid to Navigation) systems and the Manhattan Project, which developed the atomic bomb. Women did not serve in combat, but they did become gunnery instructors, mechanics, and truck drivers. By the end of the war, the Army had dropped its insistence on women staying stateside. More than 17,000 members of the WAC served overseas.

Another group of women volunteered to fly combat aircraft from their point of manufacture in the United States to bases overseas. The 1,000 members of the Women's Air Service Pilot program (WASP) encountered more official hostility from the senior ranks of the Army, partly because the traditionally male job they performed threatened gender roles much more than did the WAC or WAVES programs. The women who joined the WASP program received no military rank and no military benefits, despite serving at more than 120 air bases and logging more than 60 million miles in combat aircraft. WASP pilots also flight-tested new airplanes, a dangerous job that cost 38 WASP pilots their lives. In 1980 Congress finally authorized veteran status for the WASP pilots, but denied them full military benefits.

As the experience of the WASP showed, women who volunteered for military service in World War II faced tremendous challenges. In order to ensure that military women did not appear to challenge conventional images of women, members of the WAC and WAVES were depicted as being feminine even while they performed masculine work. This image often ran counter to women's efforts to have men take them seriously as military colleagues. Women faced harassment, condescension, and an aggressive slander campaign by those opposed to women serving in the military.

*World War II WASP pilots assigned to the 2nd Ferrying Group, Ferrying Division, at New Castle Army Air Base, near Wilmington, Delaware. (© Bettmann/CORBIS)*

The campaign spread rumors that alleged that the WAC and WAVES consisted of lesbians and, somewhat paradoxically, that these units were filled with women who were sexually promiscuous with their male peers.

Army and Navy nurses served overseas in large numbers as well. The Army employed 57,000 female nurses; the Navy, 11,000. They often served at or very near the front lines. Sixty-seven Army nurses became prisoners of war following the Philippines campaign (1941–42) and endured the brutal conditions of Japanese prisoner of war camps for three years. Despite the dangerous conditions in which they served, military nurses, operating in more traditional female roles, elicited much less controversy than did those serving in the WAC and WAVES programs.

### Postwar Debates

The end of World War II led to a significant drawdown of the American military. As in 1918, the women's programs were among the first to be cut. The numbers fell from a high of 100,000 WACs and 86,000 WAVES in 1945 to only 5,000 WACs and 1,600 WAVES by 1948, respectively. Most women, like most men, were happy to return to their prewar lives after 1945; but many women had hoped to continue their military service. Several senior military leaders and members of Congress disapproved; they recommended disbanding the WAC and WAVES altogether and returning the military to an all-male status. Women remained in administrative jobs while Congress and the services continued to debate the issue. Nursing remained an exception to the general pattern. In 1947, the Army–Navy Nurses Act permanently integrated nurses into the regular line of the armed services and opened ranks as high as lieutenant colonel/commander to nurses.

The Army–Navy Nurses Act and the growing threat of Cold War competition with the Soviet Union led to planning for a permanent role for military women. Senior military leaders like generals Dwight Eisenhower, Douglas MacArthur, and Carl Spaatz, and Adm. Chester Nimitz, all lent their support to the idea. They argued against a more conservative congressional plan to admit women only into the military reserves. Despite these high-level supporters of women in the military, Congress opposed any legislation that would create what one congressman called "an army of women." Congress also argued that providing military women with the same dependent benefits provided to military men would create an unpalatable image of women working to support their idle husbands. Still others argued that military status was incompatible with motherhood.

The result of these debates was the compromise Women's Armed Services Integration Act of 1948. Like the Army–Navy Nurses Act of the previous year, the Women's Armed Services Integration Act made women a regular and permanent part of the active and reserve portions of the American armed services. The act also set important limits on women's service, including: a ceiling on women's participation set at 2 percent of total service strength; separate promotion lists by gender; parental consent for women under the age of 21; a ban on dependent access to health care (unless a woman could claim that she was responsible for more than 50 percent of the dependent's financial support); and a ban on female service in combat aircraft and on board ships (other than hospital ships and transports outside combat areas).

The Women's Armed Services Integration Act and subsequent legislation assumed that women did not want a career in the military. In 1951, Pres. Harry S. Truman signed legislation mandating that women separate from the military if they became mothers by giving birth, by marrying a man with children, or by adopting. The services also allowed women to abandon their military commitments without penalty if they married.

As a result of the limits imposed by the Women's Armed Services Integration Act, the percentage of women in the military never exceeded 2 percent and rarely reached 1.5 percent, even during the Korean War. The low numbers of women in the military reflected the official, second-class status of women more than a lack of interest among women in military service. By another clause in the Women's Armed Services Integration Act, only the heads of the WAC, WAVES, and WAF (Women in the Air Force) programs could attain the rank of colonel or captain. The logjam of the promotion system thus limited the abilities of women to attain rank commensurate with their knowledge and experience. The poor job opportunities and continued sexual harassment that both female officers and enlisted women faced also led to high attrition rates. By the late 1950s, less than 1.3 percent of American military personnel were female.

Consequently, more than 80 percent of American military women who served in the Vietnam War were nurses. Army nurses served in areas dangerously close to the Demilitarized Zone and were often under fire. Eight Army nurses were killed in action during the war. Members of the WAC, WAVES, and WAF programs also served in Southeast Asia, most commonly at the Military Assistance Command headquarters in Saigon in South Vietnam. Despite their service in a combat zone as medical personnel, they were forbidden to take weapons training or carry side arms.

As the Vietnam War grew increasingly unpopular and Selective Service increasingly controversial, Army planners began to reconsider the use of military women. Enlisting more military women offered the possibility of reducing the number of men that the Selective Service System had to draft. As early as 1964, the armed services had officially supported a revision of the 2 percent limit on women's service legislated in the Women's Armed Services Integration Act of 1948. In 1967, Pres. Lyndon Johnson signed Public Law 90-130, which removed the 2 percent quota and also removed the limits on women's promotions, although separate promotion lists by gender remained. By 1973, women made up 2.6 percent of the Army, 2.2 percent of the Navy, and 2.9 percent of the Air Force. These modest increases were less than supporters of Public Law 90-130 had envisioned, but did demonstrate significant growth compared to the 1950s. The law, however, did not change the fundamentally unequal status of military women.

### Expanded Opportunities

The end of conscription in 1973 had a dramatic impact on the nature of women's military service. With the armed services no longer able to count on the draft to compel men to serve, and with the military now generally held in low regard among young males, the new all volunteer force had to reconsider the employment of women. In the absence of the draft, military pay and living conditions also improved, making the military a more attractive career option for women. Although many members of Congress and many in the Pentagon still hoped to keep the number of military women small, senior uniformed leaders like the Navy's chief of naval operations, Adm. Elmo Zumwalt, supported taking active and aggressive steps to improve the numbers and status of military women.

As part of his package of reforms, Zumwalt argued for the abolition of the WAVES on the grounds that a separate structure for Navy women was incompatible with the Navy's desire to offer women equal opportunity. In 1973 the WAVES were disbanded, quickly followed by the abolition of the WAF (1976) and WAC (1978) programs as well. Zumwalt and the Air Force's Theodore Marrs led the move to open up Reserve Officers Training Corps (ROTC) programs to women in the early 1970s on the same terms as men. These programs opened a large officer corps accession program to women and allowed them to take weapons training alongside men.

The success of the ROTC integration program led further to the opening of the service academies to women in 1976. Sen. Jacob Javits of New York had first recommended a woman for appointment in 1972, but the Naval Academy rejected the nomination. Congress began to take action in response to lawsuits alleging that denying women access to the academies also unfairly denied them access to senior rank. Sen. Patricia Schroeder of Colorado led a bipartisan effort to introduce an amendment to the 1975 Defense Authorization Bill that would integrate the academies. It passed by a voice vote and was signed into law by Pres. Gerald Ford with little congressional controversy.

The courts also began to take an interest in many aspects of the unequal legal status of military women. By early 1973, some 30 states had approved the Equal Rights Amendment, making its ultimate passage seem likely. The military assumed that, if passed, the Equal Rights Amendment would lead to legal challenges regarding any aspects of military service that made distinctions according to gender. Even though the amendment ultimately failed, these challenges began almost immediately. In 1973, the Supreme Court ruled that the military had to offer women the same dependent benefits offered to men. Consequently, the military decided to replace the terms "husband" and "wife" with "spouse." Other court cases led the military to change its policy requiring unwed women who became pregnant to give up their duties and declared that the Navy could not refuse women service aboard ship based solely on their gender.

The smooth integration of women into analogous institutions during the 1970s undermined the military's arguments against the further integration of women into the military. Women became successful members of police forces, fire departments, the Secret Service, and the National Aeronautics and Space Administration. Moreover, the military's own studies determined that the integration of women did not undermine unit cohesion. The Army's MAX WAC study of 1977 and REF WAC study of 1978 found that the presence of women in a unit did not impair that unit's performance. The military also discovered that women applicants had on average higher test scores than men and that women in the services missed far less time due to alcohol, drug use, and going AWOL. Even with pregnancy leave figured in, men still had nearly twice the absentee rate of women. The services soon found solutions to other problems such as restroom facilities, uniforms, and pregnancy policies.

These changes led to a dramatic rise in the numbers of military women. The administration of Pres. Jimmy Carter firmly supported the recruitment of more military women, which led to the appointment of Department of Defense officials sympathetic to the expanding the number of military women as well as their roles. Between 1973 and 1981 the percentage of female Army personnel rose from 2.6 percent to 9.4 percent. The percentage of women in the Air Force rose from 2.9 percent to 11.1 percent, in the Navy from 2.2 percent to 7.4 percent. The number of women entering the services also increased pressure to open more jobs to them. In 1978, the Coast Guard—part of the Department of Defense in times of war only—opened all sea going billets (quarters) to women on exactly the same terms as men. Although pressured to follow suit, the Navy continued to ban women from ships designated as combat vessels. The Air Force and Army also held to policies prohibiting women from combat. The Army's Direct Combat Probability Coding system coded each Army job P1 to P7, based on its likelihood of facing combat. Those at the highest end of the scale were closed to women.

The administration of Pres. Ronald Reagan supported limiting the number of women in the military but did not support the desires of some officials to roll back the military participation of women. The percentages of female military personnel thus continued to grow throughout the 1980s, though at a slower pace than in the 1970s. As a result, military operations and deployments during the Reagan years—such as those in Grenada and Panama—inevitably included women. They also showed that the Direct Combat Probability Coding system could not keep women safe from the dangers of military service. At times, the system proved to be dangerously inefficient: in some cases, unit commanders decided to deploy units to combat areas without their female soldiers, leaving the units without mission-critical personnel. In another case, an Army division commander ignored the Direct Combat Probability Coding system and sent his unit's women into combat areas.

At the same time, women were demonstrating proficiency in a wider range of military specialties. The Defense Department therefore had to deal with women performing more jobs within the context of the services' desires to keep women away from combat. In 1988 the Pentagon discarded the direct combat Probability Coding system in favor of a Risk Rule system that reduced the Army's seven classifications to two: combat and non-combat. The change opened more jobs to women but retained the presumption that women could be protected from harm by denying them the right to serve in certain jobs. But the Risk Rule failed to operate as designed in Panama, where several women came under fire.

The Persian Gulf War witnessed the deployment of more than 33,000 women overseas and demonstrated two important points that military studies had long concluded: first, that women had become a necessary and competent component of any large military operation; and second, that no amount of legislation could eliminate the risk to female military personnel. The intense media attention that accompanied the war placed these issues directly in the national spotlight.

The success of military women in the Persian Gulf War led to a movement to change the legislation governing the military service of women. On May 22, 1991, two members of Congress—Democrats Patricia Schroeder and Beverly Byron—sponsored a bill to remove the exclusions of women from combat service in the Navy and the Army. The

Pentagon initially supported the bill, but later joined Pres. George H. W. Bush's administration in opposing it. A controversial, nonbinding residential commission on the issue of women in combat issued a report opposing women in combat just after the election of Bill Clinton in 1992.

The Clinton administration ignored the report and moved quickly to open more military jobs to women. Soon after his appointment, Sec. of Defense Les Aspin, a longtime supporter of expanding roles for women, dropped the Risk Rule and opened combat aviation to women. In the early months of 1994, the Air Force welcomed its first female fighter pilot, and the Navy assigned its first women to aircraft carriers. The Clinton administration issued guidance to the Pentagon stating that women could not be banned from a military assignment based solely on the danger that the assignment posed. Aspin also announced that the Clinton administration intended to open all military jobs to women except special operations, ground combat, and service on submarines.

### Abiding Problems

The progress that women made in breaking barriers stood in marked contrast to the pervasive problems of sexual harassment and assault. In 1979, the *Baltimore Sun* ran a series of stories on sexual harassment incidents and rapes at Fort Meade in Maryland. These articles brought the issue to public attention and led to a series of congressional hearings in 1980. The Army's own investigations revealed that half of all female personnel had experienced harassment and that sexual harassment was a primary reason for women choosing not to reenlist. With the new attention came new discipline, including the Army's first-ever court martial conviction for sexual harassment.

Military studies also revealed that the problem of sexual harassment was more pronounced overseas than in the United States. A tour of European and Pacific bases by a congressionally appointed committee in 1986 and 1987 showed that sexual harassment was a commonplace occurrence that went unpunished by chains of command in Hawaii and the Philippines. The Pentagon classified the committee's report, but it was subsequently leaked to major U.S. newspapers. A new round of investigations followed, and several Philippine commanders were reassigned; but the problem remained, as evidenced by the rape of 24 women in 18 months at the Navy's Orlando, Florida, training center in 1990.

Sexual harassment jumped on to the front pages as a result of the behavior of several naval aviators at the bacchanalian 1991 Tailhook convention in Las Vegas. More than 80 women were assaulted at the conference while some officers looked on and others took pictures. Forcing women to "run the gauntlet" at Tailhook had been a feature of the conference for years. In 1991, however, the events at Tailhook stood in sharp contrast to the treatment of military women months earlier during the Persian Gulf War. A Tailhook victim and aide to an admiral publicized the events at the conference after the admiral ignored her pleas to investigate. The Tailhook scandal grew larger as some Navy officers refused to cooperate with investigators.

In 1996, a sexual assault scandal at the Army's Aberdeen Proving Ground underscored the continuing depths of the problem. In 2003, allegations of sexual assault and harassment emerged at the U.S. Air Force Academy as well. To some, the assaults and harassment are expressions of male opposition to the intrusion of women into the traditionally male world of the military. To others, they are representative of failures of leadership. One Army study concluded that sexual harassment and sexual assault cost the Army more than $500 million per year in litigation and lost work time.

The recent experiences of women in the American military is thus a history of achievement amidst abiding problems. In both world wars, women served on a temporary, emergency basis, laying a foundation for the accomplishments that followed. In the past 30 years, military women have shattered glass ceilings and demonstrated marked proficiencies in numerous jobs previously held only by males. At the same time, however, the persistence of sexual harassment and sexual assault highlights the serious issues and challenging conditions that military women continue to face.

**Bibliography**

Binkin, Martin, and Shirley Bach. *Women and the Military.* Washington, D.C.: Brookings, 1973.

De Pauw, Linda Grant. *Battle Cries and Lullabies: Women in War from Prehistory to the Present.* Norman: University of Oklahoma Press, 1998.

Holm, Jeanne. *Women in the Military: An Unfinished Revolution.* Novato, Calif.: Presidio Press, 1992.

**Further Reading**

McMichael, William H. *The Mother of All Hooks: The Story of the U. S. Navy's Tailhook Scandal.* New Brunswick, N.J.: Transaction, 1997.

Morden, Bettie. *The Women's Army Corps, 1945–1978.* Washington: United States Army Center of Military History, 1990.

Rustad, Michael. *Women in Khaki: The American Enlisted Woman.* New York: Praeger, 1982.

Stiehm, Judith Hicks. *Arms and the Enlisted Woman.* Philadelphia: Temple University Press, 1989.

Treadwell, Mattie. *The United States Army in World War II Special Studies: The Women's Army Corps*. Washington, D.C.: Office of the Chief of Military History, 1953.

U.S. Presidential Commission on the Assignment of Women in the Armed Forces. *Women in Combat.* Washington, D.C.: Brassey's, 1993.

Van Devanter, Lynda. *Home Before Morning: The True Story of an Army Nurse in Vietnam.* Reprint. Amherst: University of Massachusetts Press, 2001.

Westbrook, Robert. "I Want a Girl Just Like the Girl that Married Harry James: American Women and the Problem of Political Obligations in World War II." *American Quarterly* 42 (December 1990): 587–614.

**Related Entries**

Nurses, Military; Sampson, Deborah; Sexual Abuse and Harassment; Tailhook Convention

**Related Documents**

1759

—*Michael S. Neiberg*

# Women in the Workforce: World War I and World War II

Women in the United States have always worked, whether inside or outside the home during peacetime or wartime, but their labor-force participation received special public and government attention during the two world wars of the 20th century. Whether women worked for wages during the world wars, and in what capacity they were employed, largely depended on the duration of U.S. military involvement and the labor force needs of the military. In the case of World War I, most armed forces personnel drawn into the services for the war effort left the labor force for less than two full years, whereas in World War II the drafting of personnel began in mid-1940, and most did not return home until 1946. Thus, few women were needed to take men's places during World War I.

The conscription of millions of American men into the armed forces from December 1941 until August 1945 ended the unemployment problem of the Depression years; it provided homeland jobs to millions of women and men. During both world wars, private employers and the federal government expected women to relinquish their nontraditional wage work at the war's conclusion. All media during World War II repeated the mantra that women were replacing men only until the armed forces returned from overseas. For both national emergencies, women were considered a reserve labor force, but not all women perceived their working status as temporary. Demobilization only briefly depressed women's employment. After both world wars, married women's labor force participation continued to rise as part of a long-term secular trend throughout the 20th century.

## World War I

World War I accelerated preexisting trends in the nature and location of women's employment. Beginning in the last quarter of the 19th century, the second stage of industrialization increased mass production, distribution, and consumption. Employers sought women for unskilled and semiskilled jobs in manufacturing, sales, offices, and telephone service. Several factors determined the work options of men and women: their formal educational options and types of job training; the "appropriateness" of their wage work; their pay scales and advancement opportunities; and their entitlements to legal protections. The gender system intersected with racial, class, and ethnic barriers to circumscribe individuals' job opportunities and earning power. While the wartime labor shortage created temporary job vacancies for women in typically male-dominated fields, women's presence in such unconventional roles ended with demobilization. When the dust settled, women as a group returned to the jobs they had entered or dominated before the war.

During World War I, women sought information about job openings from the United States Employment Service, combed newspaper advertisements for job leads, and exchanged employment information with family and friends. Thousands of white women left domestic service, textile mills, and clothing shops to work in the steel, metal, chemical, lumber, glass, and leather industries. According to one detailed federal government survey of wartime production, women comprised 20 percent or more of all workers making electrical machinery, airplanes, optical goods, motion picture and photographic equipment, musical instruments, leather and rubber goods, dental supplies, and food, as well as paper, paper goods, and printed materials. Experienced clerical workers sought higher-paying jobs in government offices and telegraph and telephone exchanges.

Pervasive racism further limited African American women's job opportunities during World War I, reinforcing their concentration in domestic and personal service. Private-sector employers throughout the United States segregated workers by race, assigning the most undesirable jobs to people of color. Since Pres. Woodrow Wilson made racial segregation the official policy for all federal civilian jobs during his first term, a woman's job location within the federal bureaucracy was determined by the color of her skin. Only when a light-skinned African American was mistaken as Caucasian did she work side by side with a member of another race. In the private sector, some black women acquired factory jobs, especially in tobacco- and food-processing plants and, to a much lesser extent, in the leather, metal, paper-products, clothing, and textile industries. Because proportionally more married black women had been working for wages than had wives of other races, institutional racism during the war intensified economic hardships for families of color.

Male-dominated trade unions during World War I disliked the substitution of women for men. Invidious stereotyping and economic concerns motivated men to treat women as interlopers and adversaries. Across the social-class spectrum, most men adamantly believed that biology destined men and women to assume different social responsibilities. Male molders, foundry employees, machinists, telephone repairers, teamsters, coal miners, electrical workers, to name only a few, used bureaucratic, legal, or personal tactics to bar or discourage women from working in their fields. The barriers multiplied when middle-class female reformers joined forces with male trade unionists to lobby states for laws restricting women from jobs deemed especially risky to their physical or moral well-being. Employment in mines, quarries, shoeshine parlors, bowling alleys, and trucking firms became off-limits to women. An Ohio law prohibited women from becoming bellhops, taxi drivers, gas meter readers, freight handlers, or molders. When women succeeded in entering male-dominated industries, unions admitted women as a temporary expedient against employers hiring women to undercut men's wages. In industries under federal control, such as the transcontinental railroads, government records document men sexually harassing female co-workers in offices, machine shops, and freight yards. Male streetcar employees taunted female trolley conductors and threatened to strike unless their companies stopped hiring them. Such workplace behavior was not designated a form of unlawful sex discrimination until the passage of Title VII of the 1964 Civil Rights Act.

The so-called female interlopers strove to keep their new jobs because, contrary to popular notions about women working for pin money, women's wages in fact helped their families meet essential expenses. Such women included widows, single mothers, or daughters of low-income or debt-ridden parents. Knowing that union labor earned higher wages than non-union labor, these women embraced the opportunity to acquire union membership.

### World War II

In many important respects, the narrative of women workers during World War II resembles women's stories during the previous war: a severe labor shortage created vacancies in factories, stores, and offices; racial discrimination by employers, despite the president's executive order to the contrary, narrowed job options for women of color relative to white women; and after the war women of all races were expected to return to their prewar employment or withdraw from the work force altogether to attend to domestic duties full time. World War II differed from the first in two ways, however: a much larger number of women wage earners entered the labor force, and an explosive increase in trade union membership laid the foundation for a new wave of labor feminism among blue-collar women in the 1950s, the likes of which had not been seen in the United States since the 1910s.

According to the federal government, between 1940 and 1945 the number of women workers increased from 11 to 19.5 million. The number of women workers reported in the 1940 census under-represented the number of women who would have entered the labor force in the normal course of their lives had the United States not suffered so many years from the Great Depression. Approximately 3.5 million, or less than half, of the women who entered the job market between 1940 and 1945 took jobs because of the severe wartime labor shortage and/or government appeals to patriotism. Like their World War I counterparts, working-class women eagerly left their lower paying, often unskilled or semiskilled jobs, for higher paying, more challenging work normally reserved for men in the manufacturing, sales, clerical, and service sectors.

Family responsibilities strongly influenced which women entered the labor force. Single women, who composed almost half of the female labor force in 1940, continued wage earning during the war. Young wives without dependents rallied to the call for workers as did older married women with grown children. Employment without the benefit of substantial support services from the government or from employers discouraged mothers with children or other dependents who viewed family work as their first responsibility. When the war ended, many single women who had worked prior to the war left their jobs voluntarily, presumably to marry and raise families. Older married women did not automatically relinquish their jobs to returning soldiers; in some workplaces they stayed at their wartime posts until they were forced out. Their desire to continue working outside the home contributed to a major shift in

*Women welders at a shipbuilding plant in Mississippi in 1943. (National Archives and Records Administration)*

the expectations and options of women after World War II as the number of married mothers chose to combine domestic and wage work.

As had been the case during World War I, World War II only temporarily disrupted the long-term trends in women's employment. The wartime labor shortage brought more women into the durable goods industries of iron and steel, automobile and aircraft, shipbuilding, chemical, rubber, petroleum, and machinery manufacturing; but few women retained these jobs after the war. During and after the war, women remained dominant in the nondurable goods sectors of textiles, food, and clothing production, and their presence in the clerical and service sectors grew substantially during and after the labor shortage.

Even though the war did not change women's overall position in the labor force, it taught women of all races valuable lessons about the need for economic, social, and political reforms in American society. U.S. government propaganda against European and Asian fascism and imperialism empowered African Americans to press for legal measures that would guarantee their full citizenship in the United States. Waging a two-front war against fascism abroad and white racism at home, African American women complained to the new Fair Employment Practices Commission against employers like the Chicago State Street department stores for refusing to hire them, ostensibly because of their race, despite a severe labor shortage. The national spotlight on women's employment, their success in performing men's jobs, and the dramatic rise in trade union membership emboldened women to act collectively on their own behalf. As the labor movement grew, a new chapter in the history of class and gender politics unfolded in American society.

During the war, women trade unionists in different industries introduced a new agenda for women's rights at work. They pressured unions and employers in the private and public sectors to base their wages on their skills and performance instead of their gender. They targeted sex-based restrictive labor legislation for reconsideration, and after the war they pressed for maternity leave and child care policies in union contracts. Women's visibility and leadership increased in such unions as the United Packinghouse Workers of America, the United Automobile Workers, the United Electrical Workers and the International Union of Electrical Workers, the National Federation of Telephone Workers, and the Hotel Employees and Restaurant Employees Union. Although their efforts produced mixed results, these wartime workers should receive credit for launching a new wave of labor feminism.

Contrary to popular notions about women's postwar immersion in domesticity, married women's labor force participation rose after World War II, and public opinion slowly softened its objections to wage work for wives and mothers. The postwar economic boom attracted older married women with school-age children to take clerical, manufacturing, and service jobs. The freedoms for which the war had been fought whetted African Americans' desire for justice and fair play in all walks of American life. Profoundly dissatisfied with their designated place in American society, southern black women would soon assume key positions in the grass-roots mobilization to end racial segregation and discrimination. The ideals of a new world order based on democracy and liberty had the unintended consequence of discrediting the old world order of unequal racial and gender power relations throughout the United States.

**Bibliography**

Cobble, Dorothy Sue. *The Other Women's Movement: Workplace Justice and Social Rights in Modern America*. Princeton, N.J.: Princeton University Press, 2004.

Greenwald, Maurine Weiner. *Women, War, and Work: The Impact of World War I on Women Workers in the United States.* Westport, Conn.: Greenwood Press, 1980.

———. "Working-Class Feminism and the Family Wage Ideal." *Journal of American History* 76 (June 1989): 118–49.

Kessler-Harris, Alice. *Out to Work: A History of Wage-Earning Women in the United States.* New York: Oxford University Press, 1982.

Lemke-Santangelo, Gretchen. *Abiding Courage: African American Migrant Women and the East Bay Community*. Chapel Hill: University of North Carolina Press, 1996.

Milkman, Ruth. *Gender at Work: The Dynamics of Job Segregation by Sex during World War II*. Urbana: University of Illinois Press, 1987.

Schweitzer, Mary. "World War II and Female Labor Force Participation Rates." *Journal of Economic History* 40 (March 1980): 89–95.

**Further Reading**

Endres, Kathleen L. *Rosie the Rubber Worker: Women Workers in Akron's Rubber Factories during World War II.* Kent, Ohio: Kent State University Press, 2000.

Kesselman, Amy. *Fleeting Opportunities: Women Shipyard Workers in Portland and Vancouver during World War II and Reconversion.* Albany: State University of New York Press, 1990.

Kossoudji, Sherri A., and Laura J Dresser. "Working Class Rosies: Women Industrial Workers during World War II." *Journal of Economic History* 52 (June 1992): 431–46.

**Related Entries**

Baby Boom; Labor Strikes; Rosie the Riveter; Sexual Abuse and Harassment; Victory Gardens; War Industries Board; War Labor Board; World War I; World War II

—*Maurine W. Greenwald*

# Women's International League for Peace and Freedom

The Women's International League for Peace and Freedom (WILPF) formed in 1915 to abolish the causes of war, work for peace, and create political systems that would bring equality for all. Still in existence at the beginning of the 21st century, WILPF supports total and universal disarmament, the abolition of violence for settling conflicts, and the creation of an international economic order that is not focused on profit and privilege.

With members representing close to 40 nations from all regions of the world, WILPF is notable for its longevity as much as for its achievements. In the early days of World War I, suffragists Emmeline Pethick-Lawrence of Great Britain and Rosika Schwimmer of Hungary toured the United States to persuade American suffragists to push their neutral government to take the lead in negotiations to end the war. The image of sisterhood presented by these two women from warring countries galvanized women's opposition to the war and helped to launch the National Woman's Peace Party in Washington, D.C., in January 1915. The Woman's Peace Party would later become the U.S. section of WILPF. The progressives who founded the group were part of the first generation of women to insist that women were as capable as men. The established, mixed-sex peace groups that deferred to male authority and did not allow women to fully participate by holding leadership positions or by formulating policy had frustrated them. For this reason, WILPF was an organization of women. Feminism would always be crucially important to the group.

Pethick-Lawrence, Schwimmer, and 1,500 other suffragists met in the Netherlands on April 28, 1915 to show that women of all countries could work together in the face of a massive, worldwide war. Americans joined with Britons, Hungarians, Germans, Austrians, Italians, Poles, Belgians, Danes, Norwegians, and Swedes. The participants in the International Congress of Women at The Hague protested against World War I, suggested ways to end the conflict, and hoped to devise strategies to prevent war in the future. They rejected the theory that war was inevitable and decided to create an organization to work for peace. The group was first known as the International Committee of Women for Permanent Peace; the name changed to WILPF at their second meeting, in 1919. Conceived from the very beginning as an international organization, the umbrella committee set up 13 national committees. Although every committee was located either in Europe or North America, members of WILPF regarded themselves as citizens of the world. Jane Addams, a social worker and one of the most famous women in the United States at the time, served as the first president of the international organization.

WILPF sought to assemble a panel of neutral states for continuous mediation of conflict. The members believed that if Europe was in disorder because of deep-rooted injustices or because some nations were deprived of commercial or political opportunities, the solution could be discovered more effectively through conversation than by bloodshed. They argued that bloodshed would eventually lead to exhaustion and, at that point, nations would be forced to negotiate. WILPF believed that it made much more sense to begin with negotiations rather to than end with them after many had died.

WILPF faced considerable difficulty finding an audience during World War I. They could not persuade any country to begin the mediating process, and the entrance of the United States into the conflict in 1917 shocked American pacifists. The national climate was such that those who did not stand strongly with the U.S. government were regarded with suspicion if not outright hostility. Addams became the target of enormous public criticism for her peace activities. Undeterred, Addams and other WILPF members argued that the role of nurturer had given women a stronger sense of moral obligation than men. Therefore, she insisted, there must be equal participation by women in all levels of society if social justice is ever to be realized. In 1917, WILPF became the first secular peace organization to establish lobbying headquarters in Washington, D.C., for the purpose of establishing ongoing relations with legislators in an attempt to influence policy.

After World War I ended, WILPF saw the formation of the League of Nations as a victory for the beliefs held by women of peace. While the League never functioned in the effective way that they had envisioned, WILPF and other American peace leaders had urged its creation repeatedly upon Pres. Woodrow Wilson. Throughout the 1920s and early 1930s, WILPF concentrated on working with the League. It sent missions to trouble spots around the world with the plan of talking with all sides to head off a conflict. Emily Greene Balch, an American founder of WILPF and its general secretary, went on a mission to Haiti when U.S. Marines occupied it. Balch's 1927 book, *Occupied Haiti*, helped publicize the American presence there and spurred the withdrawal of the Marines. Balch earned the Nobel Peace Prize for her efforts.

As fascism rose in Europe, WILPF turned its attention to stopping this movement. While some national committees, particularly those with direct experience of Nazism, wanted to use aggressive tactics against fascists, others opposed any sort of violence. Many WILPF members joined other peace advocates in urging disarmament to ensure international peace. The dispute over ideological and tactical differences split WILPF. Membership declined dramatically, but the organization became the only women's peace organization to survive World War II.

WILPF's membership never regained its prewar heights. Its work after World War II centered on supporting the United Nations and opposing the threat of atomic weapons. It became one of the first groups to speak out against the Vietnam War with a 1963 campaign against military escalation in Indochina. However, the American branch soon split on whether to demand unconditional U.S. withdrawal or to back a ceasefire coupled with negotiations. By 1969, WILPF had become firmly convinced that the U.S. government's position was morally indefensible, and they called for a quick withdrawal. Yet the group remained too small to make much of an impact. It continued to work for world peace and human rights in subsequent decades but has had trouble achieving much notice.

WILPF is notable for bringing together women from around the world to work for peace. Its efforts to minimize and manage disputes before they erupted into war aimed to create a world free from bloodshed and oppression. Although not successful in ending violent conflicts, WILPF helped to create peaceful structures in the form of the League of Nations and its successor, the United Nations.

**Bibliography**


Alonso, Harriet Hyman. *Peace as a Woman's Issue: A History of the U.S. Movement for World Peace and Women's Rights.* Syracuse, N.Y.: Syracuse University Press, 1993.

Bussey, Gertrude, and Margaret Tims. *Pioneers for Peace: Women's International League for Peace and Freedom, 1915–1946.* London: Allen & Unwin, 1965.

Foster, Catherine. *Women for All Seasons: The Story of the Women's International League for Peace and Freedom.* Athens: University of Georgia Press, 1989.


**Further Reading**


Adams, Judith Porter. *Peacework: Oral Histories of Women Peace Activists.* Boston: Twayne, 1990.

Bacon, Margaret Hope. *One Woman's Passion for Peace and Freedom: The Life of Mildred Scott Olmsted.* Syracuse, N.Y.: Syracuse University Press, 1993.

Foster, Carrie A. *The Women and the Warriors: The U.S. Section of the Women's International League for Peace and Freedom, 1915–1946.* Syracuse, N.Y.: Syracuse University Press, 1995.

Randall, Mercedes M. *Improper Bostonian: Emily Greene Balch, Nobel Laureate, 1946.* New York: Twayne, 1964.

Women's International League for Peace and Freedom Website. <http://www.wilpf.org>.

**Related Entries**

American Peace Society; Antiwar Movements; Butler, Smedley Darlington; Gunboat Diplomacy; Pacifism; Wilson, Woodrow; World War I

—*Caryn E. Neumann*

# World War I

## (1917–18)

World War I cemented the importance of international trade to the nation's economic well-being, and it gave America a prominent role in bringing peace to Europe. The United States established itself as a world military power by playing a key part in the Allied victory. On the homefront, the government assumed unprecedented power over the economy, drafted a mass army, and limited civil liberties. Pres. Woodrow Wilson sought a new international role for the United States in the Fourteen Points, a document that established the major goals of American foreign policy for the rest of the century. Ultimately, World War I blazed the path for greater governmental involvement in the economy and established how the United States would mobilize for total war during the next world war.

**World War I (1917–18)**

| |
|---|
| Total U.S. Servicemembers (Worldwide): **4,734,991** |
| U.S. Population (millions): **102.8** |
| Battle Deaths: **53,402** |
| Other Deaths in Service (Non-Theater): **63,114** |
| Non-mortal Woundings: **204,002** |
| Cost (in $ current billions): **26.00** |

Source: Deaths and Nonmortal Wounds: Department of Veterans Affairs, *America's Wars*. <http://www1.va.gov/opa/fact/amwars.html>

### The United States Enters the War

World War I began in Europe in August 1914. The European conflict soon turned into a world war as Britain, France, and Germany enlisted help from their far-flung colonial empires. For the next four years the Central Powers (Germany, Austria–Hungary, Ottoman Empire, Bulgaria) faced off against the Allies (France, Britain, Belgium, Russia, Italy, Serbia). In 1914, Pres. Woodrow Wilson vowed to keep the United States neutral in thought as well as deed, but the nation's economic dependence on international trade made this a hard promise to keep. Initially, Wilson prohibited American banks from making loans to belligerent nations purchasing goods in the United States. By 1915, with the Allies running short of cash to buy American products, Wilson lifted the ban to avoid sending the American economy into recession. American banks took the first step away from neutrality by overwhelmingly loaning money to the Allied side.

A trade war that erupted between Britain and Germany also made the American position of neutrality difficult to maintain. With their armies settled into a war of attrition in the trenches along the Western Front, Britain and Germany turned to the seas to gain the advantage. The British instituted a blockade and mined the North Sea to prevent goods from reaching Germany. The Germans used a new and deadly weapon, the U-Boat, a type of submarine. Wilson expected each nation to recognize the rights of neutral nations to trade with whomever they wished, a position that became untenable as the stakes for each side rose. Wilson accepted the British mining with minimal protest and few American ships ventured into the North Sea to continue trading with Germany. The German strategy of unconditional submarine warfare, however, enraged Wilson. After 128 Americans perished aboard the British passenger ship the *Lusitania* on May 7, 1915, Wilson demanded that Germany renounce its policy of attacking any ship that entered the European war zone. Germany protested that it had warned American passengers to stay off the *Lusitania*, which indeed was carrying munitions. After two more controversial ship sinkings involving American passengers, Germany acceded to Wilson's demands in order to keep the United States out of the war. Germany issued the Arabic

Pledge on September 1, 1915, agreeing to warn passenger ships before a U-Boat attack. The Sussex Pledge made on May 4, 1916, extended this warning to merchant ships.

On February 1, 1917, Germany changed course and resumed unrestricted submarine warfare in an attempt to force Britain out of the war before the United States could come to her aid. Germany began indiscriminately sinking any merchant or naval ship headed to Britain, France, Italy, and the eastern Mediterranean. Wilson severed diplomatic relations with Germany on February 3, but still hesitated in asking Congress to declare war. On March 9, Wilson authorized the arming of merchant ships; and on March 18, the Germans sank three American merchant ships without warning, killing American citizens. In the midst of this crisis on the high seas, the American public learned the contents of the Zimmermann telegram. On January 15, 1917, the German foreign minister, Arthur Zimmermann, instructed the German ambassador in Mexico to advise the Mexican government that Germany would finance a Mexican attack on the United States to recover Texas, New Mexico, and Arizona (land lost to the United States in the 1840s). Zimmermann also suggested that Mexico encourage Japan to attack American island possessions in the Pacific. British intelligence operatives intercepted the telegram and gave it to the United States on February 23, 1917. German naval aggression and Zimmermann's attempt to incite a Mexican attack directly challenged the nation's economic and physical security. Consequently, the United States declared war against Germany on April 6, 1917.

## Mobilizing for War

Having made the decision to enter the war, the United States faced the critical task of raising an army and putting the economy on a war footing. In a mere 18 months, the U.S. Army grew from 200,000 to four million, and the government assumed unprecedented control over the civilian economy. To raise the required troops, the government instituted a national

THE NEW YORK HERALD.

PART II. NEW YORK, SATURDAY, MAY 8, 1915.—TWENTY-TWO PAGES. PRICE THREE CENTS.

THE LUSITANIA IS SUNK; 1,000 PROBABLY ARE LOST

CAPTAIN WILLIAM T. TURNER OF THE LUSITANIA

ALFRED G. VANDERBILT

LAST PICTURE OF THE LUSITANIA TAKEN AS SHE LEFT NEW YORK HARBOR.

GERMANS TORPEDO THE GIANT

MAP SHOWING WHERE THE LUSITANIA WAS SUNK.

The New York Herald *headline on May 8, 1915, the day after the* Lusitania *was sunk by a German subarine. (Getty Images)*

draft rather than rely primarily on volunteers. Eager to dispel the popular impression that a draft forced reluctant men into the Army, the government called conscription "selective service," to portray the draft as a modern management technique that selected only the best men as soldiers. Conscription in World War I was a resounding success. By the end of the war, approximately 24 million men had registered for the draft, which raised 72 percent of the wartime army. Overall, 15 percent of all adult American men served in the war, but the draft affected some groups more than others. Most married men with dependents, as well as skilled industrial workers, stayed home, while immigrants, African Americans, and Native Americans were all drafted in numbers greater than their proportional representation in the population.

The large-scale industrial warfare on the Western Front required a constant stream of supplies for the mass armies facing off along the trenches. The American government adopted a host of strategies to mobilize the economy, creating the War Industries Board (WIB) in July 1917. The WIB began as a relatively weak organization but gradually accumulated the power to set prices, standardize production codes, and purchase goods for Allied governments. To encourage compliance from business, the WIB set priority schedules that determined which industries and plants received raw materials. It also offered manufacturers easy access to credit and generous profits in government contracts. Getting industrialists on board only solved half of the economic puzzle, however. To prevent labor disputes and strikes from interrupting the flow of supplies, the government established the National War Labor Board to arbitrate labor disputes; enforce a 40-hour work week and eight hour day; ensure union recognition; and provide a living wage. These important gains for the labor movement did not, however, outlive the war.

The Food and Fuel Administration oversaw the production and distribution of these critical resources. Both agencies relied on high prices to stimulate production and propaganda to encourage conservation. Organized around the slogan "food will win the war," the Food Administration urged Americans to plant War Gardens and consume less wheat, meat, and sugar. Some government agencies took more drastic actions. On December 26, 1917, for example, the Railroad Administration took over the railroad industry after congestion, fuel shortages, and labor disputes brought rail traffic to a standstill. The government, however, amply rewarded railroad companies with generous payments for governmental use of private trains and track.

The final challenge was paying for the war. The war cost Americans over $26 billion, which amounted to $2 million an hour or 8.7 percent of the nation's estimated wealth. The government raised taxes and sold war bonds to pay for the war. War bonds came in every shape and size to reach all strata of the population, ranging from 25-cent thrift stamps to $50 certificates. Overall, the four war bond drives and one victory bond campaign raised $21.4 billion. Besides raising money, war bond campaigns also connected Americans emotionally to the war effort.

The Committee on Public Information (CPI) coordinated the dissemination of most wartime propaganda. Under the leadership of George Creel, the CPI also published an official daily bulletin of war news and organized war expositions. To accommodate the nation's large immigrant population, the CPI distributed pamphlets and posters in foreign languages. In addition, the agency sponsored lectures by volunteers called Four-Minute Men who spoke on war-related topics in movie houses, fairs, and churches.

Coercive measures played a role as well in creating unity on the home front. The Espionage Act of 1917 prohibited both aiding the enemy and discouraging men from serving in the military. The Supreme Court upheld the constitutionality of applying these prohibitions to disloyal speech as well as to behavior, arguing that circumstances determined when speech posed a "clear and present danger" to the republic. In 1918, the Sedition Act went even further and prohibited profane remarks about the government, flag, or uniform of the United States. As wartime passions rose, nearly half of the states barred teaching German in public schools, and patriots tried to purge German words from the English language by renaming hamburgers "liberty sandwiches" and sauerkraut "liberty cabbage." More ominously, occasional mobs attacked German Americans or businesses with German-sounding names. In nonpartisan fashion, the mainline Democratic and Republican party leadership in Congress and the states also targeted socialists and other dissident grassroots movements, like the northern Plains Non-Partisan League and the Oklahoma "Green Corn" tenant farmer movement.

Despite the constant drumbeat insisting on 100 percent Americanism, ethnic communities still exerted political clout during the war. Disaffected German Americans who opposed the nation's war against Germany, angry Irish Americans who hated Great Britain, and offended East Europeans who objected to the Food Administration's entreaty to eat corn instead of wheat (corn in their view was for hogs), all turned against the Democrats in the 1918 midterm election, causing them to lose control of Congress just as President Wilson prepared to travel overseas to participate in the peace treaty negotiations.

### Fighting the War

In the months it took the United States to mobilize its army and economy, the situation turned dire for the Allies along the Western Front in France. Russia signed a separate peace treaty with Germany in March 1918. Peace along its Eastern Front allowed Germany to concentrate the bulk of its army against the French and British. That same month, the Germans opened up a massive offensive along the Western Front to try to win the war before the Americans arrived in force. The few American units already in France played a pivotal role in stopping the German offensive in the battles of Chateau Thierry (May 27–June 5) and Belleau Wood (June 6–25). The American Army finally took over its own sector of the Western Front in the fall of 1918. In the battle of St. Mihiel (September 12–16), the first major operation commanded solely by American generals, 550,000 Americans fought successfully for four days to reduce a salient held by the Germans since 1914. Ten days later, the Meuse–Argonne offensive (September 26–November 11) began. This campaign was the American part of a coordinated Allied offensive along the entire Western Front. Nearly 1.2 million soldiers participated in this final American battle of the war, more soldiers than the entire Confederate Army during the Civil War.

American soldiers behind the lines made a significant contribution to the eventual Allied victory as well. For the first time in American history, the majority (60 percent) of American soldiers served in the noncombatant positions needed to supply and support troops on the front lines. Nearly 89 percent of African American soldiers served in such positions, constituting over one third of the Army's labor units.

On the high seas, the Allies made steady progress in stopping German U-Boat attacks by adopting a convoy system that sent groups of ships across the Atlantic together under the protective watch of destroyers. The convoy system, along with depth charges, dramatically reduced Allied shipping losses. Meanwhile, the continued Allied blockade of Germany made it increasingly difficult for Germany to feed its people and arm its troops.

Defeated on the battlefield and at sea, Germany sued for an armistice. On November 11, 1918 the fighting ceased. Overall, 53,000 Americans died in action and 204,000 were wounded in what amounted to six months of battle. Nearly the same number of Americans soldiers died from disease. Many were victims of the Spanish Influenza Pandemic that swept throughout the world in 1918, killing a total 25 million people, including half-a-million Americans. By comparison, over 7.5 million soldiers from all nations died during the war.

### The Versailles Peace Treaty

Active fighting ended on November 11, 1918, but negotiating the actual peace treaties lasted well into 1919. Before the United States even entered the war, Pres. Woodrow Wilson called for a peace without victory. Once America began fighting, Wilson tried to define Allied war goals in a speech to Congress that became known as the Fourteen Points. Key parts of the Fourteen Points included allowing people to choose their own government (the principle of self-determination); freedom of the seas; freedom of trade; revising national borders in Europe to reflect ethnic groupings; and settling future international disputes through a League of Nations. The Fourteen Points resonated poorly with the Allies, who expected the war to strengthen, not weaken, their colonial empires and established trading routes. The strong desire for revenge against Germany on the Allied side created another key difference between Wilson and Allied leaders as they headed to Paris to negotiate the official peace treaties with each Central Power.

The Versailles Peace Treaty ended the war between the Allies and Germany. The treaty provided for a League of

Nations and incorporated the charter for this international organization into its text. Article X of the League Covenant required member nations to come to the defense of one another, a provision that soon became controversial in the United States. American opponents to the Versailles Treaty claimed that this provision gave the League the power to control American military forces and even declare war for the United States. President Wilson embarked on a nationwide speaking tour to dispute this interpretation and rally support for the treaty. After speaking before a large, enthusiastic crowd in Colorado, Wilson fell ill and rushed back to the White House, where he suffered a severe stroke. Wilson's condition was hidden from the public, but his sudden silence on the treaty left the field open to its critics. Republican senator Henry Cabot Lodge, the main opponent of the treaty, proposed adding a reservation to the treaty that explicitly protected Congress' right to declare war. Wilson, however, refused to accept any modifications of the original treaty. As a result of this standoff, the Senate did not ratify the Versailles Treaty, and the United States never joined the League of Nations. Instead, the United States signed its own separate peace treaty with Germany on August 25, 1921, that simply ended the war.

American participation in World War I had a tremendous impact on American society. Millions of young men left their homes to fight overseas in horrendous conditions that left many physically wounded and emotionally scarred. At home, the government used a variety of techniques to rally support for a war that the nation had taken two-and-a-half years to enter. Some government agencies relied on propaganda and financial incentives to ensure cooperation, while others resorted to placing key industries and resources under direct government control. These wartime activities became important models for both the New Deal and economic mobilization during World War II.

The sudden ending of the war threw millions of Americans out of work, and the termination of the protections offered under the wartime supervision of the National War Labor Board resulted in a mass of postwar strikes in 1919. Union leaders now had a new appreciation for the role that the federal government could play in aiding their cause. At the end of the war, Americans debated the possibility of ensuring world peace through the League of Nations. Although the Senate rejected the Versailles Treaty, the government negotiated several key disarmament treaties in the 1920s. The principles articulated in the Fourteen Points lasted even longer in guiding American foreign policy. Both domestically and internationally, therefore, the legacy of World War I continued to resonate well after the guns fell silent along the Western Front.

### Bibliography

Ambrosius, L. *Woodrow Wilson and the American Diplomatic Tradition: The Treaty Fight in Perspective.* Cambridge: Cambridge University Press, 1987.

Chambers, John W., III. *To Raise An Army: The Draft Comes to Modern America.* New York: Free Press, 1987.

Clements, K. A. *The Presidency of Woodrow Wilson.* Lawrence: University Press of Kansas, 1992.

Coffman, Edward. *The War to End All Wars: The American Military Experience in World War I.* New York: Oxford University Press, 1968.

Gregory, Ross. *The Origins of American Intervention in the First World War.* NY: W.W. Norton, 1971.

Keene, Jennifer D. *The United States and the First World War.* Harlow, England; New York: Longman, 2000.

Kennedy, David M. *Over Here: The First World War and American Society.* New York: Oxford University Press, 1980.

Schaffer, Ronald. *America in the Great War: The Rise of the War Welfare State.* New York: Oxford University Press, 1991.

Trask, David F. *The AEF and Coalition Warmaking, 1917–1918.* Lawrence: University Press of Kansas, 1993.

Zeigler, Robert H. *America's Great War: World War I and the American Experience.* Lanham, Md.: Rowman & Littlefield, 2000.

### Further Reading

Barbeau, Arthur, and Florette Henri. *The Unknown Soldiers: Black American Troops in World War I.* Philadelphia: Temple University Press, 1974.

Cooper, J. M. *The Warrior and the Priest: Woodrow Wilson and Theodore Roosevelt.* Cambridge, Mass.: Harvard University Press, 1983.

Ferrell, Robert H. *Woodrow Wilson and World War I, 1917–1918.* NY: Harper & Row, 1985.

Ford, Nancy Gentile. *Americans All! Foreign-Born Soldiers in World War I.* College Station: Texas A & M University Press, 2001.

Harries, Meirion and Susie Harries. *The Last Days of Innocence: America at War, 1917–1918.* New York: Random House, 1997.

Keene, Jennifer D. *Doughboys, the Great War, and the Remaking of America.* Baltimore, Md.: Johns Hopkins University Press, 2001.

Knock, Thomas J. *To End All Wars: Woodrow Wilson and the Quest for a New World Order.* New York: Oxford University Press, 1992.

Smythe, Donald. *Pershing: General of the Armies.* Bloomington: Indiana University Press, 1986.

**Related Entries**

American Civil Liberties Union; American Legion; Committee on Public Information; Conscientious Objection; Espionage and Sedition Acts; Harlem Hellfighters; Influenza Pandemic of 1918–19; Pershing, John Joseph; Preparedness Movement; Russia, U.S. Intervention in; Selective Service System; *Stars and Stripes, The*; Tomb of the Unknown Soldier; Veterans Day; War Industries Board; Wilson, Woodrow; Women in the Workforce: World War I and World War II; York, Alvin Cullum; Young, Charles

**Related Documents**

1915 b; 1917 a, b, c, d, e, f; 1918 a, b, c, d; 1919 a, b, c, e, f; 1930; 1932; 1933

*—Jennifer D. Keene*

# World War II

## (1941–45)

World War II was fought at the height of an era of industrial mass production and intense nationalism. With military forces numbering in the millions and requiring myriad weapons, foodstuffs, vehicles, munitions, and other forms of support, the United States mobilized its material and human resources completely, causing serious dislocation of the civilian economy and way of life. Consequently, the war effort resulted in a level of civic participation as great or greater than any other war in American history. The war affected virtually every aspect of American society and culture, and marked a watershed in the history of the American people.

| World War II (1941–45) |
|---|
| Total U.S. Servicemembers (Worldwide): **16,112,566** |
| U.S. Population (millions): **133.5** |
| Battle Deaths: **291,557** |
| Other Deaths in Service (Non-Theater): **113,842** |
| Non-mortal Woundings: **671,846** |
| Cost (in $ current billions): **288.00** |

Source: Deaths and Nonmortal Wounds: Department of Veterans Affairs, *America's Wars.* <http://www1.va.gov/opa/fact/amwars.html>

### War on Two Fronts

World War II was the product of the serious economic and political dislocation in the aftermath of World War I and the 1919 Treaty of Versailles, the settlement that ended that war and was construed by many to have exacted not merely severe but vengeful measures against Germany. Within the next two decades, Nazi Germany's insistence on recovering territory lost to Poland in the Versailles settlement was the spark that ignited the tinder of the collapsing world order. On September 1, 1939, Adolf Hitler's German Army invaded Poland, setting in motion a sequence of events that led to World War II.

Germany's armored doctrine and superior military leadership were responsible for some stunning victories in the war's early years, but overconfidence prompted Hitler to order the invasion of the Soviet Union in June 1941, which heretofore had been content to remain a neutral trading partner of Germany and Italy. Six months later, the Japanese attack on Pearl Harbor brought the United States into the conflict as well. The entire complexion of the war changed with these two attacks, for now the combined resources of the Allies (consisting mainly of Great Britain, the Soviet Union, and the United States) dwarfed those of the Axis powers (principally Germany, Italy, and Japan) in most important categories. The war became a test of the Allies' ability to actualize and best employ their theoretical advantages in numbers to offset the Axis coalition's greater experience and generally superior weaponry. The Allies also faced certain territorial advantages aiding Germany's defense, that is, the classic military edge conferred by fighting on the defensive along a perimeter where it was easier for the defender than the attacker to shift forces among critical locations.

It was the large-scale confrontation on the Russian Front that gradually eviscerated the German war machine.

*People gathering around a radio outside of the Capitol building in Washington, D.C., as they listen to President Roosevelt declare war on December 8, 1941, the day after the Japanese bombing of Pearl Harbor. (© Bettmann/CORBIS)*

The Red Army ground the Wehrmacht to dust in a series of massive operations. Meanwhile, the British and Americans swept North Africa clear of Axis forces in early 1943, invaded Sicily and Italy that summer, and then mounted the largest amphibious operation in history with the Normandy invasion in June 1944. The pressures from east and west led to the collapse of German resistance in the spring of 1945.

Meanwhile, the Japanese had seized much of east and southeast Asia in the months following Pearl Harbor, but their momentum was blunted at the battles of the Coral Sea and Midway in May and June 1942, respectively. The Allies, primarily the Americans, then launched twin offensive drives through the southern and central Pacific. The relentless pressure kept the Japanese on their heels, and the two offensives finally converged in October 1944 in the Philippines. Though the Japanese resorted to the use of suicide kamikaze attackers and other desperate measures, the American-led onslaught proved overpowering. There followed the recapture of the rest of the Philippines and the seizure of Iwo Jima and Okinawa, two stepping-stones on the path to the Japanese home islands. By the summer of 1945, U.S. task forces were patrolling the waters off Japan and mercilessly pounding everything that might support further resistance.

Allied offensives on the continent of Asia were slow in developing, and plans to sweep the Japanese from the Asian land mass by reopening land communications from Burma into western China were eventually abandoned when the trans-Pacific drives proceeded ahead of the originally conceived timetables. American submarines effectively blockaded the Japanese homeland, and American bombers burned Tokyo and other cities, causing immense damage and casualties. As the Allies prepared for the invasion of Japan itself in August 1945, the twin shocks of the atomic bombings and the Soviet entry into the Pacific war at last convinced the diehards in the Japanese army and government to sue for peace.

### The American People and the War

World War II was one of the most widely supported wars in American history. Despite some antiwar sentiment from traditional pacifists, such as Congresswoman Jeanette Rankin and actor Lew Ayres, there was little organized resistance to conscription or other aspects of the war effort, which ranged from rationing and blackouts to war bond and scrap drives. This was partly the result of the national outrage over the surprise Japanese attack on Pearl Harbor; but it was also a byproduct of the public's perception of the war as a "good war," that the Axis enemies embodied an evil worthy of being defeated, no matter what the cost might be. This perception was continually fostered by the government—and the media that worked with it—to promote war aims.

Every state, and nearly every community, had its own civilian defense program, and within a month of America's entry into the war, over 5.5 million citizens were enrolled in more than 7,000 defense councils to oversee blackouts; air raid watches; and anti-espionage and anti-sabotage operations. There was, however, a difference between the public's support for the aims of the war in the abstract and the actual performance of individual sacrifices and duties in authorized government programs. The Office of Civilian Defense (OCD), for example, was organized well before Pearl Harbor, but it was decentralized and scarred by libelous accusations. First lady Eleanor Roosevelt helped organize some national programs, but under her guidance the OCD was accused of organizing frivolous and extravagant events, such as hiring disreputable performers to entertain people during blackouts. The charges were spurious, yet the OCD never overcame an image of unnecessary and wasteful officiousness.

Despite some panic at home in the first weeks after Pearl Harbor, especially on the two coasts, Americans soon understood that there was little danger of direct attack on the continental United States. Most complied as best they could with defense regulations and added them to the list of duties they looked forward to discarding with the return of peace.

Because of the need for large-scale production to support the war effort, maintaining the public's anger and commitment to victory that had been generated by the Japanese surprise attack on Pearl Harbor was a top priority of government propagandists. While most of this effort was carried out by the Office of War Information (OWI), active cooperation came from the film, music, radio, print, and other media. The propaganda, from posters and radio spots to Frank Capra's OWI *Why We Fight* film series, emphasized two principal themes. First, the enemy, whether rabid Nazi or inscrutable Japanese, bordered on the subhuman but was also cunning and dangerous—a sly, fierce animal. Hence, for the war effort to be successful, every American had to work hard at his or her job, be vigilant about spies and saboteurs, and be willing to sacrifice for the cause. Second, though the enemy might win some victories along the way, the Allies' values and virtues would in the end prove to be morally and militarily superior to the best the enemy could offer.

The propaganda effort was also notable for the images of the enemy that it constructed or reinforced among the American public. The German—and to a lesser extent, the Italian—people were in the wrong, but it was because they had allowed evil and duplicitous leadership to guide them. The implication was clear: get rid of the Nazis and the Fascists, and the Germans and Italians could be reformed into respectable citizens of the world community. But the Japanese public was represented as preternaturally militaristic, fanatical, unoriginal, and incorrigible. Such thinking had important wartime consequences, such as the internment of American citizens of Japanese descent on a far greater scale than was imposed on Italian Americans and German Americans. This perception of the Japanese also contributed to a readier acceptance of the use of atomic bombs against Japan. In the long run, such depiction of the enemy led to further problems when Japan became an important U.S. ally in the postwar world order.

### Popular Culture

After a decade or so of severe economic hardship, Americans found ready employment because of the war effort and could once again devote time and money to their own interests and pursuits. Disposable income rose substantially because of increased employment, yet the war-induced scarcity of many commodities and forms of entertainment limited how Americans spent their free time and money.

Even though nonessential travel as well as luxury items for personal consumption virtually disappeared because of the wartime demands on facilities and services, consumers found other pleasures with which to occupy themselves. Movies and radio programming became more popular than ever, despite the reduced availability of film for Hollywood and components for new radios. Even with shortages of alcohol, bars and nightclubs did a rousing business as well. Americans also resorted to simpler, stay-at-home pleasures, such as chess, checkers, and card games. Magazine subscriptions and book readership rose, too, despite cutbacks in the allotment of paper to the popular press.

Not surprisingly, the theme in music and other popular entertainment at the war's outset was national pride and the will to carry on for victory. Unabashedly patriotic songs—such as "To Be Specific, It's Our Pacific," "You're a Sap, Mr. Jap," and "Let's Put the Axe to the Axis"—dominated the popular music charts in the early months of 1942. As the war rolled on and Americans realized how many years might pass before peace and the boys could actually return, the theme in popular culture shifted to nostalgia for absent loved ones and dreams of the good old days—or how it would be in some blissful future. "White Christmas," both the song released by Bing Crosby and the movie of the same title in which he starred, were typical of this sentimental yearning for loved ones and better times, as was the movie *Casablanca* (1942) with its more strictly dramatic tone. This blended into the next phase, in which separated couples talked to each other, professing their love and asking their mates not to stray, as in the Andrews Sisters' popular hit "Don't Sit Under the Apple Tree with Anyone Else But Me." By the time the war was drawing to a close, entertainment media articulated the twin themes of war weariness and celebratory homecoming in victory.

Throughout the war there was also a subtheme of escapism, both in wild comedies (often depicting the travails of the citizen–soldier as he attempted to adapt to military life) and in westerns and adventures, such as the superheroes of the comic books. This may account for the war's most striking, popular culture phenomenon: the teen idol Frank Sinatra. Boyish and without the virility of a sex symbol such as Clark Gable, Sinatra, with his slender build and deceptively youthful face, seemed to many as the son, kid brother, or boy next door who had gone off to do his duty—and who wistfully hoped for his return one day to a better future. Although Sinatra was 27 years old in 1942, teenage girls found him irresistible, often screaming hysterically at his performances. This home front phenomenon was paralleled by the widespread resort to the "pinup" by the GIs—inspired in part from normal sexual desire, but also symbolic of the girl back home, as part of the future, for whom the boys had gone off to fight.

### Total Mobilization

The sheer scale of the forces engaged in World War II necessitated huge production efforts by the belligerents, and U.S. industrial mobilization was all the greater because of the need to support its less economically developed allies. It is no exaggeration to point out that, due to this mobilization, the nation would never be able to return to the way things were before the attack on Pearl Harbor—even years after the war had ended.

Despite the substantial economic recovery generated by French and British war orders before American entry into the war, there were still more than 3.5 million unemployed workers scattered across the country in December 1941. But the twin demands for military manpower and industrial labor quickly changed those circumstances. Nearly 15 million men and women would eventually serve in the armed forces, creating a labor shortfall that could only be bridged by granting unprecedented economic opportunities to the social groups that had traditionally suffered discrimination: women, ethnic minorities, the "Okies" displaced by the Great Depression, the uneducated, the aged, and the infirm.

The sudden plenitude of industrial jobs at decent wages touched off a vast internal migration. The largest influx was to cities of the upper Midwest and to the coasts. The Census Bureau calculated that more than 15 million Americans had changed residences to different counties by the time the war ended, and half of those were living in different states. Five-and-a-half million left farms to take large-city jobs, but many came from small towns or from among the urban unemployed. The result was chaos in the cities and the proliferation of factory towns. With the government committed to building industrial facilities, and with local property owners concerned about the influx of undesirables, there was little incentive to build proper housing or to extend sanitation and other basic services into neighborhoods settled by "transient populations." Many feared that properly accommodating these new workers would lead to crime-riddled slums.

As a result, prices of basic services, such as housing and transportation, rose precipitously, even as the quality of those services declined from overuse and shortages of investment for expansion and maintenance. The new urban citizens lived in trailers, basements, tent communities, and any other space that could be crudely modified for habitation. Longtime residents grumbled at the newcomers whenever they couldn't find a seat in a restaurant or on a bus, and they waited impatiently—both for peace and the expected end to the alien presence. But despite heavy turnover in employment owing to the overall scarcity of labor, the new workers by and large remained after the war, having established themselves as profitable consumers who boosted the local economy. The American demographic landscape was thus permanently changed—not only by the burgeoning urban population, but also because of the radical transformation of the cities' ethnic and generational composition.

Full-scale mobilization for the war intruded on Americans' lives in other ways, too. Many basic commodities became widely unavailable. Some items, such as women's hosiery made of silk (or the new nylon), became difficult or impossible to get, forcing American women simply to learn to live without. A great many more items, while not completely unavailable, were scarce, requiring the Office of Price Administration to oversee a vast rationing system, which controlled products ranging from food to gasoline.

Automobile tires provide a good example of wartime scarcity. Japanese conquests in East Asia early in the war gave Japan control of 97 percent of the world's rubber-producing areas, and American stockpiles held only about a year's supply of tires. Military needs claimed three-quarters of that supply, meaning civilians were hard pressed to keep their cars in operation. The nation's 30 million automobile owners turned to retreads or paid exorbitant prices for the few tires still left on the market. Some wooden tires were used by trucks, but they proved to be a poor substitute. Leather, cornsilk, and plastic were also investigated as replacements for rubber in tires, but none proved suitable. Myriad plants, from guayule to dandelions, were studied, but none could replace rubber. Synthetic rubber made from petroleum was more promising, but it took time and money to erect manufacturing plants. Meanwhile, a nationwide scrap rubber drive was launched, and citizens turned in 335,000 tons of old bathmats, hot water bottles, and overshoes, which was enough to make some low-grade tires, but hardly constituted a solution.

President Roosevelt finally appointed a board under the chairmanship of mobilization expert Bernard Baruch to study the situation, and their report recommended gasoline rationing as the only way to prevent the tire shortage from becoming a crisis. Accordingly, one year after Pearl Harbor, the government, in order to stretch the nation's tire supply, reduced speed limits to 35 miles per hour, banned recreational driving, and instituted a gasoline rationing system. Ration books were issued to all Americans, and gasoline had to be paid for with both cash and ration coupons. Americans grumbled and some bought black market fuel and tires, but by and large most citizens accepted these measures as a necessary sacrifice for the war effort. The same pattern held true for clothing, cigarettes, bicycles, alarm clocks, baby carriages, and all sorts of food products, from sugar and meat to vegetables and butter. Americans adjusted their diets, wardrobes, and lifestyles, and life went on.

Because of the sacrifices made and inconveniences endured by the American public, U.S. industrial mobilization in World War II was a stunning success. In the period of 1942 to 1945, the nation's gross domestic product was never less than double that of Great Britain and the Soviet Union combined, and it was anywhere from 37 to 216 percent greater than the combined GDP of the Axis powers (including Austria and Occupied France) during the same period. Through standardization of design, mass production methods, centralized planning and coordination through the War Production Board and Office of War Mobilization, and profit

*A lineup of "victory ships" at a naval shipyard on the West Coast of the United States, waiting for supplies and final outfitting before shipping off to advance bases in the Pacific—an example of the full-scale mobilization of production in the war effort. (National Archives and Records Administration)*

incentives for private industry, the American economy flooded the critical battlefields around the globe with weapons and equipment. In 1942 alone—well before the enemy believed the American economy could be converted to full-scale war production—the United States out-built the entire Axis combined in aircraft (47,000 to 27,000); tanks (24,000 to 11,000); and merchant shipping (8 million to less than 1 million deadweight tons). American production rose again in 1943 and peaked only in 1944. During the war, the Ford Motor Company produced more war material on its own than did the entire nation of Italy. Similarly, the famed Willow Run B-24 assembly plant in Michigan produced aircraft at one quarter the rate, measured by weight of airframe, of the entire Japanese aircraft industry.

The impact of American mobilization and production on the battlefield is difficult to overestimate. Not only did the United States expand its own military forces to unprecedented levels (12 million men and women were in uniform by the time the war ended), providing a major contribution to victory on battlefields seldom closer than 3,000 miles from American shores, but the United States allowed the Allies to reach their full military potential through Lend–Lease, a program of direct, uncompensated military and economic aid to any and all enemies of the Axis. Many of the impressive British and Soviet battlefield successes were won with American weapons and equipment. The United States sent the Soviet Union thousands of tanks, aircraft, and antiaircraft guns; cloth for uniforms, boots, and food; and other basic necessities for the Red Army. More beneficial in the long run were the many raw materials and capital goods the United States sent its allies through Lend–Lease. For example, U.S. Lend–Lease material dispatched to the Soviet Union included nearly half-a-million trucks, half-a-billion dollars' worth of machine tools; 2,000 railroad locomotives; and staggering sums of raw materials. Thus, even comparing national production figures will not convey the true contribution to total Allied production offered by the United States. It was the Soviets who marched into Berlin in 1945, but the Red Army did it on American boot leather, supplied by American trucks, and supported by aircraft built with American materials and machinery.

Soldiers in the Pacific routinely intoned the ditty, "The Golden Gate in 'Forty-Eight," to indicate their belief that the war would last for many years, to which the reply was, "The Bread Line in 'Forty-Nine," which embodied the widespread belief that a postwar depression would end this war boom as it had after World War I. However, American consumerism continued to expand dramatically after the war. The postwar boom was also encouraged by the Serviceman's Readjustment Act, better known as the "GI Bill," which granted various benefits to veterans as a show of the nation's gratitude for their service. In the first decade after the war, half of the veterans received professional or academic training under the bill's educational provisions, and a quarter of them built homes with government loan guarantees. The result was a major boost to the construction and education sectors and—even more important—the cultivation of an adaptable work force for the growing economy. World War II thus ushered in a quarter century of prosperity—a dramatic contrast to the 15 years of economic hardship suffered during the Great Depression and the shortages of the war years.

**Changing American Society**

The tremendous U.S. military and economic efforts in World War II carried a price for the American people. The war had an enormous impact on families. Husbands and fathers went away, sometimes for years. Alcoholism among women increased dramatically. The strain on relationships was often too much, and divorce rates hit an all-time high. One reason sociologists and psychologists gave for break-ups and marriage tensions was the returning father's distress at his wife's independence and the reluctance of the last-born child to accept this unknown father as an authority figure. Contributing to the difficulties of readjustment were post-traumatic stress disorder (though the term itself was not coined until after the Vietnam War). The discovery by servicemen that the skills and concerns that had once been so central to their existence now had little value or meaning in civilian society also made readjustment difficult. But many marriages withstood the strain, though often at great psychological cost to both partners.

The war had an impact on the institution of marriage in other ways. Many couples had rushed to the altar when the threat of separation loomed; in the first quarter of 1942, sales of wedding rings quadrupled. Romances also blossomed between soldiers in training and local women, many ending in quick marriages. The government instituted a system of monthly pay allotments for spouses of servicemen, intended to reduce the draft exemption for men with household dependents. However, this practice also spawned the nefarious "Allotment Annie" industry, whereby unscrupulous women cultivated serial romances and marriages from the procession of soldiers heading off to the front, always hoping for the ultimate jackpot of the $10,000 GI death benefit, while collecting multiple monthly allotment checks in the meantime.

America's sexual behavior was profoundly altered as well. With so many men in uniform, the demographics of most American communities changed in one of two ways: either there were far fewer young men around, or there was a base nearby that provided the community with a bounty of young men, who were periodically let loose for leave, paid well enough to have a good time, and lonely for companionship of all sorts—but especially of the female variety. The familiar British complaint that "the trouble with you Yanks is that you're overpaid, oversexed, and over here" resonated with many an American community, too, especially with parents raising a daughter near a military installation. "Khaki wacky" teenagers hung around train stations and bus depots where GIs arrived in town for a night of liberty; they came to be called "V-girls" in a society where "V" stood for victories of all sorts. Often the intent was just a pleasant evening and some attention from the handsome young men in uniform, but V-girls gained a reputation for lax sexual morality that was not entirely unfounded, though no reliable figures exist. One estimate states that only about 1/2 of 1 percent of teenage females were V-girls, yet wartime studies showed that soldiers contracted venereal diseases at a higher rate from local girls than from professional prostitutes.

There were some attempts to safeguard the morality of the young boys gone off to serve their country by closing houses of prostitution, yet some sought to contain the problem by sponsoring safe, clean houses near military bases. In the end, most of the soldiers developed a dual code of conduct: one set of values when at home with people they knew, and another altogether for the new and alien environments they came to visit during the war, whether overseas or in other parts of the United States. Given their long separation from their spouses, married men faced the same choices and often succumbed to the same temptations. For those who had lived through the morally conservative years of the Great Depression, the behavior of young people, male and female, was nothing short of shocking. Both sexes viewed morality differently after the war, even those who embraced traditional monogamy and the nuclear family in peacetime.

Children, too, endured the impact of the war. One facet of reduced adult supervision was the proliferation of the V-girls, some as young as 13; but all children inevitably experienced less control of their daily schedules because of absent fathers and working mothers. Grandparents, neighbors, and older siblings were pressed into service as babysitters; but despite those volunteer efforts, the youth of America has seldom had such free a rein as did those during World War II. Arrests among young people rose by 20 percent in 1943, and the term "juvenile delinquent" first came into common usage. Overall rates for violent crime were down, mainly because the largest single group of perpetrators, young adult males, were enlisted; but crime rates for children climbed precipitously during the war years. The foundation was laid for the hot rodders, motorcyclists, and other rebellious youth of the 1950s; the only elements missing during the war years were the leather jackets and the greater independence afforded by gas-powered vehicles.

Despite the often deleterious effects on family life caused by the war, there was much promise of lessening racial segregation and discrimination practices, thanks to the heavy demands for manpower. In the end, however, such hopes were disappointed. As early as the summer of 1941, the African American labor leader A. Philip Randolph was organizing a march on Washington to protest discriminatory hiring policies; but he called the march off when Franklin Roosevelt issued Executive Order 8802, which banned such hiring discrimination and also established the Fair Employment Practices Commission to monitor enforcement. Some 700,000 African Americans migrated to the industrial cities in search of jobs, but often found jobs difficult to come by, and often faced discrimination and segregation in their new environments. Conflicts with established white labor groups were at the root of the problem, but so too was the decline in living conditions that resulted from wartime pressures in the urban areas—conditions invariably blamed on the newcomers. Racial tensions were often high and occasionally erupted into violence, including extended "race riots" in Los Angeles, Detroit, and New York. In the end, African Americans made some gains toward equality in employment and living conditions, but the full-blown civil rights movement was still a decade away. Nonetheless, initiatives taken to deal with wartime labor shortages helped to lay the foundation for the success of the civil rights movement in a later era.

The same might be said of feminism. Six million women labored in war industries during the war, and many others worked outside the home. They faced discrimination in wages and promotion, enmity from coworkers, accusations of unprofessional or distracting behavior and dress, and lack of support at home, where everyone expected the woman of the house to keep the household and the children as safe, clean, and happy as before. Because of the paucity of support services for women—such as day care facilities at the workplace—and inflexible scheduling that made it difficult to undertake grocery shopping and other fundamental chores, the turnover rate among female employees was very high. Traditionalists decried the movement of women into the workplace; they pictured it as the first step in the disintegration of the American family, revered as the moral bedrock of society.

However, the labor shortage forced even the most reluctant employers to turn to female workers, and by mid-1942 many companies developed recruiting campaigns aimed specifically at women. Cynics grumbled, "Remember how women used to have to get married to get men's wages?" But in reality, women were paid less than men; and by the war's end, female workers had won the begrudging acceptance of most detractors. As the war industries geared down to peacetime production levels, women were usually the first to be let go, but their venture into the previously male-dominated workplace indelibly altered—for both genders—the image of the American woman. Having played her part in war and accepted reversion to her peacetime roles afterward, American women would have the self-confidence to challenge the politics of the established gender order in the not-too-distant future—or inspire their daughters to do so.

Whether one is thinking of the family or of larger social groups, the war forever altered fundamental American institutions. Ironically, upon their return to the states, the soldiers who fought to preserve American values discovered that the society they had fought to preserve had itself changed, owing in no small measure to the efforts undertaken in the homeland to ensure victory.

### World War II in History and Memory

Based on the sheer number of people directly affected, World War II remains the single most influential event in American, and world, history. Touched off by forces that had been fermenting for decades, the war was fought in an age that required total participation by the belligerent societies; it thus impacted the lives of a higher percentage of Americans than any other conflict in U.S. history, aside from the Civil War. It shaped the lives of that generation not only during the war but for decades to come, creating a set of values and beliefs that would be challenged by the nuclear culture of the Cold War, the "antiestablishment" movements of the Vietnam era, and the growing individualism and self-centeredness of the 1970s and 1980s. For the generation that experienced it, World War II would remain the single most influential factor on their political beliefs, worldviews, and personal philosophies. For them, World War II would always be the "good war," or the "big one," when Americans worked together to achieve military success for God-given righteousness and freedom for all.

**Bibliography**

Blum, John Morton. *V Was for Victory: Politics and American Culture During World War II.* New York: Harcourt Brace Jovanovich, 1976.

Dower, John. *War Without Mercy: War and Power in the Pacific War.* New York: Pantheon Books, 1986.

Goodwin, Doris Kearns. *No Ordinary Time: Franklin and Eleanor Roosevelt, The Home Front in World War II.* New York: Simon & Schuster, 1994.

Harrison, Mark, ed. *The Economics of World War II: Six Great Powers in International Comparison.* Cambridge: Cambridge University Press, 1998.

Lingeman, Richard R. *Don't You Know There's a War On?: The American Home Front, 1941–1945.* New York: Putnam, 1970.

Milward, Alan S. *War, Economy, and Society, 1939–1945.* Berkeley: University of California Press, 1977.

Murray, Williamson, and Allan R. Millett. *A War to Be Won: Fighting the Second World War.* Cambridge, Mass.: The Belknap Press of Harvard University Press, 2000.

Overy, Richard. *Why the Allies Won.* New York: W.W. Norton, 1995.

Perrett, Geoffrey. *Days of Sadness, Years of Triumph: The American People, 1939–1945.* New York: Coward, McCann & Geoghegan, 1973.

Weinberg, Gerhard. *A World at Arms: A Global History of World War II.* New York: Cambridge University Press, 1994.

### Further Reading

Crane, Conrad C. *Bombs, Cities, and Civilians: American Airpower Strategy in World War II.* Lawrence: University Press of Kansas, 1993.

Divine, Robert A., ed. *Causes and Consequences of World War II.* Chicago: Quadrangle Books, 1969.

Doubler, Michael D. *Closing with the Enemy: How GIs Fought the War in Europe, 1944–1945.* Lawrence: University Press of Kansas, 1994.

Koistinen, Paul A. C. *Arsenal of World War II: The Political Economy of American Warfare, 1940–1945.* Lawrence: University Press of Kansas, 2004.

Linderman, Gerald F. *The World Within War: America's Combat Experience in World War II.* Cambridge, Mass.: Harvard University Press, 1997.

Parillo, Mark P., ed. *"We Were in the Big One": Experiences of the World War II Generation.* Wilmington, Del.: Scholarly Resources, 2002.

Polenberg, Richard. *America at War: The Home Front, 1941–1945.* Englewood Cliffs, ed. N.J.: Prentice–Hall, 1968.

———. *War and Society: The United States, 1941–1945.* New York: J. B. Lippincott, 1972.

Roeder, George H., Jr. *The Censored War: American Visual Experience during World War II.* New Haven, Conn.: Yale University Press, 1993.

Stoler, Mark A. *The Politics of the Second Front: American Military Planning and Diplomacy in Coalition Warfare, 1941–1943.* Westport, Conn.: Greenwood, 1977.

Tuttle, William M. *Daddy's Gone to War: The Second World War in the Lives of America's Children.* New York: Oxford University Press, 1993.

Vatter, Harold G. *The U.S. Economy in World War II.* New York: Columbia University Press, 1985.

Weigley, Russell F. *The American Way of War: A History of United States Military Strategy and Policy.* Bloomington: Indiana University Press, 1973.

### Related Entries

Arnold, Henry Harley; *Best Years of Our Lives, The*; *Caine Mutiny, The*; Captain Marvel Comic Books; *Combat!*; Eisenhower, Dwight D.; *Enola Gay* Controversy; Executive Order 8802; 442nd Regimental Combat Team of Nisei; *From Here to Eternity*; German and Italian Americans, Internment of; Halsey, William F., Jr.; *Hiroshima*; Holocaust, U.S. Response to; Japanese Americans, Internment of; LeMay, Curtis Emerson; MacArthur, Douglas; Manhattan Project; Marine Corps; Marshall, George Catlett; Mauldin, Bill; Murphy, Audie; *Naked and the Dead, The*; Newsreels; Nimitz, Chester William; Oppenheimer, J. Robert; Patton, George S.; Port Chicago Mutiny; Propaganda Posters: World War II; Pyle, Ernie; Radio in World War II; Randolph, A. Philip; Roosevelt, Franklin Delano; Rosie the Riveter; *Sad Sack, The*; *Saving Private Ryan*; Spaatz, Carl; *Stars and Stripes, The*; Truman, Harry S.; *Twelve O'Clock High*; Ultra and Enigma; Victory Gardens; War Labor Board; Women in the Workforce: World War I and World War II; Zoot Suit Riot

### Related Documents

1940; 1941; 1942 a; b, c, d, e, f; 1943; 1944 a, b, c; 1945 a, b, c, d, e, f; 1946 a, b; 1947; 1948 a; 1949; 1950 a; 1953; 1964; 1975

*—Mark P. Parillo*

## York, Alvin Cullum

### (1887–1964)

### World War I Hero

In the last days of World War I, Alvin C. York came marching out of the Argonne Forest with 132 German prisoners and a remarkable story of individual daring. One of the least likely combat heroes in American history, the Tennessee-born York initially sought conscientious objector status based on his membership in the Church of Christ in Christian Union— a small, pacifist denomination founded in Ohio during the Civil War. York reluctantly accepted induction only after the Selective Service denied his pleas for deferment on religious grounds. However, his army superiors persuaded him that America was fighting God's battle in the Great War, an argument that transformed the reluctant draftee into a veritable soldier of the Lord. With a newfound confidence in the rightness of the conflict, York shipped to France in May 1918, as an infantryman in the 82nd Division.

On the morning of October 8, 1918, during the final Allied offensive in the Argonne Forest, York and the other members of a small patrol found themselves behind German lines, cut off from American forces and under heavy fire. With half of his comrades dead or wounded, York, armed with a rifle and a pistol, boldly challenged a German machine-gun nest, killing approximately two dozen men and calling on the rest to surrender. In the course of a few hours, he silenced 35 machine guns and captured four officers and 128 enlisted personnel. Promoted to the rank of sergeant for a feat that Allied commander Marshal Ferdinand Foch called "the greatest thing accomplished by any private soldier of all the armies of Europe," York received numerous decorations, including the Medal of Honor and the Croix de Guerre.

An April 1919 article in the *Saturday Evening Post*, the most widely circulated magazine in America at that time, made York a national hero virtually overnight. York's explanation that God had been with him during the firefight meshed neatly with the popular attitude that American involvement in the war was a holy crusade. As a conscientious objector turned citizen–soldier turned combat hero, York captured both the public's ambivalence about the war and its pride in military victory. York returned to the United States in the spring of 1919 amid a tumultuous public welcome and a flood of business offers from people eager to capitalize on the soldier's reputation. In spite of these lucrative opportunities, York decided to return to his Cumberland Mountain hamlet of Pall Mall, in the Valley of the Three Forks of the Wolf River, where he spent the rest of his life working to bring schools, roads, and economic development to his mountain neighbors.

York lived quietly in Tennessee until the eve of World War II, when his advocacy for military preparedness again made him prominent. Filmmaker Jesse Lasky persuaded York that a film about his World War I experiences would serve as a call to arms for the nation in a time of growing international threat. Directed by Howard Hawks with Gary Cooper in the title role, *Sergeant York* appeared in July 1941, just six months before the Japanese attack on Pearl Harbor. Cooper received an Academy Award for his portrayal of Alvin York. The film brought York a financial windfall, but by the 1950s, mismanagement of the income and Internal Revenue Service claims against his earnings brought the old soldier to the brink of bankruptcy. Prominent friends provided financial support and helped him to negotiate a settlement with the IRS a few years before his death in 1964.

At a time of domestic upheaval and international uncertainty, Alvin York's pioneer-like skill with a rifle, his homespun manner, and his fundamentalist piety endeared him to millions of Americans as a kind of "contemporary ancestor," a pioneer backwoodsman reincarnated in the midst of the 20th century to slay the nation's enemies. As such, he seemed to affirm that the traditional virtues of agrarian America still had meaning in the new era. In short, York represented not what Americans were, but what they wanted to think they were. He lived in one of the most rural parts of the country at a time when the majority of Americans lived in urban areas; he rejected riches at a time when the tenor of the nation was crassly commercial; he was pious at a time when secularism was on the rise. For millions of Americans, York embodied their romanticized understanding of the nation's past when men and women supposedly lived plainer, sterner, and more virtuous lives. Ironically, although York endured as a symbol of an older America, he spent most of his adult life working to help modernize his rural mountain region.

### Bibliography

Birdwell, Michael. *Celluloid Soldiers: The Warner Brothers Campaign Against Nazism.* New York: New York University Press, 1999.

Cowan, Samuel K. *Sergeant York and His People.* New York and London: Funk & Wagnalls, 1922.

Lee, David D. *Sergeant York: An American Hero.* Lexington: University Press of Kentucky, 1985.

Skeyhill, Thomas, ed. *Sergeant York: His Own Life Story and War Diary.* Garden City, N.Y.: Doubleday, Doran and Company, Inc. 1928.

### Further Reading

Brandt, Nat. "Sergeant York." *American Heritage* 32, no. 5 (August/September 1981): 56–64.

Perry, John. *Sergeant York: His Life, Legend and Legacy: The Remarkable Untold Story of Sergeant Alvin C. York.* Nashville: Broadman and Holman Publishers, 1997.

### Related Entries

Conscientious Objection; World War I

*—David D. Lee*

# Young, Charles

**(1864–1922)**
**African American Army Officer**

In 1889, Charles Young became the third African American to graduate from the U.S. Military Academy at West Point. Young built an impressive military resume over the next three decades, advancing to the rank of colonel in spite of ongoing racial hostility; Young's rise through the Army ranks coincided with the growing strength of white supremacy in American politics and society. Racial discrimination, ever-present in Young's career, crested in the early months of World War I when senior Army officials forced him into retirement, against his wishes and despite the protests of the African American public, to avoid the possibility of a black colonel commanding a regiment.

Young was born in Kentucky in 1864 and reared in Ripley, Ohio. After graduating from West Point, he served five years as a second lieutenant in the all-black 9th and 10th cavalries. In 1894 he transferred to Ohio's Wilberforce University to teach military science and tactics, French, and math. By the time of his promotion to first lieutenant in 1896, Young was the highest-ranking black officer in the Army, and when the Spanish–American War broke out two years later, he was the only black officer qualified to lead combat troops. The Army granted Young a wartime promotion to major and placed him in charge of training the 9th Ohio Volunteer Battalion, an African American National Guard unit. Although his men did not see action in Cuba, Young's rank and responsibilities made him an anomaly in a military establishment convinced of black soldiers' inferiority. After the war, Young received a promotion to captain and rejoined the 9th Cavalry in the Philippines where he helped to suppress the independence movement led by nationalist Emilio Aguinaldo.

Following the Spanish–American War, legislators in the South systematically disbanded their states' black militias, arguing that they did not want armed African Americans thinking themselves the equal of white men. The War Department and officials in the regular Army went along with this expansion of segregationist, "Jim Crow" policies by maligning the ability of African American officers, blocking black enlistments in combat roles, and assigning black regulars to places where their presence would not upend racial hierarchies.

Young spent much of his career out West or abroad. After the Philippine Insurrection, he was garrisoned with the 9th Cavalry at the Presidio in San Francisco, where he served in 1903 as the acting superintendent of Sequoia National Park. From 1904 to 1907, he was assigned to work with the Military Intelligence Division as an attaché in Haiti. He returned to the Philippines and the 9th Cavalry in 1908. In 1912 he left for Africa, serving as a military attaché and adviser in Liberia. Young's first opportunity to act as a superior officer to a large number of white commanders came with the 1916 Punitive Expedition against Mexican revolutionary Francisco "Pancho" Villa. By the time of the expedition, when American troops pursued Villa and his followers across the Mexico border, Young had been promoted to major and made a squadron commander in the 10th Cavalry. The squadron performed admirably under Young, saving a white squadron from almost-certain death at the hands of 600 Mexican *federales* and receiving citations and accolades for their work. His success made him a hero in the African American community.

Young's promotion to lieutenant colonel in the wake of the Punitive Expedition made him the highest-ranking African American officer in military history, but it also turned him into a more visible target for white supremacists. As the nation geared up for World War I, white officers in the 10th Cavalry rebelled against the possibility that Young, on his way to becoming a full colonel, would be put in charge of their regiment. Supported by Mississippi Sen. John Sharp Williams, they convinced Pres. Woodrow Wilson and officials in the War Department to remove Young from the regular Army. At the behest of Army Chief of Staff Gen. Tasker Bliss, a military medical board examined Young and concluded that his high blood pressure and other health problems made him unfit for active duty. He was promoted to full colonel but placed on the retired list.

Astounded and dismayed, Young maintained that he was healthy enough to serve despite the pretext used to retire him. To prove his physical fitness, he mounted a horse in Ohio, where he was acting as a military adviser to the state's adjutant general, and rode almost 500 miles to Washington, D.C. The stunt won the support of the black press and African Americans across the country, but it gained him little sympathy from the Wilson administration. Although he was disappointed, Young remained loyal to the military and urged African Americans to support the war effort unreservedly. Young stayed in retirement until five days before the Armistice on November 11, 1918, when he was returned to active duty at Camp Grant, Illinois.

Following World War I, Young accepted an assignment to once again become military attaché in Liberia. He suffered a stroke while on an investigative tour in Nigeria and died in a British military hospital in January 1922. The British government in Nigeria buried with him with military honors. In 1923, they returned his body to the United States, where he was buried in Arlington National Cemetery.

To African Americans, Col. Charles Young's military career was, as his close friend and old Wilberforce colleague W. E. B. Du Bois wrote, a "triumph of tragedy." His shoddy treatment at the hands of the Wilson administration became emblematic of the fierce discrimination experienced by thousands of African American soldiers during World War I and after. At the same time, his seemingly boundless capacity for loyalty served to inspire those African Americans determined to love America as it could be, instead of turning their backs on America as it was. Throughout his military career, Young held fast against Jim Crow with all the dignity that befitted his uniform.

#### Bibliography

Barbeau, Arthur, and Florette Henri. *The Unknown Soldiers: Black American Troops in World War I.* Philadelphia: Temple University Press, 1974.

Lewis, David Levering. *W.E.B. Du Bois: Biography of a Race, 1868–1919.* New York: Henry Holt, 1993.

———. *W.E.B. Du Bois: The Fight for Equality and the American Century, 1919–1963.* New York: Henry Holt, 2000.

Nalty, Bernard. *Strength for the Fight: A History of Black Americans in the Military.* New York: Free Press, 1986.

#### Further Reading

African American Experience in Ohio, Colonel Charles Young Collection, 1897–1931. Ohio Historical Society. <http://dbs.ohiohistory.org/africanam/mss/831.cfm>.

Buckley, Gail Lumet. *American Patriots: The Story of the Blacks in the Military from the Revolution to Desert Storm.* New York: Random House, 2001.

Kilory, David P. *For Race and Country: The Life and Career of Colonel Charles Young.* Westport, Conn.: Praeger, 2003.

Schubert, Frank N., ed. *On the Trail of the Buffalo Soldier: Biographies of African Americans in the U.S. Army, 1866–1917.* Wilmington, Del.: Scholarly Resources,1995.

**Related Entries**

African Americans in the Military; Buffalo Soldiers; Du Bois, W. E. B.; Philippine War; Spanish–American War; World War I

**Related Documents**

1900; 1919 b, c

*—Adriane D. Smith*

# Z

## Zoot Suit Riot

The Zoot Suit Riot refers to a ten-day period in June 1943 in Los Angeles, California, when civilians and servicemen clashed with young Mexican Americans, whose distinctive dress gave name to the encounter. The term "riot" is misleading because the event was actually a series of beatings and fights that continued uncontrolled for a week and a half. It was an example of how a city's social dynamics and tensions were heightened during wartime. The situation in Los Angeles was particularly contentious in this period. Increased numbers of Mexicans had been moving into Los Angeles in the aftermath of the Mexican Revolution of 1910. By the time of World War II, California faced an explosive mix between the various ethnic groups residing there, the transient military populations training in the state, and the still lingering ideology of white supremacy.

Although the zoot suit has become most identifiable with Mexican American youth because of the riot, the zoot suit itself had been popular in Europe and throughout the United States for numerous years prior to the 1940s. This distinctive style of dress involved wearing pants that were loose-fitting but tapered and cuffed at the ankles and large jackets that had wide shoulders. Large-brimmed hats often accompanied the outfit. The flamboyance of the suit itself and the brazen attitude of many of its wearers gave rise to certain terms. "Zoot suiter" referred to a young man with supposed delinquent tendencies who was shunned by much of mainstream America.

Zoot suiters demonstrated a rebellious attitude that was at odds with the patriotic spirit of the times. Tensions in the Los Angeles area towards zoot-suit wearing young men had also been exacerbated by a serious of articles published in the *Los Angeles Times* that referred to Mexican Americans in demeaning terms. Also playing a part in the tension was the constant fear that Japan might stage an attack on the West Coast. Conformity became even more important under such circumstances.

The outbreak of violence in 1943 was sparked by a street fight between sailors and young Mexican American men at the end of May. Sailors organized a few days later to retaliate against the zoot suiters. The first night, the servicemen attacked young boys (12 to 13 years of age). The following night the sailors, unable to find many zoot suiters, went into Mexican American neighborhoods, rampaging through restaurants, bars, and theaters. There was a distinct change in tactics, as any Mexican American encountered became a target, not just zoot suiters. Over the next several nights, more and more people joined in the attacks. Some were servicemen, including Army soldiers and marines; some came from installations as far away as Las Vegas. Others were citizens of Los Angeles who were eager to join in the fracas and vent their frustrations against people of color.

During the riot, thousands of off-duty servicemen were joined by hundreds of local white civilians who proceeded to attack not only Hispanic youths but also young African Americans and Filipinos. The military men beat and stripped minorities wearing zoot suits of their clothing. In this they were even encouraged by a Los Angeles newspaper, which counseled its readers to burn the seized zoot suits in fires.

The official figures stated that 112 Mexican Americans suffered serious injuries and that more than 130 others were injured who did not seek hospital care. More Mexican Americans were arrested and jailed than any other group. Ninety-four Mexican Americans were jailed, as compared to 20 servicemen and 30 non-Hispanics. The public as well as some law enforcement officers cheered the beatings and then saw to it that the victims were arrested. Police officers were quoted after the riots as stating that they did not want to arrest servicemen.

The United States military all but admitted that it could not control the sailors and servicemen who were participating in the riots. The servicemen were literally disappearing without leave from their bases for days at a time. Finally, in a desperate effort to control the situation, the military forbade sailors from even going to Los Angeles. Servicemen involved in the fights were never prosecuted for their actions, either by civil authorities or by the military. The Los Angeles City Council then banned the wearing of zoot suits on city streets, attaching a 30-day jail sentence to the offense.

Around this same time, young men wearing zoot suits were attacked in other cities as well. In California a citizens' committee investigated the riots and concluded that racism was the root cause of the melee. Other riots arose across the nation during the war years, though most were directed at African Americans. From Beaumont, Texas, to Detriot and New York's Harlem, tensions grew as both demographics and class distinctions changed. The Zoot Suit Riot clearly shows the prejudice that was at work in Southern California, and it demonstrates how a passion for patriotism can transform ordinary citizens into an uncontrollable mob.

### Bibliography

Boskin, Joseph. *Urban Racial Violence in the Twentieth Century.* 2nd ed., Beverly Hills, Calif.: Glencoe Press, 1976.

Daniels, Douglas Henry. "Los Angles Zoot: Race 'Riot,' the Pachuco, and Black Music Culture." *The Journal of Negro History* 82 (spring 1997): 201–20.

Mazón, Mauricio. *The Zoot-Suit Riots: The Psychology of Symbolic Annihilation*. Austin: University of Texas Press, 1984.

"Zoot Suit Riots." <http://www.pbs.org/wgbh/amex/zoot> (July 26, 2005).

### Further Reading

Pagán, Eduardo Obregón. *Murder at the Sleepy Lagoon: Zoot Suits, Race, and Riot in Wartime L.A.* Chapel Hill: University of North Carolina Press, 2003.

Sitkoff, Harvard. "Racial Militancy and Interracial Violence in the Second World War." *The Journal of American History* 58 (December 1971): 661–81.

White, Shane, et al. *Stylin: African American Expressive Culture from Its Beginnings to the Zoot Suit*. Ithaca, N.Y.: Cornell University Press, 1998.

### Related Entries

Latinos in the Military; Race Riots; World War II

*—Jennifer S. Lawrence*

# Chronology

**1607**
Soon after English settlers from the Virginia Company establish an outpost at Jamestown Colony, members of the Powhatan Confederacy kill two colonists and capture John Smith. After his release, Smith enforces stricter military discipline among the colonists and intensifies repression of local indigenous peoples.

**1622–32**
Chief Opechancanough's Confederation of Tidewater Indians attacks the Virginia Company's settlements in the spring of 1622, killing a quarter of the population. The company secures military aid from England and the Potomack, and fights Openchancanough's forces for nearly 11 years before the two sides agree to terms of peace.

**1637**
The Pequot War, the first serious armed conflict in New England between colonists and indigenous peoples, is fought in modern-day eastern Connecticut.

**1644–46**
Chief Opechancanough, in his 90s, leads another attack on the Virginia colonists, killing nearly 500 on the first morning. The colonists, however, now have better palisades and arms, and vastly outnumber their attackers—who are this time completely defeated.

**1675–76**
King Philip's (or Metacomet's) War, a general uprising of indigenous peoples to resist continued expansion of the English colonies in New England, leaves more than 5,000 Native Americans and some 1,500 English dead. The war ends shortly after Metacomet (his Christian name was Philip) is killed by a band of turncoat Sakonnet warriors.

**1682**
William Penn establishes the colony of Pennsylvania as a "Holy Experiment" in Quaker pacifism, following the declaration by Quaker leader George Fox 20 years earlier "against all plotters and fighters in the world."

**1689–97**
King William's War is fought. It is the first in a series of colonial conflicts between France and England for supremacy in North America.

**1702–14**
Queen Anne's War is fought in Europe and North America over the succession to the Spanish throne. In North America, fighting occurs between British and French forces in the north and between British and Spanish in the south.

**1715–18**
A confederation of Yamasee and other Muskhogean-speaking peoples in the colony of South Carolina attack colonists. South Carolinians secure the aid of North Carolinians and the Cherokee; the Yamasee are defeated and driven back into their primary area of settlement, present-day Georgia.

**1744–48**
King George's War involves military operations in North America that stem from the War of the Austrian Succession in Europe. Following King William's War and Queen Anne's War, this becomes the third major conflict between the

British and French that extends to American soil, culminating in the French and Indian War.

**1747**

In efforts to augment the ranks of their crews during King George's War, officers and men from British vessels land in Boston harbor and "press" men into service under the terms of parliamentary legislation. Bostonians react furiously, trapping several officers attending a dinner at the governor's house. Within a few days the British naval commander agrees to release most of those pressed in exchange for the release of his officers, and the Boston Press Gang Riot ends.

**1754 (May 9)**

The first American political cartoon, drawn by Benjamin Franklin, is published in the *Pennsylvania Gazette*. It depicts a snake divided into eight segments, each labeled as a colony or region of British North America, above the motto Join Or Die.

**1754–63**

The French and Indian War, the American name for the conflict in North America between Great Britain and France (in Europe known as the Seven Years' War), takes place. The war establishes British dominance of North America.

**1763**

The Royal Proclamation of 1763 prohibits settlement west of the ridge of the Appalachian Mountains, thereby inflaming backcountry settlers and colonial land speculators, who see Native American land as crucial to their economic futures.

**1765 (March 22)**

The Stamp Act, requiring all American colonists to pay a tax on every piece of printed paper they use, is passed by the British Parliament. The money thus collected is intended to help pay the costs of defending and protecting the American frontier near the Appalachian Mountains. The act, opposed by many colonists, is seen as an attempt by England to raise money from the colonies without involvement or approval of colonial legislatures.

**1770 (March 5)**

Tensions between British Redcoats and colonists lead to British troops firing on a crowd of civilians, killing five people in what becomes known as the Boston Massacre. The event has been seen by some historians as a watershed in the progress toward independence.

**1775–83**

The Revolutionary War is fought. The first shot at Lexington and Concord, Massachusetts, occurs on April 19, 1775; the Treaty of Paris recognizing American independence is signed on September 3, 1783.

**1775 (June 14)**

The 2nd Continental Congress adopts the New England militias then besieging the British Army in Boston as intercolonial, or "continental," forces.

**1775 (July 29)**

The Continental Congress authorizes ministers to serve with the rebel forces, establishing the American tradition of a military chaplaincy.

**1775 (November 29)**

The first intelligence-gathering unit in the United States, the Committee of Secret Correspondence, is established by the Continental Congress. The committee's members acquire foreign publications, hire spies, and fund propaganda activities to discover and influence the attitudes of foreign powers about the American cause.

**1776 (July 4)**

A Unanimous Declaration of the Thirteen United States of America, demanding independence from Great Britain, is adopted by Congress in Philadelphia. The Declaration of Independence begins with the words "When in the course of human events it becomes necessary for one people to dissolve the political bands which have connected them with another . . ." and establishes a clear rationale for American independence. The document would make its first newspaper appearance in the *Pennsylvania Evening Post* on July 6 and have its first public reading on July 8, in Philadelphia.

**1778**
William Billings, a tanner from Boston, composes the choral work "Chester," which combines patriotic and religious fervor. The first completely American patriotic song, it quickly becomes one of the most popular songs of the day.

**1785**
Benjamin Franklin and Frederick the Great of Prussia conclude a treaty of friendship and commerce that also codifies principles for the conduct of war. The treaty is credited with being one of the first international agreements to contain principles of the law of war in written form.

**1787**
With the United States still operating under the Articles of Confederation, the Continental Congress passes the Northwest Ordinance. One component of this law provides the framework for the distribution and use of the lands that would eventually make up the states of Ohio, Michigan, Indiana, Illinois, and Wisconsin. It also codifies the principle that the lands west of the Appalachians legally belong to Native Americans.

**1789 (April 30)**
George Washington takes office as the first president of the United States, serving two four-year terms.

**1792**
After serving in the Continental Army during the Revolution, black men are prohibited from further service in the militia by the Militia Act of 1792, inaugurating a pattern that would endure for many decades of allowing blacks to serve in the military during wartime and refusing them any military association in peacetime.

**1798**
Producing muskets for the U.S. government, Eli Whitney introduces the concept of interchangeable parts. The system is adopted by the federal arsenals, allowing faster, cheaper production and easier maintenance. Some historians have observed that this cheaper manufacturing process allowed for the rapid spread of guns throughout civilian society in the middle of the 19th century.

**1798–1800**
The federalist government of Pres. John Adams wages an undeclared naval war in the Atlantic against France (the Quasi-War) and passes the Alien and Sedition Acts (1798) to suppress media criticism.

**1802**
The United States Military Academy is established at West Point, New York.

**1803**
The United States acquires approximately 800,000 square miles of territory (mostly west of the Mississippi River) for $15 million when Pres. Thomas Jefferson and others negotiate the Louisiana Purchase from France.

**1812–15**
The War of 1812 is fought. After the Revolutionary War leaves relations between the United States and Great Britain strained, hostilities resume over a variety of issues, including the failure of the British to withdraw from American territory around the Great Lakes and British support of Native Americans on the frontiers.

**1814 (September 13)**
During a British attack on Fort McHenry in Baltimore, Maryland, Francis Scott Key writes the poem "The Defence of Fort McHenry," which seven days later would become "The Star-Spangled Banner." It receives its first public performance in Baltimore the following month. It would not become the national anthem until 1931.

# CHRONOLOGY

**1815 (January 8)**
Andrew Jackson defeats the British at the battle of New Orleans.

**1815**
Affluent merchant David Low Dodge founds the New York Peace Society. Twenty-two Protestant clerics, college presidents, and writers follow Dodge's example, founding the Massachusetts Peace Society later that year.

**1817–58**
The Seminole Wars, the longest, deadliest, and most expensive conflicts with indigenous peoples fought in the United States, are conducted in three phases (1817–18; 1835–42; 1855–58) in Florida between the United States and the Seminole.

**1819**
Norwich Military Academy is founded in Vermont by Capt. Alden Partridge, the first superintendent of the U.S. Military Academy at West Point.

**1828 (May)**
The American Peace Society is established in New York City.

**1830**
Congress passes the Indian Removal Act, which calls for the removal of all Native American peoples residing east of the Mississippi to new lands in the West.

**1838**
Abolitionist and peace activist William Lloyd Garrison exhorts New Englanders to engage in disruptive acts of civil disobedience to deprive slave-owning Southerners of federal financial, legal, and military support. Garrison, who formed the New England Anti-Slavery Society (1832) and the New England Non-Resistance Society (1838), opposed all state-sponsored violence.

**1839**
The Virginia Military Institute, the first state-supported military college in the United States, is established at Lexington.

**1842**
The government of South Carolina establishes two state military academies, The Arsenal at Columbia and The Citadel at Charleston. In 1845 The Arsenal is closed and its students and faculty merge with those at The Citadel.

**1845**
The United States Naval Academy is established at Annapolis, Maryland.

**1846 (May 13)**
After Mexican and American forces fight a skirmish north of the Rio Grande in which 11 U.S. dragoons are killed, Pres. James Polk asks for and receives a declaration of war from Congress. The Mexican–American War would continue until February 1848.

**1846–48**
Antislavery writer James Russell Lowell writes pseudonymous letters from "Ezekeil Biglow, farmer," and "Birdofredum Sawin" to the *Boston Courier*. He is critical of the war with Mexico and especially of military recruitment methods.

**1848**
Henry David Thoreau publishes "Civil Disobedience," encouraging citizens not to pay taxes that might be used to finance the Mexican–American War.

**1848 (February)**
The Treaty of Guadalupe Hidalgo is ratified, forcing Mexico to abandon title to territory in Texas north of the Rio Grande and to cede New Mexico and California to the United States.

**1853**
William Walker, the most notorious of a number of "filibusters" seeking to carve new slave states in Central America and the Caribbean, leads a body of men in his first of three failed attempts to accomplish this end, in Sonora, Mexico. After establishing a substantial foothold in Nicaragua in 1855, he is driven out in 1857. His

third attempt in 1860 in Honduras results in his execution there.

**1859 (October 16)**
John Brown leads a handful of men in a raid on the Harpers Ferry federal arsenal—a move Brown hoped would ignite a slave rebellion.

**1860 (December 20)**
South Carolina is the first state to secede from the Union following the election the previous month of Abraham Lincoln as president of the United States. From January to June 1861, Mississippi, Florida, Alabama, Georgia, Louisiana, Texas, Virginia, Arkansas, North Carolina, and Tennessee also secede, in that order.

**1861 (February 18)**
Jefferson Davis, having resigned his U.S. Senate seat the previous month upon Mississippi's announcement of its secession, is inaugurated as provisional president of the newly formed Confederate States of America in Montgomery, Alabama.

**1861 (June 13)**
Pres. Abraham Lincoln authorizes the U.S. War Department to create the U.S. Sanitary Commission. The agency was conceived by two doctors, Elizabeth Blackwell, and her sister, Emily Blackwell, to function as a national, civilian-led government relief organization. The commission contributed food, clothing, medical supplies, and other aid to the Union Army during the Civil War.

**1861 (July)**
The first battle of the Civil War, the battle of Bull Run, is fought at Manassas, Virginia.

**1861 (November)**
Representatives from a number of counties in western Virginia meet at Wheeling to begin drafting a constitution for a breakaway state. In May 1863, voters approve the constitution and the newly elected legislature petitions Congress to become the 35th state, West Virginia.

**1862**
Photographer Mathew Brady publishes two books of his Civil War photos, *Brady's Photographic Views of the War* and *Incidents of the War*.

**1862 (February 25)**
Congress passes the first Legal Tender Act, which authorizes printing of $150 million in Treasury notes. Known as "Greenbacks," these notes would remain in use in Union states throughout the Civil War and for several years thereafter.

**1862 (September 22)**
President Lincoln issues the preliminary Emancipation Proclamation, declaring that unless the rebellious states return to the Union by January 1, 1863, the slaves living therein would be "thenceforward and forever free." The rebels do not comply, and Lincoln issues the final Emancipation Proclamation on New Year's Day of 1863.

**1863 (January 26)**
President Lincoln orders the War Department to allow black troops to be raised for the 54th Regiment of Massachusetts Volunteer (Colored) Infantry. Black recruits from 24 states, the District of Columbia, Canada, the West Indies, and even Africa flock to the 54th's colors. Robert Gould Shaw is appointed the regiment's commander.

**1863 (April 24)**
General Orders, No. 100, entitled Instructions for the Government of Armies of the United States in the Field, is published. Written primarily by Francis Lieber, a German American professor of law at Columbia College, the document is regarded by many historians as the world's first official set of ethical guidelines about military conduct in the field.

**1863 (July 1–3)**
The battle of Gettysburg, in Pennsylvania, is one of the bloodiest of the Civil War. Pres. Abraham Lincoln's brief (266 words) Gettysburg Address honoring the dead of that

battle on November 19, 1863, stands among the great presidential addresses in American history.

**1863 (July)**

In New York, antidraft riots break out on July 13 and last for five days. Mobs of predominantly Irish immigrants attack government officials, wealthy white New Yorkers, and African Americans. They lynch 11 black men, injure dozens more, and destroy hundreds of buildings, including an orphanage for African Americans. The riots would rank among the most dramatic breakdowns of domestic order in the 19th century.

**1863 (August 21)**

William Clark Quantrill, a pro-Confederate Missourian, leads a force of 450 men to attack the militantly antislavery town of Lawrence, Kansas. "Quantrill's Raiders" spend three hours looting and burning the town, killing 180 of its residents.

**1863 (December)**

President Lincoln issues a Proclamation of Amnesty and Reconstruction, offering terms under which most white Southerners, excluding Confederate officials and military officers, could obtain amnesty simply by taking an oath of allegiance to the Union and by accepting emancipation. It includes a plan whereby a state in rebellion could return to the Union whenever a number of voters equivalent to at least 10 percent of those who had cast ballots in 1860 took the oath. They could then create a loyal state government.

**1864**

Several European countries draft the Geneva Convention for the Amelioration of the Condition of the Wounded in Armies in the Field. This convention, which grew out of the efforts of Swiss businessman J. Henri Dunant, is followed by others developed over the next century in Geneva, Switzerland, and The Hague, The Netherlands. All of these documents promulgate overall guidelines for the conduct of war.

**1864 (February)**

Confederate prison Camp Sumter (known by its more notorious name Andersonville) opens in Georgia.

**1864 (April 12)**

The Fort Pillow Massacre takes place. In a move to recapture the fort they had built in 1861, Confederate forces under Gen. Nathan Bedford Forrest attack Fort Pillow, near Memphis, killing more than 200 Union troops, many of them African Americans.

**1864 (September 3)**

Union forces under Gen. William T. Sherman enter Atlanta.

**1864 (November 29)**

Colorado militia colonel John Chivington leads 700 men into the Southern Cheyenne village of Black Kettle at Sand Creek in southeastern Colorado, despite having been told by U.S. Army officers at Fort Lyon that Black Kettle had surrendered. Chivington's troops kills more than 150 Native Americans. The massacre prompts a congressional investigation.

**1865 (April 9)**

Confederate general Robert E. Lee surrenders to Ulysses S. Grant and his Union forces at Appomattox Court House in Virginia.

**1865 (April 14)**

Pres. Abraham Lincoln is assassinated at Ford's Theatre in Washington, D.C., by John Wilkes Booth.

**1866 (April 6)**

The Grand Army of the Republic, the largest and most powerful organization of Union Army and Navy veterans, is founded in Decatur, Illinois, by former Army surgeon Benjamin Franklin Stephenson.

**1866–67**

Beginning as a loose affiliation of paramilitary organizations operating widely in the South during Reconstruction, the Ku Klux Klan forms and announces itself at an 1867 convention in Nashville, Tennessee, as the "Invisible Empire of the South." It is led by former Confederate general Nathan Bedford Forrest.

**1868 (May 30)**

Grand Army of the Republic (GAR) national commander John Logan enjoins all GAR posts to pay tribute to the fallen soldiers of the Civil War, thereby establishing what would become known as Memorial Day (initially known as Decoration Day).

**1870–74**

Congress passes the Force Act (1870) and the Ku Klux Klan Act (1871), directing the Army to suppress the Klan's depredations against blacks and white Republicans. Those measures prove to be effective in South Carolina, but less so elsewhere.

**1873**

The United States Naval Institute is established.

**1874**

Col. George Armstrong Custer's 7th Cavalry leads a geological expedition into the Oglala Sioux's Black Hills to determine whether gold deposits are to be found there. The report of the presence of gold leads to a flood of prospectors and the abrogation in 1876 of the treaty with the Sioux.

**1876**

The United States Coast Guard Academy is established.

**1876 (June 25)**

Gen. George Armstrong Custer's 7th Cavalry is defeated by Lakota Sioux and Cheyenne warriors led by Crazy Horse and Sitting Bull at the battle of Little Bighorn. Custer's defeat prompts the Army to redouble its campaign against the Sioux and hastens the end of indigenous people's resistance to being placed on Indian reservations.

**1877**

The U.S. Military Academy at West Point graduates its first African American, Henry Flipper.

**1877**

Labor calls strikes against railroads throughout the United States and local militia units prove unable or unwilling to protect railway property. Units of the federal armed services are ordered to perform these duties.

**1878**

The Posse Comitatus Act, restricting the circumstances under which U.S. military forces can be used to address domestic disturbances, is passed in response to Southerners' anger at the use of federal troops during Reconstruction. The act would evolve into an important foundation of in the evolution of American civil–military relations.

**1879**

National Guard officers meet in St. Louis, Missouri, to organize the National Guard Association.

**1881**

*A Century of Dishonor*, by Helen Hunt Jackson, is published, exposing the tragedies caused by the government's policies toward Native Americans. It leads to the creation of several Indian rights groups, including the Indian Rights Association (1882) and the National Indian Defense Association (1885).

**1881**

Clara Barton founds the American Red Cross.

**1884**

The Naval War College is established to serve as an advanced professional school to prepare middle- and senior-grade officers for higher command, contributing to and acknowledging the growing professionalism of the naval officer corps.

**1890 (December)**

A band of poorly armed Sioux Ghost Dancers at Wounded Knee Creek, South Dakota, is massacred in the last major engagement of the Indian Wars. For the Army this event marks the end of the military phase of the settlement of the

West. For many Native Americans, however, the Wounded Knee Massacre becomes emblematic of the ruthlessness of the frontier Army and the injustices of U.S. Indian policy.

**1895**

*The Red Badge of Courage*, a Civil War novel by Stephen Crane, is published.

**1898 (February 19)**

The USS *Maine* explodes in Havana Harbor, Cuba, amid suspicions (later shown to be unfounded) that it was sabotaged by Spanish troops. The event fuels support for a war with Spain. The Spanish–American War begins in April 1898.

**1898 (July 1)**

Establishing a symbol of the glories of imperial adventure in Cuba, Teddy Roosevelt leads the Rough Riders and units of the black 9th and 10th U.S. Army Cavalry Regiments in charges up the San Juan Heights outside Santiago de Cuba.

**1898 (December 10)**

The Treaty of Paris transfers colonial control of Guam, Puerto Rico, and the Philippines from Spain to the United States.

**1899–1902**

The Philippine War is waged, during which the United States attempts to quell Filipino insurrections in America's newly acquired colonial territory.

**1900**

The Boxer Rebellion takes place in the early months of 1900. Boxers attack foreign missionaries in the Chinese countryside and then in the diplomatic quarter in Peking (Beijing).

**1901**

With the Army Reorganization Act of 1901, a permanent female nursing corps is created.

**1903**

The first of several major U.S. interventions in Central America is instigated after Pres. Theodore Roosevelt obtains permission to build an interoceanic canal in Panama. In January, the United States negotiates with Colombia to build a canal across the Panamanian isthmus, at the time a province of Colombia. The Colombian legislature rejects the treaty even as Panama is attempting to secede and establish itself as a sovereign nation. Roosevelt then recognizes Panama as a nation and sends naval warships and members of the Marine Corps to prevent Colombia from quashing the rebellion. After successfully seceding in November 1903, Panama brokers a deal with the United States to permit the construction of the canal.

**1903**

The Militia Act of 1903 recognizes newly emergent National Guard units as the "Organized Militia" of the United States, but requires that units engage in summer training maneuvers with regular Army units, to be subject to some regular Army standards, and to submit to inspections by regular Army officers.

**1906 (August 13–14)**

Black infantrymen from the 25th Infantry Regiment in Brownsville, Texas, are accused of firing on white townspeople ("the Brownsville Riot").

**1911**

Ambrose Bierce publishes his *Devil's Dictionary*, in which he defines war as "a byproduct of the arts of peace" and peace as "a period of cheating between two periods of fighting."

**1912**

Jewish War Veterans, one of the oldest veteran's organization in the United States, forms.

**1913**

Veterans of Foreign Wars (VFW) is established.

**1914**
Panama Canal is completed under U.S. direction and remains in U.S. control until 1999.

**1914 (August)**
World War I begins in Europe.

**1914 (October)**
The American Field Service is created to provide American volunteer ambulance drivers for the war in France.

**1915**
Chicago social worker Jane Addams founds the Women's Peace Party (later the Women's International League for Peace and Freedom) to abolish the causes of war, to work for peace, and to create political systems that would bring equality for all.

**1915 (April 22)**
The German Army releases chlorine gas against British and French forces near the town of Ypres in Belgium. It it the first use of chemical weapons in warfare.

**1915 (May 7)**
The British ship *Lusitania*, with many Americans on board, is sunk by a German submarine.

**1915 (summer)**
East Coast munitions workers centered in Bridgeport, Connecticut, lead a short and successful strike, bringing the eight-hour workday to the munitions industry.

**1915 (August 9)**
Amid protests about America's lack of military preparedness in the wake of the sinking of the *Lusitania* and other incidents, a train carrying lawyers, bankers, politicians, civil servants, and the first of many students from Ivy League colleges leaves Grand Central Station for a camp in Plattsburgh, New York. The month-long session to improve the country's preparedness, to be repeated the next year in several venues, is part of a larger countrywide "Preparedness Movement."

**1915 (December 4)**
Henry Ford's Peace Ship sails from Hoboken, New Jersey, for Stockholm with a number of prominent pacifists in a vain attempt to arrange an end to the World War I.

**1916**
The Reserve Officer's Training Corps (ROTC) is established to provide military training on college campuses as part of the National Defense Act passed the same year.

**1917**
James Montgomery Flagg creates the most recognizable poster of both world wars, a picture of Uncle Sam pointing his finger at the viewer over the slogan I Want You.

**1917**
A. Philip Randolph and Chandler Owen found *Messenger*, one of the most influential African American periodicals of the war and postwar period. Through its pages, Randolph and Chandler assume the stance of conscientious objection to the war and encourage African Americans to avoid military service, prompting Justice Department officers to arrest the two for violating the 1917 Espionage Act.

**1917 (April 2)**
In a speech to Congress, Pres. Woodrow Wilson, arguing for U.S. involvement in World War I, utters the phrase "the world must be made safe for democracy."

**1917 (April 6)**
The United States declares war against Germany, officially entering World War I.

**1917 (April 13)**
Shortly after Congress declares war on Germany, President Wilson creates the Committee on Public Information—the nation's first large-scale propaganda agency—to mobilize public opinion in the United States behind the war effort, and also to gain international support.

**1917 (April 17)**
Eleven days after the formal U.S. declaration of war, the War Department creates a new federal agency, the Commission on Training Camp Activities, to protect men in uniform from moral corruption and venereal disease.

**1917 (May 18)**
Congress passes the Selective Service Act with the intent to raise a massive American army to win the war in Europe. The act requires all men between the ages of 21 and 31 (including Native Americans) to register for the draft.

**1917 (November)**
The Bolshevik Revolution in Russia overthrows the post-imperial government of Kerensky's Social Democrats. In March 1918 the Treaty of Brest-Litovsk is signed, which is favorable to Germany, and ends Russia's participation in World War I.

**1917–18**
The Espionage and Sedition acts are passed as separate pieces of legislation designed to limit treacherous behavior in wartime and to promote patriotism. The Espionage Act, approved on June 15, 1917, sets fines of up to $10,000 and prison terms for citizens who aid the enemy. The Sedition Act forbids "any disloyal, profane, scurrilous, or abusive language about the form of government of the United States, or the Constitution of the United States, or the flag of the United States, or the uniform of the Army or Navy."

**1918**
The War Labor Board is established to set wartime labor policies and secure a strong workforce.

**1918 (March)**
A strain of influenza appears in the United States as the first of three waves of a flu pandemic that continues into 1919, killing 40 million to 50 million people worldwide, and 675,000 in the United States.

**1918 (March 4)**
Pres. Woodrow Wilson issues an executive order to give the War Industries Board (WIB), under the leadership of Bernard Baruch, the power to function as a distinct agency to coordinate the channeling of civilian resources to meet the military's ever-growing industrial and transportation needs. The WIB would transform the relationship between the government and civilian society as the nation for the first time organized its resources to fight a total war.

**1918 (June)**
Under provisions in the 1917 Espionage Act, Socialist Eugene V. Debs is arrested for delivering a speech in Canton, Ohio, in which he expressed his opposition to the draft. Debs was sentenced to a 10-year prison term. In 1919 he appeals his case to the U.S. Supreme Court, which unanimously affirms his conviction in an opinion delivered by Justice Oliver Wendell Holmes. After serving three years, Debs was pardoned by Pres. Warren Harding in 1921.

**1918 (July)**
W. E. B. Du Bois publishes an editorial in the National Association for the Advancement of Colored People's magazine, *The Crisis*, urging blacks to "Close Ranks" and support the war effort. He would publish a series of impassioned editorials in *The Crisis* over the following months urging support for black soldiers, including "Returning Soldiers."

**1918 (November 11)**
An armistice is signed in the forest of Compiègne, France, ending fighting in World War I.

**1919 (March 15)**
The American Legion is established, unifying many of the newly founded veterans' groups.

**1919 (June 28)**
The Treaty of Versailles is signed, forcing Germany to pay severe war reparations and stripping it of its colonial territories.

**1919 (November 11)**
On the one-year anniversary of the end of World War I, Armistice Day is proclaimed. After 1938, November 11 was observed as a federal holiday devoted exclusively to remembering the sacrifices of that conflict. In 1954 Armistice Day became Veterans Day, a holiday honoring all U.S. veterans.

**1920 (January)**
Roger Baldwin founds the American Civil Liberties Union.

**1920**
The Disabled American Veterans of the World War (renamed Disabled American Veterans in 1941) is established.

**1920**
The last U.S. troops are withdrawn from Russia after an intervention lasting two years in Russia's civil war.

**1921**
The Veterans Bureau is established.

**1921 (November 11)**
On the third anniversary of the end of World War I, the United States lays the body of an unidentified soldier to rest at Arlington Cemetery in Virginia, designating him the country's "Unknown Soldier." It follows England and France in this gesture to recognize the thousands of soldiers unaccounted for or mutilated beyond recognition in war.

**1924**
The Indian Citizenship Act of 1924 grants citizenship to all Native Americans.

**1924**
The Army Industrial College is founded to train officers in facilitating economic mobilization in wartime.

**1925**
The Geneva Protocol for the Prohibition of the Use in War of Asphyxiating, Poisonous or Other Gases, and of Bacteriological Methods of Warfare is instituted.

**1929**
*A Farewell to Arms*, a World War I novel by Ernest Hemingway, is published.

**1929 (October)**
Stocks in America and throughout the world suffer devastating losses in value. The Crash of 1929 ushers in the Great Depression, which would last through the 1930s.

**1930 (July)**
The Veterans Administration is established to administer benefits for the nation's veterans.

**1931**
Pres. Herbert Hoover signs into law a bill that makes "The Star-Spangled Banner" the national anthem.

**1932 (May–July)**
The Bonus March takes place in Washington, D.C. Veterans of World War I march on the city to demand early payment of military bonuses owing to financial pressures brought about by the Great Depression.

**1933**
After 30 years of American military interventions in Caribbean and Central American countries, Pres. Franklin D. Roosevelt announces a "Good Neighbor Policy." Limiting interventions to assisting threatened American citizens, the Good Neighbor Policy expresses the American people's desire for international isolation.

**1933 (March)**
The American embassy in Berlin and U.S. consuls report numerous mob attacks on Jews, as well as the systematic removal of Jews from positions in government, education, and the legal profession.

**1933 (March 31)**
The Civilian Conservation Corps (CCC) is established as part of Roosevelt administration's program to provide emergency aid to unemployed youth and to revitalize the nation's natural resources.

**1935**

The first in a series of neutrality acts is signed into law, embodying America's growing isolationist impulse.

**1938**

The House Un-American Activities Committee (HUAC), also known as the Dies Committee, is established to investigate communist penetration of labor and other organizations in the United States.

**1938**

The insecticide DDT is created to kill lice and prevent the spread of such diseases as typhus; its first massive application would be with troops in World War II. DDT would become a staple insecticide in the United States after World War II.

**1939 (August)**

Émigré German scientist Albert Einstein writes Pres. Franklin Roosevelt to warn him that the Germans are on the track of creating a nuclear weapon.

**1939 (September 1)**

The German army invades Poland, setting into motion the events that would lead to World War II.

**1940 (May)**

The Selective Service and Training Act goes into effect; it exempts married men from the draft.

**1940 (September)**

After a sharp rise in the marriage rate in the wake of the May statute, Congress amends the Selective Service Act to exempt only married men with one or more children.

**1941 (March)**

In the wake of a violent strike at a Milwaukee, Wisconsin, defense plant, Pres. Franklin Roosevelt establishes the 11-member National Defense Mediation Board, later to become the National War Labor Board.

**1941 (April 1)**

Tens of thousands of Ford workers strike the massive River Rouge plant in Michigan. Faced with the prospect of losing immensely profitable government contracts, Ford signs a closed shop (union-members only) contract with the United Auto Workers—the first of its kind in the auto industry—which brings the 100,000 workers at Ford plants into the union.

**1941 (June)**

Executive Order 8802 is signed by Pres. Franklin Roosevelt. It establishes the Fair Employment Practices Commission, a body authorized to investigate complaints of racial discrimination in companies under contract to supply war materials to the government.

**1941 (August)**

The Office of Price Administration is created by Executive Order 8875.

**1941 (December)**

Representatives of gardening organizations, seed companies, the agricultural press, and other organizations meet with Sec. of Agriculture Claude Wickard to discuss how to encourage Victory Gardens in the United States. The program's goals are to increase the production and consumption of fresh vegetables and fruits, encourage the preservation of surplus vegetables and fruits by individual families, and maintain morale while offering all Americans a means of participating in the war effort.

**1941 (December 7)**

Japanese warplanes attack the U.S. Pacific fleet in Pearl Harbor, Hawaii, provoking a declaration of war by the United States.

**1941 (December 19)**

President Roosevelt establishes by executive order the Office of Censorship to monitor all civilian radio broadcasts and print media, both within the United States and across U.S. borders, to ensure that no information is transmitted or disseminated that might be of use to America's enemies.

**1942 (January 12)**
By executive order, President Roosevelt establishes the War Labor Board (WLB) to supervise and intervene in various aspects of collective bargaining. From 1942 to 1945, the WLB would settle disputed contracts and play a major role in establishing wage rates, hours, and union security. It also would help shape the nature of postwar labor relations.

**1942 (February 19)**
President Roosevelt signs Executive Order 9066, which mandates the internment of 120,000 Japanese and Japanese Americans in detention camps throughout the western United States.

**1942 (February 25)**
The Voice of America (VOA) makes its first radio broadcast, in German, commencing its mission to provide information about America and the war to international audiences. The VOA would continue spreading information to the world about U.S. culture and institutions into the 21st century.

**1942 (June 13)**
By executive order, President Roosevelt establishes the Office of War Information to coordinate news and information sent out by the U.S. government during World War II and to oversee domestic and foreign propaganda in support of the war effort.

**1942 (November 24)**
Dorothy Stratton is sworn in as first director of the Coast Guard women's organization, or SPARS, with the rank of lieutenant commander.

**1942 (December 2)**
Under the leadership of Enrico Fermi, scientists at the University of Chicago create the first nuclear chain reaction.

**1943 (February 1)**
Pres. Franklin Roosevelt announces the formation of the 442nd Regimental Combat Team, comprised of Japanese Americans. Amid doubts about the loyalty of the regiment's soldiers, the 442nd achieves one of the most outstanding records of any regiment in World War II.

**1943 (May 29)**
Norman Rockwell's *Rosie the Riveter* painting appears on the cover of *The Saturday Evening Post's* Memorial Day edition.

**1943 (mid-June)**
Following the 3rd United Mine Worker strike in just six weeks, Congress passes (over President Roosevelt's veto) the Smith–Connally War Labor Disputes Act, which authorizes the use of military force to seize struck mines and factories and provides for fines and jail terms for strike leaders.

**1943 (June)**
More than 100 Mexican Americans in Los Angeles are seriously injured, and more are jailed, during racially inspired attacks on their communities by military servicemen and Los Angeles police. The 10-day clash would become known as the "Zoot Suit" riot.

**1943 (July)**
The Women's Army Corps (WAC) is established, providing full military rank to WAC members.

**1943 (September)**
*Life* magazine publishes one of the first photographs (taken by George Strock) of American war dead, a view of three soldiers lying partly buried in the sand on Buna Beach in New Guinea.

**1943 (November 1)**
The United Mine Workers strike for the 4th time since the spring, involving all of the nation's 530,000 bituminous coal miners. Using his new powers under the Smith–Connally War Labor Disputes Act, Roosevelt sends in troops and seizes strike-bound coal mines, threatening to draft striking miners. The union refuses to back down, and Roosevelt orders Sec. of the Interior Harold Ickes to bypass the War Labor Board (which had a policy of not negotiating with a

striking union) and negotiate a contract that proves to be acceptable to the mine workers.

**1944 (May 22)**
*Life* magazine publishes a photo of a young woman seated at her desk writing a thank you note to her friend, a Navy lieutenant, who had sent her the skull of a Japanese soldier that sits before her on her desk.

**1944 (June 6)**
On D-Day, more than 100,000 Allied troops cross the English Channel and land on the beaches of Normandy in France in the largest seaborne invasion in the history of warfare. D-Day proves a decisive turning point for the Allies in World War II.

**1944 (June 22)**
President Roosevelt signs into law the Servicemen's Readjustment Act of 1944, or "GI Bill of Rights" as it is more commonly known, by which the federal government offers soldiers a wide range of benefits, including education assistance, home loans, vocational training, and business loans as a reward for military service. One of the most expansive pieces of social welfare legislation in the country's history, the GI Bill would be credited with making possible profound changes to the social fabric of postwar America.

**1944 (July 17)**
A massive explosion rocks the Port Chicago Naval Munitions Base near San Francisco, California, killing 320 servicemen and injuring another 390. The incident exposes racial discrimination given the disproportionately large number of African Americans killed; they were working under extremely dangerous conditions. The Port Chicago Mutiny follows.

**1944 (November)**
The American Veterans Committee is organized.

**1944 (December 9)**
Delegates from nine organizations meeting in Kansas City, Missouri, create the American Veterans of World War II, which becomes known as "AMVETS."

**1945 (April 18)**
War correspondent Ernie Pyle is killed by a sniper while on the front lines on Ie Shima with elements of the Army's 77th Infantry Division.

**1945 (May)**
German forces begin to surrender on European battlefields. The formal unconditional surrender is signed May 7. May 8 is declared VE (Victory in Europe) Day.

**1945 (July 16)**
The first nuclear device is detonated at Trinity Site, near Alamogordo, New Mexico.

**1945 (August 6)**
An atomic bomb is dropped from the American B-29 bomber *Enola Gay* onto the Japanese city of Hiroshima. Some 70,000 people die in the blast and thousands more die later from effects of radiation. A second bomb is dropped on Nagasaki three days later.

**1945 (August 15)**
Photographer Alfred Eisenstadt captures one of the most memorable images from World War II, "V-J Day, Times Square, 1945," showing a newly returned sailor embracing the first woman to cross his path in Times Square on Victory in Japan Day. The photo would be featured on the cover of *Life* magazine.

**1945 (September 2)**
Formal surrender of Japan onboard the USS *Missouri* in Tokyo Bay.

**1945 (December)**
Congress passes the War Brides Act, which loosens immigration laws to expedite the entry of more than 100,000 war brides, predominantly from Europe, into the United States after soldiers return home from World War II.

**1946**
*The Best Years of Our Lives*, a film directed by William Wyler about World War II veterans, premieres.

**1946**
Congress establishes the Fulbright Program for academic exchanges.

**1946 (May)**
The Doolittle Board issues its report about the relations between officers and enlisted men, leading to some improvement in the treatment of enlisted personnel and to the Uniform Code of Military Justice.

**1946 (August 31)**
*Hiroshima*, by John Hersey, is published in a single issue of *The New Yorker* magazine; the book, about the aftermath of the dropping of the atomic bomb on Hiroshima, Japan, in August 1945, is published by Alfred Knopf later in 1946.

**1947**
The U.S. Air Force is established as a distinct branch of the U.S. military.

**1947**
The National Security Act of 1947 establishes a secretary of defense, unifies the service, and creates a separate Air Force, a National Security Council, and the Central Intelligence Agency (CIA). It charges the new agency with coordinating the nation's intelligence activities and with collecting and evaluating intelligence affecting national security.

**1947**
The House Un-American Activities Committee (HUAC) investigates and puts on trial the "Hollywood Ten," communist writers in the entertainment industry. This results in the firing and blacklisting of writers, actors, and others in a widening array of industries, as well as in many schools and colleges.

**1947 (June 5)**
In a speech at Harvard University, Sec. of State George C. Marshall makes the first public announcement of the European Recovery Plan. Subsequently known as the "Marshall Plan," it would become one of the most successful government initiatives of the 20th century.

**1947**
George Kennan, a junior State Department official, provides the first widely accepted outline of a coherent American Cold War policy in his article published in *Foreign Affairs*, "Sources of Soviet Conduct."

**1948**
*The Naked and the Dead, a* World War II novel by Norman Mailer, is published.

**1948**
The first MASH (Mobile Army Surgical Hospital) units are authorized by the surgeon general of the Army to provide front-line combat care. They are the first medical units to be deployed in the Korean War in 1950.

**1948 (March)**
Activist Chicano veterans in south Texas organize the American GI Forum.

**1948 (June 24)**
A new Selective Service Act is passed by Congress.

**1948 (June 24)**
Fearing a revitalized Germany under Western influence, the Soviets foment the first major crisis of the Cold War—the Berlin Crisis of 1948. Taking advantage of a postwar arrangement guaranteeing only air access to jointly occupied Berlin, 100 miles inside the Soviet zone, the Soviet Union closes off rail and road links hoping to force out the West. Pres. Harry Truman declares that American forces will remain in Berlin, and a massive airlift supplies the city with more than two million tons of supplies. The Soviets eventually lift the blockade, effectively admitting defeat and deferring a decision on Berlin.

**1948 (July 26)**
Pres. Harry Truman signs Executive Order 9981, prohibiting racial discrimination and segregation in the U.S. armed forces.

**1949**
Radio Free Europe is established as a tool in the ongoing ideological struggle with the Soviet Union. It would provide communication services to Eastern and Southeastern Europe, the Russian Federation, and southwestern Asia in the hope of weakening the Soviet government's hold on the societies it rules by providing more open discussion of current news and events and promoting Western values.

**1949**
Local American Legion members in Westchester County, New York, mob a concert by black opera singer and civil rights activist Paul Robeson.

**1949**
The U.S. Naval Academy graduates its first African American, Wesley Brown.

**1949 (August)**
The Soviet Union tests its first nuclear device.

**1949**
*Twelve O'Clock High*, a World War II film directed by Henry King, premieres.

**1950**
National Security Council Memorandum-68 (NSC-68) calls for wholesale revision of U.S. Cold War policy. It reshaped Kennan's "containment" theory to emphasize military force over economic, diplomatic, or psychological means to preserve U.S. national security in the face of an increasingly aggressive Soviet Union. NSC-68 would emerge as the preeminent policy document of U.S. strategic thinking during the early years of the Cold War.

**1950**
The Federal Civil Defense Administration begins to produce films, pamphlets, and posters emphasizing U.S. vulnerability to enemy attack—especially from the Soviet Union.

**1950**
*Beetle Bailey*, a humorous comic strip that stars the slacker draftee whose attitudes and adventures come to represent the peacetime draft Army of the 1950s and 1960s, makes its first appearance.

**1950**
The Uniform Code of Military Justice is signed into law by Pres. Harry Truman. The code attempts to combine the command-dominated military justice system with the civilian justice system, emphasizing due process.

**1950 (June 25)**
In a move that sparks the Korean War, North Korean tanks cross the 38th parallel separating North and South Korea. The following day, Pres. Harry Truman authorizes the movement of U.S. troops to defend South Korea.

**1950 (September 9)**
The nation's first draft of doctors is signed into law to address the drastic shortage of medical personnel after post–World War II demobilization and in response to the additional requirements of the Korean War.

**1951 (April 11)**
President Truman announces the dismissal of Gen. Douglas MacArthur from his duties as Allied commander of United Nations forces in the Far East (Korea).

**1952 (July 16)**
Pres. Harry Truman signs into law the Veterans Readjustment Assistance Act of 1952, which offers education and loan benefits to veterans who served for more than 90 days during the Korean War.

**1952 (October)**
The popular and critically acclaimed documentary *Victory at Sea* begins airing on NBC. The 26-episode series, recounting the U.S. Navy's role in World War II, reinforced the idea of the "good war."

**1953**
Julius and Ethel Rosenberg are executed two years after being convicted of espionage.

**1953**
*From Here to Eternity*, a film directed by Fred Zinneman based on the 1951 novel by James Jones, premieres.

**1953**
Pres. Dwight D. Eisenhower signs Executive Order 10450, codifying sexual perversion as grounds for dismissal from federal employment, including the military.

**1953 (July 27)**
An armistice is signed ending the Korean War.

**1954**
*The Caine Mutiny*, a World War II film directed by Edward Dmytryk based on the 1951 novel by Herman Wouk, premieres.

**1954**
The United States Air Force Academy is established.

**1954**
Militant Liberty, formulated by John C. Broger of the Far East Broadcasting Company, appears. It is one of several ideological initiatives supported by the Department of Defense during the early days of the Cold War.

**1955**
*The Bridges at Toko-Ri*, a Korean War film directed by Mark Robson based on the 1953 novel by James Michener, premieres.

**1955**
*Strategic Air Command*, a film directed by Anthony Mann and starring Jimmy Stewart, premieres.

**1956**
Pres. Dwight Eisenhower's promotion of a national system of interstate highways leads to the Federal Aid Highway Act of 1956 and the National System of Interstate and Defense Highways. In 1990 it is renamed The Dwight D. Eisenhower System of Interstate and Defense Highways.

**1957**
Norman Cousins and others found the Committee for a Sane Nuclear Policy to lobby for a comprehensive test ban treaty. The organization realizes some success in 1963 when the United States, Britain, and the Soviet Union agree to stop atmospheric and underwater testing and to ban tests in space.

**1957 (October 4)**
The Soviet Union launches the first artificial satellite, *Sputnik*, into orbit.

**1958**
The civilian National Aeronautics and Space Administration (NASA) is created to promote nonmilitary, peaceful uses of space, and becomes the lead agency in the space program.

**1961 (January 17)**
In his farewell address to the American public, Pres. Dwight D. Eisenhower warns of the rise of a "military–industrial complex" and its undue legislative and economic influence. Only "an alert and knowledgeable citizenry," Eisenhower urged, can ensure that "security and liberty may prosper together."

**1961 (March 1)**
Pres. John F. Kennedy signs an executive order establishing the Peace Corps.

**1961 (June)**
At a meeting in Vienna, Soviet premier Nikita Khrushchev attempts to bully Pres. John F. Kennedy into acceding to Soviet demands for final agreements on the status of Berlin and Germany and sets a six-month deadline for formal agreements. Refusing to be bullied, Kennedy, in July 1961, announces a policy of zero tolerance for interference in Allied rights to travel across East Germany to Berlin, and at the same time begins a massive buildup of U.S. armed forces.

**1961 (August 13)**
After more than 200,000 people flee East Germany for the West during the first six months of the year, a barbed wire fence is erected to divide East and West Berlin. It is soon replaced by a stone wall. The Berlin Wall would stand as both a physical barrier and a symbol of the Cold War until November 1989.

**1962**
*Combat!,* a television series set during World War II, airs its pilot; the series runs until 1967.

**1962**
Students for a Democratic Society is founded on several U.S. college campuses.

**1962**
Rachel Carson publishes *Silent Spring,* warning against the effects of the insecticide DDT, which had been developed for use in World War II and became widely used in the United States after the war.

**1962 (October)**
The Cuban Missile Crisis is sparked when U.S. aerial surveillance on October 14 confirms Soviet missile sites in Cuba capable of delivering nuclear warheads to American soil. President Kennedy addresses the world on October 22, demanding the removal of the missiles. For a week, the United States and the Soviet Union teeter on the brink of nuclear war.

**1963**
The Treaty Banning Nuclear Weapon Tests in the Atmosphere, in Outer Space, and Under Water (often shortened as the Nuclear Test Ban Treaty) is signed by the United States, Great Britain, and the Soviet Union.

**1963**
Associated Press reporter Malcolm Browne photographs an incident in Vietnam involving Buddhist monks dousing themselves with gas and burning themselves alive, one of the first visual statements against the war in Vietnam to be circulated around the world.

**1963 (November 22)**
Pres. John F. Kennedy is assassinated in Dallas.

**1964 (August)**
After U.S. ships patrolling in the Gulf of Tonkin come under attack from North Vietnamese forces on August 2, Pres. Lyndon Johnson orders retaliatory air strikes against North Vietnamese naval installations and obtains the Gulf of Tonkin Resolution from Congress. This resolution, a major step in widening America's role in Vietnam, grants the president the authority to use whatever means necessary to protect South Vietnam and U.S. military forces in Southeast Asia.

**1964**
*Seven Days in May,* a Cold War suspense film directed by John Frankenheimer and adapted by Rod Serling from the 1962 novel by Fletcher Knebel and Charles W. Bailey, premieres.

**1964**
*Dr. Strangelove, Or How I Learned to Stop Worrying and Love the Bomb,* a film directed by Stanley Kubrick satirizing the nuclear arms race, premieres.

**1965**
The Supreme Court decision in *United States v. Seeger* establishes that a belief in a supreme being and religious membership are no longer required to claim conscientious objector (CO) status, although a CO's reasons for nonparticipation must resemble those of members of conventional religions. The Court would further refine this decision five years later in *Welsh v. United States* by removing the religious qualification, stating that an individual's "ethical and moral beliefs" that prohibit military participation are sufficient to obtain CO status.

**1965 (April 17)**
Organized by Students for a Democratic Society, more than 25,000 activists descend on Washington, D.C., to protest

the war in Vietnam—the first major demonstration against that war.

**1966 (March 3)**

Pres. Lyndon Johnson signs into law the Veterans Readjustment Benefits Act of 1966, which, unlike previous GI bills, extends benefits to veterans who served during times of war and peace. With this act, military service becomes a more viable option for economic advancement.

**1966 (April)**

The religious protest group, Clergy and Laity Concerned About Vietnam, is formed.

**1967 (April)**

Vietnam Veterans Against the War is formed by a number of American servicemen who have returned to the United States after tours of duty in Vietnam.

**1967 (June)**

Boxer Muhammad Ali is convicted for refusing induction into the U.S. Army. He is stripped of his heavyweight title, fined $10,000, and sentenced to prison for five years (though he served no time). The verdict is reversed by the Supreme Court in 1971.

**1968 (January–February)**

North Vietnamese Army and Viet Cong units launch coordinated attacks throughout South Vietnam in the Tet Offensive. Although the attacks amount to a costly military defeat for the communist forces, their scale and ferocity, coming so soon after an extensive U.S. government public relations campaign that had stressed progress in the war and the impending collapse of the communist forces, shock the American public and further erode an already declining will to continue the war.

**1968 (March 16)**

The My Lai Massacre, the slaughter of more than 500 unarmed Vietnamese civilians by soldiers of C Company, 1st Battalion, 20th Infantry, Americal Division, gives rise to highly-charged legal proceedings and fuels the public's concerns about the Vietnam War.

**1968 (April 4)**

Rev. Martin Luther King, Jr., is assassinated in Memphis, Tennessee.

**1968 (June 5)**

Sen. Robert F. Kennedy is assassinated in Los Angeles.

**1968 (August 26–29)**

Antiwar demonstrators and police engage in a violent melee outside the Democratic National Convention in Chicago.

**1968 (November)**

Richard Nixon wins the presidency with a campaign stressing law and order at home and "peace with honor" in Vietnam.

**1968**

*In U.S. v. O'Brien*, the American Civil Liberties Union argues that burning a draft card is an exercise of freedom of expression. The Supreme Court disagrees, ruling that a conviction for violating a statute prohibiting the destruction of an individual's draft card cannot be dismissed on free speech grounds.

**1969**

The Information Processing Techniques Office of the Advanced Research Projects Agency (ARPA; later the Defense Advanced Research Projects Agency, or DARPA) establishes the first wide-area network, the ARPANET, which becomes the foundation for the Internet in the early 1980s.

**1969 (August 1)**

The Military Justice Act of 1968 goes into effect.

**1969 (December 1)**

The lottery draft system replaces the Selective Service System in the United States.

## CHRONOLOGY

**1970 (April)**
President Nixon orders U.S. forces to strike at suspected enemy forces operating within the "Parrot's Beak" border area of Cambodia, unleashing a storm of protests across the United States by opponents of the war.

**1970 (May 4)**
At Kent State University in Ohio, police and National Guard troops, dispatched to quell student rioting, fire on protestors, killing four students and wounding nine others. Unrest on college campuses explodes, forcing many institutions to shut their doors. Ten days later, riots at Jackson State University in Mississippi leave two students dead from Mississippi state trooper bullets.

**1971 (June 13)**
The *New York Times* begins publication of excerpts from the "Pentagon Papers"—the first public appearance of what would eventually emerge as a 47-volume history of American involvement in Vietnam compiled by the Pentagon.

**1972 (June)**
After seven cadets and midshipmen challenge the constitutionality of mandatory chapel attendance at U.S. military academies, a federal appeals court rules that attendance must be voluntary.

**1972 (September 17)**
The television program *M*A*S*H* airs its pilot episode. The series, set during the Korean War but appearing during the Vietnam War, would run until 1983.

**1973**
The Supreme Court rules that the military must offer women the same dependent benefits offered to men.

**1973 (July)**
Military conscription (the draft) ends in the United States in favor of an All Volunteer Force.

**1973 (November)**
Congress passes the War Powers Act.

**1975 (April)**
U.S. helicopters evacuate the embassy in Saigon, South Vietnam, on April 29, and Saigon falls to North Vietnamese forces on April 30. The Vietnam War comes to an end.

**1976**
Military academies in the United States accept the first female cadets.

**1976 (February 19)**
Pres. Gerald Ford formally rescinds Executive Order 9066, which Pres. Franklin Roosevelt had signed in 1942 authorizing the internment during World War II of 120,000 Japanese Americans.

**1978**
*The Deer Hunter*, a Vietnam War film directed by Michael Cimino, premieres.

**1978**
Vietnam Veterans of America is established by Bobby Muller. The organization's founding principle is "Never again shall one generation of veterans abandon another."

**1979**
*Apocalypse Now*, a Vietnam War film directed by Francis Ford Coppola, premieres.

**1979**
Pres. Jimmy Carter commits the nation to build a national museum dedicated to the Holocaust. The museum opens in 1994.

**1979**
The first Army court-martial conviction for sexual harassment results from scandals at Fort Meade, Maryland, involving rapes and other abuse.

**1980**
The third edition of the American Psychiatric Association's *Diagnostic and Statistical Manual for Mental Disorders*

(DSM-III) officially recognizes post-traumatic stress disorder as a condition suffered by many returning soldiers.

**1980**
"Call to Halt the Nuclear Arms Race," a four-page document written by Randall Forsberg of the Institute for Defense and Disarmament Studies, is credited with launching the American nuclear freeze movement.

**1980 (June 1)**
The Cable News Network (CNN) airs its first broadcast, ushering in the era of 24-hour televised news.

**1981**
The Army introduces the Be All You Can Be recruiting campaign, one of the most highly acclaimed and recognized slogans in modern advertising.

**1982**
The Vietnam Veterans Memorial, referred to as "The Wall," designed by Maya Lin, is dedicated on the Mall in Washington, D.C.

**1982**
*First Blood,* the first in the Rambo series of films starring Sylvester Stallone as a maladjusted Vietnam veteran, is released.

**1983**
The United States intervenes in Grenada (Operation Urgent Fury).

**1983**
*WarGames*, a film about the threat of accidental nuclear war directed by John Badham, premieres.

**1984 (November 28)**
Sec. of Defense Caspar Weinberger delivers a speech (The Uses of Military Power) before the National Press Club in Washington. In the speech, he outlines six conditions that should be met before deploying U.S. troops overseas. This speech, later refined by Chairman of the Joint Chiefs Gen. Colin Powell, forms the basis of what would come to be known as the Weinberger–Powell Doctrine.

**1986**
*Platoon*, a Vietnam War film directed by Oliver Stone, premieres.

**1986 (October 1)**
Pres. Ronald Reagan signs the Goldwater–Nichols Act, which seeks to improve the quality of military advice provided to civilian decision makers, to place greater responsibility upon combat commanders, and to institute greater cooperation and coordination among the individual military services.

**1988**
After 44 years of lobbying by the American Civil Liberties Union, Congress acknowledges the government's miscarriage of justice in its wartime treatment of Japanese Americans, and offers $20,000 in reparations to each Japanese American who had been detained in one of the several internment camps in the western United States.

**1989**
*Born on the Fourth of July*, a film directed by Oliver Stone and adapted from the 1976 autobiography by disabled Vietnam veteran Ron Kovic, premieres.

**1989 (June)**
The Polish "Solidarity" trade union, which had been brutally suppressed in 1981 by the Soviet-sponsored Polish government, wins open elections, making it the first noncommunist government in Eastern Europe since the end of World War II.

**1989 (June 4)**
After weeks of student demonstrations in Tiananmen Square, Chinese troops, and tanks crack down on the demonstrators, killing hundreds in what becomes known as the Tiananmen Square Massacre.

**1989 (November 9)**
The Berlin Wall separating East and West Germany is breached, and the border is opened. The formal reunification of Germany in October of the following year marks the end of a Cold War–divided Europe.

**1990**
*The Hunt for Red October*, a Cold War suspense film directed by John McTiernan, premieres.

**1990 (July)**
Under orders of dictator Saddam Hussein, the Iraqi Army occupies neighboring Kuwait. That act prompts the sequence of events that include the mobilization under the name Operation Desert Shield and the Persian Gulf War under the name Operation Desert Storm.

**1990 (September 23–27)**
Ken Burns's documentary *The Civil War* airs on PBS. The series, featuring archival photographs and documents, contemporaneous music, interviews with historians, and narration by a wide range of well-known Americans, would be hailed as one of the most comprehensive documentary treatments of any war ever presented.

**1991 (January 16)**
The U.S. bombing of Baghdad in the Persian Gulf War begins.

**1991 (February 23)**
The ground war in Iraq begins. The cease-fire is proclaimed March 3.

**1991**
Charges of sexual abuse by women attending the Navy's annual Tailhook Convention in Las Vegas, Nevada, lead to investigations and scandal for the Navy.

**1991 (December 25)**
Mikhail Gorbachev resigns as president of the Soviet Union, effectively marking the end of the U.S.S.R.

**1992 (August 21)**
Randall Weaver, refusing to make a required court appearance, retreats with his family to their remote northern Idaho home at Ruby Ridge, beginning a 10-day standoff with U.S. marshals that ends in a bloody siege leaving several dead. The incident helps to fuel a growing antigovernment "militia movement" in the United States that lasts through much of the 1990s.

**1993**
Pres. Bill Clinton announces a more permissive policy on gays and lesbians in the military, immediately challenged in private by the military's Joint Chiefs. A compromise, known as "Don't Ask, Don't Tell," is reached.

**1993 (October 3)**
An American Rapid Reaction Force, in an effort to capture Somali warlord Mohammed Farah Aideed, loses two Blackhawk helicopters and 18 personnel in a battle with Somalis in the streets of Mogadishu. The episode—during which television broadcasts show images of a dead American being dragged through the streets of Mogadishu, along with footage of a captured U.S. airman—effectively ends U.S. involvement in Somalia. It also has a role in shaping U.S. decisions about intervening in other conflicts, including the ethnic genocide in Rwanda the following year.

**1994**
The United States Holocaust Memorial Museum opens in Washington, D.C.

**1995**
The Korean War Veterans Memorial is dedicated on the Mall in Washington, D.C.

**1995**
The *Enola Gay* controversy is prompted by an exhibit planned at the Smithsonian's National Air and Space Museum to commemorate the 50th anniversary of the dropping of an atomic bomb on Hiroshima from the B-29 *Enola Gay*. Several veterans organizations object to the

exhibit's perceived critical slant, leading to substantial revisions to the exhibit.

**1995**

Initially accepted into The Citadel, Shannon Faulkner's application is rejected once her gender becomes known. Her subsequent lawsuit paves the way for her to sign in on August 12, 1995, as the school's first female cadet. Although Faulkner leaves the school after five days, the Board of Visitors is forced to eliminate gender as a criterion for membership in the South Carolina Corps of Cadets.

**1995 (August 19)**

The Alfred P. Murrah Federal Building in Oklahoma City is destroyed by a bomb planted by "militia" enthusiast Timothy McVeigh with the help of Terry Nichols; 168 people die.

**1996**

The Wassenaar Arrangement on Export Controls for Conventional Arms and Dual-Use Goods and Technologies is established to promote transparency and greater responsibility in sales of conventional arms and to contribute to international peace and security by preventing destabilizing accumulations of conventional arms. Thirty-three countries, including the United States, participate in the agreement.

**1998**

*Saving Private Ryan*, a World War II film beginning with the D-Day landings at the beaches of Normandy, France, directed by Stephen Spielberg, premieres.

**1999**

The Panama Canal, controlled by the United States since its opening in 1914, returns to Panamanian control.

**1999 (March 24)**

The North Atlantic Treaty Organization launches Operation Allied Force to halt Serbia's "ethnic cleansing" of Albanians in Kosovo.

**2000**

The National D-Day Museum opens in New Orleans, Louisiana.

**2001 (September 11)**

Four U.S. commercial passenger jets are highjacked by terrorists associated with al Qaeda and crashed into U.S. sites, killing 2,986 people. Two planes hit the twin towers of the World Trade Center in New York, destroying both buildings; another hits the Pentagon in Arlington County, Virginia, just outside the nation's capital; a fourth crashes in a field near Shanksville, Pennsylvania—presumably headed toward a location in Washington, D.C. The September 11 attacks have profound economic, social, cultural, and military effects throughout the world.

**2001 (September 20)**

In an address to a joint session of Congress and to the American people, Pres. George W. Bush uses the phrase "war on terror" to describe the administration's intentions in the wake of the September 11 attacks, setting a seemingly long-term agenda for the country.

**2001 (October 7)**

The United States begins a military campaign against Taliban forces and al Qaeda training camps in Afghanistan.

**2001 (October 26)**

Pres. George W. Bush signs into law the USAPATRIOT Act, which permits the indefinite imprisonment without trial of any non-U.S. citizen the attorney general rules to be a threat to American national security, while relieving the government of any responsibility to provide legal counsel to detainees. The act also contains provisions criticized as infringing excessively on Americans' individual rights.

**2002 (November 25)**

The Department of Homeland Security is established in an effort to protect against terrorist attacks on U.S. soil.

**2003**
A sexual assault scandal unfolds at the U.S. Air Force Academy.

**2003 (March)**
U.S.-led forces begin the bombing of Baghdad on the night of March 21, launching the Iraq War. The ground invasion commences soon thereafter. Numerous reporters, referred to as "embeds," accompany soldiers on the march toward Baghdad, providing unprecedented coverage of war to people around the world.

**2003 (May 1)**
Pres. George W. Bush, appearing on the deck of the USS *Abraham Lincoln* under a banner that reads "Mission Accomplished," declares "major combat operations" in the Iraq War at an end. American troops, however, continue operating in Iraq, becoming more embroiled in the ensuing conflict between Iraqi factions.

**2004 (April)**
The National World War II Memorial opens in Washington, D.C.

**2004 (April 29)**
Photographs of prisoner abuse at Abu Ghraib prison in Iraq are first broadcast on CBS's *60 Minutes II*.

**2004 (July)**
The Senate Intelligence Committee reveals that the military advice given to Pres. George W. Bush about the existence of weapons of mass destruction in Iraq was predicated on faulty information.

**2004 (September)**
A federal judge overturns the USAPATRIOT Act's provision requiring telephone, Internet, and communication companies to respond to law enforcement's requests for access to customers' personal information and call records.

**2004 (September)**
The Pentagon reports that the 1,000th American soldier had been killed in Iraq.

# Documents

1609 Rev. William Symonds's Sermon Criticizing the Virginia Company's Violence against Natives
1611 John Winthrop on the Evils of Gun Ownership
1613 Defense by William Strachey of the Virginia Company's Violence against Natives
1622 Virginia Co. Sec. Edward Waterhouse Defends Company's Conduct during 1622 War
1637 Excerpt from Captain John Underhill's Account of a Raid on a Pequot Village
1654 Letter of Roger Williams
1712 John Barnwell's Expedition against the Tuscaroras of North Carolina
1737 Massachusetts's Rev. William Williams on Just Wars
1747 Massachusetts Lt. Gov. Thomas Hutchinson's Observations on the Boston Press Gang Riot of 1747 in His *History of the Colony*
1759 Petition from Army Wife Martha May for Freedom to Carry Water to Troops
1760 Lt. Col. James Grant and Gen. Jeffrey Amherst Discuss How to Subdue the Cherokees
1766 Comments from British Pamphlet on Colonies' Refusal to Pay Taxes
1768 a A Letter from Samuel Adams to the Boston Gazette
1768 b Excerpts from Tryon's Journal of the Expedition into the Backcountry
1772 Excerpt from "The Dangers of Standing Armies" by Joseph Warren
1774 North Carolina Militia Act of 1774
1775 Peter Oliver's Interview with POW William Scott
1776 a Distribution of Enlisted Men and Officers over Wealthholding Thirds of Total Ratable State Population
1776 b Gen. Washington's Letter to Continental Congress on Reenlistment Difficulties
1776 c Account of Walter Bates, Connecticut Loyalist
1777 a Petition of Samuel Townsend to New York State Convention
1777 b Account Concerning Connecticut Men's Refusal to Serve in the Revolutionary War
1777 c The Rifleman's Song at Bennington
1785 Tory Veteran's Testimony Concerning Treatment by Patriots
1797 Gov. Samuel Adam's Farewell Address
1800 Excerpt from Mason Weems's *A History of the Life and Death, Virtues & Exploits of General George Washington*
1814 Treaty of Ghent
1824 Lyrics to a Popular Song Celebrating Jackson's Victory over the British
1830 Sec. of War John Eaton on Inability to Fill Army Ranks
1833 Revolutionary War Pension Application
1835 A Crisis of Conscience and Ethan Allen Hitchcock
1838 Lyrics to "Benny Havens, Oh!"
1846 a Letter from Pres. James Polk to House of Representatives on Secrecy in Executive Branch Dealings
1846 b Excerpts from The Biglow Papers
1849 Lyrics to "I'm Off For Nicaragua"
1850 Excerpt from A. A. Livermore's *War with Mexico*

1941 Executive Order 8802: Prohibition of Discrimination in the Defense Industry
1942 a Letters from Black Soldiers in World War II
1942 b Black Serviceman Lester Simons's Account of Training Experience
1942 c Marine's Letter to Father Concerning His Experience in Guadalcanal #1
1942 d Marine's Letter to Father Concerning His Experience in Guadalcanal #2
1942 e Monica Itoi Sone's Account of Her Transfer to a Japanese Internment Camp
1942 f Interviews with Japanese-Americans Regarding Mistreatment during World War II
1943 Excerpt from Bill Mauldin's *Up Front*
1944 a Excerpt from Ernie Pyle's *Brave Men*
1944 b Excerpts from *Pacific War Diary 1942–1945* by James J. Fahey
1944 c Black Soldier's Encounter with Racism and its Psychological Effects
1945 a Black Serviceman's Account of Confrontation with Battalion Commander
1945 b Black Soldiers' Recollections of Their Experiences in World War II
1945 c Soldiers' Poems on the Horrors of War
1945 d John Ciardi's "A Box Comes Home"
1945 e Excerpt from Bill Mauldin's *Brass Ring*
1945 f Excerpts from *Company Commander* by Charles B. MacDonald
1946 a Remarks of Navajo Veteran on Serving in the Military
1946 b Excerpts from *Hiroshima* by John Hersey
1947 Excerpts from Bill Mauldin's *Back Home*
1948 a Psychiatric Case History of World War II Tailgunner
1948 b Executive Order 9981: Desegregation of the Armed Forces
1949 Attitude of Veterans and Nonveteran Fathers during World War II Toward Personality Characteristics of First-Born
1950 a World War II Veteran's Account of Experience in Service
1950 b Lyrics to the R.O.T.C. Song
1950 c Random House's Bennett Cerf Praising Military after Attending JCOC
1950 d Excerpt from Harry J. Maihafer's *From the Hudson to the Yalu: West Point in the Korean War*
1951 Recall of Gen. Douglas MacArthur
1953 Case History of World War II Psychiatric Casualty
1957 Excerpt from *Born on the Fourth of July* by Ron Kovic
1961 Pres. Dwight D. Eisenhower's Farewell Address
1964 Veteran Harold Bond's Reflections on Returning to Monte Cassino
1965 a Seymour Melman on America's Aging Metal-Working Machinery
1965 b Selective Service System's Channeling Manpower Memo
1965 c Case Report on Psychiatric Illness of Submariner's Wife
1965 d Letter Home from Serviceman on Combat Experience
1965 f Excerpts from *A Rumor of War* by Philip Caputo
1966 a Letters from Vietnam GIs on Killing Enemies in Combat
1966 b Letter from Vietnam GI Objecting to Antiwar Protesters
1966 c Air Force Officer Dale Noyd's Letter of Resignation
1966 d Excerpts from *Soldados: Chicanos in Viet Nam*
1967 a Postings to Tiger Force Website in Response to *Toledo Blade* Revelations
1967 b Environmental Effects of War in Vietnam
1968 a Accounts of Servicemen's Combat-Related Psychiatric Disorder
1968 b Defense and NASA Spending in Various States
1969 Survey of Veteran's Opinions on Effects of Service
1970 a Open Letter of Chicana GI Widow
1970 b Widow of Air Force Pilot's Account of Her Experience and Attitude Toward the War
1970 c Excerpts from "Pentagon Papers" Supreme Court Briefs

## DOCUMENTS

| | |
|---|---|
| 1971 a | Letters to Editors of *SGT Fury and His Howling Commandos* |
| 1971 b | Interview with U.S. Army Col. David H. Hackworth |
| 1971 c | Drug Use in the Army |
| 1971 d | Did Vietnam Turn GIs into Addicts? |
| 1972 | Remarks of Black Veteran on His Return to Pennsylvania |
| 1973 | War Powers Resolution |
| 1975 | Lt. Keffer's Reflections on Attending a Reunion of Buchenwald Survivors |
| 1976 a | Excerpts from Book Two (Intelligence Activities and the Rights of Americans) of the Church Committee Report |
| 1976 b | Remarks of Deserter on Eve of His Surrender to Authorities |
| 1977 | Remarks of Mother on the Death of Her Son and the Pardon of Draft Resisters |
| 1988 | Editorial on Loss of Military Service as a Rite of Passage by Gerald A. Patterson |
| 2000 | "Principles of Ethical Conduct…The Ultimate Bait and Switch" by Peter L. Duffy |
| 2001 | "The Harvest Matrix 2001" |
| 2004 a | Yale Law School Faculty Suit against Department of Defense Regarding On-campus Recruitment |
| 2004 b | Statement by Christian Leaders Condemning a "Theology of War" |
| 2004 c | Interview with Yale Graduate Tyson Belanger who Served in the Iraq War |

## 1609

### Rev. William Symonds's Sermon Criticizing the Virginia Company's Violence against Natives

*Some of the early English and Scots colonists in their North American "plantations" treated indigenous peoples with unwarranted violence. This led some of their countrymen to remind them of Christian Just War concepts. Example: word came to the spiritual leader of the Plymouth Pilgrims, Pastor John Robinson, in 1623 that the Plantation's employed military leader, Capt. Miles Standish, had led a sortie against Massachusetts Native Americans who had threatened the lives of fur trader Thomas Weston and his men, claiming that Weston had cheated them. Standish had killed several. "Oh, how happy a thing had it been," Robinson wrote, "if you had converted some before you had killed any! . . . [Y]ou being no magistrates over them were to consider [only] what by necessity you were constrained to inflict. Necessity of this . . . I see not . . . [I]ndeed I am afraid lest, by these occasions, others should be drawn to affect a kind of ruffling course in the world." Similarly, in the passage that follows, Rev. William Symonds, troubled by news of the killing of a number of Tidewaters in Virginia, delivered these admonitions during a London religious service for those about to join the first wave of colonists in 1609:*

O but, in entering of other countries, there must needs be much lamentable effusion of blood. Certainly our objector was hatched of some popish egg; & it may be in a JESUITS vault, where they feed themselves fat, with tormenting innocents. Why is there no remedy, but as soon as we come on land, like Wolves, and Lions, and Tigers, long famished, we must tear in pieces, murder, and torment the natural inhabitants, with cruelties never read, nor heard of before? must we needs burn millions of them, and cast millions into the sea? must we bait them with dogs, that shall eat up the mothers with their children? let such be the practices of the devil, of Abaddon the son of perdition, of Antichrist and his frie, that is of purple Rome. As for the professors of the Gospel, they know with Jacob and his posterity, to say to Pharaoh, To Sojourn in the land are we come; for thy servants have no pasture, &c. They can with Sampson live peaceably with the Philistines, till they be constrained by injustice, to stand upon their defence. They can instruct the barbarous princes, as Joseph did Pharaoh and his Senators; and as Daniel did Nabuchad-nezer, &c. And if these objectors had any brains in their head, but those which are sick, they could easily find a difference between a bloody invasion, and the planting of a peaceable Colony, in a waste country, where the people do live but like Deer in herds, and (no not in this stooping age, of the gray headed world, full of years and experience) have not as yet attained unto the first modesty that was in Adam, that knew he was naked, where they know no God but the devil, nor sacrifice, but to offer their men and children unto Moloch. Can it be a sin in Philip, to join himself to an Ethiopian charet? Is only now the ancient planting of Colonies, so highly praised among the Romans, and all other nations, so vile and odious among us, that what is, and hath been a virtue in all others, must be sin in us?

*NOTE: The language and typography in this excerpt have been updated to modern English.*

*SOURCE:* William Symonds, *A Sermon Preached at White-Chappel* (London: Eleazar Edgar, 1609).

*RELATED ENTRIES: Colonial Wars; Just War Theory; Religion and War*

## 1611

### John Winthrop on the Evils of Gun Ownership

*By the time that the English were beginning to colonize North America, the British Parliament had begun to limit the owning and use of firearms largely to men of property, in part to curb the poaching of game on their estates. Nevertheless, some men without property acquired firearms. In 1611 young John Winthrop (soon to become the chief magistrate of the English court at Norwich, East Anglia, and, in time, the first governor of the Puritan's Massachusetts Bay Colony) offered these entertaining thoughts in his diary on his use of his musket.*

Finding by much examination that ordinary shooting in a gun, etc: could not stand with a good conscience in my self, as first, for that it is simply prohibited by the law of the land, upon this ground amongst others, that it spoils more of the creatures than it gets: 2 it procures offence unto many: 3 it wastes great store of time: 4 it toils a man's body overmuch: 5 it endangers a man's life, etc: 6 it brings no profit all things considered: 7 it hazards more of a man's estate by the penalty of it, than a man would willingly part with: 8 it brings a man of worth and godliness into some contempt: —lastly for mine own part I have ever been crossed in using it, for when I have gone about it not without some wounds of conscience, and have taken much pains and hazarded my health, I have gotten sometimes a very little but most commonly nothing at all towards my cost and labor:

Therefore I have solved and covenanted with the Lord to give over altogether shooting at the creek; —and for killing of birds, etc: either to leave that altogether or else to use it, both very seldom and very secretly. God (if he please) can give me fowl by some other means, but if he will not, yet, in that it is [his] will who loves me, it is sufficient to uphold my resolution.

*NOTE: The language and typography in this excerpt have been updated to modern English.*

*SOURCE: Winthrop Papers, vol. 1, 1498–1628* (Boston: Massachusetts Historical Society, 1929).

*RELATED ENTRIES: Colonial Militia Systems; European Military Culture, Influence of; Gun Ownership; Militia Groups*

## 1613

### Defense by William Strachey of the Virginia Company's Violence against Natives

*Criticism of the treatment by Virginia colonists of some of their Rapahanock and Powhatan Confederacy neighbors continued to be expressed in English circles, prompting that colony's secretary, William Strachey, to include these passages in the company's defense within his report of the colony's first five years of operation.*

. . . What open and actual injury shall we do to the poor and innocent inhabitants to intrude upon them? I must ask them again, In which shall we offer them injury? for proffering them trade, or the knowledge of Christ? From one of these two or both the injury must proceed. Why? What injury can it be to people of any nation for Christians to come unto their ports, havens, or territories, when the law of nations (which is the law of God and man[)] doth privilege all men to do so, which admits it lawful to trade with any manner of people, in so much as no man is to take upon him (that knoweth any thing) the defence of the savages in this point, since the savages themselves may not impugn or forbid the same, in respect of common fellowship and community betwixt man and man; albeit I will not deny but that the savages may (without peradventure) be ignorant of as much, and (alas) of more graces beside, and particularities of humanity, the reason whereof being, because (poor souls) they know not the good which they stand in need of; but we that are Christians do know how this law (enriching all kingdoms) gives privileges to ambassadors, keeps the seas common and safe, lays open ports and havens, and allows free scales and liberal access for whosoever that will import unto them such commodities as their countries have, and they want; or export from them some of their plenty (duties and customs provincial observed). If this be so for the first, concerning the other it may fully be answered with this demand, shall it not follow, if traffic be thus justifiable (which intended nothing but transitory profit and increase of temporal and worldly goods) shall not planting the Christian faith be much more? Yes by how much the divine good (not subject to change, and under no alteration), excels, takes an account, and surveys, and surpasseth all things, and all our actions are to bend their intentions thitherward; and what way soever we make, yet miserable and wretched he whose every line he draws, every act and thought do not close and meet in the center of that. . . .

But yet it is injurious to the natural inhabitants, still say ours. Wherefore? It is because it is, now indeed, a most doughty and material reason, a great piece of injury to bring them (to invert our English proverb) out of the warm sun, into God's blessing; to bring them from bodily wants, confusion, misery, and these outward anguishes, to the knowledge of a better practice, and improving of these benefits (to a more and ever during advantage, and to a civiler use) which God hath given unto them, but involved and hid in the bowels and womb of their land (to them barren and unprofitable, because unknown); nay, to exalt, as I may say, mere privation to the highest degree of perfection, by bringing their wretched souls (like Cerberus, from hell) from the chains of Satan, to the arms and bosom of their Saviour: here is a most impious piece of injury. Let me remember what Mr. Simondes, preacher of St. Saviour's, saith in this behalf: It is as much, saith he, as if a father should be said to offer violence to his child, when he beats him to bring him to goodness. Had not this violence and this injury been offered to us by the Romans (as the warlike Scots did the same, likewise, in Caledonia, unto the Picts), even by Julius Caesar himself, then by the emperor Claudius, who was therefore called Britannicus, and his captains, Aulus Plautius and Vespatian (who took in the Isle of Wight); and lastly, by the first lieutenant sent hither, Ostorius Scapula (as writes Tacitus in the life of Agricola), who reduced the conquered parts of our barbarous island into provinces, and established in them colonies of old soldiers; building castles and towns, and in every corner teaching us even to know the powerful discourse of divine reason (which makes us only men, and distinguisheth us from beasts, amongst whom we lived as naked and as beastly as they). We might yet have lived overgrown satyrs, rude and untutored, wandering in the woods, dwelling in caves, and hunting for our dinners, as the wild beasts in the forests for their prey, prostituting our daughters to strangers, sacrificing our children to idols, nay, eating our own children, as did the Scots in those days, as reciteth Tho. Cogan, bachelor of physic, in his book De Sanitate, cha. 137, printed 1189, . . .

All the injury that we purpose unto them, is but the amendment of these horrible heathenisms, and the reduction of them to the aforesaid manly duties, and to the knowledge (which the Romans could not give us) of that God who must save both them and us, and who bought us alike with a dear sufferance and precious measure of mercy.

For the apter enabling of our selves unto which so heavenly an enterprise, who will think it an unlawful act to fortify and strengthen our selves (as nature requires) with the best helps, and by sitting down with guards and forces about us in the waste and vast unhabited grounds of theirs, amongst a world of which not one foot of a thousand do they either use, or know how to turn to any benefit; and therefore lies so great a circuit vain and idle before them? Nor is this any injury unto them, from whom we will not forcibly take of their provision and labours, nor make rape of what they cleanse and manure; but prepare and break up new grounds, and thereby open unto them likewise a new way of thrift or husbandry; for as a righteous man (according to Solomon) ought to regard the life of his beast, so surely Christian men should not show themselves like wolves to devour, who cannot forget that every soul which God hath sealed for himself he hath done it with the print of charity and compassion; and therefore even every foot of land which we shall take unto our use, we will bargain and buy of them, for copper, hatchets, and such like commodities, for which they will even sell themselves, and with which they can purchase double that quantity from their neighbours; and thus we will commune and entreat with them, truck, and barter, our commodities for theirs, and theirs for ours (of which they seem more fain) in all love and friendship, until, for our good purposes towards them, we shall find them practice violence [no more].

*NOTE: The language and typography in this excerpt have been updated to modern English.*

*SOURCE:* William Strachey, *The Historie of Travaile into Virginia Britannia* (London: Hackluyt Society, 1849).

*RELATED ENTRIES: Colonial Wars; Just War Theory*

## 1622

### Virginia Company Sec. Edward Waterhouse Defends Company's Conduct during 1622 War

*A defense similar to the one above (see document, 1613), but one more frank in its tone, was offered nine years later by Strachey's successor, Edward Waterhouse, after the Powhatan had attacked the colony in 1622, killing 25 percent of its population, in an attempt to regain lands and sovereignty.*

THUS have you seen the particulars of this massacre, out of Letters from thence written, wherein treachery and cruelty have done their worst to us, or rather to themselves; for whose understanding is so shallow, as not to perceive that this must needs be for the good of the Plantation after, and the loss of this blood to make the body more healthful, as by these reasons may be manifest.

First, Because betraying of innocency never rests unpunished: And therefore Agesilaus, when his enemies (upon whose oath of being faithful he rested) had deceived him, he sent them thanks, for that by their perjury, they had made God his friend, and their enemy.

Secondly, Because our hands which before were tied with gentleness and fair usage, are now set at liberty by the treacherous violence of the Savages not untying the Knot, but cutting it: So that we, who hitherto have had possession of no more ground than their waste, and our purchase at a valuable consideration to their own contentment, gained; may now by right of War, and law of Nations, invade the Country, and destroy them who fought to destroy us: whereby we shall enjoy their cultivated places, turning the laborious Mattock into the victorious Sword (wherein there is more both ease, benefit, and glory) and possessing the fruits of others labours. Now their cleared grounds in all their villages (which are situate in the fruitfullest places of the land) shall be inhabited by us, whereas heretofore the grubbing of woods was the greatest labour.

Thirdly, Because those commodities which the Indians enjoyed as much or rather more than we, shall now also be entirely possessed by us. The Deer and other beasts will be in safety, and infinitely increase, which heretofore not only in the general huntings of the King (whereat four or five hundred Deer were usually slain) but by each particular Indian were destroyed at all times of the year, without any difference of Male, Dame, or Young. The like may be said of our own Swine and Goats, whereof they have used to kill eight in ten more than the English have done. There will be also a great increase of wild Turkeys, and other weighty Fowl, for the Indians never put difference of destroying the Hen, but kill them whether in season or not, whether in breeding time, or sitting on their eggs, or having new hatched, it is all one to them: whereby, as also by the orderly using of their fishing Wares, no other known Country in the world will so plentifully abound in victual.

Fourthly, Because the way of conquering them is much more easy than of civilizing them by fair means, for they are a rude, barbarous, and naked people, scattered in small companies, which are helps to Victory, but hinderances to Civility: Besides that, a conquest may be of many, and at once; but civility is in particular, and flow, the effect of long time, and great industry. Moreover, victory of them may be gained many ways; by force, by surprise, by famine in burning their Corn, by destroying and burning their Boats, Canoes, and Houses, by breaking their fishing Wares, by assailing them in their huntings, whereby they get the greatest part of their sustenance in Winter, by pursuing and chasing them with our horses, and blood-Hounds to draw after them, and Mastiffs to tear them, which take this naked, tanned, deformed Savages, for no other than wild beasts, and are so fierce and fell upon them, that they fear them worse than their own Devil which they worship, supposing them to be a new and worse kind of Devils than their own. By these and sundry other ways, as by driving them (when they flee) upon their enemies, who are round about them, and by animating and abetting their enemies against them, may their ruin or subjection be soon effected. . . .

Fiftly, Because the Indians, who before were used as friends, may now most justly be compelled to servitude and drudgery, and supply the [?] of men that labour, whereby even the meanest of the Plantation may employ themselves more entirely in their Arts and Occupations, which are more generous, whilst Savages perform their inferiour works of digging in mines, and the like, of whom also some may be sent for the service of the Sommer Ilands.

Sixtly, This will for ever hereafter make us more cautious and circumspect, as never to be deceived more by any other treacheries, but will serve for a great instruction to all posterity there, to teach them that Trust is the mother of Deceit, and to learn them that of the Italian, Chi non fida, non s'ingamuu, He that trusts is not deceived; and make them know that kindnesses are misspent upon rude natures, so long as they continue rude; as also, that Savages and Pagans are above all other for matter of Justice ever to be suspected. Thus upon this Anvil shall we now beat out to our selves an armour of proof, which shall for ever after defend us from barbarous Incursions, and from greater dangers that otherwise might happen. And so we may truly say according to the French Proverb, Aquelq, chose malheur est bon, Ill luck is good for something.

Lastly, We have this benefit more to our comfort, because all good men do now take much more care of us than before, since the fault is on their sides, not on ours, who have used so-fair a carriage, even to our own destruction. Especially his Majesties most gracious, tender and paternal care is manifest herein, who by his Royal bounty and goodness, hath continued his many favors unto us, with a new, large, & Princely supply of Munition and Arms, out of his Majesties own store in the Tower, being graciously bestowed for the safety and advancement of the Plantation. As also his Royal favor is amply extended in a large supply of men and other necessaries throughout the whole Kingdom, which are very shortly to be sent to VIRGINIA.

*NOTE: The language and typography in this excerpt have been updated to modern English.*

*SOURCE:* Edward Waterhouse, *A Declaration of the State of the Colony and the Affaires in Virginia* (London, 1622).

*RELATED ENTRIES: Colonial Wars; Just War Theory; Religion and War*

## 1637

### Excerpt from Captain John Underhill's Account of a Raid on a Pequot Village

*Several thousand Puritans from England and the Massachusetts Bay Colony migrated in the mid-1630s to what is now Connecticut. In the eastern half of that region they came to loggerheads with the powerful Pequot nation whose people brooked no trespass on their domains. Violent encounters between Pequot and newcomers led to a Puritan punitive expedition in 1637. Capt. John Underhill, a Puritan settler who had gained military experience in the service of Philip William, prince of Orange, while self-exiled with his fellow Puritans in Holland, commanded the Massachusetts Bay contingent of this expedition. His account of the ensuing war includes these passages. Note the evidence of a cultural difference between the ways that Europeans their Narragansett and Mohegan allies conceived of the limits to war.*

. . . Having our swords in our right hand, our Carbines or Muskets in our left hand; we approached the Fort. Master Hedge being shot threw both arms, and more wounded; though it be not commendable for a man to make mention of any thing that might tend to his own honour; yet because I would have the providence of God observed, and his Name magnified, as well as for my self as others, I dare not omit, but let the world know, that deliverance was given to us that command, as well as to private soldiers. Captaine Mason and my self entering into the Wigwams, he was shot, and received many Arrows against his head-piece, God preserved him from any wounds; my self received a shot in the left hip, through a sufficient Buffcoat that if I had not been supplied with such a garment the Arrow would have pierced through me; another I received between neck and shoulders, hanging in the linen of my Head-piece, others of our soldiers were shot some through the shoulders, some in the face, some in the head, some in the legs; Captaine Mason and my self losing each of us a man, and had near twenty wounded: most courageously these Pequots behaved themselves; but seeing the Fort was too hot for us, we devised a way how we might save our selves and prejudice them; Captaine Mason entering into a Wigwam, brought out a fire-brand, after he had wounded many in the house, then he set fire on the West-side where he entered, my self set fire on the South end with a train of Powder, the fires of both meeting in the center of the Fort blazed most terribly, and burnt all in the space of half an hour; many courageous fellows were unwilling to come out, and fought most desperately through the Palisadoes, so as they were scorched and burnt with the very flame, and were deprived of their arms, in regard the fire burnt their very bowstrings, and so perished valiantly: mercy they did deserve for their valour, could we have had opportunity to have bestowed it; many were burnt in the Fort, both men, women, and children, others forced out, and came in troops to the Indians, twenty, and thirty at a time, which our soldiers received and entertained with the point of the sword; down fell men, women, and children, those that escaped us, fell into the hands of the Indians, that were in the rear of us; it is reported by themselves, that there were about four hundred souls in this Fort, and not above five of them escaped out of our hands. Great and doleful was the bloody sight to the view of young soldiers that never had been in War, to see so many souls lie gasping on the ground so thick in some places, that you could hardly pass along. It may be demanded, Why should you be so furious (as some have said) should not Christians have more mercy and compassion? But I would refer you to David's war, when a people is grown to such a height of blood, and sin against God and man, and all confederates in the action, there he hath no respect to persons, but harrows them, and saws them, and puts them to the sword, and the most terriblest death that may be; sometimes the Scripture declareth women and children must perish with their parents; sometime the case alters: but we will not dispute it now. We had sufficient light from the word of God for our proceedings. . . .

. . . Our Indians came to us, [sic]-eyed at our victories, and greatly admired the manner of English men's fight; but cried mach it, mach it; that is, it is naught, it is naught, because it is too furious, and slays too many men. Having received their desires, they freely promised, and gave up themselves to march along with us, wherever we would go.

*NOTE: The language and typography in this excerpt have been updated to modern English.*

*SOURCE:* John Underhill, *Newes from America; or, a New and Experimentall Discoverie of New England* (London: Peter Cole, 1638).

*RELATED ENTRIES: Colonial Wars; European Military Culture, Influence of; Just War Theory; Militarization and Militarism*

## 1654

### Letter of Roger Williams

*The founder of the Rhode Island colony, Roger Williams, maintained a lively correspondence with the government of his northern colonial neighbor, Massachusetts Bay. This included some protests against what he felt were that colony's failure to maintain some basic Just War principles in its dealings with Rhode Island's closest Native American neighbors, the Narragansett. Here he reminds the government in Boston that "all men of conscience or prudence ply to windward, to maintain their wars to be defensive. . . . "*

To the General Court of the Massachusetts Bay Colony
To the General Court of Massachusetts Bay.

Providence, 5, 8, 54. (so called.)
[October 5, 1654.]

Much Honored Sirs,—I truly wish you peace, and pray your gentle acceptance of a word, I hope not unreasonable.

We have in these parts a sound of your meditations of war against these natives, amongst whom we dwell. I consider that war is one of those three great, sore plagues, with which it pleaseth God to affect the sons of men. I consider, also, that I refused, lately, many offers in my native country, out of a sincere desire to seek the good and peace of this.

I remember, that upon the express advice of your ever honored Mr. Winthrop, deceased, I first adventured to begin a plantation among the thickest of these barbarians.

That in the Pequot wars, it pleased your honored government to employ me in the hazardous and weighty service of negotiating a league between yourselves and the Narragansetts, when the Pequot messengers, who fought the Narragansetts' league against the English, had almost ended that my work and life together.

That at the subscribing of that solemn league, which, by the mercy of the Lord, I had procured with the Narragansetts, your government was pleased to send unto me the copy of it, subscribed by all hands there, which yet I keep as a monument and a testimony of peace and faithfulness between you both.

That, since that time, it hath pleased the Lord so to order it, that I have been more or less interested and used in all your great transactions of war or peace, between the English and the natives, and have not spared purse, nor pains, nor hazards, (very many times,) that the whole land, English and natives, might sleep in peace securely.

That in my last negotiations in England, with the Parliament, Council of State, and his Highness, I have been forced to be known so much, that if I should be silent, I should not only betray mine own peace and yours, but also should be false to their honorable and princely names, whose loves and affections, as well as their supreme authority are not a little concerned in the peace or war of this country.

At my last departure for England, I was importuned by the Narragansett Sachems, and especially by Ninigret, to present their petition to the high Sachems of England, that they might not be forced from their religion, and, for not changing their religion, be invaded by war; for they said they were daily visited with threatenings by Indians that came from about the Massachusetts, that if they would not pray, they should be destroyed by war. With this their petition I acquainted, in private discourses, divers of the chief of our nation, and especially his Highness, who, in many discourses I had with him, never expressed the least tittle of displeasure, as hath been here reported, but in the midst of disputes, ever expressed a high spirit of love and gentleness, and was often pleased to please himself with very many questions, and my answers, about the Indian affairs of this country; and, after all hearing of yourself and us, it hath pleased his Highness and his Council to grant, amongst other favors to this colony, some expressly concerning the very Indians, the native inhabitants of this jurisdiction.

I, therefore, humbly offer to your prudent and impartial view, first these two considerable terms, it pleased the Lord to use to all that profess his name (Rom 12:18,) if it be possible, and all men.

I never was against the righteous use of the civil sword of men or nations, but yet since all men of conscience or prudence ply to windward, to maintain their wars to be defensive, (as did both King and Scotch, and English and Irish too, in the late wars,) I humbly pray your consideration, whether it be not only possible, but very easy, to live and die in peace with all the natives of this country.

For, secondly, are not all the English of this land, generally, a persecuted people from their native soil? and hath not the God of peace and Father of mercies made these natives more friendly in this, than our native countrymen in our own land to us? Have they not entered leagues of love, and to this day continued peaceable commerce with us? Are not our families grown up in peace amongst them? Upon which I humbly ask, how it can suit with Christian ingenuity to take hold of some seeming occasions for their destructions, which, though the heads be only aimed at, yet, all experience tells us, falls on the body and the innocent.

*NOTE: The language and typography in this excerpt have been updated to modern English.*

*SOURCE:* Roger Williams, *The Complete Writings of Roger Williams,* vol. 6 (New York: Russell & Russell, 1963).

*RELATED ENTRIES: Colonial Wars; Just War Theory; Religion and War*

## 1712

### John Barnwell's Expedition against the Tuscaroras of North Carolina

*In September 1711 the Tuscarora people of eastern North Carolina launched an attack against encroaching European colonists. The Tuscarora were particularly disturbed by the founding of New Bern in 1710, but they were also responding to a long series of aggressive actions engaged in by traders and slave raiders. The Tuscarora's initial attacks devastated the white frontier, and North Carolinians, generally powerless to respond, asked for help. South Carolina dispatched an expedition of 33 whites and about 500 allied Native Americans (mostly Yamassee) under the command of Col. John Barnwell. Barnwell marched into the southern Tuscarora towns, and, in a complicated series of sieges, truces, broken truces, and more sieges, he forced the capitulation of a major Tuscarora force defending a fort near Hancock's Town (or Catechna). Barnwell and his men and allies returned to South Carolina. Possibly because of Barnwell's actions in taking slaves from among the Tuscarora, war quickly broke out again and would continue sporadically as late as 1715. The following excerpts from his journal convey a sense of Barnwell's tactics and attitudes toward Native Americans.*

The 29th I marched hard all day and most of the night, that if possible I might surprise this great town, but to my great disappointment they discovered us, being continually upon their guard since the massacre [i.e. the Tuscaroras' initial attack]. Tho' this be called a town, it is only a plantation here and there scattered about the Country, no where 5 houses together, and then 1/4 a mile such another and so on for several miles, so it is impossible to surprize many before the alarm takes. They have lately built small forts at about a miles distance from one another where ye men sleep all night & the women & children, mostly in the woods; I have seen 9 of these Forts and none of them a month old, & some not quite finished.

*[Barnwell stormed one fort at Narhontes, and]*

Next morning ye Tuscaruro town of Kenta came to attack us, but at such a distance I could not come up with them so I ordered two of Capt. Jack's Company to cross a great Swamp that lay at the back of us and ly close untill they heard our firing, and then to come on the back or rear of the Enemy if possible to surround them, accordingly they did, but being two [too] eager, they did not time [it properly, and we took] but 9 scalps & 2 prisoners which I ordered immediately to be burned alive.

*[Now with an army of 153 whites and 128 Indians, Barnwell besieged Hancock's Fort. Progress was slow, and required the digging of zigzag approach trenches. Finally the trenches came up the palisade wall, and]*

.. . . we gained ye ditch & sevll times fired ye pallisades wch ye enemy like desperate villians defended at an amazing rate. This siege for variety of action, salleys, attempts to be relieved from without, can't I believe be parallelled agst Indians. Such bold attacks as they made at our trenches flinted the edge of those Raw soldiers, that tho' they were wholly under ground yet they would quitt their posts and with extreme difficulty be prevaled upon to resume them. The subtell Enemy finding the disadvantage they were under in sallying open to attack our works took ye same method as we did and digged under ground to meet our approaches. . .

*[Barnwell found the effort of assault too costly in lives and especially time, so he finally offered terms under which the Tuscaroras could surrender. They agreed to a list of articles that included admitting Barnwell's force into the fort. Barnwell paraded his forces through the entrance and]*

I might see by the strength of the place a good many would be killed before it could be forced. Some base people was urging to take this opportunity [to seize the Tuscaroras] but I would sooner die. In truth they were murderers, but if our Indians found that there could be no dependence on our promises, it might prove of ill consequence . . .

*NOTE: The language and typography in this excerpt have been updated to modern English.*

*SOURCE:* "Journal of John Barnwell," *Virginia Magazine of History and Biography* 5, no. 6 (1898–99): 42–55, 391–402.

*RELATED ENTRIES: Colonial Wars; European Military Culture, Influence of*

# 1737

## Massachusetts's Rev. William Williams on Just Wars

*In the 18th century, sermons on Just War were to be heard in a number of the settled British colonies of North America. A prominent Presbyterian minister, Gilbert Tennent, offered one in Pennsylvania in the 1740s. The passages below are drawn from a sermon preached before "the Honorable [Massachusetts] Artillery Company [on] the day of their [sic] election of officers" in 1737 by the Congregationalist minister William Williams.*

. . . a Christian State . . . exposed to the *Incursions and Ravages* of proud, ambitious or covetous Men . . . is needful, that they should take care for their own *Security* and *Defence*. God can indeed, make those who are disposed to be their *Enemies, to be at peace with them*. And it is the highest interest of any People to labour to be in good terms with the great Ruler and Governour of the world; and *to put their trust in Him*, as their defence. Yet since, according to the ordinary Course of Providence, his own People have seldom enjoyed *lasting peace*, but have been expos'd to Invasions and Incroachments of unreasonable Men, therefore it is needful and prudent for them to be upon their Guard and Defence, and be able to *repel force by force*. Otherwise their Civil and Sacred Liberties, their Lives and Properties, and all that is dear unto them, may be in the utmost hazard. So that by the *principles*, which the God who hath made us, hath implanted in us, it is plain that Christians need Armour of Defence against their Enemies, that they may not be made a Prey unto Devourers.

*Self-preservation* is a fundamental Law of humane Nature, and *Christianity* does not overthrow any such Laws but establish them.—This is intimated to us, by that of *our Lord* to his Disciples, *Luk.* 22, 35, 36.—*He said unto them, when I sent you without purse and scrip and shoes, lacked ye any thing? and they said nothing. Then said He unto them, But now he that hath a purse let him take it,—and he that hath no Sword let him sell his Garment and buy one:* Signifying, "that the Instruction which He gave them for the Execution of their first Commission, was but temporal, and for that time only observable, now the time requireth that you be armed to Encounter many Difficulties. Now the posture of your affairs will be much altered, you must expect Enemies and Oppositions; and the Tragedy will begin with me—. You stand concerned to make as good *preparation* as you can in these things, &c." If our Lord does not design to teach *Ministers* to take *Arms for their Defence*, nor in the least intend that the Gospel should be propagated by the *Sword*, yet he intimates to them and to all succeeding *Christians*, that they must not expect or depend on *Miracles* for their Supply or *Defence*,—but that the Sword may become as necessary as our *Cloathing*.—Nor is this at all inconsistent with that Repremand of our Saviour unto *Peter, Mat.* 26. 52. *Then said Jesus unto him, put up thy Sword now into its place; for all they that take the Sword shall perish with the Sword.* For this is to be understood, of private *Persons* taking up the Sword against the lawful *Magistrate*, or *Persons* who have not a *lawful* Call or Warrant. And thus all *Christians* are to learn the *same Lesson*. Men must have the Sword orderly put into their hands, before they may use it. It was not the Design of our Saviour to set up a *Temporal Kingdom*, or civil Dominion, as he saith, in another place, "*My Kingdom is not of this world, else would my Servants fight,*" (Joh. 18. 36.) or they might reasonably do it.

The lawfulness of *weapons of War*, and the benefit of well appointed Arms, disciplined and skilful Soldiers, has been well shew'd from this Desk,—Let it suffice therefore, now to suggest,

That the Lord himself hath this Title given Him as his great Honour: particularly in that *Song of Triumph* after the miraculous Destruction of his People's *Enemies, Exod.* 15. *Jehovah is a Man of War*—. And how often is he call'd, *The Lord of Hosts?*—The *Lord strong and mighty*:—the *Lord mighty in Battle!*—This at least, intimates that a warlike Genius, dextrous Skill and undaunted Courage, are honourable qualifications among Men.

*NOTE: The language and typography in this excerpt have been updated to modern English.*

*SOURCE:* William Williams, *Martial Wisdom Recommended; A Sermon Preached [to] the Honorable Artillery Company [on] the day of their election of officers* (Boston, 1737).

*RELATED ENTRIES: Colonial Wars; Just War Theory; Religion and War*

## 1747

### Massachusetts Lt. Gov. Thomas Hutchinson's Observations on the Boston Press Gang Riot of 1747 in His *History of the Colony*

*Britain's imperial wars of the 18th century created seasonal demands for additional naval personnel. British naval conscription measures of the day, authorized by Parliament, were simple and direct. The vessel in need sent a "press gang" of sailors under the command of an officer ashore to draft ("impress") unwary men possessed of no skill or trade that would have exempted them from such treatment. Commodore Charles Knowles, commanding a small squadron of warships in the vicinity of Boston in 1747, sent such a party ashore to find replacements for some sailors who had deserted. When they seized a number of likely candidates, word of their presence spread quickly and a number of Knowles's officers, dining with Lt. Gov. Thomas Hutchinson, found themselves besieged and threatened by a large and angry mob. The lieutenant governor's report of the incident follows.*

In 1747 (Nov. 17th) happened a tumult in the town of Boston equal to any which had preceded it, although far short of some that have happened since. Mr. Knowles was commodore of a number of men of war then in the harbour of Nantasket. Some of the sailors had deserted. The commodore

. . . thought it reasonable that Boston should supply him with as many men as he had lost and, sent his boats up to town early in the morning, and surprized not only as many seamen as could be found on board any of the ships, outward bound as well as others, but swept the wharfs also, taking some ship carpenters apprentices and labouring land men. However tolerable such a surprize might have been in London it could not be borne here. The people had not been used to it and men of all orders resented it, but the lower class were beyond measure enraged and soon assembled with sticks, clubs, pitchmops, etc. They first seized an innocent lieutenant who happened to be ashore upon other business. They had then formed no scheme, and the speaker of the house passing by and assuring them that he knew that the lieutenant had no hand in the press they suffered him to be led off to a place of safety. The mob increasing and having received intelligence that several of the commanders were at the governor's house, it was agreed to go and demand satisfaction. The house was soon surrounded and the court, or yard before the house, filled, but many persons of discretion inserted themselves and prevailed so far as to prevent the mob from entering. Several of the officers had planted themselves at the head of the stair way with loaded carbines and seemed determined to preserve their liberty or lose their lives. A deputy sheriff attempting to exercise his authority, was seized by the mob and carried away in triumph and set in the stocks, which afforded them diversion and tended to abate their rage and disposed them to separate and go to dinner.

As soon as it was dusk, several thousand people assembled in king-street, below the town house where the general court was sitting. Stones and brickbatts were thrown through the glass into the council chamber. The governor, however, with several gentlemen of the council and house ventured into the balcony and, after silence was obtained, the governor in a well judged speech expressed his great disapprobation of the impress and promised his utmost endeavours to obtain the discharge of every one of the inhabitants, and at the same time gently reproved the irregular proceedings both of the forenoon and evening. Other gentlemen also attempted to persuade the people to disperse and wait to see what steps the general court would take. All was to no purpose. The seizure and restraint of the commanders and other officers who were in town was insisted upon as the only effectual method to procure the release of the inhabitants aboard the ships.

It was thought advisable for the governor to withdraw to his house, many of the officers of the militia and other gentlemen attending him. A report was raised that a barge from one of the ships was come to a wharf in the town. The mob flew to seize it, but by mistake took a boat belonging to a Scotch ship and dragged it, with as much seeming ease through the street as if it had been in the water, to the governor's house and prepared to burn it before the house, but from a consideration of the danger of setting the town on fire were diverted and the boat was burnt in a place of less hazard. The next day the governor ordered that the military officers of Boston should cause their companies to be mustered and to appear in arms, and that a military watch should be kept the succeeding night, but the drummers were interrupted and the militia refused to appear. The governor did not think it for his honour to remain in town another night and privately withdrew to the castle. A number of gentlemen who had some intimation of his design, sent a message to him by Col. Hutchinson, assuring him they would stand by him in maintaining the authority of government and restoring peace and order, but he did not think this sufficient.

The governor wrote to Mr. Knowles representing the confusions occasioned by this extravagant act of his officers, but he refused all terms of accommodation until the commanders and other officers on shore were suffered to go on board their ships, and he threatened to bring up his ships and bombard the town, and some of them coming to sail, caused different conjectures of his real intention. Capt. Erskine of the Canterbury had been seized at the house of Col. Brinley in Roxbury and given his parole not to go aboard, and divers inferior officers had been secured.

The 17th, 18th and part of the 19th, the council and house of representatives, sitting in the town, went on with their ordinary business, not willing to interpose lest they should encourage other commanders of the navy to future acts of the like nature, but towards noon of the 19th some of the principal members of the house began to think more seriously of the dangerous consequence of leaving the governor without support when there was not the least ground of exception to his conduct. Some high spirits in the town began to question whether his retiring should be deemed a desertion or abdication. It was moved to appoint a committee of the two houses to consider what was proper to be done. This would take time and was excepted to, and the speaker was desired to draw up such resolves as it was thought necessary the house should immediately agree to, and they were passed by a considerable majority and made public.

> In the house of representatives, Nov. 19th, 1747.
>
> Resolved, that there has been and still continues, a tumultuous riotous assembling of armed seamen, servants, negroes and others in the town of Boston, tending to the destruction of all government and order.
>
> Resolved, that it is incumbent on the civil and military officers in the province to exert themselves to the utmost, to discourage and suppress all such tumultuous riotous proceedings whensoever they may happen.
>
> Resolved, that this house will stand by and support with their lives and estates his excellency the governor and the executive part of the government in all endeavors for this purpose.
>
> Resolved, that this house will exert themselves by all ways and means possible in redressing such grievances as his majesty's subjects are and have been under, which may have been the cause of the aforesaid tumultuous disorderly assembling together.
>
> T. Hutchinson, Speaker.

The council passed a vote ordering that Captain Erskine and all other officers belonging to his majesty's ships should be forthwith set at liberty and protected by the government, which was concurred by the house. As soon as these votes were known, the tumultuous spirit began to subside. The inhabitants of the town of Boston assembled in town meeting in the afternoon, having been notified to consider, in general, what was proper for them to do upon this occasion, and notwithstanding it was urged by many that all measures to suppress the present spirit in the people would tend to encourage the like oppressive acts for the future, yet the contrary party prevailed and the town, although they expressed their sense of the great insult and injury by the impress, condemned the tumultuous riotous acts of such as had insulted the governor and the other branches of the legislature and committed many other heinous offences.

The governor, not expecting so favorable a turn, had wrote to the secretary to prepare orders for the colonels of the regiments of Cambridge, Roxbury and Milton and the regiment of horse to have their officers and men ready to march at an hour's warning to such place of rendezvous as he should direct; . . . Commodore [Knowles] dismissed most, if not all, of the inhabitants who had been impressed, and the squadron sailed to the great joy of the rest of the town.

*SOURCE:* Thomas Hutchinson, *The History of the Colony of Massachusetts-Bay*, 2nd ed. (London, 1765–1828), 2: 489–92.

*RELATED ENTRIES: Colonial Militia Systems; Colonial Wars; Impressment*

## 1759

### Petition from Army Wife Martha May for Freedom to Carry Water to Troops

*European and American colonial military forces were often accompanied by women— spouses of soldiers serving in the regiment or others employed to cook, sew, and wash for the troops. When the soldier-husband of such a "camp follower" was killed, or when he ran afoul of military discipline, the man's wife could experience real distress, especially if, as in this case, she reacted in a manner that offended the power-that-was.*

Carlisle

4th June 1759

Honoured Sr/

Please to hear the Petition of your Poor unfortunate Servant Martha May now confined in Carlisle Gaol Please your Honr as my husband is an Old Soldier and Seeing him taken out of the Ranks to be Confined Put me in Such a Passion that I was almost beside myself but being informed, after that I abused Yr Honour, to a High degree for which I ask Yr Honour a Thousand Pardons, and am Really Sorrow for what I have said&done; Knowing Yr Honour to be a Compationate, and Merciful Man, I beg and hope you will take it into Consideration that it was the Love I had for my Poor husband; and no—hill will to Yr Honour, which was the cause of abusing so good a Colonel as you are. Please to Sett me at Liberty this time & I never will dis-oblige yr Honour nor any other Officer belonging to the Army for the future as I have been a Wife 22 years and have Traveld with my Husband every Place or Country the Company Marcht too and have workt very-hard ever since I was in the Army I hope yr honour will be so Good as to pardon me this [onct (stricken out)] time that I may go with my Poor Husband one time more to carry him and my good officers water in ye hottest Battles as I have done before.

I am
Yr unfortunate petitioner and Humble Servant
Mara May
[Endorsed] Petition of Martha May to carry Water to the Soldiers in the heat of Battle.
[Addressed]
To the Right Honble Colonel Bouquet

*SOURCE:* Martha May to Henry Bouquet, June 4, 1758, in *The Papers of Henry Bouquet*, vol. 2, page 30.

*RELATED ENTRIES: Camp Followers; Colonial Wars; Families, Military; Women in the Military*

## 1760

### Lt. Col. James Grant and Gen. Jeffrey Amherst Discuss How to Subdue the Cherokees

*Frontier friction between the Cherokee of the southern Appalachians and white settlers led to three expeditions against the Cherokee from 1759 to 1761. The 1760 expedition had destroyed a number of Cherokee villages, but had not ended the war. In the following excerpts, British Gen. Jeffrey Amherst and Lt. Col. James Grant, the designated commander of an expedition to begin in the spring of 1761, discuss how to defeat the Cherokee. Their discussion highlights a number of patterns in British wars against Native Americans: the intention to "chastise" rather than conquer; the reliance on devastation as a strategy; and the seemingly insoluble problem of what to do if indigenous peoples merely fled and refused to surrender or make peace.*

[Amherst to Grant to December 21, 1760.]

[Y]ou will proceed to the inland frontiers, or wheresoever the enemy may be within the Province of S. Carolina; & act against them offensively by destroying their towns & cutting up their settlements as shall occur best to you for the future protection of the Colony; the lives & the properties of the subjects; the most effectual chastisement of the Cherokees; the reducing of them to the absolute necessity of suing for pardon & peace; & the putting it out of their power of renewing hostilities with any degree of imminent danger to the Province. Immediately after you have completed this service, as I observed before, you are, with the troops under your command, to return to Charlestown, & to embark with the whole on your return here [New York], . . .

. . . No people are more easily surprised than Indians, they must at all times be pushed. If they are, they will not stand, but trust to flight and are easily conquered, so no people are more dangerous enemies when given way to, as their motions are very quick, and their howlings, with the notions the soldiers are too apt to have of their barbarities, create the greatest confusion . . .

*Grant replied to Amherst's above orders by asking a series of questions. This letter preserves both Grant's questions and Amherst's replies. One of Grant's questions asked:*

Query 3rd: After cutting up the Indian settlements, and following the Cherokees as far as troops can with any degree of safety, supposing they retire only, and don't ask for peace, what is to be done?

Answer: You are to pursue the Cherokees as far as shall be practicable; to distress them to your utmost; & not to return until you have compelled them into a peace, or that you receive orders for so doing. . . .

*SOURCE:* Edith Mays, ed., *Amherst Papers, 1756-1763, The Southern Sector,* (Bowie, Md.: Heritage Books, 1999), 153–54, 163.

*RELATED ENTRIES: Colonial Wars*

## 1766

### Comments from British Pamphlet on Colonies' Refusal to Pay Taxes

*Once the Seven Years' (French and Indian) War had ended, the Crown and Parliament, under pressure from an officer serving therein, decided to provide support for some regiments that had not been maintained in peacetime prior to that war. Several companies of men belonging to regiments that had served in the North American theater of the war were based in colonial seaport cities and taxes were levied on the colonists to pay for them. These taxes prompted widespread resistance, and a constitutional crisis emerged that led to a flurry of pamphlets supporting one side or the other. In one such pamphlet, these inflammatory passages, probably penned by a British officer and veteran of the war in America, must have infuriated colonial New Englanders who saw it.*

I take your word for it . . . and believe you are as sober, temperate, upright, humane and virtuous, as the posterity of independents and anabaptists, presbyterians and quakers, convicts and felons, savages and negro-worshippers, can be; that you are as loyal subjects, as obedient to the laws, as zealous for the maintenance of order and good government, as your late actions evince you to be; and I affirm that you have much need of the gentlemen of the blade to polish and refine your manners, to inspire you with an honest frankness and openness of behaviour, to rub off the rust of puritanism and to make you ashamed of proposing in your assemblies, as you have lately done, to pay off no more debts due to your original native country.

*SOURCE: The Justice and Necessity of Taxing the American Colonies Demonstrated* (London, 1766).

*RELATED ENTRIES: Economy and War; Revolutionary War*

## 1768 a

### A Letter from Samuel Adams to the *Boston Gazette*

*Fear of and disdain for "standing armies" came, to one degree or another, in every ship carrying successive waves of colonists from the British Isles. The earliest settlers recalled Charles I's garrisoning of his Irish regulars in English cities. Others had read of the occasional encroachments on civilian control by Rome's Praetorian Guard or the* condotierri *of the Italian city-states. When the Crown garrisoned British regulars at Boston, men like Samuel Adams (writing as "Vindex") soon raised those fears in the pages of the December 12, 1768, issue of the* Boston Gazette.

It is a very improbable supposition, that any people can long remain free, with a strong military power in the very heart of their country:—Unless that military power is under the direction of the people, and even then it is dangerous.—History, both ancient and modern, affords many instances of the overthrow of states and kingdoms by the power of soldiers, who were rais'd and maintain'd at first, under the plausible pretence of defending those very liberties which they afterwards destroyed. Even where there is a necessity of the military power, within the land, which by the way but rarely happens, a wise and prudent people will always have a watchful & jealous eye over it; for the maxims and rules of the army, are essentially different from the genius of a free people, and the laws of a free government. Soldiers are used to obey the absolute commands of their superiors: It is death for them, in the field, to dispute their authority, or the rectitude of their orders; and sometimes they may be shot upon the spot without ceremony. The necessity of things makes it highly proper that they should be under the absolute controul of the officer who commands them; who saith unto one come, and he cometh, and to another go, and he goeth. Thus being inured to that sort of government in the field and in the time of war, they are too apt to retain the same idea, when they happen to be in civil communities and in a time of peace: And even their officers, being used to a sort of sovereignty over them, may sometimes forget, that when quartered in cities, they are to consider themselves & their soldiers, in no other light than as a family in the community; numerous indeed, but like all other families and individuals, under the direction of the civil magistrate, and the controul of the common law—Like them, they are to confine their own rules and maxims within their own circle; nor can they be suppos'd to have a right or authority to oblige the rest of the community or any individuals, to submit to or pay any regard to their rules and maxims, any more than one family has to obtrude its private method of economy upon another.

It is of great importance, and I humbly conceive it ought to be the first care of the community, when soldiers are quartered among them, by all means to convince them, that they are not to give law, but to receive it: It is dangerous to civil society, when the military conceives of it self as an independent body, detach'd from the rest of the society, and subject to no controul: And the danger is greatly increased and becomes alarming, when the society itself yields to such an ill grounded supposition: If this should be the case, how easy would it be for the soldiers, if they alone should have the sword in their hands, to use it wantonly, and even to the great annoyance and terror of the citizens, if not to their destruction. What should hinder them, if once it is a given point, that the society has no law to restrain them, and they are dispos'd to do it? And how long can we imagine it would be, upon such a supposition, before the tragical scene would begin; especially if we consider further, how difficult it is to keep a power, in its nature much less formidable, and confessedly limited, within its just bounds!—That constitution which admits of a power without a check, admits of a tyranny: And that people, who are not always on their guard, to make use of the remedy of the constitution, when there is one, to restrain all kinds of power, and especially the military, from growing exorbitant, must blame themselves for the mischief that may befall them in consequence of their inattention: Or if they do not reflect on their own folly, their posterity will surely curse them, for entailing upon them chains and slavery.

I am led to these reflections from the appearance of the present times; when one wou'd be apt to think, there was like to be a speedy change of the civil, for a military government in this province. No one I believe can be at a loss to know, by whose influence, or with what intentions, the troops destin'd for the defence of the colonies, have been drawn off, so many of them, from their important stations, and posted in this town. Whether they are to be consider'd as marching troops, or a standing army, will be better determined, when the minister who has thus dispos'd of them, or G. B——d,* or the Commissioners of the customs, if he or they sent for them, shall explain the matter; as they who did send for them, assuredly will, to Britain and America. I dare challenge them, or any others to prove that there was the least necessity for them here, for the profess'd purpose of their coming, namely to prevent or subdue rebels and traitors: I will further venture to affirm, that he must be either a knave or a fool, if he has any tolerable acquaintance with the people of this town and province, nay, that he must be a traitor himself who asserts it. I know very well, that the whole continent of America is charg'd by some designing men with treason and rebellion, for vindicating their constitutional and natural rights: But I must tell these men on both sides the atlantic, that no other force but that of reason & sound argument on their part, of which we have hitherto seen but precious little, will prevail upon us, to relinquish our righteous claim:—Military power is by no means calculated to convince the understandings of men: It may in another part of the world, affright women and children, and perhaps some weak men out of their senses, but will never awe a sensible American tamely to surrender his liberty.—Among the brutal herd the strongest horns are the strongest laws; and slaves, who are always to be rank'd among the servile brutes, may cringe, under a tyrant's brow: But to a reasonable being, one I mean who acts up to his reason, there is nothing in military achievement, any more than in knight errantry, so terrifying as to induce him to part with the choicest gift that Heaven bestows on man.

But whatever may be the design of this military appearance; whatever use some persons may intend and expect to make of it: This we all know, and every child in the street is taught to know it; that while a people retain a just sense of Liberty, as blessed be God, this people yet do, the insolence of power will for ever be despised; and that in a city in the midst of civil society, especially in a time of peace, soldiers of all ranks, like all other men, are to be protected, govern'd, restrain'd, rewarded or punish'd by the Law of the Land.

*[Editor's Note: "G. B——d" refers to the Massachusetts Bay Colony's Governor, Francis Bernard; direct reference to Bernard might have invited a charge against the Boston Gazette of seditious libel.]

*SOURCE:* Article signed "Vindex," *Boston Gazette,* December 12, 1768, as given in *The Writings of Samuel Adams,* ed. H. A. Cushing (Boston, 1904), 1: 264–68.

*RELATED ENTRIES: Civil–Military Relations; Just War Theory; Militarization and Militarism; Revolutionary War*

# 1768 b

## Excerpts from Tryon's Journal of the Expedition into the Backcountry

*During the late 1760s, a vigorous protest movement developed in the piedmont counties of North Carolina. Small farmers for the most part, they called themselves "Regulators," referring to their desire to "regulate" the workings of local government, which they felt had become increasingly corrupt. In the summer of 1768 Royal Gov. William Tryon sought to raise a militia to protect the upcoming fall court session in Hillsborough—in the heart of Regulator country. In this excerpt, Tryon describes his efforts to convince the militia of Rowan County (also a piedmont county) to join his expedition. It is a vivid example of the ways in which elite leaders in the colonial era found themselves negotiating for the allegiance and support of the militia. Here Tryon pulled out all the stops, meeting separately with the officers, showing letters of support from a variety of ministers, and then manipulating the traditional militia muster to try to garner the support of the militiamen.*

July 6, 1768- October 2, 1768

Fryday 26th August. Eleven companies of the Rowan regiment marched into Town before 12 o'clock when the Governor ordered all the Captains and Field Officers to repair to Mr Montgomery's where he communicated to them the transactions that had passed between him and the Insurgents, at the same time that he read the several correspondence between them, except the Insurgents first address to the Governor and the Papers that accompanied them, which the time would not permit him to do. However the Governor explained the full extent and purport of them. The Governor also laid before these gentlemen the great necessity of a strict union of every honest man and well wisher of his Country at a juncture when the calamities of a civil war were impending. Colonel Osborn then spoke warmly in support of Government and the Liberties and Properties of the Inhabitants, which he said was in great Danger if these Insurgents should be able to overturn Hillsborough Superior Court. He then read a letter from four dissenting ministers directed to their Brethren the Presbyterians, wherein the wicked conduct and practises of the Insurgents were sensibly touched upon, the support of Government earnestly recommended and enforced—vide letter.

The Officers then desired to have a Conference among themselves and retired to a private room. In less than an hour they waited on the Governor again, when Colonel Osborn in the name of the whole returned the Governor their hearty thanks for the trouble he had taken to preserve the Peace of this Province, and told him it was at the request of those gentlemen that he assured the Governor they would unanimously assist him in the cause in hand with their utmost efforts. The Governor then marched into the field to review the regiment; as he passed along the front of the regiment, he spoke to every Company explaining to them the danger this country was in from the rash, obstinate & violent Proceedings of the insurgents, and that if every honest man and man of property would not with fortitude stand up in support of their liberties and Properties, this Province would inevitably fall into a civil war. That he should have occasion for a body of men to preserve the Peace at the next Superiour Court of Hillsborough, which was threatened to be attempted under solemn Oath by the Insurgents –That for this service he should draft no men, but receive those only who turned out Volunteers That after the Battalion had fired and a Discharge of the Artillery The Governor should order all those who were willing to serve His Majesty King George and protect the Liberties of the Country to move out of their ranks and join His Majesty's union colours in the front of the regiment, accordingly as soon as the regiment had gone through their

Fire by companies and the discharge of three pieces of artillery the Governor invited all His Majesty's Subjects, friends to the Liberties & Properties of their Country, to join the King's colours and immediately quitted his horse, took the King's colours in his hand, inviting the Volunteers to turn out to them. The first Company that joined the union Colours was Captain Dobbins', upon which the Governor took Captain Dobbins' Colours (each Company having a pair of Colours) and delivered the King's Colours into the hands of the ensign of that Company; congratulating Capt: Dobbins (who had been in service) on the honour he had obtained and merited. Other Companies immediately followed the first and in a few moments there was but one Company in the Field that declined turning out the Captain of which however honourably quitted his Company and joined the Kings Colours. Each Company as it joined the Colours was saluted with three huzzas and the whole with a discharge of the Swivel guns after which the men joined again in a battalion grounded their arms, went to the right about, and marched to refresh themselves with the Provisions His Excellency had provided for them. They were ordered to stand to their arms, when each man in the ranks had a drink of either Beer or Tody, to His Majesty's health and prosperity to North Carolina – It is to be observed that one Company (Captain Knoxes) did not turn out to join His Majesty's Colours as Volunteers but remained in their ranks and afterwards without partaking of the refreshments provided, marched out of the Field carrying that shame and disgrace with them, and the just contempt of the Regiment, which their conduct apparently incurred. The Battalion was then dismissed, and the Field Officers, Captains and Gentlemen waited on the Governor to dinner, where the health of His Majesty and the Royal Family, Prosperity to the Province and success to the Rowan and Mecklenburg Volunteers were drank.

*SOURCE: The Regulators in North Carolina: A Documentary History, 1759–1776* (Raleigh, N.C.: State Department of Archives and History, 1971).

*RELATED ENTRIES: Colonial Militia Systems; Colonial Wars; Militarization and Militarism*

# 1772

## Excerpt from "The Dangers of Standing Armies" by Joseph Warren

*The Fatal Fifth of March, 1770—also known as "The Boston Massacre"—was regarded in New England as a consequence of the stationing of British troops in colonial urban centers like Boston and New York, where off-duty soldiers competed for work with local artisans. For many years New Englanders gathered on March 5 to hear orations like this one by the man who would die commanding Massachusetts's troops at Bunker Hill three years later:*

The ruinous consequences of standing armies to free communities may be seen in the histories of SYRACUSE, ROME, and many other once flourishing STATES; some of which have now scarce a name! Their baneful influence is most suddenly felt, when they are placed in populous cities; for, by a corruption of morals, the public happiness is immediately affected; and that this is one of the effects of quartering troops in a populous city, is a truth, to which many a mourning parent, many a lost, despairing child in this metropolis, must bear a very melancholy testimony. Soldiers are also taught to consider arms as the only arbiters by which every dispute is to be decided between contending states; —they are instructed implicitly to obey their commanders, without enquiring into the justice of the cause they are engaged to support: Hence it is, that they are ever to be dreaded as the ready engines of tyranny and oppression. —And it is too observable that they are prone to introduce the same mode of decision in the disputes of individuals, and from thence have often arisen great animosities between them and the inhabitants, who whilst in a naked defenceless state, are frequently insulted and abused by an armed soldiery. And this will be more especially the case, when the troops are informed, that the intention of their being stationed in any city, is to overawe the inhabitants. That, this was the avowed design of stationing an armed force in this town, is sufficiently known; and we, my fellow-citizens have seen, we have felt the tragical effects! —THE FATAL FIFTH OF MARCH 1770, can never be forgotten—the horrors of THAT DREADFUL NIGHT are but too deeply impressed on our hearts—Language is too feeble to paint the emotions of our souls, when our streets were stained with the BLOOD OF OUR BRETHREN, —when our ears were wounded by the groans of the dying, and our eyes were tormented with the sight of the mangled bodies of the dead. —When our alarmed imagination presented to our view our houses wrapt in flames, —our children subjected to the barbarous caprice of the raging soldiery—our beauteous virgins exposed to all the insolence of unbridled passion, —our virtuous wives endeared to us by every tender tie, falling a sacrifice to worse than brutal violence, and perhaps like the famed Lucretia, distracted with anguish and despair, ending their wretched lives by their own fair hands. —When we beheld the authors of our distress parading in our streets, or drawn up in regular battallia, as though a hostile city; our hearts beat to arms; we snatched our weapons, almost resolved by one decisive stroke, to avenge the death of our SLAUGHTERED BRETHREN, and to secure from future danger, all that we held most dear; But propitious heaven forbade the bloody carnage, and saved the threatened victims of our too keen resentment, not by their discipline, not by their regular army,—no, it was royal George's livery that proved their shield—it was that which turned the pointed engines of destruction from their breasts.!!! The thoughts of vengeance were soon buried in our inbred affection to Great Britain, and calm reason dictated a method of removing the troops more mild than an immediate recourse to the sword. With united efforts you urged the immediate departure of the troops from the town—you urged it, with a resolution which ensured success—you obtained your wishes, and the removal of the troops was effected, without one drop of their blood being shed by the inhabitants.

!!! I have the strongest reason to believe that I have mentioned the only circumstance which saved the troops from destruction. It was then, and now is, the opinion of those who were best acquainted with the state of affairs at that time, that had thrice that number of troops, belonging to any power at open war with us, been in this town in the same exposed condition, scarce a man would have lived to have seen the morning light.

The immediate actors in the tragedy of that night were surrendered to justice.—It is not mine to say how far they were guilty! they have been tried by the country and ACQUITTED of murder! And they are not to be again arraigned at an earthly bar: But, surely the men who have promiscuously scattered death amidst the innocent inhabitants of a populous city, ought to see well to it, that they be prepared to stand at the bar of an omniscient judge! And all who contrived or encouraged the stationing troops in this place, have reasons of eternal importance, to reflect with deep contrition on their base designs, and humbly to repent of their impious machinations. . . .

Even in the dissolute reign of King Charles II, when the house of Commons impeached the Earl of Clarendon of high treason, the first article on which they founded their accusation was, that "he had designed a standing army to be raised, and to govern the kingdom thereby." And the eighth article was, that "he had introduced arbitrary government into his Majesty's plantations." —A terrifying example, to those who are now forging chains for this Country!

You have my friends and countrymen often frustrated the designs of your enemies, by your unanimity and fortitude: It was your union and determined spirit which expelled those troops, who polluted your streets with INNOCENT BLOOD. —You have appointed this anniversary as a standing memorial of the BLOODY CONSEQUENCES OF PLACING AN ARMED FORCE IN A POPULOUS CITY, and of your deliverance from the dangers which then seemed to hang over your heads; and I am confident that you never will betray the least want of spirit when called upon to guard your freedom. —None but they who set a just value upon the blessing of Liberty are worthy to enjoy her.

*SOURCE:* Joseph Warren, *The Dangers of Standing Armies* (Boston: Edes and Gill, 1772).

*RELATED ENTRIES: European Military Culture, Influence of; Militarization and Militarism*

# 1774

## North Carolina Militia Act of 1774

*As colonial economies and societies developed, their laws about their militias tended to change as well. A growing number of classes of artisans and professions, deemed indispensable to the vitality of the colony, were exempted from militia duties. The original militia law for the Carolinas in 1669 required "all inhabitants and freemen . . . above 17 years of age and under 60" to be "bound to bear arms, and serve as soldiers when the grand council shall find it necessary." By 1774 the law in North Carolina read as follows:*

Whereas a militia may be necessary for the defence and safety of this province.

I. Be it Enacted by the Governor, Council and Assembly and by the Authority of the same That all Freemen and Servants within this province between the Age of Sixteen and Sixty shall compose the Militia thereof and that the several Captains of the same shall Enroll the names of all such Freemen and Servants of which their several Companies consist and shall at their respective General Musters return a Copy thereof to the Colonel of their respective Regiments under the Penalty of Five Pounds Proclamation money to be levied by a Warrant of Distress from the Colonel of their Regiment directed to the Sheriff of the County to which the said Regiment belongs which Sheriff shall be paid out of the said Penalty the sum of ten Shillings: and in case any Sheriff shall neglect or refuse to serve such Warrant he shall forfeit and pay the sum of five pounds to be recovered by action of Debt in any court of Record and be applied as hereinafter directed which Copy so returned shall by every Colonel be returned to the Governor or Commander in Chief for the time being under the like Penalty and that all persons after being so Enrolled who shall at any time (Unless rendered incapable by sickness or other accident) neglect or refuse when called upon to appear at such times and places where Ordered by the Colonel or Commanding Officer, there to be mustered, Trained and exercised in Arms and be provided with a well fixed Gun shall forfeit and pay it at a private Muster five Shillings, if at a General Muster Ten Shillings and shall also be provided with a Cartouch Box, Sword, Cutlass, or Hanger, and have at least Nine Charges of powder made into Cartridges and sizeable Bullets or Swann Shot and three Spare Flints a Worm and a picker under the Penalty if at a private Muster the Sum of two Shillings and Six pence if at a General Muster Five Shillings to be levied by a Warrant of distress from the Captain of the Company directed to the Serjeant of the same who is hereby impowered to Execute the said Warrant and distrain for the said Fines and Penalties in the same manner as Sheriffs are impowered to distrain for public Taxes and shall make return thereof to the Captain which Serjeant shall deduct one Shilling and four pence out of every Fine so levied and in Case such Serjeant or Serjeants shall neglect or refuse to serve any Warrant or Warrants to him or them so directed he or they for such Neglect or refusal shall be fined Twenty Shillings to be recovered by a Warrant from the Captain directed to any other Serjeant under the same Penalty to be accounted for and applied as other fines in this Act directed. . . .

III. Provided also, That no member of his Majesty's Council, no member of Assembly, no Minister of the Church of England, no Protestant Dissenting Minister regularly called to any Congregation in this Province, no Justice of the Superior Courts, Secretary, Practising Attorney, no man who has borne a Military Commission as high as that of a Captain or Commissioned Officer who has served in the army, no Justice of the Peace, nor any Person who hath acted under a Commission of the Peace, no Clerk of the Court of Justice, Practicing Physician, Surgeon, Schoolmaster having the Tuition of ten Scholars, Ferryman, Overseer having the care of six Taxable slaves, Inspectors, Public Millers, Coroners, Constables, Overseers and Commissioners of Public Roads, Searchers, or Branch Pilots so long as they continue in office shall be obliged to enlist themselves or appear at such musters.

IV. Provided nevertheless, That in case any such Overseer having the Care of six Taxable Slaves shall be seen in the muster Field on the days of General or Private musters they shall be liable to a Fine of forty shillings to be levied by a Warrant from the Colonel or Commanding Officer and applied as other Fines in this Act directed.

V. And be it further Enacted, by the Authority aforesaid, That if the Captain, Lieutenant, or Ensign, or any Two of them shall adjudge any Person or Persons enrolled as aforesaid, to be incapable of providing and furnishing him or themselves with the Arms, Ammunition, and Accoutrements, required by this Act, every such Person shall be exempt from the Fines and Forfeitures imposed by Virtue of this Act until such Arms, Ammunition, and Accoutrements, shall be provided for and delivered him by the Court Martial; to be paid for out of the Fines already collected, and that may hereafter be collected. . . .

*SOURCE:* Walter Clark, ed., *State Records of North Carolina*, 26 vols. (Winston-Salem, N.C., 1895–1914), 23: 940–41.

*RELATED ENTRIES: Colonial Militia Systems; Conscription and Volunteerism; European Military Culture, Influence of; National Guard; Revolutionary War*

# 1775

## Peter Oliver's Interview with POW. William Scott

*Peter Oliver, a prominent Tory active in the service of "king and country," asked a Revolutionary lieutenant captured at Bunker Hill how he had decided to serve. Although we cannot know with certainty whether the lieutenant, William Scott, was being truthful, or whether he was quoted correctly, we do know that he went on to serve in a Patriot uniform (violating his parole) after having been released by the British; in any event, he is quoted as having replied:*

The case was this Sir! I lived in a Country Town; I was a Shoemaker, & got my Living by my Labor. When this Rebellion came on, I saw some of my Neighbors get into Commission, who were no better than myself. I was very ambitious, & did not like to see those Men above me. I was asked to enlist, as a private Soldier. My Ambition was too great for so low a Rank; I offered to enlist upon having a Lieutenants Commission; which was granted. I imagined my self now in a way of Promotion: if I was killed in Battle, there would an end of me, but if my Captain was killed, I should rise in Rank, & should still have a Chance to rise higher. These Sir! were the only Motives of my entering into the Service; for as to the Dispute between great Britain & the Colonies, I know nothing of it; neither am I capable of judging whether it is right or wrong.

*SOURCE:* Douglass Adair and John A. Shutz, eds., *Peter Oliver's Origin and Progress of the American Revolution* (San Marino, Calif.: Huntington Library, 1961), 130. For a discussion of Scott see *John Shy, A People Numerous and Armed* (New York: Oxford University Press, 1976), 165–79.

*RELATED ENTRIES: Conscription and Volunteerism; Prisoners of War; Revolutionary War*

# 1776 a

## Distribution of Enlisted Men and Officers over Wealthholding Thirds of Total Ratable State Population[1]

*The states' "Patriot" militias were, with a few exceptions, more representative of the socioeconomic structure of the states than were the regiments that each state raised for the Continental Line. Most of the latter contracted to serve for longer periods of time than did the members of the state militias. We know the socioeconomic composition of a few of these Continental Line units. This table is based on Mark Lender's analysis of 88 New Jersey officers and 710 enlisted men on the muster rolls between late 1776 and mid-1780 (the only period when the records were sufficiently detailed to enable him to conduct the analysis).*

| Percentage of Enlisted Men from: | | |
|---|---|---|
| Lower Third[2] | Middle Third | Upper Third[3] |
| 61% | 29% | 10% |

| Percentage of Officers from: | | |
|---|---|---|
| Lower Third | Middle Third | Upper Third[4] |
| 0 | 16 | 84 |

[1] Based on data in Lender, "Enlisted Line," chap. 4.

[2] Includes 46 percent propertyless soldiers.

[3] Includes 1 percent of the soldiers in the wealthiest tenth.

[4] Includes 31.8 percent of the officers in the wealthiest tenth.

*SOURCE:* Mark Edward Lender, "The Social Structure of the New Jersey Brigade: The Continental Line as an American

Standing Army," in *The Military in America from the Colonial Era to the Present,* ed. Peter Karsten (New York: Free Press, 1980), 70.

*RELATED ENTRIES: Colonial Militia Systems; Conscription and Volunteerism; Continental Army; Economy and War; Revolutionary War*

## 1776 b

### Gen. Washington's Letter to Continental Congress on Reenlistment Difficulties

*The following is an excerpt from a letter written by George Washington, serving as general of the Continental Army, to the Continental Congress. In it, Washington addresses the Congress's view on reenlistment difficulties and details his observations about the state militia forces, Army discipline, and the selection of officers:*

To The President of Congress
Colonel Morris's, on the Heights of Harlem,
September 24, 1776.

It is in vain to expect, that any (or more than a trifling) part of this Army will again engage in the Service on the encouragement offered by Congress. When Men find that their Townsmen and Companions are receiving 20, 30, and more Dollars, for a few Months Service, (which is truely the case) it cannot be expected; without using compulsion; and to force them into the Service would answer no valuable purpose. When Men are irritated, and the Passions inflamed, they fly hastely and chearfully to Arms; but after the first emotions are over, to expect, among such People, as compose the bulk of an Army, that they are influenced by any other7 principles than those of Interest, is to look for what never did, and I fear never will happen; the Congress will deceive themselves therefore if they expect it.

A Soldier reasoned with upon the goodness of the cause he is engaged in, and the inestimable rights he is contending for, hears you with patience, and acknowledges the truth of your observations, but adds, that it is of no more Importance to him than others. The Officer makes you the same reply, with this further remark, that his pay will not support him, and he cannot ruin himself and Family to serve his Country, when every Member of the community is equally Interested and benefitted by his Labours. The few therefore, who act upon Principles of disinterestedness, are, comparatively speaking, no more than a drop in the Ocean. It becomes evidently clear then, that as this Contest is not likely to be the Work of a day; as the War must be carried on systematically, and to do it, you must have good Officers, there are, in my Judgment, no other possible means to obtain them but by establishing your Army upon a permanent footing; and giving your Officers good pay; this will induce Gentlemen, and Men of Character to engage; and till the bulk of your Officers are composed of such persons as are actuated by Principles of honour, and a spirit of enterprize, you have little to expect from them.—They ought to have such allowances as will enable them to live like, and support the Characters of Gentlemen; and not be driven by a scanty pittance to the low, and dirty arts which many of them practice, to filch the Public of more than the difference of pay would amount to upon an ample allowe. besides, something is due to the Man who puts his life in his hands, hazards his health, and forsakes the Sweets of domestic enjoyments. Why a Captn. in the Continental Service should receive no more than 5/. Curry [5 s. currency] per day, for performing the same duties that an officer of the same Rank in the British Service receives 10/. Sterlg. for, I never could conceive; especially when the latter is provided with every necessary he requires, upon the best terms, and the former can scarce procure them, at any Rate. There is nothing that gives a Man consequence, and renders him fit for Command, like a support that renders him Independant of every body but the State he Serves.

With respect to the Men, nothing but a good bounty can obtain them upon a permanent establishment; and for no shorter time than the continuance of the War, ought they to be engaged; as Facts incontestibly prove, that the difficulty, and cost of Inlistments, increase with time. When the Army was first raised at Cambridge, I am persuaded the Men might have been got without a bounty for the War: after this, they began to see that the Contest was not likely to end so speedily as was immagined, and to feel their consequence, by remarking, that to get the Militia In, in the course of last year, many Towns were induced to give them a bounty. Foreseeing the Evils resulting from this, and the destructive consequences which unavoidably would follow short Inlistments, I took the Liberty in a long Letter, . . . to recommend the Inlistments for and during the War; assigning such Reasons for it, as experience has since convinced me were well founded. At that time twenty Dollars would, I am persuaded, have engaged the Men for this term. But it will not do to look back, and if the present opportunity is slip'd, I am perswaded that twelve months more will Increase our difficulties fourfold. I shall therefore take the freedom of giving it as my opinion, that a good Bounty be immediately offered, aided by the proffer of at least 100, or 150 Acres of Land and a suit of Cloaths and Blankt, to each non-Comd. [noncommissioned] Officer and Soldier; as I have good authority for saying, that however high the Men's pay may appear, it is barely sufficient in the present scarcity and dearness of all kinds of goods, to keep them in Cloaths, much less afford support to their Families. If this encouragement then is given to the Men, and such Pay allowed the Officers as will induce Gentlemen of Character and liberal Sentiments to engage; and proper care and precaution are used in the nomination (having more regard to the Characters of Persons, than the Number of Men they can Inlist) we should in a little time have an Army able to cope with any that can be opposed to it, as there are excellent Materials to form one out of: but while the only merit an Officer possesses is his ability to raise Men; while those Men consider, and treat him as an equal; and (in the Character of an Officer) regard him no more than a broomstick, being mixed together as one common herd; no order, nor no discipline can prevail; nor will the Officer ever meet with that respect which is essentially necessary to due subordination.

To place any dependance upon Militia, is, assuredly, resting upon a broken staff. Men just dragged from the tender Scenes of domestick life; unaccustomed to the din of Arms; totally unacquainted with every kind of Military skill, which being followed by a want of confidence in themselves, when opposed to Troops regularly train'd, disciplined, and appointed, superior in knowledge, and superior in Arms, makes them timid, and ready to fly from their own shadows. Besides, the sudden change in their manner of living, (particularly in the lodging) brings on sickness in many; impatience in all, and such an unconquerable desire of returning to their respective homes that it not only produces shameful, and scandalous Desertions among themselves, but infuses the like spirit in others. Again, Men accustomed to unbounded freedom, and no controul, cannot brook the Restraint which is indispensably necessary to the good order and Government of an Army; without which, licentiousness, and every kind of disorder triumpantly reign. To bring Men to a proper degree of Subordination, is not the work of a day, a Month or even a year; and unhappily for us, and the cause we are Engaged in, the little discipline I have been labouring to establish in the Army under my immediate Command, is in a manner done away by having such a mixture of Troops as have been called together within these few Months. . . .

Another matter highly worthy of attention, is, that other Rules and Regulation's may be adopted for the Government of the Army than those now in existence, otherwise the Army, but for the name, might as well be disbanded. For the most attrocious offences, (one or two Instances only excepted) a Man receives no more than 39 Lashes; and these perhaps (thro' the collusion of the Officer who is to see it inflicted), are given in such a manner as to become rather a matter of sport than punishment; but when inflicted as they ought, many hardened fellows who have been the Subjects, have declared that for a bottle of Rum they would undergo a Second operation; it is evident therefore that this punishment is inadequate to many Crimes it is assigned to, as a proof of it, thirty and 40 Soldiers will desert at a time; and of late, a practice prevails, (as you will see by my Letter of the 22d) of the most alarming nature; and which will, if it cannot be checked, prove fatal both to the Country and Army; I mean the infamous practice of Plundering, for under the Idea of Tory property, or property which may fall into the hands of the Enemy, no Man is secure in his effects, and scarcely in his Person; for in order to get at them, we have several Instances of People being frightend out of their Houses under pretence of those Houses being ordered to be burnt, and this is done with a view of seizing the Goods; nay, in order that the villany may be more effectually concealed, some Houses have actually been burnt to cover the theft.

I have with some others, used my utmost endeavours to stop this horrid practice, but under the present lust after plunder, and want of Laws to punish Offenders, I might almost as well attempt to remove Mount Atlas.—I have ordered instant corporal Punishment upon every Man who passes our Lines, or is seen with Plunder, that the Offenders might be punished for disobedience of Orders; and Inclose you the proceedings of a Court Martial held upon an Officer, who with a Party of Men had robbed a House a little beyond our Lines of a Number of valuable Goods; among which (to shew that nothing escapes) were four large Pier looking Glasses, Women's Cloaths, and other Articles which one would think, could be of no Earthly use to him. He was met by a Major of Brigade who ordered him to return the Goods, as taken contrary to Genl. Orders, which he not only peremptorily refused to do, but drew up his Party and swore he would defend them at the hazard of his Life; on which I ordered him to be arrested, and tryed for Plundering, Disobedience of Orders, and Mutiny; for the Result, I refer to the Proceedings of the Court; whose judgment appeared so exceedingly extraordinary, that I ordered a Reconsideration of the matter, upon which, and with the Assistance of fresh evidence, they made Shift to Cashier him.

I adduce this Instance to give some Idea to Congress of the Currt. [current] Sentiments and general run of the Officers which compose the present Army; and to shew how exceedingly necessary it is to be careful in the choice of the New Sett, even if it should take double the time to compleat the Levies. An Army formed of good Officers moves like Clock-Work; but there is no Situation upon Earth, less enviable, nor more distressing, than that Person's who is at the head of Troops, who are regardless of Order and discipline; and who are unprovided with almost every necessary.

*SOURCE:* John C. Fitzpatrick, ed., *The Writings of George Washington,* vol. 6 (Washington, D.C.: U.S. Government Printing Office, 1932), 106–16.

*RELATED ENTRIES: Colonial Militia Systems; Conscription and Volunteerism; Continental Army; Draft Evasion and Resistance; Economy and War; European Military Culture, Influence of; Revolutionary War; Washington, George*

# 1776 c

## Account of Walter Bates, Connecticut Loyalist

*Walter Bates, a young Loyalist from Darien, Connecticut, whose family was active in support of the British, was 16 years of age in 1776 when he was seized by rebels and tortured in the hope that he would inform on other Loyalists.*

At this time I had just entered my sixteenth year. I was taken and confined in the Guard House; next day examined before a Committee and threatened with sundry deaths if I did not confess what I knew not of. . . . I was taken out by an armed mob, conveyed through the field gate one mile from the town to back Creek, then having been stripped my body was exposed to the mosquitoes, my hands and feet being confined to a tree near the Salt Marsh, in which situation for two hours time every drop of blood would be drawn from my body; when soon after two of the committee said that if I would tell them all I knew, they would release me, if not they would leave me to these men who, perhaps would kill me.

I told them that I knew nothing that would save my life.

They left me, and the Guard came to me and said they were ordered to give me, if I did not confess, one hundred stripes, and if that did not kill me I would be sentenced to be hanged. Twenty stripes was then executed with severity, after which they sent me again to the Guard House. No "Tory" was allowed to speak to me, but I was insulted and abused by all.

The next day the committee proposed many means to extort a confession from me, the most terrifying was that of confining me to a log on the carriage in the Saw mill and let the saw cut me in two if I did not expose "those Torys." Finally they sentenced me to appear before Col. Davenport, in order that he should send me to head quarters, where all the Torys he sent were surely hanged. Accordingly next day I was brought before Davenport—one of the descendants of the old apostate Davenport, who fled from old England—who, after he had examined me, said with great severity of countenance, "I think you could have exposed those Tories."

I said to him "You might rather think I would have exposed my own father sooner than suffer what I have suffered." Upon which the old judge could not help acknowledging he never knew any one who had withstood more without exposing confederates, and he finally discharged me the third day.

*SOURCE:* Catherine Crary, ed., *The Price of Loyalty* (New York: McGraw-Hill, 1973), 81–82.

*RELATED ENTRIES: Conscription and Volunteerism; Prisoners of War; Revolutionary War*

## 1777 a

**Petition of Samuel Townsend to New York State Convention**

*The Patriot militia served, John Shy has observed, as a kind of thought-police, maintaining loyalty to the cause in the presence of passing enemy forces. Samuel Townsend, a farm laborer from Kingston, New York, found himself in "hot water" after he spoke critically, while "in his cups," of a Patriot Committee of Safety's order to all communities to pursue men who had enlisted in Loyalist regiments.*

Kingston Jail, April 30, 1777

To The Honorable the Representatives of the State of New York in Convention Assembled:

The petition of Samuel Townsend humbly sheweth

That ye petitioner is at present confined in the common jail of Kingston for being thought unfriendly to the American States. That ye petitioner some few days ago went from home upon some business and happened to get a little intoxicated in liquor, and upon his return home inadvertantly fell in company upon the road with a person unknown to yr petitioner and in discoursing and joking about the Tories passing through there and escaping, this person says to yr petitioner that if he had been with the Whigs, [they] should not have escaped so. . . . To which your petitioner, being merry in liquor, wantonly and in a bantering manner told him that in the lane through which they were then riding five and twenty Whigs would not beat five and twenty Tories and, joking together, they parted, and yr petitioner thought no more of it. Since, he has been taken up and confined and he supposes on the above joke.

Being conscious to himself of his not committing any crime or of being unfriendly to the American cause worthy of punishment. . . . That yr petitioner is extremely sorry for what he may have said and hopes his intoxication and looseness of tongue will be forgiven by this honorable convention as it would not have been expressed by him in his sober hours. That yr petitioner has a wife and two children and a helpless mother all which must be supported by his labor and should he be kept confined in this time his family must unavoidably suffer through want, as yr petitioner is but of indigent circumstances and fully conceives it is extremely hard to keep him confined to the great distress of his family as well as grief of yr petitioner. Yr petitioner therefore humbly prays that this honorable convention be favorably pleased to take the premises under their serious consideration so that yr petitioner may be relieved and discharged from his confinement or [granted] such relief as to the honorable house shall seem meet and ye petitioner shall ever pray.

Samuel Townsend

*SOURCE:* Catherine Crary, ed., *The Price of Loyalty* (New York: McGraw-Hill, 1973), 151–52.

*RELATED ENTRIES: Colonial Militia Systems; Conscription and Volunteerism; Revolutionary War*

## 1777 b

**Account Concerning Connecticut Men's Refusal to Serve in the Revolutionary War**

*Nathaniel Jones and 16 other Farmington men were jailed in 1777 for refusing to serve the Revolutionary cause. After a time, they recanted, were examined, and were released upon satisfying the Revolutionary government in Connecticut that "there was no such thing as remaining neuters."*

On report of the committee appointed by this Assembly to take into consideration the subject matter of the memorial of Nathl Jones, Simon Tuttle, Joel Tuttle, Nathaniel Mathews, John Mathews, Riverius Carrington, Lemuel Carrington, Zerubbabel Jerom junr, Chauncey Jerom, Ezra Dormer, Nehemiah Royce, Abel Royce, George Beckwith, Abel Frisbee, Levi Frisbey, Jared Peck, and Abraham Waters, all of Farmingon, shewing that they are imprisoned on suspicion of their being inimical to America; that they are ready and willing to join with their country and to do their utmost for its defence; and praying to be examined and set at liberty, as per said memorial on file, reporting that the said committee caused the authority &c. of Farmington to be duly notifyed, that they convened the memorialists before them at the house of Mr. David Bull on the 22d of instant May and examined them separately touching their unfriendliness to the American States, and heard the evidences produced by the parties; that they found said persons were committed for being highly inimical to the United States, and for refusing to assist in the defence of the country; that on examination it appeared they had been much under the influence of one [James] Nichols, a designing church clergyman who had instilled into them principles opposite to the good of the States; that under the influence of such principles they had pursued a course of conduct tending to the ruin of the country and highly displeasing to those who are friends to the freedom and independence of the United States; that under various pretences they had refused to go in the expedition to Danbury; that said Nathaniel Jones and Simon Tuttle have as they suppose each of them a son gone over to the enemy; that there was, however, no particular positive fact that sufficiently appeared to have been committed by them of an atrocious nature against the States, and that they were indeed grossly ignorant of the true grounds of the present war with Great Britain; that they appeared to be penitent of their former conduct, professed themselves convinced since the Danbury alarm that there was no such thing as remaining neuters; that the destruction made there by the tories was matter of conviction to them; that since their imprisonment upon serious reflexion they are convinced that the States are right in their claim, and that it is their duty to submit to their authority, and that they will to the utmost of their power defend the country against the British army; and that the said committee think it advisable that the said persons be liberated from their imprisonment on their taking an oath of fidelity to the United States: Resolved by this Assembly, that the said persons be liberated from their said imprisonment on their taking an oath of fidelity to this State and paying costs, taxed at £22 7 10; and the keeper of the gaol in Hartford is hereby directed to liberate said persons accordingly.

*SOURCE: Public Records of the State of Connecticut,* vol. 1, 259–60. John Shy's reference in an essay led the editors to this passage. See Shy, "The American Revolution: The Military Conflict as a Revolutionary Conflict," in *Essays on the American Revolution*, ed. Stephen Kurtz and James Hutson (Chapel Hill: Published for the Institute of Early American History and Culture, Williamsburg, Va., by the University of North Carolina Press, 1973), 121–56.

*RELATED ENTRIES: Antiwar Movements; Conscription and Volunteerism; Draft Evasion and Resistance; Revolutionary War*

## 1777 c

### The Rifleman's Song at Bennington

*In the summer of 1777, Gen. John Burgoyne drove south from Canada toward New York City in an attempt to link up with British forces there and cut New England off from the main Continental Army. Growing short of provisions, he sent several hundred German, Loyalist, Indian, and British troops under Lt. Col. Friedrich Baum to seize the Patriot storehouse at Bennington, Vermont, which he was led to believe was inadequately defended. It was not. Some 1,800 Patriot forces under Col. John Stark defeated both Baum and British replacements under Lt. Col. Heinrich von Breymann on August 16. The British lost 200; some 700 were captured. Burgoyne, dealt a fatal blow, surrendered at Saratoga on October 17. This "Rifleman's Song," celebrating the Patriot victory, is similar to many others written and sung throughout the next century that treat the American volunteer soldier as superior to regulars.*

Why come ye hither, Redcoats, your mind what madness fills?
In our valleys there is danger, and there's danger on our hills.
Oh, hear ye not the singing of the bugle wild and free?
And soon you'll know the ringing of the rifle from the tree.

Chorus:
Oh, the rifle, oh, the rifle
In our hands will prove no trifle.

Ye ride a goodly steed, ye may know another master;
Ye forward came with speed, but you'll learn to back much faster.
Then you'll meet our Mountain Boys and their leader Johnny Stark,
Lads who make but little noise, but who always hit the mark.

Tell he who stays at home, or cross the briny waters
That thither ye must come like bullocks to the slaughter.
If we the work must do, why, the sooner 'tis begun,
If flint and trigger hold but true, the sooner 'twill be done.

*SOURCE:* Burl Ives, *Song Book* (New York: Ballantine Books, 1966), 92–93.

*RELATED TOPICS: Music and War; Revolutionary War*

# 1785

## Tory Veteran's Testimony Concerning Treatment by Patriots

*Maurice Nowland, a Tory veteran, told a royal commission that he had served briefly as a Revolutionary soldier "by Compulsion" and/or "from attachment to a friend." These excerpts are from testimony before the commission:*

Memorial of Maurice Nowland

26th of May 1785.

Maurice Nowlan—the Claimant—sworn:

Is a Native of Ireland & went to America in 1770 to New York. He was settled in 1774 at Cross Creek & followed a Mercantile Line & carried out 200 Gas. He took part with Govt at first & rais'd a Company in 1776 & join'd Coll Macdonald at Cross Creek. Produces a Warrant for the rank of Captn with the Pay as such. He was four Years and ten Months in Captivity. He broke Gaol at Reading in Octr 1780 & got to New York from whence he went in 1781 to Charlestown. He got a Warrant from Coll Stuart to raise a Company in North Carolina but being obliged to evacuate Wilmington suddenly he was not able to raise the Company. Warrant produced dated 30th of Octr 1781. At the Evacuation of Charlestown he came to Engd. He never sign'd any Association or took any Oath. When he was in confinement he was offer'd his whole property if he would join them. He recd the pay of Captn up to this time & now receives half pay. He has an Allowance of £50 a Yr from the Treasury which he has had from the 1st of Jany 1783 & he now continues to receive it.

Neil McArthur—sworn.

Knew Mr Nowland in 1774. He was a very loyal Subject. He was a Storekeeper. He raised a Company in 1776. He was a long time confined. He married a Daur of one Wm White he married in Ireland. Wm White was an Irishman. He is not acquainted with any of [Maurice Nowlan's] Lands. He knows he had an House at Cross Creek can't tell what he gave for it. Does not know what it was worth but believes £500 S. Would have given £500 for it.

Further Testimony to the Memorial of Maurice Nowlan

2d of June 1785.

Maurice Nowlan—sworn.

Admits that he was one of the Party who went by the desire of the Rebel Committee to intercept a letter written by Govr Martin which they effected. Says however that he did not go by choice. Says he went by Compulsion & that he was taken out of his Bed. Says however that he should have been in no personal Danger if he had avoided going. Says there were two Companies in Arms in America at that time for the purpose of learning their Exercise. One Co was attach'd to America & the other to G. B. He was in that which was attached to America. He was an Assistt Lieutt. Being asked why he did not tell this Story when he spoke of his own Case he says he was confused & that he was not asked. Thinks notwithstanding this that a Man may be said to have been uniformly loyal. He chose his Co. from attachment to his friend. He join'd the British because he always meant to do it. Admits that he always thought that the British would succeed.

Alexander McKay—sworn.

Did not know that Mr Nowlan was one of the Party to take Captn Cunningham till this Day. Says in the Case of Vardy [another claimant] this affected his Opinion because he knew his Sentiments but it does not alter his opinion of Nowlan's Loyalty.

*SOURCE:* H. E. Egerton, ed., *Royal Commission on the Losses and Services of American Loyalists* (Oxford: Roxburghe Club, 1915), 368–69.

*RELATED ENTRIES: Conscription and Volunteerism; Revolutionary War*

## 1797

### Gov. Samuel Adam's Farewell Address

*Gov. Samuel Adams delivered a farewell address to the Massachusetts legislature on January 27, 1797, that left no doubt as to where he stood on the question of whether the nation should rely in the future on the states' militia systems or on the federal government's regular Army.*

PERMIT ME TO CALL your attention to the subject of the Militia of the Commonwealth. —A well regulated militia "held in an exact subordination to the civil authority and governed by it," is the most safe defence of a Republic. —In our Declaration of Rights, which expresses the sentiments of the people, the people have a right to keep and bear arms for the common defence. The more generally therefore they are called out to be disciplined, the stronger is our security. No man I should think, who possesses a true republican spirit, would decline to rank with his fellow-citizens, on the fancied idea of a superiority in circumstances: This might tend to introduce fatal distinctions in our country. We can all remember the time when our militia, far from being disciplined, as they are at present, kept a well appointed hostile army for a considerable time confined to the capital; and when they ventured out, indeed they took possession of the ground they aimed at, yet they ventured to their cost, and never forgot the battle of Bunker Hill. The same undisciplined militia under the command and good conduct of General Washington, continued that army confined in or near the capital, until they thought proper to change their position and retreated with haste to Halifax. —If the Militia of the Commonwealth can be made still more effective, I am confident that you will not delay a measure of so great magnitude. I beg leave to refer you to the seventeenth article in our Declaration of Rights, which respects the danger of standing armies in time of peace. I hope we shall ever have virtue enough to guard against their introduction. —But may we not hazard the safety of our Republic should we ever constitute, under the name of a select militia, a small body to be disciplined in a camp with all the pomp & splendor of a regular army? Would such an institution be likely to be much less dangerous to our free government and to the morals of our youth, than if they were actually enlisted for permanent service? And would they not as usual in standing armies feel a distinct interest from that of our fellow-citizens at large? The great principles of our present militia system are undoubtedly good, constituting one simple body, and embracing so great a proportion of the citizens as will prevent a separate interest among them, inconsistent with the welfare of the whole. —Those principles, however, I conceive should equally apply to all the active citizens, within the age prescribed by law. —All are deeply interested in the general security; and where there are no invidious exemptions, partial distinctions or privileged bands, every Man, it is presumed, would pride himself in the right of bearing arms, and affording his personal appearance in common with his fellow-citizens. If upon examination you shall find, that the duties incident to our present system bear harder on one class of citizens, than on another, you will undoubtedly endeavour, as far as possible, to equalize its burthens.

*SOURCE:* Harry Alonzo Cushing, ed., *The Writings of Samuel Adams* (New York, 1907), 4: 402–03.

*RELATED ENTRIES: Conscription and Volunteerism; European Military Culture, Influence of; Militarization and Militarism; National Guard*

## 1800

### EXCERPT FROM MASON WEEMS'S *A HISTORY OF THE LIFE AND DEATH, VIRTUES & EXPLOITS OF GENERAL GEORGE WASHINGTON*

*The Rev. Mason Locke Weems (known as "Parson Weems") published his famous* Life of Washington *in 1800, one year after George Washington died. It went through 59 editions before 1850. Best known for its tale of the young Washington chopping down his father's favorite cherry tree, the book contains this passage about the war in the mid-1790s with indigenous peoples of the Ohio Valley. Ask yourself whether such a passage on the loss of American military lives in a 21st century account of contemporary warfare would pass as unnoticed and unobjected to as this one did.*

Some of the Indian tribes, . . . were obliged to be drubbed into peace, which service was done for them by General Wayne, in 1794—but not until many lives had been lost in preceding defeats; owing chiefly, it was said, to the very intemperate passions and potations of some of their officers. However, after the first shock, the loss of these poor souls was not much lamented. Tall young fellows, who could easily get their half dollar a day at the healthful and glorious labours of the plough, to go and enlist and rust among the lice and itch of a camp, for four dollars a month, were certainly not worth their country's crying about.

*SOURCE:* Mason Weems, *A History of the Life and Death, Virtues & Exploits of General George Washington* (New York: Macy-Masius, 1927).

*RELATED ENTRIES: European Military Culture, Influence of; Indian Wars: Eastern Wars; Militarization and Militarism*

## 1814

### TREATY OF GHENT

*Americans who called for war with Britain in 1812 often made use of the catch-phrase "Free Trade and Sailor's Rights." The second of these two terms referred to the British practice during the Napoleonic Wars of impressing sailors found on vessels flying the flag of the United States who were suspected of being deserters from British warships. The ensuing War of 1812 was concluded with the Treaty of Ghent, which contained eleven articles. The text covers national boundaries, American conflict with Native Americans, and even slavery, but it does not mention the term impressment anywhere.*

Treaty of Peace and Amity between His Britannic Majesty and the United States of America.

His Britannic Majesty and the United States of America desirous of terminating the war which has unhappily subsisted between the two Countries, and of restoring upon principles of perfect reciprocity, Peace, Friendship, and good Understanding between them, have for that purpose appointed their respective Plenipotentiaries, that is to say, His Britannic Majesty on His part has appointed the Right Honourable James Lord Gambier, late Admiral of the White now Admiral of the Red Squadron of His Majesty's Fleet; Henry Goulburn Esquire, a Member of the Imperial Parliament and Under Secretary of State; and William Adams Esquire, Doctor of Civil Laws: And the President of the United States, by and with the advice and consent of the Senate thereof, has appointed John Quincy Adams, James A. Bayard, Henry Clay, Jonathan Russell, and Albert Gallatin, Citizens of the United States; who, after a reciprocal communication of their respective Full Powers, have agreed upon the following Articles.

ARTICLE THE FIRST.

There shall be a firm and universal Peace between His Britannic Majesty and the United States, and between their respective Countries, Territories, Cities, Towns, and People of every degree without exception of places or persons. All hostilities both by sea and land shall cease as soon as this Treaty shall have been ratified by both parties as hereinafter mentioned. All territory, places, and possessions whatsoever taken by either party from the other during the war, or which may be taken after the signing of this Treaty, excepting only the Islands hereinafter mentioned, shall be restored without delay and without causing any destruction or carrying away any of the Artillery or other public property originally captured in the said forts or places, and which shall remain therein upon the Exchange of the Ratifications of this Treaty, or any Slaves or other private property; And all Archives, Records, Deeds, and Papers, either of a public nature or belonging to private persons, which in the course of the war may have fallen into the hands of the Officers of either party, shall be, as far as may be practicable, forthwith restored and delivered to the proper authorities and persons to whom they respectively belong. Such of the Islands in the Bay of Passamaquoddy as are claimed by both parties shall remain in the possession of the party in whose occupation they may be at the time of the Exchange of the Ratifications of this Treaty until the decision respecting the title to the said Islands shall have been made in conformity with the fourth Article of this Treaty. No disposition made by this Treaty as to such possession of the Islands and territories claimed by both parties shall in any manner whatever be construed to affect the right of either.

ARTICLE THE SECOND.

Immediately after the ratifications of this Treaty by both parties as hereinafter mentioned, orders shall be sent to the Armies, Squadrons, Officers, Subjects, and Citizens of the two Powers to cease from all hostilities: and to prevent all causes of complaint which might arise on account of the prizes which may be taken at sea after the said Ratifications of this Treaty, it is reciprocally agreed that all vessels and effects which may be taken after the space of twelve days from the said Ratifications upon all parts of the Coast of North America from the Latitude of twenty three degrees North to the Latitude of fifty degrees North, and as far Eastward in the Atlantic Ocean as the thirty sixth degree of West Longitude from the Meridian of Greenwich, shall be restored on each side:-that the time shall be thirty days in all other parts of the Atlantic Ocean North of the Equinoctial Line or Equator:-and the same time for the British and Irish Channels, for the Gulf of Mexico, and all parts of the West Indies:-forty days for the North Seas for the Baltic, and for all parts of the Mediterranean-sixty days for the Atlantic Ocean South of the Equator as far as the Latitude of the Cape of Good Hope.- ninety days for every other part of the world South of the Equator, and one hundred and twenty days for all other parts of the world without exception.

ARTICLE THE THIRD.

All Prisoners of war taken on either side as well by land as by sea shall be restored as soon as practicable after the Ratifications of this Treaty as hereinafter mentioned on their paying the debts which they may have contracted during their captivity. The two Contracting Parties respectively engage to discharge in specie the advances which may have been made by the other for the sustenance and maintenance of such prisoners.

ARTICLE THE FOURTH.

Whereas it was stipulated by the second Article in the Treaty of Peace of one thousand seven hundred and eighty three between His Britannic Majesty and the United States of America that the boundary of the United States should comprehend "all Islands within twenty leagues of any part of the shores of the United States and lying between lines to be drawn due East from the points where the aforesaid boundaries between Nova Scotia on the one part and East Florida on the other shall respectively touch the Bay of Fundy and the Atlantic Ocean, excepting such Islands as now are or heretofore have been within the limits of Nova Scotia, and whereas the several Islands in the Bay of Passamaquoddy, which is part of the Bay of Fundy, and the Island of Grand Menan in the said Bay of Fundy, are claimed by the United States as being comprehended within their aforesaid boundaries, which said Islands are claimed as belonging to His Britannic Majesty as having been at the time of and previous to the aforesaid Treaty of one thousand seven hundred and eighty three within the limits of the Province of Nova Scotia: In order therefore finally to decide upon these claims it is agreed that they shall be referred to two Commissioners to be appointed in the following manner: viz: One Commissioner shall be appointed by His Britannic Majesty and one by the President of the United States, by and with the advice and consent of the Senate thereof, and the said two Commissioners so appointed shall be sworn impartially to examine and decide upon the said claims according to such evidence as shall be laid before them on the part of His Britannic Majesty and of the United States respectively. The said Commissioners shall meet at St Andrews in the Province of New Brunswick, and shall have power to adjourn to such other place or places as they shall think fit. The said Commissioners shall by a declaration or report under their hands and seals decide to which of the two Contracting parties the several Islands aforesaid do respectely belong in conformity with the true intent of the said Treaty of Peace of one thousand seven hundred and eighty three. And if the said Commissioners shall agree in their decision both parties shall consider such decision as final and conclusive. It is further agreed that in the event of the two Commissioners differing upon all or any of the matters so referred to them, or in the event of both or either of the said Commissioners refusing or declining or wilfully omitting to act as such, they shall make jointly or separately a report or reports as well to the Government of His Britannic Majesty as to that of the United States, stating in detail the points on which they differ, and the grounds upon which their respective opinions have been formed, or the grounds upon which they or either of them have so refused declined or omitted to act. And His Britannic Majesty and the Government of the United States hereby agree to refer the report or reports of the said Commissioners to some friendly Sovereign or State to be then named for that purpose, and who shall be requested to decide on the differences which may be stated in the said report or reports, or upon the report of one Commissioner together with the grounds upon which the other Commissioner shall have refused, declined or omitted to act as the case may be. And if the Commissioner so refusing, declining, or omitting to act, shall also wilfully omit to state the grounds upon which he has so done in such manner that the said statement may be referred to such friendly Sovereign or State together with the report of such other Commissioner, then such Sovereign or State shall decide ex parse upon the said report alone. And His Britannic Majesty and the Government of the United States engage to consider the decision of such friendly Sovereign or State to be final and conclusive on all the matters so referred.

ARTICLE THE FIFTH.

Whereas neither that point of the Highlands lying due North from the source of the River St Croix, and designated in the former Treaty of Peace between the two Powers as the North West Angle of Nova Scotia, nor the North Westernmost head of Connecticut River has yet been ascertained; and whereas that part of the boundary line between the Dominions of the two Powers which extends from the source of the River st Croix directly North to the above mentioned North West Angle of Nova Scotia, thence along the said Highlands which divide those Rivers that empty themselves into the River St Lawrence from those which fall into the Atlantic Ocean to the North Westernmost head of Connecticut River, thence down along the middle of that River to the forty fifth degree of North Latitude, thence by a line due West on said latitude until it strikes the River Iroquois or Cataraquy, has not yet been surveyed: it is agreed that for these several purposes two Commissioners shall be appointed, sworn, and authorized to act exactly in the manner directed with respect to those mentioned in the next preceding Article unless otherwise specified in the present Article. The said Commissioners shall meet at se Andrews in the Province of New Brunswick, and shall have power to adjourn to such other place or places as they shall think fit. The said Commissioners shall have power to ascertain and determine the points above mentioned in conformity with the provisions of the said Treaty of Peace of one thousand seven hundred and eighty three, and shall cause the boundary aforesaid from the source of the River St Croix to the River Iroquois or Cataraquy to be surveyed and marked according to the said provisions. The said Commissioners shall make a map of the said boundary, and annex to it a declaration under their hands and seals certifying it to be the true Map of the said boundary, and particularizing the latitude and longitude of the North West Angle of Nova Scotia, of the North Westernmost head of Connecticut River, and of such other points of the said boundary as they may deem proper. And both parties agree to consider such map and declaration as finally and conclusively fixing the said boundary. And in the event of the said two Commissioners differing, or both, or either of them refusing, declining, or wilfully omitting to act, such reports, declarations, or statements shall be made by them or either of them, and such reference to a friendly Sovereign or State shall be made in all respects as in the latter part of the fourth

Article is contained, and in as full a manner as if the same was herein repeated.

ARTICLE THE SIXTH.

Whereas by the former Treaty of Peace that portion of the boundary of the United States from the point where the fortyfifth degree of North Latitude strikes the River Iroquois or Cataraquy to the Lake Superior was declared to be "along the middle of said River into Lake Ontario, through the middle of said Lake until it strikes the communication by water between that Lake and Lake Erie, thence along the middle of said communication into Lake Erie, through the middle of said Lake until it arrives at the water communication into the Lake Huron; thence through the middle of said Lake to the water communication between that Lake and Lake Superior:" and whereas doubts have arisen what was the middle of the said River, Lakes, and water communications, and whether certain Islands lying in the same were within the Dominions of His Britannic Majesty or of the United States: In order therefore finally to decide these doubts, they shall be referred to two Commissioners to be appointed, sworn, and authorized to act exactly in the manner directed with respect to those mentioned in the next preceding Article unless otherwise specified in this present Article. The said Commissioners shall meet in the first instance at Albany in the State of New York, and shall have power to adjourn to such other place or places as they shall think fit. The said Commissioners shall by a Report or Declaration under their hands and seals, designate the boundary through the said River, Lakes, and water communications, and decide to which of the two Contracting parties the several Islands lying within the said Rivers, Lakes, and water communications, do respectively belong in conformity with the true intent of the said Treaty of one thousand seven hundred and eighty three. And both parties agree to consider such designation and decision as final and conclusive. And in the event of the said two Commissioners differing or both or either of them refusing, declining, or wilfully omitting to act, such reports, declarations, or statements shall be made by them or either of them, and such reference to a friendly Sovereign or State shall be made in all respects as in the latter part of the fourth Article is contained, and in as full a manner as if the same was herein repeated.

ARTICLE THE SEVENTH.

It is further agreed that the said two last mentioned Commissioners after they shall have executed the duties assigned to them in the preceding Article, shall be, and they are hereby, authorized upon their oaths impartially to fix and determine according to the true intent of the said Treaty of Peace of one thousand seven hundred and eighty three, that part of the boundary between the dominions of the two Powers, which extends from the water communication between Lake Huron and Lake Superior to the most North Western point of the Lake of the Woods;-to decide to which of the two Parties the several Islands lying in the Lakes, water communications, and Rivers forming the said boundary do respectively belong in conformity with the true intent of the said Treaty of Peace of one thousand seven hundred and eighty three, and to cause such parts of the said boundary as require it to be surveyed and marked. The said Commissioners shall by a Report or declaration under their hands and seals, designate the boundary aforesaid, state their decision on the points thus referred to them, and particularize the Latitude and Longitude of the most North Western point of the Lake of the Woods, and of such other parts of the said boundary as they may deem proper. And both parties agree to consider such designation and decision as final and conclusive. And in the event of the said two Commissioners differing, or both or either of them refusing, declining, or wilfully omitting to act, such reports, declarations or statements shall be made by them or either of them, and such reference to a friendly Sovereign or State shall be made in all respects as in the latter part of the fourth Article is contained, and in as full a manner as if the same was herein revealed.

ARTICLE THE EIGHTH.

The several Boards of two Commissioners mentioned in the four preceding Articles shall respectively have power to appoint a Secretary, and to employ such Surveyors or other persons as they shall judge necessary. Duplicates of all their respective reports, declarations, statements, and decisions, and of their accounts, and of the Journal of their proceedings shall be delivered by them to the Agents of His Britannic Majesty and to the Agents of the United States, who may be respectively appointed and authorized to manage the business on behalf of their respective Governments. The said Commissioners shall be respectively paid in such manner as shall be agreed between the two contracting parties, such agreement being to be settled at the time of the Exchange of the Ratifications of this Treaty. And all other expenses attending the said Commissions shall be defrayed equally by the two parties. And in the case of death, sickness, resignation, or necessary absence, the place of every such Commissioner respectively shall be supplied in the same manner as such Commissioner was first appointed; and the new Commissioner shall take the same oath or affirmation and do the same duties. It is further agreed between the two contracting parties that in case any of the Islands mentioned in any of the preceding Articles, which were in the possession of one of the parties prior to the commencement of the present war between the two Countries, should by the decision of any of the Boards of Commissioners aforesaid, or of the Sovereign or State so referred to, as in the four next preceding Articles contained, fall within the dominions of the other party, all grants of land made previous to the commencement of the war by the party having had such possession, shall be as valid as if such Island or Islands had by such decision or decisions been adjudged to be within the dominions of the party having had such possession.

ARTICLE THE NINTH.

The United States of America engage to put an end immediately after the Ratification of the present Treaty to hostilities with all the Tribes or Nations of Indians with whom they may be at war at the time of such Ratification, and forthwith to restore to such Tribes or Nations respectively all the possessions, rights, and privileges which they may have enjoyed or been entitled to in one thousand eight hundred and eleven previous to such hostilities. Provided always that such Tribes or Nations shall agree to desist from all hostilities against the United States of America, their Citizens, and Subjects upon the Ratification of the present Treaty being notified to such Tribes or Nations, and shall so desist accordingly. And His Britannic Majesty engages on his part to put an end immediately after the Ratification of the present Treaty to hostilities with all the Tribes or Nations of Indians with whom He may be at war at the time of such Ratification, and forthwith to restore to such Tribes or Nations respectively all the possessions, rights, and privileges, which they may have enjoyed or been entitled to in one thousand eight hundred and eleven previous to such hostilities. Provided always that such Tribes or Nations shall agree to desist from all hostilities against His Britannic Majesty and His Subjects upon the Ratification of the present Treaty being notified to such Tribes or Nations, and shall so desist accordingly.

ARTICLE THE TENTH.

Whereas the Traffic in Slaves is irreconcilable with the principles of humanity and Justice, and whereas both His Majesty and the United States are desirous of continuing their efforts to promote its entire abolition, it is hereby agreed that both the contracting parties shall use their best endeavours to accomplish so desirable an object.

ARTICLE THE ELEVENTH.

This Treaty when the same shall have been ratified on both sides without alteration by either of the contracting parties, and the Ratifications mutually exchanged, shall be binding on both parties, and the Ratifications shall be exchanged at Washington in the space of four months from this day or sooner if practicable. In faith whereof, We the respective Plenipotentiaries have signed this Treaty, and have hereunto affixed our Seals.

Done in triplicate at Ghent the twenty fourth day of December one thousand eight hundred and fourteen.

GAMBIER. [Seal]
HENRY GOULBURN [Seal]
WILLIAM ADAMS [Seal]
JOHN QUINCY ADAMS [Seal]
J. A. BAYARD [Seal]
H. CLAY. [Seal]
JON. RUSSELL [Seal]
ALBERT GALLATIN [Seal]

*SOURCE:* National Archives and Records Administration. At our.documents.gov. http://www.ourdocuments.gov/doc.php?doc=20&page=transcrip (July 22, 2005).

*RELATED ENTRIES: Impressment; Indian Wars: Eastern Wars; War of 1812*

## 1824

**Lyrics to "The Hunters of Kentucky," a Popular Song Celebrating Jackson's Victory over the British**

*This song, first performed in a Richmond, Virginia, theater, is one of a number of antebellum songs celebrating the tradition of the volunteer soldier. An instant "hit," it was often sung at political rallies supporting Andrew Jackson for president:*

Ye gentlemen and ladies fair, who grace this famous city,
Just listen, if you've time to spare, while I rehearse a ditty;
And for the opportunity conceive yourselves quite lucky,
For 'tis not often that you see a hunter from Kentucky.

Chorus:
Oh, Kentucky! the hunters of Kentucky.

We are a hardy free-born race, each man to fear a stranger,
Whate'er the game we join in chase, despising toil and danger;
And if a daring foe annoys, whate'er his strength and forces,
We'll show him that Kentucky boys are alligator horses.

I s'pose you've read it in the prints, how Packenham attempted
To make old Hickory Jackson wince, but soon his schemes repented;
For we with rifles ready cocked, thought such occasion lucky,
And soon around the general flocked the hunters of Kentucky.

You've heard, I s'pose, how New Orleans is famed for wealth and beauty
There's girls of every hue, it seems, from snowy white to sooty.
So Packenham he made his brags, if he in fight was lucky,
He'd have their girls and cotton bags in spite of old Kentucky.

But Jackson he was wide awake, and wasn't scared at trifles,
For well he knew what aim we take with our Kentucky rifles;
So he led us down to Cyprus swamp, the ground was low and mucky,
There stood John Bull in martial pomp, and here was old Kentucky.

A bank was raised to hide our breast, not that we thought of dying,
But then we always like to rest unless the game is flying;
Behind it stood our little force, none wished it to be greater,
For every man was half a horse and half an alligator.

They did not let our patience tire, before they showed their faces—
We did not choose to waste our fire, so snugly kept our places;
But when so near to see them wink, we thought it time to stop 'em,
And 'twould have done you good I think to see Kentuckians drop 'em.

They found at last 'twas vain to fight, where lead was all their booty,
And so they wisely took to flight, and left us all our beauty,
And now if danger e'er annoys, remember what our trade is,
Just send for us Kentucky boys, and we'll protect your ladies.

*SOURCE:* "The Hunters of Kentucky" (New York: Andrews, Printer).

*RELATED ENTRIES: Jackson, Andrew; Music and War*

## 1830

### Sec. of War John Eaton on Inability to Fill Army Ranks

*The disdain men like Parson Weems had in the 1790s for U.S. Army regulars persisted well into the 19th century. In 1830, John Eaton, secretary of war under Pres. Andrew Jackson, wrestled with his department's inability to find enough able men "obtained upon principles of fair contract" to fill his enlisted quota of 6,000 men. Eaton noted that there were 12 million Americans in 1830. In other words, Congress had authorized the raising of an army of 1 enlisted man for every 2,000 persons. In 2005 the U.S. population was about 296 million, and the authorized enlisted strength of the U.S. Army was about 450,000 or about 1 enlisted man for every 660 persons. In 1830 the Army had more trouble recruiting a third as many men per capita in peacetime than it would in 2005 in wartime.*

Different feelings, altered habits, higher self-respect, and honorable incentive, in some form or other, must be produced, or the evils deservedly complained of in our army, will continue. Partial remedies are mere palliatives, and cannot answer any permanent good.

The law-giver who would reach reform, must, in the adoption of his means, look for the approbation and sanction of society; and here allow me to say, that popular opinion, in the absence of war, is not with the existing law for the punishment of desertion. In time of peace, public opinion turns with abhorrence from the severity of the penalty, and renders the law a dead letter on the statute book. Milder punishments should be resorted to, carrying with them a more appropriate and certain effect.

A more important consideration, however, than the infliction of punishment as a remedy, should be looked to. If we inspirit the soldiers of our army, rather than dishonor them, and excite them through the avenues of honorable emulation, may we not expect a return more in accordance with the dignity of human nature, the character of our people, and the genius of our institutions? There is a constant proneness in man to better his condition, and every obstacle that society interposes to check this, is impolitic and unwise.

As our army is at present organized, the gallant and faithful soldier has no opportunity afforded him to rise above his enlisted condition. He may become a corporal, or sergeant, but, with that humble advance, his hopes and his ambition terminate. Knowing that impassable barriers exist, to prevent his elevation, all incentive is destroyed, and ambition is quieted. He feels that his country has placed on him the seal of abasement, and he sinks dispirited under its withering influence. But if the door to promotion be unbarred, and the law shall recognise no distinction except merit—that the highest honors may be reached by the humblest private—what a noble incentive would it create, what enthusiasm would not follow? Multitudes then would be found advancing, who now feel the stubborn interdiction which hangs upon their hopes and expectations. There is a buoyancy in hope, that sustains in adversity, and which leads on in prosperity; extend it to the soldier, and the creations of his own fancy will give a moral force and an elevated cast of character, to which, without it, he will be an alien.

The graduates of West Point Academy, from established practice, and not by authority of law, have the exclusive privilege of entering the army. All other portions of the community are excluded. The private who has served faithfully through danger and privation, and who, from experience, has learned to obey, (thereby making himself the better qualified to command) on surveying the prospects before him, finds that each year brings a stranger to command him—a junior officer from the Military Academy. This state of things must weaken the inducements to a correct and faithful course of conduct. The non-commissioned officers, knowing that no servitude, however long or faithful; no deportment, however exemplary; no valor, however distinguished; entitle them to promotion—that they but serve only as instruments for the advancement of others—feel the injustice, and sink under the despondency it produces. . . .

Another suggestion, in connexion with this subject, deserves consideration. At present, the law allows a premium to the recruiting officer for every soldier he shall enlist: this, either in whole or in part, passes to the non-commissioned officer, who superintends the performance of this duty. Under the temptation presented, it operates as a bounty for the encouragement of frauds, as it leads to active efforts to entrap the young, the inconsiderate, and the intemperate, by improper allurements and vicious devices. This regulation ought to be abrogated, that every inducement to impropriety may be removed, that the citizen may not be imposed on, and that the Army may be composed of men who seek the service voluntarily, rather than those who have been entrapped in a moment of intoxication, and who awake from the stupor with abhorrence, anxious only to devise means how they are to escape from their dread condition. If none other present, desertion becomes the alternative; and this is sustained by the fact that more than half the desertions which take place are with the new recruits.

A country possessing twelve millions of people, ought surely to be able at all times to possess itself of an Army of six thousand men, obtained upon principles of fair contract: if this cannot be effected, then will it be better to rely on some other mode of defence, rather than resort to the expedient of obtaining a discontented and besotted soldiery. To this end orders have been given to our recruiting officers forbidding any enlistments if the persons be in the least intoxicated.

*SOURCE:* Senate Doc. no. 62, vol. 2, 21st Cong., 1st Sess., 1829–30.

*RELATED ENTRIES: Conscription and Volunteerism; Jackson, Andrew; Militarization and Militarism*

## 1833

### Revolutionary War Pension Application

*In the early 19th century, Congress passed a series of laws allowing pensions for veterans of the American Revolution. To apply, veterans went to their local courthouse and swore out a statement of their service. The pension office of the War Department retained their applications on file with other supporting documentation. Depending on the state, the courthouse, and the pension law in effect, various standardized forms were also used to aid in the processing of the pension. Certain vital statistics and statements of service were required, but occasionally some veterans took the opportunity to tell longer stories. What follows is a partial transcription of South Carolina veteran James Dillard's sworn affidavit (S6797), as well as an image of a common standardized form used for his application. It is representative of an average pension application. Note that the statement was usually delivered orally and recorded by the court clerk, thus the switching of pronouns from "he" to "I" and back again. The pension records are now filed in the National Archives as the "Revolutionary War Pension and Bounty Land Warrant Application Files, 1800–1900, (M804).*

The State of South Carolina
Laurens district

To Wit

On this Eleventh day of July Anno Domini 1833 personally appeared before the Honorable Henry W. Dessaussure one of the chancellors of the said state in open Court being a Court of Chancery now sitting for the district and state aforesaid, Capt. James Dillard a resident of Laurens district in the State of South Carolina aged Seventy seven or Seventy Eight years, who being first duly sworn according to Law, doth on his oath make the following declaration in order to obtain the benefit of the provisions made by the act of Congress passed June 7 1832. That he entered the service of the United States under the following named officers and served as herein after stated.

This applicant was born in Culpepper County in the State of Virginia in the year 1755 or 1756 according to the information derived from his parents, having in his possession no record of his age. That he was living at the time he entered the service in what was then called Ninety Six District in the state of S Carolina near where he now lives and where he has continued to live to this day.

I enlisted under Capt _______ Perieuhoof [?] in Col William Thompson's Regiment of State Troops at Ninety Six otherwise called Cambridg in So Carolina for six months, some time in the month of September 1775 and at the time of Col Drayton's Campaign in that part of the State. That he was marched with a detachment of State Troops under the command of Col. Thomson from Ninety Six to Dorchester in So Carolina where he was stationed for the protection of the magazine of that place untill the expiration of his term of service which was in March 1776. Immediately upon the expiration of his first term of service, he again enlisted under Capt Perieuhoof in the same company and Regiment of State Troops commanded by the same officers for the term of eighteen months. During this term of service he was taken from Dorchester to the 10 mile house near Charleston where we were stationed for some time, and during that time Capt Perieuhoof died and was succeeded by Capt Brown. While stationed at the 10 mile house an express arrived and we were marched in the night time to Charleston where we arrived about sunrise in the morning and after receiving some refreshment we were carried over to Sullivan's Island (Fort Moultrie). Genl Lee was at this time Commander in Chief at Charlestown, Col. Moultrie had the immediate command at Fort Moultrie assisted by Maj. Marion. He was in the engagement in which Sir Peter Parker was repulsed in his attack upon Fort Moultrie in June 1776. Some time after this engagement we were removed to Charleston, from there to the 10 mile house, from the 10 mile house we were marched to Nelson's Ferry on Santee River, from thence to Purysburgh on Savannah River and after lying there a short time were were marched back to Nelsons Ferry on Santee River. From that place we were marched to [. . . .] where we remained untill he was discharged to the best of his recollection in September 1777. During the next spring this applicant volunteered his services in Capt. Josiah Greer's company of militia, in Col James William's Regt, Robert McGrary Lieut Col. and Received the appointment of Sergeant Major, and served during the expedition to Florida under the command of Genl Andrew Williamson. This expedition proceeded beoynd [sic] St. Mary's River and then returned to So Carolina after a tour of better than four months when this applicant was again discharged. After his return from Florida he again voluteered under Capt McGrary and swerved [sic] a tour of one month in pursuit of Col. Boyd who commanded a detachment of Tories. He next volunteered as a private under Capt. Thomas McGrary and served three months on the Indian frontier as a militiaman to prevent the Tories and Indians from molesting the people of the State. After the fall of Charleston he took refuge in No Carolina untill about the first of August 1780 when he joined Col. James Williams and was elected a Captain in his Regiment and received a Commission signed by Governor Rutledge, which has been lost or mislaid. With this Regiment he was marched to Kings Mountain and with the commands of Cols Campbell, Shelby, Sevier & Cleveland participated in the Victory gained over Col. Ferguson at that place where his Col. James Williams was killed. After this action Col Joseph Hays succeeded to the command of the Regiment and this applicant continued in his command as captain with the same Regiment employed in almost constant service to the close of the war. During the time Col. Hays commanded the Regiment this applicant was engaged under the command of Col. Washington of the Continental Line in a battle in which the tories were defeated at Bush River and at the taking of Williams Fort. He was also at the Battle of Cowpens under the command of Genl Morgan in which Tarleton was defeated when he received a gunshot wound. He was also at the siege of 96 under Genl Green, and was in command of the same company. In the close of the year 1781 Col. Joseph Hays was killed and was succeeded by Col. Levi Casey. Under him the Regiment proceeded under Genl Andrew Pickens to Edisto River where they defeated the tories under Col. Cunningham and this applicant was again wounded. He also received two other wounds, saber cuts, in skirmishes with the Indians. After he recovered of his wound he was sent by Col. Casey with a part of his company to join Genl Pickens in an expedition to the Cherokee Nation to compel them to deliver up Tories who had taken refuge there. This tour was about two months and during the time a treaty of peace was made with the Indians. This was the last service this applicant performed and was in the year 1783. This applicant received a discharge but it has been lost or destroyed and has no other papers relating to his services than is herewith forwarded. He hereby relingquishes [sic] every claim whatsoever to a pension or annuity except the present and he declares that his name is not on the pension Roll of any agency in any state. He refers to the Revd John B. Kennedy and Robert Lord Esquire, Golding Tinsley, James Tinsley, & Thomas Entrick [?] to testify as to his services and character. Sworn to and subscribed on day and year aforesaid.

X James Dillard [he has signed his own name, next to an X]

*SOURCE:* "Selected Records from Revolutionary War Pension and Bounty Land Warrant Application Files, 1800–1900." Microfilm in the library of the National Society of the Sons of the American Revolution, (M805).

*RELATED ENTRIES: Conscription and Volunteerism; Revolutionary War; Revolutionary War Pensions; Veterans Administration*

## 1835 (to 1854)

### A Crisis of Conscience and Ethan Allen Hitchcock

*Several 18th-century British (and late-18th-century American) Army officers not serving in active regiments declined invitations to serve in wartime with impunity on the grounds that they did not regard a war as "just." The creation of the United States Military Academy at West Point in 1803 steadily replaced the recruiting of officers in this fashion. By the 1830s officers in the U.S. Army increasingly regarded the military as a lifetime profession. Hence an officer with a troubled conscience faced a career dilemma as well as a moral one. Ethan Allen Hitchcock left a rich record of his wrestling with such moral questions in his diary, edited by W. A. Croffut. His first dilemma was with the way a fraudulent treaty with the Seminoles in 1832 (Payne's Landing) was being enforced while he served in Florida in 1835. (Others include what he viewed as the problematic nature of the war with Mexico, the treatment of Indians in the West, and possible war aimed at wresting Cuba from Spanish control in 1854.) During 1835, the Seminole treaty was sent to Gen. Wiley Thompson, the Indian agent in Florida, with orders to announce to the Indians that, in compliance with their treaty, they must go west.*

The king and his chiefs were called together at Fort King, but the moment they heard from the agent the object of the council, they loudly and earnestly denied that there was such a treaty as he alleged. The point of disagreement was upon the article in the treaty touching the deputation; and when they were informed that the six men sent to the West had signed the paper offered to them by Major Phagan, their authority to do so was utterly repudiated. It appeared to the officers of the garrison that the chiefs were entirely in the right; and it appeared also that the king had been kept in ignorance of what the deputation had done until it was disclosed by General Thompson. The Indians themselves, having been compelled to sign that paper in disobedience of the orders they had received, had maintained silence about it, never having informed the king of what they had done. At least this is the only rational solution of the matter.

Councils were then held from time to time for several weeks while a correspondence was being carried on between General Thompson and the government, in which the President insisted upon the execution of the treaty; but on each occasion when it was presented to them they stoutly denied its validity, and on one occasion, while the treaty was lying open on the council table, Miccanopy, pointing to it, exclaimed, 'That is not the treaty: I never signed that treaty!'

'You lie, Miccanopy,' said the agent Thompson, 'Interpreter, tell him he lies, for there is his signature,'—putting his finger on his mark.

But Miccanopy did not lie; for, although his mark was upon that paper, he meant only to deny that he had signed such a paper as was then interpreted to him.

By this time these councils had become quite boisterous, and a young Indian in the council name Osceola, who was called in English by the name of Powell, stood up in council, and with much gesticulation denounced the treaty and everything done about it. This General Thompson imprudently construed into a disrespect to himself, and, not regarding the freedom of debate which the Indians are even more tenacious about in council than the whites, he signified his wish to the commanding officer to have a section of the guard placed at his disposal, which soon appeared, and General Thompson ordered the guard to seize Osceola and put him into confinement, in irons. This was accordingly done, but not without some difficulty, for the young Indian became frantic with rage, and if he had had weapons about him, it would have been very dangerous to approach him; but he was overpowered and carried to prison in irons.

Upon this, General Thompson wrote desponding letters to the government, and it was uncertain for a time what was to be done or what could be done. Osceola, on his part, acted like a madman; he was perfectly furious when anybody came near him. After some days of frenzied violence he seemed to have formed his ultimate purpose and settled down into a perfect calm. He sent word to General Thompson that he wished to see him, and General Thompson, having been informed of his quiet disposition, permitted an interview. In this interview Osceola became exceedingly submissive; acknowledged himself to be entirely in the wrong; apologized for what he had done, and asked General Thompson's forgiveness; declared that he was now willing to go to the West with his people, and, as he had been made a sub-chief over a small band, he told General Thompson that if he would release him and allow him to go among his people, he would bring them all in, and deliver them to the agent.

General Thompson then addressed a letter to President Jackson direct, in which, with great exultation, he informed the President that all the difficulties were now overcome; that Osceola had gone out to bring in his people, and that the treaty would be executed. But nothing was further from Osceola's intentions than compliance with his promises. He had resorted to them only for the purpose of gaining his liberty, that he might employ it in seeking revenge upon General Thompson for the outrage put upon him by arresting him for 'words spoken in debate.'

Osceola, being at large, armed himself, and lay in wait for an opportunity of taking the life of the man whom he regarded as the foe of his people. General Thompson had been in the habit of walking between the agency house and the fort, which were separated from each other a few hundred yards, with clumps of bushes here and there along the road, affording places of concealment. An opportunity did not offer itself for the execution of Osceola's purpose for some days, and he thought it necessary to give General Thompson some evidence of his fidelity, to throw him, or keep him, off his guard. With this object he gathered up a few of the women and children of his band, and exhibiting these he told General Thompson that his people had become so much scattered that he had not been able to find them, but that he would do so as soon as possible. General Thompson had no suspicion of his purpose, and allowed him to go out again; and, as he did not care to detain the women and children, they were allowed to go also.

A few days after this, on the 28th of December, 1835, Osceola, with some of his band, concealed by bushes near the road leading from the fort to the agency house, saw General Thompson approach, accompanied by a lieutenant, Constantine Smith, and the Indians, securing their aim, at a signal fired, killing both the agent and his companion. Osceola immediately fled and took command of the Indians in the field [sending out a runner to all chiefs directing that no white woman or child should be harmed, "for this fight is between men."]

This tragedy happened on the very day on which the main body of the Indians under Miccanopy waylaid Major Dade, who was marching up from Tampa Bay to Fort King, with two companies of infantry and a piece of artillery. When within about thirty-five miles of Fort King this body of troops was ambushed, and the whole party destroyed except three who escaped from the massacre and got back to Tampa Bay.

The Indians had taken the alarm from the disclosures made in the councils at Fort King, and had banded together resolved to resist any attempt at a movement of troops in their country for their expulsion from it. Many of them knew the officers at Tampa Bay. . . .

July 8, 1836. . . . I hardly know what it is proper to do. When I left General Gaines all was quiet on the Sabine. I was temporarily attached to his staff and had his orders to return to him from Washington, but I thought the order was for my accommodation, and believing active service in that quarter at an end, I did not hesitate to avail myself of Major Smith's offer to relieve him at New York. Now I hear that General Gaines has actually crossed the Sabine and gone with his army to Nacogdoches in Texas. I am puzzled what to do. I regard the whole of the proceedings in the Southwest as being wicked as far as the United States are concerned. Our people have provoked the war with Mexico and are prosecuting it not for 'liberty' but for land, and I feel averse to being an instrument for these purposes. . . .

July 1837. . . . Report to the Secretary of War, . . .

I have crossed the purposes of a band of greedy speculators and brought upon myself the maledictions of many who will pretend an infinite degree of sympathy for the very half-breeds whom they have cheated and almost robbed by what will be boldly put forth as a legal proceeding. Be the consequences what they may, I rejoice that I have, for a few weeks at least, suspended the execution of this business. One claim of $1800 was sold under duress for $400. Can such a transaction pass in review without condemnation because it may wear the color of law? It is monstrous; and, if lawful, the law is a scourge to the innocent. . . .

June 22 [1840]. "We are ordered to St. Louis (Jefferson Barracks) and then, after the sickly season, to Florida. I saw the beginning of the Florida campaigns in 1836, and may see the end of them unless they see the end of me. The government is in the wrong, and this is the chief cause of the persevering opposition of the Indians, who have nobly defended their country against our attempt to enforce a fraudulent treaty. The natives used every means to avoid a war, but were forced into it by the tyranny of our government. . . .

Nov. 1 [1840]. . . . The treaty of Payne's Landing was a fraud on the Indians: They never approved of it or signed it. They are right in defending their homes and we ought to let them alone. The country southward is poor for our purposes, but magnificent for the Indians —a fishing and hunting country without agricultural inducements. The climate is against us and is a paradise for them. The army has done all that it could. It has marched all over the upper part of Florida. It has burned all the towns and destroyed all the planted fields. Yet, though the Indians are broken up and scattered, they exist in large numbers, separated, but worse than ever. . . . The chief, Coocoochee, is in the vicinity. It is said that he hates the whites so bitterly that 'he never hears them mentioned without gnashing his teeth.' . . .

Nov. 14. . . . General Armistead is entirely subdued and broken spirited. His confidence in his success has been boundless and his letters to Washington have doubtless been written in that temper. I cannot help thinking it is partly his own fault. If he had freely offered the Indians an ample reward to emigrate, or the undisturbed possession of the country south of Tampa Bay, he might have secured peace. I have suggested his making the overture now, but he declines. Not only did he refuse to make the offer he was authorized to make, but at the very time when Halec [Tustenugga] was here in amicable talk he secretly sent a force into his rear, threatening his people at home! . . . I confess to a very considerable disgust in this service. I remember the cause of the war, and that annoys me. I think of the the folly and stupidity with which it has been conducted, particularly of the puerile character of the present commanding general, and I am quite out of patience. . . .

29th Aug [1845]. Received last evening . . . a letter from Captain Casey and a map of Texas from the Quarter-master-General's office, the latter being the one prepared by Lieutenant Emory; but it has added to it a distinct boundary mark to the Rio Grande. Our people ought to be damned for their impudent arrogance and domineering presumption! It is enough to make atheists of us all to see such wickedness in the world, whether punished or unpunished. . . .

1st Oct. . . . [T]his morning . . . as frequently of late, [General Zachary Taylor] introduced the subject of moving upon the Rio Grande. I discovered this time more clearly than ever that the General is instigated by ambition—or so it appears to me. He seems quite to have lost all respect for Mexican rights and willing to be an instrument of Mr. Polk for pushing our boundary as far west as possible. When I told him that, if he suggested a movement (which he told me he intended), Mr. Polk would seize upon it and throw the responsibility on him, he at once said he would take it, and added that if the President instructed him to use his discretion, he would ask no orders, but would go upon the Rio Grande as soon as he could get transportation. I think the General wants an additional brevet, and would strain a point to get it. . . .

2d Nov. Newspapers all seem to indicate that Mexico will make no movement, and the government is magnanimously bent on taking advantage of it to insist upon 'our claim' as far as the Rio Grande. I hold this to be monstrous and abominable. But now, I see, the United states of America, as a people, are undergoing changes in character, and the real status and principles for which our forefathers fought are fast being lost sight of. If I could by any decent means get a living in retirement, I would abandon a government which I think corrupted by both ambition and avarice to the last degree. . . .

25th March [1846]. . . . As to the right of this movement, I have said from the first that the United States are the aggressors. We have outraged the Mexican government and people by an arrogance and presumption that deserve to be punished. For ten years we have been encroaching on Mexico and insulting her. . . .

26th March. . . . My heart is not in this business; I am against it from the bottom of my soul as most unholy and unrighteous proceeding; but, as a military man, I am bound to execute orders. . . .

*[Hitchcock became ill and was evacuated to recover in the United States.]*

Sunday, May 24. . . . I am necessarily losing, from a military point of view, all the honors of the field. I was hoping that no collision would take place. . . . My absence from my regiment at such a time as this is a species of death; yet the doctor says I must not think of going south in the hot weather, as he has another surgical operation to perform. . . .

10th Nov. I am very much disgusted with this war in all of its features. I am in the position of the preacher who read Strauss's criticism of the Gospel History of Christ. Shall he preach his new convictions? Shall he preach what his audience believes? Shall he temporize? Shall he resign? Here the preacher has an advantage over the soldier, for, while the latter may be ordered into an unjust and unnecessary war, he cannot at that time abandon his profession—at all events, not without making himself a martyr. In the present case, I not only think this Mexican war unnecessary and unjust as regards Mexico, but I also think it not only hostile to the principles of our own government—a government of the people, securing to them liberty—but I think it a step and a great step towards a dissolution of our Union. And I doubt not that a dissolution of the Union will bring on wars between the separated parts. . . .

*[Having recovered, Hitchcock was ordered to join in a expedition under the overall command of Gen. Winfield Scott.]*

New Orleans, Dec 15, 1846. High time to use my notebook. Left Louis on 21st, and got here the 31st. With other officers have since waited for a steamer to take us to the Brazos at S. Lago in western Texas. Report is fully confirmed that General Scott will take the conduct of the war, and it is considered settled that the castle of San Juan at Vera Cruz is to be assailed. My regiment is with Taylor at Monterey.

My feeling towards the war is no better than at first. I still feel that it was unnecessarily brought on by President Polk, and, not withstanding his disclaimers, I believe he expressly aimed to get possession of California and New Mexico, which I see, by his message received here today, he considers accomplished. Now, however, as the war is going on, it must, as almost everybody supposes, be carried on by us aggressively, and in this I must be an instrument. I certainly do not feel properly for such a duty, particularly as I see that my health is almost sure to fail me . . . I feel very much like making a sacrifice of myself and drawing the curtain between me and this life. I am convinced that no contingency connected with this war can affect that in me which, by its nature, is immortal, and the end must be the same be my passage to it what it may. As a matter of taste and choice, I should prefer a more quiet career, and one in which I could pursue my favorite studies, of philosophy. But this is not to be. . . .

February 27, 1847. Colonel Hitchcock to Rev. Theodore Parker in Boston: I coincide with you in your views of this abominable war. Humble as I am, I wish not to fall a victim to this war without entering my protest against it as unjust on our part and needlessly and wickedly brought about. I am here, not by choice, but because, being in this army, it is my duty to obey the constituted authorities. As an individual I condemn, I abominate this war: as a member of the government I must go with it until our authorities are brought back to a sense of justice. . . .

September 7, 1847. . . .

3 P.M. At 1, I was at the General's. He read to me his order for massing the troops by to-morrow noon. Quitman and Twiggs are ordered to Misquoique, but a brigade is this afternoon to threaten the city by the Piedad route (between San Antonio and the Chapultepec route), and to-night Worth, with his division and one brigade of Pillow's is to attack and destroy the foundry. Thus matters now stand. The foundry is under the guns of Chapultepec, and its destruction by daylight might be very difficult if not impossible without first silencing the commanding guns. Hence it is to be attempted to-night. So the orders contemplate. . . .

6 P.M. I am alone in the extensive garden attached to the house of the consul, in which I am quartered. I look upon the great variety of fruits and flowers in vast abundance and luxuriance, and I ask why the monster-genius of war is allowed to pollute such scenes.

I have often entered my protest against this war, and today I hear, from very good authority, that our commissioner has said that if he were a Mexican he would die before he would agree to the terms proposed by the United States. He ought, then, to have refused the mission he has undertaken. A degrading proposition is alike dishonorable to him who proposes as to him to whom it is proposed. . . .

*[In the early 1850s, Hitchcock commanded the army on the Pacific Coast.]*

August 5, 1852. . . . The wrong [at the headwaters of the San Joachim River] came, as usual, from white men. The Indian commissioner last year made treaties with these Indians, and assigned them reservations of land as their own. The whites have not respected the proceedings of the commissioner, but have occupied the reservation to a considerable extent and established a ferry within the lands assigned to the Indians. To this the Indians seem to have objected, and one of them told the ferryman that he was on their land and he would have to go away, because his boat and apparatus stopped the salmon from ascending the river. This, it is said, was considered a hostile threat, and a party of whites was raised to go among the Indians and demand an explanation. As what had been said to the ferryman was said by only one or two and was not advised by the tribe, the latter was taken entirely by surprise by this armed party, and, knowing nothing of its object and becoming alarmed, some it is said were seen picking up their bows, and this was considered a sign of hostile intent and they were fired on and fifteen or twenty were killed! Some of the Indians belonging to the tribe were, at the moment their friends were fired on, at work on a white man's farm some miles distant, without the smallest suspicion of existing causes of hostility.

Affairs thereupon assumed a threatening aspect, and a great council has been appointed for Aug. 15th, at which all the surrounding tribes will assemble on King's River, to discuss the question of going to war with the whites. It is to overawe this council that I have sent the troops to Fort Miller. It is a hard case for the troops to know the whites are in the wrong, and yet be compelled to punish the Indians if they attempt to defend themselves. . . .

October 24, 1852. . . . I have to-day given away my land-warrant for 160 acres of land to my cousin. I have felt some disposition to locate this land in my own name and retain it, as it is for service in the field (in the Mexican War); but as it was in a detestable war, I have concluded to put it out of my hands. . . .

May 1854. . . . [We] make a quarrel with Spain, really for the purpose of seizing the island of Cuba. I have not the smallest sympathy with the movement. I think that republican principles would be injured by the annexation of Cuba to the United States.

I have been seriously thinking of resigning from the army. . . . I consider the slavery in our country an element guided by passion, rather than by reason, and its existence among us is shaking the whole fabric of our government. Abolitionists would abolish the institution of slavery as the real evil, whereas the real evil is the want of intelligence from which slavery itself took its rise. Men in a passion, as Plato says, are already slaves.

As to leaving the army: I may do so if I choose at this time and no one to notice me, for I am unknown except to a few friends. If I wait and a war with Spain be forced on us by the headlong ambition or false policy of the Cabinet at Washington it might be hazardous to retire, even though in principle opposed to the war, not only as unjustifiable toward Spain but as impolitic and injurious as respects ourselves. I do verily believe that such a war would be a downward instead of an onward step for our republican institutions, and might easily justify my own conscience in refusing to be an instrument in the unjust campaign.

I might draw a line between my duty to remain in the army to repulse any attempt made from abroad upon us, and the questionable duty of going beyond our borders to inflict wrong upon another people, with probable injury to us in the end. I had this point in consideration on entering into the Mexican War, the grievous wrong of which was perfectly apparent to me, but I did not resign. My principles were not then so clear to me as they have since become, and it would have been more difficult to act freely then than now—in case I mean, of a war with Spain manifestly for the acquisition of Cuba. . . .

New York, May 31. I am in doubt as to leaving the army, wishing to do so, but uncertain as to the result. I do not wish to be moved by the slightest disposition to avoid service and responsibility. One point of weight with me is my personal opinions, after reading Plato, as I have, and finding myself more than ever a cosmopolite. The truth is, I am not sufficiently devoted to my profession, or even to my government, to make service a pleasure. I consider war an evil, whether necessary or not. It indicates a state of comparative barbarism in the nation engaged in it. I am also doubtful as to governments, and feel disposed to think that with my views I ought to live under what Plato, in the Statesman, speaks of as the 7th government. The question remains whether I can pass from a practical to a theoretical life, and whether, being a member of society, I am not bound to act with it. If I resign I wish to do so in such a frame of mind as to have no after regrets. This, in fact, is the principle which I wish to have guide me in whatever I do, for my eternity is here and now.

St. Louis, Oct. 6, 1855. I have prepared a letter, now on the table before me, addressed to Colonel Thomas, Asst. Adj.-General to General Scott, tendering the resignation of my commission in the army. My leave of absence terminates to-day, and I have thought for several years that if circumstances should compel me to serve under [General Harney's] orders, I would resign. It has now happened. I have been placed under the orders of a man for whom I have not the smallest respect—a man without education, intelligence, or humanity. I have not acted hastily. I have not resigned in a passion. I am not under the influence of anger or pique, nor do I feel a sense of mortification because an unworthy man has been set over me. Least of all do I suppose that I shall be missed from the army, or that my country will notice my withdrawal to private life. I know how little a great nation depends upon any mere individual, and how still less upon so humble a person as myself. I am content to be unnoticed. If I could really do some great and glorious good I should be willing to take the reputation of it, but I have not the smallest desire for mere notoriety. It is a rare thing in our service for a full colonel (brevet brigadier-general) to resign, and thereby relinquish all contingent advantages, but I voluntarily surrender them all rather than to place myself under orders of such a man as I know [General Harney] to be.

*[W.A. Croffut, the editor of Hitchcock's diary, added this paragraph of his own.]*

Shortly after these words were written a messenger came galloping across the prairies towards St. Louis telling the story that our soldiers, under [General Harney's] command, had perpetrated the bloody butchery of Ash Hollow, in which, after a treacherous parley, and while they were negotiating terms of peace, they fell upon the Brules and exterminated the tribe. The New York Tribune characterized it as "a transaction as shameful, detestable, and cruel as anywhere sullies our annals," and the St. Louis News said that the commander "divested himself of the attributes of civilized humanity and turned himself into a treacherous demon, remorseless and bloodthirsty." When he read the horrible narrative General Hitchcock congratulated himself anew on having sent his resignation.

*SOURCE:* W. A. Croffut, ed., *Fifty Years in Camp and Field* (New York: Putnam, 1909), 81–85, 111, 116, 120, 122, 123, 198, 202, 212, 214, 225, 228, 229, 237, 296, 396, 404, 411–12, 418–19.

*RELATED ENTRIES: Hitchcock; Ethan Allen; Indian Wars: Seminole Wars; Just War Theory; Osceola*

## 1838

### Lyrics to "Benny Havens, Oh!"

*Benny Havens operated a tavern in the immediate vicinity of the United States Military Academy at West Point near Buttermilk Falls some time in the 1820s. Many cadets regarded an after-hours visit to this tavern as a true measure of one's daring and skill, and a number found their way there on the sly in the 1820s, 1830s, and 1840s. The tavern was not off-limits to officers stationed at the Academy, and in 1838 Lt. Lucius O'Brien penned a number of verses, sung to Thomas Moore's song "The Wearing of the Green," that became popular with both officers and cadets. After O'Brien was killed in action in the Second Seminole War in 1841, each graduating class added a verse. The song has more than 50 known verses, but the most often sung are the first and the sixth of the nine given here:*

Come fill your glasses, fellows, and stand up, in a row,
To singing sentimentally we're going for to go.
In the Army there's sobriety, promotion's very slow,
So we'll sing our reminiscences of Benny Havens, Oh!

Chorus:
Oh! Benny Havens, Oh!
Oh! Benny Havens, Oh!
We'll sing our reminiscences of Benny Havens, Oh!

Let us toast our foster father, the Republic, as you know,
Who in the paths of science taught us upward for to go;
And the maidens of our native land, whose cheeks like roses glow,
They're oft remembered in our cups at Benny Havens, Oh!

To the ladies of our Army our cups shall ever flow,
Companions in our exile and our shield 'gainst every woe;
May they see their husbands generals, with double pay also,
And join us in our choruses at Benny Havens, Oh!

Come fill up to our Generals, God bless the brave heroes,
They're an honor to their country, and a terror to their foes;
May they long rest on their laurels, and troubles never know,
But live to see a thousand years at Benny Havens, Oh!

To our kind old Alma Mater, our rock-bound Highland home,
We'll cast back many a fond regret as o'er life's sea we roam;
Until on our last battle-field the lights of heaven shall glow,
We'll never fail to drink to her and Benny Havens, Oh!

May the Army be augmented, promotion be less slow,
May our country in the hour of need be ready for the foe;
May we find a soldier's resting-place beneath a soldier's blow,
With room enough beside our graves for Benny Havens, Oh!

And if amid the battle shock our honor e'er should trail,
And hearts that beat beneath its folds should turn or basely quail;
Then may some son of Benny's, with quick avenging blow,
Lift up the flag we loved so well at Benny Havens, Oh!

To our comrades who have fallen, one cup before we go,
They poured their life-blood freely out pro bono publico;
No marble points the stranger to where they rest below,
They lie neglected far away from Benny Havens, Oh!

When you and I and Benny, and all the others too,
Are called before the "final board" our course in life to view,
May we never "fess" on any point, but straight be told to go,
And join the army of the blest at Benny Havens, Oh!

This song, like "Army Blue," we are printing here because it is dear to our friends and rivals, the Cadets of the United States Military Academy. In addition it is beloved by every alumnus of West Point; and there are few midshipmen or naval officers who have not become acquainted with it. Benny Havens, it is understood, was originally a sutler on the West Point reservation and very popular with the cadets of earlier days; but in the course of hallowing years the name has in a way become synonymous with West Point itself.

*SOURCE:* Joseph W. Crosley and the United States Naval Institute. *The Book of Navy Songs.* Annapolis, Md.: United States Naval Academy, 1955. Reprinted by permission of the Naval Institute Press.

*RELATED ENTRIES: Military Academy, United States; Music and War*

## 1846 a

### Letter from Pres. James Polk to House of Representatives on Secrecy in Executive Branch Dealings

*This document is one of the earlier examples of the debate between the president and the Congress about the nature of executive secrecy, and the limits to which diplomatic activity could be kept secret. This letter from Pres. James K. Polk to the House of Representatives lays out one version of the executive branch's justification for preservation of at least some secrecy. The particular controversy referred to relates to the secretary of state who served under Polk's predecessor, specifically the secretary's negotiations with Britain over the northeastern boundary of the United States and Canada.*

WASHINGTON, April 20, 1846.
To the House of Representatives:

I have considered the resolution of the House of Representatives of the 9th instant, by which I am requested "to cause to be furnished to that House an account of all payments made on President's certificates from the fund appropriated by law, through the agency of the State Department, for the contingent expenses of foreign intercourse from the 4th of March, 1841, until the retirement of Daniel Webster from the Department of State, with copies of all entries, receipts, letters, vouchers, memorandums, or other evidence of such payments, to whom paid, for what, and particularly all concerning the northeastern-boundary dispute with Great Britain."

With an anxious desire to furnish to the House any information requested by that body which may be in the Executive Departments, I have felt bound by a sense of public duty to inquire how far I could with propriety, or consistently with the existing laws, respond to their call.

The usual annual appropriation "for the contingent expenses of intercourse between the United States and foreign nations" has been disbursed since the date of the act of May 1, 1810, in pursuance of its provisions. By the third section of that act it is provided—

> That when any sum or sums of money shall be drawn from the Treasury under any law making appropriation for the contingent expenses of intercourse between the United States and foreign nations the President shall be, and he is hereby, authorized to cause the same to be duly settled annually with the accounting officers of the Treasury in the manner following; that is to say, by causing the same to be accounted for specially in all instances wherein the expenditure thereof may in his judgment be made public, and by making a certificate of the amount of such expenditures as he may think it advisable not to specify; and every such certificate shall be deemed a sufficient voucher for the sum or sums therein expressed to have been expended.

Two distinct classes of expenditure are authorized by this law—the one of a public and the other of a private and confidential character. The President in office at the time of the expenditure is made by the law the sole judge whether it shall be public or private. Such sums are to be "accounted for specially in all instances wherein the expenditure thereof may in his judgment be made public." All expenditures "accounted for specially" are settled at the Treasury upon vouchers, and not on "President's certificates," and, like all other public accounts, are subject to be called for by Congress, and are open to public examination. Had information as respects this class of expenditures been called for by the resolution of the House, it would have been promptly communicated. . . .

If the President may answer the present call, he must answer similar calls for every such expenditure of a confidential character, made under every Administration, in war and in peace, from the organization of the Government to the present period. To break the seal of confidence imposed by the law, and heretofore uniformly preserved, would be subversive of the very purpose for which the law was enacted, and might be productive of the most disastrous consequences. The expenditures of this confidential character, it is believed, were never before sought to be made public, and I should greatly apprehend the consequences of establishing a precedent which would render such disclosures hereafter inevitable.

I am fully aware of the strong and correct public feeling which exists throughout the country against secrecy of any kind in the administration of the Government, and especially in reference to public expenditures; yet our foreign negotiations are wisely and properly confined to the knowledge of the Executive during their pendency. Our laws require the accounts of every particular expenditure to be rendered and publicly settled at the Treasury Department. The single exception which exists is not that the amounts embraced under President's certificates shall be withheld from the public, but merely that the items of which these are composed shall not be divulged. To this extent, and no further, is secrecy observed.

The laudable vigilance of the people in regard to all the expenditures of the Government, as well as a sense of duty on the part of the President and a desire to retain the good opinion of his fellow-citizens, will prevent any sum expended from being accounted for by the President's certificate unless in cases of urgent necessity. Such certificates have therefore been resorted to but seldom throughout our past history.

For my own part, I have not caused any account whatever to be settled on a Presidential certificate. I have had no occasion rendering it necessary in my judgment to make such a certificate, and it would be an extreme case which would ever induce me to exercise this authority; yet if such a case should arise it would be my duty to assume the responsibility devolved on me by the law.

During my Administration all expenditures for contingent expenses of foreign intercourse in which the accounts have been closed have been settled upon regular vouchers, as all other public accounts are settled at the Treasury.

It may be alleged that the power of impeachment belongs to the House of Representatives, and that, with a view to the exercise of this power, that House has the right to investigate the conduct of all public officers under the Government. This is cheerfully admitted. In such a case the safety of the Republic would be the supreme law, and the power of the House in the pursuit of this object would penetrate into the most secret recesses of the Executive Departments. It could command the attendance of any and every agent of the Government, and compel them to produce all papers, public or private, official or unofficial, and to testify on oath to all facts within their knowledge. But even in a case of that kind they would adopt all wise precautions to prevent the exposure of all such matters the publication of which might injuriously affect the public interest, except so far as this might be necessary to accomplish the great ends of public justice. If the House of Representatives, as the grand inquest of the nation, should at any time have reason to believe that there has been malversation in office by an improper use or application of the public money by a public officer, and should think proper to institute an inquiry into the matter, all the archives and papers of the Executive Departments, public or private, would be subject to the inspection and control of a committee of their body and every facility in the power of the Executive be afforded to enable them to prosecute the investigation.

The experience of every nation on earth has demonstrated that emergencies may arise in which it becomes absolutely necessary for the public safety or the public good to make expenditures the very object of which would be defeated by publicity. Some governments have very large amounts at their disposal, and have made vastly greater expenditures than the small amounts which have from time to time been accounted for on President's certificates. In no nation is the application of such sums ever made public. In time of war or impending danger the situation of the country may make it necessary to employ individuals for the purpose of obtaining information or rendering other important services who could never be prevailed upon to act if they entertained the least apprehension that their names or their agency would in any contingency be divulged. So it may often become necessary to incur an expenditure for an object highly useful to the country; for example, the conclusion of a treaty with a barbarian power whose customs require on such occasions the use of presents. But this object might be altogether defeated by the intrigues of other powers if our purposes were to be made known by the exhibition of the original papers and vouchers to the accounting officers of the Treasury. It would be easy to specify other cases which may occur in the history of a great nation, in its intercourse with other nations, wherein it might become absolutely necessary to incur expenditures for objects which could never be accomplished if it were suspected in advance that the items of expenditure and the agencies employed would be made public.

Actuated undoubtedly by considerations of this kind, Congress provided such a fund, coeval with the organization of the Government, and subsequently enacted the law of 1810 as the permanent law of the land. While this law exists in full force I feel bound by a high sense of public policy and duty to observe its provisions and the uniform practice of my predecessors under it.

With great respect for the House of Representatives and an anxious desire to conform to their wishes, I am constrained to come to this conclusion. . . .

JAMES K. POLK.

*SOURCE:* James D. Richardson, ed., *A Compilation of the Messages and Papers of the Presidents, 1789–1897,* 20 vols. (Washington D.C.: U.S. Government Printing Office, 1897), 4: 431–36.

*RELATED ENTRIES: Civil–Military Relations; Intelligence Gathering in Wart; Polk, James K.*

# 1846 b

### EXCERPTS FROM *THE BIGLOW PAPERS*

*Boston Brahmin James Russell Lowell, a foe of slavery and the Mexican War, penned a number of letters from fictitious plain Massachusetts folk upset with the Polk administration's Mexican War policies. He sent these letters to the* Boston Courier *throughout the course of the war. This, the first of them, begins with an introduction from farmer "Ezekiel Biglow," offering the Courier a poem his son "Hosea" had "thrashed out" after an unpleasant encounter with an Army recruiting sergeant.*

No. I.
A Letter

FROM MR. EZEKIEL BIGLOW OF JAALAM
TO THE HON. JOSEPH T. BUCKINGHAM,
EDITOR OF THE BOSTON COURIER,
INCLOSING A POEM OF HIS SON,
MR. HOSEA BIGLOW.

JAYLEM, june 1846.

MISTER EDDYTER: —Our Hosea wuz down to Boston last week, and he see a cruetin Sarjunt a struttin round as popler as a hen with 1 chicking, with 2 fellers a drummin and fifin arter him like all nater. the sarjunt he thout Hosea hedn't gut his i teeth cut cos he looked a kindo's though he'd jest com down, so he cal'lated to hook him in, but Hosy woodn't take none o' his sarse for all he hed much as 20 Rooster's tales stuck onto his hat and eenamost enuf brass a bobbin up and down on his shoulders and figureed onto his coat and trousis, let alone wut nater hed sot in his featers, to make a 6 pounder out on.

wal, Hosea he com home considerabal riled, and arter I 'd gone to bed I heern Him a thrashin round like a short-tailed Bull in flitime. The old Woman ses she to me ses she, Zekle, ses she, our Hosee's gut the chollery or suthin anuther ses she, don't you Bee skeered, ses I, he's oney amakin pottery. . .

EZEKIEL BIGLOW.

THRASH away, you 'll hev to rattle
On them kittle drums o' yourn,—
'Taint a knowin' kind o' cattle
Thet is ketched with mouldy corn ;
Put in stiff, you fifer feller,
Let folks see how spry you be,—
Guess you 'll toot till you are yeller
'Fore you git ahold o' me ! . . .

Ez fer war, I call it murder,—
There you hev it plain an' flat ;
I don't want to go no furder
Than my Testyment fer that ;
God hez sed so plump an' fairly,
It 's ez long ez it is broad,
An' you 've gut to git up airly
Ef you want to take in God.

'Taint your eppyletts an' feathers
Make the thing a grain more right ;
'Taint afollerin' your bell-wethers
Will excuse ye in His sight ;
Ef you take a sword an' dror it,
An' go stick a feller thru,
Guv'ment aint to answer for it,
God'll send the bill to you.

Wut 's the use o'meetin-goin'
Every Sabbath, wet or dry,
Ef it 's right to go amowin'
Feller-men like oats an' rye ?
I dunno but wut it 's pooty
Trainin' round in bobtail coats,—
But it 's curus Christian dooty
This ere cuttin' folks's throats.

They may talk o' Freedom's airy
Tell they 're pupple in the face,—
It 's a grand gret cemetary
Fer the barthrights of our race ;
They jest want this Californy
So 's to lug new slave-states in
To abuse ye, an' to scorn ye,
An' to plunder ye like sin.

Aint it cute to see a Yankee

Take sech everlastin' pains,
All to git the Devil's thankee,
Helpin' on 'em weld their chains ?
Wy, it 's jest ez clear ez figgers,
Clear ez one an' one make two,
Chaps thet make black slaves o' niggers
Want to make wite slaves o' you.

*SOURCE: The Biglow Papers* (Cambridge, Mass.: George Nichols, 1848).

*RELATED ENTRIES: Antiwar Movements; Conscription and Voluntarism; Just War Theory; Mexican War*

## 1849

### Lyrics to "I'm Off For Nicaragua"

*American "filibusters" launched several unlawful quasi-military assaults on Sonora (Mexico), Nicaragua, Cuba, and Honduras in the 1850s. Most were Southerners hoping to expand the borders of slavery. This unsympathetic ditty spoofed the "filibustering" craze.*

One day, while walking down Broadway,
What should I meet,
Coming up the street,
But a soldier gay,
In a grand array,
Who had been to Nicaragua!
He took me warmly by the hand,
And says, "old fellow, you're my man.
How would you like
A soldier's life,
On the plains of Nicaragua?
Then come with me down to the ship,
I'll quickly send you on your trip,
Don't stop to think, for there's meat and drink
On the plains of Nicaragua.

I scarcely knew what to do or say;
No money I had,
My boots were bad,
Hat was gone,
My pants were torn,
So I was off for Nicaragua.
He took me in, and did me treat,
Gave me a cigar and grub to eat;
And on his scroll did my name enroll,
A soldier for Nicaragua.
He took me down unto the ship,
Quickly sent me on my trip;
But, oh Lord! wasn't I sea-sick,
Going to Nicaragua.

But after ten days of sailing away,
We saw the land of San Juan;
My heart beat light,
For I thought it all right,
When I got to Nicaragua.
But when they got me on the shore,
They put me with about twenty more,
To fight away
Or be hanged, they say,
For going to Nicaragua.
Now, wasn't I in a pretty fix:
If I could only have cut my sticks,
You'd never caught me playing such tricks,
As going to Nicaragua.

Next morning, then, in grand array,
All fagged and jaded,
We were paraded.
At close of day,
We were marched away
To the army in Nicaragua.
Not a bit of breakfast did I see,
And dinner was the same to me.
Two fried cats
And three stewed rats
Were supper in Nicaragua.
Marching all day with sore feet,
Plenty of fighting and nothing to eat,
How I sighed for pickled pigs' feet,
Way down in Nicaragua.

The Costa Ricans tackled us one day;

In the first alarm,
I lost my arm;
But we made them yield,
On Rivas' field,
Way down in Nicaragua.
The Yankee boys fought long and well,
They gave those Costa Ricans—fits:
But wasn't I dry
And hungry,
Way down in Nicaragua!
Marching all day, and fighting away,
Nothing to eat, quite as much pay,
Do it all for glory, they say,
Way down in Nicaragua.

But when I was on duty, one day,
Give 'em the slip—
Jumped on the ship,
And bid good-by,
Forever and aye,
To the plains of Nicaragua.
And, when I got to old New York,
I filled myself with beans and pork;
My friends I cheer, and in lager beer
Drown times in Nicaragua.
And now I tread Columbia's land,
Take my friends all by the hand;
And if ever I leave 'em, may I be—blessed,
To go to Nicaragua.

*SOURCE: "I'm Off for Nicaragua"* (New York: H. De Marsan).

*RELATED ENTRIES: Filibustering; Mexican War; Music and War*

## 1850

### Excerpt from A. A. Livermore's *War with Mexico*

*Abiel Abbot Livermore won an American Peace Society prize for the best essay on how in the future the United States (and the rest of the developed world) might avoid wars like the one it had recently waged against Mexico. These excerpts are drawn from the society's publication of that essay.*

Chapter XXIX: Substitutes for War

. . . What is needed is, that the idea of a great pacific tribunal to settle the disputes of the world, should be broached, familiarized to the people, sent abroad on the wings of the press, hammered by dint of heavy and oft-repeated arguments into the mass of admitted and accredited truths, and then the work is done. We have trained mankind to war, we must now train them to peace. When the spirit of peace is largely developed in the public sentiment of Europe and America, this institution will be born in a day. The tendency of these remarks is to show that the agitation of the subject is what is now most exigent. By books and pamphlets, by the living voice and the inspired pen, this theme must be brought home to the minds and hearts of men, and they must be made to feel that every individual, be he high or low, rich or poor, is vitally concerned in having the great quarrels of kingdoms justly and amicably settled, as he is that justice should be done between man and man, and peace and order prevail in his hamlet or village. For in the earthquake shocks of war a thousand homes are overturned, and the mark of blood is left behind on ten thousand spheres of life once usefully and happily filled by fathers, sons, husbands, brothers. Let us hope, and labor, and pray, that the day may not be far distant when civilized and Christian men will see the madness of war, its bald inconsistency with the theory of a republican government, its hostility to the spirit of the present age, and its nullification of every law, and promise, and prayer of the Lord Jesus Christ.

Chapter XXX: Pacification of the World.

. . . When we consider how little has been done to prevent war, and how much to cultivate its spirit, and to invest its feats with a factitious glory; how literature and the fine arts, and politics, and, sad to confess, even professed Christians have encouraged, applauded, and diffused the passion for arms, we wonder not at the frequency of battles, and the human blood that has stained half the land and sea of the whole earth. Indeed the martial spirit has been so prevalent, mankind have drunk it so greedily as if it were as innocent as water, that we are prone to forget what a thorough education we give our children for war, and how little we do for the pacification of the world.

For when we inquire how this vast underlying passion for war has been educated and ripened in the heart of society, we shall be constrained to answer: It is by the war-songs of childhood, and the studies of the classics. It is by the wooden sword, and the tin drum of boyhood. It is by the trainings and the annual muster. It is by the red uniform and the white plume, and the prancing steed. It is by the cannon's thunder, and the gleam of the bayonet. It is by ballads of Robin Hood, and histories of Napoleon, and "Tales of the Crusaders." It is by the presentation of flags by the hands of the fair, and the huzzas for a victory. It is by the example of the father and the consent of the mother. It is by the fear of cowardice, and the laugh of the scorner. It is by the blood of youth, and the pride of manhood, and stories of revolutionary sires. It is by standing armies, and majestic men-of-war. It is by the maxims of self defence, and the cheapness of human life, and the love of excitement. It is by novels of love, and the "Pirate's Own Book." It is by the jars of home, and the squabbles of party, and the controversies of sects. It is by the misconception of the Bible, and ignorance of God. It is by the bubble of glory, and the emulation of schools, and the graspings of money-making. By one and by all, the heart of the community is educated for war, from the cradle to the coffin. When we sow the seed so copiously, we must not complain that the harvest is abundant.

*SOURCE: War with Mexico* (Boston: W.M. Crosby and H.P. Nichols, 1850).

*RELATED ENTRIES: Just War Theory; Mexican War; Militarization and Militarism; Pacifism*

## 1861 a

### Officers Staying in the U.S. Army or Joining the Confederacy, by Region of Birth*

*One old saw had it that virtually all southern-born West Point graduates "went South" when their home states seceded. In 1903 Francis Heitman found the records and "did the math." Here are the results. Officers joined the Confederacy in greater proportion the further South their home state.*

| Region | Joined CSA (%) | Stayed USA (%) | Resigned & Withdrew (%) | Total |
|---|---|---|---|---|
| Lower South (N.C., S.C., Ga., Fla., Miss., La., Texas) | 100 (79.4) | 20 (15.9) | 6 (4.8) | 126 |
| Upper South (Va., Tenn., Ark.) | 93 (58.9) | 57 (36.1) | 8 (5.1) | 158 |
| Border (Del., Md., Ky., Mo., D.C.) | 48 (27.4) | 118 (67.4) | 9 (5.1) | 175 |
| North | 28 (4.5) | 597 (95.1) | 3 (0.5) | 628 |
| **Total** | **269 (24.7)** | **792 (72.9)** | **26 (2.4)** | **1,087** |

*Foreign-born officers and officers whose places of birth are unknown have been grouped by place of appointment.

*SOURCE:* Francis B. Heitman, comp., *Historical Register and Dictionary of the United States Army, from Its Organization, September 29, 1789, to March 2, 1903* (Washington, D.C.: U.S. Government Printing Office, 1903).

*RELATED ENTRIES: Civil War; Conscription and Volunteerism*

## 1861 b

### Mark Twain's Account of His Brief Confederate Career

*Some time after the Civil War, Samuel Clemens ("Mark Twain") whimsically described his brief experience as a Confederate volunteer.*

IT WAS LATE, and there was a deep woodsy stillness everywhere. There was a veiled moonlight, which was only just strong enough to enable us to mark the general shape of objects. Presently a muffled sound caught our ears, and we recognized it as the hoof-beats of a horse or horses. And right away a figure appeared in the forest path; it could have been made of smoke, its mass had so little sharpness of outline. It was a man on horseback, and it seemed to me that there were others behind him. I got hold of a gun in the dark, and pushed it through a crack between the logs, hardly knowing what I was doing, I was so dazed with fright. Somebody said "Fire!" I pulled the trigger. I seemed to see a hundred flashes and hear a hundred reports; then I saw the man fall down out of the saddle. My first feeling was of surprised gratification; my first impulse was an apprentice sportsman's impulse to run and pick up his game. Somebody said, hardly audibly, "Good—we've got him!—wait for the rest." But the rest did not come. We waited—listened—still no more came. There was not a sound, not the whisper of a leaf; just perfect stillness; an uncanny kind of stillness, which was all the more uncanny on account of the damp, earthy, late-night smells now rising and pervading it. Then, wondering, we crept stealthily out, and approached the man. When we got to him the moon revealed him distinctly. He was lying on his back, with his arms abroad; his mouth was open and his chest heaving with long gasps, and his white shirt-front was all splashed with blood. The thought shot through me that I was a murderer; that I had killed a man—a man who had never done me any harm. That was the coldest sensation that ever went through my marrow. I was down by him in a moment, helplessly stroking his forehead; and I would have given anything then—my own life freely—to make him again what he had been five minutes before. And all the boys seemed to be feeling in the same way; they hung over him, full of pitying interest, and tried all they could to help him, and said all sorts of regretful things. They had forgotten all about the enemy; they thought only of this one forlorn unit of the foe. Once my imagination persuaded me that the dying man gave me a reproachful look out of his shadowy eyes, and it seemed to me that I would rather he had stabbed me than done that. He muttered and mumbled like a dreamer in his sleep about his wife and his child; and I thought with a new despair, "This thing that I have done does not end with him; it falls upon them too, and they never did me any harm, any more than he."

In a little while the man was dead. He was killed in war; killed in fair and legitimate war; killed in battle, as you may say; and yet he was as sincerely mourned by the opposing force as if he had been their brother. The boys stood there a half-hour sorrowing over him, and recalling the details of the tragedy, and wondering who he might be, and if he were a spy, and saying that if it were to do over again they would not hurt him unless he attacked them first. It soon came out that mine was not the only shot fired; there were five others—a division of the guilt which was a great relief to me, since it in some degree lightened and diminished the burden I was carrying. There were six shots fired at once; but I was not in my right mind at the time, and my heated imagination had magnified my one shot into a volley.

The man was not in uniform, and was not armed. He was a stranger in the country; that was all we ever found out about him. The thought of him got to preying upon me every night; I could not get rid of it. I could not drive it away, the taking of that unoffending life seemed such a wanton thing. And it seemed an epitome of war; that all war must be just that—the killing of strangers against whom you feel no personal animosity; strangers whom, in other circumstances, you would help if you found them in trouble, and who would help you if you needed it. My campaign was spoiled. It seemed to me that I was not rightly equipped for this awful business; that war was intended for men, and I for a child's nurse. I resolved to retire from this avocation of sham soldiership while I could save some remnant of my self-respect. These morbid thoughts clung to me against reason; for at bottom I did not believe I had touched that man. The law of probabilities decreed me guiltless of his blood; for in all my small experience with guns I had never hit anything I had tried to hit, and I knew I had done my best to hit him. Yet there was no solace in the thought. Against a diseased imagination demonstration goes for nothing.

*SOURCE:* Mark Twain, "The Private History of a Campaign That Failed," in *The American Claimant and Other Stories and Sketches* (New York: Collier, 1899), 276–79.

*RELATED ENTRIES: Civil War; Literature and War*

## 1861 c

### An Englishman's Memory of Enlisting in an Arkansas Regiment

*Henry Stanley, the future journalist and "rescuer" of Dr. David Livingstone in Africa, had been a young English resident of Arkansas in 1861. He later recalled the impulse that had led him to enlist in a regiment there.*

The young men joined hands and shouted, "Is there a man with soul so dead, Who never to himself hath said—'This is my own, my native land?' 'An honourable death is better than a base life,' " etc., etc. In the strident tones of passion, they said they would welcome a bloody grave rather than survive to see the proud foe violating their altars and their hearths, and desecrating the sacred soil of the South with their unholy feet. But, inflamed as the men and youths were, the warlike fire that burned within their breasts was as nothing to the intense heat that glowed within the bosoms of the women. No suggestion of compromise was possible in their presence. If every man did not hasten to the battle, they vowed they would themselves rush out and meet the Yankee vandals. In a land where women are worshipped by the men, such language made them war-mad.

Then one day I heard that enlistment was going on. Men were actually enrolling themselves as soldiers! A Captain Smith, owner of a plantation a few miles above Auburn, was raising a Company to be called the 'Dixie Greys.' A Mr. Penny Mason, living on a plantation below us, was to be the First-lieutenant, and Mr. Lee, nephew of the great General Lee, was to be Second-lieutenant. The youth of the neighbourhood were flocking to them and registering their names. Our Doctor,—Weston Jones,—Mr. Newton Story, and his brothers Varner, had enlisted. Then the boy Dan Goree prevailed upon his father to permit him to join the gallant braves. Little Rich, of Richmond Store, gave in his name. Henry Parker, the boy nephew of one of the richest planters in the vicinity, volunteered, until it seemed as if Arkansas County was to be emptied of all the youth and men I had known.

About this time, I received a parcel which I half-suspected, as the address was written in a feminine hand, to be a token of some lady's regard; but, on opening it, I discovered it to be a chemise and petticoat, such as a negro lady's-maid might wear. I hastily hid it from view, and retired to the back room, that my burning cheeks might not betray me to some onlooker. In the afternoon, Dr. Goree called, and was excessively cordial and kind. He asked me if I did not intend to join the valiant children of Arkansas to fight? and I answered 'Yes.'

At my present age [60] the whole thing appears to be a very laughable affair altogether; but, at that time, it was far from being a laughing matter. He praised my courage, and my patriotism, and said I should win undying glory, and then he added, in a lower voice, 'We shall see what we can do for you when you come back.'

What did he mean? Did he suspect my secret love for that sweet child who sometimes came shopping with her mother? From that confidential promise I believe he did, and was, accordingly, ready to go anywhere for her sake. . . .

About the beginning of July we embarked on the steamer 'Frederick Notrebe.' At various landings, as we ascended the river, the volunteers crowded aboard; and the jubilation of so many youths was intoxicating. Near Pine Bluff, while we were making merry, singing, 'I wish I was in Dixie,' the steamer struck a snag which pierced her hull, and we sank down until the water was up to the furnace-doors. We remained fixed for several hours, but, fortunately, the 'Rose Douglas' came up, and took us and our baggage safely up to Little Rock.

We were marched to the Arsenal, and, in a short time, the Dixie Greys were sworn by Adjutant-General Burgevine into the service of the Confederate States of America for twelve months. We were served with heavy flint-lock muskets, knapsacks, and accoutrements, and were attached to the 6th Arkansas Regiment of Volunteers, Colonel Lyons commanding, and A. T. Hawthorn, Lieutenant-colonel.

*SOURCE:* Dorothy Stanley, ed., *The Autobiography of Sir Henry M. Stanley* (Boston and London: Houghton Mifflin, 1909), 165–66.

*RELATED ENTRIES: Civil War; Conscription and Volunteerism*

# 1861 d

## EXAMPLES OF CONFEDERATE SOLDIERS' EXPERIENCES ON BATTLEFIELD

*A young Confederate officer and two enlisted men commented on the hardening effect of seeing dead soldiers on battlefields day after day:*

I felt quite small in that fight the other day when the musket balls and cannon balls was flying around me as thick as hail and my best friends falling on both sides dead and mortally wounded Oh Dear it is impossible for me to express my feeling when the fight was over & I saw what was done the tears came then free oh that I never could behold such a sight again to think of it among civilized people killing one another like beasts one would think that the supreme rule would put a stop to it but wee sinned as a nation and must suffer in the flesh as well as spiritually those things wee cant account for.

• • •

Up on the bluff we saw the first dead Yankee—he lay stark and cold in death upon the hillside among the trees in the gloom of the gathering twilight; the pale face turned towards us, upon which we looked with feelings mingled with awe and dread. We had heard and seen many new and strange things that day. Later on in the war, we could look upon the slain on the battlefield with little less feeling than upon the carcass of an animal. Such are some of the hardening effects of war. I don't think we were again as badly scared as on that day; I was not, I am sure.

• • •

I saw the body [of a man killed the previous day] this morning and a horrible sight it was. Such sights do not affect me as they once did. I can not describe the change nor do I know when it took place, yet I know that there is a change for I look on the carcass of a man now with pretty much such feeling as I would do were it a horse or hog.

SOURCE: W. H. Morgan, *Personal Reminiscences of the War of 1861–65* (Lynchburg, Va.: J.P. Bell, 1911), 62.

*Two barely literate privates from Alabama wrote home during the Civil War, describing their horror at what Bell Irvin Wiley called their "Baptism of fire":*

Martha . . . I can inform you that I have Seen the Monkey Show at last and I dont Waunt to see it no more I am satsfide with Ware Martha I Cant tell you how many ded men I did see . . . thay ware piled up one one another all over the Battel feel the Battel was a Six days Battel and I was in all off it . . . I did not go all over the Battel feeld I Jest was one one Winge of the Battel feeld But I can tell you that there Was a meney a ded man where I was men Was shot Evey fashinton that you mite Call for Som and there hedes shot of and som ther armes and leges Won was sot in the midel I can tell you that I am tirde of Ware I am satsfide if the Ballence is that is one thing Shore I dont waunt to see that site no more I can inform you that West Brown was shot one the head he Was sent off to the horspitel . . . he was not herte very Bad he was struck with a pease of a Bum[.]

• • •

We have had every hard fite a bout ten miles from Chat ta nooga on Chick a mog ga creak in gor ga . . . i com out safe but it is all i can say i have all ways crave to fite a lit[tle] gust to no what it is to go in to a bat tle but i got the chance to tri my hand at last anough to sad isfi me i never wan to go in to an nother fite any more sister i wan to come home worse than i eaver did be fore but when times gits better i will tri to come home thare has ben agrate meney soldiers runing a way late ly but i dont want to go that way if i can get home any other way.

SOURCE: Bell Irvin Wiley, *Life of Johnny Reb* (New York: Bobbs-Merrill, 1943), 32–33.

*RELATED ENTRIES: Civil War; Combat, Effects of; Conscription and Volunteerism; Psychiatric Disorders, Combat Related*

## 1861 e

### Excerpt from *Anglo-African* Editorial

*Northern blacks tended to see the beginning of hostilities as an opportunity to bring an end to slavery. The New York* Anglo-African *editorialized thus:*

The outbreak of the war . . . is but another step in the drama of American Progress. We say Progress, for we know that no matter what may be the desires of the men of Expediency who rule, or seem to, the affairs of the North,—the tendencies are for liberty.

God speed the conflict. May the cup be drained to its dregs, for only thus can this nation of sluggards know the disease and its remedy . . .

The free colored Americans cannot be indifferent to the progress of this struggle. . . . Out of this strife will come freedom, though the methods are not yet clearly apparent. . . . Public opinion purified by the fiery ordeal through which the nation is about to pass, will rightly appreciate the cause of its political disquiet, and apply the remedy. . . . It must be that the key to the solution of the present difficulties, is the abolition of slavery; not as an act of retaliation on the master, but as a measure of justice to the slave—the sure and permanent basis of "a more perfect Union."

*SOURCE:* Editorials, *Anglo-African,* April 20 and 27, 1861.

*RELATED ENTRIES: African Americans in the Military; Civil War*

## 1861 f

### Comments of African American Spy Allan Pinkerton

*Blacks performed important spying missions and functions for the Union Army. Allan Pinkerton, chief of the U.S. Secret Service, went to Memphis, Tennessee, posing as a Southerner in 1861. He recalled:*

Here, as in many other places, I found that my best source of information was the colored men, who were employed in various capacities of a military nature which entailed hard labor. The slaves, without reserve, were sent by their masters to perform the manual labor of building earthworks and fortifications, in driving the teams and in transporting cannon and ammunition. . . . I mingled freely with them, and found them ever ready to answer questions and to furnish me with every fact which I desired to possess. . . .

*John Scobell undertook several missions for Pinkerton in Virginia. Pinkerton described Scobell's work as follows:*

Among the many men thus employed, was a negro by the name of John Scobell, and the manner in which his duties were performed, was always a source of satisfaction to me and apparently of gratification to himself. From the commencement of the war, I had found the Negroes of invaluable assistance, and I never hesitated to employ them when, after investigation, I found them to be intelligent and trustworthy. . . .

All refugees, deserters and contrabands coming through our lines were turned over to me for a thorough examination and for such future disposition as I should recommend. John Scobell came to me in this manner. One morning I was seated in my quarters, preparing for the business of the day, when the officer of the guard announced the appearance of a number of contrabands. Ordering them to be brought in, the pumping process was commenced, and before noon many stray pieces of information had been gathered, which, by accumulation of evidence, were highly valuable. Among the number I had especially noticed the young man who had given his name as John Scobell. He had a manly and intelligent bearing, and his straightforward answers to the many questions propounded to him, at once impressed me very favorably. He informed me that he had formerly been a slave in the State of Mississippi, but had journeyed to Virginia with his master, whose name he bore. His master was a Scotchman, and but a few weeks before had given him and his wife their freedom. The young woman had obtained employment in Richmond, while he had made his way to the Union lines, where, encountering the Federal pickets, he had been brought to headquarters, and thence to me. . . .

I immediately decided to attach him to my headquarters, with the view of eventually using him in the capacity of a scout, should he prove equal to the task. . . . I resolved to send him into the South, and test his ability for active duty. Calling him into my quarters, I gave him the necessary directions, and dispatched him, in company with Timothy Webster, on a trip to Virginia. Their line of travel was laid out through Centreville, Manassas, Dumfries, and the Upper and Lower Accoquan.

John Scobell I found was a remarkably gifted man for one of his race. He could read and write, and was as full of music as the feathered songsters. . . . In addition to what seemed an almost inexhaustible stock of negro plantation melodies he had also a charming variety of Scotch ballads, which he sang with a voice of remarkable power and sweetness. . . . Possessing the talents which he did, I felt sure, that he had only to assume the character of the light-hearted, happy darky and no one would suspect the cool-headed, vigilant detective, in the rollicking negro whose only aim in life appeared to be to get enough to eat, and a comfortable place to toast his shins.

. . . Carefully noting everything that came in his way he traveled through Dumfries, Accoquan, Manassas and Centreville, and after spending nearly ten days in these localities he finally made his way to Leesburg, and thence down the Potomac to Washington. His experiences on this trip were quite numerous and varied, and only a lack of space prevents their narration. Sometimes, as a vender of delicacies through the camps, a laborer on the earthworks at Manassas, or a cook at Centreville, he made his way uninterruptedly until he obtained the desired information and successfully accomplished the object of his mission.

His return to Washington was accomplished in safety and his full and concise report fully justified me in the selection I had made of a good, reliable and intelligent operative.

*SOURCE:* Allan Pinkerton, *Spy in the Rebellion* (New York: G.W. Carleton, 1883), 194, 344–46, 366.

*RELATED ENTRIES: African Americans in the Military; Civil War; Intelligence Gathering in War*

# 1862 a

**Excerpt from Official Army Records on Impressment of Black Workers**

*During the war, slaves and free blacks did much of the work on Confederate fortifications and entrenchments, as these documents indicate.*

R. H. Chilton, Assistant Adjutant General, to General J. B. Magruder at Yorktown, Virginia, Feb. 15, 1862:

The War Department finds it necessary to impress slaves and free negroes to extend and complete the fortifications in the Peninsula. You will therefore call upon the citizens of Dinwiddie County, by direction of the Secretary of War, to send forthwith one-half of their male slaves between the ages of sixteen and fifty to execute this work on the Peninsula.

Jefferson Davis to Governor John Letcher of Virginia, Oct. 10, 1862:

In accordance with an act passed by the Legislature of Virginia October 3, 1862, I have the honor to call upon Your Excellency for 4,500 negroes to be employed upon the fortifications. . . . It is unnecessary to call Your Excellency's attention to the importance of a prompt and efficient response to this call, in view of the necessity of completing the works for the defense of Richmond.

*SOURCE: War of the Rebellion . . . Official Records of the Union and Confederate Armies,* 128 volumes (Washington, D.C.: U.S. Government Printing Office, 1880–1901), Series 1, vol. 51, part ii, 472–73, 633.

*RELATED ENTRIES: African Americans in the Military; Civil War; Conscription and Volunteerism*

# 1862 b

**Exchange between Horace Greeley and Abraham Lincoln**

*In 1862, President Lincoln threatened to veto a proposed confiscation bill that would have stripped those in rebellion of their property on the grounds of treason. The bill was criticized by moderate Republican members of Congress from slave-holding border states, but it also fell afoul, in Lincoln's eyes, of the provision in the Constitution (art. 3, sec. 3, cl. 2) that "no [congressional] attainder of treason shall work . . . forfeiture except during the life of the person attainted." In other words, slaves might be freed from their rebellious owners, but upon the death of those rebels, their children were to inherit all such "property." Incensed by Lincoln's "strict construction," Greeley excoriated him in a letter dated August 19, which was printed in the* New York Tribune *on August 20, 1862. Lincoln replied two days later.*

To ABRAHAM LINCOLN, *President of the U. States:*

DEAR SIR: I do not intrude to tell you—for you must know already—that a great proportion of those who triumphed in your election, and of all who desire the unqualified suppression of the Rebellion now desolating our country, are sorely disappointed and deeply pained by the policy you seem to be pursuing with regard to the slaves of Rebels. I write only to set succinctly and unmistakably before you what we require, what we think we have a right to expect, and of what we complain.

I. We require of you, as the first servant of the Republic, charged especially and preëminently with this duty, that you EXECUTE THE LAWS. Most emphatically do we demand that such laws as have been recently enacted, which therefore may fairly be presumed to embody the present will and to be dictated by the present needs of the Republic, and which, after due consideration have received your personal sanction, shall by you be carried into full effect, and that you publicly and decisively instruct your subordinates that such laws exist, that they are binding on all functionaries and citizens, and that they are to be obeyed to the letter.

II. We think you are strangely and disastrously remiss in the discharge of your official and imperative duty with regard to the emancipating provisions of the new Confiscation Act. Those provisions were designed to fight Slavery with Liberty. They prescribe that men loyal to the Union, and willing to shed their blood in her behalf, shall no longer be held, with the Nation's consent, in bondage to persistent, malignant traitors, who for twenty years have been plotting and for sixteen months have been fighting to divide and destroy our country. Why these traitors should be treated with tenderness by you, to the prejudice of the dearest rights of loyal men, we cannot conceive.

III. We think you are unduly influenced by the counsels, the representations, the menaces, of certain fossil politicians hailing from the Border Slave States. Knowing well that the heartily, unconditionally loyal portion of the White citizens of those States do not expect nor desire that Slavery shall be upheld to the prejudice of the Union—(for the truth of which we appeal not only to every Republican residing in those States, but to such eminent loyalists as H. Winter Davis, Parson Brownlow, the Union Central Committee of Baltimore, and to The Nashville Union)—we ask you to consider that Slavery is everywhere the inciting cause and sustaining base of treason: the most slaveholding sections of Maryland and Delaware being this day, though under the Union flag, in full sympathy with the Rebellion, while the Free-Labor portions of Tennessee and of Texas, though writhing under the bloody heel of Treason, are unconquerably loyal to the Union. So emphatically is this the case, that a most intelligent Union banker of Baltimore recently avowed his confident belief that a majority of the present Legislature of Maryland, though elected as and still professing to be Unionists, are at heart desirous of the triumph of the Jeff. Davis conspiracy; and when asked how they could be won back to loyalty, replied—"Only by the complete Abolition of Slavery." It seem to us the most obvious truth, that whatever strengthens or fortifies Slavery in the Border States strengthens also Treason, and drives home the wedge intended to divide the Union. Had you from the first refused to recognize in those States, as here, any other than unconditional loyalty—that which stands for the Union, whatever may become of Slavery—those States would have been, and would be, far more helpful and less troublesome to the defenders of the Union than they have been, or now are.

IV. We think timid counsels in such a crisis calculated to prove perilous, and probably disastrous. It is the duty of a Government so wantonly, wickedly assailed by Rebellion as ours has been to oppose force to force in a defiant, dauntless spirit. It cannot afford to temporize with traitors nor with semi-traitors. It must not bribe them to behave themselves, nor make them fair promises in the hope of disarming their causeless hostility. Representing a brave and high-spirited people, it can afford to forfeit anything else better than its own self-respect, or their admiring confidence. For our Government even to see, after war has been made on it, to dispel the affected apprehensions of armed traitors that their cherished privileges may be assailed by it, is to invite insult and encourage hopes of its own downfall. The rush to arms of Ohio, Indiana, Illinois, is the true answer at once to the Rebel raids of John Morgan and the traitorous sophistries of Beriah Magoffin.

V. We complain that the Union cause has suffered, and is now suffering immensely, from mistaken deference to Rebel Slavery. Had you, Sir, in your Inaugural Address, unmistakably given notice that, in case the Rebellion already commenced were persisted in, and your efforts to preserve the Union and enforce the laws should be resisted by armed force, you would recognize no loyal person as rightfully held in Slavery by a traitor, we believe the Rebellion would therein have received a staggering if not fatal blow. At that moment, according to the returns of the most recent elections, the Unionists were a large majority of the voters of the Slave States. But they were composed in good part of the aged, the feeble, the wealthy, the timid—the young, the reckless, the aspiring, the adventurous, had already been largely lured by the gamblers and negro-traders, the politicians by trade and the conspirators by instinct, into the toils of Treason. Had you then proclaimed that Rebellion would strike the shackles from the slaves of every traitor, the wealthy and the cautious would have been supplied with a powerful inducement to remain loyal. As it was, every coward in the South soon became a traitor from fear; for Loyalty was perilous, while Treason seemed comparatively safe. Hence the boasted unanimity of the South—a unanimity based on Rebel terrorism and the fact that immunity and safety were found on that side, danger and probable death on ours. The Rebels from the first have been eager to confiscate, imprison, scourge and kill; we have fought wolves with the devices of sheep. The result is just what might have been expected. Tens of thousands are fighting in the Rebel ranks to-day whose original bias and natural leanings would have led them into ours.

VI. We complain that the Confiscation Act which you approved is habitually disregarded by your Generals, and that no word of rebuke for them from you has yet reached the public ear. Fremont's Proclamation and Hunter's Order favoring Emancipation were promptly annulled by you; while Halleck's No. 3, forbidding fugitives from Slavery to Rebels to come within his lines—an order as unmilitary as inhuman, and which received the hearty approbation of every traitor in America—with scores of like tendency, have never provoked even your remonstrance. We complain that the officers of your Armies have habitually repelled rather than invited the approach of slaves who would have gladly taken the risks of escaping from their Rebel masters to our camps, bringing intelligence often of inestimable value to the Union cause. We complain that those who have thus escaped to us, avowing a willingness to do for us whatever might be required, have been brutally and madly repulsed, and often surrendered to be scourged, maimed and tortured by the ruffian traitors, who pretend to own them. We complain that a large proportion of our regular Army Officers, with many of the Volunteers, evince far more solicitude to uphold Slavery than to put down the Rebellion. And finally, we complain that you, Mr. President, elected as a Republican, knowing well what an abomination Slavery is, and how emphatically it is the core and essence of this atrocious Rebellion, seem never to interfere with these atrocities, and never give a direction to your Military subordinates, which does not appear to have been conceived in the interest of Slavery rather than of Freedom.

VII. Let me call your attention to the recent tragedy in New-Orleans, whereof the facts are obtained entirely through Pro-Slavery channels. A considerable body of resolute, able-bodied men, held in Slavery by two Rebel sugar-planters in defiance of the Confiscation Act which you have approved, left plantations thirty miles distant and made their way to the great mart of the South-West, which they knew to be in the undisputed possession of the Union forces. They made their way safely and quietly through thirty miles of Rebel territory, expecting to find freedom under the protection of our flag. Whether they had or had not heard of the passage of the Confiscation Act, they reasoned logically that we could not kill them for deserting the service of their life-long oppressors, who had through treason become our implacable enemies. They came to us for liberty and protection, for which they were willing to render their best service: they met with hostility, captivity, and murder. The barking of the base curs of Slavery in this quarter deceives no one—not even themselves. They say, indeed, that the negroes had no right to appear in New-Orleans armed (with their inplements of daily labor in the cane-field); but no one doubts that they would gladly have laid these down if assured that they should be free. They were set upon and maimed, captured and killed, because they sought the benefit of that act of Congress which they may not specifically have heard of, but which was none the less the law of the land—which they had a clear right to the benefit of—which it was somebody's duty to publish far and wide, in order that so many as possible should be impelled to desist from serving Rebels and the Rebellion and come over to the side of the Union. They sought their liberty in strict accordance with the law of the land—they were butchered or reënslaved for so doing by the help of Union soldiers enlisted to fight against Slaveholding Treason. It was somebody's fault that they were so murdered—if others shall hereafter suffer in like manner, in default of explicit and public direction to your generals that they are to recognize and obey the Confiscation Act, the world will lay the blame on you. Whether you will choose to hear it through future History and at the bar of God, I will not judge. I can only hope.

VIII. On the face of this wide earth, Mr. President, there is not one disinterested, determined, intelligent champion of the Union cause who does not feel that all attempts to put down the Rebellion and at the same time uphold its inciting cause are preposterous and futile—that the Rebellion, if crushed out tomorrow, would be renewed within a year if Slavery were left in full vigor—that Army officers who remain to this day devoted to Slavery can at best be but half-way loyal to the Union—and that every hour of deference to Slavery is an hour of added and deepened peril to the Union. I appeal to the testimony of your Embassadors in Europe. It is freely at your service, not at mine. Ask them to tell you candidly whether the seeming subserviency of your policy to the slaveholding, slavery-upholding interest, is not the perplexity, the despair of statesmen of all parties, and be admonished by the general answer!

IX. I close as I began with the statement that what an immense majority of the Loyal Millions of your countrymen require of you is a frank, declared, unqualified, ungrudging execution of the laws of the land, more especially of the Confiscation Act. That Act gives freedom to the slaves of Rebels coming within our lines, or whom those lines may at any time inclose—we ask you to render it due obedience by publicly requiring all your subordinates to recognize and obey it. The Rebels are everywhere using the late anti-negro riots in the North, as they have long used your officers' treatment of negroes in the South, to convince the slaves that they have nothing to hope from a Union success—that we mean in that case to sell them into a bitterer bondage to defray the cost of the war. Let them impress this as a truth on the great mass of their ignorant and credulous bondmen, and the Union will never be restored—never. We cannot conquer Ten Millions of People united in solid phalanx against us, powerfully aided by Northern sympathizers and European allies. We must have scouts, guides, spies, cooks, teamsters, diggers and choppers from the Blacks of the South, whether we allow them to fight for us or not, or we shall be baffled and repelled. As one of the millions who would gladly have avoided this struggle at any sacrifice but that of Principle and Honor, but who now feel that the triumph of the Union is indispensable not only to the existence of our country but to the well-being of mankind, I entreat you to render a hearty and unequivocal obedience to the law of the land.

Yours, . . . HORACE GREELEY.
*New-York*, August 19, 1862.

*SOURCE:* Greeley to Lincoln, August 19, 1862. Transcribed and annotated by the Lincoln Studies Center, Knox College, Galesburg, Ill. Available at Library of Congress, *Mr. Lincoln's Virtual Library, Abraham Lincoln Papers,* Manuscript Division (Washington, D.C.: American Memory Project, 2000–02), http://memory.loc.gov/ammem/alhtml/alhome.html (June 13, 2005).

Executive Mansion,
*Washington, August* 22, 1862.

DEAR SIR: I have just read yours of the 19th, addressed to myself through the New York Tribune. If there be in it any statements, or assumptions of fact, which I may know to be erroneous, I do not now and here controvert them. If there be in it any inferences which I may believe to be falsely drawn, I do not now and here argue against them. If there be perceptible in it an impatient and dictatorial tone, I waive it in deference to an old friend whose heart I have always supposed to be right.

As to the policy I "seem to be pursuing," as you say, I have not meant to leave any one in doubt.

I would save the Union. I would save it the shortest way under the Constitution. The sooner the national authority can be restored the nearer the Union will be "the Union as it was." If there be those who would not save the Union unless they could at the same time save slavery, I do not agree with them. If there be those who would not save the Union unless they could at the same time destroy slavery, I do not agree with them. My paramount object in this struggle is to save the Union, and is not either to save or to destroy slavery. If I could save the Union without freeing any slave I would do it, and if I could save it by freeing all the slaves I would do it; and if I could save it by freeing some and leaving others alone, I would also do that. What I do about slavery and the colored race, I do because I believe it helps to save the Union; and what I forbear, I forbear because I do not believe it would help to save the Union. I shall do less whenever I shall believe what I am doing hurts the cause, and I shall do more whenever I shall believe doing more will help the cause. I shall try to correct errors when shown to be errors; and I shall adopt new views so fast as they shall appear to be true views.

I have here stated my purpose according to my view of official duty; and I intend no modification of my oft-expressed personal wish that all men everywhere could be free. Yours,

A. LINCOLN

*SOURCE:* Greeley to Lincoln, August 19, 1862. Transcribed and annotated by the Lincoln Studies Center, Knox College, Galesburg, Ill. Available at Library of Congress, *Mr. Lincoln's Virtual Library, Abraham Lincoln Papers,* Manuscript Division (Washington, D.C.: American Memory Project, 2000–02), http://memory.loc.gov/ammem/alhtml/alhome.html (August 3, 2005).

*RELATED ENTRIES: Civil War; Greeley, Horace; Lincoln, Abraham*

# 1863 a

## Enlistment Speech to African Americans

*Jerry Sullivan spoke at a gathering of blacks in Nashville, Tennessee, on October 20, 1863, exhorting them to take up arms for the Union cause.*

God is in this war. He will lead us on to victory. Folks talk about the fighting being nearly over, but I believe there is a heap yet to come. Let the colored men accept the offer of the President and Cabinet, take arms, join the army, and then we will whip the rebels, even if Longstreet and all the Streets of the South, concentrate at Chattanooga. (Laughter and applause.) Why, don't you remember how afraid they used to be that we would rise? And you know we would, too, if we could. (Cries of "that's so.") I ran away two years ago. . . . I got to Cincinnati, and from there I went straight to General Rosecrans' headquarters. And now I am going to be Corporal. (Shouts of laughter.)

Come, boys, let's get some guns from Uncle Sam, and go coon hunting; shooting those gray back coons [Confederates] that go poking about the country now a days. (Laughter.) Tomorrow morning, don't eat too much breakfast, but as soon as you get back from market, start the first thing for our camp. Don't ask your wife, for if she is a wife worth having she will call you a coward for asking her. (Applause, and waving of handkerchiefs by the ladies.) I've got a wife and she says to me, the other day, "Jerry, if you don't go to the war mighty soon, I'll go off and leave you, as some of the Northern gentlemen want me to go home to cook for them." (Laughter.) . . . The ladies are now busy making us a flag, and let us prove ourselves men worthy to bear it.

*SOURCE: The Colored Citizen,* November 7, 1863.

*RELATED ENTRIES: African Americans in the Military; Civil War; Conscription and Volunteerism*

Documents

## 1863 b

### FREDERICK DOUGLASS'S COMMENTS ON THE RECRUITMENT OF HIS SONS

*Two of Frederick Douglass's sons were the first recruits from New York to join the 54th Regiment of Massachusetts Volunteer (Colored) Infantry. Douglass himself asked:*

Shall colored men enlist notwithstanding this unjust and ungenerous barrier raised against them? We answer yes. Go into the army and go with a will and a determination to blot out this and all other mean discriminations against us. To say we won't be soldiers because we cannot be colonels is like saying we won't go into water till we have learned to swim. A half a loaf is better than no bread—and to go into the army is the speediest and best way to overcome the prejudice which has dictated unjust laws against us. To allow us in the army at all, is a great concession. Let us take this little the better to get more. By showing that we deserve the little is the best way to gain much. Once in the United States uniform and the colored man has a springing board under him by which he can jump to loftier heights.

*SOURCE: Douglass's Monthly* 5, March 1863, 802.

*RELATED ENTRIES: African Americans in the Military; Civil War; Conscription and Volunteerism; 54th Regiment of Massachusetts Volunteer Infantry*

## 1863 c

### LETTER OF LEWIS DOUGLASS TO FUTURE WIFE

*The 54th Regiment of Massachusetts was nearly annihilated in a courageous but unsuccessful assault of the Confederacy's Fort Wagner at the mouth of Charleston, South Carolina, harbor. Shortly after the assault, Frederick Douglass's son Lewis, a sergeant in that regiment, described the fighting in a letter to his future wife:*

My Dear Amelia: I have been in two fights, and am unhurt. I am about to go in another I believe to-night. Our men fought well on both occasions. The last was desperate we charged that terrible battery on Morris Island known as Fort Wagoner [sic], and were repulsed with a loss of [many] killed and wounded. I escaped unhurt from amidst that perfect hail of shot and shell. It was terrible. I need not particularize the papers will give a better than I have time to give. My thoughts are with you often, you are as dear as ever, be good enough to remember it as I no doubt you will. As I said before we are on the eve of another fight and I am very busy and have just snatched a moment to write you. . . . Should I fall in the next fight killed or wounded I hope to fall with my face to the foe. . . .

This regiment has established its reputation as a fighting regiment not a man flinched, though it was a trying time. Men fell all around me. A shell would explode and clear a space of twenty feet, our men would close up again, but it was no use we had to retreat, which was a very hazardous undertaking. How I got out of that fight alive I cannot tell, but I am here. My Dear girl I hope again to see you. I must bid you farewell should I be killed. Remember if I die I die in a good cause. I wish we had a hundred thousand colored troops we would put an end to this war.

*SOURCE:* Lewis Douglass to Amelia Loguen, July 20, 1863, Woodson Collection, Manuscripts Division, Library of Congress.

*RELATED ENTRIES: African Americans in the Military; Civil War; 54th Regiment of Massachusetts Volunteer Infantry*

## 1863 d

### LETTER OF CAPTAIN M. M. MILLER TO HIS AUNT

*In early June, 1863, two regiments of recently raised Louisiana freedmen repelled a Confederate attack on Milliken's Bend, a Union outpost on the Mississippi River above Vicksburg, Mississippi. Soon after the battle, Capt. M. M. Miller of the 9th Regiment of Louisiana Volunteers of African descent wrote to his aunt in Illinois:*

We were attacked here on June 7, about 3 o'clock in the morning, by a brigade of Texas troops about 2,500 in number. We had about 600 men to withstand them—500 of them negroes. . . . Our regiment had about 300 men in the fight. . . . We had about 50 men killed in the regiment and 80 wounded; so you can judge of what part of the fight my company sustained. I never felt more grieved and sick at heart than when I saw how my brave soldiers had been slaughtered. . . . I never more wish to hear the expression, "the niggers won't fight." Come with me 100 yards from where I sit, and I can show you the wounds that cover the bodies of 16 as brave, loyal and patriotic soldiers as ever drew bead on a Rebel.

The enemy charged us so close that we fought with our bayonets, hand to hand. . . . It was a horrible fight, the worst I was ever engaged in—not even excepting Shiloh. The enemy cried "No quarter!" but some of them were very glad to take it when made prisoners. . . .

What few men I have left seem to think much of me because I stood up with them in the fight. I can say for them that I never saw a braver company of men in my life. Not one of them offered to leave his place until ordered to fall back; in fact very few ever did fall back. . . . So they fought and died defending the cause that we revere. They met death coolly, bravely—not rashly did they expose themselves, but all were steady and obedient to orders.

*SOURCE: Letter printed in the* Union, *July 14, 1863.*

*RELATED ENTRIES: African Americans in the Military; Civil War*

## 1863 e

### Account of Col. Thomas J. Morgan Concerning His African American Brigade

*Colonel Morgan, commanding a brigade of four black regiments in the battle of Nashville, gave the following account of his original regiment from the time it was organized in November 1863 until the battle of Nashville:*

November 1st, 1863, by order of Major Stearns, I went to Gallatin, Tennessee, to organize the 14th United States Colored Infantry. . . . There were at that time several hundred negro men in camp, in charge of, I think, a lieutenant. They were a motley crowd,—old, young, middle aged. Some wore the United States uniform, but most of them had on the clothes in which they had left the plantations, or had worn during periods of hard service as laborers in the army. . . .

As soon and as fast as practicable, I set about organizing the regiment. . . .

The complete organization of the regiment occupied about two months, being finished by Jan. 1st, 1864. The field, staff and company officers were all white men. All the non-commissioned officers,—Hospital Steward, Quartermaster, Sergeant, Sergeant-Major, Orderlies, Sergeants and Corporals were colored. They proved very efficient, and had the war continued two years longer, many of them would have been competent as commissioned officers. . . .

General George H. Thomas, though a Southerner, and a West Point graduate, was a singularly fair-minded, candid man. He asked me one day soon after my regiment was organized, if I thought my men would fight. I replied that they would. He said he thought "they might behind breastworks." I said they would fight in the open field. He thought not. "Give me a chance General," I replied, "and I will prove it.". . .

PULASKI, TENN.—September 27th, 1864, I reported to Major-General Rousseau, commanding a force of cavalry at Pulaski, Tenn. As we approached the town by rail from Nashville, we heard artillery, then musketry, and as we left the cars we saw the smoke of guns. [Confederate cavalry commander Nathan Bedford] Forest [sic], with a large body of cavalry, had been steadily driving Rousseau before him all day, and was destroying the railroad. Finding the General, I said: "I am ordered to report to you, sir." "What have you?" "Two regiments of colored troops." Rousseau was a Kentuckian, and had not much faith in negro soldiers. By his direction I threw out a strong line of skirmishers, and posted the regiments on a ridge, in good supporting distance. Rousseau's men retired behind my line, and Forest's men pressed forward until they met our fire, and recognizing the sound of the minie ball, stopped to reflect.

The massacre of colored troops at Fort Pillow was well known to us, and had been fully discussed by our men. It was rumored, and thoroughly credited by them, that General Forest had offered a thousand dollars for the head of any commander of a "nigger regiment." Here, then, was just such an opportunity as those spoiling for a fight might desire. Negro troops stood face to face with Forest's veteran cavalry. The fire was growing hotter, and balls were uncomfortably thick. At length, the enemy in strong force, with banners flying, bore down toward us in full sight, apparently bent on mischief. Pointing to the advancing column, I said, as I passed along the line, "Boys, it looks very much like fight; keep cool, do your duty." They seemed full of glee, and replied with great enthusiasm: "Colonel, dey can't whip us, dey nebber get de ole 14th out of heah, nebber." "Nebber drives us away widout a mighty lot of dead men," &c., &c.

When Forest learned that Rousseau was re-enforced by infantry, he did not stop to ask the color of their skin, but after testing our line, and finding it unyielding, turned to the east, and struck over toward Murfreesboro. . . .

NASHVILLE, TENN.—November 29, 1864, in command of the 14th, 16th, and 44th Regiments U.S.C.I., I embarked on a railroad train at Chattanooga for Nashville. On December 1st, with the 16th and most of the 14th, I reached my destination, and was assigned to a place on the extreme left of General Thomas' army then concentrating for the defence of Nashville against Hood's threatened attack. . . .

Soon after taking our position in line at Nashville, we were closely besieged by Hood's army; and thus we lay facing each other for two weeks. . . .

. . . [T]he first day's fight . . . had been for us a severe but glorious day. Over three hundred of my command had fallen, but everywhere our army was successful. . . . General Steadman congratulated us, saying his only fear had been that we might fight too hard. We had done all he desired, and more. Colored soldiers had again fought side by side with white troops; they had mingled together in the charge; they had supported each other; they had assisted each other from the field when wounded, and they lay side by side in death. The survivors rejoiced together over a hard fought field, won by a common valor. . . .

When the 2nd Colored Brigade retired behind my lines to re-form, one of the regimental color-bearers stopped in the open space between the two armies, where, although exposed to a dangerous fire, he planted his flag firmly in the ground, and began deliberately and coolly to return the enemy's fire, and, greatly to our amusement, kept up for some little time his independent warfare.

When the second and final assault was made, the right of my line took part. It was with breathless interest I watched that noble army climb the hill with a steady resolve which nothing but death itself could check. When at length the assaulting column sprang upon the earthworks, and the enemy seeing that further resistance was madness, gave way and began a precipitous retreat, our hearts swelled as only the hearts of soldiers can, and scarcely stopping to cheer or to await orders, we pushed forward and joined in the pursuit, until the darkness and the rain forced a halt. . . .

When General Thomas rode over the battle-field and saw the bodies of colored men side by side with the foremost, on the very works of the enemy, he turned to his staff, saying: "Gentlemen, the question is settled; negroes will fight."

*SOURCE:* Thomas J. Morgan, "Reminiscences of Service with Colored Troops in the Army of the Cumberland, 1863–65," in *Personal Narratives of Events in the War of the Rebellion* (Providence: Rhode Island Soldiers and Sailors Historical Society, 1885), 3rd series, no. 13, 11–48.

*RELATED ENTRIES: African Americans in the Military; Civil War*

## 1863 f

### Account of Black Physician on Escape from Anti-Draft/Anti-Black Riots

*William P. Powell, a black physician, barely managed to save himself and his family from an antidraft/anti-black mob in New York City. He sent the following account to a newspaper:*

On the afternoon of [July 13] my house . . . was invaded by a mob of half grown boys. . . . [They] were soon replaced by men and women. From 2 P.M. to 8 P.M. myself and family were prisoners in my own house to king mob, from which there was no way to escape but over the roofs of adjoining houses. About 4 P.M . . . the mob commenced throwing stones at the lower windows, until they had succeeded in making an opening. I was determined not to leave until driven from the premises. My family including my invalid daughter . . . took refuge on the roof of the next house. I remained till the mob broke in, and then narrowly escaped the same way. . . . We remained on the roof for an hour; still I hoped that relief would come. The neighbors, anticipating the mob would fire my house, were removing their effects on the roof—all was excitement. But as the object of the mob was plunder, they were too busily engaged in carrying off all my effects to apply the torch. . . .

How to escape from the roof of a five story building, with four females—and one a cripple—besides eight men, without a ladder, or any assistance from outside, was beyond my not excited imagination. But the God that succored Hagar in her flight, came to my relief in the person of a little deformed, despised Israelite—who, Samaritan-like, took my poor helpless daughter under his protection in his house, where I presume she now is, until friends send her to me. He also supplied me with a long rope. I then took a survey of the premises, and fortunately found a way to escape, and though pitchy dark, I took soundings with the rope to see if it would touch the next roof, after which I took a clove-hitch around the clothes line which was fastened to the wall by pulleys, and which led from one roof to the other over a space of about one hundred feet. In this manner I managed to lower my family down on to the next roof, and from one roof to another, until I landed them in a neighbor's yard. We were secreted in our friend's cellar till 11 P.M., when we were taken in charge by the Police and locked up in the Station house for safety. In this dismal place we found upwards of seventy men, women and children—some with broken limbs—bruised and beaten from head to foot. . . .

All my personal property, to the amount of $3,000, has been destroyed and scattered to the four winds. . . . As a devoted loyal Unionist, I have done all I could to perpetuate and uphold the integrity of this free government. As an evidence of this devotedness, my oldest son is now serving my country as a surgeon in the U.S. army, and myself had just received a commission in the naval service. What more could I do? What further evidence was wanting to prove my allegiance in the exigencies of our unfortunate country? I am now an old man, stripped of everything, . . . but I thank God that He has yet spared my life, which I am ready to yield in defence of my country.

*SOURCE:* Letter to the New Bedford *Standard,* reprinted in the *Pacific Appeal*, August 22, 1863.

*RELATED ENTRIES: African Americans in the Military; Civil War; Conscription and Volunteerism; New York City Anti-Draft Riots; Race Riots*

## 1863 g

### Letter from Grant to Lincoln on Recruitment of African Americans

*Gen. Ulysses S. Grant penned the following letter to President Lincoln on August 23, 1863, about the enlistment of blacks to fight as Union soldiers.*

I have given the subject of arming the negro my hearty support. This, with the emancipation of the negro, is the heavyest [sic] blow yet given the Confederacy. . . . By arming the negro we have added a powerful ally. They will make good soldiers and taking them from the enemy weakens him in the same proportion they strengthen us. I am therefore most decidedly in favor of pushing this policy to the enlistment of a force sufficient to hold all the South falling into our hands and to aid in capturing more.

*SOURCE:* Grant to Lincoln, August 23, 1863, A. Lincoln Papers, Manuscripts Division, Library of Congress.

*RELATED ENTRIES: African Americans in the Military; Civil War; Conscription and Volunteerism; Grant, Ulysses S.; Lincoln, Abraham*

## 1863 h

### Excerpts from General Orders, No. 100

*At the invitation of Gen. Henry Halleck, Francis Lieber, a German-born jurist and professor of law at Columbia University, prepared a general order on the laws of warfare for all Union Army commanders in the field. Promulgated by the adjutant general's office in April 1863, it remained the code governing U.S. forces for the next 40 years and proved to be influential in the codes adopted at The Hague in 1899 and 1907. Here are its key provisions:*

SECTION I

Martial Law—Military jurisdiction—Military necessity—Retaliation

Article 1.

A place, district, or country occupied by an enemy stands, in consequence of the occupation, under the Martial Law of the invading or occupying army, whether any proclamation declaring Martial Law, or any public warning to the inhabitants, has been issued or not. Martial Law is the immediate and direct effect and consequence of occupation or conquest. The presence of a hostile army proclaims its Martial Law.

Art. 2.

Martial Law does not cease during the hostile occupation, except by special proclamation, ordered by the commander in chief; or by special mention in the treaty of peace concluding the war, when the occupation of a place or territory continues beyond the conclusion of peace as one of the conditions of the same.

Art. 3.

Martial Law in a hostile country consists in the suspension, by the occupying military authority, of the criminal and civil law, and of the domestic administration and government in the occupied place or territory, and in the substitution of military rule and force for the same, as well as in the dictation of general laws, as far as military necessity requires this suspension, substitution, or dictation.

The commander of the forces may proclaim that the administration of all civil and penal law shall continue either wholly or in part, as in times of peace, unless otherwise ordered by the military authority.

Art. 4.

Martial Law is simply military authority exercised in accordance with the laws and usages of war. Military oppression is not Martial Law: it is the abuse of the power which that law confers. As Martial Law is executed by military force, it is incumbent upon those who administer it to be strictly guided by the principles of justice, honor, and humanity—virtues adorning a soldier even more than other men, for the very reason that he possesses the power of his arms against the unarmed.

Art. 5.

Martial Law should be less stringent in places and countries fully occupied and fairly conquered. Much greater severity may be exercised in places or regions where actual hostilities exist, or are expected and must be prepared for. Its most complete sway is allowed—even in the commander's own country—when face to face with the enemy, because of the absolute necessities of the case, and of the paramount duty to defend the country against invasion.

To save the country is paramount to all other considerations.

Art. 6.

All civil and penal law shall continue to take its usual course in the enemy's places and territories under Martial Law, unless interrupted or stopped by order of the occupying military power; but all the functions of the hostile government—legislative executive, or administrative—whether of a general, provincial, or local character, cease under Martial Law, or continue only with the sanction, or, if deemed necessary, the participation of the occupier or invader.

Art. 7.

Martial Law extends to property, and to persons, whether they are subjects of the enemy or aliens to that government.

Art. 8.

Consuls, among American and European nations, are not diplomatic agents. Nevertheless, their offices and persons will be subjected to Martial Law in cases of urgent necessity only: their property and business are not exempted. Any delinquency they commit against the established military rule may be punished as in the case of any other inhabitant, and such punishment furnishes no reasonable ground for international complaint.

Art. 9.

The functions of Ambassadors, Ministers, or other diplomatic agents accredited by neutral powers to the hostile government, cease, so far as regards the displaced government; but the conquering or occupying power usually recognizes them as temporarily accredited to itself.

Art. 10.
Martial Law affects chiefly the police and collection of public revenue and taxes, whether imposed by the expelled government or by the invader, and refers mainly to the support and efficiency of the army, its safety, and the safety of its operations.
Art. 11.
The law of war does not only disclaim all cruelty and bad faith concerning engagements concluded with the enemy during the war, but also the breaking of stipulations solemnly contracted by the belligerents in time of peace, and avowedly intended to remain in force in case of war between the contracting powers.

It disclaims all extortions and other transactions for individual gain; all acts of private revenge, or connivance at such acts.

Offenses to the contrary shall be severely punished, and especially so if committed by officers.
Art. 12.
Whenever feasible, Martial Law is carried out in cases of individual offenders by Military Courts; but sentences of death shall be executed only with the approval of the chief executive, provided the urgency of the case does not require a speedier execution, and then only with the approval of the chief commander.
Art. 13.
Military jurisdiction is of two kinds: First, that which is conferred and defined by statute; second, that which is derived from the common law of war. Military offenses under the statute law must be tried in the manner therein directed; but military offenses which do not come within the statute must be tried and punished under the common law of war. The character of the courts which exercise these jurisdictions depends upon the local laws of each particular country.

In the armies of the United States the first is exercised by courts-martial, while cases which do not come within the "Rules and Articles of War," or the jurisdiction conferred by statute on courts-martial, are tried by military commissions.
Art. 14.
Military necessity, as understood by modern civilized nations, consists in the necessity of those measures which are indispensable for securing the ends of the war, and which are lawful according to the modern law and usages of war.
Art. 15.
Military necessity admits of all direct destruction of life or limb of armed enemies, and of other persons whose destruction is incidentally unavoidable in the armed contests of the war; it allows of the capturing of every armed enemy, and every enemy of importance to the hostile government, or of peculiar danger to the captor; it allows of all destruction of property, and obstruction of the ways and channels of traffic, travel, or communication, and of all withholding of sustenance or means of life from the enemy; of the appropriation of whatever an enemy's country affords necessary for the subsistence and safety of the army, and of such deception as does not involve the breaking of good faith either positively pledged, regarding agreements entered into during the war, or supposed by the modern law of war to exist. Men who take up arms against one another in public war do not cease on this account to be moral beings, responsible to one another and to God.
Art. 16.
Military necessity does not admit of cruelty—that is, the infliction of suffering for the sake of suffering or for revenge, nor of maiming or wounding except in fight, nor of torture to extort confessions. It does not admit of the use of poison in any way, nor of the wanton devastation of a district. It admits of deception, but disclaims acts of perfidy; and, in general, military necessity does not include any act of hostility which makes the return to peace unnecessarily difficult.
Art. 17.
War is not carried on by arms alone. It is lawful to starve the hostile belligerent, armed or unarmed, so that it leads to the speedier subjection of the enemy.
Art. 18.
When a commander of a besieged place expels the noncombatants, in order to lessen the number of those who consume his stock of provisions, it is lawful, though an extreme measure, to drive them back, so as to hasten on the surrender.
Art. 19.
Commanders, whenever admissible, inform the enemy of their intention to bombard a place, so that the noncombatants, and especially the women and children, may be removed before the bombardment commences. But it is no infraction of the common law of war to omit thus to inform the enemy. Surprise may be a necessity.

Art. 20.
Public war is a state of armed hostility between sovereign nations or governments. It is a law and requisite of civilized existence that men live in political, continuous societies, forming organized units, called states or nations, whose constituents bear, enjoy, suffer, advance and retrograde together, in peace and in war.
Art. 21.
The citizen or native of a hostile country is thus an enemy, as one of the constituents of the hostile state or nation, and as such is subjected to the hardships of the war.
Art. 22.
Nevertheless, as civilization has advanced during the last centuries, so has likewise steadily advanced, especially in war on land, the distinction between the private individual belonging to a hostile country and the hostile country itself, with its men in arms. The principle has been more and more acknowledged that the unarmed citizen is to be spared in person, property, and honor as much as the exigencies of war will admit.
Art. 23.
Private citizens are no longer murdered, enslaved, or carried off to distant parts, and the inoffensive individual is as little disturbed in his private relations as the commander of the hostile troops can afford to grant in the overruling demands of a vigorous war.
Art. 24.
The almost universal rule in remote times was, and continues to be with barbarous armies, that the private individual of the hostile country is destined to suffer every privation of liberty and protection, and every disruption of family ties. Protection was, and still is with uncivilized people, the exception.
Art. 25.
In modern regular wars of the Europeans, and their descendants in other portions of the globe, protection of the inoffensive citizen of the hostile country is the rule; privation and disturbance of private relations are the exceptions.
Art. 26.
Commanding generals may cause the magistrates and civil officers of the hostile country to take the oath of temporary allegiance or an oath of fidelity to their own victorious government or rulers, and they may expel everyone who declines to do so. But whether they do so or not, the people and their civil officers owe strict obedience to them as long as they hold sway over the district or country, at the peril of their lives.
Art. 27.
The law of war can no more wholly dispense with retaliation than can the law of nations, of which it is a branch. Yet civilized nations acknowledge retaliation as the sternest feature of war. A reckless enemy often leaves to his opponent no other means of securing himself against the repetition of barbarous outrage
Art. 28.
Retaliation will, therefore, never be resorted to as a measure of mere revenge, but only as a means of protective retribution, and moreover, cautiously and unavoidably; that is to say, retaliation shall only be resorted to after careful inquiry into the real occurrence, and the character of the misdeeds that may demand retribution.

Unjust or inconsiderate retaliation removes the belligerents farther and farther from the mitigating rules of regular war, and by rapid steps leads them nearer to the internecine wars of savages.
Art. 29.
Modern times are distinguished from earlier ages by the existence, at one and the same time, of many nations and great governments related to one another in close intercourse.

Peace is their normal condition; war is the exception. The ultimate object of all modern war is a renewed state of peace.

The more vigorously wars are pursued, the better it is for humanity. Sharp wars are brief.
Art. 30.
Ever since the formation and coexistence of modern nations, and ever since wars have become great national wars, war has come to be acknowledged not to be its own end, but the means to obtain great ends of state, or to consist in defense against wrong; and no conventional restriction of the modes adopted to injure the enemy is any longer admitted; but the law of war imposes many limitations and restrictions on principles of justice, faith, and honor.

SECTION II
Public and private property of the enemy—Protection of persons, and especially of women, of religion, the arts and

sciences—Punishment of crimes against the inhabitants of hostile countries.

Art. 31.

A victorious army appropriates all public money, seizes all public movable property until further direction by its government, and sequesters for its own benefit or of that of its government all the revenues of real property belonging to the hostile government or nation. The title to such real property remains in abeyance during military occupation, and until the conquest is made complete.

Art. 32.

A victorious army, by the martial power inherent in the same, may suspend, change, or abolish, as far as the martial power extends, the relations which arise from the services due, according to the existing laws of the invaded country, from one citizen, subject, or native of the same to another.

The commander of the army must leave it to the ultimate treaty of peace to settle the permanency of this change.

Art. 33.

It is no longer considered lawful—on the contrary, it is held to be a serious breach of the law of war—to force the subjects of the enemy into the service of the victorious government, except the latter should proclaim, after a fair and complete conquest of the hostile country or district, that it is resolved to keep the country, district, or place permanently as its own and make it a portion of its own country.

Art. 34.

As a general rule, the property belonging to churches, to hospitals, or other establishments of an exclusively charitable character, to establishments of education, or foundations for the promotion of knowledge, whether public schools, universities, academies of learning or observatories, museums of the fine arts, or of a scientific character such property is not to be considered public property in the sense of paragraph 31; but it may be taxed or used when the public service may require it.

Art. 35.

Classical works of art, libraries, scientific collections, or precious instruments, such as astronomical telescopes, as well as hospitals, must be secured against all avoidable injury, even when they are contained in fortified places whilst besieged or bombarded.

Art. 36.

If such works of art, libraries, collections, or instruments belonging to a hostile nation or government, can be removed without injury, the ruler of the conquering state or nation may order them to be seized and removed for the benefit of the said nation. The ultimate ownership is to be settled by the ensuing treaty of peace.

In no case shall they be sold or given away, if captured by the armies of the United States, nor shall they ever be privately appropriated, or wantonly destroyed or injured.

Art. 37.

The United States acknowledge and protect, in hostile countries occupied by them, religion and morality; strictly private property; the persons of the inhabitants, especially those of women: and the sacredness of domestic relations. Offenses to the contrary shall be rigorously punished.

This rule does not interfere with the right of the victorious invader to tax the people or their property, to levy forced loans, to billet soldiers, or to appropriate property, especially houses, lands, boats or ships, and churches, for temporary and military uses

Art. 38.

Private property, unless forfeited by crimes or by offenses of the owner, can be seized only by way of military necessity, for the support or other benefit of the army or of the United States.

If the owner has not fled, the commanding officer will cause receipts to be given, which may serve the spoliated owner to obtain indemnity.

Art. 39.

The salaries of civil officers of the hostile government who remain in the invaded territory, and continue the work of their office, and can continue it according to the circumstances arising out of the war—such as judges, administrative or police officers, officers

of city or communal governments—are paid from the public revenue of the invaded territory, until the military government has reason wholly or partially to discontinue it. Salaries or incomes connected with purely honorary titles are always stopped.

Art. 40.

There exists no law or body of authoritative rules of action between hostile armies, except that branch of the law of nature and nations which is called the law and usages of war on land.

Art. 41.

All municipal law of the ground on which the armies stand, or of the countries to which they belong, is silent and of no effect between armies in the field.

Art. 42.

Slavery, complicating and confounding the ideas of property, (that is of a thing,) and of personality, (that is of humanity,) exists according to municipal or local law only. The law of nature and nations has never acknowledged it. The digest of the Roman law enacts the early dictum of the pagan jurist, that "so far as the law of nature is concerned, all men are equal." Fugitives escaping from a country in which they were slaves, villains, or serfs, into another country, have, for centuries past, been held free and acknowledged free by judicial decisions of European countries, even though the municipal law of the country in which the slave had taken refuge acknowledged slavery within its own dominions.

Art. 43.

Therefore, in a war between the United States and a belligerent which admits of slavery, if a person held in bondage by that belligerent be captured by or come as a fugitive under the protection of the military forces of the United States, such person is immediately entitled to the rights and privileges of a freeman To return such person into slavery would amount to enslaving a free person, and neither the United States nor any officer under their authority can enslave any human being. Moreover, a person so made free by the law of war is under the shield of the law of nations, and the former owner or State can have, by the law of postliminy, no belligerent lien or claim of service.

Art. 44.

All wanton violence committed against persons in the invaded country, all destruction of property not commanded by the authorized officer, all robbery, all pillage or sacking, even after taking a place by main force, all rape, wounding, maiming, or killing of such inhabitants, are prohibited under the penalty of death, or such other severe punishment as may seem adequate for the gravity of the offense.

A soldier, officer or private, in the act of committing such violence, and disobeying a superior ordering him to abstain from it, may be lawfully killed on the spot by such superior.

Art. 45.

All captures and booty belong, according to the modern law of war, primarily to the government of the captor.

Prize money, whether on sea or land, can now only be claimed under local law.

Art. 46.

Neither officers nor soldiers are allowed to make use of their position or power in the hostile country for private gain, not even for commercial transactions otherwise legitimate. Offenses to the contrary committed by commissioned officers will be punished with cashiering or such other punishment as the nature of the offense may require; if by soldiers, they shall be punished according to the nature of the offense.

Art. 47.

Crimes punishable by all penal codes, such as arson, murder, maiming, assaults, highway robbery, theft, burglary, fraud, forgery, and rape, if committed by an American soldier in a hostile country against its inhabitants, are not only punishable as at home, but in all cases in which death is not inflicted, the severer punishment shall be preferred. . . .

SECTION X

Insurrection—Civil War—Rebellion

Art. 149.

Insurrection is the rising of people in arms against their government, or a portion of it, or against one or more of its laws, or against an officer or officers of the government. It may be confined to mere armed resistance, or it may have greater ends in view.

Art. 150.

Civil war is war between two or more portions of a country or state, each contending for the mastery of the whole, and each claiming to be the legitimate government. The term is also sometimes applied to war of rebellion, when the rebellious provinces or portions of the state are contiguous to those containing the seat of government.

Art. 151.

The term rebellion is applied to an insurrection of large extent, and is usually a war between the legitimate government of a country and portions of provinces of the same who seek to throw off their allegiance to it and set up a government of their own.

Art. 152.

When humanity induces the adoption of the rules of regular war to ward rebels, whether the adoption is partial or entire, it does in no way whatever imply a partial or complete acknowledgement of their government, if they have set up one, or of them, as an independent and sovereign power. Neutrals have no right to make the adoption of the rules of war by the assailed government toward rebels the ground of their own acknowledgment of the revolted people as an independent power.

Art. 153.

Treating captured rebels as prisoners of war, exchanging them, concluding of cartels, capitulations, or other warlike agreements with them; addressing officers of a rebel army by the rank they may have in the same; accepting flags of truce; or, on the other hand, proclaiming Martial Law in their territory, or levying war-taxes or forced loans, or doing any other act sanctioned or demanded by the law and usages of public war between sovereign belligerents, neither proves nor establishes an acknowledgment of the rebellious people, or of the government which they may have erected, as a public or sovereign power. Nor does the adoption of the rules of war toward rebels imply an engagement with them extending beyond the limits of these rules. It is victory in the field that ends the strife and settles the future relations between the contending parties.

Art. 154.

Treating, in the field, the rebellious enemy according to the law and usages of war has never prevented the legitimate government from trying the leaders of the rebellion or chief rebels for high treason, and from treating them accordingly, unless they are included in a general amnesty.

Art. 155.

All enemies in regular war are divided into two general classes—that is to say, into combatants and noncombatants, or unarmed citizens of the hostile government.

The military commander of the legitimate government, in a war of rebellion, distinguishes between the loyal citizen in the revolted portion of the country and the disloyal citizen. The disloyal citizens may further be classified into those citizens known to sympathize with the rebellion without positively aiding it, and those who, without taking up arms, give positive aid and comfort to the rebellious enemy without being bodily forced thereto.

Art. 156.

Common justice and plain expediency require that the military commander protect the manifestly loyal citizens, in revolted territories, against the hardships of the war as much as the common misfortune of all war admits.

The commander will throw the burden of the war, as much as lies within his power, on the disloyal citizens, of the revolted portion or province, subjecting them to a stricter police than the noncombatant enemies have to suffer in regular war; and if he deems it appropriate, or if his government demands of him that every citizen shall, by an oath of allegiance, or by some other manifest act, declare his fidelity to the legitimate government, he may expel, transfer, imprison, or fine the revolted citizens who refuse to pledge themselves anew as citizens obedient to the law and loyal to the government.

Whether it is expedient to do so, and whether reliance can be placed upon such oaths, the commander or his government have the right to decide.

Art. 157.

Armed or unarmed resistance by citizens of the United States against the lawful movements of their troops is levying war against the United States, and is therefore treason.

*SOURCE:* The Avalon Project at Yale Law School, "Laws of War: General Orders No. 100," www.yale.edu/lawweb/avalon/lieber.htm (June 7, 2005).

*RELATED ENTRIES: Civil War; Geneva and Hague Conventions; Just War Theory; Philippine War; Prisoners of War; Spanish-American War*

## 1863 i

### Lyrics to "Just Before the Battle, Mother"

*Many supporters of the Union cause in the North delighted in songs written by well-known composers, including Julia Ward Howe's "The Battle Hymn of the Republic" and George Root's "The Battle Cry of*



Documents

*Freedom." Root followed up his first hit with this heart-tugger about a young lad writing to his mother on the eve of combat. Note how he folds the singing of his first song into this one:*

Just before the battle, Mother,
I am thinking most of you,
While upon the field we're watching,
With the enemy in view,
Comrades brave are 'round me lying,
Filled with thoughts of home and God;
For well they know that on the morrow,
Some will sleep beneath the sod.

Chorus:
Farewell, Mother, you may never,
Press me to your heart again,
But, oh, you'll not forget me, Mother,
If I'm number'd with the slain.

Oh, I long to see you, Mother,
And the loving ones at home,
But I'll never leave our banner,
Till in honour I can come.
Tell the traitors, all around you,
That their cruel words we know,
In ev'ry battle kill our soldiers,
By the help they give the foe.

Hark! I hear the bugles sounding,
'Tis the signal for the fight,
Now, may God protect us, Mother,
As he ever does the right.
Hear the "Battle Cry of Freedom,"
How it swells upon the air,
Oh, yes, we'll rally 'round the standard,
Or we'll perish nobly there.

*This appears to have been "a bit too much" for some of the Union soldiers themselves, for they wrote parody verses of "Just Before the Battle Mother." Here is an amalgam of the verses, sung in South Dakota by the son of a Civil War veteran to his grandson in the mid-20th century.*

Just before the battle, Mother,
I was drinking mountain dew,
When I saw the "Rebels" marching,
To the rear I quickly flew;
Where the stragglers were flying,
Thinking of their homes and wives;
'Twas not the "Rebs" we feared, dear Mother,
But our own dear precious lives.

Chorus:
Farewell, Mother, for you'll never
See my name among the slain.
For if I only can skedaddle,
Dear Mother, I'll come home again.

I hear the bugle sounding, Mother,
My soul is eager for the fray.
I guess I'll hide behind some cover,
And then I shall be OK.
Discretion's the better part of valor,
At least I've often heard you say;
And he who loves his life, dear Mother,
Won't fight if he can run away.

Do not fear for me, dear Mother,
That death shall claim your only son;
For though I'm not a fighter, Mother,
Bet your sweet life I can run.

Just behind the battle, Mother,
Foemen charge the live-long day.
'Tis bad they didn't charge me, Mother,
For when I'm charged I never pay.

Just behind the battle, Mother,
That's the safest place to be.
War and all its horrors, Mother,
Never did appeal to me.

When the enemy approaches,
I turn about and fade away;
For I'd rather live a live bum, Mother,
Than a dead hero any day.

*SOURCE:* Doug Weberg, having heard this sung by his grandfrather, shared it with the editor.

*RELATED ENTRIES: Civil War; Music and War*

## 1864 a

### Comments of Black Sailor George Reed

*George W. Reed, a black sailor serving on the U.S. gunboat Commodore Reed, Potomac flotilla, wrote this account of gunboat raids in northern Virginia:*

Sir, having been engaged in the naval service nearly six years, I have never before witnessed what I now see on board this ship. Our crew are principally colored; and a braver set of men never trod the deck of an American ship. We have been on several expeditions recently. On the 15th of April our ship and other gunboats proceeded up the Rappahannock river for some distance, and finding no rebel batteries to oppose us, we concluded to land the men from the different boats, and make a raid. I was ordered by the Commodore to beat the call for all parties to go on shore. No sooner had I executed the order, than every man was at his post, our own color being the first to land. At first, there was a little prejudice against our colored men going on shore, but it soon died away. We succeeded in capturing 3 fine horses, 6 cows, 5 hogs, 6 sheep, 3 calves, an abundance of chickens, 600 pounds of pork, 300 bushels of corn, and succeeded in liberating from the horrible pit of bondage 10 men, 6 women, and 8 children. The principal part of the men have enlisted on this ship. The next day we started further up the river, when the gunboats in advance struck on a torpedo, but did no material damage. We landed our men again, and repulsed a band of rebels handsomely, and captured three prisoners. Going on a little further, we were surprised by 300 rebel cavalry, and repulsed, but retreated in good order, the gunboats covering our retreat. I regret to say we had the misfortune to lose Samuel Turner (colored) in our retreat. He was instantly killed, and his body remains in the rebel hands. He being the fifer, I miss him very much as a friend and companion, as he was beloved by all on board. We also had four slightly wounded.

*SOURCE: Christian Recorder,* May 21, 1864.

*RELATED ENTRIES: African Americans in the Military; Civil War*

## 1864 b

### Excerpt from Sherman's Memoirs on His March from Atlanta to the Sea

*General Sherman wrote these words in his memoirs of his march from Atlanta to the sea:*

The next day [November 17, 1864, one day out of Atlanta on his march to the sea] we passed through the handsome town of Covington, the soldiers closing up their ranks, the color-bearers unfurling their flags, and the bands striking up patriotic airs. The white people came out of their houses to behold the sight, spite of their deep hatred of the invaders, and the negroes were simply frantic with joy. Whenever they heard my name, they clustered about my house, shouted and prayed in their peculiar style, which had a natural eloquence that would have moved a stone. I have witnessed hundreds, if not thousands, of such scenes; and can now see a poor girl, in the very ecstasy of the Methodist "shout," hugging the banner of one of the regiments, and jumping up to the "feet of Jesus."

*SOURCE:* William T. Sherman, *Memoirs of General William T. Sherman*, 2 vols. (New York: D. A. Appleton, 1886), 2: 180.

*RELATED ENTRIES: Civil War; Sherman, William Tecumseh*

## 1864 c

### Excerpts from the Writings of Oliver Wendell Holmes, Jr.

*Some veterans recall their time in the service as so much time lost. Those who experience the intensity of combat initially fix upon the horrors they have witnessed, but, as time passes, they tend to focus on the camaraderie associated with those moments of horror, and later remember their service as the most significant and moving periods of their lives. Oliver Wendell Holmes Jr., served in a Massachusetts regiment with the Army of the Potomac. He was wounded at Ball's Bluff and left the war in 1864. The first passage is from his Civil War diary; the second is from a speech he delivered 30 years after the war.*

Diary Entry

1864, exact date unknown

. . . I WAS QUITE FAINT—and seeing poor Sergt Merchant lying near—shot through the head and covered with blood—and then the thinking begun—(Meanwhile hardly able to speak—at least, coherently)—Shot through the lungs? Lets see—and I spit—Yes—already the blood was in my mouth. At once my thoughts jumped to "Children of the New Forest." (by Marryatt) which I was fond of reading as a little boy, and in which the father of one of the heroines is shot through the lungs by a robber—I remembered he died with terrible haemorrhages & great agony—What should I do? Just then I remembered and felt in my waist coat pocket—Yes there it was—a little bottle of laudanum which I had brought along—But I won't take it yet; no, see a doctor first—It may not be as bad as it looks—At any rate wait till the pain begins—

When I had got to the bottom of the Bluff the ferry boat, (the scow,) had just started with a load—but there was a small boat there—Then, still in this half conscious state, I heard somebody groan—Then I thought "Now wouldn't Sir Philip Sydney have that other feller put into the boat first?" But the question, as the form in which it occurred shows, came from a mind still bent on a becoming and consistent carrying out of its ideals of conduct—not from the unhesitating instinct of a still predominant & heroic will—I am not sure whether I propounded the question but I let myself be put aboard.

. . . . I was taken into the large building which served as a general hospital; and I remember . . . Men lying round on the floor—the spectacle wasn't familiar then—a red blanket with an arm lying on it in a pool of blood—it seems as if instinct told me it was John Putnam's (the Capt. Comdg Co H)—and near the entrance a surgeon calmly grasping a man's finger and cutting it off—both standing—while the victim contemplated the operation with a very grievous mug . . . presently a Doctor of (Baxter's?) Fire Zouaves* coming in with much noise & bluster, and oh, troops were crossing to the Virginia side, and we were going to lick, and Heaven knows what not—I called him and gave him my address and told him (or meant & tried to) if I died to write home & tell 'em I'd done my duty—I was very anxious they should know that— . . .

Much more vivid is my memory of my thoughts and state of mind for though I may have been light-headed my reason was working—even if through a cloud. Of course when I thought I was dying the reflection that the majority vote of the civilized world declared that with my opinions I was en route for Hell came up with painful distinctness—Perhaps the first impulse was tremulous—but then I said—by Jove, I die like a soldier anyhow—I was shot in the breast doing my duty to the hub—afraid? No, I am proud—then I thought I couldn't be guilty of a deathbed recantation—father and I had talked of that and were agreed that it generally meant nothing but a cowardly giving way to fear—Besides, thought I, can I recant if I want to, has the approach of death changed my beliefs much? & to this I answered—No—Then came in my Philosophy—I am to take a leap in the dark—but now as ever I believe that whatever shall happen is best—for it is in accordance with a general law—and good & universal (or general law) are synonymous terms in the universe—(I can now add that our phrase good only means certain general truths seen through the heart & will instead of being merely contemplated intellectually—I doubt if the intellect accepts or recognizes that classification of good and bad). Would the complex forces which made a still more complex unit in Me resolve themselves back into simpler forms or would my angel be still winging his way onward when eternities had passed? I could not tell—But all was doubtless well—and so with a "God forgive me if I'm wrong" I slept—

*The 72nd Regiment Pennsylvania Volunteers, under Colonel DeWitt Clinton Baxter, was commonly known as Baxter's Fire Zouaves.

*SOURCE:* Reprinted by permission of Harvard University Press from Diary entry No. 2, as given in *Touched with Fire: The Civil War Letters and Diary of Oliver Wendell Holmes, Jr.*, ed. Mark DeWolfe Howe, 24–28 (Cambridge, Mass.: Harvard University Press, 1946). 

THE SOLDIER'S FAITH

Memorial Day Speech, Harvard University, May 30, 1895

. . . Now, at least, and perhaps as long as man dwells upon the globe, his destiny is battle, and he has to take the chances of war. If it is our business to fight, the book for the army is a war-song, not a hospital-sketch. It is not well for soldiers to think much about wounds. Sooner or later we shall fall; but meantime it is for us to fix our eyes upon the point to be stormed, and to get there if we can.

Behind every scheme to make the world over, lies the question, What kind of world do you want? The ideals of the past for men have been drawn from war, as those for women have been drawn from motherhood. For all our prophecies, I doubt if we are ready to give up our inheritance. Who is there who would not like to be thought a gentleman? Yet what has that name been built on but the soldier's choice of honor rather than life? To be a soldier or descended from soldiers, in time of peace to be ready to give one's life rather than to suffer disgrace, that is what the world has meant; and if we try to claim it at less cost than a splendid carelessness for life, we are trying to steal the good will without the responsibilities of the place. We will not dispute about taste. The man of the future may want something different. But who of us could endure a world, although cut up into five-acre lots and having no man upon it who was not well fed and well housed, without the divine folly of honor, without the senseless passion for knowledge out-reaching the flaming bounds of the possible, without ideals the essence of which is that they can never be achieved? I do not know what is true. I do not know the meaning of the universe. But in the midst of doubt, in the collapse of creeds, there is one thing I do not doubt, that no man who lives in the same world with most of us can doubt, and that is that the faith is true and adorable which leads a soldier to throw away his life in obedience to a blindly accepted duty, in a cause which he little understands, in a plan of campaign of which he has no notion, under tactics of which he does not see the use.

Most men who know battle know the cynic force with which the thoughts of common sense will assail them in times of stress; but they know that in their greatest moments faith has trampled those thoughts under foot. If you have been in line, suppose on Tremont Street Mall, ordered simply to wait and to do nothing, and have watched the enemy bring their guns to bear upon you down a gentle slope like that from Beacon Street, have seen the puff of the firing, have felt the burst of the spherical case-shot as it came toward you, have heard and seen the shrieking fragments go tearing through your company, and have known that the next or the next shot carries your fate; if you have advanced in line and have seen ahead of you the spot which you must pass where the rifle bullets are striking; if you have ridden by night at a walk toward the blue line of fire at the dead angle of Spottsylvania, where for twenty-four hours the soldiers were fighting on the two sides of an earthwork, and in the morning the dead and dying lay piled in a row six deep, and as you rode have heard the bullets splashing in the mud and earth about you; if you have been on the picketline at night in a black and unknown wood, have heard the spat of the bullets upon the trees, and as you moved have felt your foot slip upon a dead man's body; if you have had a blind fierce gallop against the enemy, with your blood up and a pace that left no time for fear—if, in short, as some, I hope many, who hear me, have known, you have known the vicissitudes of terror and of triumph in war, you know that there is such a thing as the faith I spoke of. You know your own weakness and are modest; but you know that man has in him that unspeakable somewhat which makes him capable of miracle, able to lift himself by the might of his own soul, unaided, able to face annihilation for a blind belief.

From the beginning, to us, children of the North, life has seemed a place hung about by dark mists, out of which come the pale shine of dragon's scales, and the cry of fighting men, and the sound of swords. Beowulf, Milton, Dürer, Rembrandt, Schopenhauer, Turner, Tennyson, from the first war-song of our race to the stall-fed poetry of modern English drawing-rooms, all have had same vision, and all have had a glimpse of a light to be followed. "The end of worldly life awaits us all. Let him who may, gain honor ere death. That is best for a warrior when he is dead." So spoke Beowulf a thousand years ago.

Not of the sunlight,
Not of the moonlight,
Not of the starlight!
O young Mariner,
Down to the haven
Call your companions,
Launch your vessel,
And crowd your canvas,
And, ere it vanishes
Over the margin,
After it, follow it,
Follow The Gleam.

So sang Tennyson in the voice of the dying Merlin.

When I went to war I thought that soldiers were old men. I remembered a picture of the revolutionary soldier which some of you may have seen, representing a white-haired man with his flint-lock slung across his back. I remembered one or two living examples of revolutionary soldiers whom I had met, and I took no account of the lapse of time. It was not until long after, in winter quarters, as I was listening to some of the sentimental songs in vogue, such as—

Farewell, Mother, you may never
See your darling boy again,

that it came over me that the army was made up of what I now should call very young men. I dare say that my illusion has been shared by some of those now present, as they have looked at us upon whose heads the white shadows have begun to fall. But the truth is that war is the business of youth and early middle age. You who called this assemblage together, not we, would be the soldiers of another war, if we should have one, and we speak to you as the dying Merlin did in the verse which I just quoted. Would that the blind man's pipe might be transfigured by Merlin's magic, to make you hear the bugles as once we heard them beneath the morning stars! For to you it is that now is sung the Song of the Sword:—

The War-Thing, the Comrade,
Father of honor
And giver of kingship,
The fame-smith, the song master.
. . . . . . .
Priest (saith the Lord)
*Of his marriage with victory.*
. . . . . . .
Clear singing, clean slicing;
Sweet spoken, soft finishing;
Making death beautiful,
Life but a coin
To be staked in the pastime
Whose playing is more
Than the transfer of being;
Arch-anarch, chief builder,
Prince and evangelist,
I am the Will of God:
I am the Sword.

War, when you are at it, is horrible and dull. It is only when time has passed that you see that its message was divine. I hope it may be long before we are called again to sit at that master's feet. But some teacher of the kind we all need. In this snug, over-safe corner of the world we need it, that we may realize that our comfortable routine is no eternal necessity of things, but merely a little space of calm in the midst of the tempestuous untamed streaming of the world, and in order that we may be ready for danger. We need it in this time of individualist negations, with its literature of French and American humor, revolting at discipline, loving fleshpots, and denying that anything is worthy of reverence,—in order that we may remember all that buffoons forget. We need it everywhere and at all times. For high and dangerous action teaches us to believe as right beyond dispute things for which our doubting minds are slow to find words of proof. Out of heroism grows faith in the worth of heroism. The proof comes later, and even may never come. Therefore I rejoice at every dangerous sport which I see pursued. The students at Heidelberg, with their sword-slashed faces, inspire me with sincere respect. I gaze with delight upon our polo players. If once in a while in our rough riding a neck is broken, I regard it, not as a waste, but as a price well paid for the breeding of a race fit for headship and command.

We do not save our traditions, in this country. The regiments whose battle-flags were not large enough to hold the names of the battles they had fought, vanished with the surrender of Lee, although their memories inherited would have made heroes for a century. It is the more necessary to learn the lesson afresh from perils newly sought, and perhaps it is not vain for us to tell the new generation what we learned in our day, and what we still believe. That the joy of life is living, is to put out all one's powers as far as they will go; that the measure of power is obstacles overcome; to ride boldly at what is in front of you, be it fence or enemy; to pray, not for comfort, but for combat; to keep the soldier's faith against the doubts of civil life, more besetting and harder to overcome than all the misgivings of the battle field, and to remember that duty is not to be proved in the evil day, but then to be obeyed unquestioning; to love glory more than the temptations of wallowing ease, but to know that one's final judge and only rival is oneself—with all our failures in act and thought, these things we learned from noble enemies in Virginia or Georgia or on the Mississippi, thirty years ago; these we believe to be true.

> "Life is not lost," said she, "for which is bought
> Endlesse renown."

We learned also, and we still believe, that love of country is not yet an idle name. . . .

As for us, our days of combat are over. Our swords are rust. Our guns will thunder no more. The vultures that once wheeled over our heads are buried with their prey. Whatever of glory yet remains for us to win must be won in the council or the closet, never again in the field. I do not repine. We have shared the incommunicable experience of war; we have felt, we still feel, the passion of life to its top.

*SOURCE:* Reprinted by permission of the publisher from "The Soldier's Faith" in *The Occasional Speeches of Justice Oliver Wendell Holmes,* comp. by Mark DeWolfe Howe, 75–82 (Cambridge Mass.: The Belknap Press of Harvard University Press, 1962). 

*RELATED ENTRIES: Combat, Effects of; Memorial Day; Memory and War; Militarization and Militarism*

## 1865 a

### *New York Tribune*'s Comments on the 54th Regiment of Massachusetts

*The* New York Tribune *summarized the importance of the performance of the 54th Regiment of Massachusetts at Fort Wagner in these words*

It is not too much to say that if this Massachusetts Fifty-fourth had faltered when its trial came, two hundred thousand colored troops for whom it was a pioneer would never have been put into the field, or would not have been put in for another year, which would have been equivalent to protracting the war into 1866. But it did not falter. It made Fort Wagner such a name to the colored race as Bunker Hill has been for ninety years to the white Yankees.

*SOURCE: New York Tribune,* Sept. 8, 1865.

*RELATED ENTRIES: African Americans in the Military; Civil War; 54th Regiment of Massachusetts Volunteer Infantry; Greeley, Horace*

## 1865 b

### Lyrics to "I'm a Good Old Rebel"

*By mid-1865 all Confederate forces had surrendered and a "reconstruction" of the rebellious southern states was about to begin. One reason that Congress's planned Reconstruction ultimately failed was the intransigence of the former rebels, captured well in this song, which was popular with most white Southerners for a century after the Civil War:*

O, I'm a good old rebel,
  Now that's just what I am,
For this "Fair Land of Freedom,"
  I do not care a damn;
I'm glad I fit against it,



Documents

I only wish we'd won,
And I don't want no pardon,
For anything I done.

I hates the Constitution,
The great republic too;
I hates the Freedman's Buro,
In uniform of blue;
I hates the nasty Eagle
With all its brass and fuss,
The lyin', thieving Yankees,
I hates 'em wuss and wuss.

I hates the Yankee nation,
And everything they do,
I hates the Declaration
Of Independence too;
I hates the glorious Union,
'T is dripping with our blood;
I hates their striped banner,
I fit it all I could.

Three hundred thousand Yankees
Is stiff in Southern dust;
We got three hundred thousand,
Before they conquered us.
They died of Southern fever,
And Southern steel and shot,
I wish they was three million,
Instead of what we got.

I followed old Mas' Robert,
For four year near about,
Got wounded in three places,
And starved at Point Lookout.
I cotched the roomatism,
A-camping in the snow,
But I killed a chance o' Yankee
I'd like to kill some mo'.

I can't take up my musket
And fight 'em now no more,
But I ain't a-going to love 'em
Now that is sartin sure;
And I don't want no pardon
For what I was and am,
I won't be reconstructed,
And I don't care a damn.

*SOURCE:* National Society of Colonial Dames of America, *American War Songs* (Philadelphia: privately printed, 1925), 134–35.

*RELATED ENTRIES: Civil War; Music and War*

## 1866

### John Faller, Andersonville POW, on His Captivity

*John Faller, a Union Army captive at the notorious Confederate POW camp at Andersonville, Georgia, later recalled the long-term consequence of the inadequate rations provided to prisoners there:*

We were all more or less afflicted with scurvy, and some of us were very bad. Our teeth became loose, and in many cases would drop out. Toby Morrison's legs began to swell and turn black. One day we dug a hole in the sand, and buried him up to his waist, and tramped the sand tight about him and left him in that position for hours. We were told by an old sailor that that would draw the scurvy out of him. I don't know whether it did him any good or not, but he was very lame when we left Andersonville to go to another prison. He lived through it all and thinks he is a pretty good man yet.

Comrade Sites was afflicted with scurvy, and sinews of his limbs were drawn up so that he had to walk on his toes. He would put a little piece of wood under the ball of the foot and tie a string around it, which would relieve the pain to some extent. He, too, managed to get home alive.

J. Humer was left at Andersonville when we left in the fall on account of not being able to walk. The only meat he got to eat after we left was the half of a rat and he says he enjoyed it very much. He, too, managed to get home alive in July 1865. Broken down in health, he has since died.

Comrades McCleaf and Natcher were left back in Andersonville. McCleaf died shortly after. Natcher lived to get home but died a few years after the war from the effects of the imprisonment.

Jack Rhoads managed to pull through, after living on low diet for so long. He now lives in the country; and enjoys a good square meal, and has no more use for cow feed and water as he called it.

Comrades Harris and Elliot, after starving and almost dying for many months, and partaking of the same hospitalities in the South as we all did, managed to reach home alive. If there is anything good to eat around, they prefer it to corn meal or [Captain] Otto [Wirz's] vegetable soup.

While at Florence, Cuddy, Landis, Adams, Hefflefinger, Schlusser and the Walker boys died, and later Hal Eby died on reaching our line. Holmes died at Annapolis before reaching his home. Harkness Meloy, McCune, Natcher, Ruby, Humer have died since the war. Of those surviving today are Comrades Burkholder, Constercamp, Elliott, Faller, Gould, Harris, Morrison, Otto, Rhoads, Sites, Stoey and Vantelburg.

*SOURCE:* M. Flower, ed., *Dear Folks at Home* (Carlisle, Penn.: Cumberland County Historical Society, 1963), 140–41. Courtesy of Cumberland County Historical Society, Carlisle, Pennsylvani.

*RELATED ENTRIES: Andersonville; Civil War; Medicine and War; Prisoners of War*

## 1899 (to 1902)

### Two Songs Popular among Naval Officers Dating from the Philippine War

*The first of these songs, written by naval officers who served in the Philippine War, concerns a moment of "civil–military" tension in 1899 between the blustering and ineffective Gen. Elwell Otis, serving as U.S. governor-general of the Philippines, and Maj. Gen. Arthur MacArthur, serving as military commander, who replaced Otis in 1900. The second is an ethnic jibe at Filipinos. The sentences following the songs were provided by the Navy compiler in 1955 and speak for themselves.*

The Governor-General Or A Hobo
Oh, I've been having a helluva time, since I came to the Philippines;
I'd rather drive a bobtail mule, and live on pork and beans;
They call me Governor-General, I'm the hero of the day,
But I have troubles of my own and to myself I say—

Chorus:
Oh, am I the boss, or am I the tool?
Am I the Governor-General or a hobo?
For I'd like to know who's the boss of this show;
Is it me or Emilio Aguinaldo?

The rebels up at old Tarlac, four men to every gun—
I think the trouble is at an end, they think it's just begun,
My men go out to have a fight, the rebels fade away;
I cable home the trouble's o'er, but to myself I say—

Now General MacArthur, I have no doubt, can run the whole concern,
All right, I'll pack my trunk and go, and he can take his turn;
But when the papers "cuss him out," and lay him on the shelf,
I only ask the privilege of saying to myself—

Final Chorus:
Oh, is Mac the boss, or is Mac the tool?
Is Mac the Governor-General or a hobo?
I'd like to know who'll be boss of this show—
Will it be Mac or Emilio Aguinaldo?

This song was written on board the gunboat *Pampanga* during the winter of 1899. Aguinaldo was then the self-styled President of the Philippine Republic, and General Otis was Governor-General. The fact that an attempt was made to prevent the singing of the song only made it more popular. It was later introduced into Cornell University as a college song by one who had seen service in the Insurrection.

The Philippine Hombre
There was once a Filipino Hombre,
Who ate rice, pescado y legumbre,

His trousers were wide, and his shirt hung outside,
And this I say was costombre.

He lived in a palm-thatched bahai,
That served as home, stable and sty,
He slept on a mat with the dog and the cat,
And the pigs and the chickens close by.

His brother who was a cochero,
En Manila busco el dinero,
His prices were high when the cop wasn't nigh,
Which was hard on the poor pasajero.

His sister, a buen lavendera,
Smashed clothes in a fuerto manera,
On the rocks in the stream, where the carabaos dream,
Which gave them a perfume lijera.

His padre was buen Filipino,
Who never mixed tubig with vino,
Said, "No insurrecto, no got gun nor bolo,"
But used both to kill a vecino.

He once owned a bulic manoc,
A haughty and mean fighting cock,
Which lost him a name, and mil pesos tambien,
So he changed off to monte for luck.

His madre, she came from the Jolo,
She was half a Negrito and Moro,
All day in Manila, she tossed the tortilla,
And smoked a rotino cigarro.

Of ninos she had dos or tres,
Good types of the Tagolog race,
In dry or wet weather, in the altogether,
They'd romp, and they'd race, and they'd chase.

When his pueblo last gave a fiesta,
His familia tried to digest-a
Mule that had died with glanders inside,
And now su familia no esta.

This song is not only a wardroom favorite, but has found its way into practically every naval and military reservation in the United States and its dependencies, as well as into countless civilian homes which through friendship or blood relationship have ties with the Services. It was composed and first sung by the late Captain Lyman A. Cotten, U.S.N., about 1900, when Navy, Army and Marine Corps were busy "pacifying" the newly acquired Philippines.

*SOURCE:* Joseph W. Crosley and the United States Naval Institute, *The Book of Navy Songs.* (Annapolis, Md.: United States Naval Academy, 1955). Reprinted by permission of the Naval Institute Press.

*RELATED ENTRIES: Civil–Military Relations; Music and War; Philippine War*

## 1900

### Black Soldier's Letter to a Wisconsin Editor on American Treatment of Filipinos

*A black regular with the 24th or 25th infantry regiment poured out his anger at the racist views and conduct of his white counterparts during the Philippine War in this letter to his hometown paper in May 1900.*

Editor, New York Age

I have mingled freely with the natives and have had talks with American colored men here in business and who have lived here for years, in order to learn of them the cause of their (Filipino) dissatisfaction and the reason for this insurrection, and I must confess they have a just grievance. All this never would have occurred if the army of occupation would have treated them as people. The Spaniards, even if their laws were hard, were polite and treated them with some consideration; but the Americans, as soon as they saw that the native troops were desirous of sharing in the glories as well as the hardships of the hard-won battles with the Americans, began to apply home treatment for colored peoples: cursed them as damn niggers, steal [from] and ravish them, rob them on the street of their small change, take from the fruit vendors whatever suited their fancy, and kick the poor unfortunate if he complained, desecrate their church property, and after fighting began, looted everything in sight, burning, robbing the graves.

This may seem a little tall—but I have seen with my own eyes carcasses lying bare in the boiling sun, the results of raids on receptacles for the dead in search of diamonds. The [white] troops, thinking we would be proud to emulate their conduct, have made bold of telling their exploits to us. One fellow, member of the 13th Minnesota, told me how some fellows he knew had cut off a native woman's arm in order to get a fine inlaid bracelet. On upbraiding some fellows one morning, whom I met while out for a walk (I think they belong to a Nebraska or Minnesota regiment, and they were stationed on the Malabon road) for the conduct of the American troops toward the natives and especially as to raiding, etc., the reply was: "Do you think we could stay over here and fight these damn niggers without making it pay all it's worth? The government only pays us $13 per month: that's starvation wages. White men can't stand it." Meaning they could not live on such small pay. In saying this they never dreamed that Negro soldiers would never countenance such conduct. They talked with impunity of "niggers" to our soldiers, never once thinking that they were talking to home "niggers" and should they be brought to remember that at home this is the same vile epithet they hurl at us, they beg pardon and make some effeminate excuse about what the Filipino is called.

I want to say right here that if it were not for the sake of the 10,000,000 black people in the United States, God alone knows on which side of the subject I would be. And for the sake of the black men who carry arms and pioneer for them as their representatives, ask them not to forget the present administration at the next election. Party be damned! We don't want these islands, not in the way we are to get them, and for Heaven's sake, put the party [Democratic] in power that pledged itself against this highway robbery. Expansion is too clean a name for it.

[Unsigned]

*SOURCE:* Unsigned letter, *Wisconsin Weekly Advocate,* May 17, 1900.

*RELATED ENTRIES: African Americans in the Military; Philippine War*

## 1908 (to 1916)

### LEONARD WOOD ON PREPAREDNESS AND CIVIL OBLIGATION OF THE ARMY

*Gen. Leonard Wood, a veteran of the Indian wars in the West and the Spanish–American War in Cuba, later served as military governor of Cuba, commanding general in the Philippines, and Army chief of staff. In 1908 he offered his first call for universal military training. After the outbreak of war in Europe in August 1914, he became a Preparedness advocate as well.*

Our past military policy, so far as it concerns the land forces, has been thoroughly unsound and in violation of basic military principles. We have succeeded not because of it, but in spite of it. It has been unnecessarily and brutally costly in human life and recklessly extravagant in the expenditure of treasure. It has tended greatly to prolong our wars and consequently has delayed national development.

Because we have succeeded in spite of an unsound system, those who do not look beneath the surface fail to recognize the numerous shortcomings of that system, or appreciate how dangerous is our further dependence upon it.

The time has come to put our house in order through the establishment of a sound and dependable system, and to make such wise and prudent preparation as will enable us to defend successfully our country and our rights.

No such system can be established which does not rest upon equality of service for all who are physically fit and of proper age. Manhood suffrage means manhood obligation for service in peace or war. This is the basic principle upon which truly representative government, or free democracy, rests and must rest if it is successfully to withstand the shock of modern war.

The acceptance of this fundamental principle will require to a certain extent the moral organization of the people, the building up of that sense of individual obligation for service to the nation which is the basis of true patriotism, the teaching of our people to think in terms of the nation rather than in those of a locality or of personal interest.

This organization must also be accompanied by the organization, classification and training of our men and the detailed and careful organization of the material resources of the country with the view to making them promptly available in case of need and to remedying any defects.

In the organization of our land forces we must no longer place reliance upon plans based upon the development of volunteers or the use of the militia. The volunteer system is not dependable because of the uncertainty as to returns, and in any case because of the lack of time for training and organization.

Modern wars are often initiated without a formal declaration of war or by a declaration which is coincident with the first act of war.

Dependence upon militia under state control or partially under state control, spells certain disaster, not because of the quality of the men or officers, but because of the system under which they work.

We must also have a first-class navy, well balanced and thoroughly equipped with all necessary appliances afloat and ashore. It is the first line of defense.

We need a highly efficient regular army, adequate to the peace needs of the nation. By this is meant a regular force, fully equipped, thoroughly trained and properly organized, with adequate reserves of men and material, and a force sufficient to garrison our over-sea possessions, including the Philippines and the Hawaiian Islands. These latter are the key to the Pacific and one of the main defenses of our Pacific coast and the Panama Canal, and whoever holds them dominates the trade routes of the greater portion of the Pacific and, to a large extent, that ocean. The army must be sufficient also to provide an adequate garrison for the Panama Canal, which is an implement of commerce and an instrument of war so valuable that we must not under any conditions allow it to lie outside our secure grasp.

The regular force must also be adequate to provide sufficient troops for our coast defenses and such garrisons as may be required in Porto Rico and Alaska. The regular force must also be sufficient to provide the necessary mobile force in the United States; by this is meant a force of cavalry, infantry, field artillery, engineers and auxiliary troops sufficient to provide an expeditionary force such as we sent to Cuba in 1898, and at the same time to provide a force sufficient to meet possible conditions of internal disorder. It must also furnish training units for the National Guard, or whatever force the federal government may eventually establish in place of it, and provide sufficient officers for duty under the detail system in the various departments, instructors at the various colleges and schools where military instruction is or may be established, attachés abroad and officers on special missions.

The main reliance in a war with a first-class power will ultimately be the great force of citizen soldiers forming a purely federal force, thoroughly organized and equipped with reserves of men and material. This force must be trained under some system which will permit the instruction to be given in part during the school period or age, thereby greatly reducing the time required for the final intensive period of training, which should be under regular officers and in conjunction with regular troops. In brief, the system must be one which utilizes as far as possible the means and opportunities now available, and interferes as little as possible with the educational or industrial careers of those affected. A system moulded on the general lines of the Australian or Swiss will accomplish this. Some modifications will be required to meet our conditions.

Each year about one million men reach the military age of 18; of this number not more than fifty per cent are fit for military service, this being about the average in other countries. Far less than fifty per cent come up to the standards required for the regular army, but the minor defects rejecting them for the regular army would not reject them for general military service. Assuming that some system on the general lines of the Australian or Swiss must be eventually adopted in this country, it would seem that about 500,000 men would be available each year for military training. If the boys were prepared by the state authorities, through training in schools and colleges, and in state training areas—when the boys were not in school—to the extent that they are in Switzerland or Australia, it would be possible, when they come up for federal training, to finish their military training—so far as preparing them for the duties of enlisted men is concerned—within a period of approximately three months. We should be able to limit the period of first line obligation to the period from eighteen to twenty-five, inclusive, or seven years, or we could make the period of obligatory service begin two years later and extend it to twenty-seven. This procedure would give in the first line approximately three and one-half millions of men at the age of best physical condition and of minimum dependent and business responsibility. From the men of certain years (classes) of this period, organizations of federal forces should be built up to the extent of at least twenty-five divisions. They would be organized and equipped exactly like the regular army and would be held ready for immediate service as our present militia would be were it under federal control.

Men of these organizations would not live in uniform but would go about their regular occupations as do the members of the militia to-day, but they would be equipped, organized and ready for immediate service. If emergency required it, additional organizations could be promptly raised from the men who were within the obligatory period.

There should be no pay in peace time except when the men were on duty and then it should be merely nominal. The duty should be recognized as a part of the man's citizenship obligation to the nation. The organizations to be made up of men within the period of obligatory service, could be filled either by the men who indicated their desire for such training or by drawing them by lot. This is a matter of detail. The regular army as organized would be made up as to-day; it would be a professional army. The men who came into it would be men who had received in youth this citizenship training. They would come into the regular army because they wanted to be professional soldiers. The regular army would be to a certain extent the training nucleus for the citizen soldier organizations and would be the force garrisoning our over-sea possessions. It would be much easier to maintain our regular army in a highly efficient condition, as general military training would have produced a respect for the uniform and an appreciation of the importance of a soldier's duty.

The reserve corps of officers would be composed of men who had had longer and more advanced training, and could be recruited and maintained as indicated below, through further training of men from the military schools and colleges and those from the officers' training corps units of the nonmilitary universities and colleges. There would also be those from the military training camps and other sources, such as men who have served in the army and have the proper qualifications. This would give a military establishment in which every man would be physically fit to play his part and would have finished his obligation in what was practically his early manhood, with little probability of being called upon again unless the demands of war were so great as to require more men than those of the total first line, eighteen to twenty-five years, inclusive. Then they would be called by years as the occasion required, and would be available for service up to their forty-fifth year. It would give us a condition of real national preparedness, a much higher type of citizenship, a lower criminal rate and an enormously improved economic efficiency. Pending the establishment of such a system, every effort should be made to transfer the state militia to federal control. By this is meant its complete removal from state control and its establishment as a purely federal force, having no more relation to the states than the regular army has at present. This force under federal control will make a very valuable nucleus for the building up of a federal force of civilian soldiers. Officers and men should be transferred with their present grades and ratings. . . .

. . . As has been recommended by the General Staff, there should be built up with the least possible delay a corps of at least 50,000 reserve officers, on lines and through means recommended by the General Staff, and by means of a further development of the United States Military Training Camps for college students and older men, which have been in operation for a number of years. These plans include the coordination of the instruction at the various military college and schools and the establishment of well-thought-out plans for the nonmilitary colleges at which it may be decided to establish officers' training corps units on lines now under consideration.

This number of officers, fifty thousand, may seem excessive to some, but when it is remembered that there were one hundred and twenty-seven thousand officers in the Northern army during the Civil War, and over sixty thousand in the Southern, fifty thousand will not appear to be excessive. Fifty thousand officers will be barely sufficient properly to officer a million and a half citizen soldiers. We had in service, North and South, during the Civil War, over four million men, and at the end of the war we had approximately one and a quarter million under arms.

Under legislative provision enacted during the Civil War, commonly known as the Morrill Act, Congress established mechanical and agricultural colleges in each state, among other things prescribing military instruction and providing for this purpose officers of the regular army. There are nearly thirty thousand students at these institutions who receive during their course military instruction for periods of from one to two years. In some cases the instruction is excellent; in others it is very poor.

There are in addition a large number of military colleges and schools; at these there are some ten thousand students, so that there are approximately forty thousand young men receiving military instruction, nearly all of them under officers of the army. This means a graduating class of about eight thousand, of whom not more than forty-five hundred would be fit to undergo military training.

These men should be assembled in United States Military Training Camps for periods of five weeks each for two consecutive years, in order that they may receive that practical and thorough instruction which in the majority of instances is not possible during their college course. With these should be assembled the men who have taken the officers' training course at the various nonmilitary universities. This course, as outlined by the General Staff, will be thorough and conducted, so far as the purely military courses and duties are concerned, under the immediate control of officers of the army.

From all these sources we have practically an inexhaustible supply of material from which excellent reserve officers can be made. From the men assembled in camp each year, fifteen hundred should be selected and commissioned, subject only to physical examination, as they are all men of college type, for one year as second lieutenants in the line and in the various staff corps and departments of the regular army. They should receive the pay and allowance of second lieutenants, or such pay and allowance as may be deemed to be appropriate.

The men who receive this training would furnish very good material for reserve officers of the grade of captain and major, whereas as a rule the men who have not had this training would qualify only in the grade of lieutenant.

From this group of men could well be selected, subject to the prescribed mental and physical examination, the greater portion of the candidates from civil life for appointment in the army. We have the material and the machinery for turning out an excellent corps of reserve officers. All that is needed is to take hold of it and shape it.

The prompt building up of a reserve corps of officers is one of the most vitally important steps to be taken. It is absolutely essential. It takes much time and care to train officers. Not only should students of the various colleges, universities and schools where military training is given, be made use of to the fullest extent, but the military training camps which have been conducted so successfully during the past few years should be greatly extended and made a part of the general plan of providing officers for the officers' reserve corps. It will be necessary to place the instruction at these camps on a different basis and to combine certain theoretical work with the practical work of the camp. This is a matter of detail which can be readily arranged. The results attained at these camps fully justify their being given the most serious attention and being made a part of the general plan for the training of officers.

*SOURCE:* Leonard Wood, *Our Military History* (Chicago: Reilly & Britton, 1916), 193–213.

*RELATED ENTRIES: Civil–Military Relations; Preparedness Movement*

## 1910

### Excerpts from William James's Essay, "The Moral Equivalent of War"

*William James, a Harvard philosophy professor, offered this influential essay in 1910 at the behest of the American Association for International Reconciliation. James had absorbed considerable Social Darwinian views of humankind. Hence his view that "our ancestors have bred pugnacity into our bone and marrow, and thousands of years of peace won't breed it out of us. . . . " A realist in that sense, James nonetheless believed that these warlike propensities, not as necessary as they once had been, could and should be redirected into more productive channels by drafting young men, not for military service, but for work within the nation for the common good. This "moral equivalent of war" in time inspired others to create the American Friends Service Committee, the Civilian Conservation Corps, the Peace Corps, VISTA, Habitat for Humanity, and Americorps.*

We inherit the warlike type; and for most of the capacities of heroism that the human race is full of we have to thank this cruel history. Dead men tell no tales, and if there were any tribes of other type than this they have left no survivors. Our ancestors have bred pugnacity into our bone and marrow, and thousands of years of peace won't breed it out of us. . . .

. . . Militarism is the great preserver of our ideals of hardihood, and human life with no use for hardihood would be contemptible. Without risks or prizes for the darer, history would be insipid indeed; and there is a type of military character which every one feels that the race should never cease to breed, for every one is sensitive to its superiority. . . .

. . . I do not believe that peace either ought to be or will be permanent on this globe, unless the states pacifically organized preserve some of the old elements of army-discipline. A permanently successful peace-economy cannot be a simple pleasure-economy. In the more or less socialistic future towards which mankind seems drifting we must still subject ourselves collectively to those severities which answer to our real position upon this only partly hospitable globe. We must make new energies and hardihoods continue the manliness to which the military mind so faithfully clings. Martial virtues must be the enduring cement; intrepidity, contempt of softness, surrender of private interest, obedience to command, must still remain the rock upon which states are built—unless, indeed, we wish for dangerous reactions against commonwealths fit only for contempt, and liable to invite attack whenever a centre of crystallization for military-minded enterprise gets formed anywhere in their neighborhood. . . .

. . . If now—and this is my idea—there were, instead of military conscription a conscription of the whole youthful population to form for a certain number of years a part of the army enlisted against Nature, the injustice would tend to be evened out, and numerous other goods to the commonwealth would follow. The military ideals of hardihood and discipline would be wrought into the growing fibre of the people; no one would remain blind as the luxurious classes now are blind, to man's real relations to the globe he lives on, and to the permanently sour and hard foundations of his higher life. To coal and iron mines, to freight trains, to fishing fleets in December, to dish-washing, clothes-washing, and window-washing, to road-building and tunnel-making, to foundries and stoke-holes, and to the frames of skyscrapers, would our gilded youths be drafted off, according to their choice, to get the childishness knocked out of them, and to come back into society with healthier sympathies and soberer ideas. They would have paid their blood-tax, done their own part in the immemorial human warfare against nature, they would tread the earth more proudly, the women would value them more highly, they would be better fathers and teachers of the following generation. . . .

. . . I spoke of the "moral equivalent" of war. So far, war has been the only force that can discipline a whole community, and until an equivalent discipline is organized, I believe that war must have its way. But I have no serious doubt that the ordinary prides and shames of social man, once developed to a certain intensity, are capable of organizing such a moral equivalent as I have sketched, or some other just as effective for preserving manliness of type. It is but a question of time, of skillful propagandism, and of opinion-making men seizing historic opportunities.

The martial type of character can be bred without war. Strenuous honour and disinterestedness abound elsewhere. Priests and medical men are in a fashion educated to it, and we should all feel some degree of it imperative if we were conscious of our work as an obligatory service to the state.

*SOURCE:* William James, *The Moral Equivalent of War.* Leaflet no. 27. (New York: American Association for International Conciliation, 1910).

*RELATED ENTRIES: Antiwar Movements; Conscientious Objection; Militarization and Militarism; Pacifism*

## 1915 a

**EXCERPTS FROM *THE POET IN THE DESERT* BY CHARLES ERSKINE SCOTT WOOD**

*Charles Erskine Scott Wood graduated from West Point in 1874. He participated in campaigns in the Northwest against the Nez Percé in 1877 and the Paiute in 1878. He earned a law degree in the 1880s and resigned from the military to practice law in Portland, Oregon. A successful attorney and poet, and a self-proclaimed "social anarchist," he associated with Mark Twain, Ansel Adams, Emma Goldman, Chief Joseph of the Nez Percé, Margaret Sanger, Robinson Jeffers, Clarence Darrow, John Steinbeck, and Childe Hassam. His first major poetry collection, The Poet in the Desert, was a great success when it appeared in 1915. The first section of these excerpts, reflecting his service fighting "my brown brothers," is drawn from that edition; the second, an admonition to those facing death in the trenches, from his revised edition, published in 1918.*

XLIX

I HAVE lived with my brown brothers
Of the wilderness,
And found them a mystery.
The cunning of the swift-darting trout
A mystery, also;
The wisdom of voyaging birds;
The gophers' winter-sleep.
The knowledge of the bees;
All a mystery.
I have lain out with the brown men
And I know they are favored
As all are favored who submit
Willingly to the great Mother.
Nature whispered to them her secrets,
But passed me by.
My savage brothers instructed my civilization.
Tall, stately and full of wisdom
His face chiseled as Napoleon's,
Was Hin-mah-too-yah-laht-kt;
Thunder-rolling-in-the-mountains;
Joseph, Chief of the Nez-Perces;
Who in five battles from the Clearwater
To Bear Paw Mountain,
Made bloody protest against dishonorable Power.
Ah-laht-ma-kaht, his brother,
Who led the young men in battle
And gave his life for his brethren:
Tsootlem-mox-mox, Yellow Bull;
Cunning White Bird, a brown Odysseus,
And indomitable Too-hul-hul-soot,
High Priest, dignified; unafraid; inspired;
Standing half-naked in the Council Teepee,
Insisting in low musical gutturals,
With graceful gesture,
"The Earth is our Mother.
"From her we come;
"To her we return.
"She belongs to all.
"She has gathered into her bosom
"The bones of our ancestors.
"Their spirits will fight with us
"When we battle for our home
"Which is ours from the beginning.
"Who gave to the White Man
"Ownership of the Earth,
"Or what is his authority
"From the Great Spirit
"To tear babes from the nursing breast?
"It is contemptible to have too much where others want."
He too gave his life for his people.
And again at another time when the politicians
Once more betrayed the promise of the Republic
Squat, slit-eyed Smokhallah,
Shaman of the Wenatchies, and Chelans,
Half-draped in a red blanket,
Harangued his people to die
In brave fight on the bosom
Of the Mother who bore them.
But wily Sulk-tash-kosha, the Half Sun,
Chieftan, persuaded submission.

"The White Men are more abundant
"Than the grass in the Springtime.
"They are without end and beyond number.
"It is hopeless to fight them,
"Right is feeble against many soldiers."

Where are those many-colored cyclones
Of painted and feather-decked horses
With naked riders, wearing eagle-feathers,
And bonnets of cougar scalps;
Brandishing rifles, bows and lynx-skin quivers,
All gleaming through the yellow dust-cloud,
Galloping, circling, hallooing, whooping,
To the War Council? They are stilled forever.
The Christian Republic planted grass in their mouths.

L

Just over there where yon purple peak,
Like a great amethyst, gems the brow of the Desert,
I sprawled flat in the bunch-grass, a target
For the just bullets of my brown brothers; betrayed
By politicians hugging to their bosoms votes, not Justice.
I was a soldier, and, at command,
Had gone out to kill and be killed.
This was not majestic.
The little grey gophers
Sat erect and laughed at me.
In that silent hour before the dawn,
When Nature drowses for a moment,
We swept like fire over the smoke-browned tee-pees;
Their conical tops peering above the willows.
We frightened the air with crackle of rifles,
Women's shrieks, children's screams,
Shrill yells of savages;
Curses of Christians.
The rifles chuckled continually.
A poor people who asked nothing but the old promises,
Butchered in the dark. . . .
Young men who are about to die,
Stay a moment and take my hand,
Who am also about to die.
You have been carefully winnowed and selected
For the banqueting of a Hooded Skeleton.
Tell me by whom selected?—and for what?
Not you alone die, but the children
Who through you should enter Life.
Fathers of these expectant generations,
Tell me, for what are you selected
And by whom?
Victims stretched upon hospital cots,
You who see not the faces bending above you,
Nor shall ever see the eyes of the beloved,
Nor the face of your child.
You between whom and the world
Doors have been shut,
Who never will hear the April bird-song,
Or squirrels throwing nuts into October leaves,
Or sudden crack of a dry branch
Startling the woody silences;
You who, crumpled and twisted,
Shall be frightful to children;
You who never again shall spurn
With light, keen feet the rugged mountain-top,
The level shore,
Tell me, for what?—For what?
Shall I applaud you?
Shall I applaud gladiators
Who stain the sands with each other's blood
In a game of the Masters?

Is not Death busy enough?
None escapes his shaft.
His muffled feet creep relentlessly to all.
Why should we heap him with an unripe load?
Take War by the throat, young soldier,
And wring from his blood-frothed lips
The answer,—why?—why should we die?
Why should we die and not those who have made War?
Young men,
And even more than young men,
Young women,
Guardians of the Future,
Is one man who toils for the Masters so much better
Or so much worse than another,

So much richer or poorer,
That he must kill his brother?
Is it just to inscrutable Nature
Who with mysterious care has brought you
Down the Path Infinite
That you should kill your brother or be killed by him?
Tell me distinctly for what is the sacrifice?
I demand that you refuse to be satisfied,
That you unravel the old shoutings,
That you peer to the very bottom.
Draw in your breath delightedly,
And confidently insist:
"My life is my Own.
"A gift from the Ages,
"And to me precious
"Beyond estimation.
"I will deny Presidents, Kings, Congresses.
"I will defy authority.
"I will question all things.
"I will obstinately be informed
"Whence comes the battle?
"Whose is the combat?
"Why should I be pushed forward?"
Alas, pitiful young men, you are without intelligence
And you die.

*SOURCE:* Charles Erskine Scott Wood, *The Poet in the Desert,* 2nd ed. (Portland, Oreg.: privately printed, 1918).

*RELATED ENTRIES: Indian Wars: Western Wars; Literature and War; Religion and War*

## 1915 b

### Lyrics to "I Didn't Raise My Boy to Be a Soldier"

*Calls for greater "preparedness" in 1915 and 1916 resonated with some Americans, but met opposition from others who didn't understand why the United States need concern itself with a war between kings, kaisers, tsars, and a Britain that had yet to grant "home rule" to Ireland. This song by Al Piantadosi and Alfred Bryan, recorded by Morton Harvey (and others), was a hit with such folk, who were not an inconsequential minority. After all, President Wilson's successful reelection campaign in 1916 included this tag: "He kept us out of [the] war!"*

Ten million soldiers to the war have gone,
Who may never return again.
Ten million mothers' hearts must break,
For the ones who died in vain.
Head bowed down in sorrow in her lonely years,
I heard a mother murmur thro' her tears:

> Chorus:
> I didn't raise my boy to be a soldier,
> I brought him up to be my pride and joy,
> Who dares to put a musket on his shoulder,
> To shoot some other mother's darling boy?

Let nations arbitrate their future troubles,
It's time to lay the sword and gun away,
There'd be no war today,
If mothers all would say,
I didn't raise my boy to be a soldier.

What victory can cheer a mother's heart,
When she looks at her blighted home?
What victory can bring her back,
All she cared to call her own?
Let each mother answer in the year to be,
Remember that my boy belongs to me!

*SOURCE:* Al Piantadosi and Alfred Bryan, "I Didn't Raise My Boy to Be a Soldier." Morton Harvey., recording: Edison Collection, Library of Congress.

*RELATED ENTRIES: Antiwar Movements; Committee on Public Information; Music and War; Preparedness Movement; World War I*

## 1917 a

### MOTHER'S POEM: "I DIDN'T RAISE MY BOY" BY ABBIE FARWELL BROWN

*Once Congress declared war in April 1917, the views expressed in the song "I Didn't Raise My Boy to Be a Soldier" (see document 1915 b above) were challenged. Here was a poetic response:*

Not to be a soldier?

Did you then know what you, his mother, were raising him for?

How could you tell when and where he would be needed? When and where he would best pay a man's debt to his country?

Suppose the mother of George Washington had said, "I didn't raise my boy to be a soldier!"

Suppose the mother of General Grant, or the mother of Admiral Dewey had said it, or the mothers of thousands and thousands of brave fellows who fought for independence and liberty—where would our country be to-day?

If the mothers of heroes had clung and sniveled and been afraid for their boys, there wouldn't perhaps be any free America for the world to look to.

Mother, you are living and enjoying America now—you and the boy you "didn't raise to be a soldier."

Thanks to others, you and he are safe and sound—so far.

You may not be to-morrow, you and the other women, he and the other men who "weren't raised"—if Americans turn out to be Sons of Cowards, as the Germans believe.

You want your boy to live and enjoy life with you—to make you happy.

You don't want to risk your treasure. What mother ever wished it? It is indeed harder to risk one's beloved than one's self. But there are things still harder.

You don't want your lad to meet danger, like Washington and Grant and Sheridan, and the rest whom you taught him to admire.

You'd rather keep your boy where you believe him safe than have your country safe!

You'd rather have him to look at here, a slacker, than abroad earning glory as a patriot.

You'd rather have him grow old and decrepit and die in his bed than risk a hero's death, with many chances of coming back to you proudly honored.

You'd rather have him go by accident or illness, or worse.

There are risks at home, you know!

Are you afraid of them, too? How can you guard him?

Is it you who are keeping him back?

Shame on you, Mother! You are no true, proud mother.

It isn't only the men who have got to be brave these days. It's the women, too. We all have so much to risk when there's wicked war in the world.

Don't you know this is a war to destroy wicked war?

Don't you want your son to help make the world over?

This is a war to save our liberty, our manhood, our womanhood—the best life has to give.

Mother, what did you raise your boy for? Wasn't it to be a man and do a man's work?

Could he find a greater Cause than this to live or die for?

You should be proud if he can be a Soldier.

You must send him out with a smile.

Courage! You must help him to be brave.

We must help one another to be brave and unselfish.

For America!

*SOURCE:* Abbie Farwell Brown, "I Didn't Raise My Boy," in Albert Bushnell, ed., *Handbook of the War for Readers, Speakers, and Teachers (New York: Hart & Arthur O. Lovejoy, 1918), 100-101.*

*RELATED ENTRIES: Antiwar Movements; Committee on Public Information; Preparedness Movement; World War I*

## 1917 b

### LYRICS TO "OVER THERE," OR "JOHNNIE GET YOUR GUN"

*Popular Tin Pan Alley songwriter and performer George M. Cohan dashed off this lively tune shortly after war was declared. It was another response to the earlier Piantadosi–Bryan song (see documents 1915 b and 1917 a above).*

Johnie get your gun, get your gun, get your gun,
Take it on the run, on the run, on the run,
Hear them calling you and me,
Ev'ry son of liberty,
Hurry right away, no delay, go today
Make your daddy glad, to have had such a lad,
Tell your sweetheart not to pine,
To be proud her boy's in line.

Chorus:
Over There, over There
Send the word, send the word over There
That the Yanks are coming, the Yanks are coming
The Drums rum-tuming everywhere.
So prepare, say a pray'r
Send the word, send the word to beware.
We'll be over, we're coming over
And we won't come back till it's over, over there.

Johnie get your gun, get your gun, get your gun,
Johnie show the Hun you're a son-of-a-gun.
Hoist the flag and let her fly,
Like true heroes do or die.
Pack your little kit, show the grit, do your bit,
Soldiers to the ranks from the towns aAnd the tanks,
Make your mother proud of you,
And to liberty be true.

*SOURCE:* Lyrics found at http://www.english.emory.edu/LostPoets/OverThere.html (August 10, 2005).

*RELATED ENTRIES: Committee on Public Information; Music and War; World War I*

## 1917 c

### John Simpson's Letter to Senator

*John Simpson, head of the Farmer's Union of Oklahoma, wrote to his senator on March 31, 1917, offering a farmer's opinion on proposals to draft men to fight in France.*

My work puts me in touch with farmer audiences in country schoolhouses nearly every night. We always discuss the war question and universal military service. I know nine out of ten farmers are absolutely opposed to both. We farmers are unalterably opposed to war unless an enemy lands on our shores.

*SOURCE:* George Tindall, *The Emergence of the New South* (Baton Rouge: Louisiana State University Press, 1967), 47.

*RELATED ENTRIES: Antiwar Movements; Committee on Public Information; Conscription and Volunteerism; World War I*

## 1917 d

### "Uncle Sam's Little War in the Arkansas Ozarks," a Report of Draft Resistance in the *Literary Digest*

*Conscious that the British government had not been able to continue to raise sufficient numbers of men by relying on volunteers, the Wilson administration almost immediately secured from Congress the nation's first full-fledged conscription act. Most who were selected for service reported without incident and served honorably. But opposition to conscription was strong in rural America. Some 300,000 failed to respond to the call altogether, and over 100,000 of those who did report deserted within the first month and remained at large.*[1] *This account describes the response to conscription in rural northern Arkansas:*

When the United States entered the war with Germany, Cecil Cove did not. This little valley in the remote fastnesses of the North Arkansas Ozarks practically seceded from the Union for the duration of the war. The older men cooperated with the eligibles to resist the draft. They defied Uncle Sam, being well stocked with arms and prepared to hold out indefinitely in their hiding-places. When they finally gave up it was by no means an unconditional surrender, for the authorities accepted all the terms of the slacker gang, after a number of attempts to round them up had proved unsuccessful. A writer in the *Kansas City Star* attributes the incident to "a combination of plain ignorance, Jeff

Davis politics, *The Appeal to Reason*, and mountain religion." He adds that another fact may throw some light on the happenings in Cecil Cove, namely, that "it was a notorious hiding-place for men who were neither Federals nor Confederates in the Civil War," and who "found a refuge in the caves and fastnesses of the Cove exactly as did the slacker gang of 1917-1918."

Cecil Cove—some twelve miles long and eight miles wide—lies high up in Newton County, which has not been penetrated by the railroad. The people there form an isolated mountain community, suspicious yet hospitable, reticent, "trained and accustomed to arms," and also trained and accustomed, boys and girls, men and women alike, to using tobacco, as snuffers, smokers, and chewers. If we are to believe The *Star*, they are "unerring spitters," and "the youngest of the family is considered deserving of a reprimand if he can not hit the fireplace at ten paces."

When the news of the draft came the Cove prepared for war, but not with Germany. To quote the *Star:*

> The country roundabout was scoured for high-power rifles. Stocks of the Harrison and Jasper stores were pretty well depleted. Repeating rifles of 30-30 caliber and great range and precision began to reach the Cove from mail-order houses. Quantities of ammunition were bought—report has it that "Uncle Lige" Harp bought nearly $60 worth at one time in Harrison.

A number of young men were drafted, but refused to report for duty. The sheriff sent word he was coming after them, but seems to have thought better of it when he received the answer: "Come on, but look out for yourself!" Four United States marshals or deputies, several special investigators, and an army colonel all visited Newton County in turn, did some questioning and searching, and alike returned empty handed. We read in the *Star* that the people in the Cove were all related through intermarriage, and practically all of them were in sympathy with the slackers. They agreed to stick together, and it has been reported that some sort of covenant was signed. The Cove, we are told, "is a region of multifarious hiding places, studded with boulders and pocketed with caves; a searcher might pass within six feet of a dozen hidden men and see none of them." It is reached and penetrated only by steep mountain-trails, which are easily threaded by the "sure-footed mountain horses and mules and their equally sure-footed owners," but which are almost impassable to strangers. Moreover, continues the writer in the *Star:*

> So perfect were means of observation and communication a stranger could not enter the Cove at any point without that fact being known to all its inhabitants before the intruder had got along half a mile.
>
> Nearly all the families in the Cove have telephones. It is a remarkable fact that these mountaineers will do without the meanest comforts of life, but they insist upon having telephones. This and the other varied methods of intercourse, peculiar to the mountains, gave the Cecil Cove slackers an almost unbeatable combination. They always knew where the searchers were and what they were doing, but the searchers never were able to find anything except a blind trail.
>
> The telephone-lines might have been cut, but that would have served little purpose. News travels by strange and devious processes in the mountains. The smoke of a brush-fire high up on a peak may have little significance to the uninitiated, but it may mean considerable to an Ozark mountaineer. The weird, long-drawn-out Ozark yell, "Hia-a-ahoo-o-o" may sound the same always to a man from the city, but there are variations of it that contain hidden significances. And the mountaineer afoot travels with amazing speed, even along those broken trails. Bent forward, walking with a characteristic shuffle, he can scurry over boulder and fallen log like an Indian.

A deputy marshal "with a reputation as a killer" spent a month in Newton County, but made no arrests, telling some one that it would be "nothing short of suicide" for an officer to try to capture the slacker gang. The officer second in command at Camp Pike, Little Rock, took a hand in the affair and told the county officials that some of his men who were "sore at being unable to go across to France" would be very glad to "come up and clear out these slackers." But about this time the War Department offered something like amnesty to the Cove gang and apparently promised that a charge of desertion would not be pressed if the men were to give themselves up. Word was passed around, whether or not from official sources, that the boys would be "gone only from sixty to ninety days, that they would all get a suit of clothes and a dollar a day." At the same time a new sheriff, Frank Carlton, came into office. He knew the neighborhood and its people. He got in touch with some of the leaders of the hiding men and finally had an interview with two of them. They agreed to give themselves up if certain concessions were made and finally told the sheriff to meet them alone and unarmed and thus accompany them to Little Rock. As we read:

> The next day the gang met the sheriff at the lonely spot agreed upon. They caught a mail-coach and rode to Harrison and then were taken to Camp Pike.
>
> The morning after their arrival Joel Arnold asked the sheriff:
>
> "Do they feed like this all the time?"
>
> The sheriff replied that they had received the ordinary soldier fare.
>
> "We've been a passel of fools," Arnold replied.

The slackers are still held in custody at Camp Pike, and, according to the writer in The Star, authorities there will make no statement as to the procedure contemplated in the case. In showing how such different influences as religion, socialism, and sheer ignorance operated, the writer lets certain of the Cove leaders speak for themselves. Uncle Lige Harp backed up the slackers strongly with all of his great influence in the community. "Uncle Lige" is now an old man, but in his younger days had the reputation of being a "bad man." He tells with glee of a man who once said he would "just as soon meet a grizzly bear on the trail as meet Lige Harp." In his heyday Uncle Lige "was accounted a dead shot—one who could put out a turkey's left eye at one hundred yards every shot." Here are Uncle Lige's views:

> "We-all don't take no truck with strangers and we didn't want our boys takin' no truck with furriners. We didn't have no right to send folks over to Europe to fight; 'tain't a free country when that's done. Wail till them Germans come over here and then fight 'em is what I said when I heard 'bout the war. If anybody was to try to invade this country ever' man in these hills would git his rifle and pick 'em off."
>
> "Aunt Sary" Harp, between puffs at her clay pipe, nodded her approval of "Uncle Lige's" position.

France Sturdgil and Jim Blackwell say they are Socialists. They have read scattering copies of *The Appeal to Reason*. To be fair, it should be added that this Socialist paper, now *The New Appeal*, has taken an attitude in support of the Government's war-policy. Said Sturdgil:

> "It's war for the benefit of them silk-hatted fellers up in New York. We don't want our boys fightin' them rich fellers' battles and gittin' killed just to make a lot of money for a bunch of millionaires. Why, they own most of the country now."

To the writer of the *Star* article this sounds very much like the sort of argument which Jeff Davis used for many years in persuading the "hill billies" of Arkansas to elect him regularly to the United States Senate. George Slape, the Cove's religious leader, is "a prayin' man."

> "The good book says, 'Thou shalt not kill.' We didn't want our boys takin' nobody's life. It ain't right 'cause it's contrary to the Bible and the good Lord's teachin's," declared Slape.
>
> Asked to explain the difference between fighting Germans and preparing to resist the draft authorities, both likely to result in death, Slape said:
>
> "The boys wasn't goin' to kill nobody unless they had to. It's different killing a man who tries to make you do wrong and killin' somebody in war."

None of these leaders ever admitted they knew anything about where the boys were hiding. It was a common report that the slackers "lived at home except on those occasions when an officer was discovered to be prowling about." It is the Ozark way: "nobody ever has seen a hunted man, tho a rustling of the leaves, the crackling of a dead twig, might betray the fact that the fugitive was there only a moment before."

Cecil Cove had its loyal men. At least one young man defied home opinion and threats of violence by reporting for duty when he was drafted. He was sent to France and became an excellent soldier. Loyal citizens living on the fringe of the Cove were shot at and threatened on a number of occasions, and several were ordered to keep away from the community. "Uncle Jimmy" Richardson, a Confederate veteran, loyal and fearless, was not afraid to go straight to some of the parents of the slackers and tell them what he thought of them.

> "You're a gang of yellow bellies," he said. "If you've got any manhood in you, them boys will be made to go and serve their country."
>
> "Uncle Jimmy" got his answer one day when he ventured a little way into the Cove. A shot rang out and a bullet whistled past his ear.
>
> "The cowardly hounds wouldn't fight fair," he said. "In the old days of the Civil War them kind was swung up to the nearest tree. I'm past seventy-three now, but I'd have got down my rifle and gone in with anybody that would have went after them. I don't like to live near folks who ain't Americans."
>
> "Uncle Jimmy" does not speak to the slacker folks in the Cove now. He says he never will again. If he did, he says he would feel ashamed of the more than a dozen wounds that he received in the Civil War.

Loyalists in the Cove were forced by fear into what amounted to a state of neutrality. "We couldn't risk having our homes burned down or our stock killed, let alone anything worse," said one of them, who added "I'm not afraid of any man face to face, but it is a different proposition when you're one against thirty-six, and them with all the advantage and willin' to go anything."...

Note 1. Sec. of War Newton Baker to Woodrow Wilson, May 13, 1920, Baker Papers, Manuscript Division, Library of Congress.

*SOURCE:* "Uncle Sam's Little War in the Arkansas Ozarks," *Literary Digest,* March 8, 1919, . 107 ff.

*RELATED ENTRIES: Committee on Public Information; Conscription and Volunteerism; Draft Evasion and Resistance; World War I*

# 1917 e

## Alpha IQ Tests Administered to Recruits

*During World War I, army psychologists administered intelligence tests that they claimed measured ability. From these tests, psychologists concluded that the average mental age of the American soldier was 13. This example from a test given to literate recruits reveals that many questions measured familiarity with American culture and level of schooling.*

Test 3

This is a test of common sense. Below are sixteen questions. Three answers are given to each question. You are to look at the answers carefully; then make a cross in the square before the best answer to each question, as in the sample:

Why do we use stoves? Because

☐ they look well

☒ they keep us warm

☐ they are black

Here the second answer is the best one and is marked with a cross. Begin with No. 1 and keep on until time is called.

1. Cats are useful animals, because
   - ☐ they catch mice
   - ☐ they are gentle
   - ☐ they are afraid of dogs
2. Why are pencils more commonly carried than fountain pens? Because
   - ☐ they are brightly colored
   - ☐ they are cheaper
   - ☐ they are not so heavy
3. Why is leather used for shoes? Because
   - ☐ it is produced in all countries
   - ☐ it wears well
   - ☐ it is an animal product
4. Why judge a man by what he does rather than by what he says? Because
   - ☐ what a man does shows what he really is
   - ☐ it is wrong to tell a lie
   - ☐ a deaf man cannot hear what is said

Documents

5. If you were asked what you thought of a person whom you didn't know, what should you say?
   - ☐ I will go and get acquainted
   - ☐ I think he is all right
   - ☐ I don't know him and can't say
6. Streets are sprinkled in summer
   - ☐ to make the air cooler
   - ☐ to keep automobiles from skidding
   - ☐ to keep down dust
7. Why is wheat better for food than corn? Because
   - ☐ it is more nutritious
   - ☐ it is more expensive
   - ☐ it can be ground finer
8. If a man made a million dollars, he ought to
   - ☐ pay off the national debt
   - ☐ contribute to various worthy charities
   - ☐ give it all to some poor man
9. Why do many persons prefer automobiles to street cars? Because
   - ☐ an auto is made of higher grade materials
   - ☐ an automobile is more convenient
   - ☐ street cars are not as safe
10. The feathers on a bird's wings help him to fly because they
    - ☐ make a wide, light surface
    - ☐ keep the air off his body
    - ☐ keep the wings from cooling off too fast
11. All traffic going one way keeps to the same side of the street because
    - ☐ most people are right handed
    - ☐ the traffic policeman insists on it
    - ☐ it avoids confusion and collisions
12. Why do inventors patent their inventions? Because
    - ☐ it gives them control of their inventions
    - ☐ it creates a greater demand
    - ☐ it is the custom to get patents
13. Freezing water bursts pipes because
    - ☐ cold makes the pipes weaker
    - ☐ water expands when it freezes
    - ☐ the ice stops the flow of water
14. Why are high mountains covered with snow? Because
    - ☐ they are near the clouds
    - ☐ the sun seldom shines on them
    - ☐ the air is cold there
15. If the earth were nearer the sun
    - ☐ the stars would disappear
    - ☐ our months would be longer
    - ☐ the earth would be warmer
16. Why is it colder nearer the poles than near the equator? Because
    - ☐ the poles are always farther from the sun
    - ☐ the sunshine falls obliquely at the poles
    - ☐ there is more ice at the poles

TEST 5

The words A EATS COW GRASS in that order are mixed up and don't make a sentence; but they would make a sentence if put in the right order: A COW EATS GRASS, and this statement is true.

Again, the words HORSES FEATHERS HAVE ALL would make a sentence if put in the order ALL HORSES HAVE FEATHERS, but this statement is false.

Below are twenty-four mixed-up sentences. Some of them are true and some are false. When I say "go," take these sentences one at a time. Think what you would say if the words were straightened out, but don't write them yourself. Then, if what it would say is true, draw a line under the word "true"; if what it would say is false, draw a line under the word "false." If you can not be sure, guess. The two samples are already marked as they should be. Begin with No. 1 and work right down the page until time is called.

SAMPLES:

| | | |
|---|---|---|
| | a eats cow grass | true..false (true underlined) |
| | horses feathers have all | true..false (false underlined) |
| 1. | lions strong are | true..false 1 |
| 2. | houses people in live | true..false 2 |
| 3. | days there in are week eight a | true..false 3 |
| 4. | legs flies one have only | true..false 4 |
| 5. | months coldest are summer the | true..false 5 |
| 6. | gotten sea water sugar is from | true..false 6 |

7. honey bees flowers gather the from true..false 7
8. and eat good gold silver to are true..false 8
9. president Columbus first the was America of true..false 9
10. making is bread valuable wheat for true..false 10
11. water and made are butter from cheese true..false 11
12. sides every has four triangle true..false 12
13. every times makes mistakes person at true..false 13
14. many toes fingers as men as have true..false 14
15. not eat gunpowder to good is true..false 15
16. ninety canal ago built Panama years was the true..false 16
17. live dangerous is near a volcano to it true..false 17
18. clothing worthless are for and wool cotton true..false 18
19. as sheets are napkins used never true..false 19
20. people trusted intemperate be always can true..false 20
21. employ debaters irony never true..false 21
22. certain some death of mean kinds sickness true..false 22
23. envy bad malice traits are and true..false 23
24. repeated call human for courtesies associations true..false 24

TEST 8

Notice the sample sentence:

People hear with the eyes <u>ears</u> nose mouth

The correct word is ears, because it makes the truest sentence.

In each of the sentences below you have four choices for the last word. Only one of them is correct. In each sentence draw a line under the one of these four words which makes the truest sentence. If you can not be sure, guess. The two samples are already marked as they should be.

SAMPLES:

People hear with the eyes <u>ears</u> nose mouth

France is in <u>Europe</u> Asia Africa Australia

1. America was discovered by Drake Hudson Columbus Cabot
2. Pinochle is played with rackets cards pins dice
3. The most prominent industry of Detroit is automobiles brewing flour packing
4. The Wyandotte is a kind of horse fowl cattle granite
5. The U.S. School for Army Officers is at Annapolis West Point New Haven Ithaca
6. Food products are made by Smith & Wesson Swift & Co. W.L. Douglas B.T. Babbitt
7. Bud Fisher is famous as an actor author baseball player comic artist
8. The Guernsey is a kind of horse goat sheep cow
9. Marguerite Clark is known as a suffragist singer movie actress writer
10. "Hasn't scratched yet" is used in advertising a duster flour brush cleanser
11. Salsify is a kind of snake fish lizard vegetable
12. Coral is obtained from mines elephants oysters reefs
13. Rosa Bonheur is famous as a poet painter composer sculptor
14. The tuna is a kind of fish bird reptile insect
15. Emeralds are usually red blue green yellow
16. Maize is a kind of corn hay oats rice
17. Nabisco is a patent medicine disinfectant food product tooth paste
18. Velvet Joe appears in advertisements of tooth powder dry goods tobacco soap
19. Cypress is a kind of machine food tree fabric
20. Bombay is a city in China Egypt India Japan
21. The dictaphone is a kind of typewriter multigraph phonograph adding machine
22. The pancreas is in the abdomen head shoulder neck
23. Cheviot is the name of a fabric drink dance food
24. Larceny is a term used in medicine theology law pedagogy
25. The Battle of Gettysburg was fought in 1863 1813 1778 1812
26. The bassoon is used in music stenography book-binding lithography
27. Turpentine comes from petroleum ore hides trees
28. The number of a Zulu's legs is two four six eight
29. The scimitar is a kind of musket cannon pistol sword
30. The Knight engine is used in the Packard Lozier Stearns Pierce Arrow

31. The author of "The Raven" is Stevenson Kipling Hawthorne Poe
32. Spare is a term used in bowling football tennis hockey
33. A six-sided figure is called a scholium parallelogram hexagon trapezium
34. Isaac Pitman was most famous in physics shorthand railroading electricity
35. The ampere is used in measuring wind power electricity water power rainfall
36. The Overland car is made in Buffalo Detroit Flint Toledo
37. Mauve is the name of a drink color fabric food
38. The stanchion is used in fishing hunting farming motoring
39. Mica is a vegetable mineral gas liquid
40. Scrooge appears in Vanity Fair The Christmas Carol Romola Henry IV

*SOURCE: Memoirs of the National Academy of Sciences*, vol. 15 (Washington, D.C.: U.S. Government Printing Office, 1921).

*RELATED ENTRIES: Conscription and Volunteerism; World War I*



## 1917 f

### Beta IQ Tests Administered to Recruits

*During World War I, many men who either did not speak English or were illiterate entered the military. To test their intelligence, Army psychologists developed special exams that still required the ability to write quickly and understand directions in English. Unsurprisingly, many men who took the Beta exam were classified as morons.*

[These were the instructions given for the following Beta test for illiterate soldiers:]

Test 6, pictorial completion.

"This is test 6 *here*. Look. A lot of pictures." After everyone has found the place, "Now watch." Examiner points to hand and says to demonstrator, "Fix it." Demonstrator does nothing, but looks puzzled. Examiner points to the picture of the hand, and then to the place where the finger is missing and says to demonstrator, "Fix it; fix it." Demonstrator then draws in finger. Examiner says, "That's right." Examiner then points to fish and place for eye and says, "Fix it." After demonstrator has drawn missing eye, examiner points to each of the four remaining drawings and says, "Fix them all." Demonstrator works samples out slowly and with apparent effort. When the samples are finished examiner says, "All right. Go ahead. Hurry up!" During the course of this test the orderlies walk around the room and locate individuals who are doing nothing, point to their pages and say, "Fix it. Fix them," trying to set everyone working. At the end of 3 minutes examiner says, "Stop! But don't turn over the page."

*SOURCE: Memoirs of the National Academy of Sciences*, vol. 15 (Washington, D.C.: U.S. Government Printing Office, 1921).

*RELATED ENTRIES: Conscription and Volunteerism; World War I*

## 1918 a

### The Man's Poem and The Woman's Response

*With conscription, opportunities arose for women to take work long denied them. Their fellow male workers were, generally speaking, uncomfortable with and opposed to the presence of women at "their" worksites. When an anonymous male machinist penned a sarcastic poem about female machinists employed during World War I, an anonymous female machinist responded with revealing zest.*

The Man's Poem

**The Reason Why**

The shop girls had a meeting
They came from far and near
Some came from Bryant's, J and L
And some from Fellows Gear.

But before inside the hall
They were allowed to look
They had to take their bloomers off,
And hang 'em on a hook.

Then into the hall they went at once,
With courage ever higher
But hardly were they seated
When someone shouted "Fire."

Then out they ran all in a bunch,
They had no time to look,
And each one grabbed a bloomer
At random from the hook.

They got their bloomers all mixed up,
And they were mighty sore,
To think they couldn't have the one
They had always had before.

And that's the reason that you see
As you go 'round the streets,
Each one will stop and take a look
At every girl she meets.

And hence the reason that the girls
Who are not so very stout,
Have had to take 'em in a bit,
And the fat ones, let 'em out.

The Woman's Response

**She Hands Him a Lemon**

My man, you're really out of date
And now before it is too late,
I'll try to set you right;
We never mixed our bloomers, clown,
They fit just like a Paris gown,
They're neither loose nor tight.
The simple, tender, clinging vine,
That once around the oak did twine,
Is something of the past;
We stand erect now by your side,
And surmount obstacles with pride,
We're equal, free, at last.

We're independent now you see,
Your bald head don't appeal to me,
I love my overalls;
And I would rather polish steel,
Than get you up a tasty meal,
Or go with you to balls.
Now, only premiums good and big,
Will tempt us maids to change our rig,
And put our aprons on;
And cook up all the dainty things,
That so delighted men and kings
In days now past and gone.

Now in your talk of shouting "fire,"
You really did arouse my ire,
I tell you, sir, with pride,
That you would be the one to run
While we would stay and see the fun,
And I lend a hand beside.
To sit by your machine and chew

And dream of lovely Irish stew,
Won't work today you'll find.
Now, we're the ones who set the pace,
You'll have to bustle in the race
Or you'll get left behind.

We're truly glad we got the chance
To work like men and wear men's pants,
And proved that we made good.
My suit a badge of honor is.
Now, will you kindly mind your "biz"
Just as you know you should.

*SOURCE:* Wayne Broehl Jr., *Precision Valley: The Machine Tool Companies of Springfield, Vermont* (Englewood Cliffs, N.J.: Prentice-Hall, 1959), 98–99.

*RELATED ENTRIES: Committee on Public Information; Women in the Workforce: World War I and World War II; World War I*

## 1918 b

**VERSE OF THE AMERICAN EXPEDITIONARY FORCE, 1918–1919**

*The American Expeditionary Force headquarters created a soldier's newspaper, The Stars and Stripes, which published a number of poems written by military personnel. These are some of the more revealing ones.*

(UNTITLED)

I want to go home; I am tired of staying
Where people don't savvy my tongue,
Where I cannot tell what the waiters are saying
Nor know just how much I am stung.
I want to go back where I needn't climb stairways
Or grope to my room in the gloom.
Or shiver in chambers like chill glacial airways,
I gaze on the track to,
I long to go back to,
That better and greater place, swift elevator place,
Hot radiator place—
Home!

I want to go home; I am tired of getting
This fancy but camouflaged food,
Pale substitute eats in a Frenchified setting—
My tastes grow voracious and crude.
I'm dreaming of meals without food-card restrictions,
With much more of bodyless foam,
Where sugar and pastry meet no interdictions,
I dream of and yearn to,
I pant to return to,
That thrilling-to-utter land, makes-my-heart-flutter land,
Milk-fat-and-butter land—
Home!

Anon.
*The Stars and Stripes*
(6 June 1919)

SONG OF ST. NAZAIRE

Hurry on, you doughboys, with your rifle and your pack;
Bring along your cooties with your junk upon your back;
We'll house you and delouse you and we'll douse you in a bath,
And when the boat is ready you can take the Western Path.

For it's home, kid, home—when you slip away from here—
No more slum or reveille, pounding in your ear;
Back on clean, wide streets again—
Back between the sheets again
Where a guy can lay in bed and sleep for half a year.

Hurry on, you lousy buck, for your last advance;
You are on your final hike through the mud of France;
Somewhere in the Good Old Town, you can shift the load,
Where you'll never see again an M. P. down the road.

For it's home, boy, home, with the old ship headed west;
No more cooties wandering across your manly chest;
No more M. P.'s grabbing you—
No more majors crabbing you—
Nothing for a guy to do except to eat and rest.

Move along, you Army, while the tides are on the swell.
Where a guy can get away and not the S. O. L.
Where the gold fish passes and the last corned willy's through.
And no top sergeant's waiting with another job to do.

For it's home, kid, home—when the breakers rise and fall—
Where the khaki's hanging from a nail against the wall—
Clean again and cheerful there—
Handing out an ear full there—
Where you never have to jump at the bugle's call.

Lt. Grantland Rice
*The Stars and Stripes*
(2 May 1919)

THE WARD AT NIGHT

The rows of beds,
Each even spaced,
The blanket lying dark against the sheet,
The heavy breathing of the sick,
The fevered voices
Telling of the battle
At the front,
Of Home and Mother.

A quick, light step,
A white-capped figure
Silhouetted by the lantern's flame,
A needle, bearing sleep
And sweet forgetfulness.
A moan—
Then darkness, death.
God rest the valiant soul.

Anon.
*The Stars and Stripes*
(29 November 1918)

AS THINGS ARE

The old home State is drier now
Than forty-seven clucks
Of forty-seven desert hens
'A-chewin' peanut shucks.

There everybody's standin' sad
Beside the Fishhill store,
'A-sweatin' dust an' spittin' rust
Because there ain't no more.

The constable, they write, has went
A week without a pinch.
There ain't no jobs, so there's a gent
'At sure has got a cinch.

I ain't a-gonna beef a bit,
But still, it's kinda nice,
'A-knowin' where there's some to git
Without requestin' twice.

Anon.
*The Stars and Stripes*
(26 July 1918)

THE SHEPHERDS FEED THEMSELVES AND FEED NOT MY FLOCK

We died in our millions to serve it; the cause that you told us was ours,
We stood waist-deep in the trenches, we battled with Hell and its powers;
And you? You have gathered your millions; you have lined your pockets with pelf,
You have talked of the rights of Nations, while you worshipped the rights of self;
Do you think we shall rise and smite you? Fear not. You shall garner your gain.
And we? Will you give us our freedom, just those who have not been slain?
Fooled tho we've been by your hierlings—you know that we fought for a lie—
We fathomed a truth you see not, but one you must learn when you die,
That silver and gold and raiment are things of but little worth,
For Love is the heir of the ages, and the meek shall inherit the earth.

Maj. Guy M. Kindersley
*The Amaroc News*
(7 September 1919)

*SOURCE:* Alfred E. Cornebise, ed., *Doughboy Doggerel* (Athens: Ohio University Press, 1985).

*RELATED ENTRIES: Literature and War; World War I*

## 1918 c

### SELECTED SONGS FROM THE COMPILATIONS OF JOHN JACOB NILES

*Lt. John Jacob Niles, an Army aviator in France, was a musicologist and "song-catcher." He recorded songs as he heard them sung in bistros and trains, and was especially taken by those that black doughboys had created. These are some of the more illuminating examples of those he published in Songs My Mother Never Taught Me.*

THE HEARSE SONG

Did you ever think as the hearse rolls by
That the next trip they take they'll be lay in you by
With your boots a swingin' from the back of a roan,
And the undertaker inscribing your stone.

'Cause when the old motor hearse goes rollin' by,
You don't know whether to laugh or cry.
For the grave diggers will get you too,
Then the hearse's next load will consist of you.

They'll take you over to Field thirteen,[1]
Where the sun is a shinin' and the grass is green,
And they'll throw in dirt and they'll throw in rocks,
'Cause they don't give a damn if they break your pine box.

TELL ME NOW

I don't know why I went to war,
Tell me, oh, tell me now.
I don't know why I went to war,
Or what dese folks are fightin' for,
Tell me, oh, tell me now.

I don't know what my brown's a doin',
Tell me, oh, tell me now.
I don't know what my brown's a doin',
With all dose bucks around a wooin',
Tell me, oh, tell me now.

I don't know why I totes dis gun,
Tell me, oh, tell me now.
I don't know why I totes dis gun,
'Cause I ain't got nothin' 'gainst de Hun,
Tell me, oh, tell me now.

Note 1: Field Thirteen was the Issoudun Graveyard. We had flying fields numbered up to 12, when some humorist hit onto the idea of numbering the graveyard 13.

*SOURCE:* John Jacob Niles, *Songs My Mother Never Taught Me* (New York: Gold Label Books, 1927).

*RELATED ENTRIES: African Americans in the Military; Music and War; Niles, John Jacob*

## 1918 d

### PRESIDENT WOODROW WILSON'S FOURTEEN POINTS

*As the United States and its allies prepared for making the peace at the end of World War I, Pres. Woodrow Wilson put forth the following principles that he hoped would help to establish the new international world order. Known as the "Fourteen Points," it was a document that would help to define President Wilson's presidency and his postwar efforts at the peace conference in Paris, during which he tried to persuade his French and British allies to accept them. They did not, and neither did the Senate give its consent to the United States joining the newly-minted League of Nations.*

(Delivered in Joint Session, January 8, 1918)
Gentlemen of the Congress:

It will be our wish and purpose that the processes of peace, when they are begun, shall be absolutely open and that they shall involve and permit henceforth no secret understandings of any kind. The day of conquest and aggrandizement is gone by; so is also the day of secret covenants entered into in the interest of particular governments and likely at some unlooked-for moment to upset the peace of the world. It is this happy fact, now clear to the view of every public man whose thoughts do not still linger in an age that is dead and gone, which makes it possible for every nation whose purposes are consistent with justice and the peace of the world to avow nor or at any other time the objects it has in view.

We entered this war because violations of right had occurred which touched us to the quick and made the life of our own people impossible unless they were corrected and the world secure once for all against their recurrence. What we demand in this war, therefore, is nothing peculiar to ourselves. It is that the world be made fit and safe to live in; and particularly that it be made safe for every peace-loving nation which, like our own, wishes to live its own life, determine its own institutions, be assured of justice and fair dealing by the other peoples of the world as against force and selfish aggression. All the peoples of the world are in effect partners in this interest, and for our own part we see very clearly that unless justice be done to others it will not be done to us. The programme of the world's peace, therefore, is our programme; and that programme, the only possible programme, as we see it, is this:

I. Open covenants of peace, openly arrived at, after which there shall be no private international understandings of any kind but diplomacy shall proceed always frankly and in the public view.

II. Absolute freedom of navigation upon the seas, outside territorial waters, alike in peace and in war, except as the seas may be closed in whole or in part by international action for the enforcement of international covenants.

III. The removal, so far as possible, of all economic barriers and the establishment of an equality of trade conditions among all the nations consenting to the peace and associating themselves for its maintenance.

IV. Adequate guarantees given and taken that national armaments will be reduced to the lowest point consistent with domestic safety.

V. A free, open-minded, and absolutely impartial adjustment of all colonial claims, based upon a strict observance of the principle that in determining all such questions of sovereignty the interests of the populations concerned must have equal weight with the equitable claims of the government whose title is to be determined.

VI. The evacuation of all Russian territory and such a settlement of all questions affecting Russia as will secure the best and freest cooperation of the other nations of the world in obtaining for her an unhampered and unembarrassed opportunity for the independent determination of her own political development and national policy and assure her of a sincere welcome into the society of free nations under institutions of her own choosing; and, more than a welcome, assistance also of every kind that she may need and may herself desire. The treatment accorded Russia by her sister nations in the months to come will be the acid test of their good will, of their comprehension of her needs as distinguished from their own interests, and of their intelligent and unselfish sympathy.

VII. Belgium, the whole world will agree, must be evacuated and restored, without any attempt to limit the sovereignty which she enjoys in common with all other free nations. No other single act will serve as this will serve to restore confidence among the nations in the laws which they have themselves set and determined for the government of their relations with one another. Without this healing act the whole structure and validity of international law is forever impaired.

VIII. All French territory should be freed and the invaded portions restored, and the wrong done to France by Prussia in 1871 in the matter of Alsace-Lorraine, which has unsettled the peace of the world for nearly fifty years, should be righted, in order that peace may once more be made secure in the interest of all.

IX. A readjustment of the frontiers of Italy should be effected along clearly recognizable lines of nationality.

X. The peoples of Austria-Hungary, whose place among the nations we wish to see safeguarded and assured, should be accorded the freest opportunity to autonomous development.

XI. Rumania, Serbia, and Montenegro should be evacuated; occupied territories restored; Serbia accorded free and secure access to the sea; and the relations of the several Balkan states to one another determined by friendly counsel along historically established lines of allegiance and nationality; and international guarantees of the political and economic independence and territorial integrity of the several Balkan states should be entered into.

XII. The turkish portion of the present Ottoman Empire should be assured a secure sovereignty, but the other nationalities which are now under Turkish rule should be assured an undoubted security of life and an absolutely unmolested opportunity of autonomous development, and the Dardanelles should be permanently opened as a free passage to the ships and commerce of all nations under international guarantees.

XIII. An independent Polish state should be erected which should include the territories inhabited by indisputably Polish populations, which should be assured a free and secure access to the sea, and whose political and economic independence and territorial integrity should be guaranteed by international covenant.

XIV. A general association of nations must be formed under specific covenants for the purpose of affording mutual guarantees of political independence and territorial integrity to great and small states alike.

In regard to these essential rectifications of wrong and assertions of right we feel ourselves to be intimate partners of all the governments and peoples associated together against the Imperialists. We cannot be separated in interest or divided in purpose. We stand together until the end.

For such arrangements and covenants we are willing to fight and to continue to fight until they are achieved; but only because we wish the right to prevail and desire a just and stable peace such as can be secured only by removing the chief provocations to war, which this programme does remove. We have no jealousy of German greatness, and there is nothing in this programme that impairs it. We grudge her no achievement or distinction of learning or of pacific enterprise such as have made her record very bright and very enviable. We do not wish to injure her or to block in any way her legitimate influence or power. We do not wish to fight her either with arms or with hostile arrangements of trade if she is willing to associate herself with us and the other peace- loving nations of the world in covenants of justice and law and fair dealing. We wish her only to accept a place of equality among the peoples of the world,—the new world in which we now live,—instead of a place of mastery.

*SOURCE: U.S. National Archives & Records Administration. "Transcript of Woodrow Wilson's 14 Points." http://www.ourdocuments.gov/doc.php?doc=62&page=transcript (August 11, 2005).*

*RELATED ENTRIES: Wilson, Woodrow; World War I*

# 1919 a

## Florence Woolston Reflects on the Effect of World War I on Her Nephew Billy

*Florence Woolston, writing in The New Republic shortly after the Armistice, described how her young nephew Billy, growing up in a suburb she called "one hundred per cent patriotic," reacted to World War I.*

Billy, my nephew, is twelve years old. With the possible exception of the beef profiteers and a few superpatriots to whom life has been a prolonged Fourth of July oration, no one has got quite so much fun out of the war as Billy and his inseparable companions, Fritters, George and Bean-Pole Ross.

Clad in the khaki uniform of the Boy Scouts, with United War Campaign, Red Cross, War Saving, first, second, third and fourth Liberty Loan buttons, small American flags and service pins spread across their chests, they have lived the war from morning until night. I did not understand Billy's passionate allegiance to the Scout uniform until I discovered the great game of hailing automobiles bearing the sign, "Men in Uniform Welcome." Billy has never been willing to accompany his family on automobile rides but the pleasure of this boulevard game has been never ending.

They call the suburb in which Billy lives one hundred per cent patriotic. Everybody is in war work. Even the children under five years have an organization known as the Khaki Babes. These infants in uniform assemble, kindergarten fashion and solemnly snip for the Red Cross. Billy's crowd is indefatigable in its labors. With the other Scouts, the boys usher at meetings, assist in parades, deliver bundles and run errands. They are tireless collectors of nutshells, peach pits and tinsel paper. As Victory Boys they are pledged to earn five dollars for the United War Workers. Since most of them expect to do this shovelling snow they are praying for a severe winter.

One bit of voluntary war work was carried on through the periods of gasolineless Sundays when the four boys took positions on Commonwealth Avenue in such a way as to obstruct passing vehicles. If a car did not carry a doctor's or military sign, they threw pebbles and yelled, "O you Slacker!" It was exciting work because guilty drivers put on full speed ahead and Billy admitted that he was almost run over, but he added that the cause was worth it.

In my school days history was a rather dull subject.

. . . It is not so with Billy. Modern history is unfolding to him as a great drama. Kings and tsars and presidents are live human beings. War has nothing to do with books. It is a perpetual moving picture with reels furnished twice a day by the newspapers. Wars were as unreal as pictorial combats with painted soldiers and stationary warships. Even the Civil War belonged to historical fiction. Once a year, on the 30th of May, a veteran in navy blue came to school and in a quavering voice told stories of his war days. Thrilling as they might have been, they always seemed to lack reality. . . .

. . . Billy and his chums . . . know what boundaries mean; they pour over war maps and glibly recite the positions of the Allied troops. Billy has a familiarity with principal cities, rivers and towns that never could have been learned in lesson form. The war has created a new cosmopolitanism. The children of Billy's generation will never have the provincial idea that Boston is the centre of the world. They will see the universe as a great circle, perhaps, but all the Allies will occupy the centre.

I must confess, however, that Billy, Fritters, George and Bean-Pole Ross have a rather vague idea of what the war is about, but then so do others with more years to their credit. I asked Billy what caused the war originally, and he replied in a rather large and lofty way, "You see, the French took Alsace and Lorraine away from the Germans a long time ago and Germany wanted it back. She thought it would be nice to get hold of Paris, too, and conquer the French people, then they would have to pay taxes and indemnities to support Germany. So they started to march to Paris and then all the other countries decided to stop them."

When I compare the anemic stereopticon travel talks of my school days with Billy's moving picture shows, I have the sense of a cheated childhood. We had nothing in our young lives like *Crashing Through to Berlin*, *The Hounds of Hunland*, *Wolves of Kultur* and *The Brass Bullet*. Billy's mental images have been built by such pictures as these with the additional and more educational films of the Committee on Public Information and the Pathé weekly where actual battle scenes, aeroplane conflicts and real naval encounters are portrayed.

In the matter of books, too, Billy has had high revel. I sowed a few wild oats with Oliver Optic and Horatio Alger wherein poor lads were conducted from prairie huts to the Executive mansion. Of course we had Scott and Cooper to make medieval times or Indian days vivid. But think of reading *Over the Top* and going to shake hands with the author, a live, red-blooded officer in the army! Billy revels in *Private Peat*, *Hunting the Hun*, *Out of the Jaws of Hunland*, *From Base Ball to Boches*, and *With the Flying Corps*. I'm afraid he will never have a Walter Scott period and I am sure it will be years before contemplative literature can hold his attention.

Of course, the war has given us all an enlarged vocabulary. Billy calls his school "the trench"; he and Fritters go "over the top," "carry on," play in dug-outs, move in units, carry kits, eat mess and have elaborate systems of wig-wagging and passwords. When he is unsuccessful in a parental encounter, Billy throws up his hands and cries "I surrender!" Hun, Boche and Bolshevik are terms of terrible opprobrium. There was a bloody fist fight at recess recently, when Henry Earl was called "O you Kaiser!" The mere suggestion of a German name brings forth expressions of loud disgust and none of the boys would use a toy made in Germany.

At present it is in fashion to collect war posters. Billy has a remarkable collection of Food, Red Cross, Marine, War Savings, Navy and United War Work Campaign posters. He has trudged miles and spent much ingenuity in getting them. His room is papered with them and it is a matter of deep regret that the family is unwilling to have the entire house so placarded. A thriving business goes on in poster trading and a steady stream of small boys passes the house carrying large rolls of posters. From Billy's room, after a visitation, come delighted exclamations, "Gee! what a bute!" "Say, I'll give you a Join the Gas Hounds for a Beat Back the Huns." "Fritters has two Teufelhunden and he's going to swap it for a Clear the Way and a Tell That to the Marines."

Billy came to me with an ethical problem connected with his poster campaign. "I've got," he declared, "five Joan of Arcs, three Must Children Starves, five Blot it Outs, a

Britisher and a big Y. I can sell them and make lots of money. Would that be profiteering?" I thought it might be so considered by taxpayers. "Well," he demanded, "If I sell them and buy Thrift Stamps that would be profiteering to help the war, and that would be all right, wouldn't it?"

When a campaign is on, the boys find it hard to wait until the posters have done their work as propaganda. Sometimes a lucky boy gets a whole new set. Recently, there had been much buying and selling of addresses where posters may be obtained, five cents for a plain address, ten for a "guaranteed." I mailed a postal card for Billy addressed to the Secretary of the Navy which read, "Kindly send me a full set of your Marine and Navy posters. I will display them if you wish." Billy's collection numbers about two hundred but he knows boys who have a thousand posters. As evidence of his great delight in them, he made the following statement: "If the last comes to the last, and we couldn't get coal and we had to burn all the furniture, I'd give up one set of duplicates, but only if the last comes to the last."

Billy is a kind-hearted lad with humane instincts toward all creatures except flies. He feels, however, that the Kaiser can neither claim the protection of the S.P.C.A. nor demand the consideration usually afforded a human being. He loves to tell what he would do to the Kaiser. It is a matter of bitter disappointment that Mr. Hohenzollern is in Holland instead of in Billy's hands. At breakfast he issues bulletins of carnage. Some days he plans simple tortures like beheading, skinning, hanging, burning. At other times he concocts a more elaborate scheme such as splitting open the Kaiser's arms and putting salt on the wound, cutting his legs off at the knee and hanging his feet around his neck, or gouging out his eyes. A favorite idea is that of inoculating him with all the diseases of the world or to starve him for months and then eat a big Thanksgiving dinner in his presence.

Billy has had a full course in atrocities and is keen for reprisals. He longs to fly with an aviation unit, dropping bombs on Berlin, he aches to destroy a few cathedrals and palaces, burn all the German villages and poison the reservoirs. His description of what he would do to the Huns makes the Allied armistice sound like a presentation speech with a bunch of laurel.

There is a marked absence of patriotic sentiment with Billy and his chums. To them patriotism is action; they do not enjoy talking about it. When a Liberty Loan orator gushes about the starry banner, they roll their eyes expressively and murmur "Cut it out." Of course, some of this is the self-conscious stoicism of the small boy. But there is a matter of fact attitude toward suffering and pain which is new and due to familiarity with the idea. Boys discuss the kinds of wounds, operations and war accidents as a group of medical students might refer to a clinic.

Death seems to give them no sense of mystery and awe. "Gee! a thousand killed today," "That Ace has got his," "Say, John Bowers was gassed and he's gone now." They look over the casualty lists as grown-ups might read lists of guests at a reception. It may be because youth cannot understand the tragedy and heartache back of the golden stars on the service flags, but I think it goes deeper than that. These boys have a sense of courage and gallantry that makes the risking of life an everyday affair. Self-sacrifice is not a matter of poems and sermons and history, it is the daily news. Billy's attitude is that going to war is part of the game; when you're a little boy you have to go to school; when you're older, you draw your number and are called to camp—it's all in a day's work.

*SOURCE:* Florence Woolston, "Billy and the World War," *New Republic* (January 25, 1919): 369–71.

*RELATED ENTRIES: Committee on Public Information; Militarization and Militarism; Rationing in Wartime; World War I*

## 1919 b

### DuBois Writes of Returning Soldiers

*W. E. B. Dubois, one of the founders of the National Association for the Advancement of Colored People (NAACP) and the editor of that organization's monthly newsletter* The Crisis, *was a vigorous proponent of the Wilson administration's war aims in 1918; he believed that black service in the war might be the catalyst for change in the attitudes of whites. His editorial, "Close Ranks," in July*

*1918 advised NAACP readers that 1918 was "the great Day of Decision," a year when his readers should "forget our special grievances and close our ranks shoulder to shoulder with our own white fellow citizens" to defeat "the menace of German militarism" which represented "death to the aspirations of Negroes and all darker races for equality, freedom and democracy." He was not as sure in May 1919 after blacks, some of them returning black veterans, faced a new spate of brutal attacks in American streets.*

*The Crisis,* May 1919

We are returning from the war! *The Crisis* and tens of thousands of black men were drafted into a great struggle. For bleeding France and what she means and has meant and will mean to us and humanity and against the threat of German race arrogance, we fought gladly and to the last drop of blood; for America and her highest ideals, we fought in far-off hope; for the dominant southern oligarchy entrenched in Washington, we fought in bitter resignation.

For the America that represents and gloats in lynching, disenfranchisement, caste, brutality and devilish insult—for this, in the hateful upturning and mixing of things, we were forced by vindictive fate to fight, also.

But today we return! We return from the slavery of the uniform which the world's madness demanded us to don to the freedom of civil garb. We stand again to look America squarely in the face and call a spade a spade. We sing: This country of ours, despite all its better souls have done and dreamed, is yet a shameful land.

It lynches.

It disfranchises its own citizens.

It encourages ignorance.

It organizes industry to cheat us. It cheats us out of our land; it cheats us out of our labor. It confiscates our savings. It reduces our wages. It raises our rent. It steals our profit. It taxes without representation. It keeps us consistently and universally poor, and then feeds us on charity and derides our poverty.

It insults us.

This is the country to which we Soldiers of Democracy return. This is the fatherland for which we fought! But is is our fatherland. It was right for us to fight. The faults of our country are our faults. Under similar circumstances, we would fight again. But by the God of Heaven, we are cowards and jackasses if now that that war is over, we do not marshal every ounce of our brain and brawn to fight a sterner, longer, more unbending battle against the forces of hell in our own land.

We return.

We return from fighting.

We return fighting.

Make way for Democracy! We saved it in France, and by the Great Jehovah, we will save it in the United States of America, or know the reason why.

*SOURCE: The Crisis* 18, no. 1 (May 1919): 13–14.

*RELATED ENTRIES: African Americans in the Military; Du Bois, W. E. B.; Racial Integration of the Armed Forces; World War I*

# 1919 c

## African-American Reaction to D.C. Race Riots

*Whites viciously attacked blacks and the black community in Washington, D.C., in mid-July . Some 46 died and about 250 were wounded in these two riots.. A black woman recalled her reaction to the way blacks, a number of them returned veterans, resisted the attacks:*

The Washington riots gave me the thrill that comes once in a lifetime. I was alone when I read between the lines of the morning paper that at last our men had stood like men, struck back, were no longer dumb, driven cattle. When I could no longer read for my streaming tears, I stood up, alone in my room, held both hands high over my head and exclaimed, "Oh, I thank God, thank God!" When I remember anything after this, I was prone on my bed, beating the pillow with both fists, laughing and crying, whimpering like a whipped child, for sheer gladness and madness. The pent-up humiliation, grief and horror of a lifetime—half a century—was being stripped from me.

*SOURCE:* Francis Grimke, *The Race Problem* (Washington, D.C., 1919), 8, quoted in Arthur Barbeau and Florette Henri, *The Unknown Soldiers* (Philadelphia: Temple University Press, 1974), 182.

*RELATED ENTRIES: African Americans in the Military; Du Bois, W. E. B.; Race Riots; Racial Integration of the Armed Forces; World War I*

## 1919 d

### Facts and Questions Concerning the NREF

*The American forces stationed in North Russia (the North Russia Expeditionary Force, or NREF) were severely demoralized in 1919. Stranded in the ice-locked area until spring, soldiers petitioned in February, protesting the American involvement in the Russian Revolution. This petition includes many of the reasons that caused President Wilson to withdraw the troops in June:*

1. We officers enlisted and our men were drafted for the purpose of fighting Germany and her allies.
2. This force was sent to Russia to prevent Germany from establishing naval bases in the far North.
3. The American organisations have been split up and placed under British officers. England has undoubtedly many capable officers, but they are not in Russia. However we, ourselves, are woefully lacking in that respect. The manner in which this expedition has been mishandled is a disgrace to the civilized world.
4. Our original purpose having been accomplished we are now meddling with a Russian revolution and counter-revolution.
5. Is this consistent with the principles of American democracy?
6. The majority of the people here seem to prefer Bolshevism to British intervention. They mistrust the British. It is our opinion that British diplomats pulled the wool over the eyes of our representatives, to the end that we were sent with this expedition in an effort to take the curse off the British.
7. The few French here finally rebelled against British rule and have been given a French commander.
8. WHERE IS OUR MONROE DOCTRINE?
   If we stood by, while Mexico was torn by revolutions, the sanctity of our borders violated and Americans murdered, on what basis is our presence here justified? A British officer here, who is more human than most, quite aptly described this expedition as an effort to put on a show with two men and an orange.
9. We are fighting against enormous odds in men, artillery and material. Most of the men in the enemy forces have seen years of service. If they were not lacking in morale and discipline, we should have been wiped off the face of the earth ere this.
10. Due to a pending election in England, and the fear of antagonizing the labor parties, no reenforcements [sic] have been sent out. In fact before the election, certain British officials placed themselves on record as having no intentions [sic] of sending more troops to Russia.
11. We wonder what propaganda is at work in the States, which enables the War Department to keep troops here. It seems to us as though it is a question of potential dollars in Russia.
12. We, a porition [sic] of the civilian army of America, organized to fight Germany, wonder why we are called upon to spend American lives aiding and abetting a counter-revolution in Russia while the great majority of the people here sit idly by watching the show, not idly either, for the [sic] most of the natives here are Bolshevists in sympathy. We have no heart in the fight. We are fighting neither for Russia or for Russian wealth but for our lives. We have earnestly endeavored to find some justification for our being here, but have been unable to reconcile this expedition with American ideals and principles instilled within us.
13. We are removed 200 miles from our base, with an open country intervening, with no force except in a few villages to guard our lines and with the enemy within striking distance of the line. There is no military reason why we should be more than 20 miles from our base.

[Note from officer who confiscated the pamphlet:] The above was written by an American officer with the Dvina force and it is reported that it is widely circulated among the American troops at the front and the men consider that it fully covers their ideas regarding the reasons why American troops are kept here.

*SOURCE: National Archives, Textual Records of the War Department General & Special Staffs, Record Group 165; Office of the Director of Intelligence (G-2), 1906–49; Security Classified Correspondence and Reports, 1917–41 (Entry 65); file 24-327 (59).*

*RELATED ENTRIES: Antiwar Movements; Russia, Interventions in*

## 1919 e

### Lyrics to "How 'ya Gonna Keep 'em Down on the Farm (After They've Seen Paree?)"

*Returning veterans, having experienced a good deal of the world beyond their home counties for the first time, moved out of those counties in numbers considerably greater than had been the case in the decades before the war. The phenomenon was addressed in this popular song of 1919:*

Reuben, Reuben, I've been thinking,
Said his wifey dear;
Now that all is peaceful and calm,
The boys will soon be back on the farm;
Mister Reuben started winking,
And slowly rubbed his chin;
He pulled his chair up close to mother,
And he asked her with a grin:

> Chorus:
> How 'ya gonna keep 'em down on the farm,
> After they've seen Paree?
> How 'ya gonna keep 'em away from Broadway,
> Jazzin' aroun', and paintin' the town?
> How 'ya gonna keep 'em away from harm?
> That's a mystery.
> They'll never want to see a rake or plow,
> And who the deuce can parley vous a cow?
> How 'ya gonna keep 'em down on the farm,
> After they've seen Paree?

Reuben, Reuben, you're mistaken,
Said his wifey dear;
Once a farmer, always a jay,
And farmers always stick to the hay;
Mother Reuben, I'm not fakin',
Tho' you may think it strange;
But wine and women play the mischief,
With a boy who's loose with change.

*SOURCE:* Lyrics (Sam Lewis and Joe Young) and music (Walter Donaldson) found at http://www.musicanet.org/robokopp/usa/reubenre.htm (August 11, 2005).

*RELATED ENTRIES: Music and War; World War I*

## 1919 f

### Excerpts from the Diary of Sgt. Will Judy

*Will Judy, a young Chicago attorney, kept a rich diary of his thoughts, impressions and experiences from the day he entered the military until some time after he was discharged after war's end. These selections capture what evidence from other sources indicates: a general lack of understanding of or enthusiasm for America's war aims, the development of camaraderie among military personnel, and the veteran's problem of how to deal with media-fed conceptions of the war held by those at home:*

3 May 1917:

I fell asleep with the dread gone that in my old age the children might point to me and laugh among themselves that in the great war I stayed at home.

15 November 1917:

Hart looked up from the morning paper and inquired whether Belgium was for the Allies or Germany. I chided him but back in my thots was the belief that the heart of our people is hardly in the war. Every one tells a different reason why we are at war. Could we have a secret ballot tomorrow of the entire population, I believe the vote would be greatly in the favor of peace. Likely this is true in all wars.

27 August 1918:

. . . [W]e are not shouting loudly about making the world safe for democracy.

In truth I have not heard more than a half dozen times during my year in the army a discussion among the men or even the officers, of the principles for which we fight. We read of them here, there and everywhere but the men of their own accord and in an informal way seldom or never talk of them. . . .

Almost nine-tenths of the soldier's conversation concerns stories about women, the location of wine shops, the likelihood of being able to purchase cigarets, the next trip to the bath house, what the censor did to the last batch of letters, what is the popular song back in the United States, what's the idea of fighting for France when they charge us high prices, and above all other subjects—"when do we eat?"

18 January 1919:

We talk much of comradeship in the coming civilian life. Like mystics, we are conscious of an association that will bind us into a passionate group different and superior, as we think, to all others.

[back in garrison duty in the States:]

1 June 1919:

France has bred in us the habit of acting first and asking questions afterward. Here red tape, insolence and much ado about nothing are the order of the day. The camp officials have not learned as did we, on fields of war, where our mistakes wrought their cost first upon us, perhaps at price of our lives. They do not possess our qualities of swift action, daring effort and great labor.

3 June 1919:

Supervised the sorting and packing of the division's records for shipment to the Adjutant General of the Army at Washington for permanent file.

We hear much about ourselves as heroes. A thousand questions are asked of us and we know now the answers they wish us to make. We must say that the enemy were fiends, that they butchered prisoners, that they quaked in fear as we came upon them in their trenches, that they were not nearly as brave as ourselves, that Americans are the best and bravest fighters of all nations, and that it was only necessary to shout "We are Americans."

We are somewhat surprised but soon we learn that the populace insists upon dubbing us heroes; then we are swept into the pose against our will and wishes. We do not talk about the war unless the civilians ply us with questions and drive us into stories about our life on the battlefield. We have come back hating war, disgusted with the prattle about ideals, disillusioned entirely about the struggles between nations. That is why we are quiet, why we talk little, and why our friends do not understand. But the populace refuses to be disillusioned; they force us to feed their own delusions.

Soon we will take on the pose of brave crusaders who swept the battlefields with a shout and a noble charge. The herd among our own number will be delighted with this unexpected glory and within a few years, a cult will be made of it. An ounce of bravery on the battlefield will become a ton of daring in story as related time and again in the years to come. We as soldiers shall find ourselves made the patriotic guardians of our country, a specially honored class, against our will.

The populace is not to be blamed. They never will get away from the effects of the propaganda in the press. To them every American soldier in France was a fighter, rifle and bayonet in hand, rushing mid shot and shell across No Man's Land, and plunging the knife into the cowering enemy. Indeed, they relate to us tales of our own bravery to our surprise; we subdue our astonishment and then obligingly add little touches of exaggeration to the already dropsied story.

Four-fifths of the American soldiers in France never went over the top and scarcely a tenth of us saw a German soldier, other than a captured one. . . .

19 June 1919:

. . . The twenty-two months in the army has taught many things to me. My experiences I would not trade for any ten years of my life. I have learned to like and to hate the army. At first I saluted grudgingly; then, as the spirit of the uniform won me, I took pride in saluting promptly and snappily. It caused me to be chivalrous in the presence of women and the aged; to conduct myself creditably to the flag; and to live up to the traditions of American honor.

I could not forget that I was a civilian first and a soldier second. Perhaps I can tell best my thot of war by saying that it is as a painted woman, more attractive at some distance. I hate war, I am a man of peace; I hope there will never be another war; but if my country fights again, right or wrong, I shall be among the first to have the tailor remodel the old uniform.

*SOURCE:* Will Judy, *Soldier's Diary* (Chicago: privately published, 1931).

*RELATED ENTRIES: Committee on Public Information; World War I*

## 1929

### Lyrics to "Marines' Hymn"

*This version of the "Marines' Hymn" contains the official verses, recognized in 1929, except for one change in verse 4—from "On the land as on the sea" to "In the air, on land and sea"—made in 1942. The references in the first two verses relate to the Mexican War and the campaign against the Barbary Pirates in 1805.*

From the Halls of Montezuma
To the Shores of Tripoli;
We fight our country's battles
In the air, on land and sea;
First to fight for right and freedom
And to keep our honor clean;
We are proud to claim the title
of United States Marine.

Our flag's unfurled to every breeze
From dawn to setting sun;
We have fought in ev'ry clime and place
Where we could take a gun;
In the snow of far-off Northern lands
And in sunny tropic scenes;
You will find us always on the job—
The United States Marines.

Here's health to you and to our Corps
Which we are proud to serve
In many a strife we've fought for life
And never lost our nerve;
If the Army and the Navy
Ever look on Heaven's scenes;
They will find the streets are guarded
By United States Marines.

*SOURCE:* Marines, Marine Corps Band, http://www.ala.usmc.mil/band/hymn/hymnhistory2.asp (7/10/2005).

*RELATED ENTRIES: Marine Corps; Music and War*

## 1930

### Excerpt from *Nineteen Nineteen* by John Dos Passos

*Many World War I veterans of combat had sufficient psychological trauma to leave them with many of the symptoms of what would in the 1970s be labeled "post-traumatic stress disorder." Others were politically affected by their experiences, embittered by the hypocrisy of their leaders, and stunned by the impersonality and pointlessness of the carnage. The more articulate of these, on both sides, expressed their thoughts on paper. John Dos Passos was one of the first of such American writers in print; his Three Soldiers appeared in 1921. His trilogy, U. S. A., broke new literary ground in 1930. This passage is from the first book of that trilogy, Nineteen Nineteen.*

*The Body of an American*

Whereasthe Congressoftheunitedstates byaconcurrent resolutionadoptedon the4thdayofmarch lastauthrizedthe Secretaryofwar to cause to be brought to thunitedstatesthe body of an Americanwhowasamemberoftheamericanexpeditionaryforcesineurope wholosthislifeduringtheworldwarandwhoseidentityhasnotbeenestablished for burial inthememorialamphitheatreofthenationalcemeteryatarlington virginia

In the tarpaper morgue at Chalons-sur-Marne in the reek of chloride of lime and the dead, they picked out the pine box that held all that was left of

enie menie minie moe plenty other pine boxes stacked up there containing what they'd scraped up of Richard Roe

and other person or persons unknown. Only one can go. How did they pick John Doe?

Make sure he aint a dinge, boys,

make sure he aint a guinea or a kike,

how can you tell a guy's a hundredpercent when all you've got's a gunnysack full of bones, bronze buttons stamped with the screaming eagle and a pair of roll puttees?

. . . and the gagging chloride and the puky dirt-stench of the yearold dead . . .

John Doe was born . . .

and raised in Brooklyn, in Memphis, near the lakefront in Cleveland, Ohio, in the stench of the stockyards in Chi, on Beacon Hill, in an old brick house in Alexandria Virginia, on Telegraph Hill, in a halftimbered Tudor cottage in Portland the city of roses,

in the Lying-In Hospital old Morgan endowed on Stuyvesant Square,

across the railroad tracks, out near the country club, in a shack cabin tenement apartmenthouse exclusive residential suburb; . . .

scion of one of the best families in the social register, won first prize in the baby parade at Coronado Beach, was marbles champion of the Little Rock grammarschools, crack basketballplayer at the Booneville High, quarterback at the State Reformatory, having saved the sheriff's kid from drowning in the Little Missouri River was invited to Washington to be photographed shaking hands with the President on the White House steps;— . . .

—busboy harveststiff hogcaller boyscout champeen cornshucker of Western Kansas bellhop at the United States Hotel in Saratoga Springs office boy callboy fruiter telephone lineman longshoreman lumberjack plumber's helper,

worked for an exterminating company in Union City, filled pipes in an opium joint in Trenton, New Jersey.

Y.M.C.A. secretary, express agent, truckdriver, fordmechanic, sold books in Denver Colorado: Madam would you be willing to help a young man work his way through college? . . .

Naked he went into the army;

they weighed you, measured you, looked for flat feet, squeezed your penis to see if you had clap, looked up your anus to see if you had piles, counted your teeth, made you cough, listened to your heart and lungs, made you read the letters on the card, charted your urine and your intelligence,

gave you a service record for a future (imperishable soul)

and an identification tag stamped with your serial number to hang around your neck, issued O D regulation equipment, a condiment can and a copy of the articles of war.

Atten'SHUN suck in your gut you c-----r wipe that smile off your face eyes right wattja tink dis is a choirch-social? For-war-D'ARCH.

John Doe

and Richard Roe and other person or persons unknown

drilled hiked, manual of arms, ate slum, learned to salute, to soldier, to loaf in the latrines, forbidden to smoke on deck, overseas guard duty, forty men and eight horses, shortarm inspection and the ping of shrapnel and the shrill bullets combing the air and the sorehead woodpeckers and the machineguns mud cooties gasmasks and the itch. . . .

*Say buddy cant you tell me how I can get back to my outfit?*

Cant help jumpin when them things go off, give me the trots them things do. I lost my identification tag swimmin in the Marne, roughhousin with a guy while we was waitin to be deloused, in bed with a girl named Jeanne (Love moving picture wet French postcard dream began with saltpeter in the coffee and ended at the propho station);—

*Say soldier for chrissake cant you tell me how I can get back to my outfit?*

John Doe

heart pumped blood:

alive thudding silence of blood in your ears . . .

The shell had his number on it.

The blood ran into the ground.

The service record dropped out of the filing cabinet when the quartermaster sergeant got blotto that time they had to pack up and leave the billets in a hurry.

The identification tag was in the bottom of the Marne.

The blood ran into the ground, the brains oozed out of the cracked skull and were licked up by the trenchrats, the belly swelled and raised a generation of bluebottle flies,

and the incorruptible skeleton,

and the scraps of dried viscera and skin bundled in khaki

they took to Chalons-sur-Marne

and laid it out neat in a pine coffin

and took it home to God's Country on a battleship

and buried it in a sarcophagus in the Memorial Amphitheatre in the Arlington National Cemetery

and draped the Old Glory over it

and the bugler played taps

and Mr. Harding prayed to God and the diplomats and the generals and the admirals and the brasshats and the politicians and the handsomely dressed ladies out of the society column of the Washington Post stood up solemn

and thought how beautiful sad Old Glory God's Country it was to have the bugler play taps and the three volleys made their ears ring.

Where his chest ought to have been they pinned

the Congressional Medal, the D.S.C., the Medaille Militaire, the Belgian Croix de Guerre, the Italian gold medal, the Vitutea Militara sent by Queen Marie of Rumania, the Czechoslovak war cross, the Virtuti Militari of the Poles, a wreath sent by Hamilton Fish, Jr., of New York, and a little wampum presented by a deputation of Arizona redskins in warpaint and feathers. All the Washingtonians brought flowers.

Woodrow Wilson brought a bouquet of poppies.

*SOURCE:* John Dos Passos, *U.S.A.: Nineteen Nineteen* (Boston: Houghton Mifflin, 1930).

*RELATED ENTRIES: Antiwar Movements; Literature and War; Tomb of the Unknown Soldier; World War I*

## 1932

### "The Bonuseers Ban Jim Crow" by Roy Wilkins

*In 1924, approximately 25,000 impoverished veterans and their families converged on Washington, D.C., in the Bonus March. In this piece Roy Wilkins of the NAACP argued that the peaceful demonstration by black and white veterans revealed the possibility of immediately integrating the armed forces. Ultimately, the Army drove the bonus marchers out of the city and the military did not desegregate its ranks until 1948.*

Floating clear on the slight breeze of a hot June night in Washington came a tinkling, mournful melody, a song known by now in every corner of the globe. Lilting piano notes carried the tune that set my foot patting, in spite of myself, on the trampled grass of the little hill. Then, as I was about to start humming the words, a voice took up the cadence and rode over the Anacostia Flats on the off-key notes—

*Feelin' tomorrow,*
*Lak I feel today—*
*Feelin' tomorrow,*
*Lak I feel today—*
*I'll pack my trunk and make my get a-way*

Never, I thought, was there a more perfect setting for W. C. Handy's famous St. Louis Blues. No soft lights and swaying bodies here; no moaning trombone or piercing trumpet; no fantastic stage setting; no white shirt fronts, impeccably tailored band master or waving baton. Instead, a black boy in a pair of ragged trousers and a torn, soiled shirt squatting on a box before a piano perched on a rude platform four or five feet off the ground. A single electric light bulb disclosed him in the surrounding gloom. Skillfully his fingers ran over the keys, bringing out all the Handy secrets of the song. Plaintively he sang the well-known words. A little of the entertainer was here, for there is a little of it hidden in most of us, but the plaintive note was largely the reflection of an actual condition, not the product of an entertainer.

On the ground about and below him were grouped white and colored men listening, smoking and quietly talking. From my elevation I could see camp fires flickering here and there and hear the murmur of talk over the flats. Here was the main camp of the Bonus Army, the Bonus Expeditionary Force, as it chose to call itself, and here, in my musical introduction to it, was struck the note which marked the ill-starred gathering as a significant one for Negro Americans.

For in this army which had gathered literally to "Sing the Blues" with economic phrases, there was one absentee: James Crow. It is not strictly true, as I shall explain a little later, to say that Mr. Crow was not present at all; it is an absolute fact that he was Absent With Leave a great part of the time.

He was brought along and trotted out occasionally by some of the Southern delegations and, strange to say, by some of the colored groups themselves.

The men of the B.E.F. were come together on serious business; they had no time for North, East, South, West, black and white divisions. The main problem was not to prove and maintain the superiority of a group but to secure relief from the ills which beset them, black and white alike. In the season of despair it is foolhardy to expend energy in any direction except that likely to bring life and hope. At Washington, numbers and unity were the important factors, therefore recruits of any color were made welcome and Jim Crow got scant attention.

Here they were, then, the brown and black men who had fought (some with their tongues in their cheeks) to save the world for democracy. They were scattered about in various state delegations or grouped in their own cluster of rude shelters. A lonely brownskin in the delegation from the North Platte, Nebr.; one or two encamped with Seattle, Wash.; increasing numbers bivouacked with California and the northern states east of the Mississippi River; and, of course, the larger numbers with the states from below the Mason and Dixon line.

And at Anacostia, the main encampment, there was only one example of Jim Crow among the 10,000 men there and that, oddly enough, was started and maintained by colored bonuseers themselves, who hailed from New Orleans and other towns in Louisiana. They had erected a section of shacks for themselves and they insisted on their own mess kitchen.

A stroll down through the camp was an education in the simplified business of living, living not complicated by a maze of social philosophy and tabus. It is hard for one who has not actually seen the camp to imagine the crudity of the self-constructed accommodations in which these men lived for eight weeks.

Fairly regular company streets stretched across the flats, lined on both sides with shelters of every description. Here was a tent; here a piano box; there a radio packing case; there three doors arranged with the ground as the fourth side; here the smallest of "pup" tents; there a spacious canvas shelter housing eight or ten men; here some tin nailed to a few boards; there some tar paper.

Bedding and flooring consisted of straw, old bed ticks stuffed with straw, magazines and newspapers spread as evenly and as thickly as possible, discarded mattresses and cardboard.

At Anacostia some Negroes had their own shacks and some slept in with white boys. There was no residential segregation. A Negro "house" might be next door to a white "house" or across the street, and no one thought of passing an ordinance to "preserve property values." In the California contingent which arrived shortly before I left there were several Negroes and they shared with their white buddies the large tents which someone secured for them from a government warehouse. The Chicago group had several hundred Negroes in it and they worked, ate, slept and played with their white comrades. The Negroes shared tasks with the whites from kitchen work to camp M.P. duty.

In gadding about I came across white toes and black toes sticking out from tent flaps and boxes as their owners sought to sleep away the day. They were far from the spouters of Nordic nonsense, addressing themselves to the business of living together. They were in another world, although Jim Crow Washington, D.C. was only a stone's throw from their doors.

All about were signs containing homely philosophy and sarcasm on the treatment of veterans by the country, such as: "The Heroes of 1918 Are the Bums of 1932." I believe many of the white campers were bitter and sarcastic. They meant what they said on those signs. But disappointment and disillusionment is an old story to Negroes. They were philosophic about this bonus business. They had wished for so many things to which they were justly entitled in this life and received so little that they could not get fighting mad over what was generally considered among them as the government's ingratitude. They had been told in 1917 that they were fighting for a better world, for true democracy; that a new deal would come for them; that jobs would come to them on merit, that lynching would be stopped; that they would have schools, homes, justice and the franchise. But these Negroes found out as long ago as 1919 that they had been fooled. Some of them could not even wear their uniforms back home. So, while the indifference of the government to the bonus agitation might be a bitter pill to the whites, it was nothing unusual to Negroes. They addressed themselves to humorous take-offs in signs, to cards and to music, the latter two shared by whites.

Thus it was I came across such signs on Negro shacks as "Douglas Hotel, Chicago"; "Euclid Avenue"; "South Parkway"; and "St. Antoine St." A card game had reunited four buddies from San Francisco, Detroit and Indianapolis and they were swapping stories to the swish of the cards.

Over in one corner a white vet was playing a ukulele and singing what could have been the theme song of the camp: "In a Shanty in Old Shanty Town." On a Sunday afternoon the camp piano was played alternately by a brown lad with a New York accent, and a red-necked white boy from Florida, while a few rods away Elder Micheaux's visiting choir was giving voice, in stop-time, to a hymn, "God's Tomorrow Will Be Brighter Than Today." Negroes and whites availed themselves of the free choice of patting their feet either outdoors to the piano or in the gospel tent to the choir.

Outside the main camp (there were four settlements) James Crow made brief and intermittent appearances, chiefly because the largest Southern delegations were not at Anacostia. But even in the Southern and border contingents there was no hard and fast color line. On Pennsylvania avenue, where the men had taken over a number of abandoned buildings in the process of being torn down, were camped the Carolina, Florida, Alabama and Texas delegations as well as a scattering from Virginia, Tennessee and West Virginia.

In a five story building a company of Negroes was assigned the fifth floor, but they all received treatment from the same medical center on the first floor. At first they all ate together, but there was so much confusion and so many men (not necessarily Negroes) were coming in on the tail end of the mess line, that a system whereby each floor took turns being first in the mess line was adopted. This was an equitable arrangement, but even here whites and Negroes lined up together and ate together; no absolute separation was possible, nor was it attempted.

In a mess kitchen which served only Southerners I saw Negroes and whites mixed together in line and grouped together eating. I was told there had been a few personal fights and a few hard words passed, but the attitude of the die-hard, strictly Jim Crow whites had not been adopted officially. Such Southern whites as I met showed the greatest courtesy and mingled freely with the Negroes.

Captain A. B. Simmons, colored, who headed his company, hails from Houston, Tex. He and his men were loud in their declarations of the fair treatment they had received on the march to Washington. They were served meals in Southern towns, by Southern white waitresses, in Main Street Southern restaurants along with their white companions. They rode freights and trucks and hiked together. Never a sign of Jim Crow through Northern Texas, Arkansas, Tennessee, or Virginia. Captain Simmons attended the regular company commanders' councils and helped with the problems of administration. His fellow officers, all white Southerners, accorded him the same consideration given others of this rank.

His story was corroborated by others. A long, hard-boiled Negro from West Virginia who had just stepped out of the mess line behind a white man from Florida said: "Shucks, they ain't got time for that stuff here and those that has, we gets 'em told personally." And said a cook in the North Carolina mess kitchen (helping whites peel potatoes): "No, sir, things is different here than down home."

In general assemblies and in marches there were no special places "for Negroes." The black boys did not have to tag along at the end of the line of march; there was no "special" section reserved for them at assemblies. They were shot all through the B.E.F. In the rallies on the steps of the nation's capitol they were in front, in the middle and in the rear.

One of the many significant aspects of the bonuseers' banishment of Jim Crow is the lie it gives to United States army officials who have been diligently spreading the doctrine that whites and blacks could not function together in the army; that they could not use the same mess tents, mingle in the same companies, council together on military problems. The B.E.F. proved that Negroes and whites can do all these things together, that even Negroes and white Southerners can do them together.

How can the army higher-ups explain that? Why can't the United States army with its equipment and its discipline enlist Negroes and whites together in all branches of the service? It can, but it will not. The army is concerned with refined democracy, with tabus, with the maintenance of poses. The B.E.F. is concerned with raw democracy and with reality. But hereafter the army will have to hide behind its self-erected tradition, for the B.E.F. has demonstrated, right under the august army nose, that the thing can be done.

And right there was the tragedy of it all. I stood again on the little rise above the Anacostia Flats and looked out over the camp on my last night in town. Men and women can live, eat, play and work together be they black or white, just as the B.E.F. demonstrated. Countless thousands of people know it, but they go on pretending, building their paper fences and their cardboard arguments. Back home in Waycross, Miami, Pulaski, Waxahachie, Pine Bluff, Cairo, Petersburg, Des Moines, Cincinnati, Philadelphia, Kansas City and St. Louis they go on pretending, glaring, jabbing, insulting, fighting. In St. Louis, where I first saw daylight, they separate them in everything except street cars.

A dump of a shanty town below the majestic Washington monument and the imperious national capitol. . . . Ragged torch bearers futilely striving to light the path for the blind overlords who will not see. . . . A blue camp, its cheerfulness undershot with tragedy. . . . A blue race problem, its surface gayety undershot with poignant sorrow. . . .

As I turned away, stumbling in the dark over a hose which brought water to the camp from a nearby fire hydrant, a soft Negro voice and the tinkling piano notes came faintly to me.

*I got the Saint Louis Blues*
*Just as Blue as I can be. . .*

*SOURCE: The Crisis,* October 1932, 316–17, 332. The editors of the encyclopedia wish to thank the Crisis Publishing Co., Inc., the publisher of the magazine of the National Advancement of Colored People, for the use of this material first published in the October 1932 issue of *Crisis.*

*RELATED ENTRIES: African Americans in the Military; Bonus March; MacArthur, Douglas; Racial Integration of the Armed Forces; Veterans Administration; World War I*

## 1933

### Excerpts from *Company K* by William March

*One of the more powerful and innovative novels about World War I was written by Sgt. William March, an Alabaman who served with the 5th Marines in France at Belleau Wood, Soissons, St Mihiel, and Blanc Mont. He was wounded and gassed, and received the Distinguished Service Medal and the Navy Cross. Company K consists of the personal statements of semi-fictional members of a company of marines not unlike his own comrades:*

Private Richard Mundy

I decided to take my rifle apart and clean it thoroughly. I didn't want to think about those prisoners any more, but as I sat there with my squad in the shallow trench, with the rifle parts scattered about me, I couldn't help thinking about them. Corporal Foster was opening cans of monkey meat with a bayonet and Roger Inabinett divided the meat and the hardtack into eight equal parts.

Charlie Gordon got out his harmonica and began to play a lively tune, but Everett Qualls stopped him. Then Foster passed out the rations and each man took his share. At sight of the food, Bill Nugent took sick. He went to the edge of the trench and vomited. When he came back his face was white. Jimmy Wade had a canteen of cognac which he passed over to him and Bill took a big swig of it, but immediately he got up and vomited again. Then he lay stretched out and trembled.

"What's the matter with you, Bill?" asked Foster.

"Nothing," he said.

"They've pulled that trick on the French a thousand times, and got away with it, too!" said Foster. "These Germans are smart hombres. You got to watch them all the time."

Ahead of us, in the wheat field, the rays of the late sun lay flat on the trampled grain, but in the wood it was almost dark. Inabinett was playing with a cigarette lighter he had found in the wood. He kept snapping it with a clicking sound. "All it needs is a new flint," he said. "It'll be as good as new with another flint."

I put my rifle back together and rubbed the butt with oil. I kept seeing those prisoners falling and rising to their knees and falling again. I walked to the end of the trench and looked over the top. A long way ahead was the sound of rifle fire and to the west there was intermittent shelling, but here, in the wood, everything was calm and peaceful. "You wouldn't know we were in the war at all," I thought.

Then I had an irresistible desire to go to the ravine and look at the prisoners again. I climbed out of the trench quickly, before anybody knew what I was going to do. . . .

The prisoners lay where we had left them, face upward mostly, twisted in grotesque knots like angleworms in a can, their pockets turned outward and rifled, their tunics unbuttoned and flung wide. I stood looking at them for a while, silent, feeling no emotion at all. Then the limb of a tree that grew at the edge of the ravine swayed forward and fell, and a wedge of late sunlight filtered through the trees and across the faces of the dead men. . . . Deep in the wood a bird uttered one frightened note and stopped suddenly, remembering. A peculiar feeling that I could not understand came over me. I fell to the ground and pressed my face into the fallen leaves. . . . "I'll never hurt anything again as long as I live," I said. . . . "Never again, as long as I live. . . . Never! . . . Never! . . . Never! . . ."

Private Robert Nalls

Following the fighting at St. Mihiel, we were billeted in Blenod-les-Toul with an old French couple. They had had an only son, a boy named René, who had been killed early in the war, and they were constantly finding points in common between us and him. I had brown eyes, and René's eyes had also been brown; René had had long, slender fingers, and Sam Quillin's fingers were also long and slender. They found resemblances to René in every one: Jerry Blandford because his teeth were even and white; Roger Jones for his thick, curling hair and Frank Halligan because of the trick he had of closing his eyes and throwing back his head when he laughed. Their lives centered around their dead son. They talked about him constantly; they thought of nothing else.

After his death, the French government had sent them a small copper plaque showing in bas-relief the heroic face of a woman surrounded by a wreath of laurel, and under the woman's face were the words, "Slain on the Field of Honor." It was not an unusual decoration. It was the sort of thing that a Government would send to the next of kin of all men killed in action, but the old couple attached great importance to it. In one corner of the room they had built a tiny shelf for the medal and its case, and underneath it the old woman had fixed up an altar with two candles that burned day and night. Often the old woman would sit for a long time silent before the altar, her hands twisted and old, resting her knees. Then she would go back and scrub her pans, or walk outside to the barn and look at her cow.

We remained in Blenod for five days, and then one night we got orders to move. The old couple had become very friendly with us by that time. They walked with us to the place of assembly, offering to carry our rifles or our packs. Then they stood in the muddy road, the September wind blowing against them strongly, crossing themselves and asking God to bring us all safely back.

A few weeks later, when we were miles away from Blenod, I saw the copper plaque again: It rolled out of Bernie Glass's kit bag while he was shaving one day. He picked it up quickly, but he knew that I had seen it.

"How could you do it, Bernie?" I asked; "how could you do a thing like that?"

"I don't know that it's any of your business," said Bernie, "but I thought it would make a good souvenir to take home."

I never returned to Blenod, and I never saw that old couple again, but somehow I wish they knew that I am ashamed of the whole human race.

PRIVATE ALBERT HAYES

In addition to the chocolate and cigarettes which were sold to us at three times their regular value, the canteen put in a line of sweaters and knitted socks. It was cold in the trenches and I wanted one of the sweaters to wear next to my skin to keep me warm at nights. I picked out a yellow one because it looked comfortable, and paid the canteen ten dollars for it. After I got back to my billet, and was examining it closely, I discovered there was a tiny pocket knitted in the bottom of the sweater and that a piece of paper had been tucked into it. Here's what I read:

"I am a poor old woman, seventy-two years old, who lives at the poor farm, but I want to do something for the soldier boys, like everybody else, so I made this sweater and I am turning it over to the Ladies Aid to be sent to some soldier who takes cold easy. Please excuse bad knitting and bad writing. If you get a cold on your chest take a dose of cooking soda and rub it with mutton suet and turpentine mixed and don't get your feet wet if you can help it. I used to be a great hand to knit but now I am almost blind. I hope a poor boy gets this sweater. It's not a very good one but I have put my love in every stitch and that's something that can't be bought or sold.

"Your obedient servant,

"(Mrs.) MARY L. SAMFORD.

"P.S. Don't forget to say your prayers at night and please write regularly to your dear mother."

PRIVATE ARTHUR CRENSHAW

When I came home the people in my town declared "Crenshaw Day." They decorated the stores and the streets with bunting and flags; there was a parade in the morning with speeches afterwards, and a barbecue at Oak Grove in the afternoon.

Ralph R. Hawley, President of the First National Bank and Trust Company, acted as toastmaster. He recited my war record and everybody cheered. Then he pointed to my twisted back and my scarred face and his voice broke with emotion. I sat there amused and uncomfortable. I wasn't fooled in the slightest. There is an expressive vulgar phrase which soldiers use on such occasions and I repeated it under my breath.

At last the ceremonies were over and Mayor Couzens, himself, drove me in his new automobile to my father's farm beyond the town. The place had gone to ruin in my absence. We Crenshaws are a shiftless lot, and the town knows it. The floors were filthy, and there was a pile of unwashed dishes in the sink, while my sister Maude sat on the step eating an apple, and gazing, half asleep, at a bank of clouds. I began to wonder what I could do for a living, now that heavy farm work was impossible for me any more. All that afternoon I thought and at last I hit on the idea of starting a chicken farm. I got pencil and paper and figured the thing out. I decided that I could start in a small way if I had five hundred dollars with which to buy the necessary stock and equipment.

That night as I lay awake and wondered how I could raise the money, I thought of Mr. Hawley's speech in which he had declared that the town owed me a debt of gratitude for the things I had done which it could never hope to repay. So the next morning I called on him at his bank and told him of my plans, and asked him to lend me the money. He was very courteous and pleasant about it; but if you think he lent me the five hundred dollars you are as big a fool as I was.

PRIVATE EVERETT QUALLS

One by one my cattle got sick and fell down, a bloody foam dripping from their jaws and nostrils. The veterinarians scratched their heads and said they had never seen anything like it. I knew what was the matter, but I didn't say anything, and at last my stock was all dead. I breathed with relief then. "I have paid for what I did," I thought; "now I can start all over." But about that time a blight came upon my corn, which was well up and beginning to tassel: the joints secreted a fluid which turned red over night. The green blades fell off and the stalks withered and bent to the ground. . . . "This, too!" I thought; "this, too, is required of me!"

My crops were ruined, my cattle dead. I talked it over with my young wife. She kissed me and begged me not to worry so. "We can live some way this winter," she said. "We'll start again in the Spring. Everything will be all right."

I wanted to tell her then, but I didn't dare do it. I couldn't tell her a thing of that sort. And so I went about hoping that He had forgotten and that my punishment was lifted. Then my baby, who had been so strong and healthy, took sick. I saw him wasting away before my eyes, his legs and arms turning purple, his eyes glazed and dead with the fever, his breathing sharp and strained.

I had not prayed for a long time, but I prayed now. "Oh, God, don't do this," I pleaded. "It's not his fault; it's not the baby's fault. I, I alone am guilty. Punish me, if You will—but not this way! . . . Not this way, God! . . . Please! . . ." I could hear my baby's breath rattling in the next room; I could hear the hum of the doctor's voice, the clink of an instrument against glass and the worried words of my wife. Then the baby's breathing stopped altogether and there was my wife's intaken wail of despair.

I beat my breast and flung myself to the floor and that scene I had tried to crush from my mind came back again. I could hear Sergeant Pelton giving the signal to fire and I could see those prisoners falling and rising and falling again. Blood poured from their wounds and they twisted on the ground, as I was twisting now on the floor. . . . One of the prisoners had a brown beard and clear, sunburned skin. I recognized him to be a farmer, like myself, and as I stood above him, I imagined his life. He, too, had a wife that he loved who waited for him somewhere. He had a comfortable farm and on holidays, at home, he used to drink beer and dance. . . .

My wife was knocking on the door, but I would not let her in. Then I knew what I must do. I took my service revolver, climbed out of my window and ran to the grove of scrub oaks that divided my land. When I reached the grove, I put the barrel in my mouth and pulled the trigger twice. There came blinding pain and waves of light that washed outward, in a golden flood, and widened to infinity. . . . I lifted from the ground and lurched forward, feet first, borne on the golden light, rocking gently from side to side. Then wild buffaloes rushed past me on thundering hooves, and receded, and I toppled suddenly into blackness without dimension and without sound.

Private Sylvester Keith

I came out sullen and resentful, determined that such a thing should never happen again. I felt that if people were made to understand the senseless horror of war, and could be shown the brutal and stupid facts, they would refuse to kill each other when a roomful of politicians decided for them that their honor had been violated. So I organized "The Society for the Prevention of War" and gathered around me fifty young and intelligent men, whose influence, I thought, would be important in the years to come. "People are not basically stupid or vicious," I thought, "they are only ignorant or ill informed. It's all a matter of enlightenment."

Every Thursday the group gathered at our meeting place. They asked innumerable questions concerning the proper way to hold a bayonet, and the best way to throw hand grenades. They were shocked at the idea of gas attacks on an extended front, and the brutality of liquid fire left them indignant and profane.

I was pleased with myself and proud of my pupils. I said: "I am planting in these fine young men such hatred of war that when the proper time comes they will stand up and tell the truth without fear or shame." But someone began organizing a company of National Guard in our town about that time and my disciples, anxious to protect their country from the horrors I had just described, deserted my society and joined in a body.

*SOURCE:* William March, *Company K.* (New York: Sagamore Press, 1957). Reprinted by permission of Harold Ober Associates Incorporated. Copyright 1933 by William March. Copyright renewed 1961 by The Merchants National Bank of Mobile and Patty C. Maxwell.

*RELATED ENTRIES: Literature and War; World War I*

## 1938

### A Massachusetts Veteran Reflects on Memorial Day Ceremonies

*Many veterans feel called upon to honor those who did not return. A leader of the United Spanish[–American] War Veterans in Newburyport, Massachusetts, explained a Memorial Day ceremony in the late 1930s to those who had gathered to honor the memory and sacrifices of Newburyport men who had died in the service of their country.*

The purpose of this ceremony is to honor those who preceded us to the land of the dead. This is the true patriotic day of the nation when the children of these men honor their fathers, the flag, and all for which the flag stands—bravery, glory, courage of people. It is fitting that the men who sleep beneath the flag of the Union should have graves decked with flowers in remembrance of this trying period of suffering and sorrow which molded this nation. This was in the cause of liberty and of God. It is only right that we quicken the memories of the dead. It is our purpose to preserve and protect Memorial Day. In times of peace it is the duty of us citizens to defend the flag and fulfill the patriotism of those who preceded us.

*SOURCE:* W. Lloyd Warner, *The Living and the Dead* (New Haven, Conn.: Yale University Press, 1959), 261.

*RELATED ENTRIES: Memorial Day; Memory and War*

## 1940 (to 1943)

### War Activity, November 1943, and Civilian Population Change, 1940 to November 1, 1943

*Low per capita` defense contracting correlated with population decline during World War II in the South, as this table indicates.*

| | War contracts, dollars per capita of civilian population, 1940 | Civilian population change [%] |
|---|---|---|
| Virginia | 821.08 | +4.8 |
| Tennessee | 630.65 | -3.3 |
| Louisiana | 613.88 | -1.8 |
| Alabama | 537.88 | -3.9 |
| Georgia | 474.60 | -4.1 |
| North Carolina | 360.92 | -6.1 |
| Mississippi | 279.18 | -8.6 |
| South Carolina | 296.24 | -5.4 |
| Arkansas | 215.73 | -10.9 |

*SOURCE:* Rudolph Heberle, *The Impact of the War on Population Redistribution in the South* (Nashville, Tenn.: Vanderbilt University Press, 1945), 21.

*RELATED ENTRIES: Economy and War; World War II*

## 1941

### Executive Order 8802: Prohibition of Discrimination in the Defense Industry

*For at least a year before the beginning of U.S. involvement in World War II, the country engaged in rhetoric against our declared enemy—Nazi Germany—and its racist policies. At home, however, the social landscape was still rife with racial discrimination and segregation. Facing pressure by civil rights leader A. Philip Randolph to address this rift between rhetoric and reality, Pres. Franklin D. Roosevelt signed Executive Order 8802 on June 25, 1941. The order set up the Fair Employment Practices Commission, which was authorized to investigate racial discrimination in companies under contract to supply war materials. Only partly effective in its implementation, the order nonetheless represents one step in the federal government's efforts to use war policy to change years of segregation by race.*

Reaffirming Policy of Full Participation in the Defense Program by All Persons, Regardless of Race, Creed, Color, or National Origin, and Directing Certain Action in Furtherance of Said Policy
June 25, 1941

WHEREAS it is the policy of the United States to encourage full participation in the national defense program by all citizens of the United States, regardless of race, creed, color, or national origin, in the firm belief that the democratic way of life within the Nation can be defended successfully only with the help and support of all groups within its borders; and

WHEREAS there is evidence that available and needed workers have been barred from employment in industries engaged in defense production solely because of considerations of race, creed, color, or national origin, to the detriment of workers' morale and of national unity:

NOW, THEREFORE, by virtue of the authority vested in me by the Constitution and the statutes, and as a prerequisite to the successful conduct of our national defense production effort, I do hereby reaffirm the policy of the United States that there shall be no discrimination in the employment of workers in defense industries or government because of race, creed, color, or national origin, and I do hereby declare that it is the duty of employers and of labor organizations, in furtherance of said policy and of this order, to provide for the full and equitable participation of all workers in defense industries, without discrimination because of race, creed, color, or national origin;

And it is hereby ordered as follows:

1. All departments and agencies of the Government of the United States concerned with vocational and training programs for defense production shall take special measures appropriate to assure that such programs are administered without discrimination because of race, creed, color, or national origin;
2. All contracting agencies of the Government of the United States shall include in all defense contracts hereafter negotiated by them a provision obligating the contractor not to discriminate against any worker because of race, creed, color, or national origin;
3. There is established in the Office of Production Management a Committee on Fair Employment Practice, which shall consist of a chairman and four other members to be appointed by the President. The Chairman and members of the Committee shall serve as such without compensation but shall be entitled to actual and necessary transportation, subsistence and other expenses incidental to performance of their duties. The Committee shall receive and investigate complaints of discrimination in violation of the provisions of this order and shall take appropriate steps to redress grievances which it finds to be valid. The Committee shall also recommend to the several departments and agencies of the Government of the United States and to the President all measures which may be deemed by it necessary or proper to effectuate the provisions of this order.

Franklin D. Roosevelt
The White House
June 25, 1941

*SOURCE:* U.S. National Archives & Records Administration, "Executive Order 8802: Prohibition of Discrimination in the Defense Industry (1941)." http://www.ourdocuments.gov/doc.php?doc=72&page=transcript (August 12, 2005).

*RELATED ENTRIES: African Americans in the Military; Executive Order 8802; Executive Order 9981; Racial Integration of the Armed Forces; Randolph, A. Philip; Roosevelt, Franklin Delano*

## 1942 (to 1946) a

**LETTERS FROM BLACK SOLDIERS IN WORLD WAR II**

*The military remained segregated throughout World War II, with the exception of a number of white companies—decimated during the battle of the Bulge—that received platoons comprised of black volunteers. African Americans serving in these years found many discriminatory measures offensive; some wrote to government officials or black newspapers complaining.*

3475th Q. M. Trk Co.
Fort Ord Calif.
November 10, 1942

Mr. William H. Hastie
[Deputy to Secretary of War Henry Stimson]

Dear Sir:

It has been several months since we have passed the necessary examination and approval of the Cadet Examining Board to qualify as an aviation Cadet.

During the Course of our examination we were stationed at Fort Sill, Okla, at which time several other soldiers took the examinations and have since then received their transfers to the Air Corp; but for some unknown reason we have not received ours.

Sir, we are college men and have had Senior R.O.T.C. training. We were also members of the Enlisted Reserve

Corp. Since completing our basic training in Field Artillery we have been transferred to Fort Ord California to do basic training in the Quartermaster Corp. It seems, sir, as if we are going from one basic training to another and getting no nearer to the Air Corp. We are writing you hoping you may be able to give us either and or information so as to hasten our transfer to the Air Corp. It seems with aviation playing the vital part it is we should have hardly any trouble getting in. Our papers are in Washington awaiting disposition, as is the case of all Negro applicants. We hope you can help us. We close now awaiting your answer.

Respectfully,
Pvt. Rufus R. Johnson 15317492
Pvt. Emory A. James 15317509
Pvt. Jack Housen 15317527

78 Aviation Sqdr. (Sy)
Randolph Field, Texas
October 28, 1942

The Pittsburgh Courier

Dear Sir:

We are members of the 78 Aviation Sqdr, and its seem like we are not being treated fair. Most of us got trades of our own to help win this war.

But instead we are servant and ditch diggers and we want better, if it ever been slavery it is now, please help us because we want better.

They got us here washing diches, working around the officers houses and waiting on them, instead of trying to win this war they got us in ditches.

Please report this to the N.A.A.C.P. and tell them to do something about this slavery place, where a colored soldier haven't got a chance.

Most of us are young and want to learn something, and we even got some that, want, action to help win this war.

And the sad part about it that most of us are volunteers, but they didn't give us what we ask for, they gave us a pick.

If you want your colored brothers to get somewhere please report this to the President.

Pvt Jus Hill A Lone Soldier

Pvt. Laurence W. Harris
356 Av Sqdn S.P.A.A.T.
Lubbock, Texas
November 4, 1943

To: The Pittsburgh Courier

Dear Gentlemen:

I am writing to you in regards to my classification in the army. I have been in the army air corp for the past ten months. Gentlemen I do not feel, and in fact I know I am not doing the best I could to help win this war. I realize the army has a tough job trying to place each man where they think he is best fitted or will do the best of service for the armed forces.

In my civilian life I was a small tool maker. I worked for Silling and Spences Co in Hartford, Conn. Then I was doing much for the war effort, and was in hopes I could continue in the service. In the past ten months I feel as though I have been a complete failure to myself, and to the helping to win this war. Beside that my morale is very low because of the fact I have given the army ten months to reclassify me to something I could do much than what I am doing.

I was in hopes I could become an airplane mechanic, but the field doesn't seem to be open to negro soldiers.

I only hope and pray that I will hear from you soon as to what I could do, to get into some part of the service where I could use my trade.

Thanking you in advance.

Yours Very Truely,
Pvt. Laurence W. Harris

MEDICAL DETACHMENT, DIVISION ARTILLERY,
2nd CAVALRY DIVISION

Fort Clark, Texas
April 23, 1943

*The Atlanta Daily World*

Dear Editor:

I would like to know if your paper approves of a General calling his soldiers "Nigger" to their face? I think that we are in this war to fight for the rigts of all minority races, the morale of this organization will be low if our soldiers are not addressed in the right manner.

Our colored chaplain was run off this post by the General Johnson solely because he protested to him against using the word "Nigger" when referring to colored troops. I feel that it is my right and privilege to protect against the un-Godly ways that the men of the 2nd Cavalry Division are treated by their white Texas officers.

I hope that you will see that the colored people of this nation know that these conditions exist.

Believe me that these are true statements.

A Negro Soldier

Sgt. Ben Kiser, Jr.
Ward 22 A.
Kennedy General Hospital
Memphis, (15), Tenn.
June 20, 1944

Mr. P.L. Prattis
Executive Editor
Pittsburgh Courier
Pittsburgh, 19, Penn.

Dear Sir:

This letter is being written with a purpose of extreme importance to the Negroes stationed here at this hospital. We hope and place confidence in your giving us the information deserved.

I have been stationed here for over two (2) months as a patient. I have not been overseas but there are plenty of Negro boys here who have. Most of these boys have companions who are white. They came back together. In the time that these boys have been here they have been together. They keep in the same wards, go to the same shows without any segregation. But when going to the mess halls for chow they are segregated. [A] few of the white boys sit at the tables allowed for colored. But the Sgt tells them to move because its not permitted in the mess halls. The white boys disapprove of this measure and ask why. The Sgt tells them its orders from the Lt. When we asked the Lt. he states that this is the South. We know this is the South but also the Army. My belief is that it can be stopped with a slight push from you. We would like for you to give your opinion on the matter remembering an article published in the August edition of the Courier based on a War Dept. directive banning discrimination and segregation in army camps and hospitals. We would like to have a copy of that directive and also the numbers of it. We will appreciate all that you can do for us.

We will be awaiting your reply with great anticipation.

Sincerely yours,
Sgt Ben Kiser, Jr.
Ward 22 A.
Kennedy General Hosp.
Memphis (15) Tenn.

Napier Field, Dothan, Alabama
19 November 1944

The Pittsburgh Courier

Dear Editor:

I've just returned from the Post Theatre. Being rather disgusted over the way I was ordered out of the Post Theatre tonight; I thought I would just write this little article to show or rather let the people back home know just how we are doing down in Alabama. It is getting to the place that all colored soldiers just have to wait until there is plenty space for all whites before they can even get a seat.

I decided to take in a movie tonight. After reaching the theatre, I found that they had only five (5) seats reserved for colored, (five seats in a row), so the usher ask me to get out, so I had to get out and perhaps wait until tomorrow. Not that I mine waiting, but just the insult I got from the usher. "Get out, there isn't any seats for you colored boys." Can you picture a personnel of approximately two hundred and seventy (270) trying to see a picture at the theatre, when only twenty-five (25) can see a picture a night. Only twenty seats per night for the colored soldiers.

The Army often practice, "keep up your morale by attending movies," our morale would be very low if we had to see movies to keep it up in Napier Field.

This is something to laugh about. Two days ago a friend from Pittsburgh received a package from the Company he worked for before entering the army. It was a very nice package, he appreciated it to the highest. But one thing I notice on the outside of the package was; "To be mailed outside the limits of the continental United States." It was addressed to Napier Field, Dotham, Ala. We as colored soldiers at Napier Field readily agree with this company. When they mailed this package, they mailed it outside the limits of the continental United States.

Sgt. Jesse L. Wilkins

Pvt. John R. Wright
3252 nd. Q.M.
Ser. Co. A.P.O. 403 c/o P.M.
Munich Germany
November 16, 1946

The Pittsburgh Courier

Dear Mr. Editor:

I have just finished reading your paper, the July 7th edition and I enjoyed it very much as usual. I have eighty five points myself, and I had hoped to be home by now but, for some reason or the other, we are all still over here. My outfit has been here in Europe three years to the date yesterday. Most of these guys have 103 points. I have been over here 28 months, but here is one fellow that has 144 points and he has been over here three years. We all think that we have not been treated fair by this point system here. Isn't any kind of break for service troops. Most of us did not want to come in this army in the first place, and Mr. Eastland says we, the Negro soldier, has made America loose prestege in Europe, but it's just the other way around. There have been many times that Jim Crow and prejudice have made me very very shame to say that I was an American. And even here in Germany, the people are not as bad as we were told. The majority of the people here admire a colored man so it seems to me. I served in North Africa, Italy, France, and now Dutchland. I have worked very hard for our country. I can not understand why the people of America will let Bilbo's and others preach such hatred against the Negro citizens.

Yours Truly,
John R. Wright

*SOURCE:* Phillip McGuire, ed., *Taps for a Jim Crow Army: Letters from Black Soldiers in World War II* (Lexington: University Press of Kentucky, 1993).

*RELATED ENTRIES: African Americans in the Military; Port Chicago Mutiny; Racial Integration of the Armed Forces; World War II*

## 1942 b

### Black Serviceman Lester Simons's Account of Training Experience

*Sgt. Lester Simons had been raised in Ann Arbor, Michigan, had attended an integrated high school, and had participated in numerous integrated athletic events in the year prior to his induction. His unit was sent to Arkansas for training in 1942 and he later described the trouble his unit encountered there.*

On maneuvers we were in a wooded area. We had rifles but no ammunition, not even bayonets. Our officers had their 45s, and that was all the protection we had in an area that was getting more hostile every minute. It was decided that we would move about twenty miles down the road. As we marched along counting cadence, to our new destination, a group of mounted farmers came out of nowhere, or so it seemed. Their spokesman told our lieutenant to "Get those god-damned niggers off of the white highway and march 'em in the ditch." The ditch he spoke of had several inches of water in it; water mocassins' playground. Our lieutenant objected and told them if they weren't careful the area would be placed under martial law (which should have been done in the beginning). The rednecks rode him down with their horses, then pistol-whipped him—one of their own color! The lieutenant was later given a medical discharge because of this beating; they damned near killed him.

*SOURCE:* Reprinted from Mary P. Motley, *The Invisible Soldier: The Experience of the Black Soldier in World War II* (Detroit, Mich.: Wayne State University Press, 1987).

 Excerpt is from p. 46.

*RELATED ENTRIES: African Americans in the Military; Port Chicago Mutiny; Racial Integration of the Armed Forces; World War II*

# 1942 c

## Marine's Letter to Father Concerning His Experience in Guadalcanal #1

*Marine Lt. John Doyle speculated in a letter to his father, written on Guadalcanal in November 1942, on the effect of the combat experience on his personality and values.*

What has it done to me? What does it mean to me?

I know that I have not become cruel or callous. I am sure that I am hardened. If a man cannot produce, I'll push him into the most degrading, menial task I can find. A man that shrinks from duty is worse than a man lost. He should be thrown out of the entire outfit. He's not fit to live with the men with whom he is not willing to die. Death is easy. It happens often.

The toughest part is going on, existing as an animal. Wet, cold and hungry many times, a man can look forward only to the next day when the sun, flies and mosquitoes descend to devour him.

Few men fear bullets. They are swift, silent and certain. Shelling and bombing are more often the cursed bugaboos.

*SOURCE:* Harry Maule, ed. *A Book of War Letters* (New York: Random House, 1943), 185.

*RELATED ENTRIES: Combat, Effects of; Marine Corps; World War II*

# 1942 d

## Marine's Letter to Father Concerning His Experience in Guadalcanal #2

*Pfc. John Conroy, a Guadalcanal veteran, wrote to his father from a hospital in late 1942:*

I have been shell-shocked and bomb-shocked. My memory is very dim regarding my civilian days. . . . Of course I'm not insane. But I've been living the life of a savage and haven't quite got used to a world of laws and new responsibilities. So many of my platoon were wiped out, my old Parris Island buddies, that it's hard to sleep without seeing them die all over again. Our living conditions on Guadalcanal had been so bad—little food or hope—fighting and dying each day—four hours sleep out of 72—the medicos here optimistically say I'll pay for it the rest of my life. My bayonet and shrapnel cuts are all healed up, however. Most of us will be fairly well in six months, but none of us will be completely cured for years.

*SOURCE:* Excerpt from Dixon Wecter, *When Johnny Comes Marching Home*, pp. 545–46. 

*RELATED ENTRIES: Combat, Effects of; Marine Corps; World War II*

# 1942 e

## Monica Itoi Sone's Account of Her Transfer to a Japanese Internment Camp

*In April 1942, the Army on the West Coast was directed to relocate all Japanese Americans living in the four westernmost states to a number of internment camps in Rocky Mountain states. A young Nisei (born in the United States of Japanese immigrant parents) described her family's experience:*

General DeWitt kept reminding us that E day, evacuation day, was drawing near. "E day will be announced in the very near future. If you have not wound up your affairs by now, it will soon be too late."

. . . On the twenty-first of April, a Tuesday, the general gave us the shattering news. "All the Seattle Japanese will be moved to Puyallup by May 1. Everyone must be registered Saturday and Sunday between 8 A.M. and 5 P.M."

Up to that moment, we had hoped against hope that something or someone would intervene for us. Now there was no time for moaning. A thousand and one details must be attended to in this one week of grace. Those seven days sputtered out like matches struck in the wind, as we rushed wildly about. Mother distributed sheets, pillowcases and blankets, which we stuffed into seabags. Into the two suitcases, we packed heavy winter overcoats, plenty of sweaters, woolen slacks and skirts, flannel pajamas and scarves. Personal toilet articles, one tin plate, tin cup and silverware completed our luggage. The one seabag and two suitcases apiece were going to be the backbone of our future home, and we planned it carefully.

Henry went to the Control Station to register the family. He came home with twenty tags, all numbered "10710," tags to be attached to each piece of baggage, and one to hang from our coat lapels. From then on, we were known as Family #10710.

[On the day set for relocation] we climbed into the truck. . . . As we coasted down Beacon Hill bridge for the last time, we fell silent, and stared out at the delicately flushed, morning sky of Puget Sound. We drove through bustling Chinatown, and in a few minutes arrived on the corner of Eighth and Lane. This are was ordinarily lonely and deserted but now it was gradually filling up with silent, labeled Japanese. . . .

Finally at ten o'clock, a vanguard of Greyhound busses purred in and parked themselves neatly along the curb. The crowd stirred and murmured. The bus doors opened and from each, a soldier with rifle in hand stepped out and stood stiffly at attention by the door. The murmuring died. It was the first time I had seen a rifle at such close range and I felt uncomfortable. . . .

Newspaper photographers with flash-bulb cameras pushed busily through the crowd. One of them rushed up to our bus, and asked a young couple and their little boy to step out and stand by the door for a shot. They were reluctant, but the photographers were persistent and at length they got out of the bus and posed, grinning widely to cover their embarrassment. We saw the picture in the newspaper shortly after and the caption underneath it read, "japs good-natured about evacuation."

Our bus quickly filled to capacity. . . . The door closed with a low hiss. We were now the Wartime Civil Control Administration's babies.

About noon we crept into a small town. . . . and we noticed at the left of us an entire block filled with neat rows of low shacks, resembling chicken houses. Someone commented on it with awe, "Just look at those chicken houses. They sure go in for poultry in a big way here." Slowly the bus made a left turn, drove through a wire-fenced gate, and to our dismay, we were inside the oversized chicken farm. . . .

The apartments resembled elongated, low stables about two blocks long. Our home was one room, about 18 by 20 feet, the size of a living room. There was one small window in the wall opposite the one door. It was bare except for a small, tinny wood-burning stove crouching in the center. The flooring consisted of two by fours laid directly on the earth, and dandelions were already pushing their way up through the cracks. . . .

I stared at our little window, unable to sleep. I was glad Mother had put up a makeshift curtain on the window for I noticed a powerful beam of light sweeping across it every few seconds. The lights came from high towers placed around the camp where guards with Tommy guns kept a twenty-four hour vigil. I remembered the wire fence encircling us, and a knot of anger tightened in my breast. What was I doing behind a fence like a criminal? If there were accusations to be made, why hadn't I been given a fair trial? Maybe I wasn't considered an American anymore. My citizenship wasn't real, after all. Then what was I? I was certainly not a citizen of Japan as my parents were. On second thought, even Father and Mother. . . . had little tie with their mother country. In their twenty-five years in America, they had worked and paid their taxes to their adopted government as any other citizen.

Of one thing I was sure. The wire fence was real. I no longer had the right to walk out of it. It was because I had Japanese ancestors. It was also because some people had little faith in the ideas and ideals of democracy.

*SOURCE:* Monica Itoi Sone, *Nisei Daughter* (Seattle: University of Washington Press, 1979). Reprinted by permission of the author.

*RELATED ENTRIES: Civil–Military Relations; 442nd Regimental Combat Team of Nisei; Intelligence Gathering in War; Japanese Americans, Internment of; World War II*

## 1942 (to 1945) f

### Interviews with Japanese-Americans Regarding Mistreatment during World War II

*Two young Nisei interned in Manzanar angrily explained to government officials their refusal to attest to their loyalty to a country that had ignored their civil liberties in the passion of war:*

First Nisei

A. Here is the thing. I'm supposed to be a citizen of the United States. At the time of registration, I asked him how far my citizenship went. I don't know if there is such a thing as restricted citizenship in this country. I refused to answer because if there is such a thing as restricted citizenship, I have the right to refuse to answer. What security have we? If this can happen now, why can't the same thing happen in five years?

Q. What has happened is unfortunate. But other minorities have had to face discrimination too. In my part of the country the Germans are probably treated worse than Japanese.

A. It's all right to be of a minority as long as you're of the same race.

Q. I can't see that. If you're discriminated against because you belong to a minority group, it's as bad whatever race you belong to.

A. This is the reason you look at it differently; you are a white man. At the end of the war, animosities will be high. There will be high feelings against us. There will be a boycott of us if we start in business. At the end of the last war, the bad feeling didn't continue against the Germans. But you can't tell a German from an Englishman when he walks down the street. But when I go down the street they say, "There goes a Jap." Perhaps it will be 15 years before this feeling will die down. I disagree with you when you say that 100,000 Japanese can be assimilated now. I know the [government is] doing what [it] can. But the one hundred thirty millions in this country are hostile. (After additional discussion of this same topic) Well, you'd better write me a ticket to Tule Lake. . . .

Q. Your record doesn't show any interest in Japan and you haven't said anything that would indicate that you want to go to Japan. Why is it then that you object so strongly to question 28 [Loyalty to the United States]?

A. I have not been given citizenship rights so I don't have to answer questions like that.

Second Nisei

Q. Don't you feel that whatever has happened you should express your loyalty to the only country in which you now hold citizenship?

A. At the time of the draft I was deferred because of my dependents. At that time I said I'd die for this country in the event of war. That's the way I felt. But since I lost my business when I was young and just starting up I've changed my mind. You Caucasian Americans should realize that I got a raw deal.

Q. But things like these happen in a time of war. Evacuation was a war measure, an emergency measure.

A. They shouldn't happen to citizens. What did a war with Japan have to do with evacuating me? You've got to realize that I am an American citizen just as much as you. Maybe my dad is not, because of Congress. He couldn't naturalize. But my associates in school and college were Caucasians. It's been a hard road to take.

*A first-generation (Issei) man and a second-generation (Nisei) woman who was married to an Issei responded to questions put to them by government officials regarding their negative responses on the loyalty questionnaire:*

The Man (via a Translator)

A. He didn't register because of the rumor that those who registered would be forced to leave [Tule Lake] and he had no place to go.

Q. Does he understand now that that isn't so?

A. I guess he does.

Q. He can't understand or speak English?

A. Very little.

Q. Does he plan to return to Japan after the war?

A. Yes.

Q. Does he feel more sympathy to Japan than to the United States?

A. His sympathy lies with Japan.

Q. Why?

A. He was a law abiding citizen, worked hard, respected law, and yet he was placed here. He can't stand it any longer.

THE WOMAN

Q. Are you disloyal?

A. Yes.

Q. Why?

A. Well—no reason. If I say "loyal" will they take me or leave me here?

Q. We don't split families. If one member is on the segregation list the others in the family are given their choice of leaving or remaining. We don't want you to answer a certain way just because your husband does. This hearing is just to determine your loyalty.

A. Then it doesn't have anything to do with staying?

Q. No, you'll be given the choice of following your husband or not.

A. Then I'm loyal.

*A young Nisei woman explained to U.S. officials in September 1945 the family pressures that had led her to renounce her citizenship during the war:*

I am a Nisei girl, age 20, born and raised in Alameda, California, until the time of evacuation in Feb. 1942. My father passed away in May 1940. So there is my mother . . . 56 years old, and my brother [now] 18 years old. We were living a normal American life until we were uprooted from our beloved home. It was the home and security my father and mother worked so hard for when they came to America. This America was strange to them but they wanted to make their home here and raise us as good American citizens. Not knowing the language they had a hard time. . . . My mother was especially taken back by [evacuation] since my father passed away, so you can imagine her bitterness. Being pushed from one WRA camp to another (Pleasanton, Turlock Assembly Center, Gila Center and Tule Center) only hardened her bitterness and I myself got pretty disgusted being shoved around but I reasoned that this would not happen under normal conditions. Life was not too hard up to Gila Center, but since segregation and coming here it has been a life of turmoil, anxiety and fear. My brother and I did not want to come here but we could not go against the wishes of our mother. She isn't young anymore so this life of moving about hasn't been easy for her so we obeyed her, thinking it was the only way to make up to all her unhappiness. We had life before us but mother's life is closer to end . . . so we couldn't hurt her with any more worries. Since coming here I found out it was wrong in coming here. There are too many pro-Japanese organizations with too much influence. Naturally mother in the state of mind she was in would be greatly taken in by them. She had the family name in one of the organizations but we (my brother and I) absolutely refused to acknowledge it so she reluctantly withdrew our name. . . . When the renunciation citizenship came mother again wanted us to renounce. My brother luckily was under age but I could not fight against her this time. One [thing] that put a scare into me was that families would be separated. To me, I just had to sign on that paper, so I piled lies upon lies at the renunciation hearing. All horrid and untruthful lies they were. I didn't mean anything I said at that time, but fear and anxiety was too strong. I have regretted that I took such a drastic step—in fact I knew I would regret it before I went into it but I was afraid if I was torn away from the family I would never see them again in this uncertain world. I should have had more confidence in America but being torn away from my home and all made things so uncertain. I would never have renounced if the Administration made it clear that there would be no family separation. But the Administration could not assure us that there would be no separation.

*SOURCE:* Richard Nishimoto, and Dorothy Swaine Thomas, *Japanese-American Evacuation and Resettlement: I: The Spoilage* (Berkeley: University of California Press, 1946). 

*RELATED ENTRIES: Civil–Military Relations; 442nd Regimental Combat Team of Nisei; Intelligence Gathering in War; Japanese Americans, Internment of; World War II*

## 1943

### Excerpt from Bill Mauldin's *Up Front*

*The Army's system of replacing a unit's casualty losses with fresh troops during World War I and World War II amounted to sending both "green" privates, as well as seasoned veterans who had recovered from wounds, to replacement depots where they could expect to be "repple deppled" into the next unit in need of someone with their specific military knowledge and skills. But virtually all of those who had recovered from wounds wanted to return to their "buddies." Hence the expression: "AWOL-to-the-front." Cartoonist and commentator Bill Mauldin, who served in the war, explains:*

When a soldier gets out of an army hospital he will most likely be thrown into a "repple depple." This institution, identified in army regulations as a replacement depot, is a sort of clearinghouse through which soldiers who have been separated from their outfits or soldiers newly arrived from the States have to pass for reassignment.

I went through a repple depple at Palermo, Sicily, and my experience seems to have been typical. This establishment was operated by a paratrooper lieutenant (I don't know why, either) who spent most of his time convincing us that paratrooping had a great postwar future. Several times I interrupted him to say that my outfit was only fifteen miles away and couldn't I get over to them. Each time he told me that a truck would come within a few hours and pick me up. I believed this until I discovered two other guys from my outfit who had been waiting for this same truck for three weeks.

I guess the repple depple people didn't trust us, because the place was surrounded by a very high wall and there were guards beyond that.

We waited until night fell, then we plotted our "break." We persuaded one inmate, whose outfit had already gone and who had given up hope of salvation, to distract the guard while we went over the wall. As far as I know they still have my name and I'm still AWOL from a repple depple. I joined my outfit and caught the last boat to Salerno.

Later I learned that soldiers often languish in repple depples for months, only to be snapped up eventually by some outfit with which they are not familiar. A soldier's own outfit is the closest thing to home he has over here, and it is too bad when he has to change unnecessarily.

I heard of a soldier who spent his entire time overseas in repple depples, and went home on rotation without ever having been assigned. His home-town paper called him "a veteran of the Italian campaign."

*SOURCE:* Bill Mauldin, *Up Front* (New York: Henry Holt, 1945).

*RELATED ENTRIES: Literature and War; Mauldin, Bill; Replacement Depots; World War II*

## 1944 a

### Excerpt from Ernie Pyle's *Brave Men*

*Newsman Ernie Pyle and a GI friend watched troops passing by Italy in 1944 "after a siege in the front line." He reported his observations.*

Their clothes were muddy, and they were heavily laden. They looked rough, and any parade-ground officer would have been shocked by their appearance. And yet I said, "I'll bet those troops haven't been in the line three days."

My friend thought a minute, looked more closely as they passed, and then said, "I'll bet they haven't been in the line at all. I'll bet they've just been up in reserve and weren't used, and now they're being pulled back for a while."

How can you tell things like that? Well, I based my deduction on the fact that their beards weren't very long and, although they were tired and dirty, they didn't look tired and dirty enough. My friend based his on that too, but more so on the look in their eyes. "They don't have that stare," he said.

A soldier who has been a long time in the line does have a "look" in his eyes that anyone who knows about it can discern. It's a look of dullness, eyes that look without seeing, eyes that see without conveying any image to the mind. It's a look that is the display room for what lies behind it—exhaustion, lack of sleep, tension for too long, weariness that is too great, fear beyond fear, misery to the point of numbness, a look of surpassing indifference to anything anybody can do. It's a look I dread to see on men.

And yet to me it's one of the perpetual astonishments of a war life that human beings recover as quickly as they do. For example, a unit may be pretty well exhausted, but if they are lucky enough to be blessed with some sunshine and warmth they'll begin to be normal after two days out of the line. The human spirit is just like a cork.

*SOURCE:* Ernie Pyle, *Brave Men* (Lincoln: University of Nebraska Press, 2001).

*RELATED ENTRIES: Censorship and the Military; Combat, Effects of; Frontline Reporting; Pyle, Ernie; World War II*

## 1944 (to 1945) b

### Excerpts from *Pacific War Diary 1942–1945*, by James J. Fahey

*Seaman James Fahey's diary, the richest of its kind from the Pacific fleet during World War II, contains two revealing accounts. The first is of a kamikaze attack on November 27, 1944, and his shipmates' reactions to finding some of the remains of the kamikaze pilot; the second is of his experiences ashore in the Hiroshima area after the Japanese surrender.*

Monday, November 27, 1944: . . . One suicide dive bomber was heading right for us while we were firing at other attacking planes and if the 40 mm. mount behind us on the port side did not blow the Jap wing off it would have killed all of us. When the wing was blown off it, the plane turned some and bounced off into the water and the bombs blew part of the plane onto our ship. Another suicide plane crashed into one of the 5 inch mounts, pushing the side of the mount in and injuring some of the men inside. A lot of 5 inch shells were damaged. It was a miracle they did not explode. If that happened the powder and shells would have blown up the ship. Our 40 mm. mount is not too far away. The men threw the 5 inch shells over the side. They expected them to go off at any time. A Jap dive bomber crashed into one of the 40 mm. mounts but lucky for them it dropped its bombs on another ship before crashing. Parts of the plane flew everywhere when it crashed into the mount. Part of the motor hit Tomlinson, he had chunks of it all over him, his stomach, back, legs etc. The rest of the crew were wounded, most of them were sprayed with gasoline from the plane. Tomlinson was thrown a great distance and at first they thought he was knocked over the side. They finally found him in a corner in bad shape. One of the mt. Captains had the wires cut on his phones and kept talking into the phone, because he did not know they were cut by shrapnel until one of the fellows told him. The explosions were terrific as the suicide planes exploded in the water not too far away from our ship. The water was covered with black smoke that rose high into the air. The water looked like it was on fire. It would have been curtains for us if they had crashed into us.

Another suicide plane just overshot us. It grazed the 6 inch turret. It crashed into Leyte Gulf. There was a terrific explosion as the bombs exploded, about 20 ft. away. If we were going a little faster we would have been hit. The Jap planes that were not destroyed with our shells crashed into the water close by or hit our ships. It is a tough job to hold back this tidal wave of suicide planes. They come at you from all directions and also straight down at us at a very fast pace but some of the men have time for a few fast jokes, "This would be a great time to run out of ammunition." "This is mass suicide at its best." Another suicide plane came down at us in a very steep dive. It was a near miss, it just missed the 5 inch mount. The starboard side of the ship was showered with water and fragments. How long will our luck hold out? The Good Lord is really watching over us. This was very close to my 40 mm. mount and we were showered with debris. If the suicide plane exploded on the 5 inch mount, the ammunition would have gone up, after that anything could happen.

Planes were falling all around us, bombs were coming too close for comfort. The Jap planes were cutting up the water with machine gun fire. All the guns on the ships were blazing away, talk about action, never a dull moment. The fellows were passing ammunition like lightning as the guns were turning in all directions spitting out hot steel. Parts of destroyed suicide planes were scattered all over the ship. During a little lull in the action the men would look around for Jap souvenirs and what souvenirs they were. I got part of the plane. The deck near my mount was covered with blood, guts, brains, tongues, scalps, hearts, arms etc. from the Jap pilots. One of the Marines cut the ring off the finger of one of the dead pilots. They had to put the hose on to wash the blood off the deck. The deck ran red with blood. The Japs were spattered all over the place. One of the fellows had a Jap scalp, it looked just like you skinned an animal. The hair was black, but very short, and the color of the skin was yellow, real Japanese. I do not think he was very old. I picked up a tin pie plate with a tongue on it. The pilots tooth mark was into it very deep. It was very big and long, it looked like part of his tonsils and throat were attached to it. It also looked like the tongue you buy in the meat store. This was the first time I ever saw a person's brains, what a mess. One of the men on our mount got a Jap rib and cleaned it up, he said his sister wants part of a Jap body. One fellow from Texas had a knee bone and he was going to preserve it in alcohol from the sick bay. The Jap bodies were blown into all sorts of pieces. I cannot think of everything that happened because too many things were happening at the same time.

These suicide or kamikaze pilots wanted to destroy us, our ships and themselves. This gives you an idea what kind of an enemy we are fighting. The air attacks in Europe are tame compared to what you run up against out here against the Japs. The Germans will come in so far, do their job and take off but not the Japs. I can see now how the Japs sank the two British battleships Prince of Wales and the Repulse at the beginning of the war at Singapore. You do not discourage the Japs, they never give up, you have to kill them. . . .

Monday, October 22, 1945: We covered another landing today. The convoy consisted of about 15 transports. The Army troops wore their heavy clothing. The Montpelier again served as flagship for the gunfire support unit. All guns were manned but nothing happened. These troops will take over the Matsuyama-Shikokku area of Japan. This will be the last landing for the U.S.S. Montpelier to cover.

I saw a monster of a Jap submarine. It was much longer than one of our destroyers. It must be the largest in the world. It had a catapult on the bow for launching planes. It also carried two planes.

During the rest of our two months stay in Japan, we visited many places and met many Japanese. The most famous place we visited was Hiroshima. We were one of the first to see the extensive damage caused by the atomic bomb. Hiroshima was the first city in history to be hit with an atomic bomb.

When we saw Hiroshima, a city of approximately half a million, it was deserted except for a few people walking through with white cloths over their nose and mouths. I will never forget what I saw there. You have to see it. I cannot explain it. A few frames of buildings were the only thing that was left standing. Everything was ground into dust. The city of Hiroshima was a city of large buildings. They were made of stone, cement and steel. I bought some pictures in the next town and could see how well constructed the buildings were. We passed a mother nursing her baby in the cellar of a destroyed house. She did not pay any attention to us as she sat there in the dust. Her whole family might have been wiped out and the both of them might die later from the effects of the bomb. We felt very sorry for them. The only thing they owned was the clothes on their backs, and that was not much. We saw a few stumps of trees that were barren. They were completely black from burning. The trolley cars were blown off the tracks. Only they did not look like trolley cars anymore. They were completely destroyed. I could just see pieces of them. The fire engines were still in the building. Everything was reduced to a lot of rubble, building and trucks. The enormous buildings with walls over a foot thick were all in small chunks. Even if you were in the basement of strongly built buildings of steel and cement, you would still suffer the effects of the bomb. No place was safe to hide. As far as the eye could see, there was nothing but destruction. The force from one of these bombs is fantastic. There is only one defense against the bomb, prevent it from falling.

When we left Hiroshima, we stopped at a town not too far away. I spent some time talking to a Jap who lived in the States for 32 years. He finally returned to Japan in 1940. He said it was a warm, sunny day when the bomb was dropped, about 8 A.M. He was thrown to the ground but thought that it was an earthquake. Then a huge red flame rose high into the sky. He said that Hiroshima burnt for two days. Out of a population of half a million, two hundred thousand were killed and another two hundred thousand were injured. People were still dying. He treated many of the bomb victims. He said that there must have been poison in the bomb because it affected the victims' heads. It made them very sleepy and the next thing, they were dead. He was very angry and said the bomb never should have been dropped on Hiroshima because it did not help the war effort. He spoke very good English. While we were talking to him, some girls about 20 years old were cooking their meal over a little stove out on the sidewalk. It was a warm, sunny day but on the way back to our ship, the day became cool.

On our way back to the ship, we took a look at the damaged warships in the Kure Naval Base. It was quite a sight. Every Jap warship was severely damaged from the planes of Halsey's Third Fleet. They were hit with bombs and torpedoes. Every type of a warship was in the harbor. They even had a battleship with a flight deck on it. One of the Jap carriers we passed had some Jap sailors on it. They waved and we waved back. We also pulled alongside the Haruna. This is the ship Colin Kelley crashed into. He told his crew to bail out before he crippled the Jap battleship and lost his life for his country in the following action. The *Haruna* suffered extensive damage.

*SOURCE:* Excerpts from James J. Fahey, *Pacific War Diary: 1942–1945* (New York: Avon Books, 1963), 224–26, 379–80. 

*RELATED ENTRIES: Combat, Effects of; Hiroshima; Literature and War; Manhattan Project; World War II*

## 1944 (to 1950) c

### Black Soldier's Encounter with Racism and its Psychological Effects

*A black solider—identified here as J.G.S.—experienced racism while in the service during World War II. He developed psychoneurotic disorders, was hospitalized, and was eventually discharged. Army psychiatrists recorded his case history and noted his successful recovery upon his return to a less discriminatory and racist atmosphere.*

J.G.S. was born and raised in a small Northeastern town. A member of one of the few Negro families in that area, he experienced little discrimination and was generally accepted as an equal by his schoolmates. He completed junior college at the age of twenty with a very good scholastic record and thereafter held jobs as a public stenographer and chief clerk with the draft board. Just before his twenty-second birthday, he enlisted in the Army. Until then he had had only very limited contact with the manifestations of prejudice against his race. He had deliberately sought out an environment in which he could expect to find people, both Negro and white, who would not feel that he should act differently just because he was a member of a minority group. In this way, he was able largely to avoid discrimination and developed cultural values much closer to those of the white middle class than to those of his fellow Negroes in the South.

In the Army, however, J.G.S. found himself treated differently from other soldiers because he was a Negro. He had no choice as to where or with whom he worked. He was constantly and directly exposed to a set of values which differed radically from his own and to the manifestation of these values in discrimination, segregation, and rigidly prescribed patterns of behavior. He received his basic training in the South; later he was sent to clerical school and then assigned as a clerk, specializing in courts-martial, to an anti-aircraft artillery group.

Intelligent and relatively well educated, he was promoted rapidly and became a technician fourth grade in less than a year. Nevertheless, he was in constant conflict with many of his officers, especially those from the South. He resented any system which assigned Negroes to segregated units and on many occasions found himself in serious disagreement with his fellow Negro officers and enlisted men who accepted a second-class status. As a court stenographer he saw or heard about many instances of discrimination, which affected him in a very personal manner. Furthermore, as an educated Northern Negro he was considered by many of his white officers a troublemaker. Several times he was threatened with court-martial for treason. He was forbidden to give books to other soldiers and just before going overseas his commander denied him a pass to go to his home which was nearby; instead he received a two-hour lecture designed to make him give up his "liberal" values and accept his status as a Negro.

Early in his Army career the soldier began to develop psychiatric symptoms. During basic training he went on sick call several times with nausea, headaches, tenseness, and stuttering. While in clerical school he consulted a psychiatrist, but was not hospitalized. The symptoms continued after he joined the anti-aircraft group and became quite severe after his outfit left its former location in the Deep South and went overseas to North Africa. At times his stuttering was so incapacitating that he was unable to speak at all.

The morale of the outfit was poor primarily because of the discord between the white officers and Negro enlisted men. In May 1944, however, after about a year of overseas duty, the organization was disbanded because of reduced need for anti-aircraft protection, and J.G.S. was placed in charge of a quartermaster laundry receiving office. For two months until the replacement depot closed he supervised both white and Negro enlisted men. There was no difficulty and his headaches, nausea, and stuttering improved considerably. He was next sent to Italy and spent another two months working on courts-martial before being assigned to clerical duty with an Infantry division. Although he saw only intermittent combat, his symptoms now became quite severe. Again he was involved in a good deal of strife with white officers. Morale among the Negro troops was low and many resented being led by officers who seemed to hate them as much as the enemy. In addition there was frequent strife between Negro and white soldiers in rear areas. All this had a marked effect on J.G.S. and he spent almost a month at one time in the hospital because of his stuttering. Nevertheless, he was able to return to duty and served until returned to the States in the spring of 1945 after more than two years overseas.

Back in this country and on furlough, he became extremely disturbed over any evidence of discrimination, especially against Negro soldiers, who he felt deserved better. At that time he decided that he would never marry because he did not want a child of his exposed to the discrimination that he had experienced. On returning to camp he was hospitalized with a severe speech impediment and constant headaches. Several months later he was discharged.

Shortly after leaving service the veteran began receiving treatment for his speech disorder through the Veterans Administration while working as a government clerk in the Northeast. Free once again to avoid people who might be prejudiced against him because of his race, he gradually improved. By late 1947 when the treatment was terminated, he was making a good adjustment. He had married and had one child; he was happy in his home life. He had started taking courses with a view to obtaining a degree in business administration. By 1950 he was well on the way to accomplishing his educational objectives, although the necessity of holding a full-time job to support his family left him little time for studies.

*SOURCE:* From Eli Ginzberg, et al., eds., *The Ineffective Soldier, vol. 2, Breakdown and Recovery.* (New York: Columbia University Press), 105–08. 

*RELATED ARTICLES: African Americans in the Military; Port Chicago Mutiny; World War II*

## 1945 a

### Black Serviceman's Account of Confrontation with Battalion Commander

*Tech. Sgt. Willie Lawton recalled the means that some of his comrades used in 1945 to signal their extreme displeasure with their battalion commander.*

We had an incident in the Philippines that just missed being a bloody war; the 93rd vs. the Dixie Division. This white outfit was there when we arrived. I do not remember the name of the place but it was in the vicinity of the Dole Pineapple Company. Our men had been overseas nineteen months without seeing any women to speak of so when the guys hit the Philippines they went hog wild. The Dixie Division couldn't stand the Filipino girls going for the Negro soldiers. After several days there were small battles. The ultimate finally arrived; the Dixie Division was lined upon one side of the road for about two miles or more and the 93rd was lined up opposite them. Both sides had fixed bayonets, their guns were on-load and unlock. It took the colonels of every battalion from both divisions to get their men and bring the situation under control. They were real busy riding or running up and down that road to keep down outright war.

The next morning the colonel of my battalion called a meeting of all of the officers and NCOs. He marched us to a field and instead of talking some kind of sense we were severely reprimanded, so we knew where we stood. The thing we kept thinking about was those Dixie boys wouldn't have been caught dead with the Filipino girls back home. Anyway, we were told that anyone would be busted in rank should he become involved with the girls of the country. Neither the officers nor the NCOs liked this directive, and instead of telling the enlisted what we were supposed to we told them exactly what had been said.

The colonel, being the colonel, was the only person who had a generator to furnish light in his tent at night. That night several men cut loose with their .30 caliber rifles on that light and the upper part of his tent. Man, he came crawling out of that tent screaming bloody murder. The whole thing was settled without another word; he had gotten the message and there was no problem about our mixing with the women who came into our area.

*SOURCE:* Reprinted from Mary P. Motley, *The Invisible Soldier: The Experience of the Black Soldier in World War II* (Detroit, Mich.: Wayne State University Press, 1987).  Excerpt is from p. 101.

*RELATED ARTICLES: African Americans in the Military; Port Chicago Mutiny; World War II*

## 1945 (to 1970) b

### Black Soldiers' Recollections of Their Experiences in World War II

*Sgt. Floyd Jones, a black artilleryman in World War II and veteran of the bttle of the Bulge, recalled his decision to "set [my army experience] outside of the mainstream of my life."*

From the very beginning, when I realized there was going to be a conflict in which I would participate, I determined I was not going to allow myself to be warped by war. Therefore the time I spent in service was something I set outside of the mainstream of my life. I did my time with but one thought; in spite of hell I was going to return just as I left physically and mentally. While I was in the army I was a soldier, not an interested spectator, asking no quarter and giving none. When I stepped out of my uniform for the last time I stripped off the last vestige of army life and took up my life, to a great extent, where I had dropped it. . . .

The time I spent in service was one of the greatest experiences I ever had. I saw much of the world I would most certainly would not have seen otherwise. I did not see the victims of the war that an infantryman, or a front line man, would encounter. I saw devastation but not the victims. I am sure this helped me remain an actor who would eventually remove his makeup and become himself once more.

*Willie Lawton, a black veteran of World War II, had only unpleasant and bitter memories when interviewed in 1970:*

I most certainly think the Negro GI of World War II did play a great part in the changed overt thinking and behavior of the white military because we'd take so much and that was all. But if I had it to do over again I would take off for Canada like many of the fellows have recently done. We were supposedly sent over there to do a job, fighting for our country, when it really added up to traveling half way around the world to endure the same insults from the same people. . . .

The war was a thing I wanted to forget. I've never put on my uniform since I took it off. I've never marched in any parade. I have never applied for my citation. It is something I'd rather forget because it was a bad dream, a real nightmare.

*SOURCE:* Reprinted from Mary P. Motley, *The Invisible Soldier: The Experience of the Black Soldier in World War II* (Detroit, Mich.: Wayne State University Press, 1987). Copyright © 1975 by Mary P. Motley, ed., by permission of the Wayne State University Press. Excerpt is from pp. 103–04, 177–78.

*RELATED ARTICLES: African Americans in the Military; Combat, Effects of; Port Chicago Mutiny; World War II*

## 1945 c

### Soldiers' Poems on the Horrors of War

*Two GIs in the Italian war zone wrote poems for* The Stars and Stripes *that reveal the terror of those who experienced heavy combat:*

Battle

The blackness was in me,
Such fate and fury as I had never known:
Complete amnesia from love and spring,
And tenderness of home.
Surging through me, I could feel it rise
And lift me with it.
I was free, to lust for blood,
And I could use my hands
To tear and smash . . .
My eyes to sight for killing!
The noises, whistling, wooming
In the blackness
Became a part of me,
Spurred my passion, lashed me on,
Became fused with my mind's unwholesomeness:
I would caress, with savagery,
And put them all in hell forever.
I willed to butcher as they had butchered,
Destroy as they had destroyed.
I sobbed aloud as no man has ever cried:
Someone screamed, maybe me. I could smell
Powder, burnt flesh, maybe mine . . .
I think I died then.
I don't want to remember any more . . .
God knows—I wish I could forget.

—Sgt. S. Colker

Home from War

Who can say at war's end
"We are lucky living men?"
After so much of us has died
How can we be satisfied
That we, the so-called living men,
Will find a way to live again?
For when a man has daily faced
The brute within him, low, debased,
Can he look forward to the light,
Wipe out the memories of the fight
Forget the strange erotic bliss
That comes with some cheap purchased kiss?
Ah, no! And it will be his fateful lot
To live on and find that he lives not
Though like the living we'll behave
We'll be the dead without a grave.

—Cpl. Anthony Carlin

*SOURCE:* Charles A. Hogan and John Welsh, comps., *Puptent Poets of the "Stars and Stripes, Mediterranean"* (Naples, Italy: Stars and Stripes, 1945), 18, 109.

*RELATED ARTICLES: Combat, Effects of; Literature and War; World War II*

## 1945 d

### John Ciardi's "A Box Comes Home"

*John Ciardi flew 16 missions as a gunner on an Army Air Force B-29 over Japan. He was then assigned to write letters of condolence to next of kin. After leaving the service, he wrote several successful volumes of poetry, some of which drew upon his wartime experience.*

I remember the United States of America
As a flag-draped box with Arthur in it
And six marines to bear it on their shoulders.

I wonder how someone once came to remember
The Empire of the East and the Empire of the West.
As an urn maybe delivered by chariot.

You could bring Germany back on a shield once
And France in a plume. England, I suppose,
Kept coming back a long time as a letter.

Once I saw Arthur dressed as the United States
Of America. Now I see the United States
Of America as Arthur in a flag-sealed domino.

And I would pray more good of Arthur
Than I can wholly believe. I would pray
An agreement with the United States of America

To equal Arthur's living as it equals his dying
At the red-taped grave in Woodmere
By the rain and oakleaves on the domino.

*SOURCE:* Robert Hedin, ed., *Old Glory: American War Poems from the Revolutionary War to the War on Terrorism* (New York: Persea Books, 2004), 223. Poem reprinted by permission from Ciardi Family Publishing Trust.

*RELATED ENTRIES: American Veterans Committee; Literature and War, World War II*

## 1945 e

### EXCERPT FROM BILL MAULDIN'S *BRASS RING*

*Later in the war, after drawing several cartoons for The Stars and Stripes unflattering to officers, Bill Mauldin was ordered to report to Gen. George Patton for a "dressing down." Supreme Allied Commander Gen. Dwight Eisenhower, one of Mauldin's many appreciative readers, saw to it that this interview would not end badly for the young sergeant. In any event, this is how Mauldin reported the meeting. The passage begins with Mauldin's entertaining description of an encounter he had enroute with MPs and a provost marshal who wanted to know what a sergeant was doing, alone, in a jeep that he claimed (correctly) had been assigned to him.*

"If you'll make a couple of calls we can get all this straightened out." I offered.

"No doubt. The question is, who do we call?"

"Well, you could try General Patton's headquarters—there's a Major Quirk there—or maybe you could try Captain Harry Butcher at SHAEF."

"Butcher?"

"He's General Eisenhower's aide."

"Now we got Eisenhower in the act, with a lousy captain for an aide. If you're going to try to bullshit your way out of this, you ought to at least study the tables of organization."

"Sir, he's a captain in the navy. That's the same as a colonel in the army."

"So Eisenhower, who runs the army in Europe, has a ship's captain for his aide. . . . Listen, I'll make a deal with you, you loony bastard. I'll call this Major Quirk. I don't guarantee I'll get him, mind you, but I'll speak to his office. You got this thing on your mind about calling somebody's office, maybe it'll relieve you or something. Actually, by rules we're supposed to check all stories later anyway for a report, but as a favor I'll do it right now. Meanwhile, we're going to keep that jeep. You won't need it any more.

"It's a deal, " I said. "If I don't have an appointment with Patton you keep the jeep."

"General Patton, sergeant!"

He made the call. He didn't get Quirk, but somebody in the office straightened him out. The provost was a sport. He even laughed a little.

"We'd better get this man on his way, corporal. We've made him late."

"Oh, that's all right," I said, airily, "the appointment was pretty well open, depending on when I got there."

Patton had taken over Luxembourg's royal palace. I was scrutinized and passed by a small task force of vitamin-packed MPs with mirror-toed shoes and simonized head-gear, then directed to Quirk's office in a downstairs wing of the magnificent building. The major turned out to be a nice man—so far I was having remarkably good luck with Patton's subordinates—and although he too inspected me carefully from head to toe, I could see that he was doing it for my own good. He led me through the story-book palace, full of huge, ornate, high-ceilinged rooms. Patton's office must have been the throne room, the grandest of them all. It had great double doors. One was ajar; standing slightly behind the major as he discreetly rapped, I could see the general's desk at the far end of the room, across an acre of carpet.

There he sat, big as life even at that distance. His hair was silver, his face was pink, his collar and shoulders glittered with more stars than I could count, his fingers sparkled with rings, and an incredible mass of ribbons started around desktop level and spread upward in a flood over his chest to the very top of his shoulder, as if preparing to march down his back, too. His face was rugged, with an odd, strangely shapeless outline, his eyes were pale, almost colorless, with a choleric bulge. His small, compressed mouth was sharply downturned at the corners, with a lower lip which suggested a pouting child as much as a no-nonsense martinet. It was a welcome, rather human touch. Beside him, lying in a big chair, was Willie, the bull terrier. If ever dog was suited to master this one was. Willie had his beloved boss's expression and lacked only the ribbons and stars. I stood in that door staring into the four meanest eyes I'd ever seen.

"Come in, major," Patton said. Somehow, it broke the spell. There was that shrill voice again. Like the lower lip it brought him down to human proportions. We made the long trek across the room and came to a parade-ground halt before the desk, where I snapped out the kind of salute I used to make in high-school ROTC. Whatever of the parade-ground soldier was still left in me, Patton brought it out.

"Hello, sergeant." The general smiled—an impressive muscular feat, considering the distance the corners of his mouth had to travel—and came around the desk to offer his hand. I don't know who was more astonished, Willie or me. The dog, rising with his master, literally fell out of the chair. As we shook hands, I stole a glance at the general's famous gun belt. He was wearing only one of his pearl-handled six-shooters. Under-gunned, shaking hands, smiling—all were hopeful signs. Patton told me to sit. I appropriated Willie's chair. The dog not only looked shocked now but offended. To hell with Willie. Butcher had been right. This was going to be O.K.

"Well, sir, I'll be going," the major said.

"Going where?" Patton snapped. "Stick around. I want you to hear this."

The major hesitated for the barest instant, glanced at me—he was aware of the agreement for privacy—and took the adjacent chair. The old chill started back up my spine.

"Now then, sergeant, about those pictures you draw of those god-awful things you call soldiers. Where did you ever see soldiers like that? You know goddamn well you're not drawing an accurate representation of the American soldier. You make them look like goddamn bums. No respect for the army, their officers, or themselves. You know as well as I do that you can't have an army without respect for officers. What are you trying to do, incite a goddamn mutiny? You listen to me, sergeant, the Russians tried running an army without rank once. Shot all their leaders, all their brains, all their generals. The Bolsheviks made their officers dress like soldiers, eat with soldiers, no saluting, everybody calling everybody Comrade—and where did it get 'em? While they ran an army like that they couldn't fight their way out of a piss-soaked paper bag. Now they've learned their lesson. They put uniforms back on their officers. Some men are born to lead and don't need those little metal dinguses on their shoulders. Hell, I could command troops in a G-string. But in wartime you're bound to get some officers who don't know how to act without being dressed for it. The Russians learned you have to have rank and if some comrade looks cross-eyed at a superior today he gets his teeth kicked in. When somebody says 'frog' he jumps. And now he fights. How long do you think you'd last drawing those pictures in the Russian army?"

The question turned out to be rhetorical. I opened my mouth to say that I realized the necessity of discipline and had never thought officers should be called Comrade, chosen by popular elections among their troops, or deprived of the dinguses on their shoulders. But I quickly shut it again, and kept it shut for the next twenty minutes or so as the general reeled off examples of the necessity for rank through four thousand years of military history.

For a while it was fascinating. Patton was a real master of his subject. I have an affinity for enthusiasts, anyway, in any field of endeavor; as I sat there listening to the general talk war, I felt truly privileged, as if I were hearing Michelangelo on painting. I had been too long enchanted by the army myself—as a child listening to my father's stories, as a high-school boy dreaming of West Point—to be anything but impressed by this magnificent old performer's monologue. Just as when I had first saluted him, I felt whatever martial spirit was left in me being lifted out and fanned into flame.

At one point, somewhere around the Hellenic wars, when once again the value of stern leadership was being extolled, I absently reached out to see if Willie's ear needed scratching. I was stopped by a dog owner's reflex which reminded me never to handle another man's pet uninvited. A glance at Willie confirmed this. Had I touched his ear it would have been with my left, or working hand, and I think he would have put me out of business, accomplishing in one snap what his master was trying to do the hard way.

When Patton had worked his way back through the Russian revolution to the present again, he got around to my cartoons.

"Sergeant," he said, "I don't know what you think you're trying to do, but the krauts ought to pin a medal on you for helping them mess up discipline for us. I'm going to show you what I consider some prime goddamn examples of what I mean by creating disrespect."

He opened a drawer and came up with a small batch of cutouts from Stars and Stripes. On top was a street scene I had drawn of a French town being liberated. A convoy of motorized infantry was being deluged by flowers, fruit, and wine, handed up from the street and dropped out of windows by hysterically happy citizens. Some of the soldiers were taking advantage of the general confusion and pelting the convoy commander, in an open command car in front, with riper samples of the fruit.

"My, sir," says a junior officer, "what an enthusiastic welcome."

The general held the next one up by the tips of his thumb and forefinger as if it were contaminated. It was a night scene of a war-battered opera house with a USO show advertised on the marquee: "GIRLS, GIRLS, GIRLS. Fresh from the States!" Queued up in the snow at the front door was a long line of weary-looking soldiers of various nationalities, mostly British and American, with their coat collars turned up against the raw weather and their sad faces filled with anticipation of the charms within. It was one of my better drawings: loaded with poignancy, I thought. Queued up at the stage door were the officers, of course, all spruced up and waiting to take the girls out. Some even had bouquets.

"Now this," shrilled the general, "is the kind of goddamn . . . where are the words under this one? Somebody cut off the goddamn words!"

"Sir, there wasn't any caption under that one." Willie, the major, and I all jumped at the sound of my voice.

"No words!"

"No. sir. I didn't think it needed any."

"All right. You've got a bunch of messy goddamn soldiers in one line and a bunch of officers in another. What's it mean?"

He was going to let me speak again. It was really too much for Willie, who got up and stiffly walked to his master's side, ready for anything.

"Sir, it means the soldiers want to look at the girls and the officers want to take them out."

"Well, what the hell's wrong with that?"

"Nothing, sir," I weaseled. "I didn't imply anything was wrong. I just thought it was a humorous situation." No ordeal is worse than that of a cartoonist who has to explain his creation to a reader.

"You think the soldiers ought to get laid instead of the officers, don't you?" Patton growled.

In spite of himself he couldn't help grinning slightly at this; in spite of myself I couldn't help liking him a little for it.

"Sir, it has been my experience that when USO or Red Cross girls are to be had the officers usually get them."

"And what business is that of yours, sergeant?"

"None, sir. I just thought it was an amusing situation and I drew it as I saw it."

"It doesn't amuse me."

"To tell you the truth, sir, it doesn't seem very funny to me, either, any more," I said, honestly.

"Well, by God, now we're getting somewhere. Now, why did you draw this picture if it wasn't to create disrespect for the officers?"

He sat back in his chair, put his fingertips together in a listening attitude, and I got my chance at my only speech of the day.

"General," I said, "suppose a soldier's been overseas for a couple of years and in the line for a couple of months without a break, then he gets a few days in a rest area and goes to a USO show. He knows there's not much chance of getting next to one of the girls, but it would mean a lot to him if she'd circulate among the boys for a while after the show and at least give them the pleasure of talking to a girl from the States. Usually, there's not a chance. She arrives in a colonel's jeep two seconds before showtime and leaves in a gen . . . some other colonel's staff car before the curtain's down."

Patton's eyes glittered menacingly, but he did not interrupt.

"All right, sir, the soldier goes back to his foxhole," I said, "and he's thinking about it. He doesn't blame the girl—after all, he figures, she's a free agent, she did her bit by entertaining him, and it's her own business how she entertains herself. Nobody in her right mind would go out with soldiers when officers have better whiskey and facilities. The soldier knows all this. And he doesn't blame the officer for going after the girl, either. That's only human. . . ."

"Jesus Christ, major, does this make sense to you?" the general growled. "Well, I told Butcher I'd let this man speak his piece."

"I'm almost finished, sir. My point is, the soldier is back in his foxhole stewing about officers and thinking he's got the short end of the stick in everything, even women. Whether it makes sense or not, the fact is that he feels there's been an injustice, and if he stews long enough about this, or about any of the other hundreds of things soldiers stew about, he's not going to be thinking about his job. All right, sir, he picks up his paper and he reads a letter or sees a cartoon by some other soldier who feels the same way, and he says, 'Hell, somebody else said it for me,' and he goes back to his job."

"All I've got to say to you, sergeant," Patton said, "is that if this soldier you're talking about is stewing it's because he hasn't got enough to do. He wasn't put in that hole to stew, or to think, or to have somebody else do his thinking for him in a goddamn newspaper.

"I don't know where you got those stripes on your arm, but you'd put 'em to a lot better use getting out and teaching respect to soldiers instead of encouraging them to bitch and beef and gripe and run around with beards on their faces and holes in their elbows. Now I've just got one last thing to say to you." He looked at his watch. Forty-five minutes had gone by. "You can't run an army like a mob."

"Sir," I protested, "I never thought you could."

"Think over what I've said. All right, sergeant, I guess we understand each other now."

"Yes, sir."

We did not shake goodbye. My parting salute was at least as good as the first one, but I don't think anyone noticed. The major and I started the long hike across the carpet and I heard Willie's chair creak as he climbed back on his perch.

Will Lang was waiting outside. As one of the instigators of the meeting he felt entitled to first crack at the story. I said Patton had received me courteously, had expressed his feelings about my work, and had given me the opportunity to say a few words myself. I didn't think I had convinced him of anything, and I didn't think he had changed my mind much, either.

Years later I read Butcher's account of reading Lang's Time story to Patton over the phone. When he quoted me as saying I hadn't changed Patton's mind, there was a chuckle. When he came to the part about the general not changing my mind, either, there was a high-pitched explosion and more talk about throwing me in jail if I ever showed up again in Third Army. Time didn't print the part about the general violating the agreement by keeping the major in the office during the interview. If I'd been quoted on that I'm convinced he'd have set Willie after me.

*SOURCE:* Bill Mauldin, *The Brass Ring* (New York: W. W. Norton, 1971). Reprinted by permission of the Estate of Bill Mauldin and the Watkins/Loomis Agency.

*RELATED ARTICLES: Mauldin, Bill; Patton, George S.; World War II*

# 1945 f

### Excerpts from *Company Commander* by Charles B. MacDonald

*Charles MacDonald's Company Commander is one of the best autobiographical accounts by an American of combat in the European theater of operations. He led his advancing infantry company effectively for several months against German resistance, losing only a few of his men. His straightforward prose provides insights into two dilemmas that frontline officers like MacDonald sometimes confronted: subordinates who killed an enemy POW and superiors who proved to be disappointing.*

It seemed that since we were now in a "quiet" position every officer in the division with the rank of major or above wanted to inspect the company area. They condemned the men for not having shaved or for wearing knit wool caps without their helmets, evidently an unpardonable misdemeanor, or for untidy areas around the dugouts. The officers did not inspect my 1st Platoon area, however, usually passing it over with the excuse that it was a bit far to walk, but we laughed inwardly, knowing that it was the threat of enemy shelling that kept most of them away.

I finally protested the inspections to Captain Anderson, and a captain from regiment was sent up a few days later with the primary mission of inspecting my 1st Platoon area. That was the virtual end of the inspections, however; either from my protest or the fact that all the inspection-minded "brass" had satisfied their egos with visits to "the front." We wondered how many Silver Stars and Distinguished Service Crosses came from the visits.

• • •

"Come out with your hands up or I'll shoot your nuts off, you Nazi sonofabitch!" a soldier yelled.

He fired a single shot into the underbrush.

The fir branches stirred. A dark figure emerged slowly from the brush, and I could see that it was a German soldier with his hands raised high above his head. He wore no cap or helmet, but a dirty, blood-stained bandage stretched across his forehead. Choosing each step carefully, he advanced across the firebreak.

"Do not shoot. Do not shoot."

Two of my men grabbed him roughly and searched him for weapons.

"I have no gun," the German said in carefully chosen English. "My comrades have left me when I am wounded."

"Bring him along," I said, designating two men to walk with him. "We'll send him back when we get where we're going.". . .

I turned my attention to the prisoner, directing the two men who were with him to take him to the A Company positions. I had lost contact with the rear CP group by radio and wanted them to contact Lieutenant Smith, who should be at the A Company positions now. The men were afraid they could not find the positions. Our circuitous route through the woods had confused them, but they said they would try.

"Would you be kind to give me cigarette?" the prisoner asked.

"Why you Nazi sonofabitch," one of the guards answered, kicking the prisoner in the rear, "of all the goddamned nerve. If it wasn't for you and all your ---------- kind, all of us could be smoking now."

The patrol from the 1st Platoon returned. . . .

The two men who had taken the prisoner to the rear returned. They had made a quick trip.

"Did you get him back OK?" I asked.

"Yessir," they answered and turned quickly toward their platoons.

"Wait a minute," I said. "Did you find A Company? What did Lieutenant Smith say?"

The men hesitated. One spoke out suddenly.

"To tell you the truth, Cap'n, we didn't get to A Company. The sonofabitch tried to make a run for it. Know what I mean?"

"Oh, I see," I said slowly, nodding my head. "I see."

• • •

The buildings along the street grew in height and density until we knew that at last we were in the outskirts of Leipzig. Civilians formed in thick bunches as if to watch a parade.

A voice beckoned me from an open window, and I recognized a soldier from battalion headquarters. The Colonel was inside and wanted to see me. I halted the column, and the men sat down on the edges of the sidewalks, unperturbed by the unabashed stares of the curious civilians.

Inside the building the Colonel and the battalion staff were eating breakfast. The sight startled me at first and I said a bad word to myself. The pursuit of the war could not wait long enough for the rifle companies to eat, but there was time for battalion headquarters to breakfast in the luxury of a house that the sweat of the rifle companies had taken. I passed it off as another of the injustices to which we had become accustomed.

• • •

The battalion staff arrived on the hill, and Colonel Smith overrode my objections to firing the machine guns. I did not object because I saw the men from the patrol squad had reached the railroad tracks and four Germans jumped up from their foxholes and surrendered. I knew the town was ours. The other two squads from the 3d Platoon started down the hill, and the 1st Platoon followed.

The six machine guns chattered, their tracers spanning the town in a great fiery arc to burn themselves into the hill beyond. Lieutenant Reed called for artillery on the fleeing Germans.

An enemy machine gun opened up suddenly from the railroad tracks to the right front. The fire was high over our heads and did no damage, but the battalion staff cleared the hill as if by magic. The enemy gunner fired another burst, and I told our own machine gunners to cease firing, almost grateful to the enemy gunner who had fired and cleared the hill of the battalion staff.

• • •

We had already set up our defenses for the night in Altsattel and were delighted to find that the town still had electricity, when Colonel Smith arrived. I was dead tired from the fifteen-mile walk, and I felt that if he said to continue, I would surely fall to the ground exhausted.

He said we would continue to the next town of Prostiborg, however, and I cursed to myself, but there was nothing to do but forget our fatigue and move on.

I assembled the company at the eastern edge of town, and the machine gunners went into position in the last buildings, covering a wide expanse of valley which ended in a high tree-covered ridge which the highway crossed a mile and one-half from Altsattel. According to my map, Prostiborg lay at the foot of the ridge on the other side, two miles from Altsattel.

I sent the 3d Platoon forward initially, deciding it would be foolish to expose the entire company in the open valley until we discovered if the ridge would be defended. The battalion staff arrived and watched with me from a small knoll at the edge of town.

"Have your men push right along, Mac," the Colonel said. "There's nothing out there." The phrase had become so familiar that it was maddening.

As if it had been waiting for the cue, a round of incoming artillery whistled overhead. It was so strange to hear a round of enemy artillery, that we were almost convinced that it was one of our own rounds, but a second round a few minutes later exploded a hundred yards from the knoll and removed any doubt. It was a German gun. The battalion staff cleared the knoll in one dash, and I was left to run the attack without interruption.

"I'll bet battalion thinks we're in cahoots with the Krauts," Lieutenant Reed said, and winked.

*SOURCE:* Excerpts from Charles B. MacDonald, *Company Commander* (New York: Ballantine Books, 1947), 82–83, 141–42, 264, 300–01, 303–04. 

*RELATED ARTICLES: Literature and War; World War II*

## 1946 a

### Remarks of Navajo Veteran on Serving in the Military

*"John Nez," a Rimrock Reservation Navajo, could speak English and had been to school for 10 years before being drafted in 1941. When he returned after the war, he was unwilling to be a traditional "reservation Indian."*

I was glad at first to get back and see the folks. Then I got too lonely. It was too lonesome. I didn't like the country too well. Not only around here, but the whole New Mexico. I didn't like the people. Not only the Indians but also the Mexicans and the white people. It just seems that I didn't get along here. It was especially the Indians around here; too much government control, don't have as much freedom. I felt after being in the army and being told to do this and that, that when I got back I could make a living the way I wanted to instead of being told what to do. . . . When I was away from the reservation, I felt that I had more freedom and I can go anyplace where a white man goes like bars and places that are restricted to Indians on the reservation. I went around with white boys a lot of places where I can't do it here in New Mexico. . . . I wanted to put up some kind of business. I started thinking about it while I was in France in the hospital. Ever since they talk about getting GI loans, I thought anybody could get it. I didn't know it was so difficult. I was thinking about a small trading post. I was thinking about going to school and getting commercial training first. Eddie and I start going around asking people in government administration about it, but it didn't turn out right.

• • •

[The former headman of his community talked to an anthropologist about "John's" behavior after returning from the service:]

I heard John say that he wants to be in big cities, be with white people all the time, and keep clean like he did in the army. But that's what he said when he first got back and still had some money. Now he's broke, and I haven't heard him say it any more. And he's still living out here with the rest of us. . . . I don't know how he was acting before he go to army, but people just been telling me he came back from army and he got a little bit smart among his people when he came home. He told his people that he been to army and he got wounded over there, and white doctors got him well. And he says he's brave, he says, nobody could kill him. That's why he's drinking all the time, he says, he wants to fight with his people. He says he knows how to fight and was trained for it. That's when he's drinking he says that. . . . He thought he had lots of money, and he could drink all he wanted. Then he got broke pretty soon and lose all that money. He thought he had plenty of money to do anything, and nobody would bother him.

• • •

["John" was asked to look at some "Veteran's Apperception Test" pictures of vague, shadowy forms and to construct a story to accompany them:]

#5. This veteran just got back from overseas. The other fellow is a white man. He is trying to get him behind a house because he is a bootlegger and he knows the GI has a lot of money and he is trying to sell him some liquor at a high price. But the soldier refused to listen to him. He's got a lot of experience. He was a corporal in the army and so he went home. He is a good soldier.

#2. This soldier has been away for quite a long time and he's finally got home. He came home to the reservation and found everything about the same as when he left. He stayed around home for a few months—then he re-enlists. He went back to Europe to Germany on occupation duties. [Why did he go back into the army?] For several reasons. Because he doesn't like to stay around home and it's too lonesome and he couldn't find a job that would suit him.

#1. This soldier came home a second time. First he came home and then he re-enlist again but this time he came home for good. He came home with sergeant stripes. A lot of people were waiting for him when he came home. This time he learned mechanics job. So he got himself a job downtown. [And then what happens?] And that's where he is.

#6. (Laughs) The two brothers from somewhere in the reservation came back from the armed service. They were both in the Marine Corps in the same division. They were fighting Japs in the South Pacific. They were doing special duties in the Signal Corps. They came home after the Jap defeat. They came home and found folks and everything were the same. And they don't know just what to do yet. But they don't want to stay around home [Why?] They got a hard time getting readjusted back to civilian life. They been away too long. [Tell me a little about why they have a hard time.] They just don't feel right around home, they feel that they should go outside the reservation where they can become free. . . .

*SOURCE:* Evon Z. Vogt, "Navajo Veterans," Papers of the Peabody Museum of American Archaeology and Ethnology, Harvard University, vol. 41, no. 1, 1951: 53–54, 183–84. Reprinted courtesy of the Peabody Museum of American Archaeology and Ethnology, Harvard University.

*"John Nez" found it very difficult to live on the reservation after Army service. "Yazi Begay," who knew no English and had never been away from Rimrock before being drafted, found the post-service readjustment to reservation life easier, albeit he had changed some of his ways.*

When I came back from the army, came back home, I don't like it here very well. It's kind of quiet. Where I been there's lots of noise, lots of noise, lots of things to see. Out here there's nothing to see, just woods. Nothing going on. Just sleep on the ground, not on a bed. Long ways to go to town too. I don't like to stay around here. I felt that way for about a month. Kind of lonesome to go back over to the camps. Also the whole Rimrock area here, it seems a whole lot changed around. But now I don't feel that way. Now I'm all right. . . .

Well, when I came back from the army, my home was the same as it was when I left. But when I came back I said, "I'm going to change it a little bit different." They were living the old way when I came home. It's a whole lot different now. I made a new house and some hogans. It's a whole lot better now. The time I left, they made a fire right on the ground inside the hogan. They had it that way when I came home too. But now I don't do that. I just get hold of a big cook stove. That's what I'm using now. When I came back I said to my wife and her folks, "How come you still living the old way? You should build a hogan the new way and make it nice inside." Now I make it a whole lot different; got a new stove and everything. The old way what people used to do, they didn't put any stove in hogan. The fire made it all black inside hogan. I want it like the white people's way. Keep the hogan nice and clean. That's the way I like it.

[The headman in "Yazi's" community talked about "Yazi" with an anthropologist, Evon Vogt:]

Yazi Begay was telling me about himself. When he first went to the army, he says he know just a few words of English and it was hard when he got into the army, especially when he don't understand English. After he got used to it and learned a few words of English it wasn't so hard. First he said he was with some Mexican who taught him some English words. He got along like that. And he seen lots of things that were hard for him to do. He stay down there three years. He says he learned a lot of white people's things. Lots of different kinds of things. Machine guns, bombs, everything. He would rather be in that way he says. He wish he could understand English just as well as white people. He just wish that but he don't understand English. He says the white people are a long way ahead of us. Way ahead. We will never catch up. They are making a lot of things. Airplanes. Machine guns. And they sure know how to handle soldiers. He says he learned that when he was down there. He says he is glad that he seen all that, and he's glad he's been over the ocean. First when he start, he never did like it. But after all he liked it. He says he wish he knew more education like them other boys do. When he first came back, he says he had a little money ahead. He could have built up a little store or something else, so as to make a good living—if he only knew how to read, he says he could do that. But he can't do it now he says. He likes white ways just as much as he knows English. He would go on if he knew more English.

[The wife of the Rimrock trader talked about "Yazi" too:]

There has been more change in Yazi Begay than anybody else. He kept himself clean when he got back, and he knew a few words of English. He was a regular old Navaho when he left, but now he's not so bashful. He comes right up to the counter and tells me what he wants. When he first got back, he bought a toothbrush, toothpaste, towel, washrag, bar of soap, shaving cream—everything to keep himself clean.

*SOURCE:* Evon Z. Vogt, "Navajo Veterans," Papers of the Peabody Museum of American Archaeology and Ethnology, Harvard University, vol. 41, no. 1, 1951: 158, 160–61. Reprinted courtesy of the Peabody Museum of American Archaeology and Ethnology, Harvard University. Compare E. Vogt and J. Adair, "Navajo and Zuni Veterans," *American Anthropologist* (1949): 547 ff.

*RELATED ENTRIES: GI Bills; Native Americans in the Military; World War II*

# 1946 b

## EXCERPTS FROM *HIROSHIMA*, BY JOHN HERSEY

*John Hersey's straightforward report on his interviews with a number of survivors of the atomic bombing of Hiroshima was published in its entirety as a single issue of The New Yorker magazine on August 31, 1946. His frank style was compelling, as these passages indicate, and its impact on Americans and others throughout the world would be significant.*

Dr. Fujii sat down cross-legged in his underwear on the spotless matting of the porch, put on his glasses, and started reading the Osaka Asahi. He liked to read the Osaka news because his wife was there. He saw the flash. To him—faced away from the center and looking at his paper—it seemed a brilliant yellow. Startled, he began to rise to his feet. In that moment (he was 1,550 yards from the center), the hospital leaned behind his rising and, with a terrible ripping noise, toppled into the river. The Doctor, still in the act of getting to his feet, was thrown forward and around and over; he was buffeted and gripped; he lost track of everything, because things were so speeded up; he felt the water.

Dr. Fujii hardly had time to think that he was dying before he realized that he was alive, squeezed tightly by two long timbers in a V across his chest, like a morsel suspended between two huge chopsticks—held upright.

• • •

Everything fell, and Miss Sasaki lost consciousness. The ceiling dropped suddenly and the wooden floor above collapsed in splinters and the people up there came down and the roof above them gave way; but principally and first of all, the bookcases right behind her swooped forward and the contents threw her down, with her left leg horribly twisted and breaking underneath her. There, in the tin factory, in the first moment of the atomic age, a human being was crushed by books.

• • •

Outside the gate of the park, Father Kleinsorge found a faucet that still worked—part of the plumbing of a vanished house—and he filled his vessels and returned. When he had given the wounded the water, he made a second trip. This time the woman by the bridge was dead. On his way back with the water, he got lost on a detour around a fallen tree, and as he looked for his way through the woods, he heard a voice ask from the underbrush, "Have you anything to drink?" He saw a uniform. Thinking there was just one soldier, he approached with the water. When he had penetrated the bushes, he saw there were about twenty men, and they were all in exactly the same nightmarish state: their faces were wholly burned, their eyesockets were hollow, the fluid from their melted eyes had run down their cheeks. (They must have had their face upturned when the bomb went off; perhaps they were anti-aircraft personnel.) Their mouths were mere swollen, pus-covered wounds, which they could not bear to stretch enough to admit the spout of the teapot. So Father Kleinsorge got a large piece of grass and drew out the stem so as to make a straw, and gave them all water to drink that way.

• • •

Dr. Sasaki and his colleagues at the Red Cross Hospital watched the unprecedented disease unfold and at last evolved a theory about its nature. It had, they decided, three stages. The first stage had been all over before the doctors even knew they were dealing with a new sickness; it was the direct reaction to the bombardment of the body, at the moment when the bomb went off, by neutrons, beta particles, and gamma rays. The apparently uninjured people who had died so mysteriously in the first few hours or days had succumbed in this first stage. It killed ninety-five per cent of the people within a half mile of the center, and many thousands who were farther away. The doctors realized in retrospect that even though most of these dead had also suffered from burns and blast effects, they had absorbed enough radiation to kill them. The rays simply destroyed body cells—caused their nuclei to degenerate and broke their walls. Many people who did not die right away came down with nausea, headache, diarrhea, malaise, and fever, which lasted several days. Doctors could not be certain whether some of these symptoms were the result of radiation or nervous shock. The second stage set in ten or fifteen days after the bombing. Its first symptom was falling hair. Diarrhea and fever, which in some cases went as high as 106, came next. Twenty-five to thirty days after the explosion, blood disorders appeared: gums bled, the white-blood-cell count dropped sharply, and petechiae appeared on the skin and mucous membranes. The drop in the number of white blood corpuscles reduced the patient's capacity to resist infection, so open wounds were usually slow in healing and many of the sick developed sore throats and mouths. The two key symptoms, on which the doctors came to base their prognosis, were fever and the lowered white-corpuscle count. If fever remained steady and high, the patient's chances for survival were poor. The white count almost always dropped below four thousand; a patient whose count fell below one thousand had little hope of living. Toward the end of the second stage, if the patient survived, anemia, or a drop in the red blood count, also set in. The third stage was the reaction that came when the body struggled to compensate for its ills—when, for instance, the white count not only returned to normal but increased to much higher than normal levels. In this stage, many patients died of complications, such as infections in the chest cavity.

*SOURCE:* From John Hersey, *Hiroshima.* (New York: Alfred A. Knopf, 1985). Copyright 1946, 1985, and 1974 by John Hersey. Used by permission of Alfred A. Knopf, a division of Random House, Inc.

*RELATED ENTRIES: Literature and War; Hiroshima; Manhattan Project; World War II*

## 1947

### Excerpts from Bill Mauldin's *Back Home*

*Bill Mauldin returned from the war a Pulitzer prize-winning cartoonist syndicated in more than 100 newspapers. After practicing his trade for some time stateside, he presented a number of his observations in Back Home, published in 1947. These passages by a staunch liberal and enthusiastic member of the American Veterans Committee reflect on the benefits of the GI Bill of Rights, the Baby Boom, the problems vets with families faced in finding housing, his own "survivor guilt," his rejection of racist, anti-Semitic, and ethnocentric views rampant in the service, his championing of Japanese Americans, and his fear that Cold War America might pursue foreign and military policies that would support fascist dictatorships in the world and militarism at home.*

The people who feared that the army had created a generation of bums were in for a surprise when it turned out that veteran-students were as a rule far above their classmates in applying themselves to their work and in scholastic achievement. Many people who teach in schools where numbers of veterans have enrolled feel that most of them were sobered and matured considerably by their wartime experiences and army service and thus have a far greater appreciation of the values of an education than their classmates who, for the most part, are still dependent upon their parents for support and spending money and haven't yet been faced with the hard facts of life. Also, a hell of a lot of the college vets were married, and marital responsibility can keep a young gent's nose to the grindstone like nothing else. Carl Rose did a New Yorker cartoon in this connection which is a real masterpiece. He filled a full page with a detailed drawing of a commencement exercise, with hundreds of young men in caps and gowns looking somewhat wryly at the distinguished old speaker on the platform, who says, as dozens of young wives sit on the side lines with babies swarming over them, ". . . . and as you leave these tranquil, ivied walls to face the stern realities of life. . . ."

Two great problems beset the veterans who went back to school: money, because the GI Bill of Rights provided them with a sum that fell pitifully short of the amount required for the barest necessities; and housing. While I didn't do many drawings about the schools themselves, I spattered a lot of ink around on the housing situation.

• • •

I had had more than a speaking acquaintance with the international fracas that had just ended, and couldn't subdue a sneaking feeling of wonderment and guilt that old man Mars, who had started me in the same boat with several million other guys, had kicked most of them in the teeth, but had in the end treated me so well. I have talked with several other gents who came out of the war in better shape than when they went in, and they have told me they share that feeling. None of us has been inclined to act like a slob about it — weeping in his beer about the fortunes of war and his poor lost comrades and that sort of spectacular stuff — but we all had friends who were killed or crippled or had their lives, marriages, or careers wrecked in the past few years, and while we went ahead and enjoyed our good fortune, we did a little silent thinking to ourselves. It does throw a slight damper on your exuberance.

• • •

Somewhere in my early childhood and in the army I developed a rather suspicious and rebellious attitude toward stuffed shirts, and since it has been my experience that more stuffed shirts are to be found in the higher ranks of wealth and position than anywhere else, I find myself more often in sympathy with the people who oppose the "elite" than not.

• • •

I remember that one of the first shocks I got when I went to live in California after being discharged was the attitude among many residents toward the Japanese-Americans on the West Coast. I had grown up in New Mexico and Arizona, where I had heard some talk in my childhood about the "Japs" and the "Chinks" who "worked so cheaply and threatened the standard of living of the white men," but there hadn't been much of it, because in the places where I had lived Orientals were very scarce. The prejudices I had picked up early in life were confined to a vague feeling of aloofness toward people of Mexican extraction, who account for a good part of the population in that area, and a mild anti-Semitism, which came more from hearsay than anything else. So, because my childhood had been luckily devoid of extensive indoctrination in the glories of being a white Protestant, I came out of the army minus the few prejudices I had carried into it. During my service, I had seen some boorish Negroes, some unpleasant Jews, and some obnoxious Catholics, but I couldn't honestly say that there were any more bums in their ranks than among the "pure." The behavior of the soldiers I saw was good or bad in accordance with their upbringing and their character, rather than with their faith or ancestry.

It would be lovely if the statement, made by so many idealists, were true—that association with all races, creeds, and colors in the army cured everybody of his prejudices. Men from some areas had been taught almost from birth by family, friends, teachers, and even clergymen in some cases, to hate racial or religious groups other than their own. A few years in the army will not delouse a mind that has been that thoroughly poisoned. If a drunken Negro soldier made a spectacle of himself, he was typical of all Negroes; if a Jewish soldier was brave, he proved that Jews are troublesome; if he was timid, he proved the Jews are cowards; if he had money, he proved that Jews are selfish; if he was broke, he proved that Jews are worthless. To the minds of the indoctrinated, a bad non-Aryan was typical of his group, while a bad Aryan was nothing but a single renegade. Those of us whose indoctrination had been slight were lucky, because we were able to see all kinds of people under all kinds of conditions and were able to apply logic and come out with the conclusion that there are heels and heroes in every family.

But if my other prejudices had just sort of disappeared, I became positively lyrical about the Japanese-Americans. I saw a great deal of them in Italy where they had been formed into a battalion that fought with the 34th Division, and into two full regiments that sort of free-lanced around doing heavy fighting for everybody. Some of the boys in those outfits were from the West Coast, and some from Hawaii. A great deal has been written about their prowess, and I won't go into details, except to say that, to my knowledge and the knowledge of numerous others who had the opportunity of watching a lot of different outfits overseas, no combat unit in the army could exceed them in loyalty, hard work, courage, and sacrifice. Hardly a man of them hadn't been decorated at least twice, and their casualty rates were appalling. And if a skeptic wonders whether these aren't just "Japanese characteristics," he would do well to stifle the thought if he is around an infantry veteran who had experience with the Nisei unit.

• • •

If we must become strong in arms again, we should agitate against the professional militarists, the imperialists, the bigots, and the little Führers in our midst; it would be a terrible thing if the strength we built up fell into their hands. And we have even more reason to raise hell about our policy of buddying up with the world's worst characters – many of whom were recently our enemies – and lending support to oppressive regimes such as those in Greece and China. I think our way of life can bear inspection if it needs the world's fascists for allies.

• • •

I don't trust the army, I don't like the army, and I even poke fun at its recruiting program. Perhaps, under all the pompous and high-sounding words I have mouthed about why we should have an army, I want it around so I can draw more pictures about it.

*SOURCE:* Bill Mauldin, *Back Home* (New York: William Morrow [William Sloane], 1947), 60–61, 129, 154, 162–65, 302–03, 309–10. 

*RELATED ENTRIES: American Veterans Committee; Baby Boom; 442nd Regimental Combat Team of Nisei; G.I. Bills; Japanese Americans, Internment of; World War II*

## 1948 a

### Psychiatric Case History of World War II Tailgunner

*A psychiatrist wrote this case history of an AAF veteran whose neurosis appears to have stemmed, in large measure, from his religious sensitivity about his having killed many innocent people.*

Born to a very religious Midwestern family, P.P.T. started attending church at an early age. As well as being the religious center of his community, the church was also a major factor in much of its social life. As he grew up, graduating from high school and taking his first job, he came to accept the religious precepts as basic to his way of life. He attended services twice a week and participated actively in church affairs. Religion was his guide as well as his solace. To flout its doctrines was to flout not only his God and his family, but the whole community of which he was a part. After leaving school P.P.T. worked for four years as a truck driver and construction laborer before entering the Army at age of twenty-two.

During the first nine months of his service career he was shifted rapidly from one air field to another—Florida, Utah, Colorado, Washington, Oregon, Nebraska. By the time this training was completed he was qualified to work as a gunner on the large bombers and had attained the rank of sergeant. Although this was not the type of duty he would have chosen he accepted it. Next he was sent to England and joined a bomber squadron that had already amassed an impressive record in raids over France and Germany. His first mission was an easy one, but after that it was very difficult. The flak was almost always heavy and enemy fighters were everywhere. His pilot was killed on one raid, his bombardier on another. Once they just barely made it back to England after losing three engines and putting out a fire in the cockpit.

P.P.T. was frightened, but even more, he felt terribly guilty. Every time his plane went up its only purpose was to drop bombs on defenseless people. His job as a gunner was to kill enemy fliers and he did his job. But it seemed all wrong to him. This was contrary to his religion and everything that he had learned prior to entering the Army. He felt that he was guilty of participating in a never ending series of heinous crimes for which his family, his community, and his God must always condemn him. He became jittery, could not sleep, and vomited frequently. Yet he kept going and completed his twenty-five missions in a commendable manner. Seven months after leaving the United States he was on his way home again.

After a furlough, he returned to duty still completely obsessed with guilt. If anything, his state was worse than when he had been in combat. He didn't want to do anything, could not eat or sleep and had the sensation that ants were crawling all over his body. Hospitalized, he poured forth his preoccupations to the doctor: "There was the raid the day before Christmas. We had to go. I didn't want to kill those poor people. . . . I shot down a man, a German. I feel guilty about it. We shouldn't kill people. Here they hang people for that. . . . I guess that is what bothers me most. I killed somebody. . . . I think about that German I shot down. I know it was him or me, but I just can't forget that I saw him blow up. Up to then it was just an airplane. Then I realized that there was a man in the plane. . . . I keep trying to think that it is all behind me, but I can't. I just think about it and get upset. I can't read or go to classes without thinking about it. You have fighters coming at you in bed and you can't do anything about it. I keep dreaming about it. I just can't help it." The doctor tried to convince him that he had only been doing his duty, but to no avail, and he was finally discharged virtually unimproved by his hospital stay.

Within two months of leaving the Army P.P.T. started work in a steel plant. At first he found it difficult to work; he was plagued with frequent thoughts and dreams of combat. He did not go to church or associate with his old friends. Gradually, however, he began to participate in community activities and finally started going to church again. By 1948, although still rather restless and suffering from insomnia, he had almost fitted himself back into his old pattern of life. He enjoyed his job, went hunting and fishing for recreation, and was thinking of getting married. He felt far less guilty than he had when he returned from Europe. Later he married and had two children. He feels very much a part of his community again and has, as he sees it, returned to a religious way of life.

*SOURCE:* From Eli Ginzberg, et al., eds., *Breakdown and Recovery, vol. 11 of The Ineffective Soldier* (New York: Columbia University Press, 1959), 113–15. Copyright © 1959 Columbia University Press. Reprinted with permission from the publisher.

*RELATED ENTRIES: Combat, Effects of; World War II*

## 1948 b

### Executive Order 9981: Desegregation of the Armed Forces

*On July 26, 1948, Pres. Harry Truman signed an order banning racial discrimination in the armed forces. He later explained that his intention was to end segregation in the armed forces as well. The Committee on Equality of Treatment and Opportunity created by this order recommended such desegregation, which was quickly implemented by the Navy and Air Force. Truman's action thus became a watershed not only in military history, but in social history as well. Alongside a range of other social reforms taking effect in the middle of the century, Executive Order 9981 was instrumental in opening up opportunities to African Americans in the later decades of the 20th century.*

Establishing the President's Committee on Equality of Treatment and Opportunity In the Armed Forces.

WHEREAS it is essential that there be maintained in the armed services of the United States the highest standards of democracy, with equality of treatment and opportunity for all those who serve in our country's defense:

NOW THEREFORE, by virtue of the authority vested in me as President of the United States, by the Constitution and the statutes of the United States, and as Commander in Chief of the armed services, it is hereby ordered as follows:

1. It is hereby declared to be the policy of the President that there shall be equality of treatment and opportunity for all persons in the armed services without regard to race, color, religion or national origin. This policy shall be put into effect as rapidly as possible, having due regard to the time required to effectuate any necessary changes without impairing efficiency or morale.
2. There shall be created in the National Military Establishment an advisory committee to be known as the President's Committee on Equality of Treatment and Opportunity in the Armed Services, which shall be composed of seven members to be designated by the President.
3. The Committee is authorized on behalf of the President to examine into the rules, procedures and practices of the Armed Services in order to determine in what respect such rules, procedures and practices may be altered or improved with a view to carrying out the policy of this order. The Committee shall confer and advise the Secretary of Defense, the Secretary of the Army, the Secretary of the Navy, and the Secretary of the Air Force, and shall make such recommendations to the President and to said Secretaries as in the judgment of the Committee will effectuate the policy hereof.
4. All executive departments and agencies of the Federal Government are authorized and directed to cooperate with the Committee in its work, and to furnish the Committee such information or the services of such persons as the Committee may require in the performance of its duties.
5. When requested by the Committee to do so, persons in the armed services or in any of the executive depart-

ments and agencies of the Federal Government shall testify before the Committee and shall make available for use of the Committee such documents and other information as the Committee may require.

6. The Committee shall continue to exist until such time as the President shall terminate its existence by Executive order.

Harry Truman
The White House
July 26, 1948

*SOURCE:* U.S. National Archives & Records Administration, "Executive Order 9981: Desegregation of the Armed Forces (1948)." http://www.ourdocuments.gov/doc.php?doc=84&page=transcript (August 14, 2005).

*RELATED ENTRIES: African Americans in the Military; Executive Order 8802; Executive Order 8802; Racial Integration of the Armed Forces; Truman, Harry S.*

## 1949 (to 1950)

### Attitude of Veterans and Nonveteran Fathers during World War II Toward Personality Characteristics of First-Born

*Veterans surveyed by academics after the war complained of what they regarded as their wives' permissive rearing of their children, especially when the children had been too young to remember their fathers before the war. Fathers who had not served in the military and had not been separated from their families had few of these kinds of complaints.*

| Traits | War-separated | Non-separated |
|---|---|---|
| | Criticized | |
| Highly emotional | 7 | 5 |
| Unhappy | 2 | - |
| Stubborn | 5 | 4 |
| Disrespectful | 3 | - |
| Selfish | 3 | 1 |
| Demanding | 3 | - |
| Unresponsive | 7 | - |
| "Sissy" | 9 | 5 |
| Other | 16 | 11 |
| Total | 62 | 29 |
| | Approved | |
| Intelligent | 11 | 17 |
| Verbal | 4 | 5 |
| Creative | 1 | 3 |
| Disciplined | 3 | 5 |
| "Good" | 2 | 8 |
| Self-reliant | 2 | 5 |
| Sense of humor | 3 | 5 |
| Friendly | 3 | 10 |
| Good natured | 1 | 3 |
| Interested | 1 | 5 |
| Other | 3 | 8 |
| Total | 34 | 74 |

*NOTE: Figures indicate numbers of responses, not percentages.*

*SOURCE:* Lois Stolz and Herbert Stolz, *Father Relations of War-Born Children.* (Stanford, Calif.: Stanford University Press, 1950), 31, 66.

*RELATED ENTRIES: Baby Boom; Combat, Effects of; World War II*

## 1950 a

### World War II Veteran's Account of Experience in Service

*A World War II veteran from the Midwest wondered whether his military service had helped him to see beyond his hometown:*

The service made me see that this is rather a small-minded town. . . . Here they don't count on a person's ability. All they are interested in here is what's gone before—what the person, or people with him, have done in the past. I found this in the service, that it was the man's intelligence and ability which decided he would go ahead, and how far he would go. There's no prejudice because of your name—Romero or Smith or Brown. But here if you don't have a perfect background, it's no good. In the service a man gets ahead maybe by playing politics a bit. But there your past doesn't count a damn thing. It is your present that counts, and what you can do in the future. In this town I know I could do lots of jobs as well as perhaps half of the people here, but I wouldn't even have a chance, simply because of my [unpopular father].

I like to be left alone and do what I please, without someone forever forming a criticism of whatever I do. In a big city you get lost—or a fairly big city. But even if I hadn't been in service, I doubt if I'd ever have stayed in Midwest. I always realized that there were very few opportunities here for me. I've got a lot of ambition and so on, and even though I don't know whether my plans will come through or not, if they don't it will be simply because I'm not working. I'm not going to let this town of Midwest stop me from working them out.

*SOURCE:* Robert Havighurst, *The American Veteran Back Home* (New York: Longmans, Green, 1951), 119-20.

*RELATED ENTRIES: Geneva and Hague Conventions; Korean War*

## 1950 b

### Lyrics to the R.O.T.C. Song

*Since 1916, one of the main sources of junior officers for each of the services has been the college-based Reserve Officer Training Corps (ROTC). Until the last quarter of the 20th century, few officers who entered via ROTC made it to flag rank (general or admiral), and service academy graduates looked down upon their "Rotsie" compeers. Colin Powell, a ROTC graduate of the City University of New York, went on to become chairman of the Joint Chiefs of Staff. His success represents a growing trend away from those earlier prejudices, reflected in this song, sung to the tune "My Bonnie."*

Some mothers have sons in the Army.
Some mothers have sons o'er the sea.
But take down your service flag, Mother;
Your son's in the R.O.T.C.

Chorus:
R.—O.
R.—O.
Your son's in the R.O.T.C., T.C.
R.—O.
R.—O.
Your son's in the R.O.T.C.

Some join for the love of the Service.
Some join for the love of the Sea.
But I know a guy who's a Rotsie:
He joined for a college degree.

Oh, we are the "Weekend Commandos":
The "Summertime Sailors" are we.
So take down your service flag, Mother;
Your son's in the R.O.T.C.

These Navy versions of "My Bonnie" have become quite popular in the Fleet since the Second World War. The first expresses the Marine Pilots' unhappiness at having to operate from escort carriers (CVE's) with their small flight decks, and their envy of the Navy pilots flying from the large carriers (CVA's). "The R.O.T.C. Song" has sprung up from the good-natured rivalry between the Naval Academy midshipmen and the members of the Naval Reserve Officer Training Corps.

*SOURCE:* Joseph W. Crosley and the United States Naval Institute, *The Book of Navy Songs.* (Annapolis: United States Naval Academy, 1955).

*RELATED ENTRIES: Music and War; ROTC Programs*

## 1950 c

### Random House's Bennett Cerf Praising Military after Attending

*By 1950 the services had become skilled at promoting their usefulness to the public-opinion shapers of the nation with such programs as the Joint Civilian Orientation Conference. Bennett Cerf attended one such "dog-and-pony-show" (as these came to be called by those who staged them) and reported his "ten days with the armed forces" in the*

*Saturday Review, shortly before the beginning of the Korean War.*

It's become fashionable to remember just where you were or what you were doing when the news broke about Pearl Harbor. Should the invasion of South Korea prove an equally fateful moment in world history, I for one will have no trouble remembering where I heard about it. I was on the hangar deck of the *Midway*, the queen of the U.S. Navy's carriers, steaming to sea for a rendezvous with Task Force 23 and a brief but intensive series of naval operations in the 1950 manner. It was a stunning climax to a session of talks by top Government officials at the Pentagon Building, a display of new weapons and infantry tactics at Fort Benning, Georgia, and an inspiring show of the latest equipment and striking power of the Air Force at Eglin Base, Florida. The program was arranged for the Seventh Joint Orientation Conference, and that I was invited to be a member of it I consider one of the biggest honors and luckiest breaks of my career.

At Fort Benning, Georgia (the population of the post exceeds 30,000; the area comprises 282 square miles), the JOC had its first taste of life in the field, and the sounding of reveille at 5:45 A.M. provoked a stream of reminiscences about World War I which were, unfortunately, listened to by nobody. . . . A display of our remarkable new recoilless weapons (and other arms still considered secret) had the audience gasping. . . . The airborne troops begin their parachute training in a control tower exactly like the one that packed them in at the New York World's Fair and is now operating at Steeplechase Park. The stunt they perform just five weeks later give you goose pimples! . . .

I came home revitalized and simply busting to shout from the housetops this deep-felt conviction: when and if a war comes with Russia or anybody else this country is blessed with the basic equipment and leadership to knock hell out of them. We need more fighter planes and more carriers. We need more men in the armed forces. Our intelligence and propaganda departments need bolstering most of all. The money already allotted to defense has been, on the whole, wisely spent. In light of day-to-day news developments, increased appropriations are not only a wise investment but an absolute "must." When your life is at stake, you don't haggle over the cost.

*SOURCE: Saturday Review,* July 22, 1950, 3 ff.

*RELATED ENTRIES: Cold War; Frontline Reporting; Korean War*

## 1950 d

### Excerpt from Harry J. Maihafer's *From the Hudson to the Yalu: West Point in the Korean War*

*Lt. Harry Maihafer graduated from West Point in 1949. Within a year he was a platoon leader in the Korean War. His autobiographical account of that experience includes this insight into his humanity and professionalism.*

A cave—there appeared to be one far to my front—a dark rectangle at the base of a steep slope. I pointed it out to the leader of the 75-mm recoilless rifle crew. The gun was brought into position, sighted carefully, and fired. There was an ear-splitting roar, the characteristic sheet of flame to the weapon's rear, and an instant later a puff of smoke in the distance, about fifty yards short of the cave. The crew resighted and fired again. This time the shell hit on the hillside, a few yards to the left of the cave's mouth. I called an adjustment, and a third round was fired. This one was almost exactly on target and hit only a few yards from the opening.

I looked through my binoculars and waited for the smoke to clear so as to make another adjustment. Suddenly I saw frenzied activity. People came running from the cave, waving their arms and holding up strips of white. Soon there seemed to be a crowd, a hundred or more, apparently all civilians. They moved slightly in our direction, then stopped. Three figures detached themselves from the group and kept coming.

The three were a long time getting to us, but eventually we saw they were older, white-bearded men carrying flags of truce—bamboo poles with white articles of clothing tied to the ends. They labored up our hill and told their story to an interpreter.

When the fighting had come this way, the people of their village had taken refuge in a large cave known to all who lived in this area. Earlier in the day, enemy soldiers had come and tried to join them in the cave. But the people, especially the women, had shrieked that the Communist soldiers must go, that they would only bring trouble for all. Some of the villagers had wanted to come tell the Americans what was happening, but the Communists had threatened to kill them. Finally the soldiers had left, but only after cautioning them not to go to the Americans, who would be sure to kill any who came forth.

The leader had come to ask safe passage for his people. He and his two courageous companions were offering themselves as test cases—possible victims—in case the Communist warnings were true. I assured the leader they could pass through without harm, and the three patriarchs returned and led their people forward. Slowly the column, a ragged procession of old men, women, and children, wound its way up our mountain. I shuddered to think what would have happened had one of our shells actually entered the cave.

*SOURCE:* Harry J. Maihafer, *From the Hudson to the Yalu: West Point [Class of 1949] in the Korean War* (College Station: Texas A & M University Press, 1993), 106. Reprinted by permission of the Texas A&M University Press.

*RELATED ENTRIES: Cold War; General Orders, No. 100; Geneva and Hague Conventions; Korean War*

## 1951

### RECALL OF GEN. DOUGLAS MACARTHUR

*When the Korean War began, President Truman was empowered to appoint Gen. Douglas MacArthur to the position of commander of United Nations forces there. After MacArthur oversaw a successful end-around amphibious landing at Inchon, U.S.–UN troops routed the North Korean army and drove north towards the border with China. With increasing frequency, General MacArthur differed publicly with his commander in chief about questions of military strategy and policy. MacArthur wrote to the leadership of the Veterans of Foreign Wars of "unleashing Chang Kai-shek," the defeated Nationalist Chinese leader who had withdrawn with several hundred thousand of his troops to the island of Taiwan. After Chinese forces began flooding into North Korea (something MacArthur had assured the president would not occur), he wrote House Speaker Joe Martin, insisting that the war could only be won by going "all-out" and bombing Chinese bases and staging areas in Manchuria. The president and the Joint Chiefs of Staff, reluctant to risk widening the war, disagreed fundamentally on these issues, and Gen. Omar Bradley, Army chief of staff, told a congressional committee as much, and defended the president's decision to relieve MacArthur of command and replace him with Gen. Matthew Ridgway. Truman explained that decision to the nation, and the world:*

I want to talk plainly to you tonight about what we are doing in Korea and about our policy in the Far East.

In the simplest terms, what we are doing in Korea is this: We are trying to prevent a third world war.

I think most people in this country recognized that fact last June. And they warmly supported the decision of the Government to help the Republic of Korea against the Communist aggressors. Now, many persons, even some who applauded our decision to defend Korea, have forgotten the basic reason for our action.

It is right for us to be in Korea. It was right last June. It is right today.

I want to remind you why this is true.

The Communists in the Kremlin are engaged in a monstrous conspiracy to stamp out freedom all over the world. If they were to succeed, the United States would be numbered among their principal victims. It must be clear to everyone that the United States cannot—and will not—sit idly by and await foreign conquest. The only question is: When is the best time to meet the threat and how?

The best time to meet the threat is in the beginning. It is easier to put out a fire in the beginning when it is small than after it has become a roaring blaze.

And the best way to meet the threat of aggression is for the peace-loving nations to act together. If they don't act together, they are likely to be picked off, one by one. . . .

This is the basic reason why we joined in creating the United Nations. And since the end of World War II we have been putting that lesson into practice—we have been working with other free nations to check the aggressive designs of the Soviet Union before they can result in a third world war.

That is what we did in Greece, when that nation was threatened by aggression of international communism.

The attack against Greece could have led to general war. But this country came to the aid of Greece. The United Nations supported Greek resistance. With our help, the determination and efforts of the Greek people defeated the attack on the spot.

Another big Communist threat to peace was the Berlin blockade. That too could have led to war. But again it was settled because free men would not back down in an emergency. . . .

The question we have had to face is whether the Communist plan of conquest can be stopped without general war. Our Government and other countries associated with us in the United Nations believe that the best chance of stopping it without general war is to meet the attack in Korea and defeat it there.

That is what we have been doing. It is a difficult and bitter task.

But so far it has been successful.

So far, we have prevented World War III.

So far, by fighting a limited war in Korea, we have prevented aggression from succeeding and bringing on a general war. And the ability of the whole free world to resist Communist aggression has been greatly improved.

We have taught the enemy a lesson. He has found out that aggression is not cheap or easy. Moreover, men all over the world who want to remain free have been given new courage and new hope. They know now that the champions of freedom can stand up and fight.

Our resolute stand in Korea is helping the forces of freedom now fighting in Indochina and other countries in that part of the world. It has already slowed down the timetable of conquest. . . .

We do not want to see the conflict in Korea extended. We are trying to prevent a world war—not to start one. The best way to do this is to make plain that we and the other free countries will continue to resist the attack.

But you may ask: Why can't we take other steps to punish the aggressor? Why don't we bomb Manchuria and China itself? Why don't we assist Chinese Nationalist troops to land on the mainland of China?

If we were to do these things we would be running a very grave risk of starting a general war. If that were to happen, we would have brought about the exact situation we are trying to prevent.

If we were to do these things, we would become entangled in a vast conflict on the continent of Asia and our task would become immeasurably more difficult all over the world.

What would suit the ambitions of the Kremlin better than for military forces to be committed to a full-scale war with Red China?

The course we have been following is the one best calculated to avoid an all-out war. It is the course consistent with our obligation to do all we can to maintain international peace and security. Our experience in Greece and Berlin shows that it is the most effective course of action we can follow. . . .

If the Communist authorities realize that they cannot defeat us in Korea, if they realize it would be foolhardy to widen the hostilities beyond Korea, then they may recognize the folly of continuing their aggression. A peaceful settlement may then be possible. The door is always open.

Then we may achieve a settlement in Korea which will not compromise the principles and purposes of the United Nations.

I have thought long and hard about this question of extending the war in Asia. I have discussed it many times with the ablest military advisers in the country. I believe with all my heart that the course we are following is the best course.

I believe that we must try to limit war to Korea for these vital reasons: to make sure that the precious lives of our fighting men are not wasted; to see that the security of our country and the free world is not needlessly jeopardized; and to prevent a third world war.

A number of events have made it evident that General MacArthur did not agree with that policy. I have therefore considered it essential to relieve General MacArthur so that there would be no doubt or confusion as to the real purpose and aim of our policy.

It was with the deepest personal regret that I found myself compelled to take this action. General MacArthur is one of our greatest military commanders. But the cause of world peace is more important than any individual.

The change in commands in the Far East means no change whatever in the policy of the United States. We will carry on the fight in Korea with vigor and determination in an effort to bring the war to a speedy and successful conclusion.

The new commander, Lt. Gen. Matthew Ridgway, has already demonstrated that he has the great qualities of military leadership needed for this task.

We are ready, at any time, to negotiate for a restoration of peace in the area. But we will not engage in appeasement. We are only interested in real peace.

Real peace can be achieved through a settlement based on the following factors:

One: the fighting must stop.

Two: concrete steps must be taken to insure that the fighting will not break out again.

Three: there must be an end to the aggression.

A settlement founded upon these three elements would open the way for the unification of Korea and the withdrawal of all foreign forces.

In the meantime, I want to be clear about our military objective. We are fighting to resist an outrageous aggression in Korea. We are trying to keep the Korean conflict from spreading to other areas. But at the same time we must conduct our military activities so as to insure the security of our forces. This is essential if they are to continue the fight until the enemy abandons its ruthless attempt to destroy the Republic of Korea.

This is our military objective—to repel attack and to restore peace.

In the hard fighting in Korea, we are proving that collective action among nations is not only a high principle but a workable means of resisting aggression. Defeat of aggression in Korea may be the turning point in the world's search for a practical way of achieving peace and security.

The struggle of the United Nations in Korea is a struggle for peace.

The free nations have united their strength in an effort to prevent a third world war.

That war can come if the Communist rulers want it to come. But this Nation and its allies will not be responsible for its coming.

We do not want to widen the conflict. We will use every effort to prevent that disaster. And so in doing we know that we are following the great principles of peace, freedom, and justice.

*SOURCE:* U.S. State Department Bulletin, 16 April 1951.

*RELATED ENTRIES: Civil–Military Relations; Korean War; MacArthur, Douglas; Truman, Harry S.*

## 1953

### Case History of World War II Psychiatric Casualty

*Psychiatrists serving with the Army and Veterans Administration conducted these case histories of World War II psychiatric casualties. One case history described the experience of one veteran, including his condition a decade after combat stress had been experienced:*

The youngest of five children, U.V. left his parents' Midwestern farm shortly after completing two years of high school and secured employment as a carpenter's helper in a nearby town. Married in 1937, he continued working at this trade until inducted late in 1942. Assigned to an anti-aircraft unit, he participated in the Normandy invasion and in the campaign across northern France. He was in good health and his character and efficiency ratings were "excellent."

After about two months of combat he was knocked unconscious by the blast of an aerial bomb. Because he complained of headaches, dizziness, and a "roaring in the ears," the aid station transferred him to the evacuation hospital where his condition was at first described as "mild." However, his headaches grew worse, and his dizziness was accompanied by spells of nausea and vomiting. U.V. developed increasing nervous tension, had battle dreams, and jumped at any loud noise. Five months of hospitalization in England failed to reveal any organic basis for his persistent headaches but he showed no improvement. He was evacuated to the United States where his hospitalization continued for another seven months in general and convalescent hospitals. Finally, shortly before V-J Day, he was given a medical discharge with a diagnosis of psychoneurosis, acute, severe, anxiety state.

U.V. went back to the family farm and tried to return to the carpentry trade but could not make it. He could not tolerate the noises nor could he climb ladders. Unable to work, he puttered around the farm, and received as his only cash income the 70 percent disability compensation which the Veterans Administration had awarded him. Successive examinations failed to reveal any improvement in his emotional state. He started a liberal arts course at a junior college but soon dropped out. He was not considered suitable for training under Public Law 16 until he improved.

Over the next few years he worked occasionally at odd jobs but never for long. He had difficulties in securing jobs because he detailed his symptoms and his disabilities to any prospective employer. At times, he was able to work reasonably well but either he quit or his temporary work had ended. One employer reported (in 1950) that the veteran was "an excellent painter and carpenter but that he doesn't seem able to work. He frequently blew up on a job and went to pieces." His wife had left him and later divorced him.

He is still rated as 50 percent disabled by the Veterans Administration and the last information (1953) indicates that for the past several years he had been earning some money by working as a part-time contact man for the local post of a veterans' service organization. But his supervisor reports that he could never qualify for a service representative since he appears to be incapable of assuming responsibility. Even with close supervision he had not been doing very well since he made more promises to veterans seeking help than he could possibly fulfill. In communal activities, he would start out on a new project with great enthusiasm but soon tired and moved on to something else.

*SOURCE:* Eli Ginzberg et al., eds., *Breakdown and Recovery*, vol. 2, *The Ineffective Soldier* (New York: Columbia University Press,1959), 231-32. 

*RELATED ENTRIES: Combat, Effects of; World War II*

## 1957 (to 1958)

### Excerpt from *Born on the Fourth of July* by Ron Kovic

*The Cold War with the Soviet Union was a very real one to Americans like young Ron Kovic in the 1950s:*

We joined the cub scouts and marched in parades on Memorial Day. We made contingency plans for the Cold War and built fallout shelters out of milk cartons. We wore spacesuits and space helmets. We made rocket ships out of cardboard boxes. And one Saturday afternoon in the basement Castiglia [a friend] and I went to Mars on the couch we had turned into a rocket ship. . . . And the whole block watched a thing called the space race begin. On a cold October night Dad and I watched the first satellite, called Sputnik, moving across the sky above our house like a tiny bright star. I still remember standing out there with Dad looking up in amazement at that thing moving in the sky above Massapequa. It was hard to believe that this thing, this Sputnik, was so high up and moving so fast around the world, again and again. Dad put his hand on my shoulder that night and without saying anything I quietly walked back inside and went to my room thinking that the Russians had beaten America into space and wondering why we couldn't even get a rocket off the pad. . . .

The Communists were all over the place back then. And if they weren't trying to beat us into outer space, Castiglia and I were certain they were infiltrating our schools, trying to take over our classes and control our minds. We were both certain that one of our teachers was a secret Communist agent and in our next secret club meeting we promised to report anything new he said during our next history class. We watched him very carefully that year.

*SOURCE:* Ron Kovic, *Born of the Fourth of July* (New York: Akashic Books, 2005). Reprinted with the permission of the author and Akashic Books (website: www.akashic.com).

*RELATED ENTRIES: Born on the Fourth of July; Cold War; Film and War; Literature and War; Marine Corps; Vietnam War*

# 1961

## Pres. Dwight D. Eisenhower's Farewell Address

*Dwight Eisenhower served two terms as president of the United States. At the end of his second term, in early 1961, he gave his farewell address, which included a warning about what he called "the military–industrial complex." His experience as a student at the Army Industrial College, as a planner for the U.S. Army's mobilization prior to U.S. entry into World War II, as supreme Allied commander of European forces, and as president give his words the authority on the subject that they have enjoyed ever since.*

Delivered on January 17, 1961
Good evening, my fellow Americans.

First, I should like to express my gratitude to the radio and television networks for the opportunity they have given me over the years to bring reports and messages to our nation. My special thanks go to them for the opportunity of addressing you this evening.

Three days from now, after a half century of service of our country, I shall lay down the responsibilities of office as, in traditional and solemn ceremony, the authority of the presidency is vested in my successor.

This evening I come to you with a message of leave-taking and farewell, and to share a few final thoughts with you, my countrymen.

Like every other citizen, I wish the new president, and all who will labor with him, Godspeed. I pray that the coming years will be blessed with peace and prosperity for all. Our people expect their president and the Congress to find essential agreement on questions of great moment, the wise resolution of which will better shape the future of the nation.

My own relations with Congress, which began on a remote and tenuous basis when, long ago, a member of the Senate appointed me to West Point, have since ranged to the intimate during the war and immediate post-war period, and finally to the mutually interdependent during these past eight years.

In this final relationship, the Congress and the Administration have, on most vital issues, cooperated well, to serve the nation well rather than mere partisanship, and so have assured that the business of the nation should go forward. So my official relationship with Congress ends in a feeling on my part, of gratitude that we have been able to do so much together.

We now stand ten years past the midpoint of a century that has witnessed four major wars among great nations. Three of these involved our own country. Despite these holocausts America is today the strongest, the most influential and most productive nation in the world. Understandably proud of this pre-eminence, we yet realize that America's leadership and prestige depend, not merely upon our unmatched material progress, riches and military strength, but on how we use our power in the interests of world peace and human betterment.

Throughout America's adventure in free government, such basic purposes have been to keep the peace; to foster progress in human achievement, and to enhance liberty, dignity and integrity among peoples and among nations.

To strive for less would be unworthy of a free and religious people.

Any failure traceable to arrogance or our lack of comprehension or readiness to sacrifice would inflict upon us a grievous hurt, both at home and abroad.

Progress toward these noble goals is persistently threatened by the conflict now engulfing the world. It commands our whole attention, absorbs our very beings. We face a hostile ideology global in scope, atheistic in character, ruthless in purpose, and insidious in method. Unhappily the danger it poses promises to be of indefinite duration.

To meet it successfully, there is called for, not so much the emotional and transitory sacrifices of crisis, but rather those which enable us to carry forward steadily, surely, and without complaint the burdens of a prolonged and complex struggle—with liberty the stake. Only thus shall we remain, despite every provocation, on our charted course toward permanent peace and human betterment.

Crises there will continue to be. In meeting them, whether foreign or domestic, great or small, there is a recurring temptation to feel that some spectacular and costly action could become the miraculous solution to all current difficulties. A huge increase in the newer elements of our defenses; development of unrealistic programs to cure every ill in agriculture; a dramatic expansion in basic and applied research—these and many other possibilities, each possibly promising in itself, may be suggested as the only way to the road we wish to travel.

But each proposal must be weighed in light of a broader consideration; the need to maintain balance in and among national programs—balance between the private and the public economy, balance between the cost and hoped for advantages—balance between the clearly necessary and the comfortably desirable; balance between our essential requirements as a nation and the duties imposed by the nation upon the individual; balance between the actions of the moment and the national welfare of the future. Good judgment seeks balance and progress; lack of it eventually finds imbalance and frustration.

The record of many decades stands as proof that our people and their Government have, in the main, understood these truths and have responded to them well in the face of threat and stress.

But threats, new in kind or degree, constantly arise. Of these, I mention two only.

A vital element in keeping the peace is our military establishment. Our arms must be mighty, ready for instant action, so that no potential aggressor may be tempted to risk his own destruction. Our military organization today bears little relation to that known by any of my predecessors in peacetime, or indeed by the fighting men of World War II or Korea.

Until the latest of our world conflicts, the United States had no armaments industry. American makers of plowshares could, with time and as required, make swords as well. But now we can no longer risk emergency improvisation of national defense; we have been compelled to create a permanent armaments industry of vast proportions. Added to this, three and a half million men and women are directly engaged in the defense establishment.

We annually spend on military security more than the net income of all United States corporations.

This conjunction of an immense military establishment and a large arms industry is new in the American experience. The total influence—economic, political, even spiritual—is felt in every city, every statehouse, every office of the federal government. We recognize the imperative need for this development. Yet we must not fail to comprehend its grave implications. Our toil, resources and livelihood are all involved; so is the very structure of our society.

In the councils of government, we must guard against the acquisition of unwarranted influence, whether sought or unsought, by the military-industrial complex. The potential for the disastrous rise of misplaced power exists and will persist.

We must never let the weight of this combination endanger our liberties or democratic processes. We should take nothing for granted. Only an alert and knowledgeable citizenry can compel the proper meshing of the huge industrial and military machinery of defense with our peaceful methods and goals, so that security and liberty may prosper together.

Akin to, and largely responsible for the sweeping changes in our industrial-military posture, has been the technological revolution during recent decades. In this revolution, research has become central, it also becomes more formalized, complex, and costly. A steadily increasing share is conducted for, by, or at the direction of, the Federal government.

Today, the solitary inventor, tinkering in his shop, has been overshadowed by task forces of scientists in laboratories and testing fields. In the same fashion, the free university, historically the fountainhead of free ideas and scientific discovery, has experienced a revolution in the conduct of research. Partly because of the huge costs involved, a government contract becomes virtually a substitute for intellectual curiosity.

For every old blackboard there are now hundreds of new electronic computers. The prospect of domination of the nation's scholars by federal employment, project allocations, and the power of money is ever present—and is gravely to be regarded. Yet, in holding scientific research and discovery in respect, as we should, we must also be alert to the equal and opposite danger that public policy could itself become the captive of a scientific-technological elite.

It is the task of statesmanship to mold, to balance, and to integrate these and other forces, new and old, within the principles of our democratic system—ever aiming toward the supreme goals of our free society.

Another factor in maintaining balance involves the element of time. As we peer into society's future, we—you and I, and our government—must avoid the impulse to live only for today, plundering for, for our own ease and convenience, the precious resources of tomorrow. We cannot mortgage the material assets of our grandchildren without asking the loss also of their political and spiritual heritage. We want democracy to survive for all generations to come, not to become the insolvent phantom of tomorrow.

Down the long lane of the history yet to be written America knows that this world of ours, ever growing smaller, must avoid becoming a community of dreadful fear and hate, and be, instead, a proud confederation of mutual trust and respect.

Such a confederation must be one of equals. The weakest must come to the conference table with the same confidence as do we, protected as we are by our moral, economic, and military strength. That table, though scarred by many past frustrations, cannot be abandoned for the certain agony of the battlefield.

Disarmament, with mutual honor and confidence, is a continuing imperative. Together we must learn how to compose differences, not with arms, but with intellect and decent purpose. Because this need is so sharp and apparent I confess that I lay down my official responsibilities in this field with a definite sense of disappointment. As one who has witnessed the horror and the lingering sadness of war—as one who knows that another war could utterly destroy this civilization which has been so slowly and painfully built over thousands of years—I wish I could say tonight that a lasting peace is in sight. Happily, I can say that war has been avoided. Steady progress toward our ultimate goal has been made. But, so much remains to be done. As a private citizen, I shall never cease to do what little I can to help the world advance along that road.

So—in this my last good night to you as your president—I thank you for the many opportunities you have given me for public service in war and peace. I trust that in that service you find some things worthy; as for the rest of it, I know you will find ways to improve performance in the future.

You and I—my fellow citizens—need to be strong in our faith that all nations, under God, will reach the goal of peace with justice. May we be ever unswerving in devotion to principle, confident but humble with power, diligent in pursuit of the Nations' great goals.

To all the peoples of the world, I once more give expression to America's prayerful and continuing aspiration:

We pray that peoples of all faiths, all races, all nations, may have their great human needs satisfied; that those now denied opportunity shall come to enjoy it to the full; that all who yearn for freedom may experience its spiritual blessings; that those who have freedom will understand, also, its heavy responsibilities; that all who are insensitive to the needs of others will learn charity; that the scourges of poverty, disease and ignorance will be made to disappear from the earth, and that, in the goodness of time, all peoples will come to live together in a peace guaranteed by the binding force of mutual respect and love.

Now, on Friday noon, I am to become a private citizen. I am proud to do so. I look forward to it.

Thank you, and good night.

*SOURCE:* "Eisenhower's Farewell Address," TomPaine.com, http://www.tompaine.com/feature.cfm/ID/3749 (accessed May 27, 2005).

*RELATED ENTRIES: Cold War; Economy and War; Eisenhower, Dwight D.; Militarization and Militarism; Military-Industrial Complex*

## 1964

### Veteran Harold Bond's Reflections on Returning to Monte Cassino

*Veterans may be slow initially in associating with veterans' organizations but, as time passes, the impact of military service stands out more clearly in their memories. Harold Bond, a veteran of World War II in Italy, took his family back to the scene in the early 1960s to share with them his reminiscences.*

Monte Cassino has haunted my mind for the past twenty years. The last time I saw the abbey and the town was on a cold, wet afternoon in late February 1944, when I was being evacuated to an army field hospital. I had been an infantry soldier engaged in the bitter fighting on the German Gustav Line. This was the worst combat of the entire war for me, and during the long years of peace that followed, memories of it came back again. Scenes and incidents which I would have been happy to forget remained disconcertingly vivid. They were troublesome memories, and sometimes I brooded over them.

Like other ex-soldiers after the war, I was caught up in the business of starting a career in the workaday world and raising a family. There is little connection between a great battle and the ordinary rounds of life in peacetime, and as the war slipped further into the past I rarely heard mention of Monte Cassino and almost never had occasion to talk about it. Yet I found myself now and again reflecting on the terrible fighting. With experiences such as those I had had so deeply branded on my mind, I could not help wondering what they finally did mean to me and to the others with whom I had shared them. Had they consisted, after all, merely of senseless suffering without meaning, or was there a significance in them that I had been unable to discover?

*SOURCE:* Harold Bond, *Return to Cassino* (New York: J.M. Dent & Sons, 1964), 1.

*RELATED ENTRIES: Combat, Effects of; Memory and War; World War II*

## 1965 a

### Seymour Melman on America's Aging Metal-Working Machinery

*In 1965 Columbia University economist Seymour Melman carried President Eisenhower's warning (see document 1961 above) to the next level with a critique of the ways that massive military spending was sapping the nation's economic vitality. This brief passage from his book Our Depleted Society offers a taste of his analysis:*

In 1963, the United States reached the position of operating the oldest stock of metal-working machinery of any industrial country in the world. . . .

Here is a portrait of antiquity in American production. The percentage of machines in use that was twenty years old or older in 1963:

| | % |
|---|---|
| Machine Tools | 20 |
| Ships and Railroad Equipment | 41 |
| Construction, Mining, Materials Handling | 25 |
| Precision Instruments and Mechanisms | 15 |
| Electrical Equipment | 16 |
| Automobiles | 23 |
| Office Machines | 14 |
| Special Industry Machinery | 28 |

Since 1925 the McGraw-Hill organization has been conducting national "inventories" of the machine tools and other equipment in American industry. The following data show the proportion of metal-cutting machines in American industry found to be ten years old or older at the indicated times:

1925........44 1945........38
1930........52 1949........43
1935........67 1953........55
1940........72 1958........60
1963........64

The growing age of the machine tools in use in American factories means that 2.2 million basic manufacturing machines are not being replaced by newer equipment that could incorporate many technical improvements.

*SOURCE:* Seymour Melman, *Our Depleted Society* (New York: Rinehart & Winston: 1965), 50.

*RELATED ENTRIES: Cold War; Economy and War; Military–Industrial Complex; Vietnam War*

# 1965 b

## Selective Service System's Channeling Manpower Memo

*The Selective Service System, created in 1948 to provide military personnel that would be deployed on an as-needed basis, as well as a pool of semi-experienced reserves, was defended by President Truman when he proposed it as a measure that would "raise the physical standard of the nation's manpower, lower the illiteracy rate, develop citizenship responsibilities, and foster the moral and spiritual welfare of our young people." It also served to encourage those who preferred to acquire skills "vital to the national interest" to do so if they wished to be made exempt from military service. This memo was prepared by the director of the system's office in 1965 to provide information to new local Selective Service board members charged with determining who was to be considered exempt.*

One of the major products of the Selective Service classification process is the channeling of manpower into many endeavors and occupations; activities that are in the national interest. This function is a counterpart and amplification of the System's responsibility to deliver manpower to the armed forces in such a manner as to reduce to a minimum any adverse effect upon the national health, safety, interest, and progress. By identifying and applying this process intelligently, the System is able not only to minimize any adverse effect, but to exert an effect beneficial to the national health, safety and interest.

The line dividing the primary function of armed forces manpower procurement from the process of channeling manpower into civilian support is often finely drawn. The process of channeling by not taking men from certain activities who are otherwise liable for service, or by giving deferments to qualified men in certain occupations, is actual procurement by inducement of manpower of civilian activities which are manifestly in the national interest.

While the best known purpose of Selective Service is to procure manpower for the armed forces, a variety of related processes takes place outside delivery of manpower to the active armed forces. Many of these may be put under the heading of "channeling manpower." Many young men would have not pursued a higher education if there had not been a program of student deferments. Many young scientists, engineers, tool and die makers, and other possessors of scarce skills would not remain in their jobs in the defense effort if it were not for a program of occupational deferment. Even though the salary of a teacher has historically been meager, many young men remain in that job seeking the reward of deferment. The process of channeling manpower by deferment is entitled to much credit for the large amount of graduate students in technical fields and for the fact that there is not a greater shortage of teachers, engineers, and other scientists working in activities which are essential to the national interest.

The opportunity to enhance the national well-being by inducing more registrants to participate in fields which relate directly to the national interest came about as a consequence, soon after the close of the Korean episode, of the knowledge within the System that there was enough registrant personnel to allow stringent deferment practices employed during war time to be relaxed or tightened as the situation might require. Circumstances had become favorable to induce registrants, by the attraction of deferment, to matriculate in schools and pursue subjects in which there was beginning to be a national shortage of personnel. These were particularly in the engineering, scientific, and teaching professions.

In the Selective Service System, the term "deferment" has been used millions of times to describe the method and means used to attract to the kind of service considered to be the most important, the individuals who were not compelled to do it. The club of induction has been used to drive out of areas considered to be less important to the areas of greater importance in which deferments were given, the individuals who did not or could not participate in activities which were considered essential to the Nation. The Selective Service

System anticipates evolution in this area. It is promoting the process by the granting of deferments in liberal numbers where the national need clearly would benefit.

Soon after Sputnik I was launched it became popular to reappraise critically our educational, scientific, and technological inventory. Many deplored our shortage of scientific and technical personnel, inadequacies of our schools, and shortage of teachers. Since any analysis having any connection with manpower and its relation to the Nation's survival vitally involves the Selective Service System, it is well to point out that for quite some time the System had been following a policy of deferring instructors who were engaged in the teaching of mathematics and physical and biological sciences. It is appropriate also to recall the System's previously invoked practice of deferring students to prepare themselves for work in some essential activity and the established program of deferring engineers, scientists, and other critically skilled persons who were working in essential fields.

The Congress, in enacting the Universal Military Training and Service legislation declared that adequate provisions for national security required maximum effort in the fields of scientific research and development, and the fullest possible utilization of the Nation's technological, scientific, and other critical manpower resources. To give effect to this philosophy, the classifying boards of the Selective Service System defer registrants determined by them to be necessary in the national health, safety, or interest. This is accomplished on the basis of evidence of record in each individual case. No group deferments are permitted. Deferments are granted, however, in a realistic atmosphere so that the fullest effect of channeling will be felt, rather than be terminated by military service at too early a time.

Registrants and their employers are encouraged and required to make available to the classifying authorities detailed evidence as to the occupations and activities in which registrants are engaged. It is not necessary for any registrant to specifically request deferment, but his selective service file must contain sufficient current evidence on which can be based a proper determination as to whether he should remain where he is or be made available for service. Since occupational deferments are granted for no more than a year at a time, a process of periodically receiving current information and repeated review assures that every deferred registrant continues to contribute to the overall national good. This reminds him of the basis of his deferment. The skills as well as the activities are periodically reevaluated. A critical skill that is not employed in an essential activity does not qualify for deferment.

It is in this atmosphere that the young man registers at age 18 and pressure begins to force his choice. He does not have the inhibitions that a philosophy of universal service in uniform would engender. The door is open for him as a student to qualify if capable in a skill needed by his nation. He has many choices and he is prodded to make a decision.

The psychological effect of this circumstantial climate depends upon the individual, his sense of good citizenship, his love of country and its way of life. He can obtain a sense of well being and satisfaction that he is doing as a civilian what will help his country most. This process encourages him to put forth his best effort and removes to some degree the stigma that has been attached to being out of uniform.

In the less patriotic and more selfish individual it engenders a sense of fear, uncertainty, and dissatisfaction which motivates him, nevertheless, in the same direction. He complains of the uncertainty which he must endure; he would like to be able to do as he pleases; he would appreciate a certain future with no prospect of military service or civilian contribution, but he complies with the needs of the national health, safety, or interest—or he is denied deferment.

Throughout his career as a student, the pressure—the threat of loss of deferment—continues. It continues with equal intensity after graduation. His local board requires periodic reports to find out what he is up to. He is impelled to pursue his skill rather than embark upon some less important enterprise and is encouraged to apply high skill in an essential activity in the national interest. The loss of deferred status is the consequence for the individual who has acquired the skill and either does not use it, or uses it in a nonessential activity.

The psychology of granting wide choice under pressure to take action is the American or indirect way of achieving what is done by direction in foreign countries where choice is not allowed. Here, choice is limited but not denied, and it is fundamental that an individual generally applies himself better to something he has decided to do rather than something he has been told to do.

The effects of channeling are manifested among student physicians. They are deferred to complete their education through school and internship. This permits them to serve in the armed forces in their skills rather than as unskilled enlisted men.

The device of pressurized guidance, or channeling, is employed on Standby Reservists of which more than 2 1/2 million have been referred by all services for availability determinations. The appeal to the Reservist who knows he is subject to recall to active duty unless he is determined to be unavailable is virtually identical to that extended to other registrants.

The psychological impact of being rejected for service in uniform is severe. The earlier this occurs in a young man's life, the sooner the beneficial effects of pressured motivation by the Selective Service System are lost. He is labeled unwanted. His patriotism is not desired. Once the label of "rejectee" is upon him all efforts at guidance by persuasion are futile. If he attempts to enlist at 17 or 18 and is rejected, then he receives virtually none of the impulsion the System is capable of giving him. If he makes no effort to enlist and as a result is not rejected until delivered for examination by the Selective Service System at about age 23, he has felt some of the pressure but thereafter is a free agent.

This contributed to establishment of a new classification of I-Y (registrant qualified for military service only in time of war or national emergency). The classification reminds the registrant of his ultimate qualification to serve and preserves some of the benefit of what we call channeling. Without it or any other similar method of categorizing men in degrees of acceptability, men rejected for military service would be left with the understanding that they are unfit to defend their country, even in war time.

From the individual's viewpoint, he is standing in a room which has been made uncomfortably warm. Several doors are open, but they all lead to various forms of recognized, patriotic service to the Nation. Some accept the alternatives gladly—some with reluctance. The consequence is approximately the same.

The so-called Doctor Draft was set up during the Korean episode to insure sufficient physicians, dentists, and veterinarians in the armed forces as officers. The objective of that law was to exert sufficient pressure to furnish an incentive for application for commission. However, the indirect effect was to induce many physicians, dentists, and veterinarians to specialize in areas of medical personnel shortage and to seek outlets for their skills in areas of greatest demand and national need rather than of greatest financial return.

Selective Service processes do not compel people by edict as in foreign systems to enter pursuits having to do with essentiality and progress. They go because they know that by going they will be deferred.

Delivery of manpower for induction, the process of providing a few thousand men with transportation to a reception center, is not much of an administrative or financial challenge. It is in dealing with the other millions of registrants that the system is heavily occupied, developing more effective human beings in the national interest.

*SOURCE: The Selective Service: Its Concepts, History, and Operation* (Washington, D.C.: Government Printing Office: September 1967).

*RELATED ENTRIES: All Volunteer Force; Cold War; Conscription and Volunteerism; Draft Evasion and Resistance;Selective Service System; Vietnam War*

# 1965 c

## Case Report on Psychiatric Illness of Submariner's Wife

*Men on Polaris submarines armed with nuclear missiles were deployed for as many as six months at a time each year. This caused a strain on some of their families, as this case report indicates:*

Mrs. A., a 32-year-old mother of five, married for 15 years to a chief petty officer, had never previously had psychiatric difficulties. Two weeks before her husband was due home, she experienced a sudden onset of anxiety and was seen in the emergency room that same evening. The anxiety was intense and accompanied by uncontrollable weeping and a persistent, diffuse headache. She felt all would be well if her husband would return "tomorrow." She denied any anger at his being away, but lamented the hardship to her and her family caused by the frequent patrols. On the visit to the psychiatrist the next day, she spoke with considerable anger about the previous years of hardship. "If only I could show him what he's done to us!"

*SOURCE:* Richard Isay, "The Submariners' Wives Syndrome," *Psychiatric Quarterly* 42 (1968): 648. With kind permission of Springer Science and Business Media.

*RELATED ENTRIES: Families, Military; Medicine and War; Vietnam War*

## 1965 d

**Letter Home from Serviceman on Combat Experience**

*By the summer of 1965, thousands of Marines had been landed in the northernmost quadrant of South Vietnam, initially intended to protect the U. S. Air Force base at Da Nang. Soon they were inflicting and taking heavy casualties. A number wrote home of their experiences and feelings, as did Pfc. Richard Marks:*

When we finally get out of this it will be quite awhile to readjust to normal life, of not jumping at each sound, and just living like an animal in general. Values even change—a human life becomes so unimportant, and the idea of killing a V.C. is just commonplace now—just like a job. In a way it all scares me more than being shot at.

I am a regular combat veteran now, and I have all the hair raising stories to go with it, and I am only 19 years old. I have just grown up too fast, I wonder when it is all going to catch up to me and kick me in the teeth, and it is bound to happen.

*SOURCE:* Gloria M. Kramer, ed., *The Letters of Richard Marks, Pfc., USMC* (Philadelphia: Lippincott, 1967), 85.

*RELATED ENTRIES: Combat, Effects of; Vietnam War*

## 1965 (to 1967) e

**Excerpts from *A Rumor of War* by Philip Caputo**

*Philip Caputo was a junior officer in "I" Corps of the U.S. Marines, serving in the northern quadrant of South Vietnam from 1965 to 1966. His memoir, A Rumor of War, was one of the more eye-opening and frank accounts of combat and its consequences of those written by Vietnam veterans.*

For Americans who did not come of age in the early sixties, it may be hard to grasp what those years were like—the pride and overpowering self-assurance that prevailed. Most of the thirty-five hundred men in our brigade, born during or immediately after World War II, were shaped by that era, the age of Kennedy's Camelot. We went overseas full of illusions, for which the intoxicating atmosphere of those years was as much to blame as our youth.

War is always attractive to young men who know nothing about it, but we had also been seduced into uniform by Kennedy's challenge to "ask what you can do for your country" and by the missionary idealism he had awakened in us. America seemed omnipotent then: the country could still claim it had never lost a war, and we believed we were ordained to play cop to the Communists' robber and spread our own political faith around the world. Like the French soldiers of the late eighteenth century, we saw ourselves as the champions of "a cause that was destined to triumph." So, when we marched into the rice paddies on that damp March afternoon, we carried, along with our packs and rifles, the implicit convictions that the Viet Cong would be quickly beaten and that we were doing something altogether noble and good. We kept the packs and rifles; the convictions, we lost.

The discovery that the men we had scorned as peasant guerrillas were, in fact, a lethal, determined enemy and the casualty lists that lengthened each week with nothing to show for the blood being spilled broke our early confidence. By autumn, what had begun as an adventurous expedition had turned into an exhausting, indecisive war of attrition in which we fought for no cause other than our own survival. . . .

[In May, 1967], following a tour as the CO of an infantry training company in North Carolina, an honorable discharge released me from the Marines and the chance of dying an early death in Asia. I felt as happy as a condemned man whose sentence has been commuted, but within a year I began growing nostalgic for the war.

Other veterans I knew confessed to the same emotion. In spite of everything, we felt a strange attachment to Vietnam and, even stranger, a longing to return. The war was still being fought, but this desire to go back did not spring from any patriotic ideas about duty, honor, and sacrifice, the myths with which old men send young men off to get killed or maimed. It arose, rather, from a recognition of how deeply we had been changed, how different we were from everyone who had not shared with us the miseries of the monsoon, the exhausting patrols, the fear of a combat assault on a hot landing zone. We had very little in common with them. Though we were civilians again, the civilian world seemed alien. We did not belong to it as much as we did to that other world, where we had fought and our friends had died.

I was involved in the antiwar movement at the time and struggled, unsuccessfully, to reconcile my opposition to the war with this nostalgia. Later, I realized a reconciliation was impossible; I would never be able to hate the war with anything like the undiluted passion of my friends in the movement. Because I had fought in it, it was not an abstract issue, but a deeply emotional experience, the most significant thing that had happened to me. It held my thoughts, senses, and feelings in an unbreakable embrace. I would hear in thunder the roar of artillery. I could not listen to rain without recalling those drenched nights on the line, nor walk through woods without instinctively searching for a trip wire or an ambush. I could protest as loudly as the most convinced activist, but I could not deny the grip the war had on me, nor the fact that it had been an experience as fascinating as it was repulsive, as exhilarating as it was sad, as tender as it was cruel.

This book is partly an attempt to capture something of its ambivalent realities. Anyone who fought in Vietnam, if he is honest about himself, will have to admit he enjoyed the compelling attractiveness of combat. It was a peculiar enjoyment because it was mixed with a commensurate pain. Under fire, a man's powers of life heightened in proportion to the proximity of death, so that he felt an elation as extreme as his dread. His senses quickened, he attained an acuity of consciousness at once pleasurable and excruciating. It was something like the elevated state of awareness induced by drugs. And it could be just as addictive, for it made whatever else life offered in the way of delights or torments seem pedestrian.

I have also attempted to describe the intimacy of life in infantry battalions, where the communion between men is as profound as any between lovers. Actually, it is more so. It does not demand for its sustenance the reciprocity, the pledges of affection, the endless reassurances required by the love of men and women. It is, unlike marriage, a bond that cannot be broken by a word, by boredom or divorce, or by anything other than death. Sometimes even that is not strong enough. Two friends of mine died trying to save the corpses of their men from the battlefield. Such devotion, simple and selfless, the sentiment of belonging to each other, was the one decent thing we found in a conflict otherwise notable for its monstrosities. . . .

At times, the comradeship that was the war's only redeeming quality caused some of its worst crimes—acts of retribution for friends who had been killed. Some men could not withstand the stress of guerrilla-fighting: the hair-trigger alertness constantly demanded of them, the feeling that the enemy was everywhere, the inability to distinguish civilians from combatants created emotional pressures which built to such a point that a trivial provocation could make these men explode with the blind destructiveness of a mortar shell.

Others were made pitiless by an overpowering greed for survival. Self-preservation, that most basic and tyrannical of all instincts, can turn a man into a coward or, as was more often the case in Vietnam, into a creature who destroys without hesitation or remorse whatever poses even a potential threat to his life. A sergeant in my platoon, ordinarily a pleasant young man, told me once, "Lieutenant, I've got a wife and two kids at home and I'm going to see 'em again and don't care who I've got to kill or how many of 'em to do it."

General Westmoreland's strategy of attrition also had an important effect on our behavior. Our mission was not to win terrain or seize positions, but simply to kill: to kill Communists and to kill as many of them as possible. Stack 'em like cordwood. Victory was a high body-count, defeat a low kill-ratio, war a matter of arithmetic. The pressure on unit commanders to produce enemy corpses was intense, and they in turn communicated it to their troops. This led to such practices as counting civilians as Viet Cong. "If it's dead and Vietnamese, it's VC," was a rule of thumb in the bush. It is not surprising, therefore, that some men acquired a contempt for human life and a predilection for taking it. . . .

I came home from the war with the curious feeling that I had grown older than my father, who was then fifty-one. It was as if a lifetime of experience had been compressed into a year and a half. A man saw the heights and depths of human behavior in Vietnam, all manner of violence and horrors so grotesque that they evoked more fascination than disgust. Once I had seen pigs eating napalm-charred corpses—a memorable sight, pigs eating roast people.

I was left with none of the optimism and ambition a young American is supposed to have, only a desire to catch up on sixteen months of missed sleep and an old man's conviction that the future would hold no further surprises, good or bad.

I *hoped* there would be no more surprises. I had survived enough ambushes and doubted my capacity to endure many more physical or emotional shocks. I had all the symptoms of *combat veteranitis*: an inability to concentrate, a child-like fear of darkness, a tendency to tire easily, chronic nightmares, an intolerance of loud noises—especially doors slamming and cars backfiring—and alternating moods of depression and rage that came over me for no apparent reason. Recovery has been less than total.

*SOURCE:* Philip Caputo, *A Rumor of War* (New York: Holt, Rinehart and Winston, 1977), xii, xiv-xv, xvii-xviii, 4. 

*RELATED ENTRIES: Antiwar Movements; Cold War; Combat, Effects of; Tiger Force Recon Scandal; My Lai Massacre; Marine Cops; Vietnam War*

## 1966 a

### Letters from Vietnam GIs on Killing Enemies in Combat

*These three GIs wrote home of their thoughts upon knowing they had killed enemy personnel:*

Dear Nancee,

I received your letter yesterday evening, and it was good to hear from you again. I am fine—just a little beat. I had guard duty last night, so I am tired. We had some visitors when I was on guard the other night. About 30 V.C. tried to get into our compound. You see, what we mainly guard are helicopters. Anyway, a few tried to blow up some copters. I saw them about 20 feet from where I was. I fired a few rounds in their direction, so I might have hit one. You see, the next morning they had an investigation of the area in which I saw the V.C., and they found traces of human blood.

When I was getting off the ship, I said a silent prayer for God not to make me try to kill anyone. Because He's the only one who has the right to take a life—after all, He put us here. He can take us when He wants.

But Nancee, it was either him or me.

Sincerely,
Eddie

Hi Gram,

It was good to hear from you. I was so glad to hear from home. It felt good. My arm was giving me a little trouble this week, but okay today. Tell everyone I said hi. My back is giving me some trouble. Say, do you know when I got shot I cried, and I grabbed my gun and rifle and said *dear God don't let me die*, then I started to yell and cry and stood up. I was shooting all over, then he shot back, and I saw where he was at. I killed him. When he fell from the tree, I ran to him. I was bleeding and I was shaking very bad. When I saw him, I don't know what came over me, but I emptied all I had in him, some 87 holes they found in him. After an hour or so, I was okay. It's no fun shooting a person, and now whenever I see a person who is a Vietnamese I think of that time out there, and I start shaking and I don't know if I should kill them or what. Say, how I wish I was home. It's no fun out here. I feel lost and all alone out here so far from home. I am not doing too good. Please take care of yourself, okay? And please say a prayer for me that I get back okay. I tell you it's bad out here.

Dear Marilyn and Lowell,

Hi! How is everything going for the two of you and the kids? Just fine, I hope. Everything is going pretty good for me here at the present time.

Since the last time I wrote, a few new things have been happening. Since the last time, I've turned from a nice quiet guy into a killer. That raid I told you about that they kept canceling came off on the thirtieth, but my platoon didn't go. The next one was on the fifth, and we weren't supposed to go, either. About ten o'clock that morning we got the word to get ready.

We went in by helicopter, and after reaching shore we set up outside a village. My lieutenant after a while asked for eight guys to go on a combat patrol with him, and I of course volunteered to go.

We were supposed to search an area that was cleared earlier, but they weren't sure if any Vietcong were left or not.

While we were walking along, a shot just missed the lieutenant, and everyone hit the deck. Just before it happened, I was looking up into the trees and saw the muzzle flash from the rifle. After we hit the deck, the lieutenant yelled and asked if anyone saw him. I was raising my rifle up towards the tree just then, and I said "yeah" as I pulled the trigger. I have an automatic rifle and fired about 14 or 15 rounds into the tree where I saw the flash, and the Vietcong came falling out.

I always wondered what it would feel like to kill someone, but after it happened I didn't feel any different. It didn't bother me a bit, and I sort of felt good about it. I didn't feel proud because I killed him, but proud that I didn't freeze up when the time came. I figured his next shot might have been at me and I beat him to it.

That was the only thing that happened around me, and the next morning everyone went back to the ships. We had a couple of guys killed and some wounded, but just how many I don't know.

Well, I guess that is about it for now, so I'll close for the time being. Take care of yourself for now and don't work too hard. I'll write again soon.

All my love,
Mike

*SOURCE:* Glenn Munson, ed., *Letters from Vietnam* (New York: Parallax, 1966), 53, 73, 123.

*RELATED ENTRIES: Combat, Effects of; Vietnam War*

## 1966 b

### Letter from Vietnam GI Objecting to Antiwar Protesters

*This marine wrote home upset by the news of increasing protests against the war. He urged his family to "show your patriotism," and asked rhetorically: "After all, I am not fighting for nothing. Am I?!!"*

Hi Mom, Dad, and all,

I just received your letter. The days are getting longer, so it seems. It won't be too long and I'll be back home again. I'm so anxious to get back home that it isn't even funny. I'm so happy that Dad ordered my car, and I can't wait to see it. Thank you, Dad, I'm so very proud of you and really, Dad, you're the greatest.

It's hard to sleep, eat, or even write any more. This place has definitely played hell with us. It's been a long hard road, Mom and Dad, and I think I've proved myself so far. I know you all have a great confidence in me, and I know I can do any job assigned to me. I've engaged with the Vietcong and Hard Core so many times, I lost track of them. I've got a right to boast a little cause I know I was right in hitting the licks, just like other good Marines have done and are doing and always will. We've put long hours of sweat and blood in this soil, and we will do our best to get these people freedom. Also protect America from Communism.

I only wish I could do something to encourage the boys that are burning their draft cards to stand up and take their responsibilities for their country, family, and friends. You can't defeat Communism by turning your backs or burning your draft cards. Anyone who does it is a disgrace and plain yellow. They haven't got the guts to back up their fathers and forefathers before them. Their lives have gone to waste if the sons today are too afraid to face the facts.

There, I've said what has been on my mind! I hope this doesn't bore you but I just had to put it down on paper.

Mom, Dad, and kids, whenever the national anthem is being played, whether over TV, radio, or at a game, *please, please,* stand up. Show your patriotism. After all, I am not fighting for nothing.

*Am I?!!*

We've got to have a flag, also; do we have one?

Dad, try in every way, whether little or big, to push a little of the patriotism kick into Bob and Ron! Please! Also religion.

GO TO MASS. . .

Goodbye for now, and God bless you all.

I love you all.

Doug

*SOURCE:* Glenn Munson, ed., *Letters from Vietnam* (New York: Parallax, 1966), 106

*RELATED ENTRIES: Antiwar Movements; Conscription and Volunteerism; Draft Evasion and Resistance; Families, Military; Vietnam War*

## 1966 c

### Air Force Officer Dale Noyd's Letter of Resignation

*Troubled by what he regarded as the immoral character of the war being waged by the United States in Vietnam, Capt. Dale Noyd, U.S. Air Force, a man with 11 years of experience, refused to train pilots for service there and tendered this letter of resignation, hoping to be released before the end of his term on moral grounds. He was sentenced to a year in prison by a general court-martial:*

1. I, Dale Edwin Noyd, Captain, FR28084, under paragraph 16m, AFR 36-12, hereby voluntarily tender my resignation from all appointments in the USAF. . . .

2b. I am opposed to the war that this country is waging in Vietnam; and for the past year—since it has become increasingly clear that I will not be able to serve out my obligation and resign from the Air Force—I have considered various stratagems that would obviate my participation in, and contribution to, that war. Among other alternatives, I have considered grounding myself or seeking an assignment other than in Southeast Asia. But these choices were not an honest confrontation of the issues and they do not do justice to my beliefs. The hypocrisy of my silence and acquiescence must end—I feel strongly that it is time for me to demand more consistency between my convictions and my behavior. Several months ago I came to a decision that would reflect this consistency and sought counsel in what alternatives I might have. This letter is a result of that decision. . . .

2c. Increasingly I find myself in the position of being highly involved and caring about many moral, political, and social issues—of which the war in Vietnam is the most important—and yet I cannot protest and work to effect some change. Not only may my convictions remain unexpressed and the concomitant responsibilities unfulfilled, but I am possibly confronted with fighting in a war that I believe to be unjust, immoral, and which makes a mockery of both our constitution and the charter of the United Nations—and the human values which they represent. Apart from the moral and ethical issues, and speaking only from the point of view of the super-patriot, it is a stupid war and pernicious to the self-interest of the United States. I am somewhat reluctant to attempt an analysis of the role of this country in the affairs of Southeast Asia for two reasons: First, I have nothing to say that has not been eloquently stated by men such as Senators Fulbright and Morse, U Thant, Fall, Sheehan, Morgenthau, Goodwin, Scheer, Terrill, Raskin, Lacouture, and, of course, the spokesmen for most of the nations of the free world; and secondly, any brief statement almost of necessity will hazard the same defects that have been characteristic of our foreign policy and its public debate—simplistic and obfuscated by cliches and slogans. Nevertheless, because of the gravity of my circumstances and the unusual nature of my resignation, I shall state some of the observations and premises from which I have made my judgments. First of all, in a nation that pretends to an open and free society, hypocrisy and subterfuge have pervaded our conduct and policy in Southeast Asia at least since 1954. This is not only in relations with the

Vietnamese and in our pronouncements to the other nations of the world, but also with the American people. One need look no further than our public statements in order to detect this. I insist on knowing what my government is doing and it is clear that this right has been usurped. Although I am cognizant that an open society may have its disadvantages in an ideological war with a totalitarian system, I do not believe that the best defense of our freedoms is an emulation of that system. . . .

2g. It is an immoral war for several reasons. It is not only because our presence is unjustified and for what we are doing to the Vietnamese—as I have discussed above—but also because of our "sins" of omission. This country is capable of achieving for its people, and encouraging in other nations, enormous social advancement, but we are now throwing our riches—both of material and of purpose—into the utter waste of the maelstrom of increasing military involvement. If we as a nation really care about people, then we had best make concepts like freedom and equality real to all our citizens—and not just political sham—before we play policeman to the world. Our righteousness is often misplaced. Our behavior in Vietnam is immoral for another set of reasons which concern our conduct of that war. As many newsmen have witnessed, time and again we have bombed, shelled, or attacked a "VC village" or "VC structures" and when we later appraise the results, we label dead adult males as "VC" and add them to the tally—and fail to count the women and children. Our frequent indiscriminate destruction is killing the innocent as well as the "guilty." In addition, our left-handed morality in the treatment of prisoners is odious—we turn them over to the ARVN for possible torture or execution with the excuse that we are not in command but are only supporting the South Vietnam government. Again, this hypocrisy needs no explication. Also frighteningly new in American morality is the pragmatic justification that we must retaliate against the terrorist tactics of the VC. Perhaps most devastatingly immoral about the war in Vietnam are the risks we are assuming for the rest of the world. Each new step and escalation appears unplanned and is an attempt to rectify previous blunders by more military action. The consequences of our course appear too predictable, and although we as a people may elect "better dead than red," do we have the right to make this choice for the rest of mankind?

2h. I am not a pacifist; I believe that there are times when it is right and necessary that a nation or community of nations employ force to deter or repel totalitarian aggression. My three-year assignment in an operational fighter squadron—with the attendant capacity for inflicting terrible killing and destruction—was based on the personal premise that I was serving a useful deterrent purpose and that I would never be used as an instrument of aggression. This, of course, raises the important and pervasive question for me: What is my duty when I am faced with a conflict between my conscience and the commands of my government? What is my responsibility when there is an irreparable division between my beliefs in the ideals of this nation and the conduct of my political and military leaders? The problem of ultimate loyalty is not one for which there is an easy solution. And, unfortunately, the issues are most often obscured by those who would undermine the very freedoms they are ostensibly defending—by invoking "loyalty" and "patriotism" to enforce conformity, silence dissent, and protect themselves from criticism. May a government or nation be in error? Who is to judge? As Thoreau asked, "Must the citizen ever for a moment, or in the least degree, resign his conscience, to the legislator? Why has every man a conscience, then? I think that we should be men first, and subjects afterwards. It is not desirable to cultivate a respect for the law, so much as for the right. The only obligation which I have a right to assume, is to do at any time what I think right. . . . Law never made men a whit more just; and, by means of their respect for it, even the well-disposed are daily made the agents of injustice." The individual must judge. We as a nation expect and demand this—we have prosecuted and condemned those who forfeited their personal sense of justice to an immoral authoritarian system. We have despised those who have pleaded that they were only doing their job. If we are to survive as individuals in this age of acquiescence, and as nations in this time of international anarchy, we must resist total enculturation so that we may stand aside to question and evaluate—not as an Air Force officer or as an American, but as a member of the human species. This resistance and autonomy is difficult to acquire and precarious to maintain, which perhaps explains its rarity. Camus puts it succinctly: "We get into the habit of living before acquiring the habit of thinking." We must not confuse dissent with disloyalty and we must recognize that consensus is no substitute for conscience. As Senator Fulbright has stated, "Criticism is more than a right; it is an act of patriotism—a higher form of patriotism, I believe, than the familiar ritual of national adulation. All of us have the responsibility to act upon this higher patriotism which is to love our country less for what it is than for what we would like it to be." . . .

2j. I have attempted to sincerely state the values and beliefs that are both most meaningful in my life and relevant to my present dilemma. It would appear that I am no longer a loyal Air Force officer if this loyalty requires unquestioning obedience to the policies of this nation in Vietnam. I cannot honestly wear the uniform of this country and support unjust and puerile military involvement. Although it may be inconsistent, I have been able to justify (or rationalize) my position here at the Academy by my belief that my contribution in the classroom has had more effect in encouraging rationalism, a sense of humanism, and the development of social consciousness than it has had in the inculcation of militarism. My system of ethics is humanistic—simply a respect and love for man and confidence in his capability to improve his condition. This is my ultimate loyalty. And, as a man trying to be free, my first obligation is to my own integrity and conscience, and this is of course not mitigated by my government's permission or command to engage in immoral acts. I am many things before I am a citizen of this country or an Air Force officer; and included among these things is simply that I am a man with a set of human values which I will not abrogate. I must stand on what I am and what I believe. The war in Vietnam is unjust and immoral, and if ordered to do so, I shall refuse to fight in that war. I should prefer, and respectfully request, that this resignation be accepted.

*SOURCE: Noyd v. McNamara, Secretary of Defense, et al.*, Records and briefs, U.S. District Court, Denver, Colorado, 1967.

*RELATED ENTRIES: Antiwar Movements; Censorship and the Military; Hitchcock, Ethan Allen; Vietnam War*

# 1966 (to 1971) d

**EXCERPTS FROM *SOLDADOS: CHICANOS IN VIET NAM***

*Chicano veterans of the Vietnam Ware spoke about their background and wartime experiences in Soldados: Chicanos in Viet Nam. Excerpts from four of these accounts are reprinted here.*

Manuel "Peanuts" Marin
Seabees—Navy
Tour of Duty: August 1966 to April 1967

. . .. One of the reasons that went through my mind for joining the service was that I was once an illegal alien. I was brought over from Mexico at the age of one. Being a permanent resident, I felt that it was a good trade for being allowed to live here (U.S.) and go to school. By serving this country, I felt it was a way of paying off. It still goes, regardless of what has happened in between, whether I'd disagree with the politics of being in the service or not. I'm still sincere about this.

When I was about to finish boot camp, they told me that the school for which I had signed up, storekeeper school, was full. They told me there were a few other things I could do. I could go on sea duty and eventually I could apply for a school, or I could choose another school that was open. I wanted to go to storekeeper's school because my friend was going. I'm an impatient person. There was no way I was going on a ship. I hoped that eventually I was going to get into school. I wanted to get my training then. So I signed up for electricians' mate school. I didn't know the slightest thing about being an electrician.

I went to electrician school, and I couldn't handle it. I could do the manual part, but I couldn't handle the theory stuff. Some real nice people tried to help me pass the test, but I couldn't do it. . . . From there I was sent to Coronado, California, where they put me in the worst job possible, which was doing mess hall work. I was there for three months. It was hard work because we'd get up at four in the morning and work until seven or eight at night. After those three months, I was sent to a maintenance unit. That was a lot better because it was an eight to five job. That's when I got in the Seabees. Most of the sailors that were in maintenance were Seabees, and that's how I ended up in Vietnam.

Frank "Yogi" Delgado, Infantryman
25th Division—Army
Tour of Duty: August 1966 to February 1967

. . . The town closest to Fort Polk was Leesville. It was about the size of Corcoran. We used to call it Fleasville or Diseaseville. Louisiana is as bad as Alabama when it comes to segregation. We went to Leesville one time. It was me, a gabacho (*white man*) Jimmy Smith, and this mayate (*black man*) who went to this restaurant to eat. We were in our khaki uniforms, and we were waiting to be served. We waited for a while, and then we noticed other people were being served and waited on. Finally I asked this fat, redneck waitress, "Hey! When are you going to take my order?" She looked at us and said, "Hey! We don't serve niggers here." I have never been a person to go around fighting. I think I have only been in a couple of fights in my whole life. But I got mad in this situation and so did the gabacho. I felt that I had to do something. That's when the mayate said, "Naw, man, just look around you." We looked at the bar, and there were about ten rednecks looking at us—just staring at us. The best thing to do in that situation, which we did, was get up and leave. What are you going to do?

I'll never forget that incident. The war had been going on for two years already, and we were in our army uniforms trying to get a meal. And they pull that s--- on us?

All this time I still had the attitude, I'll take one day at a time. Somehow I knew I would make it. But I wasn't going to [sic] go ask for it. I wasn't going to join airborne. I wasn't going to volunteer for the infantry. I had a lot of camaradas (comrades) that did. That's fine, but that wasn't for me. I didn't volunteer for infantry, but that's what I got.

Larry Holguin, Infantryman
Third Marine Division
Tour of Duty: June 1968 to September 1969

At first you're scared, but after awhile the *susto* (fear) seems to go away. You will find that your fright will make you do things that you don't think you can do. Once you get past that, everything else just becomes a reflex. It's more of not thinking and just doing it. The longer you go into your tour, the sharper you get. . . .

I thought about my mom a lot—my parents, which helped me out a lot. I didn't want my mom to suffer as far as my not coming back. The way I thought about it was, if I was going to come back, I would come back whole. If I wasn't, I wouldn't come home. When I first went overseas, the only thing I wanted to do was make my mom and dad proud of me. But as things went along, it seemed to fade away. It didn't become as important. What became more important was being able to get home safely.

When you're over there (Vietnam), it's a high in itself. You figure that nobody can touch you and that nobody could even hurt you. It's just a phase of emotions that you go through, everybody goes through; and you can't change them because they're there. The only thing is to forget about them and hope the ideas don't ever come back because you're surprised at what a human body can do to another without even thinking about it. But only with the right reasons or the right surroundings can you do this. You just can't do it because you want to do it. You'd be a basket case. You'd be in trouble. Civilization and culture are made so you aren't supposed to go around blowing people up. It's like getting mad and wanting to kill the person right away. And that's what we did in Vietnam.

Freddie Delgado, Infantry
9th Mechanized Unit, 101st Airborne
Tour of Duty: April 1970 to March 1971

. . . They discharged me from Fort Lewis, Washington. They gave me my papers saying, "You, as of now, are a free man." We got there about midnight, and they paid us about three in the morning. When I left Fort Lewis, I had $600 in my pocket.

The first thing I experienced when I got back to the world was that people looked more healthy, more gordos (*fat*). They weren't as small. I said to myself, "Boy, are they feeding you people right over here."

There was an incident that happened at my sister's house. We were watching TV when I got up to change the station. At the same time a jet plane was flying over and made a sonic boom. It rattled the window and s---. I hit the ground automatically. When I got up, I felt embarrassed. My sister and my little brother didn't think it was funny. They realized what was happening to me. After a little bit we started to laugh it off.

One time I was asleep and my dad was sleeping there in the same room when all of a sudden, I gave a big, old grunt. My father told me, "Estas aquí. Ya no estas allá" (*"you are here now, you are not there anymore"*). That happened the first night I was there. I woke up relieved. I got used to it fast. There was a time people were really talking about the Vietnam War, but I didn't talk about it. Even if I would have told them what happened, they wouldn't have believed me. So I decided not to say anything about it when people would ask me questions about Vietnam.

When I came home, I saw some guys with long hair. I was pissed off at them because they didn't go where I went. I guess most of the guys were caught in the middle of the war because we were drafted. After I was home for a few months, I let my hair grow long.

*SOURCE:* Reprinted with permission of copyright holder Charley Trujillo. From Charley Trujillo, *Soldados: Chicanos in Vietnam* (San Jose: Chusma House, 1990).

*RELATED ENTRIES: Combat, Effects of; Conscription and Volunteerism; Latinos in the Military; Vietnam War*

## 1967 (and 2003) a

### Postings to Tiger Force Website in Response to *Toledo Blade* Revelations

*In the spring and summer of 1967, a platoon belonging to "Tiger Force," the elite reconnaissance battalion of the 101st Airborne Division, murdered a number of unarmed Vietnamese in the Song Ve valley and the Chu Lai area of Quang Nam province. When The Toledo Blade broke the story of the botched Army investigation in a series of investigative reports in October 2003, several veterans of Tiger Force units in Vietnam, most of them incredulous, posted communications on that unit's website (http://www.tigerforcerecon.com). Here are two such posts:*

HANK-

I would appreciate it if you would send this out to the Tigers for me.

I have been thinking about the recent story about the killing of unarmed civilians in Vietnam by members of the Tiger Force, and the one thing I keep coming back to is the fact that Vietnam was a very long time ago, and there is nothing we can do about what happened in the past.

What we can do however, is set aside our individual differences, and offer understanding and support for the Tigers who are still fighting the Vietnam War today.

I have been in touch with Rion Causey, and have read the transcript of the interview with Doug Teeters.

They (and I am sure there are more), are still suffering emotionally over what took place back then, and now the important thing is that we, as Tigers both past and present, pull together and try to help them out.

The cold reality of life is that this thing will blow over soon, and eventually be forgotten by the vast majority of people in this country, except for the people involved, and those who care about them. Let's stick together and take care of our own.

As Always,

Lance ("DOC MAT") Matsumonji

Subject: Ok, wrapping our arms around this problem

We have a forum here and I am believing it is a forum of some pretty good Vietnam veterans, men who didn't dodge the draft, men who put their lives on the line for their country, men who became soldiers. These have also been men that were faced with moral quandries that presented themselves by being put in situations where decisions of life or death, and large consequence was confronted and certainly these decisions added to our difficulty with the war. I don't care if someone was in supply or on the front lines at this stage of the game. If you went to Vietnam you were a cut above those that didn't. If you were an American soldier you had to endure the news of fellow soldiers being killed and wounded, but you also had to deal with the news of a faction of the citizens in the United States that appeared to vilify you and what you stood for and in the end, many of us found a troubling conflict about how we were going to process that.

This story won't kill us. In the end it will make us stronger as a group, in the end it will probably be good for us. I suggest everyone read as much of these links as they can stomach and talk about them.

If you look at the numbers, the number of people in this investigation at the outside, as stated, it appears to be about 18 men. The Song Ve incidents were from around May of 1967 to August 1967. Of those 18 the crimes ranged from the killing of "innocent" civilians, to the mutilating of dead bodies and on to less severe "crimes". Further of those 18 the one person that I personally found the most culpable seemed to die suffering from his own guilt and that would be Sam Ybarra, but several others who were objects of the investigation died while serving in Vietnam.

Out of the total number of men that passed through the Tiger Force Rosters over the years this represents a small percentage. As a few of you have heard, I like to draw some parallels to Columbine High School on this. Remember, many of us were just beyond High School so to place weaponry and responsibility on our heads of the magnitude we were confronting certainly became a difficult proving and testing ground. There were a lot of men that did just fine, certainly the vast majority. In the army we got used to the screw ups making our lives difficult, causing us to lose our weekend passes and those people who screwed up, lost it, tipped over, they were in the fray. Men are not perfect, we leave that distinction to God. We don't want to taint the memories of those who have lost their lives in service to their country but at the same time we don't want to ignore the accusations and attempt to hide from or cover up what may serve future soldiers and may need to be brought out.

The exploration of the Toledo Blade's activities has led me to some very interesting information and due to my knowledge and involvement in the Tiger Force there is an honest fascination and appreciation of much of the stories brought to light. Are the stories true? I can only answer for my small part of the equation. Some of what they attributed to me was accurate, but some was not. For example they said I saw P.O.W.'s being murdered. I didn't, to my present day knowledge. Further they indicated I lied to the investigator. I attempted to be honest with the investigators but we all wondered about the usefulness of the investigation in view of what the Tiger Force and it's members had already been through. In the end the investigator told me that this investigation was consuming his life and asked me to answer a few questions by saying "I don't remember". It was Oak Creek Colorado, we were standing outside an old hotel and it was near freezing at night. I told him, fine, if it would make his life easier, ask the questions, and I answered, "I don't remember." This was after I had spent several days and lost a job over this investigation.

I told Joe Mahr, of the Toledo Blade to think about it. A stint in Vietnam was more difficult than any prison sentence. It's pretty obvious that if all these soldiers had spent their years in Vietnam in prison instead we'd have over 58,000 additional people working on behalf of the United States today, educated and paying taxes. Our greatest societal punishment, the death penalty, didn't look a whole lot different than what actually happened to many of the men who were objects of this investigation. Thousands of planes fly the skies, it is only the one that crashes that makes the news and it is a good question of what could be served by this investigation. Well, I'm older now and perhaps some good could be served. Not by punishing the men further, and over the years they have demonstrated they aren't a threat to society post war, by their lives, so it was a special situation. Something should be done. Perhaps something has been done.

These stories were based upon a four and a half year investigation by the Department of the Army Criminal Investigation Department (CID). The Toledo Blade reporters were able to procure a copy of this from a person who worked in the hierarchy of the National Archives of Records who felt the story had been under reported. This person has since passed away as well. Harold Fischer, a Tiger Force medic and person that I have attempted to remain connected to, and I Dan Clint, sought to procure a copy of this report and we succeeded in getting copies. Fischer and I were not objects of the investigation, were listed as witnesses. We had the trauma of seeing these things, of reading these reports several months earlier and we kept it largely to ourselves. I didn't know how to broach the subject with the others that I had acquaintance with via this web site. Fischer kept saying, "I had no idea". Neither did I. Our initial sense of the investigation was that it centered primarily around the activities of Sam Ybarra. Sam seemed to lose it even more severely, morally, when his best friend and fellow "homey" "Boots" Green was killed. His stated hatred of the Vietnamese translated into his policy of shoot first and ask questions later and I for one was distressed that these were not always "clean" enemy confrontations.

For Fischer and I, we seemed to hold to higher moral ground, but even that higher moral ground was shaky and difficult in view of the circumstances. The two young boys working at a table in the jungles manufacturing Chi-Comm grenades. They were maybe 12 and 14 and they grabbed grenades and were dumping them on us. For them, was it playing at war? Did they know better? One of them was shot and killed and the other took off running. That was the day that Fague was shot in the arm in pursuit of the fleeing lad. Were they simply civilians doing honest work? Could we have laid our rifles down and persuaded them to stop lobbing grenades at us. You'd better laugh here. But it was interesting, Sergeant Haugh was in front of me and I could tell he didn't want to shoot them. He was looking for a way out. In a way, most of us were looking for a way out, an honorable way out. Not a draft dodging cowardice way out. Like rats in a cage, we weren't looking for food we were just wanting out.

The story countering this article needs to be told and I am confident it will be. But there is something here for us now. We can understand how these students, say, these children of Columbine High School, the young kids starting their lives, how they were going about their lives, working hard, getting good grades, thinking about their futures when two of the boys in their midst went on a killing rampage. Suddenly everything changed for these students. When someone asks them, "Where are you going to High School?" The pride of their efforts and their accomplishments suddenly becomes secondary to the larger national attention of the two schmucks that put the name "Columbine High" into an unpleasant national spotlight. Two out of how many really great kids? Well, there are parallels, but there are also certainly differences. We are older, we are men, we are paratroopers, we have demonstrated our courage under fire and in the end we will know how to understand the tragedy of these kids and how they are victims of the actions of a small minority and that will make us more compassionate and understanding and temper us a little more. In the end it will make us better friends.

As for our unit now in Iraq, these stories making the national media, the training these new soldiers are receiving as a result of our experiences in Vietnam, the difficult moral decisions of war are being addressed differently and better resultant from our having faced them. I believe the improvements are built upon the backs of us as men who waded through the streams of these complex jungles and carried our friends and our country with us.

With all of that said, Reporters are the pits eh.
Dan Clint

*SOURCE:* Two letters to the webmaster of the TigerForceRecon.com website, late 2003. Reprinted with permission from www.tigerforcerecon.com.

*RELATED ENTRIES: Combat, Effects of; My Lai Massacre; Vietnam War*

# 1967 (to 1969) b

**Environmental Effects of War in Vietnam**

*By 1967, the efforts of the United States to destroy the "cover" used by the enemy in South Vietnam heated up; the spraying of jungles, forests, and rice paddies (aiming at defoliation and crop destruction) with such plant killers as Agent Orange, rose dramatically, as this table indicates:*

Defoliation and Crop Destruction Coverage, 1962-70 (Acres)

| | Defoliation | Crop Destruction | Total |
|---|---|---|---|
| 1962 | 4,940 | 741 | 5,681 |
| 1963 | 24,700 | 247 | 24,947 |
| 1964 | 83,486 | 10,374 | 93,860 |
| 1965 | 155,610 | 65,949 | 221,559 |
| 1966 | 741,247 | 103,987 | 845,144 |
| 1967 | 1,486,446 | 221,312 | 1,706,758 |
| 1968 | 1,267,110 | 63,726 | 1,330,836 |
| 1969 | 1,198,444 | 64,961 | 1,263,405 |
| 1970 | 220,324 | 32,604 | 252,928 |
| **Total** | **4,747,587** | **481,897** | **5,229,484** |

*SOURCE:* MACV, *Command History 1970,* vol. 2, xiv-6.

*RELATED ENTRIES: Environment and War; Vietnam War*

## 1968 a

### Accounts of Servicemen's Combat-Related Psychiatric Disorders

*A psychiatrist described a typical case—from around 1968—of "pseudocombat fatigue syndrome:"*

This 22-year old LCPL USMC with 2 years of active duty and 4 months of service in Viet Nam was hospitalized aboard *Repose* after he "froze" while under enemy fire. At the time of admission he was grossly anxious, tremulous, and agitated. His speech was in explosive bursts, interrupted by periods of preoccupied silence; he reported only vague memory for his combat experiences of recent weeks and the incident which had precipitated his evacuation from the field. He was immediately treated with chlorpromazine in a dosage similar to that of Case I, and 24 hours later his symptoms had remarkably improved. He was calm and communicative, and history could be obtained. This indicated longstanding problems with emotional and impulse control which had caused difficulties in social, family, and school relationships. He enlisted in the Marine Corps after impulsively quitting high school; and his 2 years of service had been marked by frequent emotional upheavals, marginal performance of duty, and a total of nine disciplinary actions for a variety of minor offenses. His initial 2 months of Viet Nam duty had been comparatively peaceful. As his unit made more contacts with the enemy over the next 2 months, however, he grew increasingly apprehensive, and this became more severe after he received a minor shrapnel wound. On the night prior to hospitalization, he was involved in a brief but intense fire fight, and he "froze" in a state of tremulous dissociation. He was sedated, maintained in the field overnight, and then evacuated to the hospital ship in the morning. There his treatment program was very similar to that of Case I, utilizing both chemotherapy and group and individual psychotherapy; he showed early good results with almost complete initial disappearance of anxiety symptoms. It was noted that some tremulousness and apprehension recurred, however, whenever new casualties arrived aboard or when combat ashore was visible or audible from the ship. He then demonstrated acute exacerbation of symptoms when confronted with the prospect of possible return to duty, and he was finally evacuated out of the combat zone with the diagnosis of emotionally unstable personality after 10 days of hospitalization.

*SOURCE:* Robert E. Strange, "Hospital Ship Psychiatric Evacuees," in P. Bourne, ed., *The Psychology and Physiology of Stress* (New York: Academic Press, 1969), 83-84.

*Another Vietnam-era Army psychiatrist described the background of a psychiatric case from the combat zone:*

Henry was a 21-year-old enlisted man who had been in Viet Nam for some 7 months prior to his referral. He was a member of an airborne unit that had been engaged in fairly heavy combat since its arrival. Four weeks prior to his referral, the company had been surrounded while on a search and destroy operation. A saturation bombing of the area was requested. After the bombing, the enemy withdrew and the company returned to base camp. The cost, however, had been heavy. A number of Henry's close buddies had been killed or wounded. Henry did not remember talking very much about the buddies upon his return to base camp. He was all caught up with the realization that he had emerged unscathed. Besides, he was to leave on R & R the following week. The unit did not engage in combat during that week. Henry had a good deal of time to contemplate what he would be doing when he got to Thailand. His description of R & R was of a complete surrender to pleasure. There were girls and "booze." The days and nights were quiet. He had no thought of killing or being killed. However, R & R lasted only 5 days. As the time came to return to Viet Nam, he noticed that his heart was beating more rapidly, that he was sick to his stomach, and that he was restless and "all tied up in knots." Upon return, he heard that the unit had a new CO who was reputed to be a "bastard" and a "glory-hound, John Wayne type." The actual return to the unit was a lonely affair. There had been another mission in his absence. Casualties had again been high. Of the squad to which he was assigned, he was now the only "old timer." "I felt like a stranger in my own home, and that home didn't look so good either." He began to get suspicious of the new men. He thought that they were talking about him and planning to steal the things that he had brought back from Thailand. The next evening, Henry picked up an M-16. He pointed it at one of the new men, accused the man of wanting to laugh at him, and threatened to shoot. A number of men jumped on him. He was subdued and evacuated shortly thereafter.

*SOURCE:* Gary Tischler, "Combat Zone Patterns," in Peter Bourne, ed., *The Psychology and Physiology of Stress* (New York: Academic Press, 1969), 37-38.

*RELATED ENTRIES: Combat, Effects of; Vietnam War; Psychiatric Disorders, Combat-Related; Psychiatry, Military*

## 1968 b

### Defense and NASA Spending in Various States

*The impact of spending by the "military–industrial complex" during the Vietnam War, as at other times during the four decades of Cold War, varied considerably across the United States, as this table indicates. For the states listed below, defense and NASA spending in 1968 is measured in terms of the percentage of the state's total work force.*

| State | Percent |
|---|---|
| Alaska | 31.6 |
| Hawaii | 18.8 |
| District of Columbia | 15.6 |
| Virginia | 14.1 |
| Maryland | 9.9 |
| Utah | 9.9 |
| Georgia | 9.7 |
| Colorado | 9.6 |
| California | 9.3 |
| Connecticut | 9.2 |
| Arizona | 9.0 |
| South Carolina | 8.8 |
| Texas | 8.4 |
| New Mexico | 8.3 |
| Oklahoma | 8.1 |
| Washington | 8.1 |
| New Hampshire | 7.8 |
| Mississippi | 7.3 |

Note: Figures are as of June 30, 1968.

*SOURCE:* "Economies in Arms Mean Leaner Times for Many Workers," *U.S. News & World Report* (1970), reproduced in Seymour Melman, ed., *The War Economy of the United States* (New York, 1971), 231.

*RELATED ENTRIES: Economy and War; Military–Industrial Complex; Vietnam War*

## 1969

### Survey of Veterans' Opinions on Effects of Service

*Gallup pollsters asked thousands of Army veterans of World War II, Korea, and Vietnam three questions about the possible benefits they felt they had acquired as a result of their military service. Despite the popular view during the Vietnam War (and among many to this day) that Vietnam veterans were transformed by the war in ways terribly different from their predecessors, only a few differences between their experiences and those of their fellow veterans can be detected in the responses to these questions:*

**Table 1: Benefits of Military Service**

"Here is a List of Benefits Veterans Sometimes Say They Have Gained from Military Service. Please Read Through the List and Pick as Many or as Few Statements That Describe the Benefits You Feel You Gain from Your Military Service."

| | Army Veterans | | | Vietnam Veterans in |
|---|---|---|---|---|
| Total | WWII | Korea | Vietnam | College |
| **INTANGIBLE REWARDS** | | | | |
| Satisfaction of Serving my country | | | | |
| 79% | 82% | 78% | 64% | 62% |
| Chance to travel and see the world | | | | |
| 72 | 71 | 76 | 68 | 67 |
| Sense of accomplishment | | | | |
| 41 | 40 | 43 | 39 | 49 |
| **CHARACTER DEVELOPMENT** | | | | |
| Developed sense of responsibility | | | | |
| 63 | 61 | 66 | 62 | 57 |
| Discipline | | | | |
| 62 | 63 | 67 | 46 | 47 |
| Self-confidence | | | | |
| 56 | 56 | 59 | 53 | 56 |
| **SOCIAL BENEFITS** | | | | |
| Helped me to get along better with people | | | | |
| 61 | 61 | 62 | 61 | 53 |
| Personal lifetime friendships | | | | |
| 42 | 40 | 41 | 50 | 45 |
| Helped me socially | | | | |
| 23 | 22 | 25 | 24 | 15 |
| **CIVILIAN CAREER BENEFITS** | | | | |
| GI benefits for education | | | | |
| 48 | 41 | 57 | 63 | 92 |
| Became a more effective supervisor | | | | |
| 31 | 30 | 32 | 35 | 41 |
| Helped me to get a job in civilian life | | | | |
| 18 | 18 | 17 | 16 | 12 |

("None" and "no opinion" responses omitted)

TABLE 2: EFFECT ON A MAN'S CHARACTER

"In General, Do You Think Service in the Armed Forces Has a Good or Bad Effect on a Man's Character?"

| | Army Veterans | | | Vietnam Veterans in |
|---|---|---|---|---|
| Total | WWII | Korea | Vietnam | College |
| Good | | | | |
| 79% | 80% | 80% | 72% | 65% |
| Bad | | | | |
| 4 | 4 | 2 | 13 | 10 |
| Other answers | | | | |
| 14 | 13 | 16 | 11 | 20 |
| No opinion | | | | |
| 3 | 3 | 2 | 4 | 5 |

"Why Do You Say That?"*

| | Army Veterans | | | Vietnam Veterans in |
|---|---|---|---|---|
| Total | WWII | Korea | Vietnam | College |
| Percent who say army service has a good effect on a man's character | | | | |
| 79% | 80% | 80% | 72% | 65% |
| Maturity | | | | |
| 27% | 24% | 33% | 31% | 31% |
| Discipline | | | | |
| 22 | 26 | 19 | 10 | 9 |
| Responsibility/ independence | | | | |
| 20 | 19 | 21 | 20 | 15 |
| Learns how to get along with people | | | | |
| 18 | 19 | 16 | 12 | 12 |
| Learns and acquires general experience | | | | |
| 7 | 6 | 6 | 10 | 13 |
| Acquires training, special schooling, and education | | | | |
| 4 | 5 | 3 | 1 | 0 |
| Improves personal well-being, habits | | | | |
| 4 | 5 | 2 | 4 | 2 |

(Top mentions)

*Open, free-response question.

*SOURCE:* Opinion Research Corp., *The Image of the Army* (Princeton, N.J.: Opinion Research Corp., 1969), 73, 77.

*RELATED ENTRIES: American Legion; AMVETS; Korean War; Veterans of Foreign Wars; Vietnam Veterans against the War; Vietnam Veterans of America; Vietnam War; World War II*

# 1970 a

## Open Letter of Chicana GI Widow

*A Chicana widow of a GI who died in Vietnam sent an open "letter to Chicano G.I.s," printed in Right on Post, a underground GI newspaper, in August 1970:*

It is my intention in writing this letter that I will place some very important questions in your minds. It is also my most sincere hope that I may save your women, and your mothers the heartache and sorrow I have experienced.

It has been almost three years since my husband was killed in Viet Nam, leaving me without a man and my daughter without a father.

Recalling the memory of my husband, I've asked myself many times why he died in a war I knew nothing about. And the truth that I found was not easy to accept. Because I then realized my husband died for nothing. Not only did he die for nothing, but he fought and killed in the name of a government that has shamed and discriminated against our race for over two hundred years. This same government that robbed our land and kept us as slaves to work his fields. The same government that won't allow our children to speak our language in his racist schools. The same government that denied us our rights as human beings.

Every day our chicano brothers are being sent to Viet Nam and every day they're coming home in boxes. Our fight is not in Viet Nam fighting people who are fighting for their land and freedom. Our fight is here in this country; for *our land and our freedom.*

The rich white pig has used us as his slaves enough, I say. Ya Basta to the white pig politician and Ya Basta to the white pig businessman. Ya Basta! I want freedom and justice for myself and my people.

Chicana Sister

*SOURCE:* Larry Waterhouse and Mariann G. Wizard, *Turning the Guns Around* (New York: Praeger, 1971), 99. Reprinted with permission of Greenwood Publishing Group, Inc., Westport, Conn. Compare L. Nielson, "Impact of Permanent Father Loss on . . . Male War Orphans" (Ph.D. diss., University of Utah, 1971).

*RELATED ENTRIES: Families, Military; Latinos in the Military; Vietnam War*

# 1970 b

## Widow of Air Force Pilot's Account of Her Experience and Attitude Toward the War

*The wife of a young officer killed in Vietnam spoke in 1970 of her loss and of the war:*

The war came home to me on the 4th of March when I learned that my husband had been killed. I am not bitter about this war. I'm extremely shocked and grieved over his death. He was a professional officer and it seemed inevitable that he would go to war. I am the daughter of a career officer and I've grown up really all over the world. I've always had in the back of my mind that I would want to marry a military man, and while we were stationed in Germany I met my husband. On the morning of Tuesday, March the 4th, my Principal came to my classroom and asked me to go into the office with him. [She was a primary school teacher.] I did, and there were two officers who had been sent to notify me that my husband was missing in Vietnam. Of course, I had many telephone calls to make, to his parents and to the rest of our families, and I stayed at school to make those. I couldn't go home then, and shortly after that a friend came and she took me home. I spent the rest of the day at home sitting and waiting for more news, and also for the first telegram that had been promised to confirm this notification of missing. Since his death I've been surrounded by family and friends and I've also returned to my teaching job where I've been since last September.

Many people do consider this war to be an immoral war, to be unjust. I feel the United States entered this war under an agreement and we must continue there as long as we can fulfill our duty to that country, even though it does mean tremendous suffering for families and a tremendous economic strain on the country. We can't lose the ship halfway at sea. That he did not die in vain—I would never believe that nor would any one who knew him or anybody as dedicated to the military as he was. I've lived with it for two and a half years with my husband, at times I've thought maybe I should be a man so that I could also serve my country. I'm an American first and foremost even though I've lived in different countries and enjoyed different countries thoroughly. They've afforded me different experiences, but the United States is my fatherland, and I respect and admire it's Government and it's military force. My husband's death was not a useless death. It was untimely.

*SOURCE:* Robert Jones (producer), *The War Comes Home* (New Films Co., 1972). The editors are grateful for the permission to print these remarks.

*RELATED ENTRIES: Families, Military; Vietnam War*



## 1970 c

### Excerpts from "Pentagon Papers" Supreme Court Briefs

*In 1970 analyst Daniel Ellsberg leaked a rather pessimistic internal Pentagon evaluation of the Vietnam War to the New York Times. The Nixon administration secured a temporary restraining order on the publication of these documents from the 2nd Circuit Court of Appeals, and the case, involving questions of prior restraint of the press, and national security, was heard on appeal by the Supreme Court; the Court quashed the restraint, and the Times published the "Pentagon Papers."*

Excerpt from the Brief Submitted by the United States

ARGUMENT

I. The First Amendment Does Not Bar a Court From Enjoining the Publication by A Newspaper of Articles that Pose A Grave and Immediate Danger to the Security of the United States

A. The First Amendment does not provide an absolute bar to any prior restraint upon the publication by the newspaper of particular material.

1. The issue before the Court, although of great importance, is narrow. There is no question here of any blanket attempt by the government to enjoin the publication of a newspaper, or any attempt to impose a generalized prohibition upon the publication of broad categories of material. The only issue is whether, in a suit by the United States, the Frist Amendment bars a court from prohibiting a newspaper from publishing material whose disclosure would pose a "grave and immediate danger to the security of the United States."

In the *Times* case, the Court of Appeals fro the Second Court affirmed the district court's denial of a preliminary injuction, except with respect to a limited group of documents. . . . As to those documents, the court continued the preliminary injunction, but remanded the case for the district court to determine, in further *in camera* proceedings, whether any of those specified items met the standard of "grave and immediate danger" to the national security. The government has not sought review of the portion of the judgement of the court of appeals that otherwise affirmed the denial of the preliminary injunction.

In the *Post* case, the government similarly had not challenged the court of appeals' affirmance of the district court's denial of the preliminary injunction, except insofar as that court declined to impose the same condition as the Second Circuit had imposed on the *Times* case. In other words, the government is urging only that the *Post* should be prohibited from publishing those materials within the categories specified by the court of appeals in the *Times* case that pose a "grave and immediate danger" to national security.

The answer to narrow this question does not depend upon the fact that all of the material whose publication the government is seeking to prevent is classified either "top secret" or "secret", that all of the it was obtained illegally from the government and that both the Times and the Post hold such material without any authorization from the government. For whatever the classification this material has, and however the newspaper may have come into possession of it, we submit tht the First Amendment does not preclude an injunction preventing the newspaper from publishing it.

The standard adopted by the Second Circuit is that of "grave and immediate" dander to national security. Since the effect of particular action upon diplomatic relations may be extremely severe in the long run even though its immediate impact is not clear or great, we believe that, insofar as this standard involves the conduct of foreign affairs, the word "immediate" should be construed to mean "irreparable." Indeed, in the delicate area of foreign relations frequently it is impossible to show that something would pose an "immediate" danger to national security, even though the long-run effect upon such security would be grave and irreparable.

*SOURCE:* Brief for the United States, *New York Times Company v. United States of America*, the U.S. Supreme Court Reports, October Term, 1970, no. 1873. Found on National Security Archives Website, http://www.gwu.edu/~nsarchiv/NSAEBB/NSAEBB48/usbrief.pdf (accessed 7/13/2005).

EXCERPT FROM THE BRIEF SUBMITTED BY THE *NEW YORK TIMES*

CONCLUSION

This country's experience with censorship of political speech is happily almost non-existent. Through wars and other turbulence, we have avoided it. Given the choice of risks, we have chosen to risk freedom, as the First Amendment enjoins us to do.

We have not opted for some naïve insistence that all our processes of government take place in the open, or that those charged with heavy responsibilities, executive, legislative or judicial, be denied privacy in their decisional processes. But we have preserved the values of decisional privacy without resorting to censorship. We have met the needs for privacy by safeguarding it at the source, as in the Government's internal procedures for maintaining informational security. In some limited measure, we have used the deterrent force of the criminal sanction to safeguard privacy and security. But we have not censored.

As our affidavits show, press and government have a curious, interlocking, both cooperative and adversary relationship. This has been the case more or less in this country since the extension of manhood suffrage, and the rise of an idependent, rather than party-connected, or faction-connected press. It is not a tidy relationship. It is unruly, or to the extent that it operates under rules, these are unwritten and even tacit ones. Unquestionably, every so often it malfunctions from the point of view of one or the other partner to it. The greater power within it lies with the Government. The press wields the countervailing power conferred upon it by the First Amendment. If there is something near a balance, it is an uneasy one. Any redressing of it at the expense of the press, as this case demonstrates, can come only at the cost of incursions into the First Amendment.

In effect, in this case the Court is asked, without benefit of statute, to redress the balance, to readjust the uneasy arrangement which has, after all, served us well. That which the Government seeks in this case is outside the framework of both law and history.

Except as it inferentially affirms the judgment of the District Court, the judgment of the Court of Appeals should be reversed, and the case remanded with directions to dismiss the complaint.

*SOURCE:* Brief for the Petitioner, *New York Times* Company, *New York Times Company v. United States of America*, the U.S. Supreme Court Reports, October Term, 1970, no. 1873. Found on National Security Archives Website, http://www.gwu.edu/~nsarchiv/NSAEBB/NSAEBB48/nytbrief.pdf (accessed 7/13/2005).

*RELATED ENTRIES: Cold War; Media and War; Pentagon Papers; Vietnam War*

## 1971 a

**LETTERS TO EDITORS OF *SGT FURY AND HIS HOWLING COMMANDOS***

*Enthusiastic fans of the Marvel comic book series "Sergeant Fury and His Howling Commandos" wrote the series editor in 1970 and early 1971. The first letter is from a Specialist/5 in Vietnam.*

DEAR EDITOR:

I have been a regular reader of Marvel mags for many years. They have provided me with pleasure throughout my college years and afterwards. It has never occurred to me that one day I might be writing to you. However, something has come to my attention of late and I feel that I must write to you collectively.

At the present time I am serving with the "Free World Forces" in Viet Nam. As an American citizen I too feel like "Nick Fury," ". . . Fact is, the American fightin' man has always been there when the call came. . . . I ain't saying' whether we're right or wrong." I am here doing my duty. I may be opposed but I am doing my job the best way I can.

Now I'm gonna cut all this formal jazz n get to the point, And the point is . . . I've got, as we say here in the Nam, a case. Here's why.

I used to be out in the field. Not as a grunt or a Howling Commando type, but out there close to it doing the job my government trained me to do. Out there you have a lot of time to think. You pick up on things, real easy. Things you never thought about back in the world. Out there I used to pick up your mags at the PX, read em' and think about them. You guys have been saying stuff for a long time. Good things that tell it like it is. Believe me, your audience digs it. I do 'n became a legit KOF [Keeper of the Flame] turning my buddies on to you.

When your Aug. SGT. FURY came out I flipped. I bought all I could without cornering the market. I started leaving them places and passing them on to people. I left them in places where people who normally wouldn't read them would be exposed to it. Any place where guys just pick up something to read while waiting for something to happen. The ish [issue] became a real topic of rap sessions. People who never before were aware sort of got turned on to new ideas. It became sort of a collectors' item in a very short time. A lot of us were waiting for the next ish to arrive. Here's where my "case" comes in.

IT NEVER CAME.

So I figured someone screwed up . . . it is the army and it does happen. There was nothing to do but wait. Oct ish time came and still no Marvels. I got transfered to another unit cause my old unit was going home. Low and behold I was assigned to Saigon to work. Now Saigon is the New York City, Allice's Resturant, and big PX of Viet Nam. You can get it no matter what you want. N' you know what? There ain't a Marvel Mag in a PX in Nam.

Seems like you guys have stepped on some toes and hit some nerves and the "big wigs" have had you censored. How does that grab you?

It is not because there is not a market. The "other" mags are coming in and being bought. The only difference is the absence of the Marvel line.

Now I don't expect you guys to believe what follows. I have a hard time believing it myself. A couple of weeks ago I had this dream. I didn't really dig it, but you guys should know about it. It wasn't a good trip, but here goes.

I was out in the field humping an M-16 and sweatin like a polar bear in Miami. We came upon this old fort a relic of the French. It was rubble, like somebody had really done a job on the place. You could tell that whoever was hole' up in there had gotten blown away . . . but good. Being hot we dropped our gear an took ten. I went out back to check the place out and found this old fatigue shirt. I was gonna send it to you but it was so old it has fallen apart, so's I'm sending you the name tape which is all that's left . . . "Cpt. AMERIKA."

Like I said, it was a dream and a bad one. I din't like it and I hope it "never happens", God, I really do.

But, right now, I got a real bad case.

". . . you know if you gotta fight, you do . . . but it'd sure be great if we all wised up and decided to chuck all the fighting."

*Sgt. Nick Fury, August, 1970.*

RFO, TTV, KOF (in exile) Sp/5 Keith A. Mishne
275-40-5723, Co. A 519 Sp. Bn. APO S.F. 96307

[From the Editors:] Amen to that, Brother Keith—and we hope you're out of exile soon. That name tape you found sort of worried us, until we realized that it had to be a plant. Guess the Cong don't know how to spell "America."

But, seriously, we've got a stack of letters from Nam complaining that our books disappeared. We don't know what's happened yet, but we've got a guy checking it out with the distributor, and when we know something, we'll pass it on to you guys soonest.

DEAR STAN, GARY, AND JOHN:

How about having Sgt. Nick Fury, Sgt. Bob Jenkins [leader of the "Missouri Marauders"], and Captain Savage on a mission together?

Also, I would like to see the return of all the Marauders and to see the Howlers fighting the Japanese again.

*Tray Turner*, 2400 S. Frazier St.
Phila, Pa 19143

[From the Editors:] Well, Tray, we're putting it to our assemblage of battle mag buffs. What d'ya say, ya goldbricks?!

DEAR STAN, GARY, AND JOHN:

After reading an old ish last Thursday, I came to the conclusion that you guys deserve the three-star medal for your fine portrayal of our military forces. Too often our country's young criticize and deride the Armed Forces of the United States. Our boys in khaki are fighting for democracy and protecting freedom and liberty.

Your portrait of our unsung heroes is a credit to the future's hopes for our land. I thank you personally and for the men with whom I'll be serving in the ensuing months. Peace

Usher Dangerfield, 704 Roderick Mayfair House
Raploch, SCOTLAND

[From the Editors:] We're proud to receive your thanks, Usher. Even though we're not about to say that America's armed forces are always perfect, it's safe to say that we at Marvel can certainly appreciate the heroic part our men played in World War II.

*SOURCE:* Stan Lee and Al Kurzrok, *SGT Fury and His Howling Commandos,* Mag. Management Co., I, no. 88, June 1971.

*RELATED ENTRIES: Captain Marvel Comic Books; Cold War; Literature and War; Militarization and Militarism; Vietnam War; World War II*

# 1971 b

## INTERVIEW WITH U.S. ARMY COL. DAVID H. HACKWORTH

*Col. David Hackworth may have been the most decorated man in the history of the U.S. Army. He and Marine Corps general Victor Krulak were among the most perceptive military critics of the ways the Vietnam War was being waged. Aware that his next assignment would have virtually assured him of future promotion to flag rank, Hackworth boldly chose to grant a public interview on ABC's "Issues and Answers," aired nationwide on Sunday, June 27, 1971, laying out the errors being committed and explaining why he was resigning from the Army.*

Interview with U.S. Army Col. David H. Hackworth
SUNDAY, 27 JUNE 1971
GUEST: Colonel David H. Hackworth, U.S. Army
INTERVIEWED BY: Howard Tuckner, ABC News Saigon Correspondent

MR. TUCKNER: You have served in Korea, you have served in Vietnam for a long time, you have served back at the Pentagon. How do you rate the training of U.S. Army troops who came to Vietnam?

COLONEL HACKWORTH: I think in the main the training for Vietnam from the standpoint of the individual soldier, the young officer, and even the battalion, brigade, and division staff officers and senior commanders has been totally inadequate.

I think that our training was geared to the individual replacement system of World War II. The curriculum was wrong, the quality of the instructors and the leaders was—in my judgment we didn't have the type people that should have been there. The commanders there should have been—the battalion commanders should have commanded battalions in Vietnam. The company commanders should have commanded companies, here, and leaders should have been the finest leaders our country could have mustered to provide the young soldiers with the type training, the realistic training that they needed to confront a guerrilla enemy in Vietnam.

And I'd like to just make the point that when my well-trained, STRAC, one of the finest units in the U.S. Army arrived in Vietnam in June and July of 1965, the mistakes they made were criminal. The number of dead that they have killed among themselves, men that were shot by their comrades, artillery that had fallen on them. Great mistakes were made because of improper training, being not prepared for the war, even though we had from 1953 to 1965 to prepare for the war.

MR. TUCKNER: In your view did poor training lead to higher casualties in Vietnam?

COLONEL HACKWORTH: I am convinced of it. I think that our casualties were at least thirty percent higher because of—or even higher than that, but I'd say, just safely, thirty percent higher because of troops that were not properly trained.

I participated in a study group in the Pentagon in '67 and early '68 which considered U.S. casualties caused by friendly fires and the group was composed of highly experienced personnel that had served in Vietnam and it was our conclusion that fifteen to twenty percent of the casualties caused in Vietnam were the result of friendly fire—one man shooting another man; artillery, friendly artillery firing on a friendly element; friendly helicopters firing on a friendly unit; tac air striking a friendly unit; and I could count you, in my own case, countless personal examples. For example, during the battle of Dak To, June the seventeenth, a rocket ship came into my A Company's position by mistake and released its rockets right on top of the company killing the executive officer and wounding twenty-nine other troopers.

I can recall in September of 1965 as my battalion was deployed, artillery was fired in the wrong place killing seven men in one of my platoons.

MR. TUCKNER: Can it be said that the generals in the U.S. Army, many of them, did not really adjust to the tactics of this war?

COLONEL HACKWORTH: I think the average general that came to Vietnam did not have a good concept, good appreciation of the nature of guerrilla warfare. In most cases because of their lack of even reading in depth about guerrilla warfare, they were not prepared for the war and they had to fall back on Korea and World War II and they used the thought process and the techniques that worked successfully there, moving in large formations, making battalion and brigade airmobile assaults on a small LZ and having everything very tidy, artillery in position and fighting much as we did on the plains of Europe.

I don't feel that too many division commanders, or even separate brigade commanders, really understood the name of the game.

MR. TUCKNER: Did this mean more U.S. casualties, this misunderstanding of the name of the game, as you put it?

COLONEL HACKWORTH: Absolutely. Absolutely. I think probably one of the most classic examples is Hamburger Hill. Here was a hill that had to be taken. Hundreds and hundreds of casualties occurred taking this hill. They had the hill for a few days, the Americans did, and pulled off. So what was the point of taking the hill? Why not stand back if the enemy is on it and bomb, but why use infantry to take the hill?

MR. TUCKNER: Did the upper echelon of the Army really ever become changed on this war? Did they learn from their mistakes?

COLONEL HACKWORTH: I don't think so. I don't think that the top level ever developed a realistic strategic plan nor did they ever have tactics to support that strategic plan.

MR. TUCKNER: Why?

COLONEL HACKWORTH: I think that the top managers of the Army—and there is a big difference between a leader, a combat leader and a manager, the top managers were so involved in systems analysis, in the normal bureaucracy of it all that they were fighting from day to day just to move the paper that crossed their desk and they couldn't see the forest for the trees.

In February when we went into Laos, we went into Laos conventionally. The idea was to block the enemy's supply routes. So we dropped in there. We paid a horrible—the Vietnamese paid a horrible price. Tremendous mistakes were made. Again, conventional thinking. Conventional thinking put us in that operation rather than having a light, mobile guerrilla force, but a guerrilla force that belonged to the Government of Vietnam, or the American Army operating in there like guerrillas. It takes a thief to catch a thief. What we need is a thief. We don't need a conventionally trained FBI agent dashing through the woods with a large force behind him.

We need small people, well trained, highly motivated, and this is what we have not had, because what we have now among the Army is a bunch of shallow dilettantes who run from pillar to post trying to punch their card, serving minimum time at company level because the exposure—you are very close to the heat of the furnace there, meaning you can get in trouble easily.

MR. TUCKNER: Have you found that many other U.S. Army officers who have been here in Vietnam feel the way you do?

COLONEL HACKWORTH: Most of my young friends—that would be captains, majors and lieutenant colonels—who have a considerable amount of experience in Vietnam, feel as I do. A number of very highly qualified full colonels whom I know feel as I do, and I suppose there are a few generals who feel as I do, but in the main this group unfortunately—I suppose it is because of the nature of the beast—is not highly vocal regarding their views because if one would become highly vocal you might become a Billy Mitchell. It might be the end of your career.

MR. TUCKNER: Hasn't this silence meant that some who have died in this war might have been saved?

COLONEL HACKWORTH: That is right, and that is why perhaps we who have not been vocal should be charged for just criminal neglect, because it is our obligation, it is our responsibility, not only to train our soldiers well, to lead our soldiers well, but to make sure that there are no mistakes made, that they are protected as well as possible from mistakes and error and once you make mistakes they must be surfaced, critiqued, identified, and remedial action taken.

MR. TUCKNER: Colonel, I understand that because of the fact that you are considered one of the best infantry officers in the Army you have been asked a number of times to go to the War College, which is preparation for becoming general one day.

COLONEL HACKWORTH: Yes, I have been asked to go to War College for three years straight, and my reason for refusing is that I just simply felt that we were on the battlefield, we were engaged in a critical battle, and I didn't need to go to school at the time to learn anything. I was learning it on the battlefield and I was transferring the skills that I had to my men and probably saving lives.

I can recall in November of 1969 a major general here in Vietnam told me that, when I asked him, should I extend again, he said, "Hack, get out. The war for the U.S. Army is over with in Vietnam."

He said, "You've got all the right tickets and all the right credentials. Go on to War College now and prepare yourself for bigger things."

MR. TUCKNER: Colonel, we have heard a lot about body count in this war. What about it?

COLONEL HACKWORTH: Well, it has been used as a rule of measurement of success. The body count has cost us a lot. It has cost us unnecessary casualties because always in the chain of command one commander is pressuring the other commander for what is the success, what is the body count and it ends up you are calling the platoon leader, "How many have you killed?"

The platoon leader is in a firefight and he hasn't a clue of how many he has killed, but he may have to stop the fight. He may have to expose a few soldiers to go out and count the bodies during the fight. He may lose the momentum of the attack to stay on the enemy and pursue him while he is counting bodies. He may have to squat on the enemy and count the bodies.

It has also really weakened the moral fiber of the officer corps because it has taught them to lie; it has taught them to exaggerate because, again, it is a form of success. It is "How many touchdowns do you have? What is the final score of the game?" And the body count has been greatly exaggerated as a result of this and I would say it has been exaggerated to the tune of twenty to twenty-five percent.

MR. TUCKNER: Do you know of any example specifically where you were involved in trying to substantiate body count that you didn't think was accurate?

COLONEL HACKWORTH: Yes. I could give several good examples. One which comes to mind is a battle which was fought with a great number of friendly maneuver elements, found—reputedly found—an enemy force; we encircled the enemy force. All night long artillery, rockets, fighter bombers were placed on the enemy for us, and came the dawn when we swept the enemy positions there was a total of enemy dead on the battlefield of not more than twenty.

When I crossed over to the other side of the canal that we were fighting on to talk to the commander of the other battalion which was the other half of the encirclement force, the brigade commander came in and started talking about such a brilliant victory we had and that we killed something like two hundred seventy-five or two hundred eighty enemy dead, and this was a classic battle. It illustrated the techniques of mobile warfare, how we could drop on an enemy force, find them, fix them, surround them, and then destroy them, and I pointed out to the brigade commander, the acting brigade commander, I should say, that there wasn't that many dead on the battlefield. We had only killed, I would say, no more than twelve or fifteen and the colonel on the other side had told me he had six or seven, so there couldn't have been twenty or twenty-two or so and I was told there were two hundred eighty killed.*

This is what had been reported to Division. I said, "Well, it is not right. We only had—This battalion is reported to have a strength of three hundred and if we killed two hundred eighty that would leave less than twenty able-bodied men, able to remove the bodies from the battlefield," which is a normal VC technique, which was his excuse for why the bodies weren't on the battlefield.

He said, "Well, that night the survivors carried them off."

I said, "Look, we had the enemy completed surrounded; there was no corridor in which he could escape. If there were a small path that he could have gained escape through our lines that would have meant that every survivor would have had to carry seven or eight bodies plus all their individual weapons." I think there were five total individual weapons found on the battlefield, and this complete battle was a total lie in my judgment.

I was called in by the commander at the time to endorse his after-action report, this report which had all of these bodies in it, and great other irregularities and falsehood, I think designed to make this individual look like Rommel or look like some great tactician and very, very effective combat leader. And I refused to do it. And he and I had somewhat of a major confrontation.

Also during this time I was asked to sign a statement, a narrative statement to support an award for the Distinguished Service Cross for this individual who didn't even get out of his helicopter during the "battle," and I refused to do that.

It was insinuated if I would sign one or two of these documents that I would be—my unit would be considered, possibly, for a unit citation as a result of this action, which I, of course, refused to go along with.

MR. TUCKNER: Did you sign it?

COLONEL HACKWORTH: Absolutely not.

MR. TUCKNER: When leading U.S. government officials, people like former Secretary of Defense McNamara, come to Vietnam for a visit, do they get the clear, straight picture?

COLONEL HACKWORTH: I think what we do for a presentation for a senior official such as Mr. McNamara is put on a razzle-dazzle briefing, complete with charts and extremely well rehearsed briefing officers, and we try to put our best foot forward to try to look as good as possible. Perhaps a scenario would go kind of like this:

After the briefing Mr. McNamara turned to General Wheeler, who was with him, or to General Westmoreland, who I would think accompanied him, and said, "What do you think about that?" And General Wheeler said, "Great battle! We are knockin' 'em dead." And General Westmoreland would have said, "We really got 'em that time! This is a typical action in Vietnam of your U.S. modern Army in action! We have really nailed them and that is the way we are nailing them and that is why we are winning this war. Just give us a few more troops, a few more resources, and we will have 'em on the run. There's light at the end of the tunnel."

He didn't say the VC was holding the candle but he said the end is in sight.

So as a consequence, Mr. McNamara, believing this, perhaps—because it looked real enough to believe—went back and he is sitting—again part of the scenario with the President, and Mr. Johnson says, "How's it going in Vietnam?" And McNamara says, "We are winning."

MR. TUCKNER: Colonel, in 1968 you were so highly thought of that you were selected from a group of a few officers to contribute to a report to General Westmoreland. What did you say in that report?

COLONEL HACKWORTH: Well, my comments were very exciting insofar as the Army staff was concerned. I felt they were truthful and I said that in my judgment at the time this paper was written in 1968, the U.S. Army had badly botched the war in Vietnam and I had considered from a tactical standpoint we had lost the war.

And now my experience three years later only confirms those comments to General Westmoreland.

MR. TUCKNER: What's happened since then? Has there been any change? Have your comments helped anything?

COLONEL HACKWORTH: No, I don't think so. I said that I felt there have been no viable reforms. I felt that the corruption that exists in Vietnam, the graft, the failure to produce continues to exist. I felt that the military had not established any strategic goals, nor had there been any tactical concept developed to support the strategic goals which were not developed and announced.

I felt that we sent an Army to Vietnam that was not prepared to fight the war. We sent an Army that was top-heavy in administrators and logisticians and bloody thin on fighters, not trained for the war. I felt that we didn't understand the nature of the war in the military. I felt that just everything we had done in Vietnam had been done wrong.

MR. TUCKNER: Do you think it is possible, Colonel, that past United States Presidents who have been involved during the Vietnam War, the present Administration, do you think it is possible they may feel they are getting the straight truth, but that it might not be?

COLONEL HACKWORTH: Well, my thing is infantry, which I am very familiar with, and I don't know what happens at the higher echelons. I know the nature of the beast in the military is to sanitize a report to look good. I have seen what has happened at brigade level where the whole situation has been distorted.

I think it is highly probable that all of these beautiful briefings and excellent reports were so production-line Hollywoodized that by the time they got to the President and they got to the people who were making decisions, they didn't have the real facts; they didn't understand what was happening.

MR. TUCKNER: Colonel, what do you think of the Vietnamization program? Is it viable now?

COLONEL HACKWORTH: Well, my view of Vietnamization is, it is a nice word. I think that it has been glamorized; I think that it has been Madison Avenued; I think that it is perhaps a PR's dream. It is a public-relations gimmick.

I have been with the Vietnamese a long time and I have seen great improvements, significant improvement, but I haven't seen the improvements that I read about in many papers, and different magazines, and I hear leading statesmen of our nation say. I don't think the Vietnamese are that good. I don't think the whole Vietnamization thing is real.

MR. TUCKNER: If the enemy chose to react and if American troops were not here, what do you think would happen to the Vietnamese Army?

COLONEL HACKWORTH: I think if the enemy had the capability of launching a concerted attack I would think we would find ourselves in a situation as we were in in '63, '64, and early '65, really, because of the American involvement here, was to save the shattered Vietnamese Army. We were losing on the average of, as I recall, almost a battalion of Vietnamese a week in '65 and I think we would find the same situation developing. If the North Vietnamese, who I feel have the capability—they certainly proved they were pretty dangerous and tough up in Laos—and we find that we recently made a foray into Cambodia, and the enemy is much harder in Cambodia. Last April the targets we were striking along my zone in Cambodia were like taking candy from a baby. Now you go to Cambodia and you find the enemy with his stuff together. He is tough; he is moving back into the areas we used to raid with ease. I think we are going to find it more and more difficult of making these raids into Cambodia.

MR. TUCKNER: Do you think that the programs that the U.S. military and perhaps the U.S. mission had here did not fit the situation for Vietnamization?

COLONEL HACKWORTH: Exactly. We gave them a sheet of music designed by the military and that is what they had to dance by, and the whole organization of the Vietnamese Army in my judgment has been wrong; it has not been tailored or designed to fight the guerrilla in this type of warfare and we have given them a lot of sophisticated equipment, helicopters, sensor devices, radars, complicated vehicles, other complicated equipment that the Vietnamese are just incapable of using, incapable of maintaining, so we have given them now all kinds of sophisticated junk and asked them to use this. Vietnamization now will suddenly win the war because the Vietnamese have helicopters. We will suddenly win the war because the Vietnamese have the M-16 rifle, but it takes a lot more than a piece of equipment or a complicated piece of equipment such as radar and sensors and so on for them to win the war.

Instead of saying, "What you need is well-trained soldiers, what you need is highly motivated soldiers, what you need is soldiers who are similar to the Viet Cong soldiers who are fighting for an ideal, who are fighting for something—similar to Christianity; who are fighting for a cause, a crusade, not fighting to get a Honda or get a new watch or get a portable radio or to have a nice house, but fighting for a cause, and this is what has not been inculcated in the whole army of Vietnam.

MR. TUCKNER: Colonel, do you feel it is possible you have become too emotionally involved in Vietnam?

COLONEL HACKWORTH: I have become emotionally involved in Vietnam. One couldn't have spent the number of years I have spent in Vietnam without becoming emotionally involved. One couldn't see the number of young studs die or be terribly wounded without becoming emotionally involved.

I just have seen the American nation spend so much of its wonderful, great young men in this country. I have seen our national wealth being drained away. I see the nation being split apart and almost being split asunder because of this war, and I am wondering to what end it is all going to lead to.

*Clearly, during the interview my chronology as pertaining to the subject of body count at the Battle of My Phouc Tay (Thanh Phu) was confused. Though the count was inflated by almost one-third by acting Brigade CO Hunt the morning after the battle, the figure of (approximately) 280 did not come to my attention until six weeks later, when Hunt showed me the draft copy of his "History of the Battle of Thanh Phu" and attempted to get my endorsement of it. Similarly, no prolonged discussion about the battle took place between Hunt and myself until that time.

*SOURCE:* Colonel David H. Hackworth, interview by Howard Tuckner, ABC News *Issues and Answers*, ABC, 27 June 1971.

*RELATED ENTRIES: Censorship and the Military; Hitchcock, Ethan Allen; Media and War; Vietnam War*

## 1971 c

### Drug Use in the Army

*Drug use by Army personnel in Vietnam exceeded that of those stationed elsewhere in the world in 1971, but not, for the most part, by drastically different amounts, as this table indicates:*

Percentage of U.S. Army Using Drugs in the Last Twelve Months (1971) by Place of Service

| | Type of Drug | | | | |
|---|---|---|---|---|---|
| Service Location | Marijuana (%) | Other Psychedelic Drugs (%) | Stimulants (%) | Depressants (%) | Narcotic Drugs (%) |
| Continental U.S. | 41.3 | 28.4 | 28.9 | 21.5 | 20.1 |
| Europe | 40.2 | 33.0 | 23.0 | 14.0 | 13.1 |
| Viet Nam | 50.9 | 30.8 | 31.9 | 25.1 | 28.5 |
| Other S.E. Asia | 42.0 | 23.2 | 24.7 | 18.1 | 17.6 |
| Total Army | 42.7 | 29.4 | 28.0 | 20.4 | 20.1 |

*SOURCE:* U.S. Senate, *Drug Abuse in the Military: Hearing Before the Subcommittee on Drug Abuse in the Military of the Committee on Armed Services,* 92nd Cong., 2nd sess., 1972, 127, cited in Savage and Gabriel, "Cohesion and Disintegration in the American Army: An Alternative Perspective," Armed Forces and Society 2 (1975): 351.

*RELATED ENTRIES: Combat, Effects of; Medicine and War; Psychiatry, Military; Vietnam War*

## 1971 d

### Did Vietnam Turn GIs into Addicts?

*Even given the tendency of soldiers in Vietnam to use drugs slightly more frequently than soldiers elsewhere (see document 1971c above), their use did not result long-term addictions. When those returning from tours of duty in Vietnam were surveyed at a later date, it appears that only those who had used heroin, one of the most addictive drugs, were likely to have continued to use it:*

Incidence and Frequency of Drug Use Among Vietnam Enlisted Returnees, Oakland Overseas Processing Center—1—13 March 1971 (1,010 Vietnam Enlisted Separatees—E-1—6, Age 26 or Below)

| | **Before Vietnam** | **During Vietnam** | **Current (last 30 days)** |
|---|---|---|---|
| Marihuana:<br>total users | 45.80%<br>(461) | 58.50%<br>(592) | 37.10%<br>(374) |
| Amphetamines:<br>total users | 14.00%<br>(141) | 16.40%<br>(165) | 5.76%<br>(58) |
| Barbiturates:<br>total users | 11.32%<br>(114) | 15.46%<br>(156) | 7.04%<br>(71) |
| Acid (LSD, peyote, and the like):<br>total users | 12.67%<br>(127) | 9.54%<br>(96) | 4.16%<br>(42) |
| Heroin or morphine:<br>total users | 6.17%<br>(62) | 22.68%<br>(228) | 16.15%<br>(163) |
| Opium:<br>total users | 7.75%<br>(78) | 19.59%<br>(196) | 9.14%<br>(92) |

*SOURCE:* K.E. Nelson and J. Panzarella, "Prevalence of Drug Use, Enlisted Vietnam Returnees Processing for ETS Separation, Oakland Overseas Processing Center," unpublished ms., 1971, cited in John Helmer, *Bringing the War Home* (New York: Free Press, 1974), 78.

*RELATED ENTRIES: Combat, Effects of; Medicine and War; Psychiatry, Military; Vietnam War*

## 1972

### Remarks of Black Veteran on His Return to Pennsylvania

*A black Vietnam veteran from Pennsylvania talked about his moment of horror:*

Ya know, some of the fellows in Vietnam, they become hardened; ah, they develop a crustation or something that affords them the benefit of not having their conscience bother them. Now these guys might go out to the field. They might kill women, children.

Ya know, I cannot do this. I tried to develop this shield of force or whatever it was, and I really tried hard. I talked to guys who had; guys who could laugh at this, to try and formulate some way ya know, to help myself, so I could live, and on several occasions when I said I killed or was responsible for the death of my fellow man.

But, um, there's one time that really stands out in my mind, that I feel contributed greatly to my having to spend six months in a psychiatric ward. I was out on patrol and came to a village and the Cong had been there and they had killed about everyone. The ones that they hadn't killed were dying and there was one child there, and they hadn't harmed her; she was a very small child. And one of the officers said that she could inform the Cong, and that we were waiting for them we knew they'd be back because they'd left supplies here.

And he wanted this child killed, and as I looked at him I could see that this really meant something to him (to have her killed); and it was going to help him believe in what he was doing.

I could see that in his face. It was like it was unspoken. And I didn't want to help him. I didn't mind helping my fellow man, but I didn't want to help him with that. But what can you do when someone puts a gun to your head (or in your hand).

So, I killed the child. . . . and a couple of weeks later, as a result of this, my head blew up. I lapsed into a psychosis or something like this. When I was in the psychiatric ward I once saw my chart and it had "schitzophrenic reations."

I really felt as though when I was in the ward that I was an invalid. Ah, I had no physical handicap whatsoever, but some vital, ah, ah, basic, ah, central or part of my mind was affected to the extent that I really couldn't manage.

I finally left that talk about killing that person, that girl, I don't really have that much trouble providing I stay away from mirrors. But if I go out every face is a mirror, ya know what I mean?

I don't know what I see but I'll just say this, that it immediately transports me back to Vietnam. And I relive what happened over there.

I wanted to burn Pittsburgh and possibly Philly. But it's not that I'm adverse to war, it's just that I had changed so much and Pittsburgh hadn't.

*SOURCE:* Robert Jones (producer), The War Comes Home (New Film Co., 1972). The editors are grateful for the permission to print these remarks.

*RELATED ENTRIES: African Americans in the Military; Combat, Effects of; Racial Integration of the Armed Forces; Vietnam War*



## 1973

### War Powers Resolution

*An attempt by Congress to assert a more powerful role in war-making decisions, the War Powers Resolution of 1973 was enacted during a time when a public—wary from increased intelligence surveillance during the Cold War and the news of break-in of the Democratic National Committee headquarters at the Watergate Hotel—pressured elected officials to institute measures to address the possible misuse of governmental power. The resolution required presidents to inform Congress within 48 hours if U.S. military personnel were deployed in combat overseas and to withdraw them within 60 days unless sanctioned by Congress.*

Public Law 93-148
93rd Congress, H. J. Res. 542
November 7, 1973

Joint Resolution

Concerning the war powers of Congress and the President.

Resolved by the Senate and the House of Representatives of the United States of America in Congress assembled,

SHORT TITLE

SECTION 1. This joint resolution may be cited as the "War Powers Resolution".

PURPOSE AND POLICY

SEC. 2. (a) It is the purpose of this joint resolution to fulfill the intent of the framers of the Constitution of the United States and insure that the collective judgement of both the Congress and the President will apply to the introduction of United States Armed Forces into hostilities, or into situations where imminent involvement in hostilities is clearly indicate by the circumstances, and to the continued use of such forces in hostilities or in such situations.

(b) Under article I, section 8, of the Constitution, it is specifically provided that the Congress shall have the power to make all laws necessary and proper for carrying into execution, not only its own powers but also all other powers vested by the Constitution in the Government of the United States, or in any department or officer thereof.

(c) The constitutional powers of the President as Commander-in-Chief to introduce United States Armed Forces into hostilities, or into situations where imminent involvement in hostilities is clearly indicated by the circumstances, are exercised only pursuant to (1) a declaration of war, (2) specific statutory authorization, or (3) a national emergency created by attack upon the United States, its territories or possessions, or its armed forces.

CONSULTATION

SEC. 3. The President in every possible instance shall consult with Congress before introducing United States Armed Forces into hostilities or into situation where imminent involvement in hostilities is clearly indicated by the circumstances, and after every such introduction shall consult regularly with the Congress until United States Armed

Forces are no longer engaged in hostilities or have been removed from such situations.

REPORTING

SEC. 4. (a) In the absence of a declaration of war, in any case in which United States Armed Forces are introduced--

(1) into hostilities or into situations where imminent involvement in hostilities is clearly indicated by the circumstances;

(2) into the territory, airspace or waters of a foreign nation, while equipped for combat, except for deployments which relate solely to supply, replacement, repair, or training of such forces; or

(3) in numbers which substantially enlarge United States Armed Forces equipped for combat already located in a foreign nation; the president shall submit within 48 hours to the Speaker of the House of Representatives and to the President pro tempore of the Senate a report, in writing, setting forth--

(A) the circumstances necessitating the introduction of United States Armed Forces;

(B) the constitutional and legislative authority under which such introduction took place; and

(C) the estimated scope and duration of the hostilities or involvement.

(b) The President shall provide such other information as the Congress may request in the fulfillment of its constitutional responsibilities with respect to committing the Nation to war and to the use of United States Armed Forces abroad

(c) Whenever United States Armed Forces are introduced into hostilities or into any situation described in subsection (a) of this section, the President shall, so long as such armed forces continue to be engaged in such hostilities or situation, report to the Congress periodically on the status of such hostilities or situation as well as on the scope and duration of such hostilities or situation, but in no event shall he report to the Congress less often than once every six months.

CONGRESSIONAL ACTION

SEC. 5. (a) Each report submitted pursuant to section 4(a)(1) shall be transmitted to the Speaker of the House of Representatives and to the President pro tempore of the Senate on the same calendar day. Each report so transmitted shall be referred to the Committee on Foreign Affairs of the House of Representatives and to the Committee on Foreign Relations of the Senate for appropriate action. If, when the report is transmitted, the Congress has adjourned sine die or has adjourned for any period in excess of three calendar days, the Speaker of the House of Representatives and the President pro tempore of the Senate, if they deem it advisable (or if petitioned by at least 30 percent of the membership of their respective Houses) shall jointly request the President to convene Congress in order that it may consider the report and take appropriate action pursuant to this section.

(b) Within sixty calendar days after a report is submitted or is required to be submitted pursuant to section 4(a)(1), whichever is earlier, the President shall terminate any use of United States Armed Forces with respect to which such report was submitted (or required to be submitted), unless the Congress (1) has declared war or has enacted a specific authorization for such use of United States Armed Forces, (2) has extended by law such sixty-day period, or (3) is physically unable to meet as a result of an armed attack upon the United States. Such sixty-day period shall be extended for not more than an additional thirty days if the President determines and certifies to the Congress in writing that unavoidable military necessity respecting the safety of United States Armed Forces requires the continued use of such armed forces in the course of bringing about a prompt removal of such forces.

(c) Notwithstanding subsection (b), at any time that United States Armed Forces are engaged in hostilities outside the territory of the United States, its possessions and territories without a declaration of war or specific statutory authorization, such forces shall be removed by the President if the Congress so directs by concurrent resolution.

CONGRESSIONAL PRIORITY PROCEDURES FOR JOINT RESOLUTION OR BILL

SEC. 6. (a) Any joint resolution or bill introduced pursuant to section 5(b) at least thirty calendar days before the expiration of the sixty-day period specified in such section shall be referred to the Committee on Foreign Affairs of the House of Representatives or the Committee on Foreign Relations of the Senate, as the case may be, and such committee shall report one such joint resolution or bill, together with its recommendations, not later than twenty-four calendar days before the expiration of the sixty-day period specified in such section, unless such House shall otherwise determine by the yeas and nays.

(b) Any joint resolution or bill so reported shall become the pending business of the House in question (in the case of the Senate the time for debate shall be equally divided between the proponents and the opponents), and shall be voted on within three calendar days thereafter, unless such House shall otherwise determine by yeas and nays.

(c) Such a joint resolution or bill passed by one House shall be referred to the committee of the other House named in subsection (a) and shall be reported out not later than fourteen calendar days before the expiration of the sixty-day period specified in section 5(b). The joint resolution or bill so reported shall become the pending business of the House in question and shall be voted on within three calendar days after it has been reported, unless such House shall otherwise determine by yeas and nays.

(d) In the case of any disagreement between the two Houses of Congress with respect to a joint resolution or bill passed by both Houses, conferees shall be promptly appointed and the committee of conference shall make and file a report with respect to such resolution or bill not later than four calendar days before the expiration of the sixty-day period specified in section 5(b). In the event the conferees are unable to agree within 48 hours, they shall report back to their respective Houses in disagreement. Notwithstanding any rule in either House concerning the printing of conference reports in the Record or concerning any delay in the consideration of such reports, such report shall be acted on by both Houses not later than the expiration of such sixty-day period.

CONGRESSIONAL PRIORITY PROCEDURES FOR CONCURRENT RESOLUTION

SEC. 7. (a) Any concurrent resolution introduced pursuant to section 5(b) at least thirty calendar days before the expiration of the sixty-day period specified in such section shall be referred to the Committee on Foreign Affairs of the House of Representatives or the Committee on Foreign Relations of the Senate, as the case may be, and one such concurrent resolution shall be reported out by such committee together with its recommendations within fifteen calendar days, unless such House shall otherwise determine by the yeas and nays.

(b) Any concurrent resolution so reported shall become the pending business of the House in question (in the case of the Senate the time for debate shall be equally divided between the proponents and the opponents), and shall be voted on within three calendar days thereafter, unless such House shall otherwise determine by yeas and nays.

(c) Such a concurrent resolution passed by one House shall be referred to the committee of the other House named in subsection (a) and shall be reported out by such committee together with its recommendations within fifteen calendar days and shall thereupon become the pending business of such House and shall be voted on within three calendar days after it has been reported, unless such House shall otherwise determine by yeas and nays.

(d) In the case of any disagreement between the two Houses of Congress with respect to a concurrent resolution passed by both Houses, conferees shall be promptly appointed and the committee of conference shall make and file a report with respect to such concurrent resolution within six calendar days after the legislation is referred to the committee of conference.

Notwithstanding any rule in either House concerning the printing of conference reports in the Record or concerning any delay in the consideration of such reports, such report shall be acted on by both Houses not later than six calendar days after the conference report is filed. In the event the conferees are unable to agree within 48 hours, they shall report back to their respective Houses in disagreement.

INTERPRETATION OF JOINT RESOLUTION

SEC. 8. (a) Authority to introduce United States Armed Forces into hostilities or into situations wherein involvement in hostilities is clearly indicated by the circumstances shall not be inferred--

(1) from any provision of law (whether or not in effect before the date of the enactment of this joint resolution), including any provision contained in any appropriation Act, unless such provision specifically authorizes the introduction of United States Armed Forces into hostilities or into such situations and stating that it is intended to constitute specific statutory authorization within the meaning of this joint resolution; or

(2) from any treaty heretofore or hereafter ratified unless such treaty is implemented by legislation specifically authorizing the introduction of United States Armed Forces into hostilities or into such situations and stating that it is intended to constitute specific statutory authorization within the meaning of this joint resolution.

(b) Nothing in this joint resolution shall be construed to require any further specific statutory authorization to permit members of United States Armed Forces to participate jointly with members of the armed forces of one or more foreign countries in the headquarters operations of high-level military commands which were established prior to the date of enactment of this joint resolution and pursuant to the United Nations Charter or any treaty ratified by the United States prior to such date.

(c) For purposes of this joint resolution, the term "introduction of United States Armed Forces" includes the assignment of member of such armed forces to command, coordinate, participate in the movement of, or accompany the regular or irregular military forces of any foreign country or government when such military forces are engaged, or there exists an imminent threat that such forces will become engaged, in hostilities.

(d) Nothing in this joint resolution--

(1) is intended to alter the constitutional authority of the Congress or of the President, or the provision of existing treaties; or (2) shall be construed as granting any authority to the President with respect to the introduction of United States Armed Forces into hostilities or into situations wherein involvement in hostilities is clearly indicated by the circumstances which authority he would not have had in the absence of this joint resolution.

SEPARABILITY CLAUSE

SEC. 9. If any provision of this joint resolution or the application thereof to any person or circumstance is held invalid, the remainder of the joint resolution and the application of such provision to any other person or circumstance shall not be affected thereby.

EFFECTIVE DATE

SEC. 10. This joint resolution shall take effect on the date of its enactment.

*SOURCE:* Almanac of Policy Issues, http://www.policyalmanac.org/world/archive/war_powers_resolution.shtml (July 22, 2005).

*RELATED ENTRIES: Cold War; War Powers Resolution; Vietnam War*

## 1975

### Lt. Keffer's Reflections on Attending a Reunion of Buchenwald Survivors

*Fredric Keffer, a World War II veteran of the 6th Armored Division, made a different kind of trip with his son Tom to the 30th reunion of the survivors of Buchenwald; he had been a part of the first Allied unit to reach the camp. Keffer described the reunion for his "Super-Sixer" comrades, and commented on the meaning to him of what had transpired a generation before:*

On April 11, 1945, HERBERT GOTTSCHALK and I crossed through a hole in a twelve-foot-high double barbed wire enclosure and were suddenly swarmed upon and cheered and tossed up and down and madly jostled, embraced, and crushed by the 21,000 political prisoners of Buchenwald Concentration Camp. We had arrived in an M-8 scout car, just four of us, HARRY WARD and JAMES HOYT (radio operator and driver, both of whom remained with the scout car) and HERB and myself, on a side trip several kilometers away from the main body of Combat Team 9. We had come—the first American soldiers—minutes after the brutal SS guards had fled. We had come, in fact, because many of the guards had been picked up by our main body, and we wanted to find out just what it was they were fleeing. And those wonderful prisoners, those emaciated and battered skeletons of men, had somehow summoned-up a last bit of adrenalin for joyous welcome. There was little else left in them, and it didn't seem likely that any could survive another year, even in a hospital.

Yet here we were, HERB and I, over thirty years later, on September 20, 1975, being honored by nearly a hundred healthy and hearty Belgian survivors of Buchenwald, members of an organization very much like our Association, called the Amicale de Buchenwald. And we were assured that they were in close touch with many survivors from France, Netherlands, Denmark, Poland, Czechoslovakia, indeed from all over Europe—even from West and East Germany; and in fact we met one German anti-Nazi who had spent ten years, from 1935 to 1945, in various Nazi prisons. It was the first time we had seen Buchenwalders since 1945, and we were amazed and delighted by their tenacity of body and exuberence of spirit. Our Belgian hosts, together with their wives and a few fellow prisoners from outside Belgium, were assembled in the sumptuous new Congress Palace in Liège. Any Super-Sixer who had seen the crumbling town of Liège in 1945 would hardly have been prepared for the bustling, sky-scrapered, traffic-choked, steel-mill-smoked, river-polluted metropolis of 1975, complete with Holiday Inn right next door to the Congress Palace. I had trouble adjusting to the reality of today, just as my son TOM, who came with me, had trouble adjusting to a past which had produced concentration camps.

TOM and I began our journey into present and past with a drive around Bastogne, through northern Luxembourg, and across the Our River into Germany. We had to look hard to see any evidence of those awful days of 1944-45 in the cold snow. We were able, with real effort, to find one miserable little pile of rocks that looked like it might once have been part of the massive Sigfried Line. Here and there in Luxembourg one finds a German tank, an 88, or an American tank, but only because some local group has carefully maintained these relics like stuffed animals in a museum. And in Clervaux there even is a museum, yes Sir, a genuine museum, where you pay admission to look at such rare old specimens as GI helmets and OD shirts, and carbines and M1 rifles, and K rations (and even German counterparts) which were carefully collected from all that good old American (and German) litter that was left on Luxembourg battlefields. We stared in disbelief. Somehow none of this seemed to be real anymore. . . .

On Sunday noon there was a formal meeting, with speeches. [Maurice] Bolle chaired. A fiery speech with pounding on the rostrum was presented by a Frenchman who was introduced as head of the International Congress of ex-Concentration Camp Prisoners. A non-fiery, 40-minute speech in soporific French was given by the president of the Belgian group. Bolle read a "wish I could be with you" telegram from a comrade in Moscow, in French, but broken with several "STOP"s in English. I was moved to give a short speech, in English of course, to thank them all on behalf of my fellow soldiers and to say that the liberation of Buchenwald and indeed of the European continent was what World War II was all about. I didn't say so, but if I had ever had any doubts that our participation in that war was right and just, those doubts had been completely dispelled on greeting and being greeted by these wonderful men of Buchenwald. . . .

There was one little session in Liège that I have saved mention until last. Bolle brought a small group together, gave each American a handsome pewter plate memento, and then read a speech (in English, followed by translation into German by BONNIE ELDER). This Speech which expressed his worries about the future, was directed to us Americans and most specifically to TOM and to his generation. How easy it is, he said, to forget the terrors of fascism, and how hard it is to prevent fascism from arising. The principal reason he spends his time and energy keeping the Amicale de Buchenwald functioning is to educate the public and make people aware of the brutalities that might come again. He cannot rest, even at age 85. How can he get more publicity, he kept asking.

The question has no simple answer. I had already given a portion of my own answer by inviting TOM to accompany me to Liège. Another portion of my answer has been to write this account. I hope that many Super-Sixers will pass this on to their sons and daughters. Memories of evil get erased, for life must go on, and new generations cannot be locked into the past. But they would do well to remember the past.

*SOURCE:* Fredric Keffer, *The Super-Sixer* [6th Armored Newsletter] 26 (January 1976): 3-6.

*RELATED ENTRIES: Combat, Effects of; Memory and War; World War II*

## 1976 a

### Excerpts from Book Two (Intelligence Activities and the Rights of Americans) of the Church Committee Report

*During the Cold War the Federal Bureau of Investigation, the National Security Agency, the Central Intelligence Agency, and military intelligence bureaus gathered information about American citizens, manipulated the media, and plotted secret wars and assassinations overseas. One FBI operation, COINTELPRO, engaged in counter-intelligence measures against radical political groups and civil rights leaders such as Martin Luther King for some seven years (1965–1971) until its existence and conduct came to public attention. It was thereupon formally disbanded. For two decades there existed few constraints on how the information was obtained or what was done with it. With the disclosure of the break-in to the Democratic National Committee headquarters at the Watergate hotel in Washington in 1972, and the overthrow of Pres. Salvatore Allende in Chile in 1973, Congress began to act. In 1974 Congress gave teeth to the 1966 Freedom of Information Act by requiring prompt responses to requests for information held by government agencies and placing the burden of proof upon the agency for any "secret" classification of such documents. In 1975 the Rockefeller Commission reported its findings on CIA activities within the United States, and in April 1976 the public was presented with this revealing Senate report on "Governmental Operations with respect to Intelligence Activities," commonly referred to as the "Church Committee Report," after the committee's chair, Senator Frank Church (D, Idaho).*

UNITED STATES SENATE
APRIL 26 (legislative day, April 14), 1976

I. INTRODUCTION AND SUMMARY

The resolution creating this Committee placed greatest emphasis on whether intelligence activities threaten the "rights of American citizens."

The critical question before the Committee was to determine how the fundamental liberties of the people can be maintained in the course of the Government's effort to protect their security. The delicate balance between these basic goals of our system of government is often difficult to strike, but it can, and must, be achieved. We reject the view that the traditional American principles of justice and fair play have no place in our struggle against the enemies of freedom. Moreover, our investigation has established that the targets of intelligence activity have ranged far beyond persons who could properly be characterized as enemies of freedom and have extended to a wide array of citizens engaging in lawful activity.

Americans have rightfully been concerned since before World War II about the dangers of hostile foreign agents likely to commit acts of espionage. Similarly, the violent acts of political terrorists can seriously endanger the rights of Americans. Carefully focused intelligence investigations can help prevent such acts. But too often intelligence has lost this focus and domestic intelligence activities have invaded individual privacy and violated the rights of lawful assembly and political expression. Unless new and tighter controls are established by legislation, domestic intelligence activities threaten to undermine our democratic society and fundamentally alter its nature.

We have examined three types of "intelligence" activities affecting the rights of American citizens. The first is intelligence collection—such as infiltrating groups with informants, wiretapping, or opening letters. The second is dissemination of material which has been collected. The third is covert action designed to disrupt and discredit the activities of groups and individuals deemed a threat to the social order. These three types of "intelligence" activity are closely related in the practical world. Information which is disseminated by the intelligence community or used in disruptive programs has usually been obtained through surveillance. Nevertheless, a division between collection, dissemination and covert action is analytically useful both in understanding why excesses have occurred in the past and in devising remedies to prevent those excesses from recurring.

*A. Intelligence Activity: A New Form of Governmental Power to Impair Citizens' Rights*

A tension between order and liberty is inevitable in any society. A Government must protect its citizens from those bent on engaging in violence and criminal behavior, or in espionage and other hostile foreign intelligence activity. Many of the intelligence programs reviewed in this report were established for those purposes. Intelligence work has, at times, successfully prevented dangerous and abhorrent acts, such as bombings and foreign spying, and aided in the prosecution of those responsible for such acts.

But, intelligence activity in the past decades has, all too often, exceeded the restraints on the exercise of governmental power which are imposed by our country's Constitution, laws, and traditions. . . .

Our investigation has confirmed that warning. We have seen segments of our Government, in their attitudes and action, adopt tactics unworthy of a democracy, and occasionally reminiscent of the tactics of totalitarian regimes. We have seen a consistent pattern in which programs initiated with limited goals, such as preventing criminal violence or identifying foreign spies, were expanded to what witnesses characterized as "vacuum cleaners", sweeping in information about lawful activities of American citizens. . . .

*C. Summary of the Main Problems*

. . . . Too many people have been spied upon by too many Government agencies and too much information has been collected. The Government has often undertaken the secret surveillance of citizens on the basis of their political beliefs, even when those beliefs posed no threat of violence or illegal acts on behalf of a hostile foreign power. The Government, operating primarily through secret informants, but also using other intrusive techniques such as wiretaps, microphone "bugs", surreptitious mail opening, and break-ins, has swept in vast amounts of information about the personal lives, views, and associations of American citizens. Investigations of groups deemed potentially dangerous—and even of groups suspected of associating with potentially dangerous organizations—have continued for decades, despite the fact that those groups did not engage in unlawful activity. Groups and individuals have been harassed and disrupted because of their political views and their lifestyles. Investigations have been based upon vague standards whose breadth made excessive collection inevitable. Unsavory and vicious tactics have been employed—including anonymous attempts to break up marriages, disrupt meetings, ostracize persons from their professions, and provoke target groups into rivalries that might result in deaths. Intelligence agencies have served the political and personal objectives of Presidents and other high officials. While the agencies often committed excesses in response to pressure from high officials in the Executive branch and Congress, they also occasionally initiated improper activities and then concealed them from officials whom they had a duty to inform.

Governmental officials—including those whose principal duty is to enforce the law—have violated or ignored the law over long periods of time and have advocated and defended their right to break the law.

The Constitutional system of checks and balances has not adequately controlled intelligence activities. Until recently the Executive branch has neither delineated the scope of permissible activities nor established procedures for supervising intelligence agencies. Congress has failed to exercise sufficient oversight, seldom questioning the use to which its appropriations were being put. Most domestic intelligence issues have not reached the courts, and in those cases when they have reached the courts, the judiciary has been reluctant to grapple with them.

Each of these points is briefly illustrated below, and covered in substantially greater detail in the following sections of the report.

*1. The Number of People Affected by Domestic Intelligence Activity*

United States intelligence agencies have investigated a vast number of American citizens and domestic organizations. FBI headquarters alone has developed over 500,000 domestic intelligence files, and these have been augmented by additional files at FBI Field Offices. The FBI opened 65,000 of these domestic intelligence files in 1972 alone. In fact, substantially more individuals and groups are subject to intelligence scrutiny than the number of files would appear to indicate, since typically, each domestic intelligence file contains information on more than one individual or group, and this information is readily retrievable through the FBI General Name Index.

The number of Americans and domestic groups caught in the domestic intelligence net is further illustrated by the following statistics:

—Nearly a quarter of a million first class letters were opened and photographed in the United States by the CIA between 1953-1973, producing a CIA computerized index of nearly one and one-half million names.

—At least 130,000 first class letters were opened and photographed by the FBI between 1940-1966 in eight U.S. cities.

—Some 300,000 individuals were indexed in a CIA computer system and separate files were created on approximately 7,200 Americans and over 100 domestic groups during the course of CIA's Operation CHAOS (1967-1973).

—Millions of private telegrams sent from, to, or through the United States were obtained by the National Security Agency from 1947 to 1975 under a secret arrangement with three United States telegraph companies.

—An estimated 100,000 Americans were the subjects of United States Army intelligence files created between the mid 1960's and 1971.

—Intelligence files on more than 11,000 individuals and groups were created by the Internal Revenue Service between 1969 and 1973 and tax investigations were started on the basis of political rather than tax criteria.

—At least 26,000 individuals were at one point catalogued on an FBI list of persons to be rounded up in the event of a "national emergency".

*2. Too Much Information Is Collected For Too Long*

Intelligence agencies have collected vast amounts of information about the intimate details of citizens' lives and about their participation in legal and peaceful political activities. The targets of intelligence activity have included political adherents of the right and the left, ranging from activitist to casual supporters. Investigations have been directed against proponents of racial causes and women's rights, outspoken apostles of nonviolence and racial harmony; establishment politicians; religious groups; and advocates of new life styles. . . .

*3. Covert Action and the Use of Illegal or Improper Means*

(a) Covert Action.—Apart from uncovering excesses in the collection of intelligence, our investigation has disclosed covert actions directed against Americans, and the use of illegal and improper surveillance techniques to gather information. For example:

(i) The FBI's COINTELPRO—counterintelligence program—was designed to "disrupt" groups and "neutralize" individuals deemed to be threats to domestic security. The FBI resorted to counterintelligence tactics in part because its chief officials believed that the existing law could not control the activities of certain dissident groups, and that court decisions had tied the hands of the intelligence community. Whatever opinion one holds about the policies of the targeted groups, many of the tactics employed by the FBI were indisputably degrading to a free society. COINTELPRO tactics included:

—Anonymously attacking the political beliefs of targets in order to induce their employers to fire them;

—Anonymously mailing letters to the spouses of intelligence targets for the purpose of destroying their marriages;

—Obtaining from IRS the tax returns of a target and then attempting to provoke an IRS investigation for the express purpose of deterring a protest leader from attending the Democratic National Convention;

—Falsely and anonymously labeling as Government informants members of groups known to be violent, thereby exposing the falsely labelled member to expulsion or physical attack;

—Pursuant to instructions to use "misinformation" to disrupt demonstrations, employing such means as broadcasting fake orders on the same citizens band radio frequency used by demonstration marshalls to attempt to control demonstrations, and duplicating and falsely filling out forms soliciting housing for persons coming to a demonstration, thereby causing "long and useless journeys to locate these addresses";

—Sending an anonymous letter to the leader of a Chicago street gang (described as "violence-prone") stating that the Black Panthers were supposed to have "a hit out for you". The letter was suggested because it "may intensify . . . animosity" and cause the street gang leader to "take retaliatory action".

(ii) From "late 1963" until his death in 1968, Martin Luther King, Jr., was the target of an intensive campaign by the Federal Bureau of Investigation to "neutralize" him as an effective civil rights leader. In the words of the man in charge of the FBI's "war" against Dr. King, "No holds were barred." . . .

The FBI mailed Dr. King a tape recording made from microphones hidden in his hotel rooms which one agent testified was an attempt to destroy Dr. King's marriage. The tape recording was accompanied by a note which Dr. King and his advisors interpreted as threatening to release the tape recording unless Dr. King committed suicide. . . .

(b) Illegal or Improper Means.—The surveillance which we investigated was not only vastly excessive in breadth and a basis for degrading counterintelligence actions, but was also often conducted by illegal or improper means. For example:

(1) For approximately 20 years the CIA carried out a program of indiscriminately opening citizens' first class mail. The Bureau also had a mail opening program, but cancelled it in 1966. The Bureau continued, however, to receive the illegal fruits of CIA's program. In 1970, the heads of both agencies signed a document for President Nixon, which correctly stated that mail opening was illegal, falsely stated that it had been discontinued, and proposed that the illegal opening of mail should be resumed because it would provide useful results. The President approved the program, but withdrew his approval five days later. The illegal opening continued nonetheless. Throughout this period CIA officials knew that mail opening was illegal, but expressed concern about the "flap potential" of exposure, not about the illegality of their activity. . . .

*4. Ignoring the Law*

Officials of the intelligence agencies occasionally recognized that certain activities were illegal, but expressed concern only for "flap potential." Even more disturbing was the frequent testimony that the law, and the Constitution were simply ignored. . . .The man who for ten years headed FBI's Intelligence Division testifed that:

. . . "never once did I hear anybody, including myself, raise the question: 'Is this course of action which we have agreed upon lawful, is it legal, is it ethical or moral.' We never gave any thought to this line of reasoning, because we were just naturally pragmatic." . . .

*5. Deficiencies in Accountability and Control*

The overwhelming number of excesses continuing over a prolonged period of time were due in large measure to the fact that the system of checks and balances—created in our Constitution to limit abuse of Governmental power—was seldom applied to the intelligence community. Guidance and regulation from outside the intelligence agencies—where it has been imposed at all—has been vague. Presidents and other senior Executive officials, particularly the Attorneys General, have virtually abdicated their Constitutional responsibility to oversee and set standards for intelligence activity. Senior government officials generally gave the agencies broad, general mandates or pressed for immediate results on pressing problems. In neither case did they provide guidance to prevent excesses and their broad mandates and pressures themselves often resulted in excessive or improper intelligence activity. . . .

*6. The Adverse Impact of Improper Intelligence Activity*

Many of the illegal or improper disruptive efforts directed against American citizens and domestic organizations succeeded in injuring their targets. Although it is sometimes difficult to prove that a target's misfortunes were caused by a counter-intelligence program directed against him, the possibility that an arm of the United States Government intended to cause the harm and might have been responsible is itself abhorrent. . . .

*7. Cost and Value*

Domestic intelligence is expensive. We have already indicated the cost of illegal and improper intelligence activities in terms of the harm to victims, the injury to constitutional values, and the damage to the democratic process itself. The cost in dollars is also significant. For example, the FBI has budgeted for fiscal year 1976 over $7 million for its domestic security informant program, more than twice the amount it spends on informants against organized crime. The aggregate budget for FBI domestic security intelligence and foreign counterintelligence is at least $80 million. In the late 1960s and early 1970s, when the Bureau was joined by the CIA, the military, and NSA in collecting information about the anti-war movement and black activists, the cost was substantially greater.

Apart from the excesses described above, the usefulness of many domestic intelligence activities in serving the legitimate goal of protecting society has been questionable. Properly directed intelligence investigations concentrating upon hostile foreign agents and violent terrorists can produce valuable results. The Committee has examined cases where the FBI uncovered "illegal" agents of a foreign power engaged in clandestine intelligence activities in violation of federal law. Information leading to the prevention of serious violence has been acquired by the FBI through its informant penetration of terrorist groups and through the inclusion in Bureau files of the names of persons actively involved with such groups. Nevertheless, the most sweeping domestic intelligence surveillance programs have produced surprisingly few useful returns in view of their extent. For example:

—Between 1960 and 1974, the FBI conducted over 500,000 separate investigations of persons and groups under the "subversive" category, predicated on the possibility that they might be likely to overthrow the government of the United States. Yet not a single individual or group has been prosecuted since 1957 under the laws which prohibit planning or advocating action to overthrow the government and which are the main alleged statutory basis for such FBI investigations.

—A recent study by the General Accounting Office has estimated that of some 17,528 FBI domestic intelligence investigations of individuals in 1974, only 1.3 percent resulted in prosecution and conviction, and in only "about 2 percent" of the cases was advance knowledge of any activity—legal or illegal—obtained.

[Conclusion]

In considering its recommendations, the Committee undertook an evaluation of the FBI's claims that domestic intelligence was necessary to combat terrorism, civil disorders, "subversion," and hostile foreign intelligence activity. The Committee reviewed voluminous materials bearing on this issue and questioned Bureau officials, local police officials, and present and former federal executive officials.

We have found that we are in fundamental agreement with the wisdom of Attorney General Stone's initial warning that intelligence agencies must not be "concerned with political or other opinions of individuals" and must be limited to investigating essentially only "such conduct as is forbidden by the laws of the United States." The Committee's record demonstrates that domestic intelligence which departs from this standard raises grave risks of undermining the democratic process and harming the interests of individual citizens. This danger weighs heavily against the speculative or negligible benefits of the ill-defined and overbroad investigations authorized in the past. Thus, the basic purpose of the recommendations contained in Part IV of this report is to limit the FBI to investigating conduct rather than ideas or associations.

The excesses of the past do not, however, justify depriving the United States of a clearly defined and effectively controlled domestic intelligence capability. The intelligence services of this nation's international adversaries continue to attempt to conduct clandestine espionage operations within the United States. Our recommendations provide for intelligence investigations of hostile foreign intelligence activity.

Moreover, terrorists have engaged in serious acts of violence which have brought death and injury to Americans and threaten further such acts. These acts, not the politics or beliefs of those who would commit them, are the proper focus for investigations to anticipate terrorist violence. Accordingly, the Committee would permit properly controlled intelligence investigations in those narrow circumstances.

Concentration on imminent violence can avoid the wasteful dispersion of resources which has characterized the sweeping (and fruitless) domestic intelligence investigations of the past. But the most important reason for the fundamental change in the domestic intelligence operations which our Recommendations propose is the need to protect the constitutional Rights of Americans.

In light of the record of abuse revealed by our inquiry, the Committee is not satisfied with the position that mere exposure of what has occurred in the past will prevent its recurrence. Clear legal standards and effective oversight and controls are necessary to ensure that domestic intelligence activity does not itself undermine the democratic system it is intended to protect.

*SOURCE:* U.S. Senate. *Final Report of the Select Committee to Study Governmental Operations with Respect to Intelligence Activities, Book Two: Intelligence Activities and the Rights of Americans,* http://www.aarclibrary.org/publib/church/reports/book2/contents.htm.

*RELATED ENTRIES: American Civil Liberties Union; Cold War; Intelligence Gathering in Warfare; War on Terrorism*

## 1976 b

### Remarks of Deserter on Eve of His Surrender to Authorities

*Austin Hodge, a Marine Corps deserter and war resister, addressed a group gathered in a church in 1976 on the eve of his surrendering himself to authorities after living "underground" for seven years:*

"I have given up my home, my family, my wife and son, moved from city to city, taken countless menial jobs because in my heart I could not support a war so incredibly hideous that it was far beyond my capacity as a human being to conceive. [I am turning myself in because I want to confront the military with my moral opposition to the war and to actively join in the struggle for amnesty for my fellow exiles.]

You live from minute to minute. You can't be honest with friends. You can't stay in one place. You can't have a job for more than three months. . . . My father [a retired Navy Chief Petty Officer] has been my greatest supporter all along."

*SOURCE: Unitarian Universalist World 7 (March 15, 1976): 1.*

*RELATED TOPICS: All Volunteer Force; American Civil Liberties Union; Antiwar Movements; Conscientious Objection; Conscription and Volunteerism; Draft Evasion and Resistance; Pacifism; Vietnam War*

## 1977

### Remarks of Mother on the Death of her Son and the Pardon of Draft Resisters

*Alberta Mierun's son may or may not have volunteered. In any event, he was killed in Vietnam and she expressed her anger in a letter to the editor of her city's evening paper shortly after President Carter announced his pardon of Vietnam-era draft resisters:*

So President Carter is giving pardons. Maybe he will give my son a pardon.

In case he doesn't know where he is, I will give him his address:

Sgt. James Roberts, Calvary Cemetery.

If this cannot be done, then why should the evaders get pardons and come home as if they were heroes?

It's boys like my son who are the heroes, but it's the evaders who are getting the glory for not going into a war that was not declared war. Big deal!

They were nothing but cowards.

*Alberta Mierun*
Clinton

*SOURCE: The Pittsburgh Press,* January 29, 1977.

*RELATED ENTRIES: All Volunteer Force; Antiwar Movements; Conscription and Volunteerism; Draft Evasion and Resistance; Families, Military; Vietnam War*

# 1988

## Editorial on Loss of Military Service as a Rite of Passage by Gerald A. Patterson

*Veteran Gerald Patterson, father of two teenage boys and associate editor of The Pittsburgh Post-Gazette, offered his thoughts on the pluses and minuses of "the draft" some fifteen years after the institution of the all volunteer force. He argued that, while the draft may have provided vital GI Bill benefits, and the discipline to get "some kids . . . on track" that President Harry Truman had promised in 1948, a voluntary military was preferable, in that "individuality and sensitivity stood a somewhat better chance of survival under a [college] logic professor than a drill sergeant."*

### Missing the Military Rite of Passage

As someone who matured during that three-decade stretch of our history when going into "the service" was a rite of passage, I often reflect on my two sons being able to grow up without having to undergo that experience . . . and wonder how much better (or worse) off they are for having missed it.

I don't have in mind missing a war, for probably 90 percent of the 14,900,987 persons drafted into the armed forces during that period from 1940 to 1973 (with but a single, 15-month pause in the late '40s) were never exposed to hostile fire.

What I am thinking of is the exposure to the ordinary discipline and restrictions of military life at that key stage of their development. Having been exposed to three years, 11 months and 10 days of it, I have to confess that I felt a lot better seeing my guys going off to college dorms than to boot camps (in no small part because I perceived that individuality and sensitivity stood a somewhat better chance of survival under a logic professor than a drill sergeant).

But I say that not without a degree of ambivalence, an awareness that they would, indeed, be missing some worthwhile lessons. My quarrel with the military was always that it took so long to teach what it had to convey about growing up—and that you couldn't drop out if you felt satiated.

After all, I say to myself, these kids will now never know the euphoric barracks atmosphere on a once-a-month payday as a bunch of young fellows with weekend passes prepare to descend on a town (an excitement that always seemed somewhat keener to me than arrival of spring break at college). Or the awesome relief of having your discharge papers handed to you under honorable conditions after an interminable wait and being, at last, free to go.

•

Perhaps it is the absurdities of service life that remain most vivid in our memories. The sight of a hundred young men in fatigues "policing the area," stooping down to pick up cigarette butts among blades of grass and then, when those had all disappeared, spent matches, looking not unlike a flock of pigeons bobbing about Market Square. Being ordered to undergo sun-lamp treatments because our work at Strategic Air Command headquarters in England kept us underground all day and when we got out of our mountain hideaway there were rarely any rays to be absorbed.

I keep returning to the time element because that was my strongest emotion during that period, the feeling that I was marking so much time. So coiled had I become that weeks after it was over, I was enrolled in journalism school, a soon-to-be 23-year-old freshman among teen-agers. Though I had been a staff sergeant for two years, I worked full-time at night at the New York Herald Tribune as a "copy boy," so anxious was I to catch up.

But—in addition to the rich experiences of spending a summer at Barksdale Air Force Base in Shreveport, La., when the weather was so drainingly hot that life was reduced to a strange study in slow motion, after having just completed a numbing winter at Sampson Air Force Base at Geneva, N.Y., and having felt, day after day, the howling arctic wind coming off frozen Lake Seneca—what somehow made "the service" worthwhile for so many of us were the financial benefits accrued.

How many would ever have been able to go to college or get that no-down-payment first home at 5 percent interest were it not for the GI Bill? It seemed then, as it does now, more than fair payment for those who hadn't been shot up or forced to see the actual face of war.

•

It's been 15 years now since the last man was drafted and though there are some 27.5 million veterans in the country (the vast majority former enlistees), the sight of a man in military uniform, once so commonplace, is becoming less and less familiar, one almost restricted to airports and bus terminals.

Those in the armed services are there in a more purely voluntary way now. For so many of us who enlisted in other times, there wasn't really that much of a choice. The atmosphere, the peer pressure were such that one was swept up and almost carried down to the recruiting station. Few wanted to be left behind, excluded from this challenging, manly experience and the chance to get away from home, away from that familiar street corner or ice-cream parlor booth. Never mind that the terms of enlistment were for four years; when you are 18 or 19 there is time to squander.

Today those pressures—and the allure of a soldier's uniform—are much diminished and enlisting (economic need aside) appears to be more of a personal decision than a mass movement. Fortunately, the military lifestyle still attracts enough young people to make conscription unnecessary.

Though the remunerations are better than ever, it seems to me that, as long as there is a military, there will only be a certain small percentage of young men and women truly suited for the life. To the vast majority, alas, there will always be basic flaws. It will, of necessity, always be a job one cannot quit and one that demands that you either show up for work in the morning or go on sick call and demonstrate your inability to function. For sure, some kids need those restrictions to get themselves on track, but still it's a reassuring thing to see that at least now it's a path they themselves choose.

*SOURCE: Pittsburgh Post-Gazette,* 3 March 1988, C, 11.


*RELATED ENTRIES: All Volunteer Force; Cold War; Conscription and Volunteerism; Selective Service System*

## 2000

### "Principles of Ethical Conduct . . . The Ultimate Bait and Switch" by Peter L. Duffy

*Peter L. Duffy was a senior engineering manager (GS-15) at the Naval Undersea Warfare Center, Newport, Rhode Island, when, sometime in the early 1990s, he read Pres. George H. W. Bush's Executive Order 12731, "Principles of Ethical Conduct for Government Officers and Employees." In time this and the misconduct of three of his superiors inspired him to accept the order's invitation to "blow the whistle." Soon he found his career destroyed. He wrote this account of his experience while serving a two-year research fellowship with MIT's Security Studies Program.*

On October 17, 1990, President George H. W. Bush signed Executive Order 12731, entitled "Principles of Ethical Conduct for Government Officers and Employees." This order specifically requires all federal civil servants to "respect and adhere to the fundamental principles of ethical service" to include that "Employees shall disclose waste, fraud, abuse, and corruption to appropriate authorities." A little over ten years later his son, President George W. Bush, made a point to make his first presidential memorandum to the heads of all executive departments and agencies be on the subject of "Standards of Official Conduct." In that memorandum, President Bush asked his heads to ensure "that all personnel within your departments and agencies are familiar with, and faithfully observe, applicable ethics laws and regulations, including the following general principles from the Standards of Ethical Conduct for Employees of the Executive Branch." One of the fourteen principles of this executive order requires every federal employee to stand up and be a whistleblower if the situation ever presents itself. What this order does not tell you is that this is the ultimate federal "bait and switch" trick.

On 18 August 2000, I took the bait by submitting a complaint to the Navy alleging executive misconduct by the top three members of the Senior Executive Service (SES) at my command. This was not an anonymous hotline call. It was in writing, sent certified mail with my "John Hancock" at the bottom of the page. It also included evidence to back up my allegations. I was a GS-15 senior engineering manager and the actions I took in reporting this misconduct were by the book. It was an internal Navy matter and I went to the "appropriate authorities," the Naval Inspector General (IG). The allegations were made in confidence because I believe in the presumption of innocence. When the head of the Inspector General's Office for Special Inquiries told me it would be difficult for them to conduct this investigation and maintain my confidentiality I immediately waived my right to it. I did what was right and what was expected of me and assumed without question that I would be treated fairly by the Navy. This was the first of a series of bad assumptions on my part.

Over the next year and a half the Naval IG conducted an investigation and wrote its report. In the end, two of the three senior executives retired the day before they were due to be removed from federal service[1] because "the facts of this case suggest a premeditated, conspiratorial effort to defraud the Government."[2] The third executive retired after invoking his "Fifth Amendment right against self-incrimination" and declined to answer any more of the IG investigator's questions.[3] The scheme in question allowed these executives to bank their vacation time, which would then lead to a huge financial windfall, at taxpayer's expense, when they retired. Banking their vacation time however didn't stop them from still taking their vacations. These executives annually took many weeks off, claiming it was for religious observation. The estimated retirement payout to these three executives was $694,210.[4] Much of this leave was taken away from them upon their removal, saving the U.S. taxpayer hundreds of thousands of dollars.[5] [6] Subsequent investigations, because the misconduct was more widespread than I even realized, resulted in at least four more members of the SES being suspended without pay.[7] This was an unprecedented number of disciplinary actions against members of the federal government's elite SES Corps.

The switch took place the moment I submitted my complaint to the Naval IG, although I certainly didn't realize it at the time. That was the moment when I went from dutiful civil servant to institutional threat. This is because when you blow the whistle on serious executive wrongdoing you immediately create a situation where you are perceived as being potentially harmful to the very institution you set out to protect. In this case the harm comes in two forms.

First, it caused embarrassment to the Navy leadership, the very leaders who were at the helm when all this took place on their watch. The misconduct in question had gone on for more than seven years and took place right under the noses of the admirals and captains who were supposedly in command of these activities. Additionally, independent Navy audit teams with the charge to expose waste, fraud and abuse conducted regular command evaluations. Their efforts to uncover this wrongdoing were about as effective as the independent accounting audits at Enron and WorldCom. Our command received nothing but outstanding reviews.[8] By blowing the whistle, I not only uncovered the executive misconduct but also glaringly exposed the ineptitude of those in charge and the failure of the protective systems that were supposedly in place.

A second form of institutional harm is the potential liability of the agency if the whistleblower faces retaliation. This liability derives from the Whistleblower Protection Act (WPA), which purports to protect those civil servants who have the courage, or one could legitimately argue stupidity, to stand up and expose corruption. What most civil servants may not realize is that the WPA only covers very specific personnel actions taken against them. This law does not protect federal employees against some of the subtle, but no less effective, punitive tactics that retaliators employ to punish them for disclosing their wrongdoing.

As a consequence of this, once I filed my complaint and provided my evidence and testimony, the Navy lost no time in abandoning me—even though it was abundantly clear that I was vulnerable and working in a hostile environment. My whistleblower status was actually exposed by a senior Navy admiral when he betrayed to the most senior of the accused executives that I was the complainant.[9] [10] Once the IG interviews started it didn't take long for word to spread throughout the activity that hunting season was open and I had antlers. Inappropriate, subtle offers of awards and time off that were made behind closed doors quickly turned into not so subtle threats behind closed doors. To escape this situation I used personal vacation "leave" time. Then, while on leave and within 48 hours of the IG investigators interviewing the subject executives, my vacation time was backed out and I was unknowingly placed on a "Leave Without Pay" status. A coworker who became aware of what was being done to me was immediately directed not to contact me or accept any calls from me.[11] Six weeks after realizing my pay had been stopped I had to return to the same hostile environment in order to restore my family's income. Additionally, as part of my return and as further punishment for my actions, I was forced to move out of my GS-15 office and into a GS-12 cubical. My performance evaluation, for the year in question, went from the highest to the lowest with no explanation. A tire on my brand new vehicle was slashed in the parking lot. These were all classic whistleblower reprisal tactics that were meant to threaten, embarrass and humiliate. Each and every one of these incidents was reported to naval authorities at the time they occurred. Each and every one was ignored and the reprisals kept coming. The switch was real. I had been disowned and in the process the Navy leadership involved abandoned the institutional values they swore to uphold: Honor, Courage, Commitment.

Now, let's juxtapose the treatment I incurred with that of some of the players involved. The activity commander, who authorized the stoppage of my pay was transferred to a prestigious job in Washington, DC and given a meritorious medal prior to his departure. The executive director, one of the SES members forced out of the federal government, got to return three months later as an announced guest of honor at the same commander's change of command ceremony. The two most senior executives that were fired now work for a local defense contractor and at least one is regularly seen around the campus he once led.[12] Three of the four senior executives, who were suspended without pay, were authorized by the Navy to work for private contractors during their suspensions.[13] Two of them went to work for local defense contractors supporting the very activity from which they had been suspended.[14] The person who advised the senior Navy officials to authorize these executives to circumvent their pay suspensions just so happens to be responsible for the ethics program at our activity.[15] Finally, several of the subordinates to the removed executives, who participated in the corrupt scheme and who helped to facilitate its execution have now been placed in some of the most senior management positions at this command.

Numerous times throughout this difficult ordeal I reached out to various Navy leaders, both military and civilian. All, with the exception of one, ignored my plight and subordinated the principle of doing the right thing to the Darwinian principle of doing what is necessary to protect their own careers. Only one, a member of the SES and one of the few not involved in the exposed scheme, came to my aid as best he could and provided me with a safe harbor at a time when I was in dire need. In the end the corrupt scheme was exposed, the senior executives were punished and preventative corrective actions were taken. I survived a battering that no employee should be expected to endure. With my career in ruins and after being subjected to seven consecutive "120 day details" into meaningless positions I agreed to move on to a two-year Intergovernmental Personnel Act (IPA) assignment at the Massachusetts Institute of Technology. Never once, during this three-year ordeal, has any Navy official ever approached me to acknowledge, never mind recognize, the sacrifice I made by practicing the kind of ethical behavior the government disingenuously promotes.

In the final analysis, the Government needs to decide if they are truly going to get serious about ethics. Our federal commitment to ethics should not merely focus on whether accepting a cup of coffee from a contractor, pulling up CNN on your government computer or being sure to disclose to your supervisor that you own stock in IBM is the ethical thing to do. Our federal commitment to ethics should center on individuals evaluating right and wrong and choosing to do right. Lawmakers can't legislate it. Presidents can't order it. The development of this ability requires open, honest discussion at all organizational levels, about important issues that confront us in the workplace. It must be done in an environment where those that are critical should not fear being beaten for having the courage to question it. In the end we must trust that the consensus of many consciences, developed in an environment of openness, will yield sound ethical courses of action. In the meantime, until that day comes, someone needs to put a warning label on Executive Order 12731, "Following this order may be hazardous to your career and your health."

NOTES

1 Merit Systems Protection Board, Agency's Prehearing Submission, Docket Numbers BN-0752-02-0153-I-1 and BN-0752-02-0162-I-1, 7 Nov 02, Page 6

2 Naval Inspector General, Report of Investigation, Senior Official Case 20000836, 12 Feb 02, Page 5

3 Naval Inspector General, Report of Investigation, Senior Official Case 20000836, 12 Feb 02, Page 21

4 Naval Inspector General, Report of Investigation, Senior Official Case 20000836, 12 Feb 02, Page 4

5 U.S. Merit Systems Protection Board Appeal, 1 Jul 02, Page 2, Block 12

6 U.S. Merit Systems Protection Board Appeal, 12 Jul 02, Page 2, Block 12

7 Personal discussion with Executive Director NUWC Div. Newport, 3 Dec 02

8 Personal email, 19 June 00, Subj: NAVSEA IG Command Performance Inspection

9 Naval Inspector General Transcript 14 Aug 01, Pgs 4–7

10 Naval Inspector General Transcript 30 Aug 01

11 Personal discussion with former NUWCDIVNPT, Code 40 Administrator, 26 Jun 01

12 http://www.rite-solutions.com

13 Personal discussion with Executive Director NUWC Div Newport, 3 Dec 02

14 Personal discussion with Executive Director NUWC Div Newport, 3 Dec 02

15 Personal discussion with Executive Director NUWC Div Newport, 3 Dec 02

*SOURCE:* Peter L. Duffy, "Principles of Ethical Conduct . . . The Ultimate Bait and Switch," MIT Security Studies Program, *Breakthroughs* [of MIT Security Studies Program] 13, no. 1 (Spring, 2004): 8–12.

*RELATED ENTRIES: Civil–Military Relations; Cold War; Hitchcock, Ethan Allen; Military–Industrial Complex*

## 2001

### "The Harvest Matrix 2001"

*The terrorist attacks on the World Trade Center and the Pentagon on September 11, 2001, produced an upsurge of patriotic sentiment, horror, and rage within the United States, and a groundswell of sympathy and solidarity for America from abroad. It also inspired poets to react with lines like these by Margaret Shaughnessy of Pittsburgh:*

It's October, one month later,
and the bittersweet ripens on vines
hanging from maples along Pennsylvania's farm roads.
The corn maze has led us here;
it's impossible to see above the stalks.
A month later and still the acrid, burning-flesh smell
seeps into our souls,
and fires blaze randomly.

Over and over I watch the plane slide into the side of the
World Trade Center.
I could watch it a million more times
to make it real, to make it hurt.
Like the Pawnbroker slamming his splayed hand on the
spike,
I need to feel it through me.
We have been perhaps immune, too safe,
at birth inoculated against pain, against terror,
our American right.

The nuclear mushroom we so worried about in the fifties
became steel and concrete
chasing thousands down New York City streets.
How soon did they realize that steel at boiling temperatures
would melt the building into our pores,
seer our reinforced steel hearts?
Melville's Rachel weeps, searching for her lost children,
yet days later all we heard was the chirping of firemen's
alarms
buried deep in our historical dust.

Now, surreal moon men monitor our anthraxed lives.
Bible sales are up and NASDAQ is down.
Unmanned drones fly low over Afghanistan

to find Osama and burka'd women
held hostage by someone else's faith.
Poppies blooming for al-Qaida
are exchanged for our beliefs,
down payments for a honeyed jihad.
Puts on the stock market make millions for
a war against the evil West.

October in Afghanistan is grape and melon harvest.
An overlay of sadness results from
the cruel fruit of our capitalist seeds.
Freedom is
jumping from our own high buildings,
threatened by, fearful of
weapon-grade pain.

*SOURCE:* Transcript from "The Poetry of War: NPR Reviews Poems Inspired by Past Conflicts," All Things Considered, January 24, 2005. Printed with permission of the author.

*RELATED ENTRIES: Literature and War; War on Terrorism*

## 2004 a

### Yale Law School Faculty Suit against Department of Defense Regarding On-campus Recruitment

*In 2004, most of the faculty of Yale University's Law School joined in a suit against the Department of Defense. Their concern related to on-campus recruitment. The commentary of the lead plaintiff in the suit and a professor who did not join the others in the suit follow.*

#### Why we are suing

ROBERT A. BURT, Alexander M. Bickel Professor of Law

As a service to our students, Yale Law School administers an employment program that provides computerized scheduling of job interviews with, and information about, prospective employers. Since 1978, the Law School has required all employers participating in our program to pledge that they exclude no one from employment on grounds of race, gender, religion, or sexual orientation. We adopted this nondiscrimination requirement as part of our general educational mission to ensure that all of our students are treated with equal respect in any school-sponsored activity, inside or outside the classroom. In our employment program specifically, the faculty concluded that none of our students should be subjected to the indignity of encountering a discriminatory job listing ("No ______s need apply").

The United States military cannot sign our nondiscrimination pledge because it withholds employment based on sexual orientation. We have not barred the military from access to our students on this ground. For the military and other employers unwilling to sign our nondiscrimination pledge, we make available contact information for all of our students and, at the invitation of any individual student or student organization, we permit use of Law School meeting rooms. We understand that some of our students are interested in employers who do not qualify for participation in the interview program we administer. We respect the right of these students to reach their own moral judgments about prospective employers. But in our own program, we are not willing to practice, or actively to assist in the implementation of, invidious discrimination.

In May 2002, the Department of Defense announced that unless the Law School exempted the military from our nondiscrimination pledge, the entire university would lose almost all federal funds—more than $300 million, most of which goes to the School of Medicine, primarily for cancer research. (None of these funds go to the Law School.) In response to this demand, the Law School faculty voted to exempt the military temporarily, in order to protect the university against loss of federal funds while various means were pursued to vindicate our nondiscrimination policy. After this temporary exemption had lasted for three semesters, it became apparent that none of the approaches by university officials to the DOD offered any clear prospect that we would be able to reinstate our nondiscrimination policy. Accordingly, in October 2003, 44 members of the Law School faculty—two-thirds of the voting members—filed suit in Federal District Court for Connecticut seeking a declaration that the DOD had no constitutional or statutory authority for its threatened action. (The DOD invoked the Solomon Amendment, a law that authorizes the federal government to cut off federal funds if a university prevents military recruiting on campus. Our suit charges both that the DOD has misinterpreted the Solomon Amendment and that the amendment as interpreted by the DOD would itself violate the Constitution.) A few weeks later, a separate lawsuit was filed by two Law School student organizations seeking the same result.

We have gone to court to carry out our obligations as teachers and as members of the university faculty. As teachers, we have a duty to our students to protect them against unjust discrimination. The military exclusion of gays and lesbians based on their sexual orientation has no rational relationship to their capacity to perform military service. The Supreme Court recently concluded that state criminal sodomy laws are unconstitutional because they "demean the lives of homosexual persons." The military exclusion has the same wrongful implication.

As faculty members, we also have a duty to defend the autonomy of the university in carrying out its educational mission. The Supreme Court recently ruled that universities are constitutionally entitled to deference in making "educational judgments [about matters] essential to [their] educational mission." Such deference must apply not only to university decisions favoring diversity through affirmative-action admissions policies, as the Court specifically held; universities must also be free to ensure that the diverse characteristics of their students—not only race but other defining attributes such as sexual orientation—are fully respected and protected in the academic environment.

Moreover, the threat to university autonomy in our case has implications beyond our educational goal of protecting our gay and lesbian students. If the DOD action is upheld, virtually no issue of educational policy would be exempt from the government's dictate. Government control over universities' federal funding could potentially become government control over universities' admissions, courses of study, or faculty hiring.

Since World War II, American universities have become increasingly dependent on federal government funding to maintain research activities, especially in the sciences. The government does have a legitimate interest in assuring that funds given to universities for, say, cancer research are not spent for some other, unrelated purposes. But in our case the government is trying to use its cancer research funding as a lever to control the Law School faculty's decisions about matters with no conceivable relevance to the government's funding program.

We cannot properly serve as teachers and scholars if the federal government is able to exploit the financial dependence of universities in order to override educational judgments on any matter of its choosing. We cannot properly educate our students if we are forced to engage in activities that demean the equal dignity of some of our students. We look to the courts for protection against these wrongful exercises of government power.

### Why Yale should open its interview program to the military

PETER H. SCHUCK, Simeon E. Baldwin Professor of Law

There is much to applaud in the legal challenge brought by my Yale Law School colleagues. "Don't ask, don't tell" is not a principled policy of tolerance or equality. Instead, it is a political compromise between the earlier flat ban on gays in the military and the full acceptance of them that equality demands. It places both gay and straight soldiers in a painfully ambiguous situation, encourages dissimulation and exploitation (if not outright blackmail) of gays, and reinforces existing stigmas. In practice, the policy has caused the cruel outing and arbitrary discharge of many gay soldiers who boast proud records of devoted military service. DOD's refusal to clarify its own policies and interpretations under the Solomon Amendment has, moreover, created needless uncertainty, contention, and, now, litigation. At the same time, its opaque regulatory process, which seems to permit the government to cut off funds without affording Yale administrative review, raises serious questions of due process. For all these reasons, a legal test of DOD's policy is both overdue and welcome—although, like the federal court that recently ruled preliminarily against the law schools in a similar suit, I do not see how this law violates the First Amendment rights of Yale faculty and students.

Let us assume that my litigating colleagues turn out to be right on the law—either that our interviewing rules as applied to the military do not violate the Solomon Amendment or that this law violates the Constitution. This ruling would still leave us with a very important question of pedagogical policy: should Yale have adopted this policy toward military recruiters in the first place?

I have my doubts. Let me be clear about my own normative position: I oppose "don't ask, don't tell." I favor equal treatment for gays. I support the assertion of academic autonomy in the face of political pressures. My colleagues are right to defend these positions. But Yale should be dedicated to another norm as well. As a matter of principle, Yale should treat our students as mature individuals who are sufficiently well educated to be able to assess the evidence and make their own choices among potential employers without needing to be "protected" by us.

Why should Yale screen employers' practices and norms for some of the most thoughtful, critical, and well-informed young adults in the world? Can't students make up their own minds about whether they want to work for organizations whose views on sexual orientation may differ from those of their teachers? What vision of intellectuality, character, and maturity does Yale convey when it relieves students of their duty as autonomous adults and citizens to make their own moral choices? Given Yale's vaunted quest for diversity, is it not inconsistent, perhaps even intolerant, for Yale to place even small obstacles in the path of its students' exposure to a worldview—opposition to gays in the military—that was resoundingly endorsed by a democratic (and Democratic) Congress, affirmed by administrations of diverse ideological stripes, upheld by the courts, and preached by some of the great religions to which many of the students subscribe? How much liberality and subtlety of mind do Yale faculty exhibit when their interviewing rules treat all versions of that worldview as a single species of invidious homophobia to be categorically condemned and marginalized—regardless of whether it proceeds from the kind of blind hatred that murdered Matthew Shepard or from ethical traditions or prudential concerns shared by many thoughtful, morally scrupulous people?

In truth, Yale's interviewing policy is not meant to be evenhanded. Rather, it is designed to allow Yale faculty to make a political and moral statement about employers whose practices offend us. Consider an analogy. Suppose the Acme Corporation made it a bit more difficult for black applicants, but not for others, to arrange job interviews—say, by making blacks call an additional number or travel farther. Acme could not legitimately defend this practice on the ground that it did not discriminate against black applicants but instead merely denied them the benefit of the faster-track option available to other students. This analogy, I think, indicts Yale's interviewing policy a fortiori. Here, after all, Yale is disadvantaging an employment practice that unlike race discrimination is perfectly legal, a practice that reflects a hard-won political and moral consensus (although one that I do not share).

Yale's policy should be truly evenhanded. It should allow its placement resources to be used on an entirely equal basis by all employers whose policies with regard to sexual orientation are legal in the jurisdictions where their lawyers work, so long as they affirmatively disclose those policies to students and certify their legality. The real issue is not what Yale thinks about the military's refusal to hire gays—the school has already made that crystal clear—but how our students view it. Yale's moral and pedagogical duty to our students is to cultivate their capacity for independent thinking, explain the faculty's view (if, as here, it has one) on "don't ask, don't tell"—and then get out of the way. The students' duty is to listen carefully—and then make up their own minds, without their professors' thumbs on the scales.

*SOURCE:* Reprinted from "The Law Professors vs. the Military." *Yale Alumni Magazine* January/February 2004, www.yalealumnimagazine.com.

*RELATED ENTRIES: All Volunteer Force; American Civil Liberties Union; Conscription and Volunteerism; Iraq War; Militarization and Militarism; War on Terrorism*

## 2004 b

**Statement by Christian Leaders Condemning a "Theology of War"**

*Shortly before election day, on October 24, 2004, evangelist Jerry Falwell told a CNN audience that he hoped President*

*Bush would "blow [all the terrorists] away in the name of the Lord." These remarks prompted some 200 Christian theologians to take exception to Farewell's views by issuing this statement, which was published in a paid advertisement in* USA Today.

In their statement "Confessing Christ in a World of Violence," more than 200 theologians and ethicists—many from leading evangelical institutions—wrote:

"A 'theology of war,' emanating from the highest circles of American government, is seeping into our churches as well. . . . The roles of God, church, and nation are confused by talk of an American 'mission' and 'divine appointment' to 'rid the world of evil.'"

They continued: "In this time of crisis, we need a new confession of Christ."

- Jesus Christ knows no national boundaries.
- Christ commits Christians to a strong presumption against war. Christians have a responsibility to count the cost, speak out for the victims, and explore every alternative before a nation goes to war.
- Christ commands us to see not only the splinter in our adversary's eye, but also the beam in our own.
- Christ shows us that love of enemy is the heart of the gospel.
- Christ teaches us that humility is the virtue befitting forgiven sinners.
- We reject the false teaching that a war on terrorism takes precedence over ethical and legal norms.
- We reject the false teaching that America is a "Christian nation," representing only virtue, while its adversaries are nothing but vicious.
- We reject the false teaching that any human being can be defined as outside the law's protection, and the demonization of perceived enemies, which only paves the way to abuse.
- We reject the false teaching that those who are not for the United States politically are against it or that those who fundamentally question American policies must be with the "evil-doers."

Peacemaking is central to our vocation in a troubled world. We urge Christians and others to remember Jesus' teachings in making their decisions as citizens.

*SOURCE:* Sojourners Website, http://www.sojo.net/action/alerts/confessing_christ.pdf.

*RELATED ENTRIES: Iraq War; Just War Theory; Religion and War; War on Terrorism*

## 2004 c

### Interview with Yale Graduate Tyson Belanger who Served in the Iraq War

*The "Where-They-Are-Now" reporter for the Yale Alumni Magazine interviewed First Lieutenant Tyson Belanger, USMC, a veteran of the assault on Baghdad in 2003.*

Tyson Belanger '98

A first lieutenant in the Marine Corps infantry based at Camp Pendleton, California, Belanger led a platoon of marines in amphibious assault vehicles to Baghdad in the Iraq War. He expects to be redeployed to Iraq soon.

Y: Why did you decide to go into the Marine Corps?

B: I wanted to get beyond the books in my international relations studies and see international relations firsthand.

Y: The perception is that it's very unusual for an Ivy League graduate to go into the military.

B: I think that's a terrible misconception, dating from just the last 20 years. If you go to Woolsey Hall, you'll see the veterans on the wall. There's a very strong tradition at Yale of military service. I think it's only a recent phenomenon that students from Yale don't tend to be engaged in and involved in international security.

Y: And why do you think that is?

B: I think people are very interested in service, they just don't necessarily feel that service in the military is the way for them to serve. I think, however, that that's a mistake, because I think that we could use the talents and perspectives of Yale graduates in the military. And I want to make it very clear that I was far from the only Yalie who fought in the Iraq War.

Y: What was it like to be part of the war?

B: It's a bit of an understatement to say that it was memorable. Something that I was most surprised by and most impressed by was how much the Iraqi people welcomed us. We would drive down the streets and there would be thousands of them lining the streets, cheering for us.

Several of my marines mentioned—and it felt like it was true—that we were rock stars at least for that short time. And for me, that was the only explanation for how few casualties we had in the war.

Y: How did you feel after you came home?

B: I felt very good about what we did. I genuinely felt that we were liberating the people of Iraq, giving them an opportunity to live in a way that they haven't had experience with in their past, and that this was something that they wanted—the opportunity to govern themselves. I think now that the military solution has been provided, what remains is the political solution.

Y: What do you do when you are not at war? For fun?

B: Watch videos? Not much. September 11 meant a lot to me, and it's created a sense of urgency in everything I do. I've cut down to the bone a lot of what I do and I focus on my friends, my family, and my marines.

Y: Where were you on September 11?

B: I was at the infantry officers' course at the time. We cancelled our classes, we went on high alert, and we were ready to defend the FBI academy and the marine base at Quantico. There was myself on the line, with the chance that if I didn't learn something, somebody could die. With the question of life or death, there's a clarity about what's important.

Y: There does not seem to be that clarity in the country as a whole. How do you feel about the mixed reactions to the Iraq action here at home?

B: I respect it, because I know that in their hearts they do support my marines as individuals, and they recognize that they have families. And it is healthy, as a democracy, to debate, discuss, and consider the direction of the country.

Y: Any regrets?

B: I regret putting my friends and family through the experience. My poor parents were watching the television, two televisions, as often as they could during the war. It makes them upset that I keep volunteering, but they understand, they recognize that I'm following my path in doing what I'm doing.

Y: It's definitely hard to hear every day on the news that American soldiers have been killed.

B: It's easy to count American casualties. It's much more difficult to quantify the intangible benefits to the Iraqis and to feel the value of what we're doing. But the people who go, in particular me and my marines, recognize that it's a sacrifice worth making. I'm excited about the possibility of going back to Iraq. I'm studying Arabic in preparation.

*SOURCE:* Reprinted from "Where they are now: Tyson Belanger '98," *Yale Alumni Magazine* January/February 2004, www.yalealumnimagazine.com.

*RELATED ENTRIES: All Volunteer Force; Conscription and Volunteerism; Iraq War; Marine Corps; War on Terrorism*

# General Bibliography

This bibliography aims to offer researchers a substantive guide to literature on the subject of American military experience and its relationship to society. The resources are categorized by subject areas and reflect the analytical approach taken in this encyclopedia. Consequently they tie into the reader's guide found at the beginning of the set. Also, some resources may be found in more than one category.


### Art, Culture, and Memory

Adler, Kurt, ed. *Songs of Many Wars: From the Sixteenth to the Twentieth Century*. New York: Howell & Soskin, 1943.

Aichinger, Peter. *The American Soldier in Fiction, 1880–1963: A History of Attitudes Toward Warfare and the Military Establishment*. Ames: Iowa State University Press, 1975.

Anderegg, Michael A., ed. *Inventing Vietnam: The War in Film and Television*. Philadelphia: Temple University Press, 1991.

Arnold, B. *Music and War: A Research and Information Guide*. New York: Garland, 1993.

Basinger, Jeanine. *The World War II Combat Film: Anatomy of a Genre*. New York: Columbia University Press, 1986.

Beidler, Philip D. *Late Thoughts on an Old War: The Legacy of Vietnam*. Athens: University of Georgia Press, 2004.

Birdwell, Michael. *Celluloid Soldiers: The Warner Brothers Campaign Against Nazism*. New York: New York University Press, 1999.

Blair, William. *Cities of the Dead: Contesting the Memory of the Civil War in the South, 1865–1914*. Chapel Hill: University of North Carolina Press, 2004.

Blight, David W. *Race and Reunion: The Civil War in American Memory*. Cambridge, Mass.: Harvard University Press, 2001.

Boime, Albert. *The Unveiling of the National Icons: A Plea for Patriotic Iconoclasm in a Nationalist Era*. Cambridge: Cambridge University Press, 1998.

Brand, Oscar. *Songs of '76: A Folksinger's History of the Revolution*. New York: M. Evans, 1972.

Brown, Jared. *The Theatre in America During the Revolution*. Cambridge: Cambridge University Press, 1995.

Brown, Thomas J. *The Public Art of Civil War Commemoration: A Brief History with Documents*. Boston and New York: Bedford/St. Martin's, 2004.

Camus, Raoul F. *Military Music of the American Revolution*. Chapel Hill: University of North Carolina Press, 1976.

Collins, Max Allan. *For the Boys: The Racy Pin-Ups of World War II*. Portland, Ore.: Collectors Press, 2000.

Cooperman, Stanley. *World War I and the American Novel*. 1967. Reprint, Baltimore, Md.: Johns Hopkins University Press, 1970.

Cornebise, Alfred E., ed. *Doughboy Doggerel: Verse of the American Expeditionary Force 1918–1919*. Athens: Ohio University Press, 1985.

Curtin, Michael. *Redeeming the Wasteland: Television Documentary and Cold War Politics*. New Brunswick, N.J.: Rutgers University Press, 1995.

Dane, Barbara, and Irwin Silber, eds. *The Vietnam Songbook*. New York: Guardian, 1969.

Darracott, Joseph, and Belinda Loftus. *Second World War Posters*. London: Imperial War Museum Press, 1972.

Dittmar, Linda, and Gene Michaud. *From Hanoi to Hollywood: The Vietnam War in American Film*. New Brunswick, N.J.: Rutgers University Press, 1990.

Doherty, Thomas. *Projections of War: Hollywood, American Culture, and World War II*. New York: Columbia University Press, 1993.

Dubin, Stephen C. *Displays of Power: Memory and Amnesia in the American Museum*. New York: New York University Press, 1999.

# GENERAL BIBLIOGRAPHY


Engelhardt, Tom. *The End of Victory Culture: Cold War America and the Disillusioning of a Generation.* New York: Basic Books, 1995.

Fahs, Alice, and Joan Waugh, eds. *The Memory of the Civil War in American Culture.* Chapel Hill: University of North Carolina Press, 2004.

Fralin, Frances. *The Indelible Image: Photographs of War, 1846–Present.* New York: Abrams, 1985.

Fussell, Paul. *The Great War and Modern Memory.* New York: Oxford University Press, 1975.

Gabor, Mark. *The Pin-Up: A Modest History.* New York: Universe Books, 1973.

Gillis, John R. *Commemorations: The Politics of National Identity.* Princeton, N.J.: Princeton University Press, 1994.

Gilman, Owen W., and Lorrie Smith, eds. *America Rediscovered: Critical Essays on Literature and Film of the Vietnam War.* New York: Garland, 1990.

Greenway, John. *American Folksongs of Protest.* New York: Octagon, 1970.

Harrison, Brady. *Agent of Empire: William Walker and the Imperial Self in American Literature.* Athens: University of Georgia Press, 2004.

Harwit, Martin. *An Exhibit Denied: Lobbying the History of* Enola Gay. New York: Springer-Verlag, 1996.

Hass, Kristin Ann. *Carried to the Wall: American Memory and the Vietnam Veterans Memorial.* Berkeley: University of California Press, 1998.

Hawaii Nikkei History Editorial Board. *Japanese Eyes, American Heart: Personal Reflections of Hawaii's World War II Nisei Soldiers.* Honolulu: University of Hawaii Press, 1998.

Henderson, Amy, and Adrienne L. Kaeppler, eds. *Exhibiting Dilemmas: Issues of Representation at the Smithsonian.* Washington, D.C.: Smithsonian Institution Press, 1997.

Honey, Maureen. *Creating Rosie the Riveter: Class, Gender, and Propaganda during World War II.* Amherst: University of Massachusetts Press, 1984.

Jones, Peter G. *War and the Novelist: Appraising the American War Novel.* Columbia: University of Missouri Press, 1976.

Kagan, Norman. *The Cinema of Oliver Stone.* New York: Continuum, 2000.

Kammen, Michael. *Mystic Chords of Memory: The Transformation of Tradition in American Culture.* New York: Alfred A. Knopf, 1991.

Kunhardt, Dorothy Meserve, and Philip B. Kunhardt, Jr. *Mathew Brady and His World.* Alexandria, Va.: Time Life Books, 1977.

Lembcke, Jerry. *The Spitting Image: Myth, Memory, and the Legacy of Vietnam.* New York: New York University Press, 1998.

Lepore, Jill. *The Name of War: King Philip's War and the Origins of American Identity.* New York: Alfred A. Knopf, 1998.

Lewinski, Jorge. *The Camera at War: A History of War Photography from 1848 to the Present Day.* New York: Simon & Schuster, 1978.

Linenthal, Edward T., and Tom Engelhardt, eds. *History Wars: The* Enola Gay *and Other Battles for the American Past.* New York: Henry Holt / Metropolitan Books, 1996.

Lipschutz, Ronnie D. *Cold War Fantasies: Film, Fiction, and Foreign Policy.* Lanham, Md.: Rowman & Littlefield, 2001.

Lynn, John. *Battle: A History of Combat and Culture.* Boulder, Colo.: Westview Press, 2003.

MacDonald, Sharon, ed. *The Politics of Display: Museums, Science, Culture.* New York: Routledge, 1998.

Marling, Karal Ann, and John Wetenhall. *Iwo Jima: Monuments, Memories, and the American Hero.* Cambridge, Mass.: Harvard University Press, 1991.

Martignette, Charles G., and Louis K. Meisel. *The Great American Pin-Up.* Cologne, Germany: Taschen, 2002.

Masur, Louis P., ed. *The Real War Will Never Get in the Books: Selections From Writers During the Civil War.* New York: Oxford University Press, 1993.

McAdams, Frank. *The American War Film: History and Hollywood.* Westport, Conn.: Praeger, 2002.

McConachie, Bruce. *American Theater in the Culture of the Cold War: Producing and Contesting Containment, 1947–1962.* Iowa City: University of Iowa Press, 2003.

McPherson, James M. *Battle Cry of Freedom: The Civil War Era.* New York: Ballantine Books, 1989.

Meredith, Roy. *Mathew Brady's Portrait of an American Era.* New York: W. W. Norton, 1982.

Moeller, Susan D. *Shooting War: Photography and the American Experience of Combat.* New York: Basic Books, 1989.

Moltsky, Irvin. *The Flag, the Poet & the Song: The Story of the Star-Spangled Banner.* New York: Dutton, 2001.

Mosse, George L. *Fallen Soldiers, Reshaping the Memory of the World Wars.* New York and Oxford: Oxford University Press, 1990.

Murphy, Brenda. *American Realism and American Drama, 1880–1940*. Cambridge: Cambridge University Press, 1987.

———. *Congressional Theatre: Dramatizing McCarthyism on Stage, Film, and Television*. Cambridge: Cambridge University Press, 1999.

Neely, Mark, and Harold Holzer. *Mine Eyes Have Seen the Glory: The Civil War in Art*. New York: Orion Books, 1993.

Neff, John R. *Honoring the Civil War Dead: Commemoration and the Problem of Reconciliation*. Lawrence: University Press of Kansas, 2005.

Niles, John Jacob. *Singing Soldiers*. New York: Scribner & Sons, 1927.

———, and S. Moore. *The Songs My Mother Never Taught Me*. New York: Gold Label Books, 1929.

Nudelman, Franny. *John Brown's Body: Slavery, Violence and the Culture of War*. Chapel Hill: University of North Carolina Press, 2003.

O'Nan, Stewart, ed. *The Vietnam Reader: The Definitive Collection of American Fiction and Non-Fiction on the War*. New York: Anchor Books, 1998.

Panzer, Mary. *Mathew Brady and the Image of History*. Washington D.C.: Smithsonian Books, 1997.

Paret, Peter, Beth Irwin Lewis, and Paul Paret, eds. *Persuasive Images: Posters of War and Revolution from the Hoover Institution Archives*. Princeton, N.J.: Princeton University Press, 1992.

Piehler, Kurt. *Remembering War the American Way*. Washington, D.C.: Smithsonian Institution Press, 1995.

Purcell, Sarah J. *Sealed with Blood: War, Sacrifice, and Memory in Revolutionary America*. Philadelphia: University of Pennsylvania Press, 2002.

Quart, Leonard, and Albert Auster. *American Film and Society Since 1945*. 2nd ed. New York: Praeger, 1991.

———. *How the War Was Remembered: Hollywood and Vietnam*. Westport, Conn.: Praeger, 1988.

Richardson, Gary A. *American Drama from the Colonial Period Through World War I: A Critical History*. New York: Twayne, 1964.

Roeder, George H., Jr. *The Censored War: American Visual Experience During World War Two*. New Haven, Conn.: Yale University Press, 1993.

Rosenberg, Emily Smith. *A Date Which Will Live: Pearl Harbor in American Memory*. Durham, N.C.: Duke University Press, 2003.

Samuel, Lawrence R. *Pledging Allegiance: American Identity and the Bond Drive of World War II*. Washington, D.C.: Smithsonian Institution Press, 1997.

Seed, David. *Brainwashing: A Study in Cold War Demonology*. Kent, Ohio: Kent State University Press, 2004.

Shapiro, Jerome Franklin. *Atomic Bomb Cinema: The Apocalyptic Imagination on Film*. New York: Routledge, 2002.

Slotkin, Richard. *Gunfighter Nation: The Myth of the Frontier in Twentieth-Century America*. New York: Atheneum, 1992.

Smith, Kathleen E. R. *"God Bless America": Tin Pan Alley Goes to War*. Lexington: University Press of Kentucky, 2003.

Stanley, Peter, ed. *What Did You Do in the War Daddy? A Visual History of Propaganda Posters*. Oxford, Melbourne, and New York: Oxford University Press, 1983.

Suid, Lawrence H. *Guts & Glory: The Making of the American Military Image in Film*. Rev. and exp. ed. Lexington: University Press of Kentucky, 2002.

———. *Sailing on the Silver Screen: Hollywood and the U.S. Navy*. Annapolis, Md.: Naval Institute Press, 1996.

Thomas, Christopher A. *The Lincoln Memorial and American Life*. Princeton, N.J.: Princeton University Press, 2002.

Trachtenberg, Alan. *Reading American Photographs: Images as History: Mathew Brady to Walker Evans*. New York: Hill & Wang, 1989.

Turner, Fred. *Echoes of Combat: Trauma and Memory and the Vietnam War*. Minneapolis: University of Minnesota Press, 1992.

Walker, Mort. *50 Years of Beetle Bailey*. New York: Nantier Beall Minoustchine, 2000.

Wetta, Frank J., and Stephen J. Curley. *Celluloid Wars: A Guide to Film and the American Experience of War*. New York: Greenwood Press, 1992.

Wheeler, Winston Dixon. *Visions of the Apocalypse: Spectacles of Destruction in American Cinema*. London: Wallflower, 2003.

Wilson, Edmund. *Patriotic Gore: Studies in the Literature of the American Civil War*. 1962. Reprint, New York: W. W. Norton, 1994.

Wolfe, Charles K., and J. Akenson. *Country Music Goes to War*. Lexington: University Press of Kentucky, 2005.

### Media and Journalism

Bailyn, Bernard, and John B. Hench, eds. *The Press and the American Revolution*. Worcester, Mass.: American Antiquarian Society, 1980.

## GENERAL BIBLIOGRAPHY


Black, Gregory D., and Clayton R. Koppes. *Hollywood Goes to War: How Politics, Profits and Propaganda Shaped World War II Movies*. New York: Free Press, 1987.

Cohn, Lawrence. *Movietone Presents the Twentieth Century*. New York: St. Martin's Press, 1976.

Davis, Elmer, and Byron Price. *War Information and Censorship*. Washington, D.C.: American Council on Public Affairs, 1942.

Doyle, Jerry. *According to Doyle: A Cartoon History of World War II*. New York: G. P. Putnam's Sons, 1943.

Ellsberg, Daniel. *Secrets: A Memoir of Vietnam and the Pentagon Papers*. New York: Viking, 2002.

Erenberg, Lewis A., and Susan E. Hirsch, eds. *The War in American Culture: Society and Consciousness During World War II*. Chicago: University of Chicago Press, 1996.

Fahrney, Ralph Ray. *Horace Greeley and the* Tribune *in the Civil War*. 1936. Reprint, New York: Da Capo Press, 1970.

Ferrari, Michelle. *Reporting America at War: An Oral History*. New York, Hyperion, 2003.

Fielding, Raymond. *The American Newsreel, 1911–1967*. Norman: University of Oklahoma Press, 1978.

———. *The March of Time, 1935–1951*. New York: Oxford University Press, 1978.

Folkerts, Jean, and Dwight L. Teeter, Jr. *Voices of a Nation: A History of Media in the United States*. 4th ed. Boston: Allyn & Bacon, 2002.

Fox, Frank W. *Madison Avenue Goes to War: The Strange Military Career of American Advertising, 1941–45*. Provo, Utah: Brigham Young University Press, 1975.

Fyne, Robert. *The Hollywood Propaganda of World War II*. Metuchen, N.J.: Scarecrow Press, 1994.

Hallin, Daniel C. *The "Uncensored War": The Media and Vietnam*. New York: Oxford University Press, 1986.

Hammond, William M. *Reporting Vietnam: Media and Military at War*. Lawrence: University Press of Kansas, 1998.

Heil, Alan L. *Voice of America: A History*. New York: Columbia University Press, 2003.

Herring, George C. *The Pentagon Papers*. Abridged ed. New York: McGraw Hill Humanities, 1993.

Hess, Stephen, and Sandy Northrop. *Drawn and Quartered: The History of American Political Cartoons*. Montgomery, Ala.: Elliott & Clark, 1996.

———, and Marvin Kalb, eds. *The Media and the War on Terrorism*. Washington, D.C.: Brookings Institution, 2003.

———, and Milton Kaplan. *The Ungentlemanly Art: A History of American Political Cartoons*. New York: Macmillan, 1975.

Hixson, Walter L. *Parting the Curtain: Propaganda, Culture, and the Cold War, 1945–1961*. New York: St. Martin's, 1997.

Humphrey, Carol Sue. *"This Popular Engine": New England Newspapers during the American Revolution, 1775–1789*. Newark: University of Delaware Press, 1992.

Katovsky, Bill, and Timothy Carlson. *Embedded: The Media at War in Iraq*. Guilford, Conn.: Lyons Press, 2003.

Knightley, Phillip, and John Pilger. *The First Casualty: From the Crimea to Kosovo: The War Correspondent as Hero, Propagandist, and Myth Maker*. Baltimore, Md.: Johns Hopkins University Press, 2002.

Lewes, James. *Protest and Survive: Underground GI Newspapers during the Vietnam War*. Westport, Conn.: Praeger, 2003.

Library of America. *Reporting Vietnam: American Journalism 1959–1969*. Part One. New York: Literary Classics of America, 1998.

———. *Reporting Vietnam: American Journalism 1969–1975*. Part Two. New York: Literary Classics of America, 1998.

———. *Reporting World War II: American Journalism 1938–1944*. New York: Literary Classics of America, 1995.

Lipstadt, Deborah. *Beyond Belief: The American Press and the Coming of the Holocaust, 1933–1945*. New York: Free Press, 1986.

Martin, Robert W. T. *The Free and Open Press: The Founding of American Democratic Press Liberty, 1640–1800*. New York: New York University Press, 2001.

Mauldin, Bill. *Back Home*. New York: W. Sloan Associates, 1947.

_______. *Bill Mauldin in Korea*. New York: W. W. Norton, 1952.

_______. *The Brass Ring*. New York: W. W. Norton, 1971.

_______. *I've Decided I Want My Seat Back*. New York: Harper & Row, 1965.

_______. *Up Front*. New York: H. Holt, 1945.

McGurn, Barrett. Yank, *the Army Weekly: Reporting the Greatest Generation*. Golden, Colo.: Fulcrum, 2004.

Michie, Allan A. *Voices through the Iron Curtain*. New York: Dodd, Mead, 1963.

Mock, James R., and Cedric Larson. *Words That Won the War: The Story of the Committee on Public Information, 1917–1919*. Princeton, N.J.: Princeton University Press, 1939.

Nelson, Michael. *War of the Black Heavens: The Battles of Western Broadcasting in the Cold War*. Syracuse, N.Y.: Syracuse University Press, 1997.

Prados, John, and Margaret Pratt Porter. *Inside the Pentagon Papers*. Lawrence: University Press of Kansas, 2004.

Puddington, Arch. *Broadcasting Freedom: The Cold War Triumph of Radio Free Europe and Radio Liberty*. Lexington: University of Kentucky Press, 2000.

Roeder, George H., Jr. *The Censored War: American Visual Experience During World War Two.* New Haven, Conn.: Yale University Press, 1993.

Rudenstine, David. *The Day the Presses Stopped: A History of the Pentagon Papers Case*. Berkeley: University of California Press, 1996.

Short, K. R. M. *Hitler's Fall: The Newsreel Witness*. New York: Croom Helm, 1988.

Shulman, Holly Cowan. *The Voice of America: Propaganda and Democracy, 1941–1945*. Madison: University of Wisconsin Press, 1990.

Smith, Jeffery A. *War and Press Freedom: The Problem of Prerogative Power*. New York: Oxford University Press, 1999.

Starr, Paul. *The Creation of the Media: Political Origins of Modern Communications*. New York: Basic Books, 2004.

Steele, Richard W. *Free Speech in the Good War*. New York: St. Martin's Press, 1999.

Stein, Meyer L. *Under Fire: The Story of American War Correspondents*. New York: Messner, 1968.

Strobel, Warren P. *Late-Breaking Foreign Policy: The News Media's Influence on Peace Operations.* Washington, D.C.: United States Institute of Peace Press, 1997.

Sweeney, Michael S. *Secrets of Victory: The Office of Censorship and the American Press and Radio in World War II*. Chapel Hill: University of North Carolina Press, 2001.

Taylor, Philip M. *War and the Media: Propaganda and Persuasion in the Gulf War.* Manchester, England: Manchester University Press, 1992.

Tobin, James. *Ernie Pyle's War: America's Eyewitness to World War II*. New York: Free Press, 1997.

Tregaskis, Richard. *Guadalcanal Diary*. New York: Random House, 1943.

Tumber, Howard, and Jerry Palmer. *Media at War: The Iraq Crisis.* London: Sage, 2004.

Vaughn, Stephen. *Holding Fast the Inner Lines: Democracy, Nationalism and the Committee on Public Information*. Chapel Hill: University of North Carolina Press, 1980.

Voss, Frederick. *Reporting the War: Journalistic Coverage of World War II*. Washington, D.C.: Smithsonian, 1994.

Winfield, Betty Houchin. *FDR and the News Media*. Urbana: University of Illinois Press, 1990.

Winkler, Allan M. *The Politics of Propaganda: The Office of War Information, 1942–1945*. New Haven, Conn.: Yale University Press, 1978.

Wittkopf, Eugene R. *Faces of Internationalism: Public Opinion and American Foreign Policy*. Durham, N.C.: Duke University Press, 1990.

Zumwalt, Ken. *The Stars and Stripes: World War II and the Early Years*. Austin, Tex.: Eakin Press, 1989.

## Religion

Albanese, Catherine. *Sons of the Fathers: The Civil Religion of the American Revolution*. Philadelphia: Temple University Press, 1976.

Au, William A. *The Cross, the Flag, and the Bomb: American Catholics Debate War and Peace, 1960–1983.* Westport, Conn.: Greenwood Press, 1985.

Bailey, Paul. *Holy Smoke: A Dissertation on the Utah War*. Great West Indian Series 44. Los Angeles: Westernlore Books, 1978.

Bogle, Lori Lyn. *The Pentagon's Battle for the American Mind: The Early Cold War*. College Station: Texas A&M Press, 2004.

Brinsfield, John W., William C. Davis, Benedick Maryniak, and James I. Robertson, Jr. *Faith in the Fight: Civil War Chaplains*. Mechanicsburg, Penn.: Stackpole Books, 2003.

Brock, Peter. *Pioneers of the Peaceable Kingdom: The Quaker Peace Testimony from the Colonial Era to the First World War.* Princeton, N.J.: Princeton University Press, 1968.

———. *The Quaker Peace Testimony, 1660–1914.* York, England: Sessions Book Trust, 1990.

Budd, Richard M. *Serving Two Masters: The Development of American Military Chaplaincy, 1860–1920*. Lincoln: University of Nebraska Press, 2002.

Cherry, Conrad, ed. *God's New Israel: Religious Interpretations of American Destiny.* Chapel Hill: University of North Carolina Press, 1998.

Clergy and Laymen Concerned About Vietnam. *In the Name of America.* Annandale, Va.: Turnpike Press, 1968.

# GENERAL BIBLIOGRAPHY

Cooney, John. *The American Pope: The Life and Times of Francis Cardinal Spellman*. New York: New York Times Books, 1984.

Crosby, Donald F. *Battlefield Chaplains: Catholic Priests in World War II*. Lawrence: University Press of Kansas, 1994.

Furniss, Norman F. *The Mormon Conflict, 1850–1859*. 1960. Reprint, Westport, Conn.: Greenwood Press, 1977.

Gilbert, Richard R. *The Nation with the Soul of a Church: A Critical Reflection*. Washington, D.C.: American Revolution Bicentennial Administration, 1976.

Hadden, Jeffrey K. *The Gathering Storm in the Churches.* Garden City, N.Y.: Doubleday, 1969.

Hall, Mitchell K. *Because of Their Faith: CALCAV and Religious Opposition to the Vietnam War.* New York: Columbia University Press, 1990.

Helgeland, John. "Civil Religion, Military Religion." *Foundations and Facets Forum* 5, no. 1 (March 1989).

Loveland, Anne C. *American Evangelicals and the U.S. Military, 1942–1993.* Baton Rouge: Louisiana State University Press, 1996.

McNeal, Patricia. *Harder than War: Catholic Peacemaking in Twentieth-Century America.* New Brunswick, N.J.: Rutgers University Press, 1992.

Mekeel, Arthur J. *The Quakers and the American Revolution.* York, England: Sessions Book Trust, 1996.

O'Connor, John J. *A Chaplain Looks at Vietnam*. Cleveland, Ohio: World Publishing, 1968.

Polner, Murray, and Jim O'Grady. *Disarmed and Dangerous: The Radical Lives and Times of Daniel and Philip Berrigan*. New York: Basic Books, 1997.

Slomovitz, Albert Isaac. *The Fighting Rabbis: Jewish Military Chaplains and American History*. New York: New York University Press, 1999.

Walzer, Michael. *Just and Unjust Wars: A Moral Argument with Historical Illustrations*. 2nd ed. New York: Basic Books, 1992.

Zaroulis, Nancy, and Gerald Sullivan. *Who Spoke Up? American Protest Against the War in Vietnam, 1963–1975.* Garden City, N.Y.: Doubleday, 1984.

### Pacifism and Protest

Alonso, Harriet Hyman. *Peace as a Woman's Issue: A History of the U.S. Movement for World Peace and Women's Rights.* Syracuse, N.Y.: Syracuse University Press, 1993.

Barber, Lucy G. *Marching on Washington: The Forging of an American Political Tradition*. Berkeley: University of California Press, 2002.

Bennett, Scott H. *Radical Pacifism: The War Resisters League and Gandhian Nonviolence in America, 1915–1963*. Syracuse, N.Y.: Syracuse University Press, 2003.

Bernstein, Iver. *The New York City Draft Riots: Their Significance for American Society and Politics in the Age of the Civil War.* New York: Oxford University Press, 1990.

Brock, Peter. *Pacifism in the United States from Colonial Times to the First World War*. Princeton, N.J.: Princeton University Press, 1968.

———. *The Quaker Peace Testimony, 1660–1914.* York, England: Sessions Book Trust, 1990.

Bussey, Gertrude, and Margaret Tims. *Pioneers for Peace: Women's International League for Peace and Freedom, 1915–1946.* London: Allen & Unwin, 1965.

Chatfield, Charles. *The American Peace Movement: Ideals and Activism*. New York: Maxwell Maximillian International, 1992.

Curti, Merle Eugene. *The American Peace Crusade, 1850–1860.* 1929. Reprint, New York: Octagon Books, 1965.

Daniels, Roger. *The Bonus March: An Episode of the Great Depression*. Westport, Conn.: Greenwood Press, 1971.

DeBenedetti, Charles, with Charles Chatfield. *An American Ordeal: The Antiwar Movement of the Vietnam Era*. Syracuse, N.Y.: Syracuse University Press, 1990.

———, ed. *Peace Heroes in Twentieth-Century America.* Bloomington: Indiana University Press, 1986.

———. *Peace Reform in American History*. Bloomington: Indiana University Press, 1980.

Devere, Allen. *The Fight for Peace*. New York: Macmillan, 1930.

Foley, Michael S. *Confronting the War Machine: Draft Resistance During the Vietnam War*. Chapel Hill: University of North Carolina Press, 2003.

Foster, Carrie A. *The Women and the Warriors: The U.S. Section of the Women's International League for Peace and Freedom, 1915–1946.* Syracuse, N.Y.: Syracuse University Press, 1995.

Foster, Catherine. *Women for All Seasons: The Story of the Women's International League for Peace and Freedom.* Athens: University of Georgia Press, 1989.

Frazer, Heather T., and John O'Sullivan. *"We Have Just Begun to Not Fight": An Oral History of Conscientious Objectors in the*

*Civilian Public Service During World War II.* New York: Twayne, 1996.

Gilje, Paul A. *Rioting in America*. Bloomington: Indiana University Press, 1996.

Hagan, John. *Northern Passage: American Vietnam War Resisters in Canada*. Cambridge, Mass.: Harvard University Press, 2001.

Heineman, Kenneth J. *Campus Wars: The Peace Movement at American State Universities in the Vietnam Era.* New York: New York University Press, 1993.

_____. *Put Your Bodies Upon the Wheels: Student Revolt in the 1960s*. Chicago: Ivan Dee, 2001.

Kohn, Stephen M. *Jailed for Peace: The History of American Draft Law Violators, 1658–1985.* New York: Praeger, 1987.

Lewes, James. *Protest and Survive: Underground GI Newspapers during the Vietnam War.* Westport, Conn.: Praeger, 2003.

Lynd, Staughton, and Alice Lynd. *Nonviolence in America: A Documentary History*, Rev. ed. Maryknoll, N.Y.: Orbis Books, 1995.

Meltzer, Milton. *Ain't Gonna Study War No More: The Story of America's Peace Seekers*. New York: Harper & Row, 1985.

Merton, Thomas. *Passion for Peace: The Social Essays*. Edited by William Shannon. New York: Crossroads Publishing, 1996.

Moskos, Charles C., and John W. Chambers, eds. *The New Conscientious Objection: From Sacred to Secular Resistance*. Oxford: Oxford University Press, 1993.

Polner, Murray, and Jim O'Grady. *Disarmed and Dangerous: The Radical Lives and Times of Daniel and Philip Berrigan*. New York: Basic Books, 1997.

Small, Melvin, and William D. Hoover, eds. *Give Peace a Chance: Exploring the Vietnam Antiwar Movement.* Syracuse, N.Y.: Syracuse University Press, 1992.

Wells, Tom. *The War Within: America's Battle Over Vietnam.* Berkeley: University of California Press, 1994.

Whitney, Edson Leone. *The American Peace Society: A Centennial History*. Washington, D.C.: American Peace Society, 1928.

Wittner, Lawrence S. *Rebels Against War: The American Peace Movement, 1933–1983.* Philadelphia: Temple University Press, 1984.

Zaroulis, Nancy, and Gerald Sullivan. *Who Spoke Up? American Protest Against the War in Vietnam, 1963–1975.* Garden City, N.Y.: Doubleday, 1984.

Ziegler, Valarie H. *The Advocates of Peace in Antebellum America*. Macon, Ga.: Mercer University Press, 2001.

## Education

Ambrose, Stephen. *Duty, Honor, Country: A History of West Point.* Baltimore, Md.: Johns Hopkins University Press, 1999.

Andrew, Rod, Jr. *Long Gray Lines: The Southern Military School Tradition, 1839–1915*. Chapel Hill and London: University of North Carolina Press, 2001.

Atkinson, Rick. *The Long Gray Line*. Boston: Houghton Mifflin, 1989.

Cooling, Benjamin Franklin. *Gray Steel and Blue Water Navy: The Formative Years of America's Military Industrial Complex, 1881–1917*. Hamden, Conn.: Archon Books, 1979.

Crackel, Theodore J. *Mr. Jefferson's Army: Political and Social Reform of the Military Establishment 1801–1809*. New York: New York University Press, 1987.

———. *West Point: A Bicentennial History.* Lawrence: University Press of Kansas, 2002.

Fagan, George. *The Air Force Academy: An Illustrated History*. Boulder, Colo.: Johnson Books, 1988.

Forney, Todd. *The Midshipman Culture and Educational Reform: The U.S. Naval Academy, 1946–76*. Newark: University of Delaware Press, 2004.

Hattendorf, John. *Sailors and Scholars: The Centennial History of the U.S. Naval War College*. Newport, R.I.: Naval War College Press, 1984.

Kinkead, Katharine T. *Walk Together, Talk Together: The American Field Service Student Exchange Program.* New York: W. W. Norton, 1962.

Lipsky, David. *Absolutely American: Four Years at West Point*. Boston: Houghton Mifflin, 2003.

Lovell, John P. *Neither Athens Nor Sparta? The American Service Academies in Transition*. Bloomington: Indiana University Press, 1979.

Manegold, Catherine S. *In Glory's Shadow: Shannon Faulkner, The Citadel, and a Changing America.* New York: Alfred A. Knopf, 1999.

Masland, John, and Laurence Radway. *Soldiers and Scholars: Military Education and National Policy*. Princeton, N.J.: Princeton University Press, 1957.

Morrison, James L. *"The Best School in the World": West Point, the Pre–Civil War Years, 1833–1866.* Kent, Ohio: Kent State University Press, 1986.

Neiberg, Michael S. *Making Citizen-Soldiers: ROTC and the Ideology of American Military Service.* Cambridge, Mass.: Harvard University Press, 2000.

Simons, William E. *Professional Military Education in the United States.* Westport, Conn.: Greenwood Press, 2000.

Spector, Ronald. *Professors of War: The Naval War College and the Development of the Naval Profession.* Newport, R.I.: Naval War College Press, 1977.

Sweetman, Jack. *The U.S. Naval Academy: An Illustrated History.* Annapolis, Md.: Naval Institute Press, 1995.

Vlahos, Michael. *The Blue Sword: The Naval War College and the American Mission, 1919–1941.* Newport, R.I.: Naval War College Press, 1981.

### Race and Ethnicity

Barbeau, Arthur, and Florette Henri. *The Unknown Soldiers: Black American Troops in World War I.* Philadelphia: Temple University Press, 1974.

Bendersky, Joseph W. *The "Jewish Threat": Anti-Semitic Politics of the U.S. Army.* New York: Basic Books, 2000.

Berlin, Ira, et al. *Free at Last: A Documentary History of Slavery, Freedom, and the Civil War.* New York: New Press, 1992.

———. *Slaves No More: Three Essays on Emancipation and the Civil War.* New York: Cambridge University Press, 1992.

Boskin, Joseph. *Urban Racial Violence in the Twentieth Century.* 2nd ed. Beverly Hills, Calif.: Glencoe Press, 1976.

Brooks, Jennifer E. *Defining the Peace: World War II Veterans, Race, and the Remaking of Southern Political Tradition.* Chapel Hill: University of North Carolina Press, 2005.

Buckley, Gail Lumet. *American Patriots: The Story of the Blacks in the Military from the Revolution to Desert Storm.* New York: Random House, 2001.

Burchard, Peter. *One Gallant Rush: Robert Gould Shaw and His Brave Black Regiment.* New York: St. Martin's Press, 1965.

Burton, William L. *Melting Pot Soldiers: The Union's Ethnic Regiments.* Ames: Iowa State University Press, 1988.

Christian, Garna L. *Black Soldiers in Jim Crow Texas, 1899–1917.* College Station: Texas A&M University Press, 1995.

Cornish, Dudley Taylor. *The Sable Arm: Black Troops in the Union Army, 1861–1865.* 1956. Reprint, Lawrence: University Press of Kansas, 1987.

Dalfiume, Richard M. *Desegregation of the U.S. Armed Forces.* Columbia: University of Missouri Press, 1969.

Daniels, Roger. *The Decision to Relocate the Japanese-Americans.* Philadelphia: Lippincott, 1975.

Davis, Daniel S. *Behind Barbed Wire: The Imprisonment of Japanese-Americans During World War II.* New York: Dutton, 1982.

DiStasi, Lawrence. *Una Storia Segreta: The Secret History of Italian American Evacuation and Internment during World War II.* Berkeley, Calif.: Heyday Books, 2001.

Dobak, William A., and Thomas D. Phillips. *The Black Regulars 1866–1898.* Norman: University of Oklahoma Press, 2001.

Du Bois, W. E. B. *Black Reconstruction in America, 1860–1880.* New York: Harcourt, Brace, 1935.

Dudziak, Mary L. *Cold War Civil Rights: Race and the Image of American Democracy.* Princeton, N.J.: Princeton University Press, 2002.

Fletcher, Marvin E. *The Black Soldier and Officer in the United States Army, 1891–1917.* Columbia: University of Missouri Press, 1974.

Foner, Jack D. *Blacks and the Military in American History.* New York: Praeger, 1974.

Ford, Nancy Gentile. *Americans All!: Foreign-born Soldiers in World War I.* College Station: Texas A&M University Press, 2001.

Fox, Stephen. *America's Invisible Gulag: A Biography of German American Internment and Exclusion in World War II—Memory and History.* Vol. 23 of New German American Studies/Neue Deutsch-Amerikanisch Studien. New York: Peter Lang, 2000.

———. *The Unknown Internment: An Oral History of the Relocation of Italian Americans During World War II.* Twayne's Oral History Series 4. Boston: Twayne, 1990.

Glatthaar, Joseph. *Forged in Battle: The Civil Alliance of Black Soldiers and White Officers.* New York: Free Press, 1990.

Harris, Stephen L. *Harlem's Hell Fighters: The African-American 369th Infantry in World War I.* Washington, D.C.: Brassey's, 2003.

Hawaii Nikkei History Editorial Board. *Japanese Eyes, American Heart: Personal Reflections of Hawaii's World War II Nisei Soldiers.* Honolulu: University of Hawaii Press, 1998.

Horton, James Oliver, and Lois E. Horton. *Slavery and the Making of America*. New York: Oxford University Press, 2005.

Keith, Jeanette. *Rich Man's War, Poor Man's Fight: Race, Class, and Power in the Rural South during the First World War*. Chapel Hill: University of North Carolina Press, 2004.

Kilory, David P. *For Race and Country: The Life and Career of Colonel Charles Young*. Westport, Conn.: Praeger, 2003.

Kornweibel, Theodore, Jr. *No Crystal Stair: Black Life and* The Messenger, *1917–1928*. Westport, Conn.: Greenwood Press, 1975.

Krammer, Arnold. *Undue Process: The Untold Story of America's German Alien Internees*. London and Boulder, Colo.: Rowman & Littlefield, 1997.

Lanning, Michael Lee. *The African-American Soldier: From Crispus Attucks to Colin Powell.* Secaucus, N.J.: Carol Publishing, 1997.

Leak, Jeffrey B., ed. *Rac[e]ing to the Right: Selected Essays of George S. Schuyler.* Knoxville: University of Tennessee Press, 2001.

Leckie, William A., with Shirley A. Leckie. *The Buffalo Soldiers: A Narrative of the Black Cavalry in the West.* Rev. ed. Norman: University of Oklahoma Press, 2003.

Lewis, David Levering. *W. E. B. Du Bois: Biography of a Race, 1868–1919.* New York: Henry Holt, 1993.

———. *W. E. B. Du Bois: The Fight for Equality and the American Century, 1919–1963*. New York: Henry Holt, 2000.

MacGregor, Morris J., and Bernard C. Nalty, eds. *Blacks in the United States Armed Forces: Basic Documents.* 13 vols. Wilmington, Del.: Scholarly Resources, 1977.

Marqusee, Mike. *Redemption Song: Muhammad Ali and the Spirit of the Sixties*. New York: Verso, 2000.

Mazón, Mauricio. *The Zoot-Suit Riots: The Psychology of Symbolic Annihilation*. Austin: University of Texas Press, 1984.

Mershon, Sherie, and Steven Schlossman. *Foxholes and Color Lines: Desegregating the U.S. Armed Forces*. Baltimore, Md.: Johns Hopkins University Press, 1998.

Morin, Paul. *Among the Valiant: Mexican-Americans in World War II and Korea.* Los Angeles: Bottden, 1963.

Moskos, Charles C., and John Sibley Butler. *All That We Can Be: Black Leadership and Racial Integration the Army Way*. New York: Basic Books, 1996.

Nalty, Bernard. *Strength for the Fight: A History of Black Americans in the Military.* New York: Free Press, 1986.

Pagán, Eduardo Obregón. *Murder at the Sleepy Lagoon: Zoot Suits, Race, and Riot in Wartime L.A.* Chapel Hill: University of North Carolina Press, 2003.

Pfeffer, Paula F. *A. Philip Randolph: Pioneer of the Civil Rights Movement*. Baton Rouge: Louisiana State University Press, 1990.

Reed, Merl. *Seedtime for the Modern Civil Rights Movement: The President's Committee on Fair Employment Practice, 1941–1946.* Baton Rouge: Louisiana State University Press, 1991.

Roberts, Frank E. *The American Foreign Legion: Black Soldiers of the 93rd in World War I.* Annapolis, Md.: Naval Institute Press, 2004.

Schubert, Frank N., ed. *On the Trail of the Buffalo Soldier: Biographies of African Americans in the U.S. Army, 1866–1917*. Wilmington, Del.: Scholarly Resources, 1995.

_____. *Voices of the Black Soldiers: Records, Reports and Recollections of Military Life and Service in the West*. Albuquerque: University of New Mexico Press, 2003.

Schuyler, George S. *Black and Conservative: The Autobiography of George S. Schuyler*. New Rochelle, N.Y.: Arlington House Publishers, 1966.

Shaffer, Donald R. *After the Glory: The Struggles of Black Civil War Veterans*. Lawrence: University Press of Kansas, 2004.

Smith, John David, ed. *Black Soldiers in Blue: African-American Troops in the Civil War Era.* Chapel Hill: University of North Carolina Press, 2004.

Sterba, Christopher M. *Good Americans: Italians and Jewish Immigrants During the First World War*. New York: Oxford University Press, 2003.

Takaki, Ronald. *Double Victory: A Multicultural History of America in World War II.* Boston: Little, Brown, 2000.

Trudeau, Noah Andre. *Like Men of War: Black Troops in the Civil War, 1862–1865* Boston: Little, Brown, 1998.

Trujillos, Charley. *Soldados: Chicanos in Vietnam*. San Jose, Calif.: Chusma House. 1993.

### Native Americans

Ambrose, Stephen. *Crazy Horse and Custer: Parallel Lives of Two American Warriors*. New York: Doubleday, 1975.

# GENERAL BIBLIOGRAPHY


Antal, Sandy. *Wampum Denied: Procter's War of 1812*. Ottawa: Carleton University Press, 1997.

Bernstein, Alison. *American Indians in World War II: Toward a New Era in Indian Affairs.* Norman: University of Oklahoma Press, 1991.

Brandao, Jose Antonio. *'Your fyre shall burn no more': Iroquois Policy toward New France and Its Native Allies to 1701*. Lincoln: University of Nebraska Press, 1997.

Britten, Thomas A. *American Indians in World War One: At Home and At War.* Albuquerque: University of New Mexico Press, 1997.

Brown, Dee. *Bury My Heart at Wounded Knee: An Indian History of the American West*. New York: Holt, Rinehart & Winston, 1974.

Calloway, Colin. *The American Revolution in Indian Country: Crisis and Diversity in Native American Communities.* Cambridge: Cambridge University Press, 1995.

———. *New Worlds for All: Indians, Europeans, and the Remaking of Early America.* Baltimore, Md.: Johns Hopkins University Press, 1997.

Cave, Alfred. *The Pequot War.* Amherst: University of Massachusetts Press, 1996.

Chalfant, William Y. *Cheyennes and Horse Soldiers: The 1857 Expedition and the Battle of Solomon's Fork*. Norman: University of Oklahoma Press, 1989.

Debo, Angie. *Geronimo: The Man, His Time, His Place*. Norman: University of Oklahoma Press, 1976.

Dowd, Gregory Evans. *A Spirited Resistance: The North American Indian Struggle for Unity.* Baltimore, Md.: Johns Hopkins University Press, 1992.

———. *War Under Heaven: Pontiac, the Indian Nations, and the British Empire*. Baltimore, Md.: Johns Hopkins University Press, 2002.

Dunlay, Thomas W. *Wolves for Blue Soldiers: Indian Scouts and Auxiliaries with the United States Army, 1860–1890.* Lincoln: University of Nebraska Press, 1982.

Edmunds, R. David. *Tecumseh and the Quest for Indian Leadership*. Boston: Little, Brown, 1984.

Foreman, Grant. *Indian Removal.* Norman: University of Oklahoma Press, 1972.

———. *A Traveler in Indian Country: The Journal of Ethan Allen Hitchcock.* Cedar Rapids, Iowa: Torch Press, 1930.

Gilbert, Bill. *God Gave Us This Country: Tekamthi and the First American Civil War*. New York: Athenaeum, 1989.

Graymont, Barbara. *The Iroquois in the American Revolution.* Syracuse, N.Y.: Syracuse University Press, 1972.

Hauptman, Lawrence M. *Between Two Fires: American Indians in the Civil War.* New York: Free Press, 1996.

Heidler, David S., and Jeanne T. Heidler. *Old Hickory's War: Andrew Jackson and the Quest for Empire.* Mechanicsburg, Penn.: Stackpole Books, 1996.

Hitchcock, Ethan Allen. *Fifty Years in Camp and Field: The Diary of Major-General Ethan Allen Hitchcock*. Edited by W. A. Croffut. New York: G. P. Putnam's Sons, 1909.

Holm, Tom. *Strong Hearts, Wounded Souls: Native American Veterans of the Vietnam War.* Austin: University of Texas Press, 1996.

Jackson, Donald, ed. *Black Hawk: An Autobiography*. Urbana: University of Illinois Press, 1955.

Knetsch, Joe. *Florida's Seminole Wars, 1817–1858*. Charleston, S.C.: Arcadia Publishing, 2003.

Langellier, John P. *American Indians in the U.S. Armed Forces, 1866–1945.* Mechanicsburg, Penn.: Greenhill Books, 2000.

Laumer, Frank. *Dade's Last Command.* Gainesville: University of Florida Press, 1995.

Mahon, John K. *History of the Second Seminole War, 1835–1842*. Rev. ed. Gainesville: University of Florida Press, 1992.

Malone, Patrick M. *The Skulking Way of War: Technology and Tactics Among the New England Indians.* Baltimore, Md.: Johns Hopkins University Press, 1991.

Meadows, William C. *The Comanche Code Talkers of World War II.* Austin: University of Texas Press, 2002.

_____. *Kiowa, Apache and Comanche Military Societies: Enduring Veterans, 1800 to the Present*. Austin: University of Texas Press, 1999.

Merritt, Jane T. *At the Crossroads: Indians and Empires on a Mid-Atlantic Frontier, 1700–1763*. Chapel Hill: University of North Carolina Press, 2003.

Missall, John, and Mary Lou Missall. *The Seminole Wars: America's Longest Indian Conflict.* Gainesville: University Press of Florida, 2004.

Nester, William R. *"Haughty Conquerors": Amherst and the Great Indian Uprising of 1763*. Westport, Conn.: Praeger, 2000.

Peckham, Howard H. *Pontiac and the Indian Uprising*. New York: Russell & Russell, 1970.

Porter, Kenneth W. *The Black Seminoles: History of a Freedom-Seeking People.* Revised and edited by Alcione M. Amos and Thomas P. Senter. Gainesville: University Press of Florida, 1996.

Remini, Robert V. *Andrew Jackson and His Indian Wars*. New York: Viking Press, 2001.

Richter, Daniel K. *Facing East from Indian Country: A Native History of Early America.* Cambridge, Mass.: Harvard University Press, 2001.

Russell, Charles M., III. *A Good Year to Die: The Great Sioux War.* New York: Random House, 1995.

Skaggs, David Curtis, and Larry L. Nelson, eds. *The Sixty Year's War for the Great Lakes, 1754–1814.* East Lansing: Michigan State University Press, 2001.

Sprague, John T. *The Origin, Progress and Conclusion of the Florida War.* 1848. Reprint, Gainesville: University Press of Florida, 1964.

Starkey, Armstrong. *European and Native American Warfare, 1675–1815.* Norman: University of Oklahoma Press, 1998.

Steele, Ian K. *Warpaths: Invasions of North America.* New York: Oxford University Press, 1994.

Stephanson, Anders. *Manifest Destiny*. New York: Hill & Wang, 1995.

Sugden, John. *Tecumseh: A Life*. New York: Henry Holt, 1997.

Tate, Michael L. *The Frontier Army in the Settlement of the West.* Norman: University of Oklahoma Press, 1999.

Townsend, Kenneth W. *World War II and the American Indian.* Albuquerque: University of New Mexico Press, 2000.

Utley, Robert M. *Frontier Regulars: The United States Army and the Indian, 1866–1891.* Lincoln: University of Nebraska Press, 1974.

———. *Frontiersmen in Blue: The United States Army and the Indian, 1848–1865.* New York: Macmillan, 1967.

———. *The Indian Frontier of the American West, 1846–1890.* Albuquerque: University of New Mexico Press, 1974.

Wallace, Anthony F. C. *The Long, Bitter Trail.* New York: Hill & Wang, 1993.

Washburn, Wilcomb, ed. *Garland Library of Narratives of North American Indian Captivities*. 112 vols. New York: Garland, 1977–83.

Weisman, Brent Richards. *Unconquered People: Florida's Seminole and Miccosukee Indians*. Gainesville: University Press of Florida, 1999.

White, Richard. *The Middle Ground: Indians, Empires, and Republics in the Great Lakes Region, 1650–1815*. Cambridge: Cambridge University Press, 1991.

Wickman, Patricia R. *Osceola's Legacy.* Tuscaloosa: University of Alabama Press, 1991.

### GENDER AND SEXUALITY

Alonso, Harriet Hyman. *Peace as a Woman's Issue: A History of the U.S. Movement for World Peace and Women's Rights.* Syracuse, N.Y.: Syracuse University Press, 1993.

Attie, Jeanie. *Patriotic Toil: Northern Women and the American Civil War*. Ithaca, N.Y.: Cornell University Press, 1998.

Belkin, Aaron, and Geoffrey Bateman, eds. *Don't Ask, Don't Tell: Debating the Gay Ban in the Military.* Denver, Colo.: Lynne Rienner Publishers, 2003.

Bérubé, Allan. *Coming Out Under Fire: The History of Gay Men and Gay Women in World War II.* New York: Free Press, 1990.

Binkin, Martin, and Shirley Bach. *Women and the Military*. Washington, D.C.: Brookings Institution Press, 1973.

Blacksmith, E. A. *Women in the Military.* New York: Wilson, 1992.

Braudy, Leo. *From Chivalry to Terrorism: War and the Changing Nature of Masculinity*. New York: Alfred A. Knopf, 2003.

Bussey, Gertrude, and Margaret Tims. *Pioneers for Peace: Women's International League for Peace and Freedom, 1915–1946.* London: Allen & Unwin, 1965.

Campbell, D'Ann. *Women at War with America: Private Lives in a Patriotic Era.* Cambridge, Mass.: Harvard University Press, 1984.

Carpenter, Stephanie A. *On the Farm Front: The Women's Land Army in World War II.* Dekalb: Northern Illinois University Press, 2003.

Clinton, Catherine, and Nina Silber, eds. *Divided Houses: Gender and the Civil War.* New York: Oxford University Press. 1992.

De Pauw, Linda Grant. *Battle Cries and Lullabies: Women in War from Prehistory to the Present*. Norman: University of Oklahoma Press, 1998.

# GENERAL BIBLIOGRAPHY


Ebbert, Jean, and Marie-Beth Hall. *Crossed Currents: Navy Women from WWI to Tailhook.* Washington D.C.: Brasseys / Macmillan, 1993.

Ender, Morton, ed. *Military Brats and Other Global Nomads.* Westport, Conn.: Praeger, 2002.

Endres, Kathleen L. *Rosie the Rubber Worker: Women Workers in Akron's Rubber Factories during World War II.* Kent, Ohio: Kent State University Press, 2000.

Faust, Drew G. *Mothers of Invention: Women of the Slaveholding South in the Civil War.* Chapel Hill: University of North Carolina Press, 1995.

Foster, Catherine. *Women for All Seasons: The Story of the Women's International League for Peace and Freedom.* Athens: University of Georgia Press, 1989.

Garrison, Nancy S. *With Courage and Delicacy: Civil War on the Peninsula: Women and the U. S. Sanitary Commission.* New York: Perseus Books, 2003.

Giesberg, Judith Ann. *Civil War Sisterhood: The United States Sanitary Commission and Women's Politics in Transition.* Boston: Northeastern University Press, 2000.

Godson, Susan H. *Serving Proudly: A History of Women in the U.S. Navy.* Annapolis, Md.: Naval Institute Press, 2001.

Goossen, Rachel Waltner. *Women Against the Good War: Conscientious Objection and Gender on the American Home Front, 1941–1947.* Chapel Hill: University of North Carolina Press, 1997.

Halley, Janet E. *Don't: A Reader's Guide to the Military's Anti-Gay Policy.* Durham, N.C.: Duke University Press, 1999.

Herek, Gregory M., J. B. Jobe, and R. M. Carney, eds. *Out in Force: Sexuality and the Military.* Chicago: University of Chicago Press, 1996.

Höhn, Maria. *GIs and Frauleins: The German-American Encounter in 1950s West Germany.* Chapel Hill: University of North Carolina Press, 2002.

Holm, Jeanne. *Women in the Military: An Unfinished Revolution.* Novato, Calif.: Presidio Press, 1982.

Honey, Maureen. *Creating Rosie the Riveter: Class, Gender, and Propaganda during World War II.* Amherst: University of Massachusetts Press, 1984.

Jarvis, Christina S. *The Male Body at War: American Masculinity during World War II.* Dekalb: Northern Illinois University Press, 2004.

Kesselman, Amy. *Fleeting Opportunities: Women Shipyard Workers in Portland and Vancouver during World War II and Reconversion.* Albany: State University of New York Press, 1990.

Lehring, Gary L. *Officially Gay: The Political Construction of Sexuality by the U.S. Military.* Philadelphia: Temple University Press, 2003.

Leonard, Elizabeth D. *Yankee Women: Gender Battles in the Civil War.* New York: W. W. Norton. 1994.

Mann, Herman. *The Female Review: Life of Deborah Sampson the Female Soldier in the War of the Revolution.* 1866. Reprint, New York: Arno Press, 1972.

McMichael, William H. *The Mother of All Hooks: The Story of the U.S. Navy's Tailhook Scandal.* New Brunswick, N.J.: Transaction, 1997.

Meyer, Leisa D. *Creating G.I. Jane: Power and Sexuality in the Women's Army Corps During World War II.* New York: Columbia University Press, 1996.

Milkman, Ruth. *Gender at Work: The Dynamics of Job Segregation by Sex during World War II.* Urbana: University of Illinois Press, 1987.

Monahan, Evelyn, and Rosemary Neidel-Greenlee. *And If I Perish: Frontline U.S. Army Nurses in World War II.* New York: Alfred A. Knopf, 2003.

Morden, Bettie. *The Women's Army Corps, 1945–1978.* Washington, D.C.: United States Army Center of Military History, 1990.

National Defense Research Institute. *Sexual Orientation and U.S. Personnel Policy: Options and Assessment.* Santa Monica, Calif.: RAND, 1993.

Norman, Elizabeth M. *Women at War: The Story of Fifty Military Nurses Who Served in Vietnam.* Philadelphia: University of Pennsylvania Press, 1990.

Rupp, Leila. *Mobilizing Women for War: German and American Propaganda, 1939–1945.* Princeton, N.J.: Princeton University Press, 1978.

Rustad, Michael. *Women in Khaki: The American Enlisted Woman.* New York: Praeger, 1982.

Sarnecky, Mary T. *A History of the U.S. Army Nurse Corps.* Philadelphia: University of Pennsylvania Press, 1999.

Schultz, Jane E. *Women at the Front: Hospital Workers in Civil War America.* Chapel Hill: University of North Carolina Press, 2005.

Shilts, Randy. *Conduct Unbecoming: Gays and Lesbians in the U.S. Military*. New York: St. Martin's Press, 1993.

Sterner, Doris. *In & Out of Harm's Way: A Navy Nurse Corps History*. New York: Peanut Butter Publishing, 1996.

Stiehm, Judith. *Arms and the Enlisted Woman*. Philadelphia: Temple University Press, 1989.

———. *It's Our Military, Too!: Women and the U.S. Military*. Philadelphia: Temple University Press, 1996.

Strum, Phillippa. *Women in the Barracks: The VMI Case and Equal Rights*. Lawrence: University Press of Kansas, 2002.

Treadwell, Mattie. *The United States Army in World War II Special Studies: The Women's Army Corps*. Washington, D.C.: Office of the Chief of Military History, 1953.

United States Presidential Commission on the Assignment of Women in the Armed Forces. *Women in Combat*. Washington, D.C.: Brassey's, 1993.

Van Devanter, Lynda. *Home Before Morning: The True Story of an Army Nurse in Vietnam*. 1983. Reprint. Amherst: University of Massachusetts Press, 2001.

Virden, Jenel. *Goodbye Piccadilly: British War Brides in America*. Urbana: University of Illinois Press, 1996.

Weatherford, Doris. *American Women and World War II*. New York: Facts On File, 1990.

Willenz, June A. *Women Veterans: America's Forgotten Heroes*. New York: Continuum, 1983.

Young, Alfred. *Masquerade: The Life and Times of Deborah Sampson, Continental Soldier*. New York: Alfred A. Knopf, 2004.

Yuh, Ji-Yeon. *Beyond the Shadows of Camptown: Korean Military Brides in America*. New York: New York University Press, 2002.

Zeiger, Susan. *In Uncle Sam's Service: Women Workers with the American Expeditionary Force, 1917–1919*. Ithaca, N.Y.: Cornell University Press, 1999.

Zimmerman, Jean. *Tailspin: Women at War in the Wake of Tailhook*. New York: Doubleday, 1995.

### Daily Life and the Home Front

Abrahamson, James L. *The American Home Front: Revolutionary War, Civil War, World War I, World War II*. Washington, D.C.: National Defense University Press, 1983.

Bentley, Amy. *Eating for Victory: Food Rationing and the Politics of Domesticity*. Urbana: University of Illinois Press, 1998.

Blum, John Morton. *V Was for Victory: Politics and American Culture During World War II*. New York: Harcourt Brace Jovanovich, 1976.

Boswell, Victor R. *Victory Gardens*. Washington, D.C.: U.S. Department of Agriculture, 1943.

Boyer, Paul. *By the Bomb's Early Light: American Thought and Culture at the Dawn of the Atomic Age*. Chapel Hill: University of North Carolina Press, 1994.

Gilman, John, and Robert Heide. *Home Front America: Popular Culture of the World War II Era*. San Francisco: Chronicle Books, 1983.

Goodwin, Doris Kearns. *No Ordinary Time: Franklin and Eleanor Roosevelt, the Home Front in World War II*. New York: Simon & Schuster, 1994.

Hayes, Joanne Lamb. *Grandma's Wartime Kitchen: World War II and the Way We Cooked*. New York: St. Martin's Press, 2000.

Hill, Reuben, et al. *Families under Stress: Adjustment to the Crises of War Separation and Reunion*. New York: Harper & Row, 1949.

Jeffries, John W. *Wartime America: The World War II Home Front*. Chicago: Ivan R. Dee, 1996.

Kains, M. G. *The Original Victory Garden Book*. New York: Stein & Day, 1978.

Kerr, Thomas J. *Civil Defense in the U.S.: Bandaid for a Holocaust?* Boulder, Colo.: Westview Press, 1983.

Lingeman, Richard R. *Don't You Know There's a War On?: The American Home Front, 1941–1945*. New York: Putnam, 1970.

May, Elaine Tyler. *Homeward Bound: American Families in the Cold War Era*. New York: Basic Books, 1988.

McEnaney, Laura. *Civil Defense Begins At Home: Militarization Meets Everyday Life in the Fifties*. Princeton, N.J.: Princeton University Press, 2000.

Rose, Kenneth D. *One Nation Underground: The Fallout Shelter in American Culture*. New York: New York University Press, 2001.

Ware, Caroline F. *The Consumer Goes to War: A Guide to Victory on the Home Front*. New York: Funk & Wagnalls, 1942.

Weart, Spencer R. *Nuclear Fear: A History of Images*. Cambridge, Mass.: Harvard University Press, 1988.

Winkler, Allan M. *Life Under a Cloud: American Anxiety About the Atom*. Oxford: Oxford University Press, 1993.

# GENERAL BIBLIOGRAPHY


## Economics and Labor

Black, Edwin. *IBM and the Holocaust: The Strategic Alliance Between Nazi Germany and America's Most Powerful Corporation.* New York: Crown, 2001.

Brandes, Stuart D. *Warhogs: A History of War Profits in America.* Lexington: University Press of Kentucky, 1997.

Briody, Dan. *The Halliburton Agenda: The Politics of Oil and Money.* Hoboken, N.J.: Wiley, 2004.

Cuff, Robert D. *The War Industries Board: Business–Government Relations During World War I.* Baltimore, Md.: Johns Hopkins University Press, 1973.

Dobak, William A. *Fort Riley and Its Neighbors: Military Money and Economic Growth, 1853–1895.* Norman: University of Oklahoma Press, 1998.

Dubofsky, Melvyn, ed. *American Labor Since the New Deal.* Chicago: Quadrangle Books, 1971.

Eklund, Robert B., and Mark Thornton. *Tariffs, Blockades, and Inflation: The Economics of the Civil War.* New York: Rowman Littlefield, 2004.

Engelbrecht, H. C., and Frank Cleary Hanighen. *Merchants of Death: A Study of the International Armament Industry.* New York: Dodd, Mead, 1934.

Foner, Eric. *America's Reconstruction: People and Politics After the Civil War.* New York: HarperCollins, 1995.

Frazer, Robert W. *Forts and Supplies: The Role of the Army in the Economy of the Southwest, 1846–1861.* Albuquerque: University of New Mexico Press, 1983.

———. *Forts of the West: Military Forts and Presidios and Posts Commonly Called Forts West of the Mississippi River to 1898.* Norman: University of Oklahoma Press, 1965.

General Accounting Office. *Report to Congress: Military Bases, Lessons Learned From Prior Base Closure Rounds.* Washington, D.C.: U.S. Government Printing Office, 1997.

Gimbel, John. *The Origins of the Marshall Plan.* Stanford, Calif.: Stanford University Press, 1976.

Hackemer, Kurt H. *The U.S. Navy and the Origins of the Military-Industrial Complex, 1847–1883.* Annapolis, Md.: Naval Institute Press, 2001.

Higham, Charles. *Trading with the Enemy: An Expose of the Nazi–American Money Plot, 1933–1949.* New York: Delacorte Press, 1983.

Hogan, Michael J. *The Marshall Plan: America, Britain, and the Reconstruction of Western Europe, 1947–1952.* New York: Cambridge University Press, 1987.

Jackson, Donald. *Custer's Gold: The United States Cavalry Expedition of 1874.* New Haven, Conn.: Yale University Press, 1966.

Johnson, Russell L. *Warriors into Workers: The Civil War and the Formation of Urban Industrial Society in a Northern City.* New York: Fordham University Press, 2003.

Koistinen, Paul A. *Arsenal of World War II: The Political Economy of American Warfare, 1940–45.* Lawrence: University Press of Kansas, 2004.

———. *Beating Plowshares Into Swords: The Political Economy of American Warfare, 1606–1865.* Lawrence: University Press of Kansas, 1996.

———. *The Military-Industrial Complex: A Historical Perspective.* New York: Praeger, 1980.

———. *Mobilizing for Modern War: The Political Economy of American Warfare, 1865–1919.* Lawrence: University Press of Kansas, 1997.

———. *Planning War, Pursuing Peace: The Political Economy of American Warfare, 1920–1939.* Lawrence: University Press of Kansas, 1998.

Kuznets, Simon. *National Product in Wartime.* New York: NBER, 1945.

LaFeber, Walter. *The New Empire: An Interpretation of American Expansion, 1860–1898.* Ithaca, N.Y.: Cornell University Press, 1963.

Lichtenstein, Nelson. *Labor's War at Home: The CIO in World War II.* Cambridge: Cambridge University Press, 1982.

———. *State of the Union: A Century of American Labor.* Princeton, N.J.: Princeton University Press, 2002.

Lynch, John E. *Local Economic Development after Military Base Closures.* New York: Praeger, 1970.

Markusen, Ann, and Joel Yudken. *Dismantling the Cold War Economy.* New York: Perseus Books, 1993.

Miller, Sally M., and Daniel A. Cornford, eds. *American Labor in the Era of World War II.* Westport, Conn.: Praeger, 1995.

Milward, Alan S. *The Reconstruction of Western Europe, 1945–51.* Berkeley and Los Angeles: University of California Press, 1984.

———. *War, Economy and Society.* London: Alan Lane, 1977.

Nelson, Donald M. *Arsenal of Democracy. The Story of American War Production*. New York: Harcourt, Brace, 1946.

Phillips, Kevin P. *American Dynasty: Aristocracy, Fortune, and the Politics of Deceit in the House of Bush*. New York: Viking, 2004.

Pierre, Andrew J. *The Global Politics of Arms Sales*. Princeton, N.J.: Princeton University Press, 1982.

Prucha, Francis Paul. *Broadax and Bayonet: The Role of the United States Army in the Development of the Northwest, 1815–1860*. Madison: State Historical Society of Wisconsin, 1953.

———. *The Sword of the Republic: The United States Army on the Frontier, 1783–1846*. New York: Macmillan, 1969.

Ransom, Roger L. *Conflict and Compromise: The Political Economy of Slavery, Emancipation, and the American Civil War*. Cambridge: Cambridge University Press, 1989.

Rockoff, Hugh. *Drastic Measures: A History of Wage and Price Controls in the United States*. New York: Cambridge University Press, 1984.

Rosecrance, Richard N. *The Rise of the Trading State: Commerce and Conquest in the Modern World*. New York: Basic Books, 1986.

Rundquist, Barry S., and Thomas M. Carsey. *Congress and Defense Spending: The Distributive Politics of Military Procurement*. Norman: University of Oklahoma Press, 2002.

Schubert, Frank N. *Buffalo Soldiers, Braves, and the Brass: The Story of Fort Robinson, Nebraska*. Shippensburg, Penn.: White Mane Publishing, 1993.

Sharkey, Robert P. *Money, Class, and Party: An Economic Study of Civil War and Reconstruction*. Baltimore, Md.: Johns Hopkins University Press, 1967.

Sorenson, David S. *Shutting Down the Cold War: The Politics of Military Base Closure*. New York: Palgrave Macmillan, 1998.

Tate, Michael. *The Frontier Army in the Settlement of the West*. Norman: University of Oklahoma Press, 1999.

Unger, Irwin. *The Greenback Era: A Social and Political History of American Finance, 1865–1879*. Princeton, N.J.: Princeton University Press, 1964.

Vatter, Harold G. *The U.S. Economy in World War II*. New York: Columbia University Press, 1985.

### Science and Technology

Arnold, David C. *Spying from Space: Constructing America's Satellite Command and Control Systems*. College Station: Texas A&M University Press, 2004.

Bartlett, Merrill L., ed. *Assault from the Sea: Essays on the History of Amphibious Warfare*. Annapolis, Md.: Naval Institute Press, 1983.

Biddle, Wayne. *Barons of the Sky—From Early Flight to Strategic Warfare: The Story of the American Aerospace Industry*. Baltimore, Md.: Johns Hopkins University Press, 2001.

Boslaugh, David L. *When Computers Went to Sea: The Digitization of the United States Navy*. Los Alamitos, Calif.: IEEE Computer Society and the Society of Naval Architects and Marine Engineers, 1999.

Bromberg, Joan Lisa. *NASA and the Space Industry*. Baltimore, Md.: Johns Hopkins University Press, 1999.

Brown, Frederick J. *Chemical Warfare: A Study in Restraints*. Princeton, N.J.: Princeton University Press, 1968.

Campen, Alan D., contributing ed. *The First Information War: The Story of Communications, Computers, and Intelligence Systems in the Persian Gulf War*. Fairfax, Va.: AFCEA International Press, 1992.

Cecil, Paul Frederick. *Herbicidal Warfare: The Ranch Hand Project in Vietnam*. New York: Praeger, 1986.

Citino, Robert M. *Armored Forces: History and Sourcebook*. Westport, Conn.: Greenwood Press, 1994.

Conant, Jennet. *109 East Palace: Robert Oppenheimer and the Men and Women Who Followed Him to the Secret City of Los Alamos*. New York: Simon & Schuster, 2005.

Cooling, B. Franklin. *Gray Steel and Blue Water Navy: The Formative Years of America's Military-Industrial Complex, 1881–1917*. Hamden, Conn.: Archon Books, 1979.

DeVorkin, David H. *Science With a Vengeance: How the Military Created the U.S. Space Sciences After World War II*. New York: Springer-Verlag, 1992.

Dux, John, and P. J. Young. *Agent Orange: The Bitter Harvest*. Sydney: Hodder & Stoughton, 1980.

Gifford, Jonathan Lewis. *Planning the Interstate Highway System*. Boulder, Colo.: Westview Press, 1998.

Hanlon, Martin. *You Can Get There From Here: How the Interstate Highways Transformed America*. New York: Palgrave Macmillan, 2002.

Harris, Robert, and Jeremy Paxman. *A Higher Form of Killing: The Secret History of Chemical and Biological Warfare*. New York: Random House, 2002.

Heller, Charles E. *Chemical Warfare in World War I: The American Experience, 1917–1918*. Fort Leavenworth, Kan.: U.S. Army Command and General Staff College, 1984.

Herken, Gregg. *Brotherhood of the Bomb: The Tangled Lives and Loyalties of Robert Oppenheimer, Ernest Lawrence, and Edward Teller*. New York: Henry Holt, 2002.

Hunnicutt, R. P. *Bradley: A History of American Fighting and Support Vehicles*. Novato, Calif.: Presidio Press, 1999.

Jacobs, John F. *The Sage Air Defense System: A Personal History*. Bedford, Mass.: MITRE Corporation, 1986.

Johnson, David E. *Fast Tanks and Heavy Bombers: Innovation in the U.S. Army, 1917–1945.* Ithaca, N.Y.: Cornell University Press, 1998.

Kahn, David. *Seizing the Enigma: The Race to Break the German U-Boat Codes, 1939–1943.* New York: Barnes & Noble, 1991.

Knox, MacGregor, and Williamson Murray, eds. *The Dynamics of Military Revolution, 1300–2050.* Cambridge: Cambridge University Press, 2001.

Koistinen, Paul A. C. *The Military Industrial Complex: A Historical Perspective.* New York: Praeger, 1980.

Levidow, Les, and Kevin Robins, eds. *Cyborg Worlds: The Military Information Society*. London: Free Association Books, 1989.

Macksey, Kenneth, and John H. Batchelor. *Tank: A History of the Armoured Fighting Vehicle*. New York: Scribner & Sons, 1974.

Markusen, Ann. *The Rise of the Gunbelt: The Military Remapping of Industrial America.* New York: Oxford University Press, 1991.

Mauroni, Albert J. *America's Struggle with Chemical-Biological Warfare*. Westport, Conn., and London: Praeger, 2000.

Murray, Williamson, and Allan R. Millett, eds. *Military Innovation in the Interwar Period.* Cambridge: Cambridge University Press, 1996.

Norberg, Arthur L., and Judy O'Neill. *Transforming Computer Technology: Information Processing for the Pentagon, 1962–1986*. Baltimore, Md.: Johns Hopkins University Press, 1996.

Pursell, Carroll W., ed. *The Military-Industrial Complex.* New York: Harper & Row, 1972.

Redmond, Kent C., and Thomas M. Smith. *From Whirlwind to MITRE: The R&D Story of the SAGE Air Defense Computer.* Cambridge, Mass.: MIT Press, 2000.

Russell, Edmund. *War and Nature: Fighting Humans and Insects with Chemicals from World War I to* Silent Spring. Cambridge and New York: Cambridge University Press, 2001.

Sherry, Michael S. *The Rise of American Air Power: The Creation of Armageddon.* New Haven, Conn.: Yale University Press, 1987.

Singer, P. W. *Corporate Warriors: The Rise of the Privatized Military Industry.* Ithaca, N.Y.: Cornell University Press, 2003.

Spiers, Edward M. *Chemical and Biological Weapons: A Study in Proliferation*. New York: St. Martin's Press, 1994.

Stares, Paul B. *The Militarization of Space*. Ithaca, N.Y.: Cornell University Press, 1985.

### Environment, Medicine, and Health

Apel, Otto F., and Pat Apel. *MASH: An Army Surgeon in Korea*. Lexington: University Press of Kentucky, 1998.

Bayne-Jones, Stanhope. *The Evolution of Preventive Medicine in the United States Army, 1607–1939*. Washington, D.C.: U.S. Government Printing Office, 1968.

Brandt, Allan. *No Magic Bullet: A Social History of Venereal Disease in the United States Since 1880.* New York: Oxford University Press, 1985.

Bristow, Nancy. *Making Men Moral: Social Engineering in the Great War*. New York: New York University Press, 1996.

Byerly, Carol R. *The Fever of War: The Influenza Epidemic in the U. S. During World War I*. New York: New York University Press, 2005.

Cirillo, Vincent J. *Bullets and Bacilli: The Spanish-American War and Military Medicine*. New Brunswick, N.J.: Rutgers University Press, 2004.

Cooter, Roger. "War and Modern Medicine." In *Companion Encyclopedia of the History of Medicine,* edited by W. F. Bynum and Roy Porter. New York: Routledge, 1993.

Crosby, Alfred. *America's Forgotten Pandemic: The Influenza of 1918.* Cambridge: Cambridge University Press, 1989. First published 1976 by Greenwood Press as *Epidemic and Peace, 1918.*

Dean, Eric T., Jr. *Shook over Hell: Post-Traumatic Stress, Vietnam, and the Civil War*. Cambridge, Mass.: Harvard University Press, 1997.

Dulles, Foster Rhea. *The American Red Cross: A History*. New York: Harper, 1950.

Fenn, Elizabeth. *Pox Americana: The Great Smallpox Epidemic of 1775–82*. New York: Hill & Wang, 2001.

Gabriel, Richard A., ed. *Military Psychiatry: A Comparative Perspective*. New York: Greenwood Press, 1986.

———. *The Painful Field: The Psychiatric Dimension of Modern War*. Westport, Conn.: Greenwood Press, 1988.

Grob, Gerald N. *The Deadly Truth: A History of Disease in America*. Cambridge, Mass.: Harvard University Press, 2002.

Hanlon, Martin. *You Can Get There From Here: How the Interstate Highways Transformed America*. New York: Palgrave Macmillan, 2002.

Hardaway, Robert M. *Care of the Wounded in Vietnam*. Manhattan, Kan.: Sunflower University Press, 1988.

Hill, Reuben, et al. *Families under Stress: Adjustment to the Crises of War Separation and Reunion.* New York: Harper & Row, 1949.

Long, Lisa A. *Rehabilitating Bodies: Health, History and the American Civil War*. Philadelphia: University of Pennsylvania Press, 2004.

Martin, James A., Linette R. Sparacino, and Gregory Belenky, eds. *The Gulf War and Mental Health: A Comprehensive Guide*. Westport, Conn.: Praeger, 1996.

Meyerson, Harvey. *Nature's Army: When Soldiers Fought for Yosemite*. Lawrence: University Press of Kansas, 2001.

Neel, Spurgeon. *Medical Support of the U.S. Army in Vietnam 1965–1970*. Washington, D.C.: U.S. Government Printing Office, 1973.

Neushul, Peter. "Fighting Research: Army Participation in the Clinical Testing and Mass Production of Penicillin during the Second World War." In *War, Medicine and Modernity*, edited by Roger Cooter, Mark Harrison, and Steve Sturdy. Somerset, England: Sutton, 1998.

Oates, Stephen B. *A Woman of Valor: Clara Barton and the Civil War*. New York: Free Press, 1994.

Phillips, Howard, and David Killingray, eds. *The Spanish Influenza Pandemic of 1918–1919: New Perspectives.* New York: Routledge, 2003.

Pryor, Elizabeth Brown. *Clara Barton: Professional Angel*. Philadelphia: University of Pennsylvania Press, 1988.

Russell, Edmund. *War and Nature: Fighting Humans and Insects with Chemicals from World War I to* Silent Spring. Cambridge and New York: Cambridge University Press, 2001.

Shay, Jonathan. *Achilles in Vietnam: Combat Trauma and the Undoing of Character*. New York: Scribner & Sons, 1995.

Shealy, Gwendolyn C. *A Critical History of the American Red Cross, 1882–1945: The End of Noble Humanitarianism*. Lewiston, N.Y.: Edwin Mellen Press, 2003.

Shephard, Ben. *A War of Nerves: Soldiers and Psychiatrists in the Twentieth Century*. Cambridge, Mass., and London: Harvard University Press, 2001.

Tucker, Richard P., and Edmund Russell, eds. *Natural Enemy, Natural Ally: Towards an Environmental History of War.* Corvallis: Oregon State University Press, 2004.

War Department, Office of the Surgeon General. *Medical Department of the United States Army in the World War.* 15 vols. Washington, D.C.: U.S. Government Printing Office, 1921–29.

### Law and Justice

Anderson, David L., ed. *Facing My Lai: Moving Beyond the Massacre*. Lawrence: University Press of Kansas, 1998.

Best, Geoffrey. *Humanity in Warfare: The Modern History of the International Law of Armed Conflicts*. London: Methuen, 1983.

Bishop, Joseph. *Justice Under Fire: A Study of Military Law*. New York: Charterhouse, 1974.

Byrne, Edward M. *Military Law*. Annapolis, Md.: Naval Institute Press, 1981.

Clark, Robert D., Andrew M. Egeland Jr., and David B. Sanford. *The War Powers Resolution*. Washington, D.C.: National Defense University Press, 1985.

Cottrell, Robert C. *Roger Nash Baldwin and the American Civil Liberties Union*. New York: Columbia University Press, 2000.

Cramer, C. E. *For the Defense of Themselves and the State: The Original Intent and Judicial Interpretation of the Right to Keep and Bear Arms.* Westport, Conn.: Praeger, 1994.

DeConde, Alexander. *Gun Violence in America: The Struggle for Control.* Boston: Northeastern University Press, 2001.

Department of the Army. *Fundamentals of Military Law*. Washington, D.C.: Department of the Army, 1980.

Dinstein, Yoram. *The Conduct of Hostilities Under the Law of International Armed Conflict*. New York: Cambridge University Press, 2004.

Fleck, Dieter, ed. *The Handbook of Humanitarian Law in Armed Conflicts*. New York: Oxford University Press, 1995.

Flory, William E. S. *Prisoners of War: A Study in the Development of International Law*. Washington. D.C.: American Council on Public Affairs, 1942.

Generous, William T., Jr. *Swords and Scales: The Development of the Uniform Code of Military Justice*. Port Washington, N.Y.: Kennikat Press, 1973.

Green, L. C. *The Contemporary Law of Armed Conflict*. Manchester, England: Manchester University Press, 2000.

Greenberg, Milton. *The G.I. Bill: The Law That Changed America*. New York: Lickle Publishing, 1997.

Grimmett, Richard. *Conventional Arms Transfers to Developing Nations, 1996–2003*. Washington, D.C.: Congressional Research Service, August 26, 2004.

Halbrook, Stephen P. *That Every Man Be Armed: The Evolution of a Constitutional Right and Social Philosophy*. Albuquerque: University of New Mexico Press, 1984.

Hartigan, Richard Shelly. *Lieber's Code and the Law of War*. Chicago: Precedent, 1983.

Howard, Michael, George J. Andreopoulos, and Mark R. Shulman, eds. *The Laws of War: Constraints on Warfare in the Western World*. New Haven, Conn.: Yale University Press, 1994.

Kalshoven, Frits, and Liesbeth Zevgeld. *Constraints on the Waging of War*. Geneva: International Committee of the Red Cross, 2001.

Kennett, Lee, and James LaVerne Anderson. *The Gun in America: The Origins of a National Dilemma*. Westport, Conn.: Greenwood Press, 1975.

Kohn, Richard H. *Military Laws of the United States from the Civil War through the War Powers Act of 1973*. New York: Arno Press, 1979.

Lumpe, Lora, and Jeff Donarski. *The Arms Trade Revealed: A Guide for Investigators and Activists*. Washington, D.C.: Federation of American Scientists Arms Sales Monitoring Project, 1998.

Lurie, Jonathan. *Arming Military Justice: The Origins of the U.S. Court of Military Appeals, 1775–1950*. Princeton, N.J.: Princeton University Press, 1992.

———. *Military Justice in America: The U.S. Court of Appeals for the Armed Forces, 1776–1980*. Lawrence: University Press of Kansas, 2001.

———. *Pursuing Military Justice: The History of the United States Court of Appeals for the Armed Forces, 1951–1980*. Princeton, N.J.: Princeton University Press, 1998.

Maguire, Peter. *Law and War: An American Story*. New York: Columbia University Press, 2001.

Malcolm, Joyce Lee. *To Keep and Bear Arms: The Origins of an Anglo-American Right*. Cambridge, Mass.: Harvard University Press, 1994.

May, Robert E. *Manifest Destiny's Underworld: Filibustering in Antebellum America*. Chapel Hill: University of North Carolina Press, 2002.

O'Connell, Mary Ellen. *International Law and the Use of Force*. New York: Foundation, 2004.

Rehnquist, William H. *All the Laws but One: Civil Liberties in Wartime*. New York: Alfred A. Knopf, 1998.

Rivkin, Robert. *The Rights of Servicemen: The Basic ACLU Guide to Servicemen's Rights*. New York: Baron Publishing, 1973.

Schlueter, D. A. *Military Criminal Justice: Practice and Procedure*. 6th ed. Newark, N.J.: LexisNexis / M. Bender, 2004.

Stone, Geoffrey R. *Perilous Times: Free Speech in Wartime from the Sedition Act of 1798 to the War on Terrorism*. New York: W. W. Norton, 2004.

Sullivan, John H. *The War Powers Resolution: A Special Study of the Committee on Foreign Affairs*. Washington, D.C.: U.S. Government Printing Office, 1982.

Twine, Robert F. *The War Powers Resolution: Its Implementation in Theory and Practice*. Philadelphia: Foreign Policy Research Institute, 1983.

Walker, Samuel. *In Defense of American Liberties: A History of the ACLU*. New York: Oxford University Press, 1990.

Westerfield, Donald L. *War Powers: The President, the Congress and the Question of War*. Westport, Conn.: Praeger, 1996.

Winthrop, William. *Military Law and Precedents*. 2nd ed. Buffalo, N.Y.: S. Hein, 2000.

### Civil–Military Relations

Baskir, Lawrence, and William Strauss. *Chance and Circumstance: The Draft, the War, and the Vietnam Generation*. New York: Vintage, 1978.

Carr, Caleb. *The Lessons of Terror: A History of Warfare Against Civilians: Why It Has Always Failed and Why It Will Fail Again*. New York: Random House, 2002.

Coakley, Robert W. *The Role of Federal Military Forces in Domestic Disorders, 1789–1878*. Washington, D.C.: U.S. Army Center of Military History, 1988.

Cohen, Eliot. *Citizens and Soldiers: The Dilemmas of Military Service*. Ithaca, N.Y.: Cornell University Press, 1985.

Cooper, Jerry. *The Militia and the National Guard in America Since Colonial Times: A Research Guide*. Westport, Conn.: Greenwood Press, 1993.

———. *The Rise of the National Guard: The Evolution of the American Militia, 1865–1920*. Lincoln: University of Nebraska Press, 1997.

Corcoran, James. *Bitter Harvest: Gordon Kahl and the Rise of the Posse Comitatus in the Heartland*. New York: Penguin, 1990.

Cress, Lawrence Delbert. *Citizens in Arms: The Army and the Militia in American Society to the War of 1812*. Chapel Hill: University of North Carolina Press, 1982.

Cunliffe, Marcus. *Soldiers and Civilians: The Martial Spirit in America, 1775–1865*. Boston: Little, Brown, 1968.

Dees, Morris, and James Corcoran. *Gathering Storm: America's Militia Threat*. New York: HarperCollins, 1996.

Desch, Michael C. *Civilian Control of the Military: The Changing Security Environment*. Baltimore, Md.: Johns Hopkins University Press, 1999.

Feaver, Peter D. *Armed Servants: Agency, Oversight, and Civil-Military Relations*. Cambridge, Mass.: Harvard University Press, 2003.

———, and Christopher Gelpi. *Choosing Your Battles: American Civil–Military Relations and the Use of Force*. Princeton, N.J.: Princeton University Press, 2004.

———, and Richard H. Kohn, eds. *Soldiers and Civilians: The Civil–Military Gap and American National Security*. Boston: MIT University Press, 2001.

Flynn, George. *America and the Draft, 1940–1973*. Lawrence: University Press of Kansas, 1993.

Gillis, John, ed. *The Militarization of the Western World*. New Brunswick, N.J.: Rutgers University Press, 1989.

Holsti, Ole R. *Public Opinion and American Foreign Policy*. Rev. ed. Ann Arbor: University of Michigan Press, 2004.

Huntington, Samuel P. *The Soldier and the State: The Theory and Politics of Civil–Military Relations*. Cambridge, Mass.: Harvard University Press, 1957.

Kohn, Richard H., ed. *The United States Military under the Constitution of the United States, 1789–1989*. New York: New York University Press, 1991.

Larson, Eric V. *Casualties and Consensus: The Historical Role of Casualties in Domestic Support for U.S. Military Operations*. Santa Monica, Calif.: RAND Corporation, 1996.

Levitas, Daniel. *The Terrorist Next Door: The Militia Movement and the Radical Right*. New York: St. Martin's Press, 2002.

May, Robert E. *Manifest Destiny's Underworld: Filibustering in Antebellum America*. Chapel Hill: University of North Carolina Press, 2002.

Mueller, John. *War, Presidents and Public Opinion*. New York: Wiley, 1973.

Segal, David R. *Recruiting for Uncle Sam: Citizenship and Military Manpower Policy*. Lawrence: University Press of Kansas, 1989.

Singer, P. W. *Corporate Warriors: The Rise of the Privatized Military Industry*. Ithaca, N.Y.: Cornell University Press, 2003.

Sinisi, Kyle S. *Sacred Debts: State Civil War Claims and American Federalism, 1861–1880*. New York: Fordham University Press, 2003.

Sobel, Richard. *The Impact of Public Opinion on U.S. Foreign Policy Since Vietnam: Constraining the Colossus*. New York: Oxford University Press, 2001.

Stern, Kenneth S. *A Force Upon the Plain: The American Militia Movement and the Politics of Hate*. Norman: University of Oklahoma Press, 1996.

Stewart, Gail B. *Militias*. San Diego, Calif.: Lucent Books, 1998.

Tap, Bruce. *Over Lincoln's Shoulder: The Committee on the Conduct of the War*. Lawrence: University Press of Kansas, 1998.

Vagts, Alfred. *A History of Militarism: Civilian and Military*. New York: Meridien Books, 1959.

Whisker, James Biser. *The Rise and Decline of the American Militia System*. London: Associated University Press, 1999.

Wittkopf, Eugene R. *Faces of Internationalism: Public Opinion and American Foreign Policy*. Durham, N.C.: Duke University Press, 1990.

# GENERAL BIBLIOGRAPHY


**Planning, Strategy, and Command and Control**

Borgiasz, William S. *The Strategic Air Command: Evolution and Consolidation of Nuclear Forces, 1945–1955.* Westport, Conn.: Praeger, 1996.

Callahan, David. *Dangerous Capabilities: Paul Nitze and the Cold War.* New York: HarperCollins, 1990.

Cohen, Eliot. *Supreme Command: Soldiers, Statesmen, and Leadership in Wartime.* New York: Free Press, 2002.

Crane, Conrad C. *Bombs, Cities, and Civilians: American Airpower Strategy in World War II.* Lawrence: University Press of Kansas, 1993.

Doubler, Michael D. *Closing with the Enemy: How GIs Fought the War in Europe, 1944–1945.* Lawrence: University Press of Kansas, 1994.

Etzold, Thomas H., and John Lewis Gaddis, eds. *Containment: Documents on American Policy and Strategy, 1945–1950.* New York: Columbia University, 1978.

Fishel, Edwin C. *The Secret War for the Union: The Untold Story of Military Intelligence in the Civil War.* Boston: Houghton Mifflin, 1996.

Freedman, Lawrence. *The Evolution of Nuclear Strategy.* 3rd ed. Houndmills, England: Palgrave, 2003.

Gaddis, John Lewis. *Strategies of Containment: A Critical Appraisal of Postwar American National Security Policy.* New York: Oxford University Press, 1982.

Gartner, Scott. *Strategic Assessment in War.* New Haven, Conn.: Yale University Press 1997.

Gibson, Andrew, and Arthur Donovan. *The Abandoned Ocean: A History of United States Maritime Policy.* Columbia: University of South Carolina Press, 2000.

Hagan, Kenneth. *This People's Navy: The Making of American Seapower.* New York: Free Press, 1991.

Hagerman, Edward. *The American Civil War and the Origins of Modern Warfare: Ideas, Organization, and Field Command.* Bloomington: Indiana University Press, 1988.

Haycock, D. J. *Eisenhower and the Art of Warfare: A Critical Appraisal.* Jefferson, N.C.: McFarland, 2004.

Huelfer, Evan A. *The "Casualty" Issue in American Military Practice: The Impact of World War I.* Westport, Conn.: Praeger, 2003.

Iriye, Akira. *The Globalizing of America, 1913–1945.* New York: Cambridge University Press, 1993.

James, D. Clayton. *Refighting the Last War: Command and Crisis in Korea, 1950–1953.* New York: Free Press, 1993.

———. *A Time for Giants: Politics of the American High Command in World War II.* New York: Franklin Watts, 1987.

Keegan, John. *Intelligence in War: Knowledge of the Enemy from Napoleon to al-Qaeda.* New York: Alfred A. Knopf, 2003.

Kennedy, Paul. *Freedom from Fear: The American People in Depression and War, 1929–1945.* New York: Oxford University Press, 1999.

Kimball, Warren F. *The Juggler: Franklin Roosevelt as a Wartime Statesman.* Princeton, N.J.: Princeton University Press, 1991.

Knock, Thomas J. *To End All War: Woodrow Wilson and the Quest for a New World Order.* Princeton, N.J.: Princeton University Press, 1995.

Korb, Lawrence J. *The Joint Chiefs of Staff: The First Twenty-Five Years.* Bloomington: Indiana University Press, 1976.

Latimer, Jon. *Deception in War: The Art of the Bluff, the Value of Deceit, and the Most Thrilling Episodes of Cunning in Military History, from the Trojan Horse to the Gulf War.* Woodstock, N.Y.: Overlook Press, 2001.

Lavoy, Peter, Scott Sagan, and James J. Wirtz. *Planning the Unthinkable: How New Powers Will Use Chemical, Biological and Nuclear Weapons.* Ithaca, N.Y.: Cornell University Press, 2000.

Lederman, Gordon Nathaniel. *Reorganizing the Joint Chiefs of Staff: The Goldwater–Nichols Act of 1986.* Westport, Conn.: Greenwood Press, 1999.

Locher, James R., III. *Victory on the Potomac: The Goldwater-Nichols Act Unifies the Pentagon.* College Station: Texas A&M University Press, 2001.

Long, Gavin. *MacArthur as Military Commander.* London: B. T. Batsford, 1969.

Lowenthal, Mark N. *Intelligence: From Secrets to Policy.* Washington, D.C.: Congressional Quarterly, 2000.

Mahnken, Thomas G. *Uncovering Ways of War: U. S. Intelligence and Foreign Military Innovation, 1918–1941.* Ithaca, N.Y.: Cornell University Press, 2002.

May, Ernest, ed. *American Cold War Strategy: Interpreting NSC-68.* Boston: Bedford, 1993.

Miller, Nathan. *Spying for America: The Hidden History of U.S. Intelligence.* New York: Paragon, 1989.

Murray, Williamson. *The Emerging Strategic Environment: Challenges of the Twenty-first Century.* Westport, Conn.: Greenwood, 1999.

Ninkovich, Frank. *The Wilsonian Century: U.S. Foreign Policy since 1900.* Chicago: University of Chicago Press, 1999.

Nitze, Paul, with Ann M. Smith and Steven L. Rearden. *From Hiroshima to Glasnost: At the Centre of Decision.* New York: Grove, 1989.

O'Toole, G. J. A. *Honorable Treachery: A History of U.S. Intelligence, Espionage, and Covert Action from the American Revolution to the CIA.* New York: Atlantic Monthly Press, 1991.

Pape, Robert A. *Bombing to Win Air Power and Coercion in War.* Ithaca, N.Y.: Cornell University Press, 1996.

Perry, Mark. *Four Stars: The Inside Story of the Forty-Year Battle Between the Joint Chiefs of Staff and America's Civilian Leaders.* Boston: Houghton Mifflin, 1989.

Ranelagh, John. *The Agency: The Rise and Decline of the CIA.* Rev. ed. New York: Simon & Schuster, 1987.

Shulimson, Jack. *The Marine Corps' Search for a Mission, 1880–1898.* Lawrence: University Press of Kansas, 1993.

Simmons, Edwin Howard. *The United States Marine Corps: A History.* 4th ed. Annapolis, Md.: Naval Institute Press, 2003.

Skelton, William, B. *An American Profession of Arms: The Army Officer Corps, 1784—1861.* Lawrence: University Press of Kansas, 1993.

Stoler, Mark A. *Allies and Adversaries: The Joint Chiefs of Staff, the Grand Alliance, and U.S. Strategy in World War II.* Chapel Hill: University of North Carolina Press, 2000.

———. *The Politics of the Second Front: American Military Planning and Diplomacy in Coalition Warfare, 1941–1943.* Westport, Conn.: Greenwood, 1977.

Sumida, Jon. *Inventing Grand Strategy and Teaching Command: The Classic Works of Alfred Thayer Mahan Reconsidered.* Baltimore, Md.: Johns Hopkins University Press, 1997.

Takaki, Ronald. *Hiroshima: Why America Dropped the Atomic Bomb.* New York: Little, Brown, 1995.

Talbot, Strobe. *Master of the Game: Paul Nitze and the Nuclear Peace.* New York: Vintage, 1989.

Weigley, Russell F. *The American Way of War: A History of United States Military Strategy and Policy.* New York: Macmillan, 1973.

Zegart, Amy. *Flawed by Design: The Evolution of the CIA, JCS, and NSC.* Stanford, Calif.: Stanford University Press, 1999.

### Soldiering and Veterans' Experience

American Veterans of World War II, Korea, and Vietnam. *AMVETS: Fifty Years of Proud Service to America's Veterans.* Lanham, Md.: American Veterans of World War II, Korea, and Vietnam, 1994.

Appy, Christian. *Working Class War: American Combat Soldiers and Vietnam.* Chapel Hill: University of North Carolina Press, 1993.

Barker, A. J. *Prisoners of War.* New York: Universe Books, 1974.

Bonior, David, Stephen Champlin, and Timothy Kolly. *The Vietnam Veteran: A History of Neglect.* New York: Praeger, 1984.

Brende, Joel Osler, and Erwin Randolph Parson. *Vietnam Veterans: The Road to Recovery.* New York: Plenum Press, 1985.

Chambers, John Whiteclay, II. *To Raise an Army: The Draft Comes to Modern America.* New York: Free Press, 1987.

Coffman, Edward M. *The Old Army: A Portrait of the American Army in Peacetime, 1784–1898.* New York: Oxford University Press, 1986.

Cohen, Eliot. *Supreme Command: Soldiers, Statesmen, and Leadership in Wartime.* New York: Free Press, 2002.

Cox, Caroline. *A Proper Sense of Honor: Service and Sacrifice in George Washington's Army.* Chapel Hill: University of North Carolina Press, 2004.

Davies, Wallace. *Patriotism on Parade: The Story of Veterans and Hereditary Organizations in America, 1783–1900.* Cambridge, Mass.: Harvard University Press, 1955.

Dearing, Mary R. *Veterans in Politics: The Story of the G.A.R.* Baton Rouge: Louisiana State University Press, 1952.

Dinter, Elmar. *Hero or Coward: Pressures Facing the Soldier in Combat.* London and Totowa, N.J.: Frank Cass, 1985.

Ebert, James R. *A Life in a Year: The American Infantryman in Vietnam, 1965–1972.* Novato, Calif.: Presidio Press, 1993.

Flory, William E. S. *Prisoners of War: A Study in the Development of International Law* Washington. D.C.: American Council on Public Affairs, 1942.

Flynn, George Q. *The Draft, 1940–1973.* Lawrence: University Press of Kansas, 1993.

# GENERAL BIBLIOGRAPHY


Fredland, J. Eric, Curtis Gilroy, Roger D. Little, and W. S. Sellman, eds. *Professionals on the Front Line: Two Decades of the All-Volunteer Force.* Washington, D.C.: Brassey's, 1996.

Frey, Sylvia R. *The British Soldier in America: A Social History of Military Life in the Revolutionary Period.* Austin: University of Texas Press, 1981.

Fullinwider, Robert. *Conscripts and Volunteers: Military Requirements, Social Justice and the All-Volunteer Force.* New York: Rowman & Littlefield, 1983.

Gerber, David, ed. *Disabled Veterans in History.* Ann Arbor: University of Michigan Press, 2000.

Gray, J. Glenn. *The Warriors: Reflections on Men in Battle.* New York: Harper & Row, 1959.

Greenberg, Milton. *The G.I. Bill: The Law That Changed America.* New York: Lickle Publishing, 1997.

Griffith, Robert K., Jr. *The U.S. Army's Transition to the All-Volunteer Force, 1968–1974.* Washington, D.C.: U.S. Army Center of Military History, 1997.

Hillerman, Tony. *Kilroy Was Here: A GI's War in Photographs from the Collection of Frank Kessler.* Kent, Ohio: Kent State University Press, 2004.

Holm, Tom. *Strong Hearts, Wounded Souls: Native American Veterans of the Vietnam War.* Austin: University of Texas Press, 1996.

Holmes, Richard. *Acts of War: The Behavior of Men in Battle.* New York: Free Press, 1985. First published 1986 by Jonathan Cape as *Firing Line.*

Hunt, Andrew. *The Turning: A History of Vietnam Veterans Against the War.* New York: New York University Press, 1999.

Hynes, Samuel. *Soldier's Tale: Bearing Witness to Modern War.* New York: Penguin, 1998.

Janowitz, Morris. *The Professional Soldier: A Social and Political Portrait.* New York: Free Press, 1971.

Keeley, John B., ed. *The All-Volunteer Force and American Society.* Charlottesville: University of Virginia Press, 1978.

Kellett, Anthony. *Combat Motivation: The Behavior of Soldiers in Battle.* Boston and The Hague: Kluwer Nijoff Publishing, 1982.

Knight, Amy W., and Robert L. Worden. *Veterans Benefits Administration: An Organizational History, 1776–1994.* Washington, D.C.: Veterans Benefits Administration, 1995.

Lifton, Robert Jay. *Home from the War: Vietnam Veterans—Neither Victims Nor Executioners.* New York: Touchstone Press, 1973.

Linderman, Gerald F. *Embattled Courage: The Experience of Combat in the American Civil War.* New York: Free Press, 1987.

Logue, Larry. *To Appomattox and Beyond: The Civil War Soldier in War and Peace.* Chicago: Ivan R. Dee, 1996.

McConnell, Stuart. *Glorious Contentment: The Grand Army of the Republic, 1865–1900.* Chapel Hill: University of North Carolina Press, 1992.

Meadows, William C. *Kiowa, Apache and Comanche Military Societies: Enduring Veterans, 1800 to the Present.* Austin: University of Texas Press, 1999.

Millet, Allan. *Semper Fidelis: The History of the United States Marine Corps.* New York: Free Press, 1991.

Moser, Richard. *The New Winter Soldiers: GI and Veterans Dissent During the Vietnam Era.* Piscataway, N.J.: Rutgers University Press, 1996.

Mosesson, Gloria A. *The Jewish War Veterans Story.* Washington, D.C.: Jewish War Veterans of the United States of America, 1971.

Moskos, Charles C., John Allen Williams, and David R. Segal, eds. *The Postmodern Military: Armed Forces After the Cold War.* Oxford: Oxford University Press, 2000.

Myers, Minor. *Liberty Without Anarchy: A History of the Society of the Cincinnati.* Charlottesville: University Press of Virginia, 1983.

Nicosia, Gerald. *Home to War: A History of the Vietnam Veterans' Movement.* New York: Crown Press, 2001.

O'Neill, Robert, and Jerome Corsi. *Unfit for Command: Swift Boat Veterans Speak Out Against John Kerry.* Washington, D.C.: Regnery Publishing, 2004.

Pencak, William. *For God and Country: The American Legion, 1919–1941.* Boston: Northeastern University Press, 1989.

Resch, John. *Suffering Soldiers: Revolutionary War Veterans, Moral Sentiment, and Political Culture in the Early Republic.* Amherst: University of Massachusetts Press, 1999.

Riconda, Harry P. *Prisoners of War in American Conflicts.* Lanham, Md: Scarecrow Press, 2003.

Ross, Davis R. B. *Preparing for Ulysses: Politics and Veterans During World War II.* New York: Columbia University Press, 1969.

Rumer, Thomas. *The American Legion, 1919–1989.* Indianapolis, Ind.: American Legion Publishing, 1990.

Scott, Wilbur J. *Vietnam Veterans Since the War: The Politics of PTSD, Agent Orange, and the National Memorial*. Norman: University of Oklahoma Press, 2003.

Severo, Richard, and Lewis Milford. *The Wages of War: When America's Soldiers Came Home, from Valley Forge to Vietnam.* New York: Simon & Schuster, 1989.

Shaffer, Donald R. *After the Glory: The Struggles of Black Civil War Veterans*. Lawrence: University Press of Kansas, 2004.

Shay, Jonathan. *Odysseus in America: Combat Trauma and the Trials of Homecoming.* New York: Scribner & Sons, 2002.

Skelton, William. *An American Profession of Arms: The Army Officer Corps.* Lawrence: University Press of Kansas, 1996.

Skocpol, Theda. *Protecting Soldiers and Mothers: The Social Origins of Welfare Policy in the United States.* Cambridge, Mass.: Belknap Press of Harvard University Press, 1992.

Stacewicz, Richard. *Winter Soldiers: An Oral History of the Vietnam Veterans Against the War*. Boston: Twayne, 1997.

Van Ells, Mark D. *To Hear Only Thunder Again: America's World War II Veterans Come Home.* Lanham, Md.: Lexington Books, 2001.

Verrone, Richard Burks, and Laura M. Calkins. *Voices from Vietnam.* London: David & Charles, 2005.

Willenz, June. *Women Veterans: America's Forgotten Heroes.* New York: Continuum, 1983.

## Specific Wars

### Pre-Revolutionary

Anderson, Fred. *Crucible of War: The Seven Years' War and the Fate of Empire in British North America, 1754–1766*. New York: Alfred A. Knopf, 2000.

———. *A People's Army: Massachusetts Soldiers and Society in the Seven Years' War*. Chapel Hill: University of North Carolina Press for the Institute of Early American History and Culture, 1984.

Dederer, John Morgan. *War in America to 1775: Before Yankee Doodle*. New York: New York University Press, 1990.

Dowd, Gregory Evans. *War under Heaven: Pontiac, the Indian Nations, and the British Empire*. Baltimore, Md.: Johns Hopkins University Press, 2002.

Ferling, John E. *Struggle for a Continent: The Wars of Early America*. Arlington Heights, Ill.: Harlan Davidson, 1993.

———. *A Wilderness of Miseries: War and Warriors in Early America*. Westport, Conn.: Greenwood Press, 1980.

Gallay Alan. *The Indian Slave Trade: The Rise of the English Empire in the American South, 1670–1717*. New Haven, Conn.: Yale University Press, 2002.

Leach, Douglas Edward. *Arms for Empire: A Military History of the British Colonies in North America, 1607–1763*. New York: Macmillan, 1973.

Lenman, Bruce. *Britain's Colonial Wars, 1688–1783*. New York: Longman, 2001.

———. *England's Colonial Wars 1550–1688: Conflicts, Empire and National Identity*. New York: Longman, 2001.

Lepore, Jill. *The Name of War: King Phillip's War and the Origins of American Identity*. New York: Alfred A. Knopf, 1998.

Richter, Daniel K. *Facing East from Indian Country: A Native History of Early America*. Cambridge, Mass.: Harvard University Press, 2001.

Starkey, Armstrong. *European and Native American Warfare, 1675–1815*. Norman: University of Oklahoma Press, 1998.

Steele, Ian K. *Betrayals: Fort William Henry and the "Massacre."* New York: Oxford University Press, 1990.

———. *Warpaths: Invasions of North America.* New York: Oxford University Press, 1994.

### Revolutionary War

Cogliano, Francis D. *Revolutionary America, 1763–1815: A Political History*. London: Routledge, 2000.

Duffy, Christopher. *The Military Experience in the Age of Reason.* New York, Athenaeum, 1988.

Ellis, Joseph J. *His Excellency: George Washington*. New York: Alfred A. Knopf, 2004.

Frey, Sylvia R. *The British Soldier in America: A Social History of Military Life in the Revolutionary Period.* Austin: University of Texas Press, 1981.

Higginbotham, Don. *George Washington: Uniting a Nation*. Lanham, Md.: Rowman & Littlefield, 2002.

———. *George Washington and the American Military Tradition.* Athens: University of Georgia Press, 1985.

———. *The War of American Independence: Military Attitudes, Policies, and Practice, 1763–1789.* New York: Macmillan, 1971.

Linebaugh, Peter, and Marcus Rediker. *The Many-Headed Hydra: Sailors, Slaves, Commoners, and the Hidden History of the Revolutionary Atlantic*. Boston: Beacon Press, 2000.

Martin, James Kirby, and Mark E. Lender. *A Respectable Army: The Military Origins of the Republic, 1763–1789*. Wheeling, Ill.: Harlan Davidson, 1982.

Mayer, Holly A. *Belonging to the Army: Camp Followers and Community during the American Revolution*. Charleston: University of South Carolina Press, 1996.

Neimeyer, Charles Patrick. *America Goes to War: A Social History of the Continental Army*. New York: New York University Press, 1996.

Purcell, Sarah J. *Sealed with Blood: War, Sacrifice, and Memory in Revolutionary America*. Philadelphia: University of Pennsylvania Press, 2002.

Royster, Charles. *A Revolutionary People at War: The Continental Army and American Character, 1775–1783*. Chapel Hill: University of North Carolina Press, 1979.

Shy, John. *A People Numerous and Armed: Reflections on the Military Struggle for American Independence*. Rev. ed. Ann Arbor: University of Michigan Press, 1990.

Thomas, Evan. *John Paul Jones: Sailor, Hero, Father of the American Navy*. New York: Simon & Schuster, 2003.

Wright, Robert K. *The Continental Army*. Washington, D.C.: Center of Military History, 1983.

War of 1812

Elting, John R. *Amateurs to Arms!: A Military History of the War of 1812*. Chapel Hill, N.C.: Algonquin Books, 1991.

Hickey, Donald R. *The War of 1812: A Forgotten Conflict*. Urbana: University of Illinois Press, 1989.

Remini, Robert V. *The Battle of New Orleans: Andrew Jackson and America's First Military Victory*. New York: Viking, 1999.

Skeen, C. Edward. *Citizen Soldiers in the War of 1812*. Lexington: University Press of Kentucky, 1999.

Mexican War

Bauer, K. Jack. *The Mexican War, 1846–1848*. New York: Macmillan, 1974.

Eisenhower, John D. *So Far From God: The U.S. War with Mexico, 1846–1848*. New York: Random House, 1989.

Foos, Paul. *A Short, Offhand, Killing Affair: Soldiers and Social Conflict During the Mexican-American War*. Chapel Hill: University of North Carolina Press, 2002.

Francaviglia, Richard V., and Douglas W. Richmond. *Dueling Eagles: Reinterpreting the U. S.-Mexican War, 1846–1848*. Fort Worth: Texas Christian University Press, 2000.

Haynes, Sam W. *James K. Polk and the Expansionist Impulse*. New York: Longman, 1997.

Hietala, Thomas R. *Manifest Design: Anxious Aggrandizement in Late Jacksonian America*. Ithaca, N.Y.: Cornell University Press, 1985.

Johannsen, Robert W. *To the Halls of the Montezumas: The Mexican War in the American Imagination*. New York: Oxford University Press, 1985.

Pletcher, David M. *The Diplomacy of Annexation: Texas, Oregon, and the Mexican War*. Columbia: University of Missouri Press, 1973.

Winders, Richard Bruce. *Mr. Polk's Army: The American Military Experience in the Mexican War.* College Station: Texas A&M Press, 1997.

Civil War

Bernstein, Iver. *The New York City Draft Riots: Their Significance for American Society and Politics in the Age of the Civil War*. New York: Oxford University Press, 1990.

Blight, David W. *Race and Reunion: The Civil War in American Memory*. Cambridge, Mass.: Harvard University Press, 2001.

Boritt, Gabor S., ed. *Lincoln, the War President*. New York: Oxford University Press, 1992.

Foner, Eric. *Reconstruction: America's Unfinished Revolution, 1863–1877*. New York: Harper & Row, 1988.

Fowler, William M. *Under Two Flags: The American Navy in the Civil War*. New York: W. W. Norton, 1990.

Gallagher, Gary W. *Lee and His Army in Confederate History*. Chapel Hill: University of North Carolina Press, 2001.

———. *Lee the Soldier*. Lincoln: University of Nebraska Press, 1996.

Geary, James. *We Need Men: The Union Draft in the Civil War*. Dekalb: Northern Illinois Press. 1991.

Hattaway, Herman, and Archer Jones. *How the North Won: A Military History of the Civil War*. Urbana: University of Illinois Press, 1983.

Kennett, Lee. *Sherman: A Soldier's Life*. New York: HarperCollins, 2001.

Kunhardt, Dorothy Meserve, and Philip B. Kunhardt, Jr. *Mathew Brady and His World*. Alexandria, Va.: Time Life Books, 1977.

Marvel, William. *Andersonville: The Last Depot*. Chapel Hill: University of North Carolina Press, 1994.

McPherson, James M. *Battle Cry of Freedom: The Civil War Era*. New York: Oxford University Press, 1988.

Meredith, Roy. *Mathew Brady's Portrait of an American Era*. New York: W. W. Norton, 1982.

Nolan, Alan T. *Lee Considered: General Robert E. Lee and Civil War History*. Chapel Hill: University of North Carolina Press, 1991.

Paludan, Phillip Shaw. *A People's Contest: The Union and Civil War, 1861–1865*. New York: Harper & Row, 1988.

Panzer, Mary. *Mathew Brady and the Image of History*. Washington, D.C.: Smithsonian Books, 1997.

Simpson, Brooks D., and Jean V. Berlin. *Sherman's Civil War: Selected Correspondence of William T. Sherman, 1860–1865*. Chapel Hill: University of North Carolina Press, 1999.

Thomas, Emory M. *The Confederate Nation: 1861–1865*. New York: Harper & Row, 1979.

Tucker, Spencer C. *A Short History of the Civil War at Sea*. Wilmington, Del.: Scholarly Resources, 2002.

Weigley, Russell F. *A Great Civil War: A Military and Political History, 1861–1865*. Bloomington: Indiana University Press, 2000.

Williams, T. Harry. *Lincoln and His Generals*. New York: Alfred A. Knopf, 1952.

**Spanish–American War**

Dobson, John. *Reticent Expansionism*. Pittsburgh, Penn.: Dusquesne University Press, 1988.

Gould, Lewis L. *The Spanish-American War and President McKinley*. Lawrence: University Press of Kansas, 1999.

Morgan, H. Wayne. *America's Road to Empire*. New York: Wiley, 1965.

Musicant, Ivan. *Empire by Default*. New York: Henry Holt, 1998.

O'Toole, G. J. A. *The Spanish War*. New York, W. W. Norton, 1984.

Trask, David F. *The War with Spain in 1898*. New York: Macmillan, 1981.

**Philippine War**

Boot, Max. *The Savage Wars of Peace: Small Wars and the Rise of American Power*. New York: Basic Books, 2002.

Gates, John Morgan. *Schoolbooks and Krags: The United States Army in the Philippines, 1899–1902*. Westport, Conn.: Greenwood Press, 1975.

Linn, Brian McAllister. *Guardians of Empire: The U.S. Army and the Pacific, 1902–1940*. Chapel Hill: University of North Carolina Press, 1997.

———. *The Philippine War, 1899–1902*. Lawrence: University Press of Kansas, 2000.

Welch, Richard E. *Response to Imperialism: The United States and the Philippine-American War, 1899–1902*. Chapel Hill: University of North Carolina Press, 1979.

**World War I**

Coffman, Edward. *The War to End All Wars: The American Military Experience in World War I*. New York: Oxford University Press, 1968.

Ferrell, Robert H. *Woodrow Wilson and World War I, 1917–1918*. New York: Harper & Row, 1985.

Fussell, Paul. *The Great War and Modern Memory*. New York: Oxford University Press, 1975.

Gregory, R. *The Origins of American Intervention in the First World War*. New York: W. W. Norton, 1971.

Harries, Meirion, and Susie Harries. *The Last Days of Innocence: America at War, 1917–1918*. New York: Random House, 1997.

Keegan, John. *The First World War*. New York: Alfred A. Knopf, 1997.

Keene, Jennifer D. *Doughboys, the Great War and the Remaking of America*. Baltimore, Md.: Johns Hopkins University Press, 2001.

———. *The United States and the First World War*. Harlow, England; New York: Pearson, 2000.

Kennedy, David M. *Over Here: The First World War and American Society*. New York: Oxford University Press, 1980.

Knock, Thomas J. *To End All Wars: Woodrow Wilson and the Quest for a New World Order*. Princeton, N.J.: Princeton University Press, 1995.

Schaffer, Ronald. *America in the Great War: The Rise of the War Welfare State*. New York: Oxford University Press, 1991.

Trask, David F. *The AEF and Coalition Warmaking, 1917–1918*. Lawrence: University Press of Kansas, 1993.

Zeigler, Robert H. *America's Great War: World War I and the American Experience*. Lanham, Md.: Rowman & Littlefield, 2000.

### World War II

Blum, John Morton. *V Was for Victory: Politics and American Culture During World War II*. New York: Harcourt Brace Jovanovich, 1976.

Dower, John. *War Without Mercy: War and Power in the Pacific War*. New York: Pantheon Books, 1986.

Harrison, Mark, ed. *The Economics of World War II: Six Great Powers in International Comparison*. Cambridge: Cambridge University Press, 1998.

Jeffries, John W. *Wartime America: The World War II Home Front*. New York: Ivan Dee, 1996.

Kennedy, Paul. *Freedom from Fear: The American People in Depression and War, 1929–1945*. New York: Oxford University Press, 1999.

Kimball, Warren F. *The Juggler: Franklin Roosevelt as a Wartime Statesman*. Princeton, N.J.: Princeton University Press, 1991.

Linderman, Gerald F. *The World Within War: America's Combat Experience in World War II*. Cambridge, Mass.: Harvard University Press, 1997.

Lingeman, Richard R. *Don't You Know There's a War On?: The American Home Front, 1941–1945*. New York: Putnam, 1970.

Milward, Alan S. *War, Economy, and Society, 1939–1945*. Berkeley: University of California Press, 1977.

Murray, Williamson, and Allan R. Millett. *A War to Be Won: Fighting the Second World War*. Cambridge, Mass.: Belknap Press, 2000.

Overy, Richard. *Why the Allies Won*. New York: W. W. Norton, 1995.

Parillo, Mark P., ed. *"We Were in the Big One": Experiences of the World War II Generation*. Wilmington, Del.: Scholarly Resources, 2002.

Perrett, Geoffrey. *Days of Sadness, Years of Triumph: The American People, 1939–1945*. New York: Coward, McCann & Geoghegan, 1973.

Polenberg, Richard. *America at War: The Home Front, 1941–1945*. Englewood Cliffs, N.J.: Prentice-Hall, 1968.

———. *War and Society: The United States, 1941–1945*. New York: J. B. Lippincott, 1972.

Tuttle, William M. *Daddy's Gone to War: The Second World War in the Lives of America's Children*. New York: Oxford University Press, 1993.

Weinberg, Gerhard L. *A World at Arms: A Global History of World War II*. Cambridge: Cambridge University Press, 1994.

### Korean War

Blair, Clay. *The Forgotten War: America in Korea, 1950–1953*. New York: Times Books, 1987.

Futrell, Robert F. *The United States Air Force in Korea, 1950–1953*. Rev. ed. Washington, D.C.: U.S. Government Printing Office, 1983.

Goulden, Joseph. *Korea: The Untold Story of the War*. New York: Times Books, 1982.

Hastings, Max. *The Korean War*. New York: Simon & Schuster, 1987.

Ridgway, Matthew B. *The Korean War*. Garden City, N.Y.: Doubleday, 1967.

### Vietnam War

Bilton, Michael, and Kevin Sim. *Four Hours in My Lai: A War Crime and Its Aftermath*. New York: Viking, 1992.

Davidson, Phillip B. *Vietnam at War: The History: 1946–1975*. Novato, Calif.: Presidio Press, 1988.

Ebert, James R. *A Life in a Year: The American Infantryman in Vietnam, 1965–1972*. Novato, Calif.: Presidio Press, 1993.

Gilbert, Marc Jason, ed. *Why the North Won the Vietnam War*. New York: Palgrave, 2002.

Halberstam, David. *The Best and the Brightest*. New York: Random House, 1972.

Herring, George C. *America's Longest War: The United States and Vietnam, 1950–1975*. New York: Alfred A. Knopf, 1986.

Hersh, Seymour M. *My Lai 4: A Report on the Massacre and Its Aftermath*. New York: Random House, 1970.

Isaacs, Arnold R. *Without Honor: Defeat in Vietnam and Cambodia*. Baltimore, Md: Johns Hopkins University Press, 1983.

Karnow, Stanley. *Vietnam: A History*. New York: Penguin Books, 1997.

Lehrack, Otto J. *No Shining Armor: The Marines at War in Vietnam: An Oral History*. Lawrence: University Press of Kansas, 1992.

MacPherson, Myra. *Vietnam and the Haunted Generation*. New York: Doubleday, 1984.

McMaster, H. R. *Dereliction of Duty: Lyndon Johnson, Robert McNamara, the Joint Chiefs of Staff and the Lies That Led to Vietnam*. New York: HarperCollins, 1997.

Nicosia, Gerald. *Home to War: A History of the Vietnam Veterans' Movement*. New York: Crown Publishers, 2001.

Olson, James S., and Randy Roberts. *My Lai: A Brief History with Documents*. Boston: Bedford Books, 1998.

Palmer, Bruce. *The 25-Year War: America's Military Role in Vietnam*. Lexington: University Press of Kentucky, 1984.

Record, Jeffery. *The Wrong War*. Annapolis, Md.: Naval Institute Press, 1998.

Wells, Tom. *The War Within: America's Battle over Vietnam*. Berkeley: University of California Press, 1994.

Young, Marilyn. *The Vietnam Wars, 1945–1990*. New York: HarperPerrenial, 1991.

### Cold War

Allison, Graham, and Philip Zelikow. *Essence of Decision: Explaining the Cuban Missile Crisis*. 2nd ed. New York: Longman, 1999.

Betts, Richard. *Soldiers, Statesmen, and Cold War Crises*. 2nd ed. New York: Columbia University Press, 1991.

Crockatt, Richard. *The Fifty Years War*. London: Routledge, 1995.

Freedman, Lawrence. *Kennedy's Wars: Berlin, Cuba, Laos, and Vietnam*. New York: Oxford University Press, 2000.

Fursenko, Aleksandr, and Timothy Naftali. *"One Hell of a Gamble": Khrushchev, Castro, and Kennedy, 1958–1964*. New York: W. W. Norton, 1997.

Gaddis, John Lewis. *We Now Know: Rethinking Cold War History*. New York: Oxford University Press, 1998.

George, Alice L. *Awaiting Armageddon: How Americans Faced the Cuban Missile Crisis*. Chapel Hill: University of North Carolina Press, 2003.

Herring, George C. *America's Longest War*. 4th ed. Boston: McGraw-Hill, 2002.

Isaacs, Jeremy, and Taylor Downing. *Cold War: An Illustrated History, 1945–1991* Boston: Little, Brown, 1998.

LaFeber, Walter. *America, Russia, and the Cold War, 1945–1990*. 8th ed. New York: McGraw-Hill, 1997.

May, Elaine Tyler. *Homeward Bound: American Families in the Cold War Era*. New York: Basic Books, 1988.

Offner, Arnold A. *Another Such Victory: President Truman and the Cold War, 1945–1953*. Stanford, Calif.: Stanford University Press, 2002.

Sagan, Scott D., and Kenneth Waltz. *The Spread of Nuclear Weapons: A Debate Renewed*. New York: W. W. Norton, 2003.

Smyser, W. R. *From Yalta to Berlin: The Cold War Struggle Over Germany*. New York: St. Martin's Press, 1999.

Weldes, Jutta. *Constructing National Interests: The United States and the Cuban Missile Crisis*. Minneapolis: University of Minnesota Press, 1999.

### Persian Gulf War

Atkinson, Rick. *Crusade: The Untold Story of the Persian Gulf War.* Boston: Houghton Mifflin, 1993.

Freedman, Lawrence, and Efraim Karsh. *The Gulf Conflict: Diplomacy and War in the New World Order*. Princeton, N.J.: Princeton University Press, 1993.

Friedman, Norman. *Desert Victory: The War for Kuwait*. Annapolis, Md.: Naval Institute Press, 1991.

Gordon, Michael, and Bernard Trainor. *The Generals' War: The Inside Story of Conflict in the Gulf.* Boston: Little, Brown, 1995.

McCain, Thomas, and Leonard Shyles, eds. *The 1,000 Hour War: Communication and the Gulf War*. Westport, Conn.: Greenwood Press, 1994.

Mueller, John. *Policy and Opinion in the Gulf War.* Chicago: University of Chicago Press, 1994.

Woodward, Bob. *Bush at War.* New York: Simon & Schuster, 2002.

### Iraq War

Cordesman, Anthony H. *The Iraq War: Strategy, Tactics, and Military Lessons.* Washington, D.C.: Center for International and Strategic Studies, 2004.

Hersh, Seymour H. *Chain of Command: The Road from 9/11 to Abu Ghraib*. New York: HarperCollins, 2004.

Keegan, John. *The Iraq War*. New York: Alfred A. Knopf, 2004.

Murray, Williamson, and Robert H. Scales. *The Iraq War: A Military History*. Cambridge, Mass.: Harvard University Press, 2003.

Woodward, Bob. *Plan of Attack*. New York: Simon & Schuster, 2004.

Zucchino, David. *Thunder Run: The Armored Strike to Capture Baghdad*. New York: Atlantic Monthly Press, 2004.

### U.S. Overseas Interventions (Pre– and Post–Cold War)

Andrew, Graham Yooll. *Imperial Skirmishes: War and Gunboat Diplomacy in Latin America.* Brooklyn, N.Y.: Olive Branch Press, 2002.

Boot, Max. *The Savage Wars of Peace: Small Wars and the Rise of American Power*. New York: Basic Books, 2002.

Bowden, Mark. *Black Hawk Down: A Story of Modern War.* New York: Atlantic Monthly Press, 1999.

Cable, James. *Gunboat Diplomacy: Political Applications of Limited Naval Force.* New York: Praeger, 1971.

Daniel, Donald C., Bradd C. Hayes, and Chantal de Jonge Oudraat. *Coercive Inducement and the Containment of International Crises.* Washington, D.C.: United States Institute of Peace Press, 1999.

Findlay, Trevor, and Stockholm International Peace Research Institute. *The Use of Force in U.N. Peace Operations.* Solna, Sweden, and New York: SIPRI/Oxford University Press, 2002.

Fleitz, Frederick H. *Peacekeeping Fiascoes of the 1990s: Causes, Solutions, and U.S. Interests.* Westport, Conn.: Praeger, 2002.

Haass, Richard. *Intervention: The Use of American Military Force in the Post–Cold War World.* Rev. ed. Washington, D.C.: Brookings Institution Press, 1999.

Iriye, Akira. *The Globalizing of America, 1913–1945*. New York: Cambridge University Press, 1993.

Johnson, Chalmers. *The Sorrows of Empire: Militarism, Secrecy and the End of the Republic*. New York: Metropolitan Books, 2004.

LaFeber, Walter. *The United States in the Caribbean*. 2nd ed. New York: W. W. Norton, 1993.

Langley, Lester D. *The Banana Wars: United States Intervention in the Caribbean, 1898–1934.* Lexington: University Press of Kentucky, 1985.

Munro, Dana. *Intervention and Dollar Diplomacy, 1900–1921.* Princeton, N.J.: Princeton University Press, 1964.

Shawcross, William. *Deliver Us From Evil: Peacekeepers, Warlords, and a World of Endless Conflict.* New York: Simon & Schuster, 2001.

# Contributors

**Angevine, Robert G.**
Project Director, Strategic Assessment Center
Hicks and Associates, Inc.
McLean, Virginia

**Arnold, David**
Independent Writer
Washington, D.C.

**Baugess, Jim**
Instructor, Humanities Department
Columbus State Community College
Columbus, Ohio

**Beall, Jonathan A.**
Ph.D. Candidate, Department of History
Texas A&M University
College Station, Texas

**Bednarek, Janet R. Daly**
Professor, Department of History
University of Dayton
Dayton, Ohio

**Belknap, Michal R.**
Professor, California Western School of Law
Adjunct Professor of History,
University of California, San Diego
San Diego, California

**Binker, Mary Jo**
Associate Editor and Project Co-Director,
The Eleanor Roosevelt Papers
The George Washington University
Washington, D.C.

**Bland, Larry I.**
Senior Director, Marshall Papers Project
George C. Marshall Foundation
Lexington, Virginia

**Bogle, Lori**
Associate Professor, Department of History
United States Naval Academy
Annapolis, Maryland

**Boulton, Mark**
Assistant Director, Center for the Study of War and Society,
Department of History
University of Tennessee
Knoxville, Tennessee

**Brady, Lisa**
Assistant Professor of History
Boise State University
Boise, Idaho

**Bristow, Nancy K.**
Professor, Department of History
University of Puget Sound
Tacoma, Washington

**Britten, Thomas A.**
Assistant Professor, Department of History
University of Texas at Brownsville—Texas Southmost College
Brownsville, Texas

**Brown, Thomas J.**
Associate Professor, Department of History
University of South Carolina
Columbia, South Carolina

## CONTRIBUTORS


**Brown, William H.**
Editor, Governors' Documentaries
N.C. Office of Archives and History
Raleigh, North Carolina

**Budreau, Lisa M.**
Ph.D. Candidate
St. Antony's College
Oxford University, England

**Buescher, John**
Chief, Tibetan Broadcast Service
Voice of America
Washington, D.C.

**Burgess, Mark**
Research Analyst, Center for Defense Information
World Security Institute
Washington, D.C.

**Burke, Laurence**
Ph.D. Candidate, Department of History
Carnegie Mellon University
Pittsburgh, Pennsylvania

**Burke, Michael**
Instructor, Department of English Language and Literature
Southern Illinois University, Edwardsville
Edwardsville, Illinois

**Byerly, Carol R.**
Ph.D., Independent Writer
Boulder, Colorado

**Calkins, Laura**
Oral Historian and Assistant Archivist, Vietnam Archive
Texas Tech University
Lubbock, Texas

**Campbell, D'Ann**
Dean of Academics
U.S. Coast Guard Academy
New London, Connecticut

**Campbell, Jacqueline G.**
Assistant Professor, Department of History
University of Connecticut
Storrs, Connecticut

**Cirillo, Vincent J.**
Ph.D., Independent Scholar
North Brunswick, New Jersey

**Cooper, Jerry**
Professor Emeritus, Department of History
University of Missouri-St. Louis
St. Louis, Missouri

**Cox, Amy A.**
Ph.D. Candidate, Department of History
University of California
Los Angeles, California

**Cox, Caroline**
Associate Professor, Department of History
University of the Pacific
Stockton, California

**Crothers, A. Glenn**
Assistant Professor of History, University of Louisville
Director of Research, Filson Historical Society
Louisville, Kentucky

**Davin, Eric Leif**
Lecturer, Department of History
University of Pittsburgh
Pittsburgh, Pennsylvania

**Desnoyers, Ronald C., Jr.**
Graduate Student, School of Justice Studies
Roger Williams University
Bristol, Rhode Island

**Dobbs, Charles M.**
Professor, Department of History
Iowa State University
Ames, Iowa

**Dobson, John**
Professor, Department of History
Oklahoma State University
Stillwater, Oklahoma

**Eaton, George**
AFSC/JMC Command Historian
U.S. Army Field Support Command
Rock Island, Illinois

**Ehrman, James**
Visiting Professor, Department of History
and Political Science
Norwich University
Northfield, Vermont

**Faith, Thomas**
Teacher, Social Studies
U.S. House of Representatives Page School
Washington, D.C.

**Feaver, Peter D.**
Alexander F. Hehmeyer Professor of Political Science
and Public Policy
Duke University
Durham, North Carolina

**Finger, Laura**
Independent Writer
Galveston, Texas

**Foglesong, David S.**
Associate Professor, Department of History
Rutgers University
New Brunswick, New Jersey

**Foley, Michael S.**
Associate Professor of History,
The College of Staten Island
The City University of New York
Staten Island, New York

**Forney, Todd**
Adjunct Professor, Department of Humanities
Columbus State Community College
Columbus, Ohio

**Frykman, Niklas**
Ph.D. Candidate, Department of History
University of Pittsburgh
Pittsburgh, Pennsylvania

**Gardiner, Steven L.**
Visiting Assistant Professor, Department of Anthropology
Miami University
Oxford, Ohio

**Gelpi, Christopher F.**
Associate Professor, Department of Political Science
Duke University
Durham, North Carolina

**Ginchereau, Eugene T.**
CAPT, MC, USNR (Ret.)
Associate Clinical Professor, Department of Medicine
University of Pittsburgh
Pittsburgh, Pennsylvania

**Gingell, Reginald**
Teaching Fellow, Department of History
University of Pittsburgh
Pittsburgh, Pennsylvania

**Godin, Jason**
Ph.D. Student/Teaching Assistant, Department of History
Texas A&M University
College Station, Texas

**Goldstein, Donald M.**
Professor, Graduate School of Public
and International Affairs
University of Pittsburgh
Pittsburgh, Pennsylvania

**Gormley, Dennis M.**
Senior Lecturer, Graduate School of Public
and International Affairs
University of Pittsburgh
Pittsburgh, Pennsylvania

**Gray, Christopher M.**
Independent Writer
Alexandria, Virginia

**Greenwald, Maurine**
Associate Professor, Department of History
University of Pittsburgh
Pittsburgh, Pennsylvania

**Grenier, John**
Associate Professor, Department of History
United States Air Force Academy
Colorado Springs, Colorado

**Grimsley, Mark**
Associate Professor, Department of History
The Ohio State University
Columbus, Ohio

**Hagerty, Bernard**
Lecturer, Department of History
University of Pittsburgh
Pittsburgh, Pennsylvania

**Haggerty, Tim**
Director, Humanities Scholars Program
Carnegie Mellon University
Pittsburgh, Pennsylvania

**Hammill, Gail Sullivan**
Independent Writer
Cherry Hill, New Jersey

**Harper, Judith**
Independent Scholar
Canton, Massachusetts

**Harrington, Peter**
Curator, Anne S. K. Brown Military Collection
Brown University
Providence, Rhode Island

**Heineman, Kenneth J.**
Professor, Department of History
Ohio University
Lancaster, Ohio

**Hemmerle, Oliver Benjamin**
Doctor of Philosophy
Chemnitz University
Germany

**Hendrix, Scott N.**
Ph.D. Candidate, Department of History
University of Pittsburgh
Pittsburgh, Pennsylvania

**Herrera, Ricardo A.**
Assistant Professor, Department of History
Mount Union College
Alliance, Ohio

**Hillman, Elizabeth L.**
Associate Professor, Law
Rutgers University School of Law
Camden, New Jersey

**Hinshaw, John Hendrix**
Associate Professor of History and American Studies,
Department of History and Political Science
Lebanon Valley College
Annville, Pennsylvania

**Hogg, Gordon E.**
Director, Academic Liaison Deptartment
University of Kentucky Libraries
Lexington, Kentucky

**Horky, Roger**
Graduate Assistant Non-Teaching, Department of History
Texas A&M University
College Station, Texas

**Houston, W. Robert**
Associate Professor, Department of History
University of South Alabama
Mobile, Alabama

**Hoyt, Marguerite**
Independent Writer
Ellicott City, Maryland

**Hutchinson, Daniel**
Graduate Student, Department of History
University of Alabama at Birmingham
Birmingham, Alabama

**James, Jeffrey**
Adjunct Professor, School of Public Policy
George Mason University
Fairfax, Virginia

**James, Pearl**
Visiting Assistant Professor, Department of English
Davidson College
Davidson, North Carolina

**Janda, Lance, Ph.D.**
Associate Professor, Department of History and Government
Cameron University
Lawton, Oklahoma

**Jay M. Parker, Ph.D.**
Colonel, United States Army
Professor of Political and International Affairs, Director of International Relations and National Security Studies; Department of Social Sciences
United States Military Academy
West Point, New York

**Junco, Reynol**
Assistant Professor, Department of Academic Development and Counseling
Lock Haven University of Pennsylvania
Lock Haven, Pennsylvania

**Kaplan, Edward**
Assistant Professor, Department of History
United States Air Force Academy
Colorado Springs, Colorado

**Karsten, Adam**
Independent Writer/Director of Stage and Screen
New York, New York

**Karsten, Bonnie Klein, Esquire**
Independent Writer
Pittsburgh, Pennsylvania

**Karsten, Peter**
Professor, Department of History
University of Pittsburgh
Pittsburgh, Pennsylvania

**Keene, Jennifer D.**
Associate Professor and Chair, Department of History
Chapman University
Orange, California

**Kelly, Lorelei**
Senior Associate
Henry L. Stimson Center
Washington, D.C.

**Kinder, John M.**
Ph.D. Candidate, Department of American Studies
University of Minnesota
Minneapolis, Minnesota

**Kindsvatter, Peter S.**
U.S. Army Ordnance Center & Schools Historian
Aberdeen Proving Ground, Maryland

**Krebs, Ronald R.**
Assistant Professor, Department of Political Science
University of Minnesota
Minneapolis, Minnesota

**Kroll, Douglas, Ph.D.**
Assistant Professor of History, Division of Social Science
College of the Desert
Palm Desert, California

**Laberge, Martin**
Lecturer, Department of History
University of Montreal
Montreal, Quebec, Canada

**Lambert, Laura**
Independent Writer
New York, New York

# CONTRIBUTORS

**LAWRENCE, JENNIFER S.**
Assistant Professor, Department of History, Geography, Religion
Tarrant County College – Southeast Campus
Arlington, Texas

**LEE, DAVID**
Dean, Potter College of Arts, Humanities
and Social Sciences
Western Kentucky University
Bowling Green, Kentucky

**LEE, WAYNE**
Assistant Professor of History
University of Louisville
Louisville, Kentucky

**LINN, BRIAN M.**
Professor, Department of History
Texas A&M University
College Station, Texas

**LIPPMAN, MATTHEW**
Professor, Department of Criminal Justice
University of Illinois at Chicago
Chicago, Illinois

**MAASS, JOHN**
Ph.D. Candidate, Department of History
The Ohio State University
Columbus, Ohio

**MCCOLLOCH, MARK**
Vice President for Academic Affairs,
Queensborough Community College
City University of New York
New York, New York

**MCCONACHIE, BRUCE**
Professor of Theatre
University of Pittsburgh
Pittsburgh, Pennsylvania

**MCCONNELL, STUART**
Professor of History, History Field Group
Pitzer College
Claremont, California

**MCDONALD, ROBERT M. S.**
Associate Professor, Department of History
United States Military Academy
West Point, New York

**MILLETT, ALLAN R.**
Mason Professor of Military History, Department of History
The Ohio State University
Columbus, Ohio

**MISSALL, JOHN AND MARY LOU**
Independent Writers
Ft. Myers, Florida

**MITCHELL, PATRICIA PUGH**
Graduate Student, Department of History
University of Pittsburgh
Pittsburgh, Pennsylvania

**MORROW, JOHN H., JR.**
Franklin Professor of History
University of Georgia
Athens, Georgia

**MROZEK, DONALD J.**
Professor, Department of History
Kansas State University
Manhattan, Kansas

**MUELLER, JOHN**
Woody Hayes Chair of National Security Studies,
Mershon Center
Professor of Political Science,
The Ohio State University
Columbus, Ohio

**MUNDEY, LISA M.**
Ph.D. Candidate, Department of History
Kansas State University
Manhattan, Kansas

**MURRAY, WILLIAMSON**
Senior Fellow, Joint Advanced Warfighting Program
Institute for Defense Analyses
Alexandria, Virginia

**Neiberg, Dr. Michael S.**
Professor of History
University of Southern Mississippi
Hattiesburg, Mississippi

**Neumann, Caryn E.**
Ph.D. Candidate, Department of History
The Ohio State University
Columbus, Ohio

**O'Connell, Mary Ellen**
William B. Saxbe Designated Professor of Law
Moritz College of Law, The Ohio State University
Columbus, Ohio

**Ortiz, Stephen R.**
Assistant Professor, Department of History
East Stroudsburg University
East Stroudsburg, Pennsylvania

**Oyos, Matthew M.**
Associate Professor, Department of History
Radford University
Radford, Virginia

**Parillo, Mark P.**
Associate Professor, Department of History
Kansas State University
Manhattan, Kansas

**Parker, Jay M.**
Colonel, U.S. Army
Professor of Political and International Affairs, Director of International Relations and National Security Studies
Department of Social Sciences, United States Military Academy
West Point, New York

**Pencak, William**
Professor of History
Penn State University
University Park, Pennsylvania

**Phillips, Jonathan F.**
Postdoctoral Fellow, Institute for Southern Studies
University of South Carolina
Columbia, South Carolina

**Phillips, Thomas**
Independent Writer
Raymond, Mississippi

**Piehler. G. Kurt**
Director, Center for the Study of War and Society
The University of Tennessee
Knoxville, Tennessee

**Rafuse, Ethan S.**
Associate Professor of Military History, Department of Military History
U.S. Army Command and General Staff College
Fort Leavenworth, Kansas

**Reardon, Carol**
Associate Professor, Department of History
Pennsylvania State University
University Park, Pennsylvania

**Reaves, Stacy**
Director, Sand Springs Cultural and Historical Museum
Sand Springs, Oklahoma

**Reins, Thomas**
Lecturer, Department of History
California State University, Fullerton
Fullerton, California

**Resch, John**
Professor of History
University of New Hampshire-Manchester
Manchester, New Hampshire

**Ridler, Jason S.**
Instructor, Department of History
Royal Military College of Canada, Kingston
Ontario, Canada

**Riker-Coleman, Erik**
Instructor, Department of History
Lake Superior College
Duluth, Minnesota

**Rockoff, Hugh**
Professor, Department of Economics
Rutgers University
New Brunswick, New Jersey

**Rohall, David**
Assistant Professor, Department of Sociology and Anthropology
Western Illinois University
Macomb, Illinois

**Rose, Kenneth D.**
Lecturer, Department of History
California State University, Chico
Chico, California

**Sankey, Margaret**
Assistant Professor, Department of History
Minnesota State University Moorhead
Moorhead, Minnesota

**Sargent, Walter**
Instructor, Department of History
Winona State University
Winona, Minnesota

**Saxe, Dr. Robert Francis**
Assistant Professor, Department of History
Rhodes College
Memphis, Tennessee

**Scully, Beth**
Independent Writer
Brooklyn, New York

**Sheftall, Mark**
Visiting Professor, Department of History
North Carolina State University
Raleigh, North Carolina

**Shiman, Philip**
Historian, Defense Acquisition History Project
U.S. Army Center of Military History
Washington, D.C.

**Simpson, Brooks D.**
Professor, Department of History
Arizona State University
Tempe, Arizona

**Smith, Adriane D.**
Postdoctoral Fellow, History
The University of North Carolina at Chapel Hill
Chapel Hill, North Carolina

**Smith, Barbara Clark**
Curator, Division of Politics and Reform
National Museum of American History
Washington, D.C.

**Smith, Colonel Daniel, USA (Ret.)**
Senior Fellow on Military Affairs
Friends Committee on National Legislation
Washington, D.C.

**Speelman, Jennifer L.**
Assistant Professor, Department of History
The Citadel
Charleston, South Carolina

**Springer, Paul**
Ph.D. Candidate/Lecturer, Department of History
Texas A&M University
College Station, Texas

**Stohl, Rachel**
Senior Analyst
Center for Defense Information
Washington, D.C.

**Stokes, Brian**
Adjunct Professor, Department of History
Camden County College
Blackwood, New Jersey

**Tiro, Karim M.**
Assistant Professor, Department of History
Xavier University
Cincinnati, Ohio

**Valentine, Janet**
Historian, U.S. Army Center of Military History
Ft. McNair
Washington, D.C.

**van de Logt, Mark**
Research Scholar, American Indian Studies Research Institute
Indiana University
Bloomington, Indiana

**Van Ells, Mark D.**
Associate Professor, Department of History
Queensborough Community College (CUNY)
Bayside, New York

**Vaughn, Stephen L.**
Professor, School of Journalism and Mass Communication
University of Wisconsin
Madison, Wisconsin

**Wala, Michael**
Professor of North American History, Department of History
Ruhr-Universität-Bochum
Bochum, Germany

**Watts, Tim J.**
Humanities Librarian, Hale Library
Kansas State University
Manhattan, Kansas

**Wetherington, Mark V.**
Director
The Filson Historical Society
Louisville, Kentucky

**Wettemann, Robert, Jr.**
Assistant Professor of History
McMurry University
Abilene, Texas

**Whit, George, Jr.**
Assistant Professor of History and African American Studies
University of Tennessee
Knoxville, Tennessee

**Whitmer, Mariana**
Center for American Music
University of Pittsburgh
Pittsburgh, Pennsylvania

**Williams, Chad L.**
Assistant Professor, Department of History
Hamilton College
Clinton, New York

**Wills, Brian S.**
Asbury Chair of History
University of Virginia's College at Wise
Wise, Virginia

**Wirtz, Jim**
Professor, Department of National Security Affairs
Postgraduate Naval School; Monterey, California
Visiting Professor, Center for Security and Cooperation
Stanford University; Stanford, California

**Woodworth, Steven E.**
Professor, Department of History
Texas Christian University
Fort Worth, Texas

**Yockelson, Mitchell**
Reference Archivist
National Archives and Records Administration

**Zboray, Mary Saracino**
Visiting Scholar, Department of Communication
University of Pittsburgh
Pittsburgh, Pennsylvania

**Zboray, Ronald J.**
Associate Professor, Department of Communication
University of Pittsburgh
Pittsburgh, Pennsylvania

**Zyla, Benjamin**
Ph.D. Candidate, Department of Politics and Economics
The Royal Military College of Canada
Kingston, Ontario

# Index

Page numbers in **boldface** type indicate article titles. Page numbers in *italic* type indicate illustrations or charts and graphs.

# INDEX

# INDEX

# INDEX